THE MAGINOT LINE

THE MAGINOT LINE

A New History

Kevin Passmore

YALE UNIVERSITY PRESS
NEW HAVEN AND LONDON

Excerpts in Chapter 3 first appeared in Kevin Passmore, 'Organizing the terrain: the Maginot Line in the natural world, 1919–1939', *Environmental History*, 29:1 (2024), pp. 86–116. Republished by permission of the publisher: Chicago University Press.

Excerpts in Chapter 10 first appeared in Kevin Passmore, 'The *Drôle de Guerre* on the Maginot Line: Soldiers and Civilians in Alsace-Lorraine, September 1939 to June 1940', in *French Historical Studies*, 48:1, pp. 101–137. Copyright 2025, Society for French Historical Studies. All rights reserved. Republished by permission of the publisher: www.dukeupress.edu

Excerpts in Chapter 11 first appeared in Kevin Passmore, '"Au contact": French tactics in the Maginot Line advance posts during the phoney war, 3 September 1939 to 9 May 1940', *War in History*, 2025, 0:0, 1–22, https://doi-org.cardiff.idm.oclc.org/10.1177/09683445251329056. Republished by permission of the publisher: Sage.

For information about this and other Yale University Press publications, please contact:
U.S. Office: sales.press@yale.edu yalebooks.com
Europe Office: sales@yaleup.co.uk yalebooks.co.uk

Set in Adobe Garamond Pro by IDSUK (DataConnection) Ltd
Printed and bound in the UK using 100% renewable electricity at CPI Group (UK) Ltd

Library of Congress Control Number: 2025939086
A catalogue record for this book is available from the British Library.
Authorized Representative in the EU: Easy Access System Europe, Mustamäe tee 50, 10621 Tallinn, Estonia, gpsr.requests@easproject.com

ISBN 978-0-300-27704-3

10 9 8 7 6 5 4 3 2 1

MIX
Paper | Supporting responsible forestry
FSC www.fsc.org FSC® C013604

CONTENTS

PLATES AND FIGURES

Plates

13. A *corps franc* patrol in the Northern Vosges. © Auteur inconnu / ECPAD / Défense.
14. The view from one of the cloches on La Ferté's Bloc 2. Associated Press / Alamy.
15. The destroyed GFM cloche on La Ferté's Bloc 2. Sueddeutsche Zeitung Photo / Alamy.
16. German soldiers at La Ferté's entrance. Service historique de la Défense, 29N91.
17. General Weygand, Paul Baudouin, Paul Reynaud and Marshal Pétain, 10 June 1940. World History Archive / Alamy.
18. A wounded German soldier at PO-Kerfent. Musée de la Moselle en 1939–45 (ASCOMEMO).
19. The destruction of Bloc 3 of Kerfent *petit ouvrage*, June 1940. © Auteur inconnu / ECPAD-collection Bruge / Défense.
20. Colonel Fabre learns that he is considered to be a prisoner of war, June 1940. © Auteur inconnu / ECPAD-collection Bruge / Défense.
21. German soldiers inspect a turret in RF-Metz. Musée de la Moselle en 1939–45 (ASCOMEMO).
22. Wehrmacht soldiers at Hackenberg Bloc 8, June 1940. Musée de la Moselle en 1939–45 (ASCOMEMO).

Figures

Unless otherwise stated, all figures are by Kirsty Harding, Cardiff University.

ABBREVIATIONS

Military Units

AK	Armee-Korps (German corps)
AOK	Armeeoberkommando (equivalent of an army, between corps and army group)
BAF	Bataillon alpin de forteresse (Alpine Fortress Battalion)
BCA	Bataillon de chasseurs alpins (Alpine Light Infantry Battalion)
BCP	Bataillon de chasseurs à pied (Light Infantry Battalion)
BCPyr	Bataillon de chasseurs pyrénéens (Pyrenean Light Infantry Battalion)
BEF	British Expeditionary Force
CAF	Corps d'armée de forteresse (Fortress Corps, replaced the fortified regions (RFs) from January to March 1940)
DBAF	Demi-Brigade alpin de forteresse (Half-Brigade of Alpine Fortress Infantry)
DC	Division de cavalerie (Cavalry Division)
DCLI	Duke of Cornwall's Light Infantry
DCr	Division cuirassée (Armoured Division; wrongly, '. . . de réserve' – a lower-case 'r' was added to distinguish these units from cavalry divisions, DC)
DI	Division d'infanterie (Infantry Division)
DIA	Division d'infanterie alpine (Alpine Infantry Division)

DIC	Division d'infanterie coloniale (Colonial Infantry Division)
DIF	Division d'infanterie de forteresse (Fortress Division, replaced certain fortified sectors (SFs) from January to March 1940)
DIM	Division d'infanterie motorisée (Motorised Infantry Division)
DINA	Division d'infanterie nord africaine (North African Infantry Division)
DIP	Division d'infanterie polonaise (Polish Infantry Division)
DLM	Division légère mécanique (Light Armoured Division)
GRCA	Groupe de reconnaissance de corps d'armée (Corps Reconnaissance Group)
GRDI	Groupe de reconnaissance de division d'infanterie (Divisional Reconnaissance Group)
GRM	Garde républicaine mobile (Mobile Republican Guard, responsible for policing public order and the frontier)
ID	Infanterie Division (German)
RAMF	Régiment d'artillerie mobile de forteresse (Mobile Fortification Artillery Regiment)
RAP	Régiment d'artillerie de position (Fortification Artillery Regiment; sometimes wrongly, '. . . à pied')
RARF	Régiment d'artillerie de région de forteresse (Regional Fortification Artillery Regiment, the equivalent of corps artillery)
RI	Régiment d'infanterie (Infantry Regiment)
RIA	Régiment d'infanterie alpine (Alpine Infantry Regiment)
RIC	Régiment d'infanterie coloniale (Colonial Infantry Regiment, naval infantry)
RIF	Régiment d'infanterie de forteresse (Fortress Infantry Regiment; wrongly, '. . . fortifié')
RMIC	Régiment de mitrailleurs d'infanterie coloniale (Regiment of Colonial Machine Gunners, formerly Régiment mixte d'infanterie colonial)
RRT	Régiment régional de travailleurs (Regional Labour Regiment)
RTA	Régiment de tirailleurs algériens (Algerian Infantry Regiment)

RTT Régiment de tirailleurs tunisiens (Tunisian Infantry Regiment)
SD Secteur défensif (defensive sector)
SES Section d'éclaireurs-skieurs (Ski Scouting Platoon)
SF Secteur fortifié (fortified sector)
SSF Sous-secteur fortifié (fortified sub-sector)

Other Abbreviations

AEF Administration des eaux et forêts (Forest and Water Administration)
CDF Commission chargée de l'étude de défense des frontières (Commission for Frontier Defence, 1925–35)
CDT Commission chargée d'études de l'organisation de la défense du territoire (Commission for the Study of the Organisation of the Territory, 1922–3)
CEFZ Commission d'études des zones fortifiées (Commission for the Study of Fortified Zones, 1939–40)
CEP Charles Serre, ed., *Rapport fait au nom de la Commission chargée d'enquêter sur les événements survenus en France de 1933 à 1945 par M. Charles Serre: Annexes (Témoignages)* (9 vols, 1951)
CORF Commission d'organisation des régions fortifiées (Committee for the Organisation of Fortified Regions, 1927–36)
CP Contrôle postal (postal censorship and monitoring)
CSDN Conseil supérieur de la défense nationale (Supreme Council of National Defence, a body in which military ministers and heads of the army and navy advised the government on preparation for war)
CSG Conseil supérieur de la guerre (Supreme War Council, responsible for advising the government on military policy in peacetime)
DGSAL Direction générale des services d'Alsace et de Lorraine (General Department for Alsace-Lorraine Services, Paris-based administrative body responsible for the province, 1925–35)

DGSN	Direction générale de la sécurité nationale (General Department of National Security, formed 1934 to oversee national criminal and special police forces)
EMA	État-major des armées (Army General Staff)
GO	*Gros ouvrage* (large fort with artillery)
GQG	Grand quartier général (General Headquarters in the Army Zone in wartime; the EMA and military regions retain responsibility for the 'interior')
IEE	Institut d'études européennes (state-subsidised private intelligence agency in Alsace-Lorraine)
IGU	*Instruction sur l'emploi tactique des grandes unités* (Instructions on the tactical employment of large units, published in 1936)
IPGU	*Instruction provisoire sur l'emploi tactique des grandes unités* (Provisional instructions on the tactical employment of large units, published in 1921)
IPS	*Instruction personelle et secrète* (Personal and Secret Instruction)
JMO	Journal de marches et d'opérations (War Diary)
JODC	*Journal officiel: Débats parlementaires: Chambre* (Official Record, Chamber of Deputies, Debates)
JODS	*Journal officiel: Débats parlementaires: Sénat* (Official Record, Senate, Debates)
JOLD	*Journal officiel: Lois et décrets* (Official Record, Laws and Decrees)
LMG	Light machine gun
MOM	*Main d'œuvre militaire* (Military labour)
NCO	Non-commissioned officer
OKH	Oberkommando des Heeres (land army high command)
OKW	Oberkommando der Wehrmacht
PO	*Petit ouvrage* (smaller fort armed with infantry weapons – antitank guns, mortars, machine guns)
POW	Prisoner of war
PV	*Procès-verbaux* (minutes)
RF	Région fortifiée (fortified region)
SCAL	Service central des services d'Alsace et de Lorraine (Central Department for Alsace-Lorraine Services, Paris-based administrative body responsible for the province, 1935–40)

SMG	Submachine gun
SNI	Syndicat national des instituteurs (National Union of Primary-School Teachers)
STG	Service technique du génie (Engineers' Technical Department)
UPR	Union populaire républicaine / Elsässische Volkspartei (Popular Republican Union / Alsatian People's Party)

ACKNOWLEDGEMENTS

Researching and writing this book would have been impossible without the award of a Leverhulme Trust Major Research Fellowship (2014–17). I also benefited from three British Academy/Leverhulme Small Research Grants and from a Cardiff University Research Fellowship. Big thanks are due to my colleagues in the History Department at Cardiff University for their commitment to covering rotational research leave, often in challenging circumstances. Gratitude is also due to Kirsty Harding, who drew the figures.

I am extremely grateful to the staff of the Bibliothèque nationale de France, the Dépot Central des Archives de la Justice Militaire at Le Blanc, the Images-Défence at Fort d'Ivry, the Archives du Sénat, and the departmental archives of the Alpes-Maritimes, Alpes de Haut-Provence, Ardennes, Côte d'Or, Moselle, Meuse, Nord and especially of Bas-Rhin at Strasbourg. Particular thanks are due to Caroline Piketty at the Archives nationales and to Nicolas Texier, Anne-Aurore Inquimbert, Pascal Carré, Luc Binet and Justine Chevigny at the Service historique de la défense. Philippe Wilmouth, president and founder of the Association pour la conservation de la mémoire en Moselle en 1939–1945 and of its wonderful museum at Hagondage, helped me to locate photographs for the book. Thanks also to Andrew Sims at the DCLI Museum and Archive in Bodmin, Cornwall, a museum which many years ago did so much to awaken my interest in history. Thanks to Sergeant Bethany Keenan PhD for explaining the physiological and psychological impact of bombardment. My brother, Colonel (retd) J.E. Passmore (late RE) read the manuscript and made insightful comments and suggestions.

Thanks are due to Joanna Godfrey for supporting this project and for sympathetic reading of the manuscript, and to all the staff at Yale University Press London, including Stuart Weir, Rachael Lonsdale and Katherine Powell, have contributed to the finished book.

My greatest debt is owed to my wife, Professor Garthine Walker, brilliant historian and psychotherapist, for her intellectual stimulation and love over three decades. Besides serving as an incisive and encouraging reader of the manuscript, she revealed an unsuspected talent for locating obscure Maginot Line installations in the thick forests of the beautiful Northern Vosges – pushing on where I would have given up.

INTRODUCTION

At dawn on 10 May 1940, Adjutant-chef Robert Lavergne, commander of the enormous Hackenberg fort's Bloc 24, saw some five hundred aircraft flying into the interior. Later, he heard the sound of combat at the Maginot Line advance posts a few kilometres forward on the Franco-German border and of growling motors in the distance northwest towards Luxembourg. There, unknown to him, the flank guard of a huge Panzer force was pushing back French cavalry. Lavergne, who had recently observed the combat systems of the aircraft-carrier Béarn, initiated the well-honed alert procedure. Observation cloches were manned, airlocks closed, gas alarms and turrets tested and light machine guns set up to defend underground communication galleries against infiltrators. By the 13th, the sector had quietened. Over the following weeks, the men had little to do besides test their weapons and await the electric trains bringing their rations – doubtless cold.[1]

Life underground was challenging. A few months previously, parliamentary inspectors had found a well-organised crew with good morale 'in this artificial atmosphere, difficult despite all the improvements'. They urged the purchase of ozonisers to neutralise 'smells of all origins' – they meant the kitchens and latrines.[2] Over the eight months of the phoney war, damp, cold and artificial light produced a mental condition that the men labelled '*bétonite*' – 'concretitis'.

Hackenberg was the largest artillery fort, *gros ouvrage*, on the Maginot Line. Sited between the Moselle and Nied river valleys, it covered the most direct route from Germany to Paris. Laws of 14 January 1930 and 6 July 1934 funded nineteen such forts plus thirty-two infantry forts, *petits ouvrages*, and numerous interval casemates and shelters. They defended the border from Longuyon opposite Luxembourg to the Rhine at Lauterbourg. The Rhine itself was covered by machine-gun casemates. The 1930 law also funded forts in the mountain passes and coastal plain on the Italian border, while the 1934 programme fortified a few key points in the north (Figures 1, 2 and 3). Individual forts such as Hackenberg were just one part of a huge military complex, consisting of special barracks for troops, garden cities for officers, military roads, narrow-gauge railways, electrical and telephone cables, command posts, planned flooding, thousands of miles of barbed wire and antitank rails and supply chains reaching across the French empire and the world. During the war, nearly half of France's two million front-line soldiers served on the Maginot Line at any given time and all the best divisions served tours there.

Hackenberg alone cost over 170 million francs to build – 135 million euros in 2024 prices – not including armament. Unusually, it consisted of two half-forts joined by an escarpment. In other respects, Hackenberg differed from other *gros ouvrages* only in the size of its crew – around one thousand men – and in the number of its individual fighting blocs, of which there were seventeen. They were numbered up to twenty-four, however, for seven blocs never got beyond the drawing board. Four blocs were armed with rapid-fire 75mm guns with a range of up to twelve kilometres; two more housed 135mm indirect-fire howitzers. The other blocs were armed with combinations of antitank guns, mortars and light machine guns in cloches, machine guns in turrets and artillery casemates firing to the flanks.

Men and supplies all entered the Hackenberg through the misleadingly named munitions entrance, for its personnel entrance was actually an emergency entrance (see Plate 1). Narrow-gauge railways led directly from a valley, through the munitions entrance down a slope under the hill, ninety-six metres underground at the deepest point. Near the entrance were an infirmary, power plant, magazines, kitchens, officers' mess and sleeping quarters. The main gallery then forked towards the two half-forts and then to the base of each combat bloc, several hundred

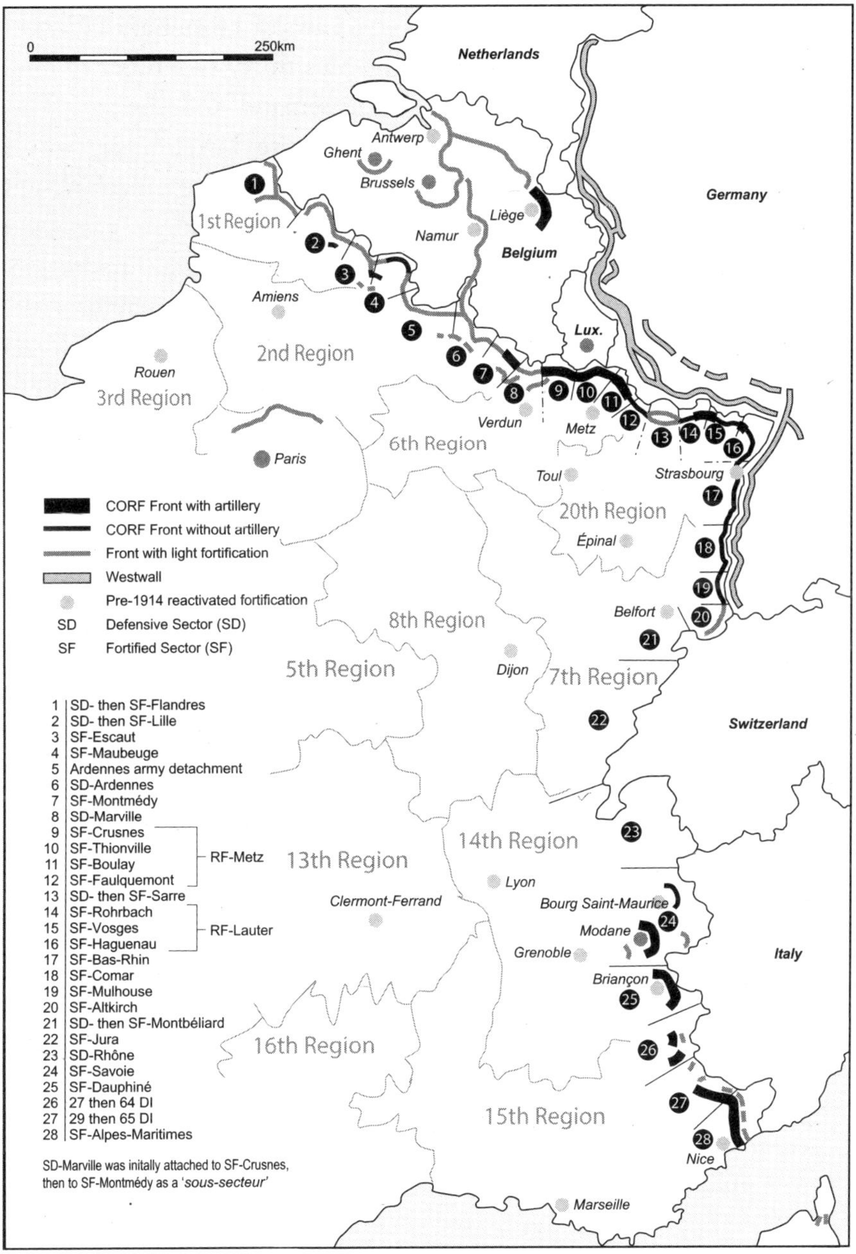

1. Fortified and defensive sectors and military regions.

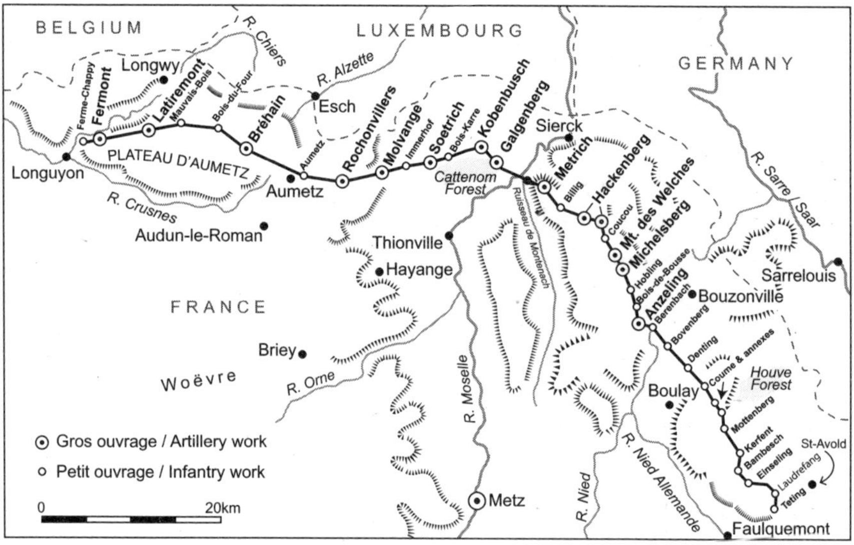

2. RF-Metz.

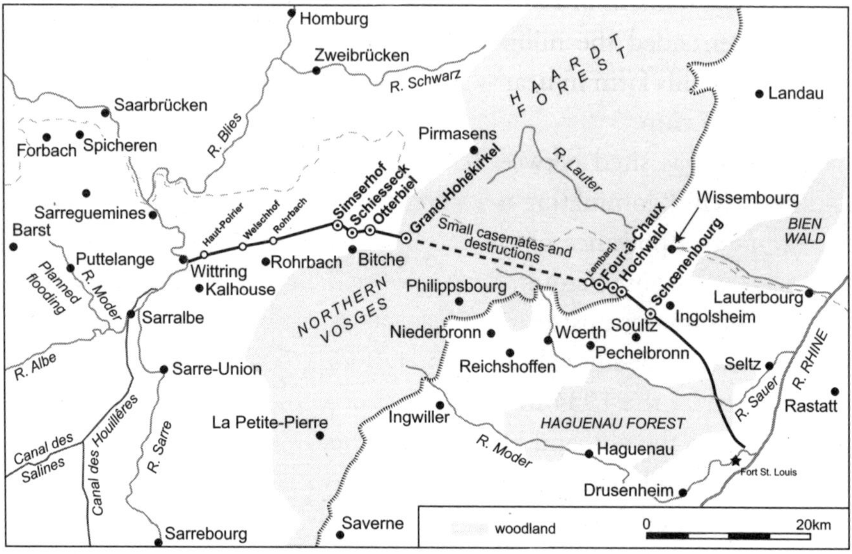

3. RF-Lauter.

metres forward. Shafts with elevators and steps led up to the turrets and casemates of the combat blocs at the surface (Figure 4).

Like almost all Maginot Line forts and Rhine casemates, Hackenberg was positioned in Alsace-Lorraine, which had returned to France in 1918 after forty-seven years of annexation to Germany. The local inhabitants were overwhelmingly first-language speakers of various German dialects and had multiple linguistic, economic and cultural ties to those across the border. Many of the soldiers serving in specially trained fortress artillery and infantry regiments were recruited from this population.

On 10 May 1940, further north on the Belgian border, the 106 soldiers manning *petit ouvrage* La Ferté, the last fort on the Maginot Line, also heard guns and aircraft. The alert shattered their dreams of relief from the crushing boredom of their 'troglodyte life' below ground, as one soldier put it.[3] The next day, the authorities ordered the inhabitants of neighbouring villages to evacuate. The sad spectacle prompted thirty-three-year-old Lieutenant Maurice Bourguignon, La Ferté's commander, to remind his wife that as natives of the region, they too had fled the Germans in 1914. One soldier, who had seen his own family pass by, persuaded the military postmaster – a mobilised priest – to escort him to his farm in nearby Auflance, from where he returned with a shoulder of ham.[4]

La Ferté was sited between the villages of Villy and La Ferté-sur-Chiers on a hill dominating the River Chiers, a tributary of the Meuse, the military importance of which all aspirant officers learned in their topography lessons. Verdun, the scene of the battle of the Great War, was fifty kilometres upstream on the Meuse. La Ferté was part of fortified sector Montmédy (SF-Montmédy), an extension to the Maginot Line funded by the 1934 fortification law. These 'new fronts' were less powerful than the old, and La Ferté was their weakest link, armed only with antitank and machine guns. Its galleries were narrow and its rooms were too cramped for the crew.

On 12 May, Bourguignon, 'courteous as ever', allowed a local priest to say mass in one of the fort's fighting blocks, for open-air services were now too dangerous. The priest reminded the congregation of its duty to defend the Ardennes people's lives and property and asked them whether they were 'ready in this just war that is now beginning to meet

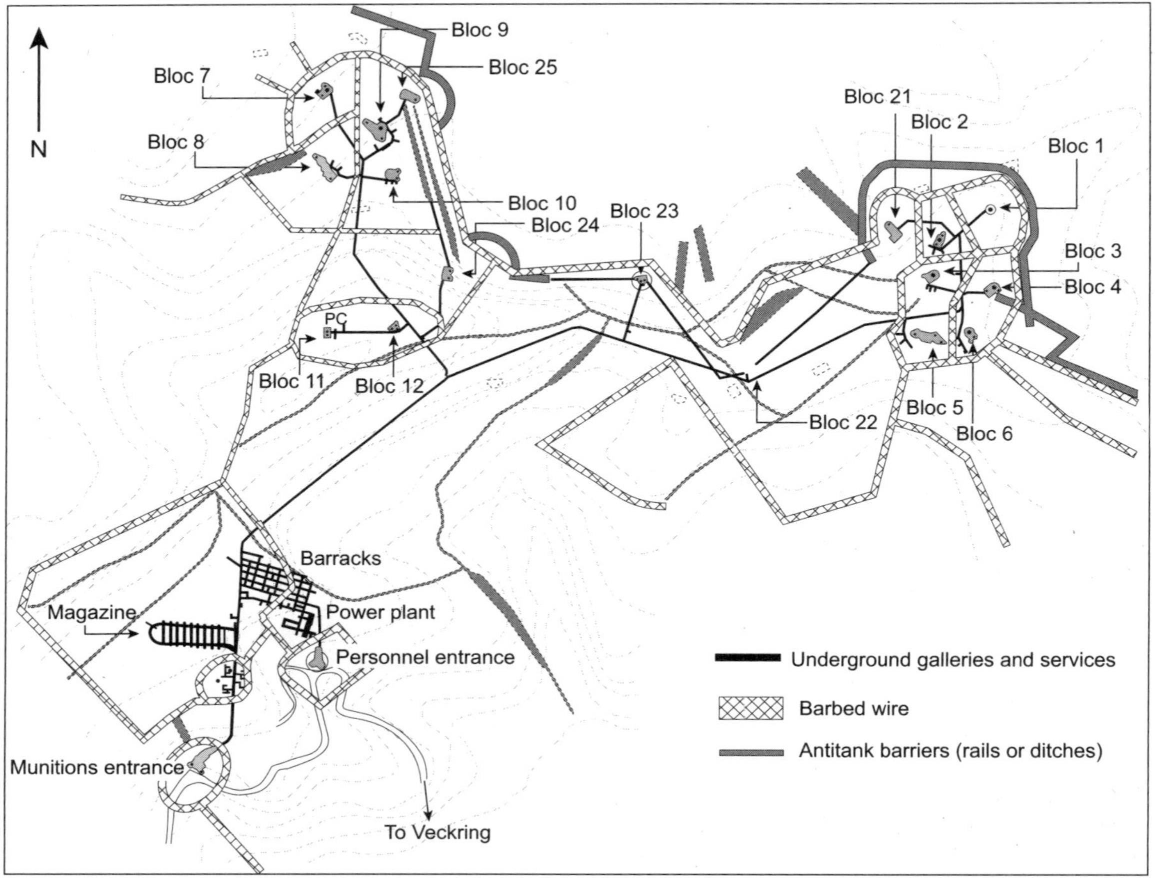

4 Schematic plan of GO-Hackenberg

God'.[5] The next day, gunfire was audible towards Sedan, thirty minutes northwest. That was puzzling. The high command did not consider the area to be vulnerable, for it was covered by thick forest and the River Meuse. Its fortifications were intended merely to delay the enemy long enough to bring up reinforcements. Bourguignon told the priest not to return because the Germans were coming. The young lieutenant did not know that French plans were already unravelling. Arguably, within another day, the Battle of France was lost.

On 10 May, German forces, for whom the high command had ordered 35 million methamphetamine pills, had crossed the Luxembourg, Belgian and Dutch frontiers. Commander-in-Chief General Maurice Gamelin sent the best allied forces to meet what he thought was the main enemy effort in central Belgium and the Netherlands – the Dyle–Breda operation. As Dutch resistance faded, the Germans broke the Belgian centre on the first day and quickly advanced towards the Allies. Although the Allies held the Panzers on the Belgian Plains, it counted for little, for they had entered a trap (Figure 5).

The main German thrust came further south through the Ardennes Forest. On 13 May, infantry crossed the Meuse at three points – Dinant in Belgium and Monthermé and Sedan in France. Panzer divisions then headed west and northwest to the Channel, thus encircling Allied forces in Belgium. Prime Minister Paul Reynaud's replacement of Gamelin with General Maxime Weygand (Gamelin's predecessor as head of the army) did not change Allied fortunes. The armies trapped in Belgium fell back to Dunkirk, from where 338,000 troops were evacuated. The Battle of Dunkirk over, the Germans assaulted French lines on the Rivers Somme and Aisne. They quickly broke through and fanned out over the country. Now the Maginot Line too was encircled. On 10 June, Italy declared war on France. A week later, Marshal Philippe Pétain, hero of the Great War, formed a new government and sued for peace. In July, the marshal became head of the dictatorial and collaborationist Vichy regime.

In the ninth decade after this catastrophe, the Maginot Line remains a symbol of an expensively useless response to real or perceived danger. The myth is used to discredit policies from Donald Trump's wall on the Mexican border, through the US Army's response to artificial-intelligence-powered weaponry and Ukrainian defences against the Russian invasion, to the

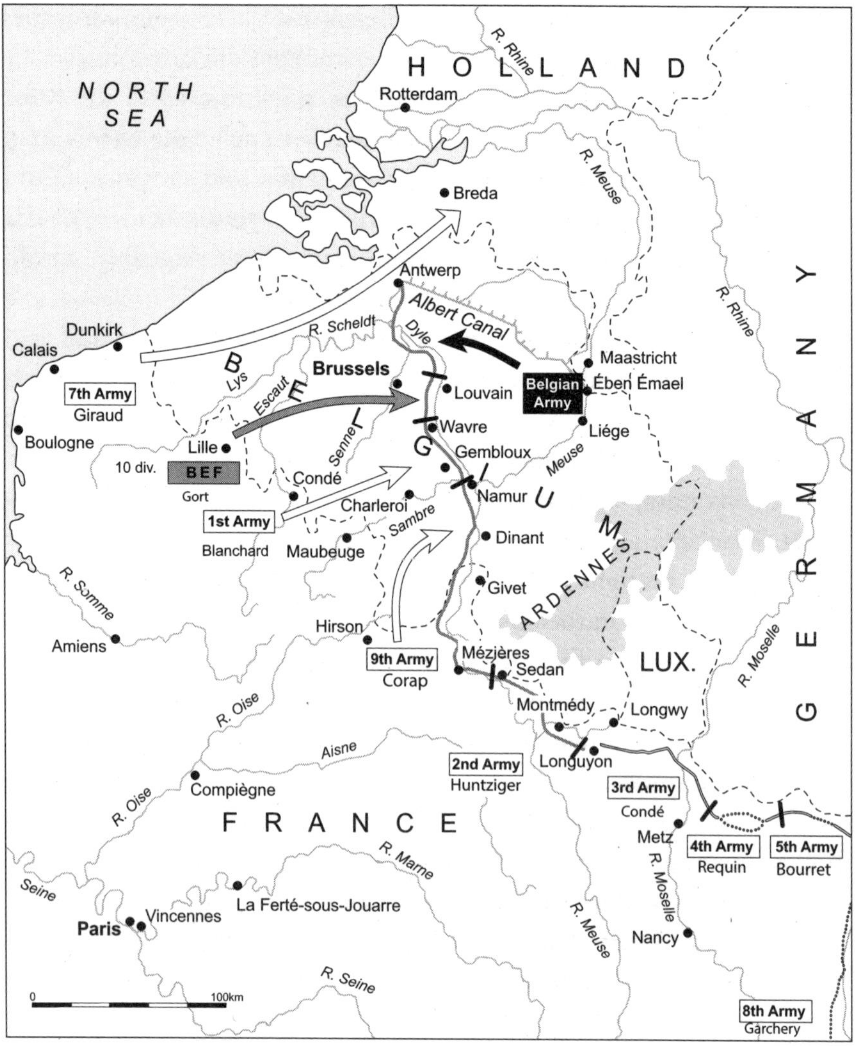

5. Dyle–Breda plan, 10 May 1940.

EU's proposed tariffs on Chinese electric vehicles.[6] As this book went to press, readers of the *Guardian* newspaper's sports pages learned that the Latvian soccer team had erected Maginot Lines in a vain attempt to prevent their English opponents from scoring.[7] According to the myth, French soldiers sat behind invulnerable fortifications, only to be outflanked by a Blitzkrieg armoured attack. Often, the Maginot Line symbolises more than military disaster: it is a sign of French or any other nation's 'decadence', its collective failure to face the challenges of the modern world. The reality is more complex.

The concept of decadence is problematic. It relies on untenable assumptions derived from late nineteenth-century fascination with social biology, evolution and race. It assumes that nations are organisms with bodies, brains and unique mentalities, which evolve through cycles of decay and rebirth – both Pétain and the Resistance saw the world in these terms, and claimed to regenerate decadent, defeated France. A particularly relevant example of this narrative is Jean-Louis Crémieux-Brilhac's monumental study of the defeat, *Les Français de l'an 40*, for its author served on the Maginot Line himself before being captured, escaping from POW camp and joining the Resistance.[8] He declared that 'our country after the physical haemorrhage of '14–'18 and the mental haemorrhage of the interwar years no longer had the "biological" strength to fight a second world war'.[9] But nations do not have collective minds. On the contrary, the following pages reveal that deep divisions among the French shaped the history of the Maginot Line. The fortifications were not even straightforwardly French, for they borrowed from German models and international architectural and construction trends.

Another problem with the decadence concept is that it reads history backwards from the defeat. It falls victim to the *post hoc ergo propter hoc* fallacy, which assumes that one event causes another simply because it comes first. After any failure of a complex society or organisation, it is too easy to find 'a disaster waiting to happen'. Julian Jackson shows that had France lost in 1914 or Britain in 1940, as both nearly did, it would have been easy to find cracks as serious as those supposedly responsible for the French debacle.[10] In reality, it is one thing to identify shortcomings, another to demonstrate that they influenced the course of the battle, and another again to show that those events were decisive. The best accounts of the defeat drop generalisations about French mentalities to illuminate specific issues such as the failure to anticipate the German plan, the advance into Belgium and the Netherlands, poor battlefield intelligence, inflexible command systems and lack of air superiority. Most important was that the Germans concentrated their best divisions against the weakest French forces.[11]

Building on these insights, the first purpose of this book is to ask what part the Maginot Line really played in the defeat. There has been surprisingly little research on this topic. Since it figures in the decadence narrative only as the reflection of a national mentality, it is usually disposed of with a few generalisations. Critics of the decadence thesis show that fortification was a logical response to the circumstances of the time, not an expression of national decline, and that it achieved its objective of forcing the Germans into a risky attack through the Low Countries. Since this narrative focuses on the decisive events in the north, it too marginalises the fortifications. Yet given its immense scale, it is implausible that the Maginot Line was irrelevant to the campaign.

This book's second objective is to widen the question beyond why the French lost, to how and why French military policy and forces assumed the shape they did and why decision-makers made the choices they did. Besides setting aside hindsight, answering these questions requires understanding the relationship between military policy and the political, social and cultural circumstances of the time.

It does not follow from the untenability of the decadence concept that the French (or Allied) defeat can be attributed simply to the generals' mistakes, as some argue. Indeed, the idea of 'mistakes' too easily leads to speculation and even to fantasies about what generals and politicians 'should have done'.[12] In fact, the decadence thesis rightly relates military matters to French politics, society and culture, even if its method of doing so is crude. Both the generals' decisions and their context matter. The hard part is bringing them together. The task is harder still because, as the above short account of the campaign shows, both the role of the static Maginot Line in French plans *and* the dash 200 kilometres into Belgium and the Netherlands must be explained.

The answer proposed here is that French plans, doctrines, weaponry and deployments were the outcome of politicised power struggles and compromises among protagonists with clashing ideas and objectives in which the intentions of French allies and enemies were at best partially known. In this respect, France was not so different to Germany. It is now known that the Blitzkrieg was not pre-planned, but emerged during the battle from conflict within the Wehrmacht about the nature of warfare and indeed of German society.[13] Although the balance of contending parties in France was different, controversies in the two countries were not entirely dissimilar, for no country monopolised key military principles – all agreed that fortification of one type or another was necessary – and armies closely observed one another.

We shall see that although few people rejected fortification in principle, its place in French plans was permanently controversial and evolving. The French did not regard fortification as urgent until at least 1927. Even then, heated debates about its nature delayed construction for years. What was actually built was a compromise, not entirely what anyone had wanted. As the fortifications were completed around 1933–5, priorities shifted towards tanks, planes and manoeuvre, without displacing fortification. By 1939, attitudes to military doctrine and planning were increasingly polarised, with many interjacent positions. New manoeuvrable armoured units were formed and doctrine became more flexible, just as those who favoured appeasing Hitler advocated remaining behind the Maginot Line unless France was directly threatened. Arguably, the disastrous advance into Belgium was a consequence of this conflict.

Notwithstanding, to write the story of the Maginot Line only to refine explanations of the defeat in the north would be to impoverish its history. Abandoning hindsight brings the otherwise irrelevant combat on the Maginot Line into view – after all, it was the site of one of the greatest encirclement battles of the Second World War, possibly second only to Kyiv in 1941 in terms of numbers captured. Much that is most fascinating about the fortifications has a tangential relation to the defeat and to the campaign, or none at all.

The book's third purpose is to tell the story of one of the most significant engineering projects, military or civil, of the early twentieth century. The Maginot Line belongs to histories other than that of the defeat – the transformation of the army into a professionalised, technically trained force in a period of democratisation and rapid technological change. It also belongs to the centralising neoclassical tradition of the French state, updated with modern managerial methods and the architectural genres of the time. It was part of the fight against communism and regional minorities within the army and society. Fortification confronted the technical difficulties of regulating air, water and geomorphology.

These stories had major consequences for the millions of people – and horses – who built and manned the fortifications and fought in them or lived in their shadow.

At this point, it is impossible to avoid the journalist Roger Bruge's eight-volume contribution to the history of the Maginot Line. Bruge was a resister, internee in Buchenwald camp and veteran of the Indochinese and Algerian wars. The commemorative nature of his books, his presentation of the fortifications as 'unconquered' and of the troops as the first resisters, should not detract from their great historical merit. And unlike much of the academic work, Bruge takes seriously the human experience of the Maginot Line.[14]

A fourth purpose of this book is to use a fuller range of contemporary historical methods to understand the history of the Maginot Line and thus bring them to a wider audience. While there is nothing new about using political, cultural and social methods to understand armies and war, *The Maginot Line* integrates histories of the natural environment, technology, emotions, and of architectural, literary and cinematic genres into the narrative.

From a social perspective, the fortifications combined defence of the frontier with an attempt to restore and modernise top-down military command in the face of the upheaval of the Great War and its aftermath. In the military sphere, this revolution took the form of tactical devolution of command to junior officers and NCOs, democratisation of the officer corps and, in 1917, mutinies on the part of ordinary soldiers. In the background was the Russian Revolution and the spread after the war of communist antimilitarism to France, where it met socialist and liberal pacifism. Fortification was the military dimension of a wider conservative response, which paralleled responses in the factories and the political system. It was designed to buttress hierarchical command and to regulate and synchronise human beings and the natural environment in the interests of military, national, social and political defence.

This project was impossible in practice. Many political and military experts opposed the construction of permanent fortifications. Ordinary officers resented serving in them. Rank-and-file soldiers contested top-down command, usually as citizens with democratic rights, sometimes as pacifists or communists. The resulting conflicts among officers and men were complicated by the psychological scars of the Great War on veterans and their families. France as a 'body' was not traumatised, but many individuals were. It proved impossible to 'perfect', as one general put it, the natural environment, air, water and the landscape for military purposes. New technology was fallible.

Many of the inhabitants of Alsace-Lorraine were hostile to fortification, which they believed undermined their province's role as a bridge between France and Germany. They resented the fortification's impact on their livelihoods and the presence of the many 'interior French', foreign and colonial labourers and troops who built and manned them. And while the French authorities saw fortification as a contribution to reintegrating Alsace-Lorraine into France, their suspicion of German speakers led to increasingly authoritarian surveillance that prepared the way for the summary justice of the Vichy dictatorship. Fortifications that were intended to seal the frontier concentrated the tensions of French society and its empire into a strip of land thirty to forty kilometres wide.

Amidst catastrophe in May–June 1940, fortifications originally shaped by conservative political objectives became an obstacle to Pétain's and Weygand's endeavour to rescue the army as the spine of regenerated, authoritarian France. The 400,000-plus soldiers left on the Maginot Line became pawns in their schemes. As the victorious Wehrmacht reduced its pressure on other fronts, Hitler insisted on conquering the famous Maginot Line, capturing its defenders and restoring German rule in Alsace-Lorraine. To repurpose the expression of General Gaston Prételat, who commanded the Maginot Line, that was its tragic destiny. This book tells its story.[15]

Part I
BUILDING THE MAGINOT LINE

1

THE DISPUTED LESSONS OF THE GREAT WAR

One of the most durable clichés regarding the Maginot Line is that generals and politicians wanted to refight the Great War. Hypnotised by their own victory, they supposedly neglected new technologies or incorporated them into old thought systems and ignored the development of Blitzkrieg in Germany. This stereotype reduces the Great War to massacre by shellfire of soldiers cowering in waterlogged holes or advancing in dense lines into machine-gun fire. It makes the fortifications a glorified trench system.

Understandably, the army was keen to learn from the Great War. Yet as former chief of the État-major des armées (EMA – Army General Staff) General Marie Debeney wrote in 1931, 'People talk a lot about the "lessons of the war" and they apply to this expression many contestable conclusions.'[1] Agreement was difficult because the war witnessed unprecedented innovations in tactics, operational methods and weaponry. The conflict evolved through several phases, each marked by debate about how to win or avoid defeat.[2] Fortification was a subject of controversy before, during and after the conflict.

Fortification before 1914

The architects of the Maginot Line worked with a millennial legacy of fortification. It was not simply that, as the future general Charles Gaulle put it, a vulnerable frontier made fortification 'a permanent necessity' for France.[3] Fortifications were comparatively less susceptible to technological obsolescence than other military equipment. To this day, fortifications from trenches to missile silos remain standard elements of the military repertoire.

In the fourteenth century, the invention of artillery rendered obsolete castles with high walls to prevent scaling. Forts were thereafter constructed with lower, thicker walls, protected by earth ramparts and ditches. During his time as Louis XIV's general inspector of fortifications, Sebastien Le Prestre de Vauban (1633–1707) oversaw the construction of no fewer than 160 such strongpoints. He added bastions and crescents, which enabled defenders to fire into the flanks of those approaching the walls and ditches. The V-shaped pincers (*tenailles*) that gave his works their symmetrical star shape enabled defenders to sally forth without being shot at.

Military priorities alone did not determine the design of Vauban's individual forts. Their neoclassical, harmonious architectural forms symbolised the absolute, centralising monarchy's desire to delimit its boundaries and rationalise its administrative structures in the tangle of feudal jurisdictions, religious and ethnic groups that characterised Europe in the days before the creation of nation states. However, fortification was not simply a means to defend and consolidate the royal realm. It was also a jumping-off point for further expansion – hence fortification of Kehl opposite Strasbourg on the Rhine.[4]

Before the late nineteenth century, the French built little new fortification. Revolutionary and Napoleonic armies used existing fortification where serviceable. When besieged, they defended aggressively and broke out if possible. The Napoleonic doctrine of manoeuvre persisted into the nineteenth century, and defeated France could not in any case afford fortification. The only major new strongpoints were the mutually supporting forts constructed in the early 1840s around Lyon and Paris, doubled in the capital with a thirty-eight-kilometre wall. Their value soon became questionable. The improved range of rifled artillery meant that forts close to cities could not prevent bombardment of the population. Air-burst shells disrupted the complex systems within Vauban's forts.

That was the situation in 1870–1, when Prussia and its German allies defeated France. The newly founded German state annexed

Alsace-Lorraine along with Vauban's frontier fortifications. Given France's diplomatic isolation and military weakness, protection of the territory became urgent. Moreover, defence of Vauban's fortifications at Belfort and Bitche were rare successes, which earned German respect. When peace was concluded, their defenders marched out, heads high. Belfort was not annexed with the rest of Alsace, and still retains independent administrative status within France.

In 1874, the government assigned the newly appointed director of military engineers (the Génie militaire), General Raymond Séré de Rivières, the task of rebuilding defences. His 'iron barrier' comprised 166 forts and 43 smaller works stretching along the whole frontier. To keep enemy artillery out of the range of cities, satellite forts were aligned in inner and outer rings. Although Séré's forts abandoned bastions, which Vauban himself had shown were vulnerable to enfilading fire, they retained the neoclassical ethos, often adorned with useless embellishments such as pilasters. They were harmonious polygons with a glacis and ditch. Like Vauban's forts, they dominated the landscape and visibly projected state power.

Strategically, they were designed to keep the enemy away from Paris. Attackers were to be channelled into pockets between 'defensive curtains' – the Stenay Pocket between Verdun and the frontier, and the Charmes Pocket between Verdun and Belfort–Épinal. A second line stopped enemies who penetrated the pockets. Forests were integral to the system, for they provided cover, attenuated the effectiveness of shrapnel and helped to block and channel the enemy. In 1875, the Administration des Eaux et Forêts (AEF – Forest and Water Administration) was militarised, and charged with enhancing the military value of forests and waterways, clearing, planting and diverting where necessary.[5]

No sooner were Séré de Rivières's forts completed than improvements in artillery threatened to make them redundant. Breech-loading steel guns with recoil mechanisms increased range up to six kilometres, while steel shell casings allowed increased powder charges. Powerful new explosives made possible projectiles that exploded on impact. The German 'torpedo-shell' precipitated the 'crisis of 1885'. Masonry could not withstand these projectiles and troops were vulnerable to their toxic gases and the reverberations of explosions.

The invention of industrial-scale concrete and then reinforced concrete provided the solution. Layers of sand, concrete and earth protected forts from at least 210mm shells. Nothing could be exposed directly to shellfire, so infantry required underground galleries, while artillery needed armoured casemates and turrets. The Verdun–Toul and Belfort–Épinal complexes were modernised.[6] Fortification remained an essential part of the syllabus at Saint-Cyr military academy – de Gaulle got his best mark in the subject – and at the École supérieure de guerre.[7]

Yet fortification was no longer a priority, for since the 1890s the doctrine of all-out attack had been in the ascendant. Its theorists attributed the Prussian victory of 1870 to aggressive tactics. A developing alliance with Russia ended France's military isolation, thus making recovery of Alsace-Lorraine feasible. The feats of the colonial army convinced officers that French society required a dose of adventure and daring; the offensive appeared to be the antidote to 'democratic levelling' and to the 'mediocrity' of modern life, supposedly symbolised by the victory of the left-wing Radical-Socialists and their Socialist allies in the 1902 legislative elections.

In the mid-1900s, young staff officers, known as the 'Young Turks' after the nationalist movement of the time, held that the destructive power of automatic artillery and machine guns was exaggerated, or, inconsistently, that new weapons increased attackers' advantage. Troops would form up one pace apart and strike frontally at the heart of the enemy line, firing in salvoes rather than individually, ultimately driving the enemy off with the bayonet. Cover, hiding and crawling were spurned as unmanly. Whereas other European armies adopted less visible khaki or grey uniforms, the French stuck to bright colours.

General Ferdinand Foch, professor of military history at the École supérieure de guerre in 1895–1901, advocated a more cautious form of the offensive, conforming more closely to the Napoleonic doctrine of outflanking and/or concentrating forces on the enemy's weak point. As an artillery officer trained at the elite engineering school, the École polytechnique, he did not rely on élan alone. Although like many officers Foch was a Catholic conservative, unsympathetic to the anticlerical Republic, in 1908, moderate-left Premier Georges Clemenceau made him commander of the École supérieure de guerre.[8] The appointment in 1911 of General Joseph Joffre to lead the army confirmed the triumph of offensive doctrine, though it was always contested.

Colonels Pétain and Debeney, professors at the École de guerre, advocated careful forward movement covered by artillery. Citing the precedent of the recent Russo-Japanese War, they highlighted the defensive power of machine guns and rapid-fire artillery and advocated dispersal of troops, cover and camouflage.[9] Since these officers favoured improvised field fortification, they were no more interested in permanent fortifications than their opponents. Those on the Belgian frontier were especially neglected, despite Séré de Rivières's warning that failure to fortify the north would encourage the Germans to invade through Belgium.[10]

The Offensive and the Defensive, 1914–1918

In August 1914, Joffre concentrated the army in front of Séré's fortifications rather than under their protection, thus underlining their irrelevance. His forces advanced into the Ardennes, Lorraine and Alsace. Commanders attacked recklessly, often without prior reconnaissance or artillery cover. Red-trousered waves were cut down by hidden machine guns and long-range artillery. The Germans then attacked their flanks and destroyed them. Attackers proved more vulnerable than defenders to modern firepower.

As the French faltered in Alsace, the Germans progressed rapidly in Belgium, easily overcoming unmodernised fortifications. In September, they nearly reached Paris, but were stopped on the Marne, for their supply lines were overstretched and they were obliged to send troops to the eastern front. Also, the French imitated German tactics, making better use of artillery and machine guns and of field fortification. After the Marne, the opposing armies tried and failed to outflank each other in a race to the sea. By the end of the year, the front had settled down into lines of trenches.

Field fortifications became increasingly elaborate. Trenches zigzagged to protect occupants from enfilading fire and to enable sealing in case of enemy infiltration. Fortified, often concrete, machine-gun and light-artillery posts were built at key points. Perpendicular or transversal communication trenches (*boyaux*) permitted movement between lines of trenches and command posts. Shelters for infantry, magazines and command posts were dug metres into the ground and covered with earth, rails, logs, concrete and stones. The army abandoned red trousers, but only for the somewhat less visible sky blue, for France did not have the dyes required for khaki. The French pioneered camouflage, calling on artists from cubists to art nouveau interior designers.[11]

The imperatives of dispersal and camouflage appeared to confirm that visible permanent fortification was outmoded. In the north, the unmodernised Belgian forts of Liège and Namur fell rapidly. Séré's neglected forts of Maubeuge, Longwy and Lille proved no match for the Germans' huge 420mm Big Bertha artillery. On the German frontier, the modernised fort of Manonvillier also fell, though it was an isolated strongpoint designed only to delay enemy entry into the Charmes gap. Guns and garrisons were removed from forts, including those of Verdun, and sent to the campaign army. Joffre's instruction of 9 August 1915 stipulated that forts must become strongpoints within continuous fronts – if they were not so integrated, they had no role.

In reality, the supposed obsolescence of permanent fortification was debatable, as Foch's experience showed. On mobilisation, his XX Corps was ordered to improve the defences of Nancy. Dismissive of fortification, he complied half-heartedly. When the offensive began, he rashly advanced into a pocket within German fortifications – exactly the kind of trap set by Séré de Rivières for the Germans. Disaster was avoided only by the enemy's impatience to attack before the jaws closed.

As for French fortifications, Verdun–Toul held out with the exception of Saint-Mihiel. French armies retreating from Alsace-Lorraine held on at neglected second-line fortifications. After the war, two senior officers were court-martialled for having surrendered Maubeuge too easily, but Joffre testified that its resistance diverted German troops from the Marne and helped the French to prevail. Ironically, after their Marne defeat, the Germans retreated to French fortifications on the Brimont and Brimu massifs, where they stayed until 1917.[12]

Some French officers were impressed by German field fortifications, sometimes so elaborate that they resembled permanent structures. Staff officer Colonel Edmond Buat, once a Young Turk, became an enthusiast. He visited a captured concreted gallery lit by electrical generators at Mort-Homme near Verdun, 'the Kronprinz'. It was six metres wide, up to three metres high and over a kilometre in length. Through it ran a narrow-gauge railway. He compared it favourably with French trenches.[13] For the French, trenches were temporary expedients prior to expelling the invader.

The offensive remained in the ascendant, albeit represented chiefly by the more prudent Foch. Subsequent counterattacks restored credit lost in his near disaster in Alsace. He was promoted to command the 9th Army on the Marne, where he implemented his theories of counterattack. After this success, Joffre gave Foch command of the northern armies, effectively making him his deputy.[14]

Rather than rely simply on the élan of the attacking infantry, Foch advocated the 'methodical' and 'scientific conduct of the battle'. This doctrine entailed massing light artillery close to the front, often mounted in motor vehicles, and using mortars to lob shells into trenches.[15] In September 1915, however, simultaneous attacks in Artois and Champagne failed, the last offensives in which troops advanced with bands and standards led by senior officers armed with rifles and fixed bayonets. In both cases, German defence in depth – echeloned defence in successive lines – frustrated the attackers. Bombardment permitted infantry to take the first lines, but second and third lines were sited out of range, often on reverse slopes. Taking them required moving up artillery, reorganisation and another long bombardment, by which time the Germans had constructed new second and third lines. Each preparation took several days because the French lacked rapid-fire heavy guns. (The Germans achieved the same in a few hours.)

Pétain, now a general, was among the first on the French side to imitate defence in depth. In the first years of the war, troops were ordered never to cede terrain. Men were packed into the first line, where they were vulnerable to artillery and frequently overrun.[16] In August 1915, Buat recorded a visit to second and third lines in Pétain's sector. Hitherto neglected, they were now 'prettied up with blockhouses and machine guns under concrete, which singularly strengthen the defence'.[17] In the front line, he found a field of barbed wire, up to 500 metres deep – 'the passive obstacle in all its value; no human force could clear it without the defenders knowing; a few men were enough to guard it'.[18]

Pétain soon won a reputation for being 'economical' with the lives of his men.[19] President of the Republic Raymond Poincaré, who met Pétain then, described him as 'reserved' but was impressed by the 'calm, force, and clarity' of his explanations, and remarked that 'only a slight nervous movement of the eyelids shows from time to time that underneath his very cold appearance the general hides an ardent and secretly emotive nature'.[20] Those who knew Pétain, even the most favourably disposed, agreed that he was also pessimistic and inclined to focus on obstacles. He would attack only when all conditions had been fulfilled. However, Joffre and Foch planned new offensives for 1916, in the hope that British forces, now present in substantial numbers, would tip the balance.

In February 1916, the German attack at Verdun, where they captured the almost undefended Douaumont fort, pre-empted French plans. To stem the ensuing panic, Joffre sent for Pétain, inadvertently making the reputation of the man who became his most serious rival. Pétain did launch an attempt to recapture Douaumont – in which de Gaulle was wounded and captured – but did not repeat the experience. Other generals began to doubt his attacking spirit.[21] In April, the irate Joffre promoted Pétain to command Army Group Centre, which included Verdun. To Verdun itself, he sent the more offensively minded General Robert Nivelle. Despite Pétain's micro-management, Nivelle and his successor General Charles Mangin retook the lost ground.[22]

Verdun's consequences for the future of permanent fortification were open to dispute. On the one hand, the battle seemingly confirmed the validity of Joffre's August 1915 instruction, for Verdun was merely one strongpoint in a continuous front. Furthermore, soldiers disliked permanent fortification. Conditions inside were atrocious.[23] A junior officer described a railway tunnel within the Verdun fortifications, the 'antechamber to hell':

> Two or three thousand men living in there without air, without light, ambulances and troops mixed up, satisfying all their needs including life's most intimate, in the long corridor. Horses, mules

> piled up. A fetid mud, sometimes up to the ankles, giving off a hideous odour, a heavy air, opaque. Anyone who hasn't heard the death rattles of the wounded on the battlefield, without medical help, drinking their urine to relieve their thirst, and the life of men in the Metz–Verdun tunnel, has seen nothing of war.[24]

A few weeks after the officer's visit, between four and five hundred men were killed by an ammunition explosion in the tunnel. However difficult conditions in trenches were, soldiers felt less vulnerable there.

On the other hand, the ease with which the Germans captured Douaumont did not necessarily show its weakness. It was held only by a token force. General Adolphe Guillaumat, future architect of the Maginot Line, was convinced that the Germans attacked Verdun only because the sector was weak.[25] Moreover, the French held the Vaux satellite fort for longer than they had Douaumont, and ultimately the Germans failed before the rearmed Souville satellite. Modernised forts proved their resistance even to 420mm artillery. Turreted artillery was never silenced.

The French were impressed by the Germans' improvement of Douaumont during their short tenure. The writer Henri Bordeaux, mobilised as a reserve officer, entered the fort after its recapture. He mentioned the smell of corpses, but also newly installed telephone and radio and a fat grey cat. Yet in his book *La délivrance de Verdun*, published seventeen years later, he depicted filth and chaos. In response, Capitaine du Génie Fernand Ducom wrote,

> I must admit that I didn't see Douaumont in this unengaging condition. In reality, the Germans had organised their conquest admirably. Electric lamps with reflectors spread a brilliant light; comfortable beds were installed in all the rooms; all sorts of equipment was installed (telephones, radios, oxygen machines to combat gas, all of German manufacture); the corridors were clean, and the air did not stink, contrary to what has been written. The fort had a power plant, a 'Lazarett' (sick bay) and even an officers' mess.[26]

On 12 March 1916, Joffre ordered that fortifications were to be repaired and rearmed. Field commanders also improvised improvements. At the

Moulainville satellite fort, the commander ordered the men to dig deep shafts and galleries to link combat positions and a 700-metre tunnel to enable troops to leave the fort during bombardments. In 1917, the high command carried out improvements at Verdun. Following the explosion at the aforementioned Metz–Verdun tunnel, commanders installed lighting, duckboards, latrines and a triple rank of bunks below which men and supplies could circulate.[27] All this foreshadowed the Maginot Line. Yet operationally, attack remained the priority.

Thanks to the demands of Verdun, the Somme offensive was scaled down and British divisions outnumbered French. Rather than send successive waves into the same point, the new plan was to wear the enemy down by massive attacks over a lengthy period at different points along a forty-kilometre front. Heavy artillery, repositioned after each wave, would destroy successive enemy positions. Only then would the infantry advance.[28] The attack stalled with enormous losses. The British repeated many of the mistakes that the French had made in 1914–15 and suffered accordingly. The French usually dispersed their infantry, but artillery preparation was still too slow for surprise and second lines remained nearly impossible to breach.[29]

Criticism of Joffre for failures at Verdun and on the Somme intensified. Pétain and Foch probably criticised their chief to politicians.[30] Yet neither benefited. When Joffre was finally replaced in December 1916, Foch went too. Much to his displeasure, Pétain was passed over in favour of Nivelle, impenitent believer in the offensive. Indeed, advocates of the offensive claimed that overreliance on artillery on the Somme had deprived the infantry of 'élan'.

Nivelle prepared a new offensive for April 1917 with still greater resources. Infantry would advance behind another innovation, the rolling barrage. Field commanders were given more room to exploit successes. Senegalese troops – who, according to racist prejudice, were brave in the attack – were dispersed in the line to encourage French units to advance. Other French units ensured that Senegalese troops did not run, for racist thinking also held that reckless attack quickly descended into panic.[31]

Nivelle's catastrophic Chemin des Dames offensive caused a deep crisis of command. Nivelle's order to resume the attack provoked soldiers in around 60–70 of 110 divisions to refuse to go into the line. Mutinies coincided with strikes in the war industries and calls for a negotiated peace. The February Revolution in Russia raised hopes for an end to the war. At the same time, junior officers and NCOs criticised the high command for failure to understand that modern war required devolved tactical command. This latter conflict, never resolved, requires attention, for it shaped the Maginot Line.

Devolved Command and Organisational Science

In his brilliant study, *La chair et l'acier*, General Michel Goya, a former NCO, described the delegation of tactical command during the war. Before 1914, a few officers insisted that defence against automatic weapons required dispersal of troops, cover and camouflage. Yet the high command remained convinced that troops would fight only if the certainty of punishment incited more fear than the possibility of death in combat – as General Adolphe Messimy, war minister in August 1914, put it: 'Give me the guillotine, and I'll give you victory.' Executions for 'cowardice' were most numerous during the 1914 war of manoeuvre, during which sword- and revolver-waving officers encouraged their men to attack, with the consequences we know.

Units spontaneously adapted their tactics. They organised soldiers into smaller groups commanded by junior officers and even sergeants. More use was made of light machine guns; assaulting infantry were less densely packed, and advanced in bounds under cover fire. Specialist groups reconnoitred enemy positions and raided them to capture prisoners for interrogation. Infantry units included 'specialist' grenadiers, telephonists, machine gunners and so forth alongside traditional riflemen.[32] Polytechnic-trained junior officers, reserve officers unaware of military orthodoxy and mobilised peasants and workers used their ingenuity and practical experience to cobble together new weapons. In January 1916, a high-command circular endorsed these innovations and admitted that men could not charge into automatic fire. On receiving it, a captain wrote home that he was astonished that it had taken eighteen months to recognise this truth.[33]

Tactical revolution coincided with displacement of career officers, for by late 1915 over half were dead or invalided, and over half of those remaining were non-combatants. They were replaced at the front by reserve officers, young graduates of the military schools and NCOs promoted from the ranks, whose relationship with soldiers was different. In the front line, discipline became more relaxed. The 'community of the trenches' was not entirely mythical; soldiers' letters show much mutual praise of officers and men.[34] The war experience of two politicians who later played vital roles in the construction of the Maginot Line illustrates the changing complexion of the army.

In 1914, André Maginot, already a centre-right republican deputy, was mobilised as a sergeant, despite his upper-bourgeois background. His lowly rank earned him an enduring reputation for republican egalitarianism, but might have had more to do with his superiors' opinion of him during his military service: 'very vigorous, very intelligent, very good swimmer and fencer', but 'hardly the military type'.[35] During the war, Maginot's issue with discipline proved useful. He formed a reconnaissance group from local hunters, poachers and daredevils and won the Médaille militaire for bravery. Then, on 9 November 1914, German troops ambushed his men. Six were killed and Maginot received two bullets in his left leg. He dragged himself behind a farmyard trough and was rescued only when the Germans were hit by friendly fire. Maginot was invalided out of the army with the Légion d'honneur and a citation signed by Pétain. He forever walked with two sticks.[36] He never experienced trench warfare and was never emotionally committed to fortification or even defence.

As a baker's son from Carpentras in Provence, Édouard Daladier, future prime minister and immovable war minister, was a pure product of republican and democratic meritocracy. He had been ranked first nationally in the demanding Agrégation examination, and his appointment as history professor in a Nîmes lycée in 1909 might have been the first step in a fine academic career. Politics attracted him more, however. He stood unsuccessfully for parliament in 1914 as an opponent of three-year military service. After he was mobilised as a sergeant, his first unit was decimated in the Arras sector. In 1916, serving in the Bois d'Avocourt on the Verdun battlefield, he was wounded, decorated and promoted to lieutenant. By the end of the war, he had been wounded several more times, winning three citations and the Légion d'honneur. Throughout his political life, Daladier celebrated the cult of the *poilu* (hairy one), the ordinary soldier, and the republican ideal of the armed nation and citizen army, but spoke little of his personal experience.[37] He did claim that in the Bois d'Avocourt he had fraternised with German soldiers, with whom he evoked the possibility of a better postwar world.[38]

The democratisation and devolution of tactical command epitomised by Maginot and Daladier coincided with a quite contrary trend: the use of top-down managerial techniques, the 'sciences of organisation'. These emerged in the decade before the war in the growing state administration, new mass armies and big corporations. For different reasons, organisational science appealed across the political spectrum. For conservatives, it was an alternative to 'socialist' planning. It regulated the market while preserving the power of managers and officers in the face of free education, trade-union pressure for workers' self-government and demands for democratisation of the officer corps. Some socialists were also attracted to organisational science as a step towards a planned economy, run in the interests of the people. Their leader, Jean Jaurès (murdered in August 1914), envisaged a technically trained, meritocratic, democratically recruited officer corps, better equipped to lead citizen-soldiers than the distant, poorly trained traditional officer.[39] Both versions of organisational science shaped the postwar army and the Maginot Line.

The leading theorist of management was Henri Fayol, director-general of a big mining and metallurgy firm. He applied monarchical and military models to the factory, updated with fashionable ideas about the importance of the 'leader' (the 'chef'), who supposedly possessed a special ability to direct the 'crowd'. For Fayol, the businessman-manager alone had the foresight and wide outlook necessary to understand the strategy of the organisation. He therefore insisted on 'unity of command', and that the leader should transmit orders downwards through heads of department and supervisors with limited room for initiative to workers who simply executed orders.[40] Fayol was responsible also for a keystone of managerial science: that leadership skills were transferable between military, economic and political organisations.[41]

Fayol's ideas complemented the American F.W. Taylor's methods of rationalised, standardised mass production, known in France as 'the organisation of work'. Time-and-motion studies broke complex tasks into simply executed gestures, easily learned and performed quasi-automatically at the pace of the machine. Besides increasing productivity (*rendement*), this subdivision reinforced the manager's monopoly on knowledge of the whole. As in Fayol's system, workers were reduced to unreflecting extensions of the machine. However, organisers held that efficiency and mass production would improve workers' prosperity and conditions, thus turning them away from socialism. Before 1914, neither Fayolist nor Taylorist methods were widely implemented, though they were used in the War Ministry. They became integral to the prosecution of total war.

Initially, neither generals nor politicians had expected total war. Having staked everything on the standing army winning a quick victory, they prioritised neither reserves (unlike the Germans) nor the war economy. To meet these challenges and mobilise the entire nation for a long war, generals and politicians turned to organisational science.

Fayol's *Administration industrielle et générale*, published in 1916, was an immediate success. Military officers rarely endorsed Fayolism explicitly, for they did not see themselves as 'administrators'. Nonetheless, organisational science vocabulary became so common in military documents that it would be tedious to point out each recurrence. Officers spoke of industrialising the army, just as huge war factories employed mobilised workers under military discipline. Staff officers measured the productivity of weapons and calculated the number of shells required to neutralise different types of position.[42] Digging trenches was 'organising the terrain'. One journalist described the army as 'a sort of Taylor system: we know that this system rests on a minute division of labour, specialisation and training of all workers, and constant surveillance of the accomplished task'.[43] Although 'industrial warfare' was often criticised as socialist, bureaucratic and ponderous, its purpose was efficient, rapid execution without waste.

In the first two years of the war, Joffre as commander-in-chief and the centre-right Alexandre Millerand as war minister ran the sort of military–state–business partnership that conservative organisationalists envisaged. The Grand quartier général (GQG – General Headquarters in the Army Zone) enjoyed powers extending well beyond the military field, negotiating contracts for production with business organisations, notably in the steel industry. Subsequently, the Socialist Albert Thomas, as under-secretary for armaments and then minister, built state-owned, Taylorised factories, which he ran in partnership with business and the trade unions.

Colonel Buat epitomised the officer-organiser. He began the war as head of Millerand's military cabinet. After Millerand's fall in October 1915, he briefly commanded in the field before returning to the GQG as deputy major-general, where his superior, General Noël de Castelnau, a very right-wing Catholic officer whom Buat despised, dismissed him as a 'poet' with chimerical ideas.[44] In May 1916, promoted to general, Buat left again to command a division in the field.[45] In January 1917, he developed his organisationalist skills as commander of the General Artillery Reserve. He praised his chief of staff, a reserve major, for having brought his experience as an 'organiser' from the gas and electricity industry.[46] By the end of the war, Buat was major-general at the GQG, a body he described in Fayolist and Taylorist terms as a 'division of labour with coordination at a higher level'.[47]

Organisationalism was not just an academic and technical doctrine: it was part of avant-garde culture. It was epitomised by futurist fascination with the speed of motor vehicles and aircraft, and by cubism, which abandoned the single viewpoint to capture the way in which the appearance of objects changed with the position of the viewer. Futurism and cubism foreshadowed abstraction, but in fact the machinery, motor vehicles and aircraft they depicted depended on mathematics, scientific rigour and standardised production. Cubist paintings of the same object from different perspectives shared a purpose with the mechanical blueprint.

Before the war, thirty-five-year-old painter Fernand Léger enjoyed a reputation in futurist and cubist circles. He was mobilised in 1914, originally as a sapper, then as a stretcher-bearer, and served at Verdun in 1916. He sketched military equipment and later claimed that the mere 'sight of the breech of a 75mm gun in the sunlight' had caused him to leave abstraction behind.[48] He developed the 'machine-art' for which he is best known. Among his most impressive works is *La partie de cartes* (The card game), painted in 1917 while recovering from gassing, which blurs the distinction between man and machine. There is another side to this painting, however, which is that Léger was traumatised by his experience, for the players' exposed internal organs and the partial figures in the background recall the mangled bodies he collected from the battlefield. He remarked darkly that the war made him even more cubist, for battle was perfect for more or less cleanly dividing a chap into several parts and scattering them to the four points of the compass.[49] Even so, Léger's paintings testify to the pervasiveness of the industrial, Taylorised aesthetic – as do the increasingly numerous celebratory images of tanks, aircraft and artillery pieces in the illustrated magazine *Miroir*.[50]

Organisational science conflicted with the devolution of command. By 1916, junior officers were highly critical of the 'unreality' of the high command's methods. While they also decried politicians, many complained to them. Mobilised parliamentarians, including Maginot, future centre-right Prime Minister André Tardieu and the Catholic conservative Émile Driant (killed at Verdun), became the core of a 'national opposition'. Another of their number, Abel Ferry (killed on parliamentary inspection in 1917), dismissed the general staff as 'professors' and 'theoreticians', writing in his diary,

> We need to make experience on the ground penetrate above.
>
> It's a war of details, of little victories. The war in the trenches is a war of small commands, platoon commanders, company commanders and colonels at most.
>
> The officers of the general staff who did not imagine this war, who did not study it, who have not experienced it, know nothing about it.[51]

Senior field commanders such as Guillaumat agreed that the high command possessed a theoretical view of war derived from map exercises.[52] To appease critics, the high command floated plans to exchange officers between the front and the field. Buat objected that only the 'competent' could manage the war. He attributed the contrary view that anyone could do so to 'regimental commanders' and 'parliamentary mediocrities'.[53]

These schemes did not assuage discontent. The national opposition largely opposed Nivelle's appointment. For Ferry, he was the candidate of the general staff. His own preference was for Pétain, whom he claimed was the choice of the army – meaning junior officers and NCOs. Pétain, who had not hidden his opposition to Nivelle's offensive, was praised in the press for having made the 'least costly' contribution. And although Pétain criticized politicians, he cultivated War Minister Paul Painlevé, the two men's careers remaining linked into the years in which the Maginot Line was planned. In the War Cabinet, Painlevé's support for Pétain prevailed over Interior Minister Louis Malvy's denunciation of him as a danger to the Republic. Only one member of the national opposition opposed Pétain's appointment: Minister of Colonies Maginot dismissed the Painlevé–Pétain tandem as defeatist. When on 15 May 1917 the Comité de guerre appointed Pétain general-in-chief, Maginot threw his crutch on the table in disgust.[54]

Pétain owed his appointment to the support of key political figures, the appeal of his defensive methods amidst military crisis and his willingness to take up the grievances of junior officers and ordinary soldiers. His solutions to the crisis fundamentally marked his priorities for the rest of his life and are vital to understanding the history of the Maginot Line. He attributed the mutinies to exploitation of the genuine grievances of patriotic soldiers by socialist 'agitators'. To fight these agitators, he combined repression with improving troop conditions. 'Bad apples' were supposedly eliminated by 26–30 executions and 2,870 other sentences. He simultaneously facilitated leave, and improved billets and food (while restricting the sale of wine). Commanders tolerated relaxed discipline at the front, thus acknowledging the practical devolution of command and social transformation of the army, but reinforced discipline in depots, trains and railway stations. To meet troops' demand for 'fairness' in sacrifice and appease junior officers, he made staff officers serve at the front.[55]

Pétain assured the troops that while there would be no compromise peace, there would be no more attempts at the decisive breakthrough. Victory would await British and American reinforcements and sufficient tanks, aircraft and rapid-fire long-range artillery. He endorsed devolved command but subjected it to strict rules, borrowing from Foch the doctrine of the scientific, conducted and methodical battle minus expectation of a breakthrough. Offensive operations were limited to attrition of the enemy with minimum losses. Pétain's three offensives of 1917 were each preceded by six days of artillery preparation and used large numbers of aircraft and tanks. They won relatively little ground, but German losses were far greater than French.

From October 1917, defence became the priority, for Lenin's seizure of power put Russia out of the war and freed the Germans to take the offensive in the West. Pétain ordered army intelligence, the Deuxième Bureau, to publicise defence in depth. Directive no. 4 of 22 December ordered lightly held front lines and second and third lines well back. Behind these defences, a network of light railways, roads and telephone lines facilitated command, troop movement and resupply from an economy totally mobilised for war. Without being a theoretician, Pétain embraced the organisationalist vocabulary of efficiency and rapidity.

Pétain's tactics were contested. Foch, despite being his chief of staff, criticised defensiveness. Many officers refused to envisage evacuating terrain that had been recaptured at great cost.[56] Controversy intensified in the crisis of the German offensives of spring 1918. On 21 March, the enemy threatened to split the British and French armies at Amiens. Pétain hesitated between reinforcing the British and retreat to cover Paris, but the government backed Foch's insistence on sending all reserves to reinforce the British. On 26 March, the Allies made Foch commander of an allied reserve and then supreme commander of allied forces, leaving Pétain to command French operations.

The Germans resumed their offensive on 27 May, this time breaking through the French. The results of Directive no. 4 were mixed. General Henri Gouroud, who implemented the instructions fully, held out. On the Aisne, General Denis Duchêne, with Foch's connivance, overloaded his first line, which was overrun.[57] As foreseen by Pétain's critics, units hastily brought into the line lacked the time as much as the will to execute his complex instructions. Pétain ordered retreat to the second position, once again advising the government to quit Paris. Poincaré demanded Pétain's resignation, but Clemenceau stood by him, hoping that sacking some of his advisors would break the spell of pessimism.

Relations between Pétain and Foch deteriorated. As individuals, they had little in common. Pétain was a religiously lukewarm womaniser of peasant origin, whereas Foch was a bourgeois, Jesuit-educated family man. While Pétain had hardly left France, Foch had long experience of working with the British during his command on the northern front. According to Lloyd George, 'In the March crisis, Haig and Pétain were disconcerted and incapable of any decision and Foch stood up like a giant.'[58] The Allies were saved by greater mobility. Lack of horses had forced the French artillery, infantry and even the cavalry to motorise, allowing mobile reserves to block the Germans. Decentralisation allowed lower commanders to call up artillery support.[59]

In late June, the Germans once more pressed on the Marne and Pétain was again accused of excessive caution. To encourage him, Foch and Clemenceau made Buat his major-general.[60] When the Germans attacked, Buat persuaded Pétain to counterattack. This turning point also owed something to devolved command. On 14 July 1918, a raid brought back twenty-seven prisoners and other intelligence that permitted disruption of the German offensive. Among the most courageous participants was 'elite grenadier' Sergeant Joseph Darnand, of whom we shall hear more.[61]

On 18 July, counterattack Villars–Cottet took place after a shorter than usual artillery preparation using 800 aircraft and 300 tanks. For the first time, US troops participated on a large scale and helped to turn the tide. Whereas in 1914 the Germans had been able to retreat safely from the Marne, the Allies' mobility and air superiority now allowed them to stick to their tails. The Allies implemented a series of limited attacks designed to disorganise German lines rather than achieve breakthrough. The German offensive was in any case a desperate gamble with a crumbling war machine and home front. On 19 October, Foch ordered a general offensive, and in less than a month the war was over. French troops entered Alsace-Lorraine. On 7 December, in Metz, Pétain received his marshal's baton from Poincaré, whose speech, according to one journalist, showed that the national soul had passed into him. The left-wing socialist and future communist, Marcel Cachin, heard the cry of enslaved Alsace-Lorraine 'acclaiming the return of liberty', but warned administrators, soldiers and chauvinists to be sensitive to the province's difference.[62]

Contested Legacies

The foregoing pages reveal the crudeness of the notion that the Maginot Line reflected a desire to refight the Great War. The conflict bequeathed multiple possibilities, open to reinterpretation in new circumstances, technological innovation, social and political conflict and personal rivalries. Few disputed that the next war should not be fought on French soil but in occupied Germany or failing that, Belgium. Otherwise, debate between offence and defence persisted in the Pétain–Foch rivalry, institutionalised after the war in patronage and promotions. Nevertheless, doctrinal controversies burst the bounds of a binary opposition between defence and manoeuvre.

Tactical devolution conflicted with top-down organisational science. While most senior officers wished to re-establish hierarchical command, junior officers trained in the old military schools were torn between antipathy to the high command and dislike of reserve officers and those promoted from the ranks. The war also established the cult of the democratic, republican citizen-soldier, of the *poilu*, institutionalised in the veteran movement. Pétain's compromise between organisational control, the methodical and conducted battle and tactical devolution was fragile.

As for fortification, the war demonstrated the value both of fieldworks integrated into the landscape and of modernised permanent fortification dominating it. The dispute between advocates of strong front lines and echeloned defence continued into the French defeat in 1940 and in other armies thereafter. The supposed lessons of Verdun were endlessly disputed. The recovery of Alsace-Lorraine enabled study of German fortifications, which, unlike centralised French fortifications, were dispersed in the terrain. Little wonder that agreeing a fortification programme required ten years of controversy.

2

THE DECISION TO FORTIFY, 1919–1930

In his brief victory speech to the Chamber of Deputies on 11 November 1918, Prime Minister Clemenceau rendered homage to 'our great dead' and declared that he welcomed in advance the survivors as they marched along the boulevards to the Arc de Triomphe. He expected of them a great work of social reconstruction.[1] Newspapers reminded the Chamber that he was the sole survivor of the deputies who in 1871 had protested against the cession of Alsace-Lorraine to Germany. His speech over, the entire chamber sang the national anthem, 'La Marseillaise', which Claude-Joseph Rouget de Lisle had composed in Strasbourg. Outside the Chamber, ceremonial guns sounded. Across the Seine on the Place de la Concorde, flowers replaced the black drapes that had hitherto shrouded the statues of Strasbourg and Metz.[2]

France's leaders now faced the task of winning the peace and defending Alsace-Lorraine – a challenge, given the cost of victory. Besides the 1,375,800 men killed, another 3 million were wounded, 1.1 million of them severely. Disabled veterans begged on the streets. In the ten liberated departments, vast tracts of agricultural land and whole towns and villages were ruined, perhaps wiped from the map. As they retreated, the Germans flooded mines, dismantled factories and machine-gunned forests to make timber unusable. France had sold its gold reserves and contracted enormous debts. Tax income had hardly increased, yet the state faced unprecedented demands for reconstruction and support for war victims. Twenty-two per cent of mobilised primary school teachers had been killed. Many men, women and children were traumatised. In 1922, War Minister Maginot told parliament, 'If there is one thing that's henceforth agreed about modern warfare, it's that victory is insufficient to compensate a people for the damage of invasion.'[3]

It is sometimes said that the Maginot Line derived from the trauma of war, and there is no denying its psychological and political legacy. There was much antiwar sentiment. The growing Communist Party was antimilitarist, though not against political violence or war waged by communist states. Pacifism, opposition to war itself, was widespread in the Socialist and moderate-left Radical-Socialist parties, though most accepted that France must defend itself if attacked. The veteran movement also contained a strong pacifist tendency, and its identification with the ordinary soldier shaded into dislike of regular officers. Even the right accepted that military service must be reduced.

The extent of pacifism should not obscure the widespread desire to maintain military superiority over Germany, which was anyway weakened by its massive death toll, economic crisis and near civil war. The Versailles Treaty, signed on 28 June 1919, imposed reparations on Germany and confirmed the cession of Alsace-Lorraine to France and the loss of other lands to Poland, Belgium and Denmark. Britain and France received German colonies under League of Nations mandate, supposedly to prepare them for independence. Although France did not obtain the desired annexation, detachment or permanent occupation of the left bank of the Rhine (present-day Rhineland–Palatinate/Rheinland–Pfalz), the Allies were to jointly occupy it until 1935, or 1930 if Germany proved cooperative. After evacuation, the German banks of the Rhine were to be permanently demilitarised, while the French were entitled to fortify their bank in Alsace-Lorraine. The German army, the Reichswehr, was reduced to a professional force of 100,000 men without tanks, planes or general staff. Germany's chief ally, the Austro-Hungarian Empire, collapsed, and its successor states – Poland, Yugoslavia and Czechoslovakia – were allied to France. Belgium, neutral before 1914, became France's ally. The French were understandably reluctant to fight another war on national territory, but were quite ready to do so in Germany. And France appears even less pacifist in light of the unbroken series of vicious colonial wars it fought in Morocco, Indochina and Syria. Maintaining control over the empire was vital for supplying men and raw materials needed to sustain French military capabilities in Europe – whether defensive or offensive.

Fortification was not the reflex of a defensive nation. Until around 1929–30, all the generals considered defensive war unlikely because Germany was weak. In the long controversy about fortification, the debate was not about *strategic* offence or defence, but about the *tactics* appropriate to a defensive war that was unlikely in the near future. If some years thence, however, Germany were to recover, a reasonable supposition, France might initially face a superior enemy alone.

It quickly became clear that fortification was controversial. Would the next war be a long, attritional conflict behind fortified fronts, or could manoeuvre bring a quick victory? Must fortification ensure the absolute inviolability of national territory? Did it entail a continuous front or intervals in which to trap the enemy, as in Séré de Rivières's system? Did it require echelons or a single strong line? What were the implications of fortification for command? Personal rivalries and a fragmented decision-making process complicated the answers.

The Deciders

In the victory parade of 14 July 1919, the three marshals marched side by side in uniforms that symbolised their leverage in the postwar world (see Plate 2). Joffre, who preferred to remember the Marne rather than subsequent disappointments, wore his uniform with red trousers of 1914. Foch sported the dark-blue uniform he wore as supreme allied commander. Pétain chose his sky-blue uniform, expressing identification with the *poilu*.[4] The celebrations over, a quiet but bitter combat of memoirs and proxy publications claimed credit and attributed blame.

In January 1920, the marshals became life members of the Conseil supérieur de la guerre (CSG – Supreme War Council). This body was responsible, within the government's strategic and budgetary parameters, for advising the War Ministry on the shape of French land and air forces. It was presided over by the president of the Republic and attended by the prime minister and war minister along with the generals who commanded individual arms and military regions in peacetime and corresponding corps and armies in wartime. As vice-president of the CSG, Pétain was commander-in-chief designate.

One general commented retrospectively that contact between CSG members was rare 'for a thousand reasons, of which not least was barely disguised antipathy between certain of them'.[5] Buat, as chief of the general staff, the EMA, thought 'nothing could be gained from this kind of assembly; the members are men of experience with personal views on everything and little inclination to nuance their arguments'. He lamented that the CSG would be rid of the marshals only when they died.[6]

Joffre's health did not long survive the peace. Although Foch too was failing by 1927, his record as Allied supreme commander continued to count. In 1919, his near-insubordinate campaign for detachment of the Rhineland from Germany made him unpopular with the left and popular with the right. He remained Pétain's major rival until 1927, when his baton passed to Weygand, his former chief of staff, whom Pétain disliked.

Pétain's relative youth and physical health ensured that he outlasted his rivals. Furthermore, he cleverly constructed a broad popular appeal by identification with the ordinary veteran. To maintain his above-party image, he rarely expressed controversial views publicly, so that when he did speak, his words appeared weighty. He was not at his best in face-to-face meetings, but he was well informed on detail, stubborn when he chose, and not above political scheming. Pétain's power was limited by a dilemma: maintaining independence from factions compromised his ability to decide. Buat complained that the marshal's desire to please everyone caused him often to reverse his position – 'it's the decadence of a great man', he noted in his diary.[7]

At a point impossible to determine precisely, Pétain's calculated reticence shaded into cognitive impairment preceding dementia. By the late 1930s, early symptoms were plain, but subtler signs may have dated back ten or even fifteen years. Such impairment includes difficulty with new information, indecisiveness, apathy and tiredness, all of which

Buat and others saw in Pétain. Sufferers may also mask symptoms by repeating strongly held ideas, however inappropriate they are to specific situations – in Pétain's case, for instance, his dislike of primary school teachers and commitment to echeloned defence. Yet he remained capable of embracing new ideas into the 1930s, notably in his enthusiasm for strategic bombing.[8]

Pétain's room for manoeuvre was anyway limited. EMA chiefs Buat (1919–23) and Debeney (1923–9) were responsible not to him but to the war minister. Neither was the creature of Pétain sometimes depicted by historians.[9] Both owed their positions to their competence, political reliability and republicanism. The EMA's four Bureaux (offices or desks) constituted powerful agencies in their own right – the first was responsible for organisation and personnel, the second for intelligence, the third for operations and the fourth for supply.

The War Ministry, staffed by officers and civilians, constituted another power centre. Its four directorates – the first responsible for infantry, the second for artillery, the third for cavalry and the fourth for engineers – were charged with financial oversight, but often encroached on policy. The minister's civil and military cabinets advised him and dealt with promotions.

The centrality of parliament in the constitution of the Third Republic further complicated decision making. Its power to make and break governments was much greater than in the US or British systems. During the Great War, the army commissions of the Chamber of Deputies (lower house) and Senate, in which retired generals were prominent, reinforced oversight of the army.

Furthermore, the many deputies who had served in the trenches – unlike most members of the CSG – claimed a special right to pronounce on military matters. As one historian ironically put it, the war massively conferred 'certificates of expertise in strategy and tactics' on politicians.[10] Veterans, such as the future military ministers Maginot, Pierre Cot and Daladier, presented themselves as the voices of republican citizen-soldiers who had defended France with their chests. Cot held that 'men who have experienced five years of war seem capable of understanding all the technical issues relevant to the organisation of our frontiers'. Daladier agreed that Cot expressed the infantry veteran outlook.[11] Both were close to the mainstream veteran movement, which, despite its distrust of the high command, admired Pétain as friend of the *poilu*. Conservative generals criticised the cult of the *poilu*. In an echo of the conflict about command, Castelnau maintained that the real artisans of victory were not the *poilus*, but 'the educated youth which led the troops and organised production'.[12]

The high command was closer, not surprisingly, to the right, to which the handful of retired generals in parliament belonged. Castelnau, Foch and Weygand were Catholic nationalists, probably monarchists. Yet the days when such men dominated the officer corps were gone. Officers such as Buat and Debeney were republican, if of conservative inclination. A handful, such as Nivelle, favoured the left.

Pétain's position was anomalous. Although barely republican, he aligned with Daladier and Cot in disputes about fortification, for all three preferred field fortification to permanent works. Most of the right, in contrast, favoured permanent artillery works, which it saw as guaranteeing hierarchical command. For some years, these debates were hypothetical, for a German attack on France was unlikely and French plans were resolutely offensive.

First Discussions, 1919–1924

German resistance to signature and then implementation of the Versailles Treaty made it impossible to rule out renewal of hostilities. Plans T (Transitional) and P (Provisional) of 1919–23 imagined concentration of French and Belgian forces in the occupied Rhineland, from where they would advance to meet Polish and Czech forces and cut Germany in two. Plan A (1924–6) increased the force of the attack, and to profit from Germany's lack of easily mobilised trained reserves it prioritised mobility.

The army planned to counter a limited German assault on French occupation troops, for until 1924 Germany resisted treaty fulfilment. The so-called 'attaque brusquée' was a surprise attack designed to seize bargaining chips or bridgeheads, perhaps prior to a long war. The army did not believe such an attack on France itself to be imminent, given that weak German forces would first have to break through the occupation army, but it evoked the danger to win better funding.[13] Although Franco-German relations subsequently improved, noisy German nationalists still clamoured for revenge, including Hitler's National Socialists. If a revanchist government were to win power, Germany would have significant advantages over France, which are too easily forgotten.

The French frontier was hard to defend. In 1815, the second Treaty of Paris punished defeated Napoleonic France with a border cut by perpendicular river valleys through which invaders could easily reach Paris. Blocking these 'invasion routes' was central to all discussions of fortification (Figure 6). On the Belgian border, they were the Escaut (Scheldt in Flemish) and its tributaries, the Scarpe and Lys (via Valenciennes), the Sambre (through Maubeuge) and the Oise (the Chimay Gap, via Laon and Soissons) The Ardennes Forest in Belgium and Luxembourg was a significant barrier, but not impassable.

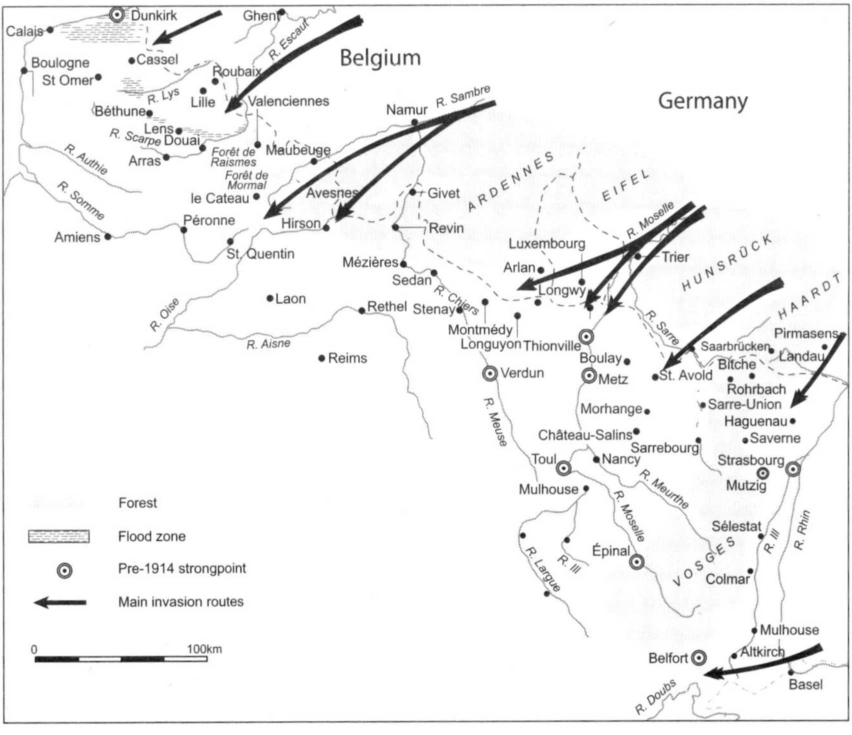

6. Invasion routes.

On the Franco-German border, the Moselle Valley led to Paris through Thionville, Metz and Nancy. Further east, the River Sarre offered another route into France, but fortification was problematic there because the peace treaty placed the German Saarland opposite under French control until 1935, when a referendum would decide its fate. Further east again, the hilly northern Vosges Forest was unsuited to a large-scale German attack. Then, from Wissembourg to the Rhine, only the thirty-eight kilometres of the Lauter, little more than a stream, prevented the enemy sweeping into the Alsatian plain to take Strasbourg from the rear. The return of Alsace-Lorraine gave France the Rhine from Lauterbourg to Switzerland, but it had been crossed many times in the past and could be outflanked from the north or south through Switzerland.

Significant French coal, steel and engineering industries occupied vulnerable positions on the frontier from Lille to the Moselle. Paris, in which administration, war industries and communications were concentrated, was within easy reach of the frontier. This centralisation would make resistance difficult if Paris fell. German industries and cities were dispersed and protected by mountain ranges, rivers and bogs, though an offensive launched from Belgium could threaten the Ruhr.

The Italian frontier was more defensible, for the Alps were 200 kilometres deep on the French side and only seven mountain passes were crossable by motor vehicle. On the Italian side, the mountain barrier was narrower and passes led directly to the Lombard plain. Italian forces advancing along the coastal plain towards Nice would be vulnerable to artillery in the foothills.[14]

Germany possessed substantially greater human and economic resources than France. True, as the historian Adam Tooze shows, neither Germany nor France was by modern standards a wealthy country. German per capita national income in the late 1920s ranked with present-day Tunisia, South Africa and Iran, and France was only a little better off.[15] After seventeen years of further development since 2007 when Tooze wrote, the comparison remains roughly valid with Tunisia. Yet in absolute terms, German military and economic potential was substantially greater than that of the French. In 1921, despite territorial losses, sixty-one million Germans faced thirty-eight million French. In

1933, the German population reached sixty-five million, while the French, thanks to a low birth rate, remained stable. France was able to some extent to compensate with colonial soldiers and resources, but with empire went overstretch. Without a fleet, the Germans did not threaten the colonies, but the Italian and Japanese navies did. Colonial rebellion was endemic, and was encouraged by President Woodrow Wilson's commitment to national self-determination. His Fourteen Points were cited not only by anticolonialists but by Breton and Alsatian minorities in France itself.

France's wartime allies proved unreliable. Neither the USA nor Britain fulfilled their promise to guarantee French territory. Yet to defend its Mediterranean communications, France was reliant on the British to protect its Atlantic ports, and the latter's naval power was in turn now conditional on American goodwill. Another consequence of the Great War was that France and even Britain were dependent on American finance.[16] Yet the United States intervened in European affairs only to encourage the French to compromise on German reparations and repay French debts to America. The Americans and British wanted Germany reintegrated into the world economy. While Britain would certainly assist France if attacked, help would be slow to arrive, for until 1937–9, British land forces were terribly neglected. Pacts with quarrelling states in eastern Europe were no substitute for the Russian alliance, which had saved France in 1914. Belgium was now an ally, but meaningful military agreement proved elusive. Fortification might compensate for French disadvantages, but type, location and principle were militarily and politically controversial.

On 25 February 1919, shortly after the armistice, the War Ministry invited Pétain to give his views on defence of the territory.[17] As Pétain's major-general at the wartime GQG (still operational under the state of siege), Buat asked senior commanders for their views on fortification. They unanimously replied that national territory must be defended on the Rhine and that permanent occupation of the left bank was better than financially ruinous fortification.

Further consultations confirmed these views. The fullest response ruled out a 'Great Wall of China' and permanent fortification on the frontier as a waste of money and a burden on frontier regions, 'which already see themselves as everyone's battleground'. Instead, it advocated field fortification close to the frontier or in occupied Germany. Troops were expected to push forward either to give depth to defence or to undertake wide-ranging armoured and motorised offensive operations.[18]

Some respondents to the first consultation did envisage fortification if France failed to get the Rhineland. Even offensively minded General Mangin, deputy commander of the Army of the Rhine, admitted that fortification might be needed to cover manoeuvre and block the invasion routes. Practical proposals ranged from stocking trenching tools near the border, through enhancement with concrete shelters and command posts, to the construction of artillery forts (*gros ouvrages*). The ingredients of future conflict were present, but defence was not an obsession.[19] Pétain approved the report, but refused submission to the minister until the peace conference had determined French frontiers.[20] German resistance to the treaty ruled out complete inaction. On 18 November 1919, the Interior Staff requested its Troisième Bureau (operations) to produce a defensive programme to support Plan T. It responded again that since France's military frontier was on the Rhine, fortification must be integrated with 'organisation of the battlefield' in Germany. The model was Pétain's defence in depth.[21]

This doctrine was to become part of the 1921 *Instruction provisoire sur l'emploi tactique des grandes unités* (IPGU – Provisional Instructions on the Tactical Employment of Large Units), formalised in the 1929 Infantry Regulations and a revised manual for NCOs.[22] It has often been seen as the embodiment of defensiveness and passivity, and thus of 'Maginot thinking'. Closer examination reveals institutionalisation of Pétain's 1917 compromise, which combined tactical devolution with strict rules.

Devolution of command was formalised in the division of infantry sections (platoons) into three eleven-man combat groups, each with a light machine gun. This disposition was more suited to defending continuous fronts than to manoeuvre. Improvisation was explicitly forbidden. Nonetheless, in a 1925 consultation, five of eight corps commanders objected to the degree of responsibility given to reserve NCOs and corporals (the latter were part of the troop).[23] The command issue remained unresolved.

Defensively, the IPGU prescribed lightly held advance posts, a resistance position and second line. Should the enemy break through locally, transversal lines permitted defenders immediately to counterattack enemy flanks and re-establish the continuous front. More serious breaches required retreat to second and third positions and corps-level counterattacks. Defensive lines consisted of field positions and small bunkers, not large permanent fortifications. Offensively, forces were to advance prudently under artillery cover from one terrain 'compartment' bounded by natural obstacles and field fortification to the next.[24] This was the doctrine that Pétain defended in debates about fortification.

Yet his influence on French doctrine was not unlimited.[25] Although Foch was no less likely than Pétain to quote the maxim that modern warfare depended on firepower, and did not oppose fortification in principle, he advocated offensive and defensive manoeuvre around permanent or field fortifications.[26] Pétain's proposals were attacked on all sides, and their final shape was the product of conflict.

In March 1920, War Minister André Lefebvre ordered studies of the defence of Alsace-Lorraine. Probably thanks to Pétain, now vice-president of the CSG, they were to be inspired by Joffre's wartime instruction concerning the integration of permanent fortifications into the continuous front and Pétain's instruction on echeloned defence. Lefebvre's instruction also introduced Pétain's idea of 'prepared battlefields' on French and German soil, on which trenching equipment, barbed wire and suchlike would be stocked ready for use. The strongest positions, designated 'fortified regions', included concrete shelters and observation and command posts, but not large permanent forts.[27]

The EMA responded with an ambitious study that departed significantly from Pétain's.[28] Rather than depth, it proposed fortified regions, necessary because modern war required dense supply networks, airfields and mutually supporting artillery forts with underground galleries and a 'resistance line' close to the frontier. Fortification of the Belgian and Swiss frontiers with Germany would prolong the French line. One suspects the hand of EMA chief Buat, for he consistently advocated this system thereafter.[29] Pétain refused to submit the report to the minister.[30]

Nevertheless, the EMA report formed the basis of a shorter report presented to a meeting of the CSG on 17 May 1920.[31] Pétain perhaps hoped for consensus, for a few days previously Foch had urged him to act, given that fortification would take years to build.[32] Yet Foch continued to insist that fortification should facilitate manoeuvre and was rarely inclined to agree with Pétain. Along with Guillaumat and Nivelle, he decried the report's defensiveness. Foch condemned the 'prepared battlefield', for it implied obligation to fight there and constrained manoeuvre; even in fifteen years, when the Rhineland would be evacuated, he insisted that the French must meet the Germans in the demilitarised zone, not simply move forward under the cover of fortifications. Nivelle added that a long war must be avoided at all costs.

Pétain defended the proposal weakly. He realised too late that contrary to the ministerial instruction it included permanent fortification, and wrongly claimed that it only envisaged prepared battlefields. He conceded willingly that preparation must be minimal, and that money could be saved on concrete and armour. He also urged the CSG to prepare for departure from the Rhineland and protested that protecting the territory did not rule out the offensive or counterattack.

Besides resurrecting the old offence/defence controversy, the meeting showed that fortification was not a priority, one member remarking that there was presently nothing to fear from Germany. Writing in his diary that evening, Buat did not mention the meeting, despite often lambasting Pétain for letting him down. The outcome was simply to confirm, in accordance with a ministerial instruction, that CSG members would produce studies of specific parts of the frontier.

The generals expressed diverse views, if they bothered at all.[33] In his study of the north, Guillaumat advocated advance into Belgium, but felt that if fortification proved necessary Dunkirk and Maubeuge should be priorities. Nivelle pleaded that he had insufficient documentation to study the Alpine frontier and reiterated that the offensive was the only way to avoid a ruinous long war. Joffre proposed echeloned fortified regions similar to Séré de Rivières's system without new forts, given that finance was so uncertain.[34] General Henri Berthelot, commander in Alsace-Lorraine, imagined simultaneously defensive and offensive fortifications on the German border. Military engineers began studies of 'modern fortification'.

Pétain meanwhile inspired a revised instruction of 10 December 1920, which again rejected permanent fortification in favour of 'equipping' the whole frontier (including the north) with material to construct echeloned field defences on mobilisation.[35] To appease Foch, the instruction described defence as a 'worst case'. Yet the expression 'fortified region' was replaced by 'Great Wall of France', which Pétain thought better expressed the doctrine of the continuous front. The minister approved further study. Accordingly, the EMA's Troisième Bureau developed fuller proposals, but in June and December 1921 Pétain rejected its drafts. Since it was difficult to impose his views on the EMA, he asked his own cabinet for a proposal.[36]

The new document reinforced Pétain's doctrine of defence in depth. It assumed a stalemate war, in which the offensive was limited to troubling the enemy mobilisation. Battlefields were to be 'prepared' on the frontier itself and, in the Rhineland, integrated with Belgian fortifications. The whole supposedly formed a 'muraille de France'. Yet the decisive battlefield, as Figure 7 shows, was sited well back on prewar French and German positions.[37]

Pétain dared not ask Foch to comment. Other CSG members were harsh. Guillaumat condemned a triple Great Wall of China, financial fantasy and military danger, subordinating manoeuvre to fortification and turning France into a vast fortified camp. Buat pointed out that the question of permanent fortification was unresolved.[38] Mangin opposed fixed fortification as 'always expensive and sometimes useless', but liked the emphasis on mobility, communications and campaign fortification.[39] Pétain's redraft was cosmetic,[40] and another stiff exchange of letters revealed only that the generals remained entrenched.[41] Pétain took the document to Maginot, war minister since January 1922.

Maginot was in a delicate position. In 1917, he had abandoned his national opposition allies to back the Nivelle offensive and had opposed Pétain's appointment, thus excluding himself from subsequent governments. Then there was his private life: for the Communists, he was always 'le sergent de chez Maxim's', the famous Parisian nightclub. Marshal Hubert Lyautey, a famous colonial soldier and resident-general in Morocco, used the familiar 'tu' form with Maginot and partied with him in Morocco, but saw him as an 'opportunist'.[42]

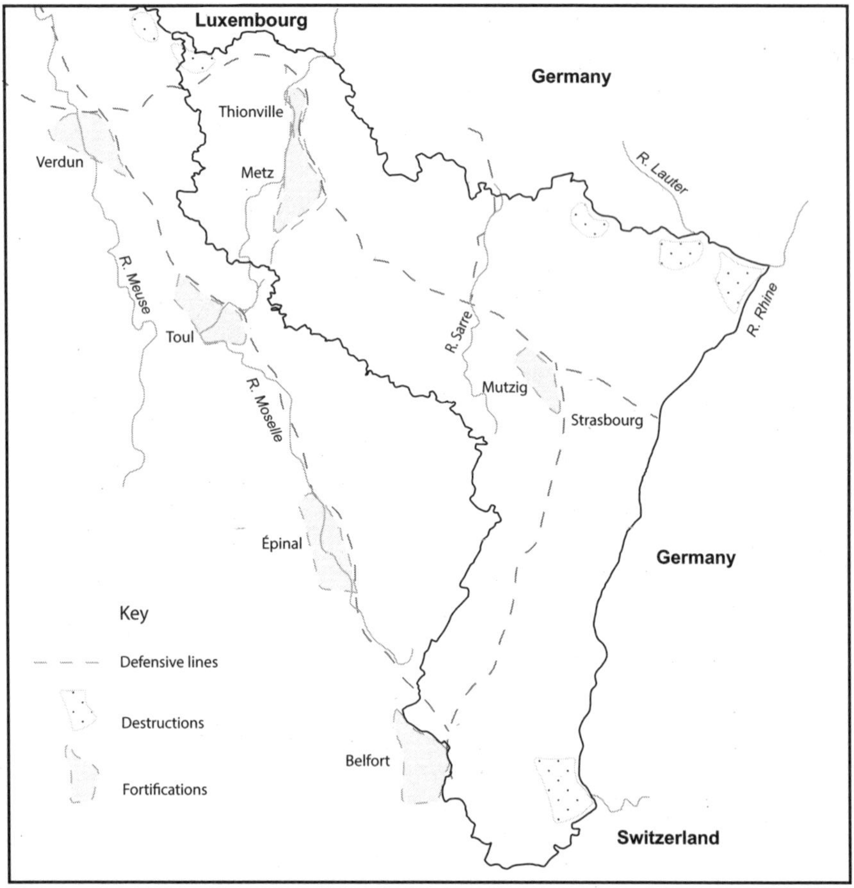

7. Pétain's proposal for defence in depth.

Maginot recovered his political standing by supporting the reconstruction of his devastated Meuse constituency and by advocacy for wounded veterans, heading an association known simply as 'La Fédé [Federation] Maginot'. He thus made himself the obvious choice to lead the wounded veterans in the victory parade, and from 1920 to serve as minister of pensions. In November he went to Verdun to organise the choice of remains of the unknown soldier.

Maginot's credit within the army remained weak. Buat told him to his face that officers did not welcome his appointment.[43] From Buat's perspective, association with the veterans was not advantageous. Indeed, Maginot backed veteran demands for revision of the sentences of soldiers executed 'as an example', including the notorious case of Lucien Bersot, shot for refusing to wear bloodstained trousers taken from a corpse. The execution was illegal, since the incident took place in the rear, where disobedience was not a capital crime. Maginot compensated, however, by appointing General Maurice Auroux, prosecution, judge and jury in Bersot's trial, to his cabinet. He won credit with Pétain by listening to his complaint that he was excluded from ministry decisions. He made the marshal inspector-general of the army, so that Buat had to submit papers to him before the minister saw them. Buat admitted a personal setback, but rightly suspected that Pétain would not enforce this requirement vigorously.[44] Ultimately, Buat developed genuine affection for Maginot.[45]

Maginot rejected Pétain's revised instruction – whether because he did not feel strong enough to decide between Pétain and Buat or because he remained attached to the offensive, we cannot say. Instead, Maginot called a meeting of the CSG for 22 May 1922 in the hope of dispelling 'equivocation'.[46] The day before the meeting, Buat travelled with Foch to attend the consecration of the mass grave above which the ossuary of Notre-Dame-de-Lorette was to be constructed. In Foch's private carriage, Buat revealed that Pétain had excluded both Foch and Joffre from the consultation. They agreed that the following day's meeting should name a commission headed by Joffre, whose views were closer to Foch's. The next day, as members arrived, Buat quietly told his old friend President of the Republic Millerand how matters would proceed.[47]

Opening the meeting, Pétain ventured optimistically that everyone was agreed on the principle of inviolability of the frontier, but not whether 'defensive organisations' were necessary.[48] Cutting through confused discussion of definitions and competence, Foch criticised inviolability as a 'new doctrine'. Until now, he said, armies had defended the territory through manoeuvre and if necessary had temporarily sacrificed land. (In fact, Pétain too was prepared to sacrifice territory in echeloned defences.) Foch advocated field fortification constructed with the flow of the battle and permanent fortification if it allowed multiple possibilities. His private jottings show that he was open-minded about whether physical obstacles and permanent fortifications were required to cover manoeuvre, and that he wanted to put off constructing a defensive barrier until this question had been resolved.[49] Guillaumat added that inviolability was a dangerous idea to share with the public, for it encouraged a false sense of security. Millerand's attempt to persuade the generals to vote on Pétain's proposal succeeded only in provoking muddled argument about the distinction between permanent and campaign fortification and about the necessity for continuity. Finally, Pétain himself proposed a commission under Joffre – 'after a wasted hour', as Buat told his diary. Pétain claimed that the meeting had identified guiding principles for the commission.[50] In fact, it had ignored Pétain's proposals.

At any rate, fortification remained a secondary concern. In June 1922, the opening sentence of the agenda for the first meeting of the Commission chargée d'études de l'organisation de la défense du territoire (CDT – Commission for the Study of the Defence of the Territory) stated that 'organisation of the defence of the territory is only one branch of the organisation of national defence and not the most important'. It was subordinate to the organisation of the army, industrial mobilisation and protection of communications with North Africa.[51] Low importance, however, did not prevent bitter doctrinal quarrels.

At the first meeting on 19 June 1922, Buat and Guillaumat clashed. Unlike Pétain, both advocated powerful *gros ouvrages* on the frontier, not depth. Buat wanted these forts integrated into a continuous front completed by campaign fortification, while Guillaumat wanted to fortify only the invasion routes, leaving the intervals between regions left open with pockets, as Séré de Rivières had advocated. Neither general, it should be noted, envisaged a defensive *strategy*: fortification was an insurance if advance into Germany failed. Guillaumat thought that pockets would allow immediate counterattack; Buat thought that a disorganised retreating army should dig in for a long war.[52]

Since other duties prevented Buat from attending the next meeting, the participants ignored his views. They proposed fortified fronts on the Lauter, at Metz–Thionville and at Belfort on the Swiss frontier, and delegated Berthelot, as Alsace-Lorraine commander, to carry out practical studies. Outraged, Buat informed Pétain, who insisted that the CDT agree principles before practical positioning. Joffre took it as a disavowal and promptly resigned.[53]

Buat, who assumed that Pétain would take over as president of the CDT, was surprised to learn that Guillaumat had taken on the post.[54] The choice was probably Maginot's, who perhaps saw Guillaumat as more inclined towards manoeuvre and closer politically. Then approaching sixty, Guillaumat was notorious for his brusqueness. Buat described him as 'never happy' and 'venomous'.[55] Guillaumat nevertheless possessed the qualifications necessary to preside over the CDT. He had been professor of military doctrine and history at Saint-Cyr before holding senior field commands during the war, which he ended by leading the 5th Army into the Ardennes. He was connected to the powerful centre politicians Foreign Minister Aristide Briand and Clemenceau, who, like Buat, were alumni of the Lycée de Nantes.

Buat saw Guillaumat as stuck in 1914, unaware that modern war depended on material and technology. Guillaumat later wrote that his divergences with Buat 'concerned more an opposition between two ways of making war than between two conceptions of fortification'.[56] Guillaumat admired Séré de Rivières, whose principles he had taught at Saint-Cyr, whereas Buat advocated the continuous front.[57]

In the CDT, Buat and Guillaumat somehow compromised: fortification of the Franco-Belgian frontier was unnecessary, for if the Germans came that way the French would advance to meet them; isolated strongpoints were outdated except in the Alps; there must be fortified regions with mutually supporting artillery forts. As a fudge, the intervals between forts were to be left open as Guillaumat preferred, but their 'organisation' would be studied in peacetime, with a view either to defence or to attack. Members agreed on the necessity for underground forts, but not whether they should be armed with artillery. Buat wrote in his diary that agreement had been reached in practice if not with the heart.[58]

Yet the CDT's report of 27 March 1923 entirely reflected Guillaumat's preferences.[59] Buat wrote a counter-report advocating continuity and absolute defence of the territory, principles which, he claimed, had been established by Vauban and confirmed by Séré de Rivières and total war. For Buat, in modern warfare, individual strongpoints could not resist if surrounded. They must form a mutually supporting chain, protecting the whole nation as a besieged fortress. He rejected

Guillaumat's preference for defensive manoeuvre; money spent on giving fortified regions deep flanks would be better used for breadth.[60]

Maginot declined to choose, and Buat failed to persuade Pétain to decide. Buat noted in his diary, 'once again we witness the CSG divided on essential questions and the effect is deplorable'. Pétain, he asserted, does not act like a leader and 'people are saying it'.[61] That was his last diary entry. A few days later he took to his bed, and on 27 December 1923 he died of an unknown illness.

Pétain did not see fortification as a priority. In October 1922, the CSG had reaffirmed the necessity of striking at the heart of Germany, and in January 1923 French and Belgian armies occupied the Ruhr in an attempt to force the Germans to pay reparations. Pétain urged the government to take the chance to separate the Rhineland from Germany. Buat's diaries show that through 1923 the Ruhr, not fortification, was his and Pétain's principal concern.[62]

Fortification was not a direct response to war and invasion. While Pétain attempted to promote his doctrine of echeloned defence, and his defensive and pessimistic inclinations sometimes came through, he did not insist, and discussion of fortification remained hypothetical. The right-wing governments of these years preferred to force weakened Germany to fulfil the treaty, and Maginot made no effort to drive fortification policy forward.

The Cartel, June 1924–July 1926

In September 1923, the Germans ended their passive resistance to the Ruhr occupation. Yet this apparent French victory marked the end of strict treaty enforcement. A financial crisis and the need for an American loan obliged Prime Minister Poincaré to accede to their demands for conciliation of Germany. He accepted the Dawes Commission's recommendation of reduced reparations payments and effectively agreed to abandon use of force.[63]

Then, in May 1924, the Cartel des gauches (Left Cartel) won a narrow electoral victory. It endeavoured to enmesh Germany in a network of treaties overseen by the League of Nations, which it expected Germany eventually to join.[64] The Cartel's crowning achievement was the Locarno Treaty, ratified in March 1926, under which Britain, France, Germany and Italy guaranteed Germany's western frontiers (not its eastern borders). These developments are sometimes said to explain France's shift towards a defensive military strategy and thus to fortification. In reality, Cartel security policy was mixed.

On the one hand, the left possessed a strong pacifist element, convinced that since Germany had become a republic, the elimination of the old aristocratic militarist leadership meant that French arms spending could be reduced. On the other hand, most leftists accepted that the country must defend itself if attacked. Practical policy looked back to the *levée en masse* (mass rising/mobilisation) of 1792, when, according to myth, the people rushed to the frontier to defend *la patrie en danger* against the aristocratic enemies of the French Revolution and their European allies. The modern equivalent was short universal male military service and a long reserve period. The left, and indeed republicans of the right, saw universal male military service as a pillar of democracy.

The Cartel's first war minister, General Charles Nollet, was more interested in reforming the army along these lines than in fortification. He did not allow the CSG to discuss fortification and halted tests on prototype *ouvrages*.[65] Nollet's tenure of the ministry ended with the collapse of the government in April 1925. One-year service plus reserve service to age forty-eight was nevertheless enacted in 1927–8, and we shall see that it became entangled with renewed debate about fortification.

On 17 April 1925, Paul Painlevé became prime minister and war minister. His tenure of the premiership was brief, but he remained war minister almost continuously until November 1929. A famous scientist, Painlevé still held the Chair in Fluid Mechanics at the Polytechnique, albeit no longer on the cutting edge, having hitched his intellectual chariot to the anti-Einstein cause. Painlevé, it should be remembered, had appointed Pétain as general-in-chief in the dark days of 1917. Painlevé's fortunes quickly waned, for he fell in the crisis that eventually brought to power Georges Clemenceau, the 'father of victory'. Painlevé attempted restore his reputation by linking himself to the victorious generals, publishing in 1923 a book entitled *How I Appointed Foch and Pétain*.

Pétain had less to gain from association with the ageing, non-combatant Painlevé, a tireless advocate of the League of Nations and reconciliation with Germany. Painlevé nevertheless considered the danger of German militarism to be real.[66] And unlike the left's military experts, Daladier, Cot and Joseph Paul-Boncour, he was willing to follow the generals' lead on fortification, so long as it was not too expensive. Pétain respected Painlevé, with whom he probably shared a dislike for Foch and his protégé Weygand.[67]

Soon after taking office, Painlevé instructed Debeney, Buat's successor as EMA chief, to review the fortification dossier. Yet on 12 April 1925 the outbreak of the Rif Rebellion in Morocco pushed fortification to the bottom of the agenda. Painlevé sent Pétain to fight the rebels, so the CSG could not meet. In May, Painlevé refused funds for test fortifications and advised making older fortifications gas-resistant instead.[68]

Three considerations encouraged Painlevé to reopen the dossier. First, General Messimy, for the Senate Army Commission, complained that it was 'inadmissible' not to have produced a defence plan six years after the armistice.[69] Second, Painlevé was committed to 'disarmament', a misleading term which in practice meant outlawing offensive weapons. According to the League of Nation's definitions of December 1925, fortification was 'defensive'.[70] Third, government and army were sensitive to British accusations that they were delaying fortification to avoid evacuating the Rhineland.[71] Pétain returned from Morocco on 6 November 1925, telling journalists falsely that the Rif Rebellion was over.

The government called a meeting of the CSG for 15 December. Debeney's short introduction backed Guillaumat's preference for discontinuity and manoeuvre over Buat's continuity. It also emphasised common features – inviolability of the territory, equipment of the frontier for either defence or offence, fortified regions close to the frontier with powerful permanent fortification, independent of the plan of campaign but cooperating with the field army.[72]

The meeting was as ill-tempered as ever. Pétain continued to oppose both alternatives in favour of the equipped battlefield and depth without permanent fortification, continuous from the North Sea to Basel. Foch, Guillaumat and Nollet advocated permanent fortification of the northeast alone. By seven votes to five, members rejected Pétain's proposal – even Pétain voted against! Guillaumat's plan for discontinuous fortified regions in the northeast with permanent fortification passed unanimously, but the interval–continuity question was unresolved. The CSG charged the revived CDT, renamed the Commission chargée de l'étude de la défense des frontières (CDF – Commission for Frontier Defence), with determining the outline of the fortified regions and producing preliminary designs for permanent fortifications.

On 31 December 1925, Painlevé confirmed Guillaumat's victory by choosing him to preside over the CDF and recommended that he consult the archives of the Séré de Rivières Commission.[73] The ministry gave the CDF a budget and secretariat headed by the inspector of military engineers, General Étienne Fillonneau. CDF members reconnoitred the frontier while local delegations undertook detailed research.[74] The ministry ordered the technical department of the military engineers, the Service technique du génie (STG), to test the resistance of prototype fortifications. Although much remained to be settled, investment of resources and time created momentum.

In his 1941 hagiography, General Émile Laure wrote that Pétain retreated because he expected that continuity would develop in practice.[75] And so it eventually did on the northeastern front. Yet Pétain had consistently opposed the choice of permanent works. More likely, he was unable to prevail against the war minister, EMA chief and majority of the CSG. In conformity with his military doctrine, Pétain executed a tactical withdrawal to maintain his above-faction image. His reversals of position also suggest growing indecisiveness. Yet any cognitive impairment was mild, for in the months that followed he attempted to undermine the CSG's decision.

Fortification Becomes a Priority, July 1926–1928

In July 1926, the Cartel des gauches collapsed, unable to resolve a financial crisis and faced by far-right demonstrations in the streets. The moderate-left Radical-Socialists and Painlevé's Republican Socialists switched support to a government of national union under the conservative Poincaré. Reversal of majorities did not alter the policy of reconciliation with Germany, however, as the continued presence of Briand, who had negotiated the Locarno Treaty, and Painlevé at the foreign and war ministries respectively confirmed. The right embraced détente on condition that France remained militarily pre-eminent on the continent. Coercion having failed, Plan A bis (Plan A Revised) of June 1926 scaled back the objectives of the advance into Germany. The emphasis on rapid transport and manoeuvre remained, but on the Italian frontier 'passive' defence of the national soil appeared for the first time.[76] Foch's increasing enthusiasm for permanent fortification helped tip the scales in its favour. He pointed out the urgency of some kind of work because German treaty compliance meant that the Rhineland could be evacuated early.[77]

Fortification also compensated for overstretch. Colonial troops earmarked for service in France had to be used to suppress rebellions in other parts of the empire, while by October 1925 51,990 metropolitan troops were in Morocco. Italian demands for Nice, the Savoie and Tunisia created southeastern and Mediterranean commitments. In the CSG, General Gouroud proposed warning the government that the army could not simultaneously 'defend victoriously' the northeast and the southeast, given that it would initially fight without allied support. Painlevé and Pétain saw such a declaration as dangerous. The marshal pessimistically ruminated that in 1914 France had been attacked only in the north yet had prevailed only after four years with the assistance of numerous allies.[78] The army also considered that without fortification, conscripts serving for only one year from 1929 would be insufficiently well trained to hold the frontier until reserves arrived.[79]

The emergence of autonomism in Alsace-Lorraine made it imperative to signal to enemies within and without that the province would be defended. The retired generals prominent in the leadership of nationalist parties in Alsace-Lorraine joined the Senate Army Commission, from where they took the campaign for fortification into civil society. In June 1927, Alsatian senator General Auguste Hirschauer presided at the inaugural meeting at Nancy of the Union lorraine pour la protection de la frontière du Nord-Est. Backers included the far-right, neo-royalist Action française, which was in the forefront of the anti-autonomist movement.[80] In December 1928, sixty delegates from the Chambers of Commerce of the eastern economic region (linked to the corresponding military region) endorsed the campaign.[81]

On 6 November 1926, the CDF produced proposals for three fortified regions with *gros ouvrages* close to the frontier: Metz–Longwy, Lauter–Vosges and Belfort. Between the first two regions was an interval, the Sarre Gap, into which the enemy would be channelled and where it would be counterattacked. The Rhine was to be defended by machine-gun casemates. Fortification would be sufficiently powerful to counter a lightly armed *attaque brusquée*, and, once reinforced by campaign troops, to withstand full-scale attack and cover manoeuvre. It would oblige the enemy either to make costly frontal attacks or to attempt outflanking through Switzerland or Belgium. Since the army planned to meet a violation of Belgian neutrality beyond the frontier, permanent fortification was unnecessary in the north. In both the northeast and the north, mobile fortification equipment and weaponry (*parcs mobiles de fortification*) would be used to dig in on the spot or follow the advancing army.

The report did not reflect consensus. In his covering letter, Guillaumat reminded the minister of the commitment of 'certain generals' – i.e. the late Buat and Pétain – to continuous defensive positions. Another CDF member, Debeney, thought that the report saw fortification as a worst-case scenario and was more concerned with movement into Germany and Belgium.[82]

The CSG meeting of 17 December 1926 showed that Pétain had not disarmed.[83] Despite the ailing Foch's absence, acrimony persisted and sticking to the agenda remained challenging. Pétain rehashed the arguments against permanent works, stating that 'the best fortification is field fortification'. He thought that a light covering position on the frontier sufficed to allow the army time to concentrate on a resistance line, which, we saw, was positioned at Metz, Toul and Verdun (Figure 7 page 50). He was prepared to sacrifice the Longwy–Briey industrial regions, and, it seemed, much of Alsace-Lorraine. He also criticised the CDF for providing only one very expensive model fort. Painlevé too wanted cheaper, 'less perfect' forts.

Guillaumat objected that Pétain was undermining everything that had been done. The old marshal failed to persuade members to postpone discussion of the CDF report pending further study, for they insisted on approving the outline of the fortified regions. But despite earlier votes, they did not confirm the CDF's proposals for siting works within them – a victory for Pétain.

On 6 January 1927, Painlevé instructed the CDF to resolve matters. Pétain was probably pleased that he also ordered it to consult officers not on the CDF, which was done in February and April.[84] The task of summarising the results went to Fillonneau, secretary of the CDF and strongly committed to its view. Interviewees, he said, agreed on the necessity of adaptation to terrain, underground communications and immunity to artillery – in other words, they approved *gros ouvrages* – but claimed that 'the harvest of original ideas advanced during these two days was not abundant'.[85] He spoke disingenuously and too soon.

In the CDF, generals Jean Degoutte, commander of the Alpine front, and Jean Maurin, inspector of artillery, claimed, with some justice, that interviewees had criticised the lack of depth (one of Pétain's key concerns). Degoutte advocated instead a large number of mutually supporting small blockhouses. The CDF majority rejected this proposal as a revival of Pétain's prepared battlefield, but in fact it required construction of far more blockhouses than Pétain had envisaged. The CDF conceded that on 'less exposed' fronts Degoutte's method might work, and agreed to trials at Belfort. Otherwise, the CDF's note of 16 May 1927 restated its first proposal.[86] Stalemate was complete.

In June, in a further attempt to force the issue, Pétain visited the frontier himself, starting with five days in Alsace-Lorraine. Every four to ten kilometres he stopped his car and climbed the high points. His reconnaissance broadly confirmed the outlines of the CDF's proposed fortified regions and, predictably, his own preference for depth.[87]

On his return, Pétain demonstrated both his ability to manoeuvre within the decision-making apparatus and his indecisiveness. He persuaded Painlevé to allow him to present his proposals to an extraordinary 'preparatory meeting' of the CSG generals alone, then on a revised agenda to the CSG meeting already scheduled for 4 July, and then to preside himself at a special session of the CDF. In the first preparatory meeting, Nollet and another member of the CSG, General Antoine Targe, backed Pétain's criticisms of *gros ouvrages*. Both these generals sympathised with the left and as artillery officers they doubted whether their arm could spare men for artillery works – Targe condemned excessive mechanisation for that reason. Fillonneau defended the CDF position.[88]

Although the CSG meeting had originally been called simply to discuss the technical specifications of individual forts, on the assumption that the general outline had already been agreed, Pétain presented his new agenda the evening before.[89] As chair, President of the Republic Gaston Doumergue was legitimately annoyed. Pétain brushed his protests aside and laid out his proposals. On the resistance line, he accepted only a few artillery works and on the second line even fewer of them. The marshal's strongest support came from Degoutte and Maurin, who repeated that the officers interviewed in February and April had 'undermined' the CDF's proposals. Degoutte claimed that numerous small blockhouses provided denser fire with more weapons more cheaply and required few specialists, which, he considered, would be impossible to recruit. He presented the results of another trial east of Boulay.[90]

Fillonneau, Guillaumat and Debeney urged members to stick to the original agenda. Foch advocated closing the frontier immediately with permanent works and thinking about a second position later, for in eight years' time the Rhineland would be evacuated. General Edmond Boichut, commander in Alsace-Lorraine, implied that Pétain's proposal would lose the province. Fillonneau added that manpower was insufficient for a dispersed system. Frustrated at the confusion, Doumergue urged members to work 'methodically' and vote on the original agenda. Pétain summoned all his authority to say that he could not chair the following day's CDF meeting unless the CSG answered his questions – i.e. unless it approved his proposal. Unwilling to risk Pétain's resignation, members agreed.

When it came to a vote, the marshal retreated – as so often. He withdrew a motion to reserve artillery works for the shorter second position, allowing members to approve positioning *ouvrages* on the frontier. As an empty concession to Pétain, the resolution stated that positions would be 'nuanced' according to conditions. Foch ensured that Pétain's proposal that the frontier regions 'must' be prepared in depth was changed to 'could be'. Pétain's *volte face* permitted the CSG to endorse the CDF proposal for a line of *gros ouvrages* on the frontier. Closing the meeting, Doumergue reminded participants that the Senate Army Commission was getting impatient.

The following day, 5 July, Pétain confirmed his retreat in the CDF meeting. If he felt any embarrassment, it was softened by minor concessions. As he wished, the CDF withdrew the line covering the Longwy's steel complex behind it – an easy concession, for Longwy's proximity to the frontier made it hard to defend. The CDF also conceded the withdrawal further back of the right flank of RF-Lauter and cancellation of *gros ouvrages* on its left at Rohrbach.[91] Purchase of land, transport of construction material and preliminary work were expected to begin within months.[92]

Why did Pétain back down again? The faithful Laure's subsequent claim that he had always advocated permanent artillery works was incorrect.[93] In reality, Pétain's commitment to echeloned campaign fortification had not hitherto wavered.[94] More likely, to preserve his mediating position, Pétain again applied his doctrine of tactical withdrawal, and it is hard to avoid the suspicion that his mental faculties were declining. This time, however, he did not attempt to undermine the CSG decision. Two developments convinced him of the merits of permanent artillery forts.

The first was that the CDF had produced new designs for individual forts. In the CSG meeting of 17 December 1926, Pétain had regretted that the CDF proposed only one model fort. The CDF duly produced a 'sample' (the commercial term was not accidental) of ten model forts and shelters. Most were Verdun-style centralised forts, but they included a major innovation, the *ouvrage palmé* – the 'webbed fort'.[95] This possibility had been included in the CDF's original report, but no model design had yet been produced. Much controversy was necessary before such forts became standard. For now, the point is that they met one of Pétain's objections to permanent fortification. Rather than siting all the weapons in a single massive concrete bloc, they were dispersed in the terrain in smaller blocs, linked by underground galleries. Pétain had always advocated dispersal, camouflage and cover. In its 4 July meeting, the CSG accepted the sample forts without discussion. Pétain became an enthusiast for the *ouvrage palmé*.

Another reason for Pétain's change of heart was the disappointing result of studies of small blockhouses. On 18–21 July 1927, Pétain toured the Belfort region, where he inspected the CDF's experiment on Degoutte's system of small works.[96] He learned that the sheer number of blockhouses and the need to expropriate huge expanses of land made the scheme more expensive than *gros ouvrages*. Small blockhouses were vulnerable to gas and artillery, and even a very large number could not ensure a continuous line of fire. They required more officers to command a greater number of dispersed troops.

Like most officers, Pétain was sensitive to the latter point, and ultimately rallied to the majority view that *gros ouvrages* best guaranteed command.[97] Command was a recurring theme for advocates of *gros ouvrages*. The CDF's first report had criticised multiple blockhouses on the grounds that each would soon become isolated.[98] Pétain subsequently told Degoutte that his system of small blockhouses would leave defence in the hands of combat groups.[99]

On 23 August, Pétain revealed his latest reversal to the CDF, which agreed to mix large and small fortifications depending on local conditions. To assuage the marshal's fears over the lack of specialists at a time when France was short of labour and recruitment of career soldiers was difficult, intermediate works could if necessary be delayed until credits were available. On 11 October, perhaps to avoid re-enacting military quarrels in front of politicians and spare Pétain's blushes, a preparatory meeting of the CSG approved a lightly modified version of the CDF note, which was rubber-stamped by the full CSG the following day.[100] On 29 December, Painlevé signed the programme. He thus approved the outline of the fortifications, the construction within them of *gros ouvrages* close to the frontier and the general principles on which technical forms would be based.

Practical work was beginning. Regional military engineer units, Chefferies de travaux de fortification, had been created in April. Then, on 30 September, a decree established the Commission d'organisation des régions fortifiées (CORF) – on which more later – which was charged with drawing up detailed plans.[101] In February 1928, the ministry approved a pre-project for the northeast and in March technical specifications for fortifications.

'Now we enter the stage of realisation,' said President Doumergue, closing the 12 October CSG meeting. He was too optimistic. The CSG vote was not quite unanimous. Three members opposed artillery-proof underground galleries and thus *gros ouvrages*. Advocates of small works remained vociferous, notably generals Targe, Degoutte, Nollet and Maurin.[102] That Nollet and Maurin were past and future war ministers in left-wing and centre-right governments respectively revealed the politicisation of the fortification question. The right-wing Prime Minister Poincaré's backing for small-scale fortification also contributed to politicisation.

Politicisation, 1928–January 1930

For Poincaré, cheaper fortification solved a dilemma. On the one hand, through Hirschauer's lobby group, influential figures in his own Meuse constituency demanded fortification of their short frontier with Belgium. Poincaré himself saw fortification as a way to counter Alsace-Lorraine autonomism – a few days after the CSG meeting, his police arrested leading autonomists. On the other hand, he was committed to saving money, for he had come to power to solve a financial crisis and doubled as finance minister. His reservations about the cost of *gros ouvrages*, which to some extent Painlevé and Pétain shared, gave their opponents another chance.

In the first weeks of 1928, Painlevé had divided the fortification programme into tranches and provided the basic parameters for planning on the ground. Yet in July, on Poincaré's instruction, he charged General Alfred Normand with finding savings: as director of engineers at the War Ministry, cost was his responsibility. Although the EMA and CORF only found out about the review through the grapevine, they had little to fear. Normand broadly approved the plan and suggested only 330 million francs of savings: elimination of some counterscarp antitank barriers, and the replacement of some second-line forts with field artillery, of some delicate machine-gun turrets with casemates and LMG cloches and of some concrete galleries with masonry.[103] (All these measures had consequences for those manning the forts.) The proposed fortified region at Belfort was quietly shelved.

Normand's report did not break the deadlock. When in late July 1928 he presented his findings to Painlevé, Targe, also present, seized the chance to resuscitate Degoutte's system. Normand conceded only that flexibility was possible. Painlevé was struggling to find a way forward. He wondered whether it would be better to reduce the length of the front rather than its strength. Rather desperately, he considered asking Poincaré to tour the frontier. In a senate hearing, the Alsace-Lorraine nationalists Hirschauer and General Jean Stuhl pressed Painlevé and Debeney to hasten construction, even though, according to Stuhl, the population from Boulay to Bitche opposed the work already underway. Painlevé asked Pétain to decide, but he refused to reopen the question.[104] Pétain too had doubts. Although no longer opposed in principle to *gros ouvrages*, he told the Conseil supérieur de la défense nationale (CSDN – Supreme Council of National Defence) that he was ready to reduce spending on fortification to remedy the sorry state of the army.[105]

In autumn 1928, preparatory works were beginning, but the CDF's grand designs were far from realisation. On 22 October, the ministry authorised the construction of three prototype *gros ouvrages* in the northeast: Rochonvillers and Hackenberg in RF-Metz and Hochwald in RF-Lauter.[106] Expropriation of land and recruiting contractors began. Haste was most noticeable in the southeast, for Mussolini had recently repeated that Nice and Savoie were Italian. The first pick-axe blow was struck on 4 September 1928 on the Rimplas *gros ouvrage* on a spectacular peak overlooking the confluence of the Tinée and Valdeblore valleys.[107] Painlevé ensured that the War Ministry budget for 1929 included initial funding, but the outlook for the whole was unclear.[108]

In November, Pierre Cot brought controversy into the public sphere. Nationalists ridiculed his 'bleating pacifism'. In fact, with the authority of a decorated veteran, he advocated a legal framework for international relations with a clear definition of self-defence and sanctions against aggressors, military if necessary.[109] In his article 'Fortifications or machine guns? Vauban or Hotchkiss' he argued that while disarmament was the best way to ensure national security, fortification was an insurance policy.[110] He saw concrete *ouvrages* as 'ruinous and ineffective' relics of Vauban and argued that the Hotchkiss machine gun, fieldworks, mobility and camouflage were the most effective means of protection and of concentrating fire in modern war. Field fortification was also compatible with disarmament and cheaper. He pictured a new *levée en masse*: military-age male citizens would rush to the frontier in uniform while older civilians constructed field fortifications using stocks stored on site.

There is some truth in Laure's remark that the debate set left against right: 'One would almost have thought that there was a sumptuous and reactionary fortification, the *gros ouvrages*, and an another that was economical and doubtless democratic, that of *petits ouvrages*.'[111] Yet the dichotomy requires qualification. Right-wing politicians such as Poincaré backed field fortification, while in the army Targe endorsed the militia and many officers preferred field to permanent fortification, which they associated with the Génie's abstractions.[112]

At the end of November 1928, a cross-party alliance of Cot and right-wing members of the Chamber Army Commission pressed the government for action. Days later, the Senate echoed their concerns. In the Chamber, Painlevé, either disingenuously or because he was undecided, declared that the question of fortification remained open and that he would consult reserve officers. Construction would begin in such a way that the final form need not be decided.[113] Meanwhile, Cot's article provoked a vigorous secret rebuttal by the EMA, which reprised its earlier critique of Degoutte's system: Cot's proposal was costly, required huge numbers of men and undermined command.[114]

A few weeks later, an anonymous serving officer echoed Cot's case in the military newspaper *La France militaire*. The author probably had inside knowledge, for he implicitly refuted the army's secret response. And since articles had to be approved by the EMA, the high command too must have been uncertain.[115] Two weeks later, another anonymous article countered that only fortification could resist the more numerous and better-trained German army.[116] (In fact, the Reichswehr was limited to 100,000 men.) For two months, contributors to *La France militaire* rehearsed the familiar arguments and disputed the lessons of the war. In January 1929, Painlevé told the Senate and Chamber Army Commission presidents that argument had resumed 'in a very lively manner, propagated by its very dissemination'.[117]

Painlevé nonetheless allowed construction to gather momentum. In January 1929, he sent Debeney to the conservative parliamentary leader

André Tardieu to convince him of the plan's merits. On the 7th, as public controversy raged, he formally approved the CORF's project (which matched the CDF's), while prudently downplaying the role of *gros ouvrages* when presenting it to the Council of Ministers and commission presidents. Implicitly repudiating Cot, he denied that the plan returned to Vauban.[118] Contractors for the first three *ouvrages* were agreed, yet since detailed specifications were lacking, directors of works improvised.

Poincaré's financial concerns remained a major obstacle to progress. On 12 January, he chaired a meeting at which Degoutte again presented his plan.[119] Those present rejected it yet again, but agreed that further cuts in the CORF plan were essential.[120] Pétain insisted that the general principles could not be changed, but told General Charles Belhague, who had just succeeded Fillonneau as inspector of engineers, to find savings. The marshal's long-standing concerns came to the fore again, for he laid down that *ouvrages* on the RF-Metz right flank should be downgraded from artillery to more numerous but cheaper infantry forts, thus providing a continuous line of fire more cheaply. Artillery works on the right flank of RF-Lauter had already been cancelled – thus weakening both flanks of the Sarre Gap (another decision with consequences). In the following months, the ministry issued further instructions on matters such as armament, communications and supply. Local delegations drew preliminary plans for Hackenberg, Rochonvillers and Hochwald.[121]

Poincaré still blocked Painlevé's efforts to secure long-term funding, despite the budget for once being in surplus. In January 1929, Poincaré rejected Painlevé's suggestion to use 'extra-budgetary resources' – a special account – thus countering foreign attacks on French militarism by reducing the military budget proper.[122] The situation changed in July 1929, when ill health obliged Poincaré to resign. A month later, agreement at the Hague that the Rhineland must be evacuated by 30 June 1930 focused minds.

Remaining at the War Ministry in a brief government headed by Briand, Painlevé persuaded Finance Minister Henry Chéron to accept long-term funding. The projected cost was 2.7 billion, despite the CDF estimate of seven (probably the final cost).[123] Belhague warned that the fortifications would not have the power envisaged in 1928; Pétain reassured him that new blocs could be added to the *ouvrage palmé*.[124] Belhague probably heard rumours that the Finance Ministry planned to renege on the agreement and not disburse money promised for 1929.[125]

That was how matters stood on 3 November 1929, when a new administration with Tardieu at its head and Maginot at the War Ministry took office. According to Tardieu, he immediately called Maginot and Finance Minister Chéron to his office in the Interior Ministry on Place Beauvau. They agreed that including fortification in the war budget would have 'repercussions in international opinion' and allow cuts in future years. Maginot told the press that he planned a special account.[126] In fact, the bill presented to the Chamber of Deputies on 16 December did not include such an account, probably because the Finance Ministry blocked it. Instead, it authorised spending up to 2.9 billion on fortification plus 400 million for air defence over five years, of which one billion was authorised in 1930–1.

Introducing the bill on 17 December, Maginot told the Chamber that fortification was essential for reconciliation with Germany.[127] Listeners might have been surprised, for Maginot enjoyed a reputation as a foreign-policy hawk, and his presence at the War Ministry was indeed meant to reassure nationalists. In fact, like most conservatives, Maginot approved Briand's peace policy. The new Plan B of 1929 abandoned the invasion of Germany for a fighting retreat by the Rhine occupation army to defensive positions on the frontier.[128]

In the short debate, the principal political protagonists, with the exception of Painlevé, rehearsed the old arguments: Maginot, Daladier, Cot and Colonel Jean Fabry (an influential member of the Senate Army Commission and friend of Maginot). As was usual in the French parliament, which valued consensus through debate, Maginot reassured deputies that Cot's interventions had not been futile. He described disputes concerning fortification as about 'means' and the bill as a compromise between *gros ouvrages* and continuous field fortification. To give an impression of national unity, the president of the Chamber engineered acceptance by raised hands rather than by a formal vote. On the 28th, the bill passed in the Senate, and it became law on 14 January 1930. It was known as 'la loi du 14 janvier', not 'la loi Maginot', for at the time Painlevé's role was universally acknowledged. Subsequently,

Maginot was responsible for setting up a special account (law of 20 July 1931), for he feared that once credits ran out, the Finance Ministry would cut the programme.[129]

Thus, only in the later 1920s, in the context of reconciliation with Germany, did fortification become a priority, and even then some still saw it as cover for offensive manoeuvre. Neither did fortification derive directly from a doctrine framed by the last war, for there was little agreement as to what that war's lessons were. Pétain's proposal for successive lines of field fortifications on the entire frontier was roundly rejected in favour of permanent works on the Franco-German border. Furthermore, we shall see that the form of the *ouvrages* remained controversial and ultimately owed much to German innovations.

Neither was there a national consensus in favour of fortification. Voting the law by acclamation disguised disagreement. After the Chamber vote, four groups complained that trickery had prevented them voting against.[130] The Communists and Alsace-Lorraine autonomists were probably telling the truth, as their small parliamentary groups were easily outmanoeuvred. We may doubt the sincerity of the Socialists and Radical-Socialists, for these wily parliamentary operators could have demanded a nominal vote at the time. Most likely they did not because it would have revealed that they were torn between pacifism and defensive war and that they had doubts about *gros ouvrages*. In the 1930s, they became increasingly influential and had significant support within the army.

General Stuhl, reporting the bill in the Senate, expressed the mood in the army better than Maginot. Rather than 'compromise', he evoked the 'bitterest of quarrels between technicians charged with studying the organisation of the frontier'. He remarked that 'everyone wanted to apply the lessons of the war, but nobody agreed' what they were.[131] The final shape of the fortifications was far from settled.

3

ORGANISING THE FRONTIER, 1930–1935

The 'armes savantes', the 'learned arms', the artillery and engineers who dominated the CORF, played the primary role in designing the fortifications. These elite officers acquired advanced scientific knowledge in the École polytechnique, which trained France's senior civil and military engineers – the Génie civil and the Génie militaire. Graduates from the Polytechnique's military pathway completed their training at the École d'application de l'artillerie et du génie at Fontainebleau, which, as its name suggests, taught them to apply their theoretical training. There, they joined direct entrants, Saint-Cyrians and others, who constituted the great majority of Génie officers. Direct entrants had little hope of a senior position, for in 1939 all but one of the generals of military engineers were polytechnicians.

The Polytechnique and CORF were ramifications of the notoriously centralised French administration, which had persisted through revolutions and coups, absolute and constitutional monarchies, two empires and three republics. This administration gave France its geographically uniform departments headed by appointed prefects and communes administered by elected mayors. It oversaw the regularisation of rivers, laid out forests in squares, and oversaw construction of telephone, road, waterway and rail networks and an electrical grid converging on Paris.[1] Since war industries were also concentrated around Paris, blocking routes from the porous frontier to the capital was the condition of winning a war. Officers often quoted Vauban's saying that whereas most forts defended provinces, Metz defended the state.[2]

Culturally, polytechnicians were rooted in the neoclassical tradition epitomised by Vauban, fortifier, besieger, hydrologist and founder of the corps of engineers. The ideal proportions of his fortifications reflected mathematical calculability and the benevolent, harmonious, rational power of the state, as did thousands of prefectures and town halls (*mairies*). In the 1920s, polytechnicians updated neoclassicism with organisational science, with its commitment to command and downward transmission of orders, and with some openness to modernist simplicity. Fortification was routinely known as 'organisation of the frontier', while digging a trench was 'organising the terrain'. Organisation extended to the humans – and animals – who manned new, technically trained fortification units. This was the ethos of the CORF.

The CORF was charged with ensuring that each *ouvrage* fulfilled its mission within the whole as defined by the CDF. It inherited the latter's technical secretariat and local delegations, and was directly responsible to the ministry via the engineer directorate within it. Successive chiefs of the EMA – Debeney, Weygand (January 1930–February 1931) and Gamelin (from February 1931) – had some say in construction, as did Pétain as vice-president of the CSG until he retired in 1931. Other members of the CSG, to their annoyance, were sidelined.

Initially, the artillery and engineers feared that the CORF would encroach on their technical prerogatives. In practice, their officers dominated it, for they monopolised the requisite technical knowledge and resources. Its presidency fell by right to the inspector of military engineers, initially to Fillonneau, who had done so much to ensure the choice of *gros ouvrages*, and then, from December 1929, to Belhague. In 1928–9, representation of artillery and engineer officers was increased. Infantry officers were outnumbered and to prevent special pleading were forbidden to hold field commands.[3]

Guided by the CDF's programme, the CORF established preliminary projects for siting groups of *ouvrages*. Once the ministry approved these projects, its local delegations drew up plans for individual forts. These plans were submitted to the CORF, which took advice from the technical sections of the engineers and sent representatives to check conformity to the general schema. Once the CORF gave the green light, territorial engineer units (*chefferies*) began to expropriate land, put out tenders to private contractors and clear forests in liaison with the AEF. CORF delegations then became directorates of works, which supervised civilian contractors and workers.[4]

The fortifications did not turn out as the CDF and CORF planned them. Even the *gros ouvrage*, the embodiment of organisational science, fell short of the ideal. The younger engineers responsible for the actual construction of the *ouvrages* did not necessarily share their elders' neoclassical and modernist commitment to uniformity and centralisation. Although fortification was designed to protect the country's economic resources for a possibly long war, reconciling business and military priorities was complicated. The forest and water authorities complained that the CORF sacrificed the short to the long term. The senior officers designated to command on the frontier in wartime accused the CORF, with its unrealistic plans, of encroaching on their prerogatives. The sheer scale and cost of the CORF's ambition and the practical ability of contemporary engineering to control rock, water and air made the project impossible.

The Age of Organisation

The *gros ouvrages* were designed in what some historians call the 'age of organisation'.[5] After the Great War, social conservatives saw organisational science as a way to re-establish authority in the face of industrial unrest and challenges from socialism and communism. Organisers accepted that unrestrained market forces caused inefficiency, degraded workers' conditions and pushed them into the embrace of communism. As an alternative to the left's solutions of state planning and socialisation, they advocated partnership between business, administrative and military leaders to 'organise' economy and society using Fayolist and Taylorist principles. These methods were expected to improve productivity and ensure that workers' allegedly basic needs were met, thus reconciling them to capitalism. The moderate left agreed with much of this, differing only in advocating a greater role for trade unions in industry and democratisation of the officer corps.

This was also the age of leaders, of the 'chef' (chief). Leadership theory assumed that society was chaotic and purposeless unless organised by an elite. It justified the primacy of business, administrative, academic and military leaders on grounds of superior character and leadership qualities rather than those of birth or wealth.[6]

André Tardieu, prime minster when funding for fortification was approved, was a leading organiser. Following a brief period at the front, he occupied a senior position in the war economy. In peacetime, he participated in various Fayolist and Taylorist groups, of which the best-known was Redressement français. Foch and Lyautey were honorary presidents, while Pétain, Debeney and Laure attended its meetings.[7] Tardieu's administrations of 1929–32 implemented a 'prosperity policy', of which the centrepiece was a Plan d'outillage national (National Re-tooling Plan) funded by budget surpluses and war reparations. It subsidised road building, port improvement and electrification, all of which were integral to fortification.[8]

Although officers were reluctant to see themselves as administrators, Fayol's vocabulary was ubiquitous in military documents. Pétain used Fayol's concept of unity of command in his campaign for a single defence ministry and commander-in-chief, writing, 'Productivity in implementation and organisation must be sought at the highest echelon; it is above all at this echelon that it is essential to organise administration and command.'[9] He claimed that 'the progress of armaments has transformed the battlefield into an immense factory, where the role of technique is affirmed'.[10]

The moderate socialist deputy Joseph Paul-Boncour saw the efficiency of organisational science as the necessary condition for the reduction of service to one year.[11] Continuing Jaurès's campaign for modernisation of the army and democratisation of the officer corps, he mocked the 'useless gestures' (Taylorist language) of ceremonial guards in front of empty quarters whose only duty was to salute passing officers. Invoking his own war experience, he wrote, 'We pay the price of inefficiency: we have seen the machine work; we know its cogs.'[12] Regular officers were doubtful about democratisation, but agreed that short-service conscripts required rationalised training and strong leadership. General Jean-Joseph Rouquerol wrote that 'cohesion resulting from rigorously identical training takes the modern machine as its model' and that training 'has no more military value than the machine, good or bad, depending on the skill of him who operates it'.[13]

Politicians and the army agreed that reduction in the length of military service was conditional upon professionalisation. The military laws prescribed an increase in the number of career soldiers from around 78,000 in 1926 to 115,000 as a spine for the army. To free these cadres for training, civilian auxiliaries were hired for routine administrative work – an innovation known as 'industrialising the army'. A new professional Garde républicaine mobile (GRM), part of the gendarmerie, took over the army's tasks of public order and watching the frontier. Debeney explained that professionalisation strengthened leadership and along with fortification compensated for the reduced number of covering troops on the frontier.[14]

Observation of the German Treaty Army, the Reichswehr, reinforced the movement for professionalisation. General Nollet, war minister in 1924, who had observed the Reichswehr closely as president of the inter-allied control commission in Berlin, feared that this highly trained 100,000-strong force was capable of carrying out a surprise attack and then quickly mobilising a mass army.[15] Debeney rejected Reichswehr chief General Hans von Seekt's claim that his professionals could defeat the French conscript force, but agreed on 'the excellence of German organisation and the mediocrity of current French organisation'.[16]

Advocates of fortification also saw mechanisation as compensation for inferior French resources. They were as fascinated by machinery as were campaigners for armoured divisions. In his 'La guerre moderne et les machines' (1922), Debeney likened machine operators to medieval knights, going into battle like armoured meteors, with the irresistible power of the lance.[17] The CDF stated that 'the price per cubic metre of concrete means that armament must have the highest possible productivity, thanks to its very rapid rate of fire'. Since multiplying weaponry increased the size and vulnerability of *ouvrages*, sufficient firepower could 'only be achieved using all the resources of modern technology'.[18] The model for individual forts was the Taylorised factory, one journalist describing them as 'commercial enterprises with several branches, selling firepower'.[19] Those who manned them were not the peasant soldiers of traditional France, but skilled workers, technicians and engineers.

The high command borrowed organisationalist methods from the navy, which had pioneered them. A Fayolist course was taught in the naval school well before Fayol set foot in the École de guerre, for warships were readily assimilated to factories and maritime engineers knew Fayol's work on coal combustion. From 1927, Fillonneau, Guillaumat, Pétain and others visited coastal batteries, warships, naval laboratories and Schneider's Creusot works to study naval artillery.[20] Naval officers were attached to the fortifications. They advocated a single commander, and below him single medical, supply and communication 'départements' (services) as on a warship and in a big factory, rather than the traditional division into arms.[21]

Organisational science was also a cultural movement with military ramifications, prefigured in Léger's idealisation of military weaponry and heroic machine-soldiers. In the 1920s, organisation was intrinsic to the 'call to order', an artistic movement which rejected the alleged confusion and near-abstraction of prewar cubism. Simplified, 'organised' landscapes were the best-selling paintings of the period. They reasserted the wholeness – the organisation – of the French countryside after the devastation of the war.[22] A key figure was the modernist painter and architect Charles-Édouard Jeanneret, better known as Le Corbusier. Just as managers and officers aspired to organise workers and troops, Le Corbusier sought what he called 'the pure element in order to reconstruct organised paintings that seem to be facts from nature itself'. The geometrical exactness of his paintings contrasts with 'messy' cubism. Painters and architects saw themselves as experts and leaders, uniquely competent to organise disorder, just like managers.

In his architecture, Le Corbusier is best known for modernist skyscrapers, but the general principles he advocated were present in the design of the *gros ouvrages*, not least because modernism and neoclassicism had much in common. He advocated simplification, industrialisation, mechanisation, Taylorisation and construction with standard concrete and steel modularised components. He imagined buildings that provided workers with 'modern comfort' and thus countered the appeal of communism.[23] His unrealised plans for the reconstruction of central Paris imagined a total society, with separate zones for bourgeois and working-class housing, factories and commercial districts linked by high-speed transport. Concentrating dwellings and offices in skyscrapers made more land available for healthy green spaces.[24] Separation of work from home and integration of the latter into green spaces linked Le Corbusier to the older garden-city movement, which rejected skyscrapers in the name of traditional styles but advocated using industrial methods to adapt regionalism to modern life.[25]

These schemes had a military dimension. In 1930, Le Corbusier wrote that for ten years he had been 'developing plans for urbanisation and habitation that respond to most of the requirements of anti-aircraft defence'.[26] Although Le Corbusier's specific designs for buildings were too radical for most military engineers, a vaguer modernism was attractive to the Génie for its order, efficiency and anticommunist potential and even its military advantages. Officers wrote in avant-garde architectural reviews that skyscrapers and wide avenues were better able to withstand bomb blasts and gas attacks than densely packed cities.[27] The popular science magazine *La Nature* predicted that in future all cities and even villages would be fortified against air attack, complementing fortification of the frontier.[28]

Military–Business Partnership

In accordance with conservative organisational science, the Maginot Line was built by a partnership of army, state and big business. The CORF advocated employment of 'very large contractors' with the resources to purchase the 'most modern equipment', build accommodation for thousands of workers and borrow privately, pending repayment by the state. With their engineers and research departments, it added, these firms guaranteed quality work; their experience in supervising large numbers of workers would lighten Génie officers' load.[29] Openly favouring big business was difficult in the French parliament, which prided itself on protecting small concerns. The latter were permitted to form consortiums, but construction of the *ouvrages* was largely the work of big contractors. They were at the forefront of the public campaign for fortification, for besides wishing to defend frontier assets, they foresaw lucrative revenue streams. The Union lorraine pour la protection de la frontière du Nord-Est, which lobbied for fortification, was backed by the Chambers of Commerce affiliated to the eastern economic region.[30]

Although bidding for contracts was restricted to firms able to meet financial and technical standards, competition was fierce. Eleven firms submitted for GO-Rimplas; the successful company, Faraut, agreed a rebate of 28.5 per cent and paid a deposit of 150,000 francs.[31] In April 1930, in response to complaints that parliamentarians were secretly aiding their clients, Maginot introduced public bidding in the presence of local mayors. There were now between twenty and sixty bidders per contract. Yet government oversight was limited, not least because the true cost was not known in advance. Ministerial approval of huge contracts was reduced to five working days, provoking the colonel responsible to remark that any less time would render accountability illusory.[32] The largest contracts still went to firms such as the Grands travaux de Marseille, the number one firm in France. Another winner was the number seven company, Les Établissements André Borie, whose eponymous boss enjoyed a reputation as an organiser and was close to Daladier.[33]

The construction effort was huge (see Plate 3). The first step was to improve or build road and narrow-gauge rail links, so that material could be brought on site. Combat and entrance blocs consisted of immense reinforced-concrete cubes. Once excavation was complete, a reinforced-concrete slab was laid. When wooden frames and steel rods were in place, interior and exterior walls and roof slabs were usually poured together. Galleries were excavated with mechanical or compressed-air drills. They were lined with masonry, but close to the surface they were reinforced with concrete. In 1933, turrets, embrasure protection for casemates, cloches, power plants and ammunition loaders were installed.[34] New machinery was invented in the course of construction, from automatic loaders for gravel to special tractors for transporting turrets and machinery for laying barbed wire and trenching.

Nevertheless, the work remained hard and labour-intensive. Geological conditions were rarely entirely known in advance. On one site in the Meuse department, a contractor sued the state because work had been delayed by rocky ground.[35] Given that France was short of labour, the CORF and government stressed that immigrant workers were required, just as heavy industry employed them for menial tasks.[36] Foreign workers were necessary because French peasants were reluctant to leave the land, which, differently from British agricultural labourers, they often owned. France had long been a country of immigration, and in 1930 nearly three million foreigners were working mainly in agriculture, heavy industry and construction.

Building the fortifications was thus a mirror of interwar organised capitalism: a state–private partnership operating in a system of limited competition, combining advanced technology with recourse to a mass of skilled and unskilled labour, often immigrant. Yet the army struggled to reconcile military priorities with protection of the nation's factories for the long war that fortification was supposed to defend.

Defending the steel industries at Longwy was particularly difficult. They were situated in a vulnerable salient at the intersection of the French, Luxembourg and Belgian borders, with forest cover through which the enemy could approach. Yet it was psychologically difficult to abandon an area that had suffered German occupation in 1914–18 and which since then had expanded to produce almost all France's iron ore and over half its steel. The CDF tentatively proposed a line close to the frontier englobing Longwy and culminating at Longuyon but postponed a definitive choice.[37] In 1929, the Union lorraine, national press, and Meurthe-et-Moselle senator and Chamber Army Commission president Albert Lebrun pressed Maginot for fortifications on the frontier. Weygand, Pétain and Guillaumat rejected this idea along with a 'bound' into Luxembourg. Instead, they agreed a line further back (GOs Bréhain, Latiremont and Fermont).[38] It would not have been constructed at all without political and business pressure, but Longwy was effectively sacrificed.

A disadvantage of the chosen line was that it traversed the Boulay–Faulquemont–Saint-Avold coalfield, which companies planned to exploit to compensate for the expected loss of Saar mines following the 1935 plebiscite. Pétain modified the line, hoping that in return the companies would accept the restrictions that accompanied fortification.[39] In fact, the companies complained that planned airfields would render mining impossible.[40] In this case, the army prevailed. Its relations with the AEF, however, were more complex.

Organising Nature

Organising the frontier required remodelling the landscape – organising the terrain.[41] As Buat put it, 'when nature failed, military art created artificial frontiers designed to achieve the same security', and, along with the troops, 'the whole constituted a coherent, organised system'.[42] Nature, like the human crowd, was thought to be dangerous unless organised and led. Otherwise, the enemy might turn it against France, just as communist agitators turned the human crowd against its country. Thus, General Pierre Klein, a fortification expert consulted in 1919, remarked presciently that forests on the Belgian frontier could just as easily mask the enemy's movements as defend the nation.[43]

Rivers too were dangerous. History showed that even the Rhine was crossable. In an extended metaphor, Klein claimed that Germany and the Rhine were 'liable to overflows that threatened the rich Alsatian plain; [the Alsatians] have built dykes to protect it against this invasion when the waters are inflated from upstream'. Yet, Klein warned, dykes were cut by roads; there were fissures even in the best, and leaks could isolate the guard posts.[44]

To counter such dangers, command was essential.[45] Colonel Louis Chauvineau, who taught fortification to engineer cadets, stressed that 'tactics, topography, cunning, technique and the organisation of work, constitute an indissociable bloc'. He likened ad hoc entrenching to 'spontaneous vegetation'. Nothing required officers' coordination more than 'organisation of the terrain'.[46]

Organisation meant dividing the terrain into compartments bounded by crests, rivers and forests. These limits were often referred to as 'môles de résistance' (breakwaters), which broke 'the impetuosity of the waves', as one general put it.[47] Fortification provided compartments with boundaries where nature did not.[48] Since fortification required substantial modification of the terrain, the cooperation of the AEF was essential.

As another emanation of the centralising state, the AEF assumed that to serve the national interest nature required the guiding hands of expert foresters and hydrologists. To facilitate commerce, foresters laid out woodlands in squares. Hydrologists calculated water flows and reinforced banks with masonry to give them single beds to make them navigable and prevent flooding. As the AEF was semi-militarised in peacetime and wholly in wartime, and many officials were reserve officers, it was sympathetic to military priorities, while the army understood the need for long-term management. Yet the AEF sometimes saw the army's immediate demands as conflicting with the interests of the state, as the long-running controversy concerning CORF fortifications in the Mormal Forest showed.[49]

Works there were among the few approved on the northern frontier in 1930. Guarding the southern flank of the Escaut/Scheldt invasion route, the Mormal Forest had long been valued as a military strongpoint. Far from natural, it was cut by clearings, paths and pastures, overexploited for game, firewood, pitprops and clog-making, and degraded by cattle and by fires sparked by trains. In 1914–18, the occupying Germans cleared two-thirds of it and machine-gunned trees they had not felled, making the timber unusable. In 1930, there remained considerable unemployment in the timber and clog-making industries, and the hunting on which poor families relied to supplement meagre incomes was still not restored. However, Mormal's status as a national domain forest ensured regeneration. White oaks reseeded themselves, and the AEF encouraged them with planting and thinning. By 1930, the forest was reconstituting, though not yet productive.[50]

In February, the AEF was alarmed to learn of the CORF's plans for thirteen casemates on the forest's northern limit, re-siting a small firing range to permit use of modern weapons and a 1,850-hectare camp for fortification troops – around one-fifth of the forest. In June 1934, the proposed construction of a *petit ouvrage* at Eth to the northwest of the forest made building a barracks for two thousand fortress troops still more urgent.

The AEF could not stop construction of the CORF works, but resisted cession of land for the firing range and especially the camp. With the support of the agriculture and finance ministries, it complained about loss of revenue from the regenerating forest, the danger to navigation and the potential flooding of the Escaut and Sambre rivers. It predicted that clog-makers would protest against the loss of raw materials. That the AEF did not mention that the camp would be built on

France's first bird sanctuary underlines that it defended the forest for the good of the state, not for the beauty of nature. The army reiterated the priority of defending the frontier. When the mayor of Locquignol in the middle of the forest objected, a military engineer retorted that the camp would be built 'come what may'.

The AEF eventually ceded the necessary land, not least because most local elected officials were pressing for completion of fortification to relieve unemployment. Among local politicians was the moderate-left Deputy Charles Daniel-Vincent, mayor of the forest commune of Le Quesnoy, and a war veteran who happened to be a member of the Senate Army Commission, which he chaired in 1936.

Yet construction was delayed to a time when the army prioritised tanks and aircraft rather than fortification. Only some access roads, light training facilities and a water tower without a pump were ever built. Nature itself, the spontaneous regeneration of the forest, coupled with the opposition of the AEF, stymied organisation of the frontier, despite the combined power of the army and Senate.[51]

AEF and army cooperated more effectively in hydrological works, for they agreed on the necessity of regularisation. The most important project was the planned flooding of the twenty-kilometre Sarre Gap. Until 1935, when a referendum returned it to Germany, French control of the German Saarland made fortification there impolitic. The zone was hard to defend anyway because it was dominated by heights on the German side and surface clay made the ground too wet for underground *ouvrages*. The same geological conditions also facilitated flooding.

The military flooding project originated in 1927 with Monsieur Pariset, a military engineer turned chief civil engineer of the Moselle department. Small structures designed to dam the Sarre and its left tributaries, the Moderbach and Albe, were complete by 1935. Beds were deepened and banks strengthened. To regulate flow, rivers were linked to three modified natural lakes and six artificial pools controlled by locks. The works were disguised as fishing improvements and carried out by civil engineers.[52] This successful partnership did not, however, make France an exception to the rule that 'improving' a river on one stretch had consequences elsewhere.

Such was the case on the Rhine, where the army failed to prevail against navigation authority, commercial and diplomatic interests. In the nineteenth century, German engineers had eliminated meanders and islands on the Rhine downstream from Strasbourg and constructed two dykes on each bank to contain flooding.[53] The hitherto wandering Rhine gained a single bed and was on the way to becoming the concrete canal of the present. However, these works speeded up flow upstream from Strasbourg, forming alluvial bars, exposing rocks and creating rapids at Istein and a potential crossing point at Saint-Louis, thus making the river unnavigable from Strasbourg to Basel.

At the turn of the century, the Alsatians and Swiss proposed a lateral canal to circumvent Istein, but Baden blocked a project that competed with its railways and threatened to harm agriculture by lowering the water table.[54] The Versailles Treaty having given the French the sole right to develop the river, they pushed through plans for a 'Grand canal d'Alsace' on French soil. The first stage, constructed between 1928 and 1931, was a dam, canal pound and hydro-electric station at Kembs and locks at Istein.[55] The German press portrayed the canal as a plot to turn Baden into steppe and integrate the river into French fortifications.[56]

In fact, the French army complained that the canal substituted the 'real and indestructible barrier of the Rhine [for] an obstacle of less value and essentially vulnerable', for it would drain water from the river. Another difficulty was that the Kembs installations, which controlled the level of the river, lay just outside a zone in which fortification was forbidden under the 1815 Treaty of Paris. The army ensured that points for explosives were built into the bridge over the dam so that it could be blown if necessary and the full flow of the Rhine restored. Even then, officers worried that this process would take thirty-six hours.[57] Ultimately, the army had to defend the river as the navigation authorities constructed it.

Defending the Rhine was even more difficult because it proved impossible to camouflage the casemates on the banks with embankments and trees. The Navigation Department pointed out that these modifications would divert summer meltwater floods and alter the course of the river. Doubtless the army accepted the advice because diversion would have rendered the blockhouses useless. Instead, the

Génie modified the (already artificial) banks upstream and downstream. The blockhouses resembled bridge piers and were more visible than ever – with serious consequences in 1940.[58] Thus, commercial interests and politics coupled with the properties of rivers and forests sometimes frustrated the centralising CORF's plans for the general outline of the fortifications. In the course of construction, the CORF's preference for centralised *gros ouvrages* also faced challenges from officers with different ideas about military architecture and tactics.

From *ouvrage centralisé* to *ouvrage palmé*

The senior officers on the CORF attended the Polytechnique in the late nineteenth century, when neoclassicism reigned supreme. Fillonneau graduated in 1887. Then, at the École d'application, he studied the *Cours de fortification*, according to which any modern fort contained the same elements – a central redoubt and a polygonal perimeter folding into the terrain, perhaps with pseudo-bastioned form at the gorge, covering mathematically calculated fields of fire.[59] Séré de Rivières's fortifications dispensed with bastions, but their centralisation, regular shapes, classical ornamentation and domination of the terrain remained. After constructing civil and military infrastructure in the colonies, Fillonneau commanded the Polytechnique before entering the CSG as inspector of engineers.[60] Belhague, his successor as inspector and president of the CORF, graduated in 1892.

When the fortifications were conceived, neoclassical principles had been updated with the use of industrial methods and with modernist simplicity. In 1928, Normand stated that the École d'application, which he had previously commanded, was infused with the spirit of Vauban, subtly modernised. He praised the unparalleled allure of the school's stables, achieved 'without decoration, by the simple character of its lines and the art of its proportions, which are the essence of architecture'.[61] The son and brother of eminent architects, Normand rejected the avant-garde international style of Le Corbusier in favour of the French classical tradition. He nevertheless held that reinforced concrete 'allowed new audacities – but evolution, not revolution'.[62] Classical language informed the CDF report: although individual *ouvrages* lacked bastions, whole forts were bastions just in advance of the line, covering each other's flanks.[63]

The report's accompanying model fort leaned towards neoclassicism. In accordance with the *Cours de fortification*, it centralised weaponry in a single bloc of concrete with a counterscarp to the front. The whole was surrounded by a lozenge-shaped dry ditch, barbed wire and antitank obstacles. The fort itself differed from prewar designs in having a 120-metre-wide front, but only 25 metres of depth, so that it was less likely to be hit by shells arriving frontally. It also added the improvements pioneered at Verdun, notably a gallery leading to the rear. This was the model that Pétain criticised. Most designs in the CDF's revised catalogue of May 1927 were similar, but included an important innovation, originally conceived by Lieutenant-Colonel Tricaud, commander of 6 Génie Regiment: the *ouvrage palmé*.[64] The *ouvrage palmé* overcame a major disadvantage of centralisation, which was that every hit was a bullseye, damaging the armour somewhat and troop morale more significantly. The new design solved this problem by dispersing weapons in separate reinforced-concrete blocs, each linked by galleries to the main gallery. From above, the plan resembled a bird's foot – hence the name 'webbed work'.

Fillonneau initially dismissed Tricaud's design because it lacked a ditch and howitzers, and positioned barracks and air intakes in the fort itself. These deficiencies were remedied in the CDF's new catalogue, and Fillonneau told the CSG the unlikely story that he had conceived the *ouvrage palmé* himself in February 1918 while standing on the destroyed Verdun glacis.[65] In fact, he continued to prefer centralised forts. After Fillonneau's retirement at the end of 1928, Belhague proved just as committed to them. In March 1929, the CORF stipulated that centralised forts were appropriate in flat, open terrain and sometimes in lumpier areas too; *ouvrages palmés* were a last resort, for they were said (mistakenly) to be two or three times more expensive.[66] Centralisers also claimed that the length of the rear gallery undermined command.[67] Yet most forts turned out to be *ouvrages palmés*.

Take for instance GO-Simserhof on the left flank of RF-Lauter on the fringe of the northern Vosges Forest near Bitche. Work on the plans began in the summer of 1928. The first definitive version, dated 7 June

1929, was the work of Colonel Charles Frossard, head of the CORF's Strasbourg delegation, an old-school polytechnician. It was nearly identical to Plan no. 2 in the CORF catalogue, itself a slightly elongated version of the CDF's original centralised model. It was chosen on the debatable grounds that the terrain was flat (Figure 8).

In July, CORF members concluded that Simserhof's proposed field of fire was inadequate, despite 'rectifying' the edge of the forest by felling thirty-eight hectares of trees. Belhague brushed aside Infantry General Robert Guitry's suggestion of constructing an *ouvrage palmé* in favour of two centralised half-forts from the CORF catalogue. After a site visit had confirmed Belhague's solution, Frossard drew a second plan, which the CORF and ministry approved on 24 September.[68] The plans were then returned to the Strasbourg delegation, now transformed into a directorate of works. Yet the latter broke the half-forts into eight individual blocs linked by a Y-shaped central gallery – an *ouvrage palmé* far removed from the original proposal (Figure 9).

Although we have no direct evidence of how or why that happened at Simserhof, extrapolation from wider contexts provides possible answers. Cost-cutting mattered, for in December 1929 counterscarps and ditches were eliminated from all Model 2 forts, as Normand had suggested to Painlevé the previous year. In fact, the cost of the *ouvrage palmé* could easily be reduced simply by not constructing specific blocs. At the Hochwald in RF-Lauter, which was similar to Simserhof, the first plans for a pair of *ouvrages* and redoubt potentially swallowed one-sixth of the funds available for the entire sector. Pétain initially approved them, but when construction began in August 1929 the redoubt was scaled back and only part of its entrance bloc was ever completed. The Hochwald forts lost their separate entrances, and so were linked by a single one, thus becoming two half-forts. Forty metres of galleries were never faced with coating. Some blocs were never constructed.[69]

Cost-cutting went further in the Sarre Gap. *Ouvrages* on its right were cancelled altogether. On its left, in RF-Metz, *ouvrages* were downgraded from artillery to infantry works. They too became *ouvrages palmés*, but lost their rear entrances. Air intakes and accommodation were therefore within the forts themelves. On RF-Lauter's right flank, a *gros ouvrage* planned at Oberroedern was replaced by casemates.

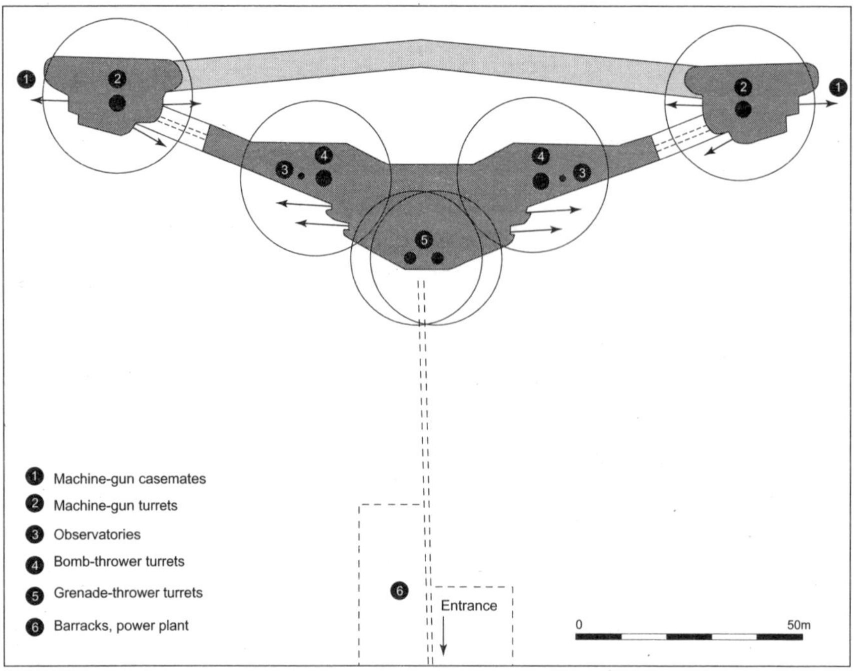

8. GO-Simserhof, first plan.

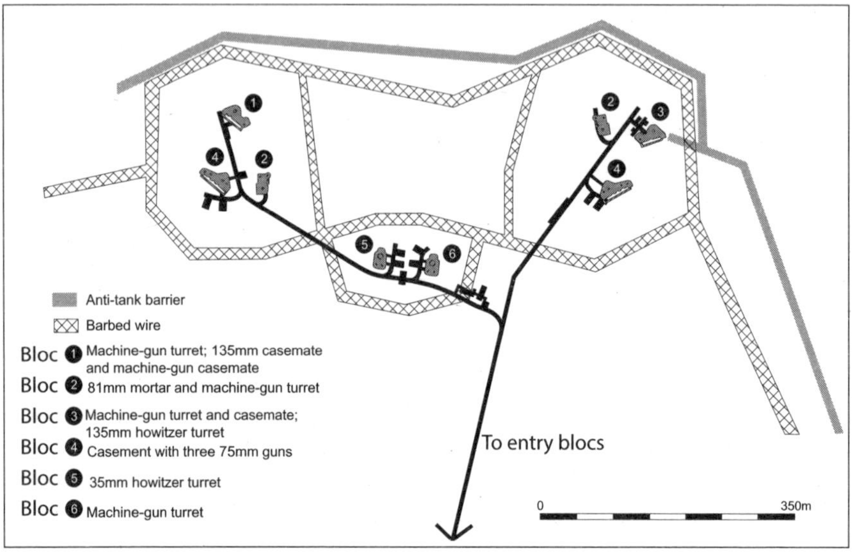

9. GO-Simserhof, final form.

The shafts and galleries already constructed were simply abandoned. There were only two fixed artillery pieces between Schœnenbourg and the Rhine.[70]

A second reason for the adoption of *ouvrages palmés* was that the engineers of the local directorates had room to reshape the designs, for the CORF lacked formal authority over the construction process. CORF instructions were often vague, for it relied on 1:20,000 German maps and incomplete geological and hydrological surveys, and guidance on the nature and range of armament was slow to arrive. At Hochwald, evolution of the plans resulted from toing and froing between the Génie's topographical surveyors and draughtsmen, without the intervention of the CORF, which never globally approved them but did issue dozens of notices.[71]

The CORF worried that construction was escaping its oversight. In May 1929, it asked the ministry to decree that important changes should be submitted to the CORF so that it could provide 'useful instructions to ensure consistency of views', following which plans would be approved again by the artillery directorate at the ministry.[72] In 1934, it vainly pressed the ministry again to grant it a greater role in supervising works.[73]

The younger generation of engineers responsible for construction were less rooted in neoclassicism and modernism than their elders. As the global depression hit France, protectionism, nationalism and regionalism ended the brief flirtation with international architectural modernism of the years during which the forts were planned. In the army, moreover, modernism had long been contested. From the 1900s, under the influence of Gaston Umbdenstock, the Polytechnique's architectural syllabus evolved away from classicism, especially after he returned from the trenches to become professor of architecture. The charismatic Umbdenstock was an advocate of romanticism, dismissive of 'soulless' modernism but also critical of neoclassicism insofar as it anticipated modernism. His goal was to integrate 'popular' neo-Gothic architecture into the national tradition together with 'elitist' neoclassicism.[74] In 1936, Major André Metz, director of the Génie's technical review, who had experienced Umbdenstock's teaching in 1910–12, remembered that he had taught officers to be artists in the purest sense, and that aesthetically sound military architecture should produce an emotional response and 'act on the soul'.[75] Umbdenstock urged military engineers to inspire heroism using 'secant effects' – dissymmetrical combinations of curves and straight lines, like bandoliers on uniforms. Napoleon urging his troops forward, standard in hand, had understood better than Vauban what the troops wanted, he argued. Practically, he advocated traditional regional styles, more in harmony with the landscape than modernism.[76]

From 1932, the Association of War Veteran Architects, in which Umbdenstock was involved, published *L'Art national*, which attacked modernism in terms that might have resonated with critics of top-down organisational science. One contributor denied that 'a + b means that you must live in a barracks and admire [modernists] on command'. He added that a 'free man can only laugh when in pseudo-artistic milieux he hears [architects] cry, "Left! Right!" like corporals teaching new recruits to goose-step' – implying that modernism was also German.[77] Some Génie officers might have read *L'Art national*, but many more read the mass-circulation daily, *Le Matin*. In October 1930, its editor, Stéphane Lauzanne, was one of the first journalists to visit the fortifications. He saw – or probably heard from Génie officers – that 'each casemate has its own plan and arrangement: it's not mass production; it's magnificent and ingenious individual work'.[78]

Younger officers, polytechnicians or not, were also aware of the German *Festen* of the Moselstellung in recovered Alsace-Lorraine, which they visited as trainees or on subsequent courses.[79] A CORF note described the *Festen* as 'just armoured, turreted artillery batteries submerged in concrete blocks [which in their] dimensions, habitability and mechanics, are very similar to our *ouvrages palmés*'. The German forts differed in firing frontally, whereas French forts supported each other with flanking fire, thus protecting vulnerable embrasures. The *Festen* did not have galleries leading to services in the rear.[80]

Another reason for evolution from centralised to dispersed forts was Pétain's influence, which remained strongest in tactical matters. He often modified designs, in the case of Simserhof to ensure that barracks were well to the rear. On the question of dispersal, he was at one with many infantry officers, who also preferred integration of forts into the terrain, as did Guitry in the CORF.

Ultimately, the design of individual *ouvrages* blended attention to the terrain and the *Feste* model with modernist architecture and urbanism, neoclassicism and organisational science. Rather than dominate the landscape, forts were integrated into it and camouflaged; perimeters were not geometrical, but moulded into the topography. Unlike Séré de Rivières's forts, entrances and casemates lacked embellishment, but resembled them in that retaining walls each side of the massive concrete facades were neatly faced with local stone.

Like Vauban's forts, entrances projected state power. Troops paraded ceremonially into them, recalling the procession of sovereign princes through the gates of medieval walled towns. The detective movie *Double crime sur la ligne Maginot* is framed by a ceremonial entrance into the fort at the beginning and exit at the end, for which the army provided a battalion of infantry with its band.[81] When the war began, foreign dignitaries were photographed in ceremonies outside the entrances.

Underground, the separation of living from fighting blocs echoed modern urbanists' advocacy of functionally segregated urban zones linked by high-speed transport, as in Le Corbusier's planned cities. Forts resembled upside-down versions of his skyscrapers, for they contained barracks for up to a thousand men, clinics, kitchens and power plants in a small surface area, well away from fighting blocs (see Plate 4). Troops' conditions were better than at Verdun, but could not be too easy, for soldiers had to prove their soldierliness by overcoming hardship. Fillonneau told the CSG that although troops would not be provided with 'modern comfort', fortification must be 'habitable'. In response, Pétain recalled the sickening conditions at Verdun.[82] Military engineers agreed that to protect morale, the garrison must live in healthy conditions, segregated from workspaces, 'with all the facilities indispensable for a prolonged stay – air, water, latrines, hospitals, protection from bombardment, etc.'.[83] The fortifications included elevators, central heating, air conditioning and electric ovens well before they appeared in homes or public buildings.

In the novel from which *Double crime sur la ligne Maginot* was adapted (written by a serving military officer), a character reflects on this subterranean town, 'minutely regulated, without useless effort, and without undue haste', with its trains running in underground galleries, and an electricity generating station supplying 'power, light and life'.[84] The fort was the antithesis not only of Verdun, but also of the disordered cities of the 1930s, to which organisation was the antidote.

Modernism was also evident in the design of furniture, at least in theory. In bourgeois modernist housing, simple steel furniture suited clean lines and airy spaces. In working-class housing, it saved space in tiny apartments, thus permitting higher-density occupation and rescuing the maximum number of workers from slums. In the *ouvrages*, where space was also at a premium, engineers stipulated that furniture should be reduced to a minimum, movable and foldable.[85] Consequently, folding metal chairs and tables were used in the fortifications well before domestic settings (though photographs show that in reality many chairs were wooden Thonet-style chairs – as it happened, the only style modernists accepted).[86] The stacking principle reached its high point in triple-tier, metal-framed bunks for troops (see Plate 5). Yet nowhere was the failure of the *ouvrages* to provide 'modern comfort' clearer than in their sleeping arrangements.

In many *ouvrages*, damp was a serious problem. Water proved hard to 'organise', not least on account of the geologically complex nature of the region. In simple terms, the border coincides with the upturned rim of the Paris Basin, the strata of which, from bottom to top, are formed of limestones, marls and sandstones, which, as a result of folding, volcanic events and differential erosion, created varied geological and hydrological conditions. Sufficiently dry ground was abundantly available to the west of the Moselle on the limestone plateau and on around half the ground to the east of the river, where clays were present. Ground was rarely suitable through the Northern Vosges to the Rhine, where permeable sandstones overlying clays ensured that the ground was often waterlogged.[87] Multiple difficulties appeared during construction. For instance, all three geological strata were encountered within the limits of the Hochwald *ouvrage*. At Bloc 7, iridescent clay marls inflated on contact with the air and buckled supporting props.[88]

The problems became evident after construction. Properly poured, with a final layer consisting of a high cement-to-fine-sand-and-gravel ratio, concrete was waterproof. But mistakes occurred. At PO-Einseling, pouring in two stages created a crack through which rainwater ran.[89] Often, surface water ran into the blocs, especially in southeast France, where they crossed fault lines in the limestone, and in the impermeable clay soil around GO-Anzeling on the aforementioned Moselle right bank. Grassing embankments to bind the surface soil so that water did not create channels often failed because contractors had not foreseen that soil excavated for the foundations would have to cover the blocs.[90]

Masonry galleries and the rooms leading from them were even more vulnerable to water. Although *ouvrages* were not constructed within the water table, infiltration from underground springs was common. Top-down solutions did not work. Belhague recognised that local knowledge must be respected regarding the precise combination of pressurised cementation, waterproof coatings and drainage. He urged dissemination of best practice. The Génie's experts, through the STG, ruled that waterproofing should be complete in all shafts, galleries and underground installations except for latrines, washrooms and galleries and shafts not containing machinery, where 'slight seepage' could be tolerated on cost grounds.[91] Central heating was installed in underground sleeping quarters, which raised the temperature there to twenty degrees, but was not completed everywhere.

Air quality was another problem. Air was renewed by electrical ventilation through rear entrances in *gros ouvrages* or in the forts themselves in many *petits ouvrages*. Noxious gases from weapons and soiled air from kitchens and latrines were expelled through surface vents. During combat, *ouvrages* were sealed and kept in a state of slight overpressure, so that gas from explosions did not enter. Incoming air was filtered in the event of a gas attack. Air intakes were potential weaknesses, especially if sited within the *ouvrage* itself.

In summer, warm, damp air arriving through ventilators from outside condensed on colder surfaces inside, although this could be prevented by cooling air as it entered. Yet in winter, warmer air in the depths of the *ouvrage* condensed as it rose into cooler blocs nearer the surface. The problem was tackled by pumping between different parts of the *ouvrage*, thus mixing the air, and by installing air conditioning.[92] Circulation of fresh air nevertheless remained difficult because cost and military considerations dictated that underground works were as small as possible. Circulation was further inhibited by compartmentalisation to protect against gas attack and to prevent the spread of gases produced within the *ouvrage*.

In June 1935, the Senate Army Commission urged the army to solve the problem of damp.[93] War Minister Colonel Jean Fabry complained that in RF-Metz damp had caused considerable damage to equipment.[94] The engineers were not optimistic. General Joseph Alleau, director of engineers in the War Ministry, told Belhague that sealing the *ouvrages* would 'never be complete'. Commander-in-Chief Gamelin was informed that 'whatever measures were implemented previously, we will always be obliged to implement new ones to ensure that *ouvrages* are watertight', and that the ability to do so depended on funds.[95]

Opposition to the CORF

In 1935, General Émile Alléhaut presciently argued that it was intrinsically impossible to 'perfect the terrain' and cover all angles of attack. The journalist Robert Poulaine, writing in *Le Temps*, summarised Alléhaut's views more pithily: 'You might well have marked out in advance all possible fields of fire, taken the precaution of covering all the terrain from all angles. But during the battle the churning up of soil by enemy artillery will modify your field of vision and annul all your adjustments.'[96] Poulaine nevertheless thought that interval troops and mobile artillery would prove Alléhaut wrong.[97]

In 1929, the anonymously published *Feue l'armée française* (The late French army) was particularly critical of industrial warfare. From a perspective well to the right, its author, Captain Lucien Souchon, claimed that the high command's doctrine derived from having spent the war calculating productivity in the GQG rather than at the front. He criticised methodical doctrine and called for greater devolution of command to small teams with modern weapons, each capable of improvisation under the guidance of elite soldiers. He criticised fortification and advocated the offensive, though led by horse cavalry rather than armour.

Souchon saw war as an art dependent on intuition, not as a science. Like contemporary philosophers, such as Henri Bergson, he held that rationalist science could not grasp the flux of modern life. The officer, he wrote, required 'divination, to experience at each moment the phases of the battle, weigh his feeling for the strength of the enemy against that of his own forces, discern beyond analysis what is possible, what is useful, what is fertile, and choose what is opportune'.[98] Most officers had not read Bergson, but Souchon's ideas resonated, as widespread interest in the pseudo-science of radiesthesia shows.

Radiesthesia, invented in 1930, involved using pendulums to detect the energy supposedly given off by bodies and objects. The idea seemed plausible when research into radio and radar was in its infancy and when the army was investigating the paranormal. Academic scientists debunked radiesthesia, but their own lack of rigour blurred the boundaries between science and pseudoscience.[99] Some engineers were interested, and in 1934 one of them invented a machine supposedly able to detect the waves emitted by human bodies. The *Revue du génie militaire* published an enquiry into radiesthesia, which indicated that four of five officers were open to it – another sign of the decline of neoclassicist rationality. André Metz's editorial combined scepticism with goodwill.[100] But it was infantry officers who were most favourable. The most prominent advocate was General Gaston Prételat, future commander on the Maginot Line. Whether officers saw radiesthesia as a science accessible to themselves, as an alternative to science or because contemporary leadership theory offered no sophisticated way of linking doctrine to tactics, it challenged the 'armes savantes' and the CORF.

Meanwhile, the CSG members who were designated as wartime corps commanders criticised the CORF's refusal to allow them a say in the fortification of their sectors. In his memoirs, Prételat claimed that the CORF's system would have been more coherent had local commanders been able to position the *ouvrages* and determine intervals according to the nature of the terrain within the agreed plan. The 'jealous' CORF, he said, echoing Alléhaut, saw only the technical aspects of fortification, and so sited forts on hills, creating dead zones that made surface defence difficult.[101]

Particularly recalcitrant was General Degoutte, the opponent of *gros ouvrages*. As commander-designate of the Army of the Alps, he constructed small works on the frontier itself, using a small sum advanced by the government in response to Italian threats. However, the CDF, CORF and EMA rejected his global programme for the southeast, citing its cost, manpower requirements and incompatibility with the northeastern system. Degoutte grumbled that three years of work had been summarily ditched. Pétain laid down the law to Degoutte in a sharp face-to-face meeting, but allowed him to construct two or three more blockhouses on the frontier as an experiment.[102]

The CDF and CORF both attempted to preserve the coherence of their system. For the former, Guillaumat stated that premature decentralisation to frontier commanders would undermine the 'harmony' of the system, which was the 'primary quality of such a complex organisation'. Belhague, for the CORF, protested that corps commanders' interference was useless and harmful; fortification could not, he wrote, be the work of individuals, however high-ranking. Field commanders should be updated only by himself as president of the CORF. Pétain reminded commanders that the CORF's plans were approved by the ministry and could not be changed.[103]

The Maginot Line was not the concrete expression of a national mentality or a refusal to face the modern world. On the contrary, it blended modern technology and management methods with changing aesthetic fashions and the German fortification model. Moreover, the *gros ouvrages* were constructed despite field commanders' hostility to the 'industrial warfare' they epitomised. The decision to build them was the product of specific circumstances in 1928–31 – reconciliation with Germany, relative economic prosperity and, culturally, a brief modernist moment. These conditions hardly survived the time it took to complete the major *ouvrages*.

Yet Foch's prediction that if you built them you would have to defend them was becoming a reality. In the following years, as they were completed and manned, individual *ouvrages* became models of organisational science, integrated into semi-independent administrative and territorial structures. This happened despite widespread criticism of industrial warfare and a shift in spending priorities away from fortification.

4

FORTIFICATION CONTESTED

Enthusiasm for *gros ouvrages* was waning even as they were constructed, and from around 1934–5, fortification in any form definitively ceased to be the top military spending priority. Pétain's successors, Weygand and especially Gamelin, oversaw substantial modernisation of the army's equipment – tanks, planes, motorisation, modern mortars, antitank guns – and of its field regulations. These changes significantly shaped French operations in May 1940, but did not mean that fortification became irrelevant or that it ceased to be controversial.

The last years of peace witnessed a three-way conflict. First, Weygand and Gamelin saw fortifications – field or permanent – as adjuncts to defensive or offensive manoeuvre, and so preferred strongpoints to continuous lines. Second, from 1932, war ministers across the political spectrum wished to incorporate permanent fortifications into a continuous line of light fortification, ultimately from the North Sea to the Tunisia–Libya border. Pétain – war minister himself in 1934 – was their chief military backer. Cultural trends were moving in the same direction, for the neoclassical and modernist international styles that had initially shaped the *gros ouvrages* were giving way to sensitivity to the landscape. The third actor in the debate about fortification was the CORF, which fought a losing battle to defend the coherence of its system. Nevertheless, the fortifications became a semi-independent 'organised' structure within the army.

By 1938–9, the fortification question was politicised and polarised. On one side stood appeasers, who saw fortification as a symbol of France's willingness to fight only if directly attacked. At the other pole stood the communists and some socialists and Radical-Socialists, whose objective was to fight fascism domestically and internationally. As neophytes in military matters, however, anti-appeasers had little that was militarily practical to offer besides alliance with the Soviet Union. The army's position was uncertain: anticommunist and open to appeasement, but anti-German, torn between manoeuvre and defence and constrained by past choices and strategic disadvantages.

Weygand

On 3 January 1930, a few days before parliament approved the fortification law, Maginot appointed Weygand, Foch's former deputy, to succeed Debeney as chief of the EMA. Maginot passed over the Painlevé–Pétain tandem's preference for General Maurin, acceptable to Pétain for his belief in the continuous front and to Painlevé as a moderate republican.[1] On 10 February 1931, Maginot also secured Weygand's appointment to succeed Pétain as vice-president of the CSG. However, his plan for Weygand to combine his new position with his old one of EMA chief failed, for, not without reason, republicans considered Weygand to be too reactionary to be trusted with such power.[2] Painlevé spoke against the idea in parliament. As a counterweight, the republican Gamelin took over the EMA. His doctrinal views were more eclectic than Weygand's, but he too promoted manoeuvre.

Although Weygand had no alternative to initial defence, he was conscious that the enemy might concentrate overwhelming force at any point on strung-out French lines. Consequently, he wished to combine fortification of the northeast with a *masse de manoeuvre* capable of counterattack from the Low Countries to Switzerland. As Weygand put it, the continuous front in the northeast guaranteed 'the manoeuvre of our great campaign units' in the north.[3]

To this end, in 1933, Weygand initiated the formation of motorised infantry and mechanised cavalry divisions, perhaps seeing the daring of the cavalry as the antidote to republican decadence. The first Division légère mécanique (DLM – Light Armoured Division), similar to German Panzer divisions, became operational in July 1935, shortly after his retirement.[4] Weygand also launched a discussion of the IPGU (regulations), which revealed much dissatisfaction with its rigidity. He was particularly impressed with Gamelin's response, in which he saw Foch's spirit. Gamelin brought reform to fruition.[5]

Meanwhile, *La France militaire* published articles from multiple perspectives on topics from fortification to armoured warfare. Some officers discussed unorthodox ideas at retired Lieutenant-Colonel Émile Mayer's Sunday morning salon on the Boulevard de Beauséjour in Paris. The left-wing Mayer's own ideas were eclectic and inconsistent. His historical significance lies more in having encouraged Charles de Gaulle to publish in 1933 his first article on the professional armoured corps.[6]

In the same year, de Gaulle also published his *Vers l'armée de métier* (Towards the professional army). Although de Gaulle was later lionised as an outsider prophet of Blitzkrieg, the book was primarily written to prove the superiority of a professional force over the conscripted *armée nationale*. The book is vague on technical detail, but clear on the need to combine fortification with an armoured corps able to support France's eastern allies. This corps would seize 'bargaining chips' (*gages*) behind German lines and sow confusion in the rear.

De Gaulle's critics found the concentration of professionals in a single corps unacceptable, for most officers and politicians insisted that the elite must be dispersed through the army. Others doubted the feasibility of manoeuvrable heavy tanks. De Gaulle's major contribution was to publicise wider debates in engaging language.[7] In 1935, he conceded that the principle of armoured divisions was gaining ground in all milieus.[8] In 1936, Weygand pointed out that France already possessed the DLM.[9]

It was nevertheless hard for Weygand to turn his ideas into practice, for his personal position was not unassailable. As a naturalised citizen, born in Belgium to unknown parents, he was a victim of snobbery. One officer commented on his election to the Académie française, in which leading writers (loosely defined) established the rules of the French language, that 'if the Academy has got past the word "fascism", it hasn't yet arrived at "to be an upstart" [*parvenir*]'.[10] Weygand was essentially a staff officer, despite not having attended the École de guerre. Buat, among others, alluded to his not having commanded in the field.[11] One wonders whether Weygand's dismissal of front-line veteran Daladier as a 'Café de Commerce politician' betrayed insecurity about his own military status and a secret political ambition.

Most members of the CSG were senior to Weygand. Lacking the counterweight of popularity in the army that he acquired in retirement, he could not compete with Pétain's influence among politicians and the public. Indeed, rather than retire, Pétain accepted Painlevé's offer to become inspector of air defence. Then, in 1934, as war minister, he prevented the CSG from meeting, thus depriving Weygand of leverage. Weygand later admitted how difficult he found it to disagree publicly with Pétain, given the marshal's immense popularity.[12] Money was in any case so short that until 1936 most funds went on maintaining the troops.[13] Even so, the Pétain–Weygand opposition is important because it was integral to power struggles in the army and disputes about doctrine and policy, as the question of the fortification of the north shows.

Defence of the North

The CDF's final report expressed military orthodoxy when it stated that 'since an invasion through the north is most dangerous, the mass of the French army will necessarily be stationed there'. Indeed, it saw such an attack as more likely than in 1914 because the recovery of Alsace-Lorraine made the German border more defensible. The CDF chose Longuyon as the endpoint of fortifications because outflanking them necessitated violation of Belgian neutrality.[14] Although by 1930 the army had abandoned plans to invade Germany immediately, it still preferred to fight in Belgium, thus shortening the front, threatening the Ruhr, and ensuring Belgian and British support. Even if Belgium did not call in French troops, the army expected to 'bound' to a defensive position beyond Lille. The CDF proposed mobile fortification depots (*parcs mobiles de fortification*) – stores of equipment near railway hubs for digging, camouflage and communication, ready for use in Belgium.[15]

For the CDF, fortification of the north was unnecessary. It proposed declassification of the Maubeuge strongpoint, which had anyway been largely destroyed during the previous war. The 1930 law allocated a mere 40 million francs for permanent works in the Raismes and Mormal forests and for flooding coastal areas. In any case, fortification of the Belgian border was problematic, given the length of the frontier, the presence of numerous towns and industries and, in Flanders, the high water table. Permanent installation of artillery able to fire into Belgium was politically problematic.

The CDF did not reckon with pressure from serving officers, retired generals, frontier politicians, veterans and business. As parliament approved funding for fortification, deputies interrupted Maginot with cries of 'What about the north?' Through his lobby group and in the Senate Army Commission, General Hirschauer pressed for fortification of the whole frontier. In 1932, as an 'old sapper', he reminded the ministry of his faith in 'solidly held lines' and claimed that the Germans had invaded via Belgium in 1914 because they knew that Maubeuge and the Belgian fortifications were weak.[16] Northern interests including Chambers of Commerce, Chambers of Agriculture, the Union of Heads of Family of the Dunkirk region and the local councillors and parliamentarians of the Nord department all demanded fortifications.[17]

The ministry and EMA retorted that fortification depended on parliament's readiness to vote funds. They reiterated the CDF's view that the northeast was a higher priority, and that a few small works and campaign fortification were sufficient in the north given that the Germans would take time to cross Belgium. Painlevé, more politically astute, reassured senators that the government understood the necessity of preserving the region from invasion.[18] Doubts about Belgian support increased pressure for fortification.

True, the Anglo-French guarantee of Belgium was written into the Versailles Treaty, a Franco-Belgian military convention had been signed in 1920 and in 1923–4 the two countries had jointly occupied the Ruhr to compel Germany to pay reparations. In 1928, in view of the Allies' imminent departure from the Rhineland, the Belgian General Émile-Joseph Galet planned three possible lines on which they expected French support, which remained the basis of Allied planning up to May 1940. Furthest forward was the new Albert Canal, covered by a planned modern fort at Ében-Émael. Further back was a line from Antwerp along the River Dyle to Namur, and further back still, saving a corner of Belgian territory, was the River Escaut/Scheldt line. The Ardennes Forest, which lay on the right flank of these lines, would be defended only by destructions and delaying actions. By spring 1932, the Liège fortifications were being modernised, tendering was underway for the modernisation of Namur and land had been purchased on the frontier.

Galet's proposals faced criticism from the neutrality-inclined Flemings in western Belgium, who feared that the second line would turn their towns into battlefields. Walloons feared that Galet was not serious about defending the francophone east and the Ardennes. The pro-Walloon Albert Devèze, war minister from 1932, pushed for better defence of Wallonia. French frontier politicians were not reassured.

In September 1931, Maginot, sensitive to the question as deputy for the frontier Meuse department, ordered a reconnaissance of the Belgian frontier. It concluded that the CDF's proposal for light defences constructed on mobilisation should be replaced by moles (defensive 'breakwaters') in the invasion routes able to provide refuge for retreating troops or start lines for advance. They were probably Gamelin's idea, for he consistently advocated such strongpoints. He saw Maubeuge as one such mole and therefore opposed declassification. Like Foch and Weygand, he saw strongpoints as bases for manoeuvre.[19]

In December, General Messimy, president of the Senate Army Commission, protested to Maginot that the 'few mediocre works' members had seen on the northern frontier were a mere 'facade' designed to appease the population. Senators were unsure, he added, that Belgium would repeat its heroic gesture of 1914, given the stance of the Flemish population, the potential speed of a German motorised attack and the industrial worth of northern France. He pleaded for the construction of at least two fortified regions.[20] Gamelin replied that 'more complete' proposals were on the way.[21]

The Senate Finance Commission forced the issue. It invoked a 1922 law allowing 240 million francs of emergency military spending on condition that it was used to fortify the north. On 29 March 1932, Nord department Senator Daniel-Vincent, with the support of the Army Commission, proposed inclusion of the funding in an amendment to the finance bill, a step which obliged the Chamber to discuss the issue. Fearful that a debate would criticise Belgium and expose French military weakness, the government accepted the amendment.[22]

The CORF proposed a fortified region with moles at Condé-sur-l'Escaut and the Monts de Flandres defending the Lille region, Maubeuge defending the Sambre valley and small works elsewhere, mostly infantry works without artillery. The CSG eventually discussed the proposals on 28 May.[23] The summary presentation, probably Weygand's work, reminded members that defence of the north 'is entirely based on movement'.[24] Although Weygand did not consider northern fortification to be a priority, he was nevertheless prepared to use the money for that purpose if it could not be used for anything else. Gamelin optimistically felt that since nobody now believed in continuous defence, the money could be used to construct moles in the north.[25]

Pétain's unprecedented intervention scuppered the proposal. Having accepted permanent works reluctantly, he did not want more. Supposedly not wishing to embarrass Weygand, he did not attend the meeting. Yet his scruples did not prevent him from sending a letter stating that extending the fortifications would swallow too many campaign troops. As inspector of air defence, he preferred to fund a powerful independent offensive and defensive air force. Influenced by Colonel Paul Vauthier, a member of his cabinet, he had embraced General Giulio Douhet's theory that wars could be won by strategic bombing alone.[26] He combined Douhetism with his own doctrine: the land army would attack when bombing had degraded the psychological, military and industrial capacity of the enemy.[27]

Weygand hammered another nail into the proposal's coffin. Despite awareness that the money could only be used for fortification, his rivalry with Pétain and conviction that the air force should apply itself to ground support rather than strategic bombing got the better of him. He opined that the real priority was reconstituting the army's stocks of mortars, helmets and gas masks – more important even than motorisation or planes!

As the discussion derailed, a minister detected 'a sort of hostility against the fixed defences that have parliamentary favour'. Weygand replied that, for the army, France's military frontier was the Germano-Belgian border, to which the French must advance.[28] The question was sent for further study.[29]

Debates in the reconvened CSG are interesting only because they confirmed disagreements between Pétain on the one hand and Weygand and Gamelin on the other on the Belgian question and on doctrine. Members unanimously insisted that fortification of the north was less important than tanks, aircraft and improving the northeastern fortifications, but did not agree about where and how to fight in Belgium. On that, the council voted seven–six for Pétain's choice of using *parcs mobiles* to construct a continuous front a short distance into Belgium. Only the oldest member (Gouroud) and the four youngest, including EMA chief Gamelin, backed Weygand. The latter therefore stood on his prerogative as general-in-chief designate to decide French deployment. He dismissed *parcs mobiles* as unproven and French and Belgian conscripts as unreliable and added that any fortifications in the north should, like those in the northeast, leave the terrain clear for manoeuvre.[30]

The debate was academic, for on 8 May 1932 the moderate-left Radical-Socialists and their Socialist allies (the Cartel des gauches), who were committed to continuous light fortification of the north, triumphed in the second round of elections to the Chamber of Deputies. In Germany, Hitler's National Socialism was on the march, and the world economic crisis, which had hitherto spared France, arrived. The rest of Weygand's tenure witnessed an inconclusive conflict between Daladier and Pétain's commitment to continuous light defence, Weygand's attempt to balance fortification with mobility and the CORF's attempts to preserve its position.

The Return of the German Question

Until 1934–5, the left hoped to appease German nationalism through concessions on reparations and armaments within the framework of international disarmament (i.e. limitation of offensive weapons). Its military experts, Paul-Boncour, Cot and Daladier, therefore stuck to their preference for continuous defensive fronts largely constructed on mobilisation – still more attractive as tax revenues fell. France's European and imperial commitments remained huge. Even under one-year service, there were between 540,000 and 610,000 men to be fed, quartered and paid. Some deputies pressed for fortification to alleviate unemployment, but military spending fell.[31] In 1932, Paul-Boncour, the Cartel des gauche's first war minister, asked Gamelin for studies of the northern question, but prioritised disarmament.[32] Moreover, he secured the passage of a law effectively reducing service to ten months. The army was relieved when he lost office in December.

Daladier succeeded him, and in January 1933 he also took over as prime minister, a few days before Adolf Hitler became German chancellor. On his first day at the War Ministry, Daladier found a report from Weygand stating that the army had 'sunk to the lowest level for ensuring the security of France'. After meeting Daladier, Weygand noted, 'the former [Paul-Boncour] always courteous and shifty. The new one more likeable; gives an impression of uprightness . . . He has read my report . . . He is already very up to date on many things; his mind seems free from limitations. He gives the impression of a simple, frank man of conviction.'[33] Daladier's commitment to savings and disarmament soon caused Weygand to change his mind. Moreover, his views on military doctrine and fortification were closer to Pétain's than to Weygand's.[34]

Included in Weygand's report was a request to fund improvements in the northeastern defences. They included construction of *ouvrages* on the Rohrbach plateau on the left flank of RF-Lauter, which had been cut from the CDF's original proposal, and of smaller works in the Belfort region to block invasion via Switzerland. In the north, Weygand proposed a fortified region covering Montmédy.

Weygand saw strongpoints as bases for manoeuvre, while Daladier prioritised continuity and defence. One of the latter's first actions was to approve the creation of static fortification regiments. Whereas an instruction of 1931 on occupation of the fortifications subordinated fortification troops to the field army, Daladier's decree made them organisationally independent – albeit to permit them to reach the frontier more quickly than the ponderously mobilised field army.[35] Daladier also issued plans to divide the entire frontier into Secteurs fortifiés (SFs – fortified sectors) with permanent works and Secteurs défensifs (SDs – defensive sectors) in which field fortification would be organised on mobilisation. Each sector was to be defended permanently or on mobilisation by fortification troops, rapidly reinforced by local reserves – the *levée en masse*.[36] Weygand saw these measures as attacks on the manoeuvrability of the campaign army.[37]

A compromise nevertheless emerged. In September, Daladier reconnoitred the frontier. He agreed to Weygand's proposals for the north-east and Montmédy, perhaps because the Senate Army Commission was pressing for the 240 million for the north to be added to the ministry's plans.[38] However, Daladier wanted new works in Montmédy and RF-Metz downgraded from *gros* to *petits ouvrages* and those on the Rohrbach plateau to Vosges-type casemates. For most of the north, he revived the left's old demand for continuous field fortification constructed by the military regions using their own labour.[39]

Daladier's intervention annoyed the CORF. An unsigned scribbled note, probably by an officer attached to a directorate of works, complained that during his inspection the prime minster's 'ill-informed entourage' (doubtless the officers of his military cabinet) encroached on the prerogatives of the high command and its technical advisers. Daladier, the note added, should have been accompanied by Belhague for the CORF and Gamelin for the EMA. Through Gamelin, the CORF pointed out that it had already substantially cut its programme. It dismissed the proposed Vosges casemates as too weak and pointed out that military labour was incapable of constructing works resistant to 280mm artillery. The CORF saw fundamental change to the system as unnecessary.[40] Belhague wrote personally to Daladier in defence of *gros ouvrages*, attaching supporting statements from officers who had served at Verdun to appeal to Daladier's war experience.[41] These efforts were in vain, for Daladier's ministry marked the end of new *gros ouvrages*. In the project deposed in parliament, his preference for Vosges-type casemates did not survive, but with one exception all new works were *petits ouvrages* without artillery.[42]

Despite these measures and public pronouncements in favour of continuous defences from the Mediterranean to the North Sea, it is difficult to say where Daladier really stood. Like many infantry veterans, he regarded trench warfare as less costly than 1914-style offensives. He reminded the EMA that, since France was a peaceful nation, strategy must initially be defensive; the army must prepare a long war behind fortifications in which the economy would count as much as battles.[43] Yet there was always a discrepancy between Daladier's utterances and the paltry resources accorded to the north. Indeed, he told a relatively private Senate Army Commission hearing that fortification of the north was less important than 'the accord with Belgium, which permits you not only to make an important saving of several hundreds of millions, and to take the war outside our own territory, but perhaps even to engage in battles that could be decisive'.[44]

Neither was Daladier's broader policy entirely defensive. In 1933, along with Cot, the new air minister, he embraced Douhet's bombing theory. As one of the first on the left to advocate military resistance to Germany, Cot saw bombing as a way to support France's eastern allies.[45] Strategic bombing was not viewed as 'defensive' by the League of Nations.[46]

For the moment, Daladier no longer counted. On 6 February 1934, fifteen members of far-right leagues were killed on the Place de la Concorde as they protested against a financial scandal involving Daladier's Radical-Socialist Party. The next day Daladier resigned, fearing a military coup (which in fact only retired Marshal Lyautey considered). Pétain became war minister in the new right-wing government, which was headed by ex-president of the Republic Gaston Doumergue. Nobody remarked on the irony that Pétain owed his position to a deadly clash on improvised fortifications outside parliament.

Pétain, War Minister

Pétain's remarkable good health allowed him to outlast all his rivals. From nine to five each day, he worked through immense heaps of files, summarised for him by his devoted staff. He began to picture himself as a crisis recourse, called on to rescue catastrophic situations created by incompetent generals and/or politicians. He had carefully cultivated his prestige, keeping his anti-republicanism private while telling others what they wanted to hear.[47] When he spoke in parliament, even some on the far left applauded him. Left-wing admirers would have been alarmed to learn that he presented Doumergue with a programme 'inspired by what is happening in Germany and Italy'.[48]

On 14 October 1933, Germany withdrew from the League of Nations and Disarmament Conference. The Doumergue government effectively followed suit. During 1934, Foreign Minister Louis Barthou toured France's eastern allies in the hope of shoring up support and began negotiations for agreements with Italy and the Soviet Union. Pétain approved these efforts from the sidelines, but spoke rarely in the Council of Ministers.

As war minister he achieved little, despite the government having the right to legislate by decree. Even his acolytes pleaded 'circumstances' in his defence. He refused Weygand's requests to convene the CSG. He evaded military demands for longer service and better funding, for the government was in power precisely to cut spending.[49] A series of emergency decrees reduced the defence budget by 20 per cent.

Pétain did save the Weygand–Daladier programme, which, on 14 June, he presented to the Chamber (Figure 10). Speaking, the press said, as if issuing the order of the day, he claimed that the proposed SFs Montmédy and Maubeuge would guarantee continuity between the northeastern and northern fronts and that it represented 'proof, inscribed in the terrain, of France's pacific intentions'. Daladier, in his first Chamber speech since his 6 February humiliation, praised the proposal's combination of great sunken battleships and smaller fortifications.[50] This New Fronts Law, signed on 6 July, provided 3,120 million francs of special credits. Of this sum, the northeastern fortifications received 1,275 million to cover overspends, weaponry, barracks to house troops near the forts, and for the Rohrbach extension. Only 292 million was allocated to the north. (Plan I for the modernisation of the air force was additionally approved.)

This New Fronts Law marked the beginning of a shift in funding priorities away from fortification altogether. Speakers in the debate were as concerned about tanks and aircraft as they were about fortification, if not more so. Radical-Socialist Marc Rucart, intervening for the Chamber Army Commission, wanted fast tanks for reconnaissance and exploitation of a breakthrough. The Socialists pointed out that the funds did not cover overspends in the northeast, and in late 1935 the EMA admitted that, despite this money, most scheduled new works had been shelved.[51] The already weaker new front fortifications were cut further. An *ouvrage* at Vaux-les-Mouzon that would have covered little La Ferté's left was cancelled.[52]

Pétain visited the northeast twice, urging commanders to construct simpler infantry works and rely on field rather than fixed artillery.[53] He

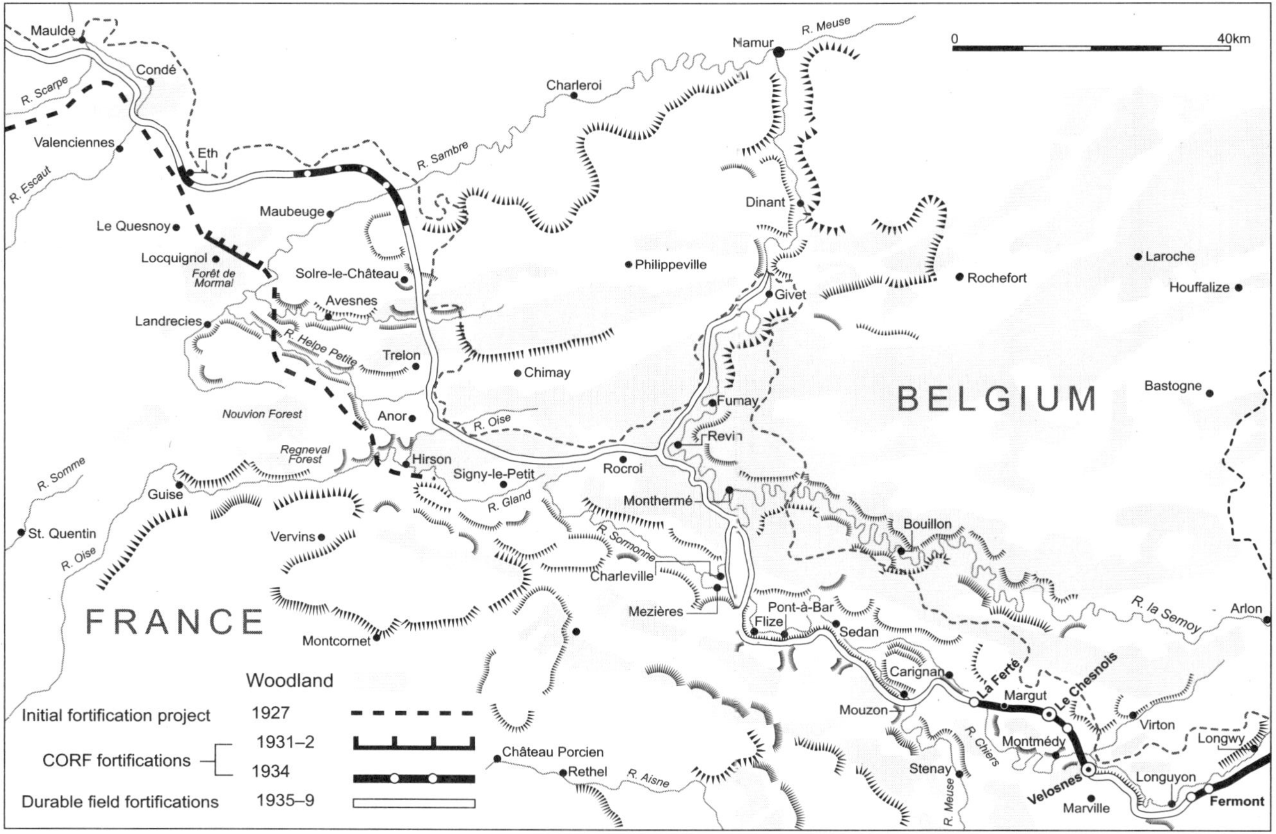

10. The northern fortifications.

issued a decree implementing Daladier's division of the frontier into SDs and SFs (see Figure 1, page 3).[54] Weygand protested again that the army would be 'deprived of any element of manoeuvre', adding that the use of North African troops on the frontier was not a 'solid foundation' for the defence of 'French soil'.[55]

Despite his caution, Pétain responded to pressure from Weygand and Gamelin to fund new equipment in a 'special account'. While this 3,415 million included only 445 million of new credits spread over five years, it provided the first serious credits for gas masks, antitank guns, motorisation and armoured vehicles.[56] Yet there were simultaneous cuts in the finance law's allocation for new equipment. In October 1934, Pétain left the government before his plan was approved.[57] The following January, Weygand retired.

Gamelin

Gamelin, Weygand's successor, was the first general since Joffre to combine vice-presidency of the CSG with heading the EMA. General Maurin, war minister from 8 November 1934 to 7 June 1935 and from 24 January to 4 June 1936, entrusted Gamelin with these powers because, having entered Saint-Cyr with him in 1899, he could be sure of his republicanism. Weygand, in his farewell to the CSG, demanded 'spiritual equipment of the nation' and a 'dictatorial will' in central government.[58]

Of the many charges levelled against Gamelin, one at least is unjustified: that he was 'the quintessential staff officer and bureaucrat'.[59] He combined intellectual and organisational abilities with far greater field experience than Weygand. His career began with achieving first place at Saint-Cyr and second at the École de guerre.[60] Aside from brief periods on Joffre's staff, he served at the front during the Great War, initially as a major in a demi-brigade of chasseurs (light infantry). Afterwards, he served until 1925 as head of the military mission to Brazil, then suppressed a Druze rebellion in Syria before commanding the prestigious 20th Region at Nancy. In 1933, as EMA chief, he worked better with Daladier than Weygand did. Their partnership resumed in 1936, when Daladier returned to the War Ministry.

Although Gamelin consciously imitated Joffre's legendary unflappability – a subordinate alleged that his limp handshake was intended to make him appear distant – he never identified as closely with his mentor as Weygand did with Foch.[61] While he advocated manoeuvre, his military ideas were less firmly established than those of his predecessors. Whether he was indecisive, opportunist or flexible is unclear. We can be sure that, like Foch and Weygand, he prioritised tanks and motorisation, linked fortifications to manoeuvre and opposed construction of further CORF fortifications.

Gamelin took over at a difficult time. The army had little modern equipment, including only thirty-four modern tanks. The air force's Plan I was failing thanks to lack of mass-production facilities. Although in January 1935 Maurin secured parliamentary approval of the first tranche of Pétain's special plan – increased to 800 million – mass production of equipment was a long way off. The international situation deteriorated further. In January 1935, Saarlanders, predictably, voted to rejoin Germany, though the area remained demilitarised. On 16 March, Hitler officially announced rearmament and the introduction of one-year military service. There was no time, money or military desire for more *gros ouvrages*. Further works would have to be small-scale.

We must linger on the Gamelin–Maurin spring 1935 programme, for it established the framework of fortification until the outbreak of war without eliminating disagreement about its nature or its place in French plans.[62] The two authors of the programme agreed on field fortification and cheapness, but were not otherwise of one mind. Whereas Gamelin backed moles and manoeuvre, Maurin elevated the continuous front to a dogma. He wanted to construct an unbroken line of defences along the entire frontier using innovations such as mechanical diggers and barbed-wire-laying machines.[63] Gamelin's note, issued two days after Hitler's rearmament announcement, consisted of two parts.

First, on the CORF fronts, new and old, designated as 'fortified sectors', the programme planned to establish a continuous barbed-wire and antitank barrier reinforced with roadblocks in front of the *ouvrages* plus field fortification to provide depth behind them. Reinforcing planned flooding in the Sarre Gap was another priority. All these works were to be constructed by military labour, *main d'œuvre militaire* (MOM).

Secondly, the note instructed regional commanders to draw up plans for continuous antitank and barbed-wire obstacles in the 'defensive sectors' on the rest of the frontier, covered by one or two mutually supporting blockhouses per kilometre. This 'durable campaign fortification' would be constructed as money became available, using MOM labour and material from the *parcs mobiles.* Since MOM labour could only construct weaker structures, the note ordered commanders to prioritise camouflage over tactical positioning, to begin with key points and to undertake nothing that could not be completed within two months. Priority was accorded to the Meuse from its confluence with the Chiers, where work on La Ferté was beginning, northwards through Sedan and Mézières to Givet. Taken together, the two parts of Gamelin's instruction ultimately involved construction of a continuous barbed-wire barrier running through fortified and defensive sectors from Mulhouse to Givet, doubled where necessary with antitank rails or ditches. For the moment, little was planned north of there, and work had begun hardly anywhere. Only 51 million of extra funds were granted to the regions (see Figure 1, page 3).[64]

In July 1935, War Minister Colonel Fabry, a firm believer in the continuous front, informed Belhague in the passive-aggressive style dear to the French administration that he would 'doubtless agree that the dissolution of the CORF could be implemented without inconvenience'. Belhague vainly protested that the CORF should retain oversight of ongoing works.[65] As a sop, his remit as inspector of military engineers was extended to include fortifications. He soon found that he had been sidelined and that Gamelin, to whom he reported his inspections, was indifferent. In his memoirs, Gamelin wrote that urgency had made it essential to be liberated from the 'hierarchy of special Génie organisms' and that local variations were justified by the nature of the terrain. In August 1936, Belhague retired. He became honorary inspector of engineers, but his interventions in this capacity were dismissed as attempts to reinvent the CORF.[66] By then, the political, diplomatic and military situation had changed significantly.

Fortification and Rearmament

In 1934, France and the Soviet Union began negotiations for a military pact. To facilitate agreement, the Communist International encouraged the French communists to drop revolutionary agitation in favour of defending the Republic against domestic fascism. Over the following months, the Communists, Socialists and Radical-Socialists – the latter led by Daladier – came together in the Popular Front. In March 1935, shortly after Foreign Minister Pierre Laval signed the pact, Moscow ordered the French communists to endorse national defence and put an end to antimilitarism – though a campaign against 'fascist officers' did not reassure the army.

Rather than welcoming communist prodigal sons into the national community, the French right and some left-wing pacifists viewed the new strategy as a plot to provoke war, extend communist influence in eastern Europe and incite revolution in France. Most conservatives still wished to resist Germany through alliance with Italy, but some began to excuse Italian and even German expansionism. For appeasers, the fortifications were a symbol of order against communist subversion and proof that France would fight only if attacked rather than undertake an ideological crusade against Fascist Italy or Nazi Germany.

The army too preferred alliance with Italy to the Franco-Soviet Pact, and ensured that the latter did not lead to serious military agreement. For some senior figures, notably Pétain, anticommunism, appeasement and defensive doctrine went together. Others, perhaps the majority, did not go so far. They were pessimistic about the present state of the army and exaggerated German capabilities. Yet three invasions in 150 years could not easily be forgotten and the army's entire structure, weaponry and deployment were designed to defeat Germany. Ultimately, Italian expansionism exposed the difference between military and political priorities.

In January 1935, Laval and Mussolini signed the Rome Agreement, and Gamelin quickly negotiated a military convention directed against Germany. Fortification work in the southeast was suspended. However, Laval, who headed a right-wing government from June 1935, was a pacifist who favoured understanding with Germany as well as Italy. His government scuppered a proposal to extend Plan I to 1,500 planes. Fabry, Laval's war minister, pressed for funding for the Pétain–Maurin special rearmament plan, increased to 3,620 million, but no money was released and the defence budget itself was cut.[67]

On 3 October 1935, the Italian invasion of Abyssinia sank the Italian alliance. Laval reluctantly implemented League of Nations sanctions, for the British were strongly opposed to Italian expansion in the Mediterranean. Yet Laval's own majority justified Italian actions. War Minister Fabry who also opposed sanctions, linked appeasement to fortification. He opposed the formation of armoured divisions and dismissed the idea that they could operate in advance of the army – which was precisely what the field regulations that were shortly to appear laid down. In a meeting that took place at the height of the crisis, he urged storing ammunition for a long war, whereas Gamelin wanted to accumulate equipment for the first battle.[68] A few days later, Gamelin was deeply disturbed to hear Laval, Pétain and Fabry declare their willingness to agree to German demands for arms equality in return for a lasting peace. Gamelin expressed his views only in a private note that evening, however, not in the meeting.[69] In fact, he too was pessimistic about the present state of the army, as his response to the Rhineland crisis showed.

Support for sanctions having helped to cement the left's unity around antifascism, in February 1936, a mostly left-wing parliamentary majority ratified the Franco-Soviet Pact. On 7 March, on the spurious grounds that ratification of the pact breached the Locarno Treaty, German troops entered the demilitarised Rhineland. A German garrison established itself at Saarbrücken, just opposite the fortifications.[70] Prime Minister Albert Sarraut, head of a caretaker Popular Front government pending imminent elections, declared it unacceptable that Strasbourg should come within artillery range. He ordered partial mobilisation and permanent occupation of the CORF *ouvrages*. The British withheld their support, however, as did the Belgians, who were moving towards neutrality.

The high command's pessimistic advice helped tip the balance against resistance. Gamelin told the government that countermeasures required total mobilisation and that if the Germans did not give way, only British intervention would break the inevitable stalemate. This advice rested on a huge inflation of German troop numbers by including labour battalions, police forces and Nazi Brownshirts.[71] In reality, the German army remained weak, though the French would probably have faced popular resistance of the kind witnessed during the disastrous Ruhr occupation of 1923, for civilians were improvising fortifications to block a French invasion.

The presence of German troops on the frontier focused the government and army's attention on French defences without changing priorities. Of the 350 million francs of emergency funding made available immediately after remilitarisation, only 50 million went to fortification, the rest to munitions, equipment and industrial mobilisation. For fortification, the priority was improvement of existing CORF works. At the end of March, Gamelin proposed a wider programme of improvements in RFs Metz and Lauter, rapid completion of SF-Montmédy, motorisation of seven infantry divisions and mechanisation of the cavalry as a mobile reserve able to intervene rapidly in Belgium. Construction of durable campaign fortification from Sedan to Mézières remained a second priority. Subsequently, a series of study sessions of the CSG confirmed Gamelin's proposals.[72] In August, Inspector of Engineers General Antoine Huré reaffirmed that the imminence of the danger made the construction of further *gros ouvrages* impossible. Any new works must simply be shelters for machine and antitank guns and field artillery; they would not have air filters; ventilation would rely on the natural circulation of air or hand pumps.[73] The ministry also ordered that, since the Germans were so close, older reserves in the fortified zones should on mobilisation reinforce GRM frontier posts to help them warn of and delay a surprise attack. This was the first step towards organising a corps of frontier guards (Gardes frontaliers).[74]

Hitler's mixed messages reassured those who wanted to be reassured. He accompanied remilitarisation with a proposal for a new Locarno agreement based on equal rights, Germany's return to the League of Nations and demilitarisation of both sides of the Franco-Belgian–German border. Negotiations failed because the French would not dismantle their fortifications, as Hitler surely expected.[75] The Germans soon began to erect the first bunkers of what became the Westwall, thus leaving them free, as Gamelin put it, to 'contain us with minimum force' while attacking our eastern allies.[76] On 24 August 1936, German military service was increased to two years.

In May 1936, the Popular Front won a majority in the lower-house elections, which included seventy communists. Soon afterwards, a huge wave of strikes and factory occupations broke out. As the communists became increasingly bellicose and abandoned even their campaign against 'fascist officers', the right became even more convinced that communist patriotism covered provocation of war and revolution.

The new prime minister, Léon Blum, hesitated. He still hoped to achieve pacification through negotiation with Germany, and refused to defend the Spanish Republic against a military insurrection. He also attempted to bolster the Soviet alliance and declared his willingness to risk war against Germany.

In September, the government announced a massive 14 billion rearmament programme (plus the new Plan II for aircraft). For the first time, priority went to new equipment, not to fortification or troop maintenance. Forty per cent was allocated to mechanisation. Of the rest, the biggest sums were allocated to motorisation, artillery and re-equipping the infantry. The programme included only 1.2 billion (8.5 per cent) for fortification, all of which was allocated to armament of CORF forts.

Blum, who two years previously had condemned de Gaulle's armoured corps as a revival of aggressive warfare, now granted him an audience. Years later, keen to preserve his status as sole critic of orthodoxy, de Gaulle claimed that nothing came of the meeting.[77] In fact, it confirmed that debate was widespread and that de Gaulle was not an outsider. His promotion did not suffer, and in 1938 he was chosen to command the 507th tank regiment ahead of an officer who saw tanks as subordinate to the infantry.[78] A wide-ranging review submitted to Daladier insisted on the danger of German mechanised forces. Gamelin and Daladier agreed that since France could not compete with Germany quantitatively, it must prioritise technology.[79] The strategy these weapons served did not change – initial defence, fortification, movement into Belgium and/or Switzerland and assault on Germany once the war industries had mobilised – but defence became more mobile and flexible tactically and therefore potentially extended its reach.

This evolution informed new field regulations, too easily dismissed as superficial reworkings of the 1921 IPGU.[80] In fact, revision was a response to the appearance of new weapons: antitank guns, tracked supply vehicles (*chenillettes*), 60 and 81mm mortars, faster tanks and aircraft and motorcycles.[81] The French were also impressed by the emphasis on initiative and manoeuvrability in the new German regulations of 1933–4, the *Truppenführung* (which also stipulated continuous echeloned defence, nearly identical to French doctrine).[82] Observation of German methods fed criticism of the inflexibility of French infantry tactics. The EMA authorised a general discussion in the *Revue d'infanterie* and *La France militaire*, which revealed polarisation. Older officers were particularly inclined to attack the devolution of command to combat groups led by 'poorly educated' men, while younger officers advocated greater autonomy, less reliance on light machine guns and thus greater manoeuvrability.[83] In 1935, Alléhaut in his *Être prêts* criticised the primacy of firepower and the continuous front and pleaded for modernisation of the infantry by giving it sporty uniforms and equipment plus mechanisation and motorisation of ten divisions. For years, he had urged the French to study German infantry tactics.

The new 1936 *Instruction sur l'emploi tactique des grandes unités* (IGU) expressed these debates rather than a coherent point of view. For instance, it explained that while methodical preparation was appropriate for attacking solidly established fronts, 'sudden and brutal action is more important than minute preparation' where the enemy is less well established. Speed, 'the essence of warfare', depended on the celerity and clear orders of the commander, well informed by subordinates. Execution of orders could be accelerated by troops' 'capacity for manoeuvre, physical training, morale, etc.'. Yet 'methodical reconnaissance, artillery support and coordination of arms must never be sacrificed to impatience to act'.[84] These regulations were not merely academic, for they contained a new section on using light-armoured forces to seize the best terrain before the enemy – the doctrine applied in the Low Countries in 1940.[85] A commentary in *La France militaire* saw both change and conservatism; it regretted failure to recognise that celerity and surprise were 'inversely proportional to centralisation'.[86]

Critics of defensiveness were more impressed by a new manual for NCOs, revised in light of the IGU. An anonymous contributor to *La France militaire* saw it as a product of the 1935 debate, proving that critics were not isolated. Whereas the old regulations emphasised firepower, the new expected commanders to manipulate the poles of firepower, terrain and offensive movement, thus restoring their autonomy.[87]

This is not to deny the significance of defensive doctrine, for which it is easy to find evidence in military publications and training.[88] By 1939, moreover, there were forty-six battalions of fortress infantry, four machine-gun battalions, seven battalions of Alpine fortress infantry, nine fortress artillery regiments, divisional artillery in the Lille sector and the staffs and organic elements of twenty-eight fortified and defensive sectors and of two fortified regions. Additionally, frontier engineer regiments created specialist companies and detached men to *ouvrages* and fortification sectors and regions. Fortification units remained static. As they became operational, the fortifications were becoming a ponderous bureaucracy, albeit created, like all bureaucracies, in the name of efficiency. Yet the same decree of 24 July 1935 that substantially increased the number of fortress battalions also established the first DLM.

In fact, old-fashioned factories were incapable of mass production of complex modern weapons. And because they relied on irreplaceable skilled workers, they were vulnerable to industrial unrest. Furthermore, fear of technological obsolescence meant that the army constantly changed specifications. Although the French created another DLM in 1937, formation of a heavy-armoured division had to await January 1940, thanks to slow production of heavy tanks. Pierre Cot's plans for planes also failed on account of production difficulties and doctrinal controversy. In 1936–7, strategic-bombing theory was abandoned in favour of ground support – too late. Even so, the 1936 rearmament plan confirmed the shift in priorities away from fortification. Yet soon after its announcement the danger in the unfortified north increased.

On 14 October 1936, the Belgian king declared that to avoid fighting a war on behalf of international communism, his country would henceforth be neutral. To reassure the French, he promised to strengthen Belgium's fortifications and encouraged the French to fortify the north so that the Germans would be deterred from invading

Belgium. Nevertheless, Belgian neutrality meant that France could no longer respond to a German attack on its eastern allies by moving from the Belgian frontier to the Ruhr (although theoretically France could have invoked Article 16 of the League of Nations Covenant, which allowed troops enforcing collective security passage through third countries). Backchannels alone provided Gamelin with fragmentary information on Belgian plans.[89]

An EMA survey provoked by the new Belgian policy revealed that permanent work on RFs Metz and Lauter was complete except for the installation of antitank guns, while construction of a second position covering the planned flooding in the Sarre was also beginning. In the north, the old fronts in the forests of Raismes and Mormal were ready, while 50 per cent of the forts and 80 per cent of the casemates were complete on the new fronts at Rohrbach, Montmédy and Maubeuge and on the Escaut.

As for fieldworks, antitank and barbed-wire barriers were around 60 per cent complete from Basel through the Ardennes to Hirson on the Belgian border. From the Ardennes to the Escaut, about two-thirds of the infantry casemates planned in 1935 were complete. In the Sedan–Mézières sector, General Jean de Barbeyrac Saint-Maurice's plan for one to four blockhouses per kilometre was finished by the end of 1936.[90] Northwards to the sea, little had been done and even studies were incomplete. In 1935–7, a mere 120 million francs were allowed for completion of the few permanent CORF works in the north, and another 26 million for fieldworks.[91]

Daladier and Gamelin toured the frontier. The minister's preference for continuity on the whole frontier apparently prevailed, for which 50 million was immediately promised. Daladier's instructions of 6 November 1936 reiterated the importance of defensive and fortified sectors. The northern SDs, the Escaut and Flanders, were upgraded to SFs, and therefore permanently manned by fortification regiments. Further work in the Ardennes and Montmédy was planned. On 21 October, Daladier requested 560 million francs, of which 100 would be immediately available. Of the total, 360 million would be allocated to the northern frontier and 200 to the Jura (for the danger of a German violation of Swiss neutrality increased now that Italy was hostile).[92] Inspired by his infantry experience in Flanders in 1914 and the defence of Madrid during the Spanish Civil War, Daladier saw the towns and cities on the northern frontier as defensive barriers, reinforced by specially constructed fortified houses.[93]

Everywhere, there was a contrast between the publicly expressed desire for a continuous barrier and the resources allotted to it. In fact, the northern programme was behind schedule. Daladier recognised the huge cost of continuity and accepted in practice Gamelin's alternative of moles.[94] Furthermore, in 1937 he told parliament that 'France will not remain immobile behind its ramparts while fire rages on the plain'.[95] He referred to Hitler's threats to Austria and Czechoslovakia.

The stories of the Anschluß, the incorporation in March 1938 of Austria into the Reich, and the destruction of Czechoslovakia in September are well known. How integral fortification was to these crises is less so. Since the French and British had long been resigned to the Anschluß, they responded feebly to German threats. Yet the annexation fundamentally weakened the military position of Czechoslovakia, France's major ally in the east. With French help, the Czechs had fortified their German but not their Austrian border. Their fortifications could now be outflanked.[96]

Gamelin stated in his memoirs that he responded to the Anschluß with a request for 171 million to construct further strongpoints, but heard 'nothing more'.[97] Political lobbying for fortification of the north increased. In April, Nord department Senator Rotours demanded fortifications as strong as those in the northeast. Deputies Parmentier and Thiébut demanded respectively strengthening of fortifications in Flanders and on the Meuse. The army evaded the question of *gros ouvrages* and insisted that works were 'in hand'.[98]

German publicity for its own Westwall fortifications added to pressure for fortification in France. In mid-1938, to secure his rear while he crushed Czechoslovakia, Hitler ordered intensification of construction. To ensure speedy completion, he abandoned plans for powerful fortified regions in favour of lighter works, while a major propaganda effort lauded their strength.[99] At Nuremberg on 12 September, Hitler declared that expansion of the German army and 'construction of one of the most gigantic fortresses of all time' were the conditions of defending the Sudeten-German minority in Czechoslovakia against 'aggression'. After this speech, disturbances began in the Sudetenland.

By this time, Daladier had abandoned the Popular Front to become prime minister as well as war and defence minister in a right-wing anticommunist government. Although he was personally probably in favour of defending Czechoslovakia against Hitler's demands for the Sudetenland, his parliamentary majority was convinced that war served only the communists (and the Jews), while the British were determined not to let French commitment to Czechoslovakia drag them into war. Hitler's demands were so excessive, however, that on 24 September the British rejected them and mobilised the fleet. The Czechs mobilised and the Soviet Union promised support – though purges had just decapitated the Red Army. The French called up 750,000 reservists and mobilised fortress troops. They were ordered to dig trenches, lay barbed wire and build blockhouses.[100] On 30 September at Munich, however, Mussolini (as mediator), Hitler, Daladier and Chamberlain agreed to staged occupation of the Sudetenland, which the Czechoslovaks, who were not invited to Munich, had little choice but accept (see Plate 6).

The army's role in this climbdown was ambiguous. On the one hand, Gamelin saw Czechoslovakia as essential to French strategy. He probably envisaged an offensive against Germany once the war industries had mobilised but had nothing to offer in the short term other than the faint hope that a better agreement would preserve Czech military power. On the other hand, intelligence reports exaggerated the number of combat-ready German troops, while General Joseph Vuillemin stressed the catastrophic state of the French air force. German propaganda regarding the Westwall had some impact, with agents reporting imaginary deep galleries and an underground airport at Etzenhofen.[101] At lower levels, too, officers were impressed by the Westwall. The crisis over, Colonel Max Creskens (23 RIF – Régiment d'infanterie de forteresse) admitted that officers were troubled by German fortifications on the Rhine, which he described as a 'model of organisation, decision and rapidity in execution'. Officers, he said, feared that the means available to the enemy might paralyse French fortifications.[102]

The crisis over, Pétain was not alone in thinking that Hitler might turn his attention to Alsace-Lorraine.[103] On 9 October, National

Socialists from all over Germany celebrated again in Saarbrücken. Typically, Hitler's speech mixed pacification with threats. He denied claims on Alsace-Lorraine, but in a barely disguised message to Mosellans across the border, he declared that Saarlanders were especially aware of what it meant to be separated from the Reich. He added that fortification 'that no power in the world will be able to break' was necessary for protection against the British war machine.

On the French side, controversy about whether to construct continuous defences or moles as bases for manoeuvre continued. Gamelin had plans drawn up for moles armed with artillery casemates on the northern frontier at Maubeuge, Révin, Mézières, Sedan–La Marfée, Mouzon and Cappel. They were to be manned by machine-gun battalions if within a secure sector and campaign troops if not. They were expected to resist if the front was broken, and thus permit the establishment of new defences and counterattacks.[104] CSG member Prételat, however, whom Gamelin charged with reconnoitring the frontier, preferred continuous obstacles and covering blockhouses everywhere. His tour found that works had advanced since the last survey in 1936. There was a continuous line of antitank ditches and rails from Lille south to Maubeuge, supported by blockhouses 'of real value'. From there to Sedan, Barbeyrac's blockhouses were complete, but few in number and weak. There were ten artillery casemates on the whole Ardennes front, but only two of them were between Mézières and Sedan.[105]

On 20 December 1938, the CSG approved Prételat's proposals, which were funded by 300 million francs in two tranches. In his summing up, Gamelin nevertheless insisted that since a surprise attack was impossible on the Belgian border, moles were more important than continuity. Specific instructions reflected his views. He also insisted that the Ardennes should be fourth priority behind the Alps, Belfort and the Sarre – despite having witnessed Prételat's cadre exercise showing that the Germans could cross the Ardennes in sixty hours (it took fifty-eight). Funding was used primarily to block the gap between SF-Montmédy and the Maginot Line – not Sedan.[106]

On 17 March 1939, the Germans invaded the rump Czechoslovakia. Gamelin again proposed accelerating the existing fortification programme and beginning some new works. Of the 439 million francs requested, 109 million were assigned to northern fortification. From April to July, a further 350 million were made available. The money was to be shared between metropolitan regions, Corsica and Tunisia's Libyan frontier.[107] It represented a minimal proportion of military expenditure, which had reached over 93 billion francs by March 1939. Moreover, fortification was constructed on the cheap, as a closer look at field fortifications confirms.

Organising the Terrain

Fieldworks, including blockhouses small enough to be constructed by MOM labour, had always been the responsibility of frontier commanders. In 1930, the EMA ordered them to reconnoitre the terrain and prepare plans for works to be begun when funds were available and to be completed on mobilisation.[108] In 1935, the Gamelin–Maurin note provided precise instructions, while the introduction of two-year military service made available the necessary MOM labour – pioneer units and detachments from fortress or campaign regiments. Work was supervised by divisional and corps Génie officers. *Parcs mobiles* provided the material.

Field commanders saw themselves as sole possessors of the intuitive feeling required to 'organise' the terrain. In the Ardennes region, Barbeyrac himself criss-crossed the terrain, often lying flat on his belly to point out positions.[109] Dislike of scientific generalisations and enthusiasm for radiesthesia had not dimmed. An engineer who taught at the École de guerre on the eve of war found radiesthesia to be almost the orthodoxy among its majority infantry officers and a few polytechnicians who, he said, had forgotten their science.[110] In June 1939, Prételat persuaded the CSG, with Gamelin's approval, to resume research into radiesthesia.[111]

Regional commanders were no less keen to modify and perfect the terrain than was the CORF. Each year, weather permitting, conscripts cleared land, dug foundations and poured concrete. They felled hectares of trees, cratered paths and constructed barbed-wire barriers. In 1936, for instance, 250,000 francs were allocated for this purpose in the

Haguenau Forest, so that it could fulfil its role as the grandly named 'Môle de Résistance de Bas-Alsace'.[112] Numerous small works modified rivers, notably in the Haguenau and Vosges forests in RF-Lauter, and in the Boulay and Saint-Avold sectors of RF-Metz.

These efforts led to quarrels between infantry and engineers. At PO-Haut-Poirier, the 20th Region command used credits for MOM labour to construct an emergency exit through the drain and a covering blockhouse without informing the EMA. This blockhouse had less than half the standard protection and no armoured door to prevent enemy incursion. The structure was mentioned in no report and figured on no map. Tipped off by Inspector of Engineers and Fortifications General Charles Griveaud, the ministry warned the region that all modifications to CORF *ouvrages* must be approved by itself.[113] In neighbouring SF-Vosges, the Génie protested that 37 RIF had constructed fieldworks without informing it. The regiment's commander retorted that work had been ordered verbally by the 'doers' – a not-so-veiled criticism of the engineers' impracticality.[114] More pettily, an infantry officer complained that 'grunts' (*fantassins*) were fed up with seeing Génie NCOs circulating in automobiles.[115]

The opposition between infantry and engineers should not be exaggerated. As we have seen, younger Polytechniciens educated by Umbdenstock were less influenced by classicism than their elders and more sensitive to local conditions. And during the 1930s, anticommunism intensified a reaction against the allegedly Bolshevik international style in the name of French national and regional traditions. Since the engineers who supervised blockhouse construction were often reserve officers, perhaps with a background in civil engineering, they were necessarily aware of contemporary construction trends.

Contemporary aesthetic trends were visible in the fortified houses (*maisons fortes*) constructed in advance of the fortifications. These were Daladier's idea, inspired by the improvised fortification he had witnessed in Lille-Roubaix city in 1914. In 1933, as part of his plans for light fortification, he requested 'a defensive blockhouse to provide flanking fire on a light barrier'.[116] The result was a structure resembling a forest dwelling in the modern regionalist style, housing antitank and machine guns in a ground floor bunker and lodgings for three to six soldiers above. A sapper described the *maisons fortes* of Alsace as 'fortified *ouvrages* capped with maisonettes', marvelling at their telephones, running water and electricity.[117] The level of 'modern comfort' was indeed high for the period. Coffee grinders were standard.

Engineers showed much imagination in their varied designs for blockhouses. At Wissembourg, a blockhouse was disguised in the base of the thirteenth-century Tour de La Poudrière (Plate 7). The Weihersthal-Sud blockhouse at the junction of the D87 and D87A near Philippsbourg was simply a hollow in the rocky roadside, protected with a camouflaged reinforced-concrete front. The nearby Falkenstein observatory consisted simply of accommodation for a handful of men in the base of the sandstone outcrop with a ladder to the top, connected by military telephone to local *ouvrages*.

This diversity was problematic. Successive commanders imposed different ideas. Since no blockhouse resembled another, parts such as armoured doors and protection for machine-gun apertures were likely to arrive in the wrong sizes, provoking manufacturers to complain of lack of standardisation.[118] Directors of works often purchased material on their own initiative, thus undermining 'homogeneity and uniformity'.[119] More blockhouses were constructed than could be maintained and many were of dubious value. A staff officer remembered that 'with all the enthusiasm of his spiky character', Barbeyrac imposed well-camouflaged blockhouses, but with only one-metre protection, hardly able to resist a 105mm shell, and with wide frontal embrasures facing the enemy. His men called them 'pill-boxes'.[120]

The AEF also complained. Units felled trees without permission from either their superiors or the AEF, thus undermining the industrial production on which the long war depended and the coherence of the system. The commander of SF-Vosges admonished subordinates for constructing a relief trench through the domain forest to the Rothenbourg casemate without informing the AEF.[121] In June 1939, an AEF inspector protested that fortification troops had felled fifteen oaks and thirty beeches in Rayerswiller Forest, costing the commune 1,556 francs.[122]

While the AEF had no power, legal or practical, to enforce its views, nature remained intrinsically hard to organise and potentially vulnerable to enemy exploitation. The army had little faith in its river works.

For instance, despite 'improvement' the flow of the River Nied Allemande remained too feeble to be trustworthy. Military engineers installed concrete weirs, but soon removed them because they caused silting; they then deepened the bed between Biding and Folschviller villages and at Grossberg to make an antitank barrier.[123] In the Sarre Gap, the army feared that even if flood installations were not wrecked by a surprise attack, releasing water too quickly would destroy the dykes. Consequently, flooding would have to be spread over two days – hence the plan to protect the area with thirty-one casemates, twelve of which were constructed by December 1938.[124] In the sandy soil of the northern Vosges Forest, the ground was too unstable to dig reliable trenches. There was no money to concrete them, so wattle was substituted or camouflaged pathways used instead.[125]

Pétain, despite favouring field fortification in principle, recognised the problems. Inspecting the fortifications in November 1937, he was pleased that works in the Belfort region had been carefully researched, and that blockhouses were standardised, small, easy to engineer and methodically constructed. Elsewhere, he attributed poor artillery positioning to deficient MOM work: some infantry weapons could fire only within the position and were lost to the continuous barrage, he complained.[126]

On his 1938 inspection, Prételat was accompanied by Griveaud, who, as president of the Génie's technical committee, was particularly aware of the problems. They were disappointed to find no clear plan or technical specifications for blockhouse construction in the Sarre Gap and Ardennes.[127] In December, they persuaded the CSG to issue 'firm and precise technical directives', from which emerged the Génie's model STG blockhouse.[128] Griveaud's successor from 1939, General Louis Philippe, who also possessed a strong technical background, sponsored a cheaper STG model and distributed a catalogue to the regions. These innovations enabled mass production of standardised parts – so long as local commanders used the specifications and industry could produce the parts.[129]

The Last Days of Peace

After Munich, public opinion opposed further concessions to Germany and Italy. One reason was that in the eyes of the right, the collapse of the Popular Front weakened communism and made war appear less likely to benefit it. Then, in December, Mussolini renewed claims on Nice, Savoie, Corsica and Tunisia, provoking a wave of nationalist feeling in France. In March 1939, Hitler's destruction of the rump Czechoslovakia showed that he did not respect the Munich agreement. These developments neither discouraged diehard appeasers, albeit now fewer in number, nor produced consensus on the role of fortification in French plans.

Since the army assumed that Italy would attack France only in concert with Germany, it planned to remain behind fortified fronts in the southeast and Tunisia until Germany had been defeated. It therefore responded to Italian threats by ending the pause in work on the south-eastern fortifications. Since 1936, engineers had also been constructing eight artillery and forty-five infantry casemates and fifteen command posts on the Tunisia–Libya border from Mareth to the Matmata mountains. In early 1938, Gamelin flirted with using metropolitan and colonial fortifications as bases for an offensive against Italy. In fact, they were purely defensive, despite insufficient power and density for continuity. Since reinforcement was unlikely, they were expected to hold out for two years.[130]

For appeasers, fortification of Tunisia was integral to retreat into the empire away from the British alliance. Senate Army Commission President Fabry asked, 'Isn't it possible that tomorrow, overturning all the usual rules of strategy, we might have to face the adversary on a front established on our own soil, straddling the Mediterranean, with installations on Corsica, extending to North Africa and reaching the edge of the Sahara?'[131] Pétain too was committed to appeasement. He accepted that Hitler's insatiability would ultimately mean war, but given British unreliability and the state of French society and its army, he was prepared to make further concessions to delay it.[132]

In contrast, Gamelin and others saw fortification in the Mediterranean theatre as a way to strengthen the British alliance through common defence against Italy. He was not entirely convinced that France could win a long war. In October 1938, he told Daladier that 'it is through the cohesion of its empire that France will remain a great nation', but immediately added the condition that French authority be re-established in

Africa and the Levant. Gamelin's focus remained on victory in the Low Countries.[133]

Ironically, given his mythical status as a prophet of Blitzkrieg, de Gaulle was moving in the opposite direction. He was still pressing for the formation of heavy-armoured divisions, but no longer saw them as professional forces and dropped the idea of seizing bargaining chips across the frontier. He was now just as interested in organisation of the country and empire for a long war.[134]

The best evidence of conflict within the army is Pétain's notorious preface to the book of 1939 in which General Chauvineau denied that an invasion was possible.[135] The marshal endorsed the author's view that industrial construction methods rendered the continuous front still more solid than in the previous war. Chauvineau's book both provides evidence of a 'Maginot mentality' and shows that it was not universally shared. When Pétain received a draft in 1935, he refused to endorse it. He changed his mind in late 1938 because he feared the return of offensive doctrine. He concluded his preface with a warning that the experience of 1914 was too costly for that to be allowed to happen. Pétain exaggerated, but implicitly highlighted the modernisation of the army's equipment and doctrine initiated by Weygand and extended under Gamelin, designed for counterattack and intervention in Belgium and Switzerland.

At the same time, as Gamelin recognised, what had been conceived as a system of fortified regions supporting manoeuvre became a continuous barrier of unequal value.[136] Insofar as it conformed to any of the plans approve in 1926–7, it was closest to those of Buat, who had envisaged a continuous line of *ouvrages* close to the frontier without depth. Yet it lacked the strength that Buat had imagined. Furthermore, the fortifications were becoming a bureaucracy greedy for human and technical resources, manned by static fortification units. A few weeks before the outbreak of war, Prételat proposed breaking the fortified regions up and converting fortification units into field units once mobilisation was complete. In the following chapter we shall see that the officers who manned the fortifications were also ambivalent about the industrial warfare they represented.

Part II

MANNING THE MAGINOT LINE

5

OFFICERS AND NCOs ON THE MAGINOT LINE, 1933–1939

From August 1933, as Hitler consolidated his power, newly formed fortification infantry and artillery regiments began to occupy sectors in which the construction of *ouvrages* and camps was sufficiently advanced. Accustomed to traditional garrison-town life, officers and men were disconcerted to find themselves on isolated Alpine peaks or in poor industrial or sparsely populated rural and forest areas on the German frontier, where locals were largely first-language German speakers. Damp, darkness and poor air quality made the *ouvrages* unfit for long-term occupation and camps were rudimentary.

Although material life improved as construction progressed, resources never matched the CDF's aspiration in 1926 for *gros ouvrages* in which conditions were 'as perfect as possible', or the 1937 fortification regulations' stipulation that the greatest attention must be paid to hygiene, lodgings, food, sports and other distractions. Even when material conditions did improve, the perceived social and cultural isolation of fortification service and its traditionally low status were harder to remedy.

Difficult conditions were not necessarily problematic. Coping with adversity was intrinsic to training and military manliness, and expectations were relative to social position. Thus, in a society in which access to education was limited by class and wealth, NCOs found fortification service attractive, and they were relatively well integrated into local culture. For officers, poor conditions were not compensated by improved career prospects.

Besides seniority, advancement for officers depended firstly on the acquisition of general culture, which supposedly provided the broad outlook necessary for command. Generalist education was acquired in secondary schools, which only gradually abolished fees during the 1930s. It was sustained by study and participation in bourgeois culture – impossible on the frontier. Secondly, advancement depended on heroism, self-sacrifice and bravery. In peacetime, training for combat and/or the suppression of colonial rebellion permitted demonstration of these qualities, but that was impossible in the fortifications. As a technically trained elite, fortification infantry and artillery regiments (RIFs and RAPs respectively) supposedly differed from prewar fortress regiments, to which disgraced officers were allegedly sent to finish their careers austerely.[1] In practice, fortification service never shook off the reputation of being bureaucratic and unmilitary. Fortification officers not incorrectly suspected that field officers regarded them as second-rate. They both defended the status of their arm and complained about the difficulty of their lives while fearing that those lives were too bourgeois.

Fortifications as Corporations

As a product of organisational science, the fortifications were a hybrid of military hierarchy and business corporation. At the summit, commanders resembled factory managers and/or naval captains. Advised by 'technicians', they passed orders downwards to junior officers and NCOs equivalent respectively to middle managers and supervisory personnel. The fortifications were meant to provide homes, social lives and careers for officers and NCOs appropriate to their status in garden cities. Troops, the workers, were divided into skilled specialists and the unskilled. Reserves were recruited from counterpart civilian occupations. Factory managers commanded combat blocs as reserve officers; skilled metalworkers maintained turrets as reserve sergeants and corporals; Paris Métro personnel looked after generators and narrow-gauge railways.

Initially, the army expected only a handful of men to serve continuously in the *ouvrages*, where they would install, test and maintain equipment, perfect procedures, keep watch and patrol the area. Outside training periods, only a corporal and half a dozen men might be found in a *gros ouvrage*, while *petits ouvrages* were often locked and empty. Experimental mobilisations in 1935–6, however, demonstrated the advantages of a fuller complement. When remilitarisation of the Rhineland brought German troops to the frontier, instant readiness became a necessity. Commanders were ordered to constitute permanent crews within fortification units, strong enough to respond to a surprise attack using half the fort's armament. By 1938, the *ouvrages* were almost fully operational and many smaller works were permanently occupied too. Most fortress troops rotated between short periods in the *ouvrages* and longer periods in the intervals and camps.

To repel a surprise attack with their peacetime complement alone, fortress units possessed a substantial core of regular officers and a high proportion of specialist NCOs and corporals. GO-Hackenberg's full complement in September 1939 comprised 297 infantrymen, 466 gunners, 238 engineers and eleven medics. Artillery regiments required gun-layers, calculators, observers, armourers, loaders and gunners. Génie regiments added electro-mechanics to their traditional radio-telegraphists, railway sappers and miners (responsible for building blockhouses and countering enemy attempts to mine into *ouvrages*).[2]

Fortress artillery and infantry also served in the intervals. Artillery regiments (RAPs – Régiments d'artillerie de position) differed from conventional artillery only in lacking transport. RIFs were divided into specialist casemate and *ouvrage* crews, companies of traditional riflemen, and sufficient men to serve up to 48 machine guns and 130 LMGs per battalion, plus mortars and antitank guns. Infantry and artillery regiments also included the usual administrators, cooks, saddlers and those caring for carrier pigeons. They relied on horses rather than motor transport – a cruel deficiency, it turned out.

To underline elite status and modernity, the RIFs, but not the RAPs, were the first to receive the new khaki uniforms. (Despite *ouvrage* crews having no need for invisibility, they received them before field units.)[3] Khaki replaced the dilapidated, all-too-visible sky-blue uniforms, which, one general remarked, 'quickly faded to a piss colour, giving troops a dishevelled look' – as any period photograph confirms.[4] Although khaki uniforms referenced the old-fashioned cut of the sky blue of the Great War, they reflected the simplification associated with modernist practicality. Uniforms were adorned with patches indicating specialism, together with another modern innovation – enamel regimental badges.[5]

The organisationalist ethos of the fortifications is particularly clear in the eighty security camps (*camps de sûreté*) built near the *ouvrages*. New camps were essential because existing barracks were notoriously dilapidated and too far from the *ouvrages* for instant response to a surprise attack. They were a cross between fortified and company towns and garden cities (*cités-jardins*). As distant offspring of Vauban's neoclassical ideal towns, they were strongpoints, surrounded by barbed wire and studded with gun emplacements and bomb shelters. Wives and children were provided with gas masks.[6] One journalist described them as 'warrior cities'.[7]

Like company towns, camps were divided into zones segregated by function, class, rank and marital status. The commander of SD-Thionville (a steel-producing region) thought that 'as in any industrial enterprise, the "villas" of the engineers and the foremen's houses should be constructed along with workers' housing'.[8] Within the *cité-jardin*, married officers lived in semi-detached houses while married NCOs occupied flats in apartment blocks. Unmarried officers and NCOs shared rooms in apartment blocks, where, to the annoyance of older colleagues, they pursued bachelor lifestyles. Conscripts and corporals occupied barracks, just as unskilled immigrant labourers, such as those who constructed the fortifications, often lived in barracks too.

The first instructions for the camps reflected the centralism of the CORF. Belhague's 1930 guidelines envisaged that most training would happen under officers' eyes in central barracks in Metz, Thionville and Haguenau. The new camps would provide accommodation only for permanent small crews and for battalions rotated for periods of training close to the *ouvrages*. Camps would require only one or two semi-detached houses for officers up to captain rank and their families and three or four blocs for a dozen or so NCOs. The camps were to reconcile comfort sufficient to attract officers with simple and economical construction. Furthermore, the CORF proposed that, to save money, only accommodation for permanent detachments should initially be built.[9]

Just as the *ouvrage palmé* replaced the monobloc fort, the camps became more integrated into the region. Fortification officers criticised centralised training for having no relation to real fortification service and for rendering the *ouvrages* vulnerable to a surprise attack by depleting their crews. By 1935, the army had accepted the need for larger crews and therefore camps. Most were commanded by majors, not captains, and as commanders of sectors, RIF colonels resided there too.

Architecturally, just as in the early 1930s modernist architects softened their international aesthetic with regionalist touches, camp buildings were often harmonised with local styles. Although standardised modern buildings were not uncommon, accommodation conformed more to the garden-city style advocated in military circles by Camille Rougeron, a Polytechnique-trained naval engineer. Rougeron attacked what he called the reinforced-concrete carcasses of modernist buildings 'that were supposed to last for centuries and adapt to changing artistic tastes by redesigning their facades', which, he added, are 'rendered passé between two art deco exhibitions'. (Le Corbusier's modernist plans for Paris were first displayed in the 1924 art deco exhibition.) Rougeron considered that *cités-jardins* dispersed in the countryside were better equipped to resist bombardment than modernist 'tower-cities'. *Cités-jardins*, he wrote, would be protected like the 'dispersed machine guns under concrete in the east' – the fortifications.[10] As manning requirements increased, officers' accommodation evolved into genuine *cités-jardins* built in the modern regionalist style of the suburbs.

Construction in bricks and mortar was permitted, but steel frame with concrete-block filling was preferred for its relative cheapness and because deadly fires and epidemics had stirred up antimilitarism.[11] Although there was no attempt to use the freedom that steel-frame construction allowed, there was enough leeway for junior Génie officers to add regionalist touches.

The Elzange camp was a fine example of the genre. It was situated on the territory of the communes of Elzange ('Elsingen' for its overwhelmingly germanophone inhabitants) and Koenigsmacker. The *cité-jardin* was set among lawns, trees, allotments, tennis courts, a school, a dispensary, garages and stables.[12] With the exception of its functional, modern entrance building, Elzange structures referenced the Moselle (see Plate 8). The Germanic style is evident in the hip roofs of the officers' houses, while the arches on the facades evoke the barns of the terraced farmhouses of Lorraine village streets – without the usual heaps of manure. The steps were common in wine-growing villages, where habitations were built over cellars. Following the principle of rank – Vauban's 'convenance' – the exteriors of the NCOs' blocks were less elaborate than officers' houses, for they lacked arches.[13] Typically of modern regionalist buildings, regional features were confined to facades. Interiors did not conform to the Lorraine pattern of three rooms leading successively from one side of a corridor perpendicular to the street, with a kitchen as the second room. Rather, unimaginative use of the steel frame dictated that each floor was divided into equal square rooms.

Journalists detected the fashionable suburban rustic look even in blockhouses, which they described as 'maisonettes', 'villas' and 'country cottages'. A communist journalist described a Rhine casemate semi-ironically thus: 'veranda, green shutters, nice whitewash, the whole fenced off, but with barbed wire, and with the signs "entrance and photography forbidden – military terrain" '.[14] For the novelist Henry de Montherlant, the flowerpots decorating entrances to *ouvrages* were a reminder of 'villas' in the Parisian suburb of Arcueil-Cachan – 'typical embourgeoisement of tragedy by the French'.[15] In fact, officers and men used fashionable styles to humanise their difficult environment.

Living in the Fortifications

It quickly became clear that cold, damp and poor air quality in the *ouvrages* undermined comfort and efficiency. An inspection of GO-Anzeling found that sleeping conditions were acceptable in the underground barracks, but because of condensation were 'mediocre or frankly bad' in the fighting blocs. The crew were reminded to close the airtight doors. At GO-Soetrich, on the drier left bank of the Moselle, the inspector found everything perfectly clean, and conditions of 'comfort and even luxury'. Even there, food had to be protected from condensation and stored clothing and mattresses rotted.[16] Cold was another issue. The temperature was usually 13°C, often lower – at which point bodies do not function at full capacity. Those who served in the Alps, where generators caused a deafening vibration of the mountain rock, complained for years afterwards of hearing problems. Belhague reported that kitchens were struggling as a result of rising crew numbers, and more beds were forced into already cramped spaces. He feared that men were so tightly packed that the objective of economy of effort was proving illusory.[17]

In July 1935, War Minister Fabry sent the governor of Metz a litany of issues: damp, poor ventilation, lack of drinking water, cold food, no electricity to power loaders and turrets, poor telecommunications, poor placement of command and observation posts and poor sleeping conditions. He demanded urgent action to prevent a decline in morale and a loss of confidence in fortification.[18] Even the right-wing press did not entirely disguise the truth. In *Le Matin*, veteran and journalist Léo Gerville-Réache wrote that he found men 'pallid, doubtless thanks to their termite life' in a 'monstrous cold sap'.[19]

The CDF did not foresee that many soldiers would serve in casemates and blockhouses rather than in the *ouvrages*. Material conditions were acceptable in summer, but in winter frigid draughts penetrated through apertures.[20] During the especially cold winter of 1933–4, parliamentary inspectors persuaded Gamelin to order that casemates should be left unoccupied and visited by patrols or guarded by one or two soldiers in simple posts outside the entrances – that was often the case anyway.[21] In the Rhine casemates, where periodic flooding made electrification impossible, storm-lantern smoke poisoned the air. The EMA therefore recommended that troops leave their barracks only to patrol the area.[22] As the international situation deteriorated, the requirement for permanent lookout overrode concern for the troops. Gerville-Réache wrote that long days and nights in glacial casemates were passed watching terrain in which nothing happened.[23]

Officers and men, we have seen, took matters into their own hands by improvising buildings above ground. While they were often decorated and surrounded by vegetable plots and livestock pens, they did not provide suburban amenities. At GO-Hackenberg, the previously mentioned medical inspector found a leaky chipboard structure serving as restroom, refectory and kitchen. The tin hut serving as a latrine, which was emptied manually and the contents buried, was 'far from ideal'.[24]

Although life in the camps was easier than below ground, conditions were mixed, especially in the first years. The cadres of 155 RAP, for instance, found Drachenbronn camp (SF-Haguenau) facilities 'too summary'. Bedrooms were tiny and the officers' mess was too close to the troops' lodgings. Heating repeatedly failed and water pressure was too low for infantry and artillery cadres to turn the taps on simultaneously.[25]

There was insufficient accommodation in the camps. Cadres and their families often had to rent expensive lodgings in poor villages without hotels and commute daily on difficult roads in uncomfortable lorries. Officers, able to pay more, lodged closer to the barracks. Married NCOs often lived so far away that they preferred to live apart from their families. At Zimming, Bockange and Veckring camps, all but a few married men were shuttled by coach from Metz to the camp, and consequently worked very long days.[26] In the Alps, elevated heating costs and the competition of tourists for accommodation pushed up the cost of living. Officers of 70 BAF (Bataillon alpin de forteresse) at Bourg-Saint-Maurice found their lodgings comfortable, but colleagues at Vaulnix did not like theirs.[27]

In 1936, remilitarisation of the Rhineland stimulated spending on security barracks, but the picture remained uneven.[28] Some improved dramatically. Léon Rodier remembered that in May 1938, IV/149 RIF moved into the 'ultramodern' Saint-Jean-lès-Marville camp in SF-Montmédy: 'Magnificently well arranged, there reigned in these camps a certain luminosity with spaces for life, leisure, study or sport, with all-arms firing ranges close by. There was a soldiers' club, well-equipped officers' and NCOs' messes, magazines and clothing stores equipped according to the most modern norms, garages for automobiles etc.' The only disadvantages were that soldiers spent too little time there and that the camp was distant from the station, 'the only way to go on leave'.[29]

Lieutenant-Colonel Jean-Marie Reyx (153 RIF) saw officers' accommodation at Oermingen as 'too uniform', with a concern for alignment that made it resemble too closely the barracks or workers' cottage (*coron*). (It is now a prison.) The apartments themselves were nevertheless well designed and more comfortable than private lodgings. Reyx thought the mess-hotel for single officers was 'the best-designed and the most luxurious of the type that has been built in a security barracks'. Colleagues at Rohrbach were less fortunate: single officers' rooms, used for sleeping and working, were 'veritable cells and sound boxes thanks to the cold metallic cladding on partition walls'.[30]

NCOs

NCOs often embraced the opportunities offered by the creation of fortification regiments. In 1933, parliament approved the recruitment of 15,000 infantry specialists, mostly to administer fortification and motorised units and maintain and operate their equipment. Initially, it was difficult to recruit sufficient technicians. In 1934, Weygand complained that some of those serving in smaller *ouvrages* were specialists in name only – their answer to a power cut was a petrol lamp.[31] By early 1936, there were 1,750 specialists in fortification units, and it was expected that there would be 4,000 by the end of the year, almost entirely recruited among conscripts, who were then obliged to serve beyond the legal term.[32] The following year saw the creation of a legal category of specialists, mostly NCOs, armed with diplomas.[33] In 1938, eleven NCOs of 172 RIF became specialists, while forty-two chief corporals were promoted to sergeant.[34] Career corporals requested transfer to the east in the expectation of quick promotion to NCO. Several commanders remarked upon the rising quality of NCOs, charged with tasks from bookkeeping through commanding casemates to radio operation.[35]

Typical was Albert Laumonier, the offspring of a family of peasant proprietors in the Vienne department. Despite showing himself to be a gifted child, he left school at thirteen to work on his parents' and neighbours' farms. Aged eighteen, he joined 151 RAP at Thionville, just as it expanded to supply crews for the *ouvrages*. He was immediately allocated to corporal and then NCO training. By 1938, he proudly remembered, he was a sergeant, earning 1,000 francs per month, substantially more than a primary-school teacher – 'the fine life began'. He bought a fashionable suit and profited from the social life of the area. In 1939, aged twenty, he trained as a mechanic at GO-Rochonvillers, responsible for all its artillery equipment, which, he said, 'represented millions, indeed, billions [*sic*, of francs]'. In his evenings, he studied for the platoon-leader certificate, a step to becoming an officer.[36]

NCOs were better integrated into village society than officers, though not, as Colonel Herique (37 RIF) thought, because their needs were less.[37] In SF-Rohrbach, the NCOs of 153 RIF were said to find social and living conditions corresponding to their desires, though schools and transport were lacking.[38] Relations with locals in Alsace-Lorraine were relatively good, for many hailed from the region, spoke dialect and had married local women.[39] Of course, NCOs were as likely as anyone to suffer from boredom, stress and depression, but either the sources are silent, or, as in Laumonier's case, the picture really is positive.

NCOs were less attracted to the Alpine fortifications, for they did not benefit from bonuses for difficult conditions. Many requested transfers away, while commanding officers attempted to unburden fortification regiments of older men, recruited in the days when demand was superior to supply. One Alpine commander lamented that his unit had suffered from the tradition of using the creation of new units to rid themselves of 'doubtful and even frankly undesirable NCOs'. General Joanny Garchery advocated the promotion of the best NCO administrators to officer, but saw it as a 'mistake to keep in uniform men who wear it so lamentably and who are no more than pen-pushers'.[40] This comment reflects officers' concern that the bureaucratic character of fortification service was demilitarising.

Indeed, the army was somewhat ambivalent about NCOs' family life. On the one hand, as an institution it endorsed the national campaign to stimulate the notoriously sluggish French birth rate and thus increase the supply of conscripts. On the other hand, officers often preferred single subordinates, for they were easier to transfer and supposedly more committed to the army. One colonel rejoiced over the 'epidemic' of NCO marriages, but regretted that it had been provoked by a life deprived of comfort and pleasure in the security camps.[41]

This ambivalence is evident in the layout of NCO houses. Homes at the internationally famous *cité-jardin* at Ungemach (Strasbourg) were built with kitchen-diners, in order to integrate the wife into the family while she cooked, thus encouraging family life and childbirth in the lower middle class, to which NCOs were usually assimilated. Although a general served on the Ungemach council, there were no kitchen-diners in the security camps.[42] Of course, kitchen-diners were hardly appropriate for officers, for they normally had maids or orderlies to cook and clean. But officers too were ambiguous about family life.[43]

Officers

The army attempted to meet fortification officers' expectations of marriage, education for their children, domestic comfort and bourgeois social and cultural life. To attract 'officers of choice', it promised bonuses, enhanced promotion, choice of post following their fortification tour, award of the Légion d'honneur, high-quality food and schools for their children. In 1937, the fortification regulations specified that, for officers, peacetime occupation of the *ouvrages* must conciliate 'the necessities of service with the obligations of family life'.[44]

Yet nowhere in France was pay sufficient for officers without private means easily to sustain a bourgeois lifestyle. Colonel André Caille (168 RIF) commented that while officers were respected in Thionville – a garrison and steel town with a significant francophone population – their workload and straightened budgets meant that they could hardly mix socially.[45] In 1935, complaints were intensified by the financially hard-pressed government's 10 per cent pay cut for all state employees. Almost every report stated that while cadres happily shared in sacrifice, budgets were tight. Pay was an obsession in the military press. De Gaulle saw that as evidence of greed, yet insisted that officers needed enough income not to have to worry about money.[46]

Complaints about the absence of secondary schools were ubiquitous. In 1900, the future general Heinz Guderian had left Saint-Avold for boarding school for that reason. Primary education was more often available, but the nearest school to Mont-Agel *gros ouvrage* (SF-Alpes Maritimes, altitude 1,450 metres) was at Turbie (altitude 480 metres), ten kilometres down a hazardous uneven military road, often impassable in winter.[47]

Officers missed the facilities of the old barracks towns. In December 1934, two batteries of 157 RAP were given forty-eight hours' notice to leave Nice to man Mont-Agel *ouvrage* in the Corniches sub-sector. They found no local resources, no transport and no way of leaving the military installations to buy essentials or for a change of air. Water and electric light were lacking, as were lodgings for married cadres.[48] The Bitche camp (constructed before 1914 by the Germans) was notoriously difficult. The commander of SF-Vosges described the area as a 'little Siberia'. The town provided few resources at high prices; public transport was non-existent. The regiment lacked horses and its two soft-top touring cars were wholly unsuited to the climate.[49]

Officers saw border communities as beneath them. Whereas in barracks towns, officers socialised with the sub-prefect, doctors and notaries and their children attended lycées, that was not possible on the germanophone frontier. In 1935, Colonel Charles-Auguste Potier (171 RIF), recently installed on the Rhine, wrote that certain officers were 'disoriented' by the change of scenery and the German language of the locals, and could not hide their desire for garrisons more compatible with their habits, origins and affections.[50] Colonel Vital Fonlupt (42 RIF) claimed that there was no society to speak of in Neuf-Brisach; although locals respected officers, relations were impossible for 'a variety of reasons'.[51] For Caille, whose 168 RIF was stationed in the Elzange, Cattenom and Anzeling camps, 'no social relations are possible with locals, who lack education'.[52] Chef de bataillon Devevey (30 BCP, Bataillon de chasseurs à pied) reported that relations in Sarreguemines were good, but limited because 'even the educated' largely speak German.[53]

Complaints about promotion were not confined to the fortifications. The number of officers had expanded during the Great War through temporary promotion from the ranks, and postwar measures to reduce their numbers had only partially restored balance. NCOs who lost their temporary officer status often passed the entrance examination for the Saint-Maixent school, which trained those from the ranks who aspired to officer status.[54] In the infantry, there were five generals for every division and 236 colonels for 100 infantry regiments. The proportion of Saint-Cyriens in the officer corps fell from 40 per cent in 1913 to 25 per cent in 1928, while that of officers promoted from the ranks had risen from 4 to 24 per cent.[55] Regulars grumbled that Saint-Maixentais lacked the general culture required for command. De Gaulle complained that the army accepted three quarters of applicants to Saint-Maixent, of whom 'very few possess an education that is really elevated and complete'.[56]

For RIF and RAP officers, the low status of fortification service intensified anxiety about promotion. Although in theory the French army had no elite units, assignments to Parisian formations, chasseurs, Alpine troops and certain line regiments were prized. In such units, prestige and promotion compensated for difficult conditions. Thus, when an officer wrote that service was as difficult in the Alps as in the northeast, another pencilled in the margin, 'There's all the attraction of the mountains – besides, no officer in the Alps would swap with an officer in the security camps of the northeast.'[57] Alpine fortress brigades were less prestigious: Colonel Dessaux (157 DBAF – Demi-Brigade alpin de forteresse) reported multiple transfer requests.[58] In the northeast, Colonel Max Creskens (23 RIF) attempted to convince subordinates that fortification service 'envelops all the actions of military life with an atmosphere of reality and creative action, from which officers can draw great profit'.[59] Most officers considered that such conditions were worthwhile only if they aided promotion.

Colonel Herique (37 RIF) reported that the fortifications received only sub-lieutenants who had graduated in last place, and that 'the cadres of the fortified region aspire only to leave the frontier, while those of the interior do everything they can to avoid coming here'. Numbers were made up by reserve officers, 'whose military spirit remains to be confirmed'.[60] The future general Alberich Vaillant was posted to Einseling *ouvrage* because his graduation ranking at Saint-Cyr was too low for the colonial posting he wanted.[61]

Although Daladier forbade the practice, disgraced officers were often sent to the fortifications.[62] Despite repeated protests, 23 RIF received two officers with heavy pasts – crimes against honour, significant debts, drunkenness in uniform in the street.[63] For the commander of SF-Faulquemont, it was 'too much' that those guilty of failure in the interior should be stationed on the frontier, where officers were permanently on half-alert. The general commanding the Saverne sector saw disciplinary transfers as dangerous, given the activity of spies on the frontier, and lamented that these officers gave all cadres a bad name.[64]

The new khaki uniform, which was meant to promote elite status, was unevenly distributed.[65] Those who got it complained of the great variety of shades.[66] To their annoyance, fortification artillery units had to make do with the old sky blue, which, as commented by the commander of 39 RARF (Régiment d'artillerie de région de forteresse), was 'faded and unbecoming, a reason why the men no longer had pride in their uniform. The "new khaki", which could be tailored, would have a positive impact.'[67]

The EMA summary of morale reports for 1933 warned that fortification units were not attracting elite officers.[68] The 1935 survey confirmed discontent all along the German and Italian frontiers. Suffice it to quote Colonel Baudouin's report on 146 RIF (SF-Faulquemont), in which he described 'a very harsh life, in regions where the climate is severe during a great part of the year, organised without comfort in the summary installation of the camps, isolated from entertainment and material or intellectual relaxation and lastly faced by great obstacles to family life. Cadres certainly make very bitter comparisons with their colleagues in the interior.'[69] Such reports persuaded the ministry to act. In July 1935, it agreed to improvements in pay for cadres, and on 6 December officers serving in security barracks in the northeast (but not the southeast) became eligible for an indemnity for service in 'disinherited garrisons'. Most importantly, from January 1936 newly minted sub-lieutenants aspiring to promotion were liable to be assigned to fortress units, and from 1937 all officers were expected to serve such a tour.[70] The return of two-year service in July 1935 improved officers' morale, for it potentially improved the training of troops.

Better-qualified officers came, if not entirely by choice. The 2nd Region commander wrote that the new rules had 'brought from the interior remarkable individuals, who have sensibly raised units' standard of encadrement'.[71] Some married officers now came voluntarily, at least to 168 RIF.[72] Yet most 153 RIF officers did not wish to stay too long, and the opportunity of a choice garrison afterwards was said to be a comfort.[73]

From 1936, inflation further eroded salaries at a time when spending on rearmament did not incline the army to raise wages. Some thought that the Popular Front government in power from 1936 privileged the workers: Colonel Grisot (SF-Boulay) claimed that the allowance of 83.33 francs for the family expenses of a senior officer was less than daily tips earned by a waiter in a second-rate Parisian café. He compared NCOs' poverty with conditions for workers in the 'week of two Sundays' (the recently introduced forty-hour week).[74]

At least several camps now had primary schools. Children of 168 RIF officers and NCOs benefited from a school in Elzange camp, but those of colleagues in Hettange-Grande and Cattenom were obliged to attend local schools, which could not cope with 80–100 extra pupils. Education suffered, and many children were incapable of passing the *Certificat d'études* at thirteen years. Colonel Tournade (168 RIF) saw that problem as harming future recruitment of 'excellent elements traditionally animated by the military spirit' who were capable of becoming NCOs.[75]

Secondary education, still largely the preserve of officers' children, remained difficult everywhere. In SF-Boulay, the offspring of 168 RIF's officers faced a twelve-kilometre trip to Thionville, which obliged parents to pay for midday meals. Lieutenant-Colonel Fonlupt (42 RIF) said that his children had lost one to four years of schooling thanks to a previous posting in 'the minuscule garrison of Neuf-Brisach'.[76]

Integration into local society sometimes improved. In the Wissembourg area, interior French active officers and Alsatian reserve officers got to know each other militarily and socially, in one case because a school teacher reserve officer taught an active's daughter.[77] Further south, on the outskirts of Strasbourg, locals and interior French socialised in reserve-officer and NCO associations.[78] In January 1939, an intelligence survey concluded that while in some (unspecified) areas officers found 'intellectual possibilities' and a certain social and even 'society life' appropriate to their status, in others conditions were more akin to those in the colonies – a recurrent comparison.[79] Colonel Auguste Cochinard reported that although the provision of libraries improved officers' general culture, it was still limited by the absence of 'normal life', seen as involving lectures and relations with educated civilians.[80]

Promotion remained an issue. Typically, Grisot claimed that officers left because they disliked promotion prospects and found travel from their quarters too expensive.[81] The noisiness of single officers' accommodation made it hard to study for promotion.[82] The officers of 42 RIF on the Rhine thought that the high command did not value fortification troops, for none had been nominated for promotion.[83]

General Désiré Sivot, commander of RF-Metz, complained again that fortified regions were receiving disciplinary transfers. In 1938, 168 RIF was allocated four such reprobates, two lieutenants and two captains, one of whom, to his colonel's surprise, had recently been promoted. He saw this as proof that the high command saw fortress troops as second-rate.[84]

In 1938, the army still believed that officers needed encouragement to come to the fortifications. In a feature film made with army support, *Trois de Saint-Cyr* (Three men of Saint-Cyr), the hero, having graduated in first place, has the right to choose his garrison. Implausibly, he wants to choose a fortification regiment, but having fallen on hard times opts for the better-paid colonies. The desperate defence of a desert outpost depicts fortress service as heroic.

Shortly before the film appeared, the RF-Metz staff reiterated the reality of overwork, shortages of officers, the creation of new units, detachments for other duties, the training of conscripts, reserves and frontier guards, learning new weapons, running reserve-officer and NCO schools, constructing fieldworks, administering camps and guarding *ouvrages*.[85] In September 1938, partial mobilisation during the Munich crisis tested cadres to the full. Commanders generally praised the devotion of their subordinates, but there were many hiccoughs. The EMA concluded that overwhelmed cadres suffered from extreme exhaustion, leading to a few cases of 'madness or at least moral derangement, suicides and sudden deaths'.[86]

The Psychological Dangers of Fortification Service

How officers experienced life in the fortifications is as ungraspable as the experiences of anyone who lived in the past. However, the psychology of emotions can help us understand how officers made sense of their feelings in words. Physiologically, emotions consist of degrees of arousal plus levels of comfort and discomfort, while the meaning ascribed to these feelings varies culturally and contextually. Thus, the physiological experience of fortification officers varied from high arousal due to overwork to low arousal on watch, and from discomfort during freezing dark nights on watch or on the lorry taking them to work to cosiness in the garden-city family home. Potentially, a single capacious military slang expression encapsulated all these feelings: 'le cafard'.

Literally, 'cafard' refers to a type of beetle, and in the nineteenth century it was a slang term for a hypocritical, falsely devout person. By the 1890s, it had begun to acquire its modern meaning, akin to depression but much more. It was first used in the Foreign Legion, where it denoted a not wholly negative emotion. It harked back to 'nostalgia', a bitter-sweet regret for home experienced by Swiss mercenaries when they heard certain songs. But legionnaires accepted their *cafard*: they proved their manliness by overcoming the physical and emotional challenges of the colonies where they served, and rhetorically preserved their humanity in brutal circumstances. Yet *le cafard* also encompassed over-sensitivity, violence against indigenous people and even between soldiers, which was supposedly unknown on 'civilised' French soil. Soon, civilian colonists also embraced the term, which they associated with alleged diseases such as 'Africanitis' or Sudanitis'.

During the Great War, the expression *le cafard* was used by troops to make sense of the front as an alien, war-ravaged landscape like that of the colonies.[87] It retained the connotation of homesickness for the families for whom one fought, thus preserving the humanity of men whose duty it was to kill. Use of the word spread to civilian society without losing its primarily military and colonial connotations. It was part of the slang ritually transmitted to each military generation. The colonial meaning was kept alive in films about the Foreign Legion.

In the fortifications, '*le cafard*' retained its colonial connotation with its combination of depression and potential for conflict. In November 1938, Colonel Cochinard reported that 'for some [officers], the very restricted social life and [interpersonal] friction due to lack of privacy [in the camps] has created a sad state of mind that is analogous to "le cafard colonial"'. He regretted that it was necessary to 'confront all the little vexations and maliciousness that one finds in little towns'.[88] Another officer compared the camps to living like legionnaires in 1910, without the relief of the African sun. Even underground *ouvrage* life was preferable.[89]

Some officers who had served in the colonies thought that conditions in the fortifications were just as difficult.[90] Colonel Potier (171 RIF) wrote that some cadres suffered from nostalgia for overseas service, where material existence had been rendered easy for them. They therefore struggled to accept the life of a frontier garrison, especially in Neuf-Brisach, where the 'rough' Germanic language of the population had caused some surprise.[91] This attitude linked Alsace-Lorrainers to colonised peoples. Their villages were often referred to as '*le bled*' – an Arab term for country/village of origin, with negative connotations for the French.

In the fortifications, *cafard* was also attributed to the stress of industrial warfare. Colonel Reyx reported that while the duties of the fortification officer were always absorbing, they demanded more sustained mental effort than duties in the interior. Even the best-intentioned officers risked slackening in the long term.[92] But life in the camps could also be too comfortable. In March 1939, long extracts from an anonymous article in an unnamed magazine reached Gamelin, warning of the supposed dangers of too much comfort and family life in the *cité-jardin*.[93] The authors were reserve RIF officers in a camp somewhere in RF-Metz. They describe the lives of married officers, who, finishing work early, retreat into the family milieu:

> In each garden, whenever the weather is good, we see officers in pyjamas fervently digging their vegetable plots.

> Good little neighbourly relations are created between households, which live on gossip and exchanging seeds and recipes; it's a life of slippers in winter and gardening and fishing in summer.
>
> In short, everyone's ambition is to make their nice little functionaries' lives a little more comfortable.
>
> Consequently, working or not, the officers of the security camps see no reason to summon or maintain the energy or desire for good that they should all possess. In most officers, we see weakening of professional and moral qualities.

The authors were also shocked to find quite different attitudes among the unmarried, many of whom left their beds in daytime only to eat. They had no interest in card games, reading, training or in ensuring that their men had something to occupy their leisure time. Single officers had only the mess, where they alternated between drunken excess, depression, twelve-hour nights and afternoon siestas.

The anonymous reserve officers attributed the problems they described to the fortifications' 'eternally defensive' character. The infrequency of exercises paralysed enthusiasm, for they amounted to hardly more than 'waiting with blank weapons for an imaginary enemy'. RIF officers' preference for field units is confirmed by their tendency to omit the 'F' in the regimental title in their written communications. The commander of 149 RIF was frustrated that the formation in 1937 of specialist *ouvrage* companies and machine-gun battalions had not freed the regiment's rifle battalions (*voltigeurs*) to manoeuvre like campaign units. Young officers, he said, were too specialised in the defensive and unable to acquire the skills of manoeuvrability.[94]

The crime novel *Double crime sur la ligne Maginot* (1936), which we encountered in chapter 3, dramatises the ambiguous place of fortification service in military culture. On the one hand, it denies that fortification service is 'industrial' and presents it in traditionally heroic military terms. When a lieutenant reflects that fortification officers risk death as if they were merely factory foremen, his superior, Captain Ardant, retorts that 'as soon as bullets begin to fly, your role as technicians will give way to your tasks as leaders [*chefs*]'. Yet Ardant's status as the novel's hero depends on his secret role as a Deuxième Bureau intelligence officer, for which his fortification officer uniform is only a cover. It is telling that author Pierre Nord did not choose to serve in the fortifications himself, but in Paris.

The extent of dislike of fortification service certainly contradicts the view that the army was entirely suffused with a defensive Maginot mentality. De Gaulle's criticism of defensive warfare and desire for action were widely shared among ordinary officers. However, the point is not simply to pile up evidence that the French were not decadent after all, for the attitudes and conflicts described here are too complex to squeeze into such simple categories. Officers' complaints about being treated as second-class were compatible with defence of their interests as fortification officers and thus of the fortifications as another organised interest in the army. And as seen in previous chapters, the fortifications were based on the idea that it was possible to cover every possible angle of attack, an impossible task that could never be complete, but which required ever greater resources.

While the social and psychological challenges of fortification service potentially throw new light on the role the fortifications played in the battle of 1940, they belong primarily to the history of the Maginot Line itself. In the next chapter, we shall see that despite lamenting the unmilitary nature of fortification service, career officers largely bought into the absolute command model that the *ouvrages* were supposed to buttress. Yet ordinary soldiers proved as hard to 'organise' as the natural environment.

6

COMMAND AND DISOBEDIENCE ON THE MAGINOT LINE

In 1926, the CDF insisted that since command was of 'capital importance', all *ouvrages* must be commanded by an officer at the head of at least a sixty-strong platoon. It rejected small works on the grounds that they dispersed the troops and removed them from officers' authority.[1] Two years later, the EMA's refutation of Pierre Cot's last-ditch appeal for fieldworks breathlessly declared that 'gathering together conscripts in the powerful *ouvrages* of the fortified regions entails facilities for command and immediate and direct action of officers and NCOs on the troop, the importance of which is fundamental for giving units that are not yet battle-hardened all the cohesion and solidity required to resist attacks of which suddenness and vigour are the essential characteristics'.[2] The conflict between backers of *gros ouvrages* and of field fortification was the latest episode in decades of debate about command, in which the 1921 field regulations, the IPGU and its annexes, figured as a compromise. These manuals endorsed the division of infantry regiments into eleven-man combat groups, but subjected them to strict rules to prevent improvisation. Likewise, the authority of the *ouvrage* commander, which equated to that of a ship's captain, compensated for the objection that the long galleries of the *ouvrages palmé* dispersed the crew.

In reality, top-down command was difficult in a closed *ouvrage*, problematic in the camps and impossible in the hundreds of construction sites and dispersed blockhouses in which soldiers actually served.

In any case, command rarely spoke with one voice. The transmission of orders depended on reserve officers, NCOs and corporals with ideas of their own, the latter caught between loyalty to the troops with whom they lived and the hierarchy above. Absolute command also conflicted with the ethos of the democratic army, the republican idea that soldiers were citizens with rights as well as duties. The latter principle was embodied in the 1928–9 military laws, which made the army a semi-militia in which young men served for only one year but remained in the reserve until age forty-eight.

The Military Justice Law of 1928, a response to wartime abuses, was based on the same principle. The commission responsible for drafting it stated that, in view of 'short service, stable garrisons and frequent leaves generally spent with family thanks to rapid transport, we may say that the soldier no longer has a life apart, but is merely an ordinary citizen with a supplementary military duty to accomplish'.[3] Courts martial were replaced by military tribunals, presided over by civilian judges and served by trained military prosecutors. Punishments for officers (who hardly ever appeared in these courts anyway) remained more or less unchanged, while those for soldiers were softened, especially in peacetime.[4] The high command objected that the new law lowered officers' authority. General Rouquerol regretted the old 'paternal and benevolent' courts.[5] In fact, the army obtained a number of concessions; for instance, military rather than civilian courts continued to judge common-law crimes such as theft committed on military premises. Officers, NCOs and corporals could still punish summarily.

There was much potential for conflict between officers who believed that military authority extended into a conscript's whole life, on duty and in their 'organised leisure', in the barracks or in the street, and the democratic principle that authority was confined to the time and place of duty. And while many conscripts came to the fortifications with an ethos of patriotic conformity and work discipline learned in factory and field, others brought violent youth culture and political opinions from communism to Alsace-Lorraine autonomism. That so many individuals were psychologically damaged also complicated command.

Command and Its Limits

Organisational science placed the *chef* (chief/leader) at the summit of the *ouvrage*. Although advised by deputies with specialist knowledge, he was the sole guardian of its purpose, for his 'general culture' gave him an overview that specialists lacked. He transmitted orders downwards through 'heads of departments', as in the corporate firm, through galleries, electric trains and telephone wires, to subordinates who in the small realm of the combat blocks were *chefs* too. In theory, ordinary soldiers mechanically executed simple tasks (Plate 4).

Officers routinely employed the language of crowd psychology, according to which the *chef*, as member of an 'elite', was able to direct the crowd because he (always he) could use his reason and superior character to master his own emotions, possibly his fear, whereas the crowd could not. De Gaulle, typically, saw creative action as the monopoly of the commander.[6] Without the *chef*'s firm leadership, the mass was vulnerable to panic and to exploitation by 'agitators', i.e. communists. Colonel Chateignon (149 RIF) warned that agitators with precise instructions could 'act more easily in a milieu that is certainly not sympathetic on the whole [to communism] but which is susceptible to following as the crowd follows, without understanding exactly, just to make a noise. The cadres' task is to counter their action.'[7] Officers prided themselves on their ability to do so. The commander of an RAP said that 80 per cent of new recruits feared 'terrible military discipline', but were reassured when they saw that those already serving were smiling and that the officers spoke to them civilly. Only three teachers – the agitators – were not won over.[8]

The naval model was another pillar command. For General Guitry, both warship and *ouvrage* had a 'chef' and specialist combatants who fought from the alert 'to the final sacrifice' – neither an *ouvrage* nor a warship could ever surrender.[9] Naval officers were seconded to the fortifications. In RF-Metz, Capitaine de Corvette Ollivier, according to one fortification commander, 'incontestably gave to the organisation of our garrisons the unity it had hitherto lacked'.[10] In exercises at GO-Anzeling, Ollivier divided the crew into duty and relief twelve-hour watches, corresponding to port and starboard. The fruit of these trials was the provisional fortification regulations of 7 October 1937 – 109 pages plus an organigramme of which Fayol would have been proud.[11] War Minister Daladier's preface, stuffed with organisationalist and mechanical vocabulary, explained that the principle of economy of force would produce a 'veritable *fusion of the elements of all arms* charged with defence of the *ouvrages* under the authority of the single chief who is "the Commander" '.[12]

Daladier also stressed that the precise functioning of the *ouvrage* mechanism and impersonality of roles within it should not mean neglect of its 'personality' and 'allure'. To attach troops to *their ouvrage*, training should include explanation of the military purpose of the fort and of the historical and geographical importance of the position.[13] By 1935, each RIF had a name, signifying 'for each soldier the frontier zone with whose defence he had been entrusted'.[14] For instance, 162 RIF was named 'le Régiment de la Nied' after the river. This identity was often depicted in an enamel badge.

The apparently insignificant right of fortification regiments to wear these insignia underlines the importance of command. Fortress regiment officers, whatever their arm, wore a standard badge on their oversized berets, depicting a stylised gun barrel protruding from the embrasure of a casemate, with an observation cloche in the background. Around the edge was a barbed-wire barrier and the legend 'On ne passe pas' (they shall not pass). Its modernist simplicity reflected the primacy of artillery and engineers, and thus of the system as a whole.

In the past, the army had been ambivalent about unit insignia, for they were often frivolous and irreverent. During the Great War, unofficial emblems painted on vehicles and equipment proliferated as part of the devolution of command, increased specialisation and the citizen ethos of the reserve army. For instance, an image of 'La vache qui rit' (the laughing cow, a play in French on 'Valkyrie'), immortalised as a make of ultra-processed cheese, adorned vehicles supplying beef to the front.

In the early 1930s, the invention of high-quality cheap enamel badges caused the high command to worry that soldiers would design inappropriate insignia and facilitate enemy identification of units.[15] Yet insignia potentially reinforced unit cohesion, for as crowd psychology supposedly taught, simple soldiers understood images better than reason.[16] The solution was to confine enamel insignia to motorised and fortress regiments.[17] They were designed by amateurs in the regiments, but approved by commanding officers.

Far removed from the black humour of the Great War, these insignia depicted episodes from regimental history, regional motifs and/or the equipment and armament of the *ouvrage*. For instance, that of 168 RIF, the Régiment de la Moselle, was crenellated along the top edge to signify fortification. The right diagonal depicted in bright colours the river flowing between a casemate and factories. The left, in sombre colours, showed in silhouette a cross, broken trees and a wolf's head. The inscription 'Bois-le-Prêtre' along the bottom linked the regiment to the famous battle of the previous war, when its predecessor was part of 128 DI (Division d'infanterie), the Division des loups (Wolves Division). Unlike the standard fortress badge, it referenced the infantry.

In the case of the Gardes frontaliers – reserve units charged with reinforcing the advance posts on mobilisation – the right to special insignia did enhance cohesion, for some men proudly wore their badges off duty. Some men designed standards on their own initiative, adorned with slogans such as 'Touch me and I'll sting!'[18] In Alsace-Lorraine, frontier guards had been subject to particularly strong vetting to ensure their loyalty. Insignia were more controversial in RIFs. Prior to the 1935 circular, they were reluctant to reference the fortifications in them, for they wished to preserve their identity as field units.

Sometimes, rivalry between arms prevented command from speaking with one voice. Artillery and engineer officers were annoyed that individual *ouvrages* were usually commanded by infantry officers, a consequence of the belief that unlike 'specialist' artillery and Génie officers, infantry officers possessed the general culture required for overall command. In 1935, an EMA inspection of GO-Sœtrich found constant friction between artillery, engineers and intendancy, 'each jealously reserving their prerogatives'. The inspector underlined that 'beginning in peacetime a modern *ouvrage* requires a crew adapted to its task and a *chef*. It is an illusion to expect good productivity of the *ouvrage* if this condition is not fulfilled.'[19] Four years later, the EMA regretted that assimilation of the *ouvrage* to the warship was not yet total. Artillery and infantry were simply juxtaposed, thus undermining the authority of the *ouvrage* commander, with potentially terrifying military consequences. The author's recommendation to merge infantry and artillery into single regiments had no chance of success. Neither did the EMA proposal to grant the *ouvrage* commander certain prerogatives of a corps general, including authority over training, maintenance, administration and mobilisation.[20]

Professionalisation and technical training created alternative hierarchies that potentially undermined command. Specialists often had knowledge that the commander lacked, and their autonomy was enhanced by the permanent necessity of maintaining breakdown-prone machinery. Colonel Candé (2 Génie) wrote that electro-mechanical officers would have nothing to do even with fellow sappers. They supposedly disdained the military part of their duties and anything that was not technical. Candé regretted that electro-mechanics escaped the 'direct action of the commander'.[21]

Older officers' tendency to criticise the rising generation is a cliché of any period. But in the fortifications it was linked to professionalisation. The commander of an Alpine fortress regiment (71 BAF) complained that whereas officers trained before and during the war possessed a vocation, professionalisation undermined the military spirit of 'certain young officers', who did not have a precise idea of 'external signs (uniform, precision)'.[22] Lieutenant-Colonel Baldoni (30 DBAF) lamented that young officers lacked basic politeness, neglected to present themselves to superiors in meetings, forgot to salute when in civvies and showed seniority insufficient respect.[23]

Another complexity was that career officers disparaged reserve officers' aptitude for command.[24] Whether the latter really were less effective is impossible to say, but since up to 20 per cent of the officers in some regiments were primary-school teachers – the backbone of the democratic republic – it is likely that many embraced the ethos of the citizen army.[25] Furthermore, there was more than one model of masculinity in interwar France. The stereotype of the distant career officer competed with the brave but vulnerable character of reserve officer Maréchal in *La grande illusion*, the great film of 1937. Its director, the veteran Jean Renoir, had served in the air force, where discipline was more relaxed.[26]

Officers' obsession with command concealed the reality that the more senior they were, the less often they ordered small groups or individuals to carry out specific tasks. Face-to-face command of the troop usually fell to corporals, who were the weak link in the chain of command, for they were not NCOs but part of the troop. Under three-year service, it had been possible to choose corporals from among the best conscripts. In his *Feue l'armée française*, Captain Souchon considered such men to be the nation's elite.[27] With shorter service, corporals were more likely to be professionals unsuited to NCO or specialist training in the modern army. Reyx thought that many had failed in civilian life and sought refuge in the army.[28] General Charles Condé (a commander on the Maginot Line) was harsher still: unless proven criminals, career soldiers were recruited blindly and were 'mediocre subjects from all points of view, incapable of doing anything in civilian life, rejected by their families and all employers'. Many ended up in punishment battalions, he added (correctly).[29] Colonel Grisot (153 RAP) opined that a crisis of authority in society explained NCOs' and corporals' 'tolerance of minor offences against discipline (uniform contraventions, exterior signs of respect)'.[30]

Colonels universally complained that dispersal of troops in multiple blockhouses and construction sites compromised command and training. The colonel of 155 RIF on the Meuse negatively compared his well-trained *ouvrage* crews with the five battalions dispersed over several dozen kilometres.[31] Colonel Creskens (23 RIF) reported that owing to dispersal, transfers and reliefs, 'officers cannot properly know all their men, exert a moral influence or make a durable impression on their troops'.[32] The commander of 172 RIF asked that soldiers not be transferred from punishment battalions and military prisons to fortification regiments because of the influence these 'defective' elements had on young soldiers in isolated casemates.[33]

The consequences of dispersal were vividly described by the anonymous reserve officers encountered in the previous chapter.[34] In their unnamed RIF, a lieutenant who wished to see his whole platoon had to make a huge round trip, on which he would find one man working as a mason on a blockhouse, another pile-driving antitank rails, another painting walls in an *ouvrage* and yet another doing heavy lifting for the artillery. Even within the *ouvrages*, part of the crew was absent on training courses. The whole regiment was never together in camp. Commanders allegedly recognised that although they signed papers as 'unit commander', they no longer commanded.

That a significant proportion of fortification troops were Alsace-Lorrainers with an imperfect grasp of French complicated command. The question of how well conscripts spoke French was politically controversial, since statistics were reported publicly each year as a measure of the reintegration of the recovered provinces. In 1928, a CSG inspector reported progress among the most recent recruits, who had received francophone teaching in their last four years of schooling, but admitted that results were uneven.[35] In June 1932, a *France militaire* article stated that nearly all of those who had supposedly learned French spoke an incomprehensible gibberish, and that interior French conscripts could not understand Alsace-Lorraine NCOs' poor French. The journalist added the old chestnut that some who supposedly could not speak French had been caught surreptitiously speaking it to trusty comrades.[36]

In 1935, the army reported that almost all conscripts knew some French.[37] The autonomist press suggested that the real figure was 15 per cent and doubted that asking basic questions of naked conscripts undergoing medical examination was an adequate test of linguistic competence.[38] Evidence from the regiments shows that proficiency in French was uneven. In 1936, fifty of ninety-eight conscripts in 37 RIF had a weak or non-existent knowledge of French. This regiment was recruited from the Northern Vosges, in which French speaking was especially limited and autonomism strong.[39] The class of 1938 was the first to have begun schooling after the province returned to France. There are no statistics for that year, but almost all conscripts spoke French well enough to dispense with an interpreter in military tribunals. Everyone knew how to swear in French.

Older reservists called up during the Munich crisis rarely knew French. One of them told an autonomist meeting that Alsatians 'understood not a word of what their officers said'.[40] The army's own investigator confirmed that 'numerous reservists did not understand French well enough to be of any use'. Moreover, the roads were clogged with wives and girlfriends visiting their menfolk, while some reservists left to work their fields – easy to do, given that so many lacked uniforms. The investigator suggested permanent manning of *ouvrages* so that they would not depend on 'the untrained *frontalier* unable to speak French'.[41] The War Ministry reminded mobilisation centres to assign cadres who knew 'patois or German', but they were in short supply.[42]

Organised Leisure

Command in the fortifications was not simply about passing on orders and ensuring their execution. It also meant attending to troops' allegedly simple material and cultural needs and stirring their latent patriotism. Failure to do so compromised efficiency and enabled 'agitators' to exploit legitimate grievances by promising impossible utopias. This task extended command into conscripts' off-duty time.

We have already seen that the CDF's desire for something like 'modern comfort' in the *ouvrages* was unrealisable. Even at their best, conditions were poor. A medical visit to PO-Coume, then occupied by 180 men for just two weeks, revealed there had been only one evacuee (for angina), that ventilators, functioning for fifteen minutes per hour, provided good-quality air and did not trouble sleep, and that the men did not complain of cold. Lighting was adequate and fresh running water was drawn from a spring. Sleeping in the two levels of bunks was a different matter. Each mattress was permanently occupied by three men in turn, with no separation from neighbours. The inspector thought this arrangement 'susceptible to favour the propagation of infection by microorganisms and parasites'. He added that there were too few sinks; chemical toilets were adequate, 'but the men were being trained in their use' – which suggests that the air was not entirely pure.[43] Heating in the *ouvrage* sleeping quarters was gradually improved, but not everywhere. In many *ouvrages*, the only antidote to poor conditions was to take the air at the surface.[44] Off-duty entertainment was limited to cards, music and reading – if there was sufficient light.

Better conditions could be provided in the camps, but they had to contend with the competition of local cafés. Condé wrote that a 'new organisation' was vital because 'streets, cafés, factories and shops glimmering with light' in modern cities contrasted painfully with the 'dark hole of the barracks', which 'throw the men into the streets and into shady bars of ill-repute' where they meet professional (i.e. communist) antimilitarists.[45] A contributor to *La France militaire* thought new barracks were vital because conditions in the east were too hard for today's weakling soldier.[46]

In the first years of occupation, the camps remained primitive. Colonel Balourdet, amongst others, called for games and reading rooms and sports grounds, so that the men would not feel a troublesome sense of isolation. Lighting was so poor that the men could not read or write in the long winter evenings, and trainee corporals could not study the regulations. (The regulation maximum for dormitories was a 19-watt bulb!)[47] Colonel Denis (162 RIF) reported that provision of entertainment was urgent to ensure that 'the men were not left to their own devices either on Sundays or on the long winter evenings'.[48]

A year later, matters were already improving. At Zimming, Bockange and Veckring security camps there were twenty men in well-lit, centrally heated rooms in either light brick structures or metallic prefabricated huts. The refectories and toilets, aside from 'small problems', were adequate. In the summer, some conscripts were accommodated in tents.[49]

In 1936, Daladier, as the Popular Front's war minister, instructed commanders to 'prioritise everything concerning the physical and moral health of the troop'. While officers were probably not reassured by his view that patriotism had reached its highest point under the Convention (the Jacobin terror of 1793), Daladier's practical proposals were similar to the army's.[50] In fact, the left had always felt that working-class leisure should be 'organised', so that lives were not dissipated in the bistro, which is why the Popular Front created a new ministry responsible for 'organising leisure'. Now, organisation appeared still more important to the left because street violence and mass strikes in 1935–6 provoked fear that the masses were escaping their leaders' control. Then, in 1937, introduction of the forty-hour week gave workers more leisure.[51] The communists were particularly concerned because unrest undermined their objective of uniting the country to resist German expansionism. The once antimilitarist communists now advocated 'humane discipline' in the army.

On the eve of war, conditions in the barracks were almost always good. In the southeast, Garchery reported 'considerable' enhancements to refectories, the installation of showers, barbers' shops, heating, lighting, reading rooms, libraries and infirmaries, even if the primitive furniture of the dormitories and refectories was 'no longer in harmony with that in the homes of very modest peasants and workers'.[52] Reyx reported as positively on Oermingen barracks, but regretted that despite the proximity of the electrical grid, troops had only petrol lighting at night.[53]

As a product of both left and right, the camps balanced individual comfort, unit cohesion and military authority with some concessions to the republican ideal of the citizen-soldier. The latter priority is evident in a sapper's remark that the Légeret camp was 'modern and less austere' than old camps. Its barracks resembled well-equipped suburban 'pavillons', set in a park enclosed by a low wall with railings, without the feeling of separation from civilian life experienced within the 'high walls of our old prisons'.[54]

Usually, the 'suburban look' amounted to no more than light regional touches on basically neoclassical barracks. The barracks reminded troops of the power of the state while referencing the more regionalist officers' houses and thus their own place in the hierarchy – officers were housed as individuals with a family, while the troops were a collective. Whereas only the most radical modernist architects advocated communal living, the army never doubted its necessity for troops. Conscripts' individuality was limited to the space around their beds, in which storage of kit was strictly regulated. Officers saw collective living as particularly important within the fortified zone, given the extent of dispersal in casemates and construction sites.[55] In the social club at Elzange, rural and desert landscapes in false arches on the walls reminded troops of their duty to defend the frontier and that their fort was part of an imperial defence system; they were painted in the 'organised landscape' style of the École française, the most popular genre of art in the interwar years.

The army opposed making troops *too* comfortable, for it saw military service as the antidote to the decadent softness of modern society. Colonel Herique – the same Herique who bemoaned poor conditions for officers – claimed that conscripts' 'proximity to the frontier maintains good morale'.[56] The frontier reminded troops of the glorious wars that had made the nation, isolated them from agitators and provided opportunities for physical fitness that turned conscripts into men. Thus, Colonel Balourdet (155 RAP) reported that despite the extension of service to two years and serving in 'incompletely organised, very uncomfortable *ouvrages*, no word of revolt, or even of ill temper has been heard in the regiment. They are conscious of the great mission of guarding the frontier for which they are responsible.'[57] The reality of obedience and disobedience was more complex, for conscripts came to the army with diverse views of military life gained from school and popular culture.

Obedience and Disobedience

Most peasant, lower middle-class and working-class conscripts were inclined to obey, whether because they accepted the army's claim on them or simply because obedience was easier than disobedience. For many conscripts, military service was a rite of passage on a journey to work, manhood, family life and respectability. After leaving school at thirteen (fourteen from 1936), adolescents usually worked while living with parents or relatives. Many conscripts were already habituated to routine in the factory, where Taylorist and piecework production processes mirrored military discipline, especially in the *gros ouvrages*. Young peasant soldiers were used to hard work and the routine of the seasons. For some, work in the army hardly differed from their civilian occupations, from caring for horses through repairing machinery to digging foundations for blockhouses.

But military service as a right of passage also entailed rituals and behaviour that the army only half tolerated – such as drunkenness en route to camp or threatening cadres at the end of service. And while most soldiers were probably patriotic, their idea of patriotism was not necessarily the same as that of their officers. Some were not patriotic at all. Some were traumatised. Conscripts came to the army with ideas more complex than their officers' view that they were simple souls inclined to follow leaders. Their education and popular culture provided multiple messages.

The first conscripts to serve in the Maginot Line in 1933–5 had been educated from 1917 to 1925, when they more likely experienced the nationalist textbooks and anti-German propaganda of the war and its aftermath than pacifism. Many of the numerous teachers who returned to their classrooms after demobilisation embraced the ambiguous pacifism of the veterans' movement, which depicted soldiers as victims of war and of inhumane officers while valorising their own heroism in suffering and victory.[58] Some teachers were so marked by their military experience that they enforced iron discipline in the classroom.[59] Schools played a significant part in remembrance.

In the later 1920s, pacifism dominated the primary-school teachers' union, the Syndicat national des instituteurs (SNI), and many primary-school teachers and some secondary-school colleagues (notably the philosopher Jean-Paul Sartre) refused to undertake reserve-officer training. Forty per cent of primary-school teachers were not members of the SNI, however, and many were reserve officers. The conscript class of 1938, educated from 1923 to 1931, experienced the high point of teacher pacifism (after which, divisions appeared).

Teachers were not the only source of ideas about the army. It was ever-present in cinema newsreel images of manoeuvres and parades, commemorations and inaugurations with close-ups of uniforms and medals.[60] War films presented more diverse messages. Léon Poirier's *Verdun* (1928), a battle in which the director had fought, depicted veteran pacifism. Abel Gance's *J'accuse* (1919) was remade with sound in 1938 and a pro-appeasement message. Colonial films, of which sixty-two were made in the 1930s, were another source of ideas about the army. In some, criminals or unfortunate individuals join the Foreign Legion and wind up dead. Others show the colonies as a place in which heroes regenerate themselves through combat and participation in the empire's 'civilising mission'.[61]

Immensely popular military vaudevilles, some forty of which were released during the 1930s, explicitly represented command on the screen. Major Pierre Calvet, head of the army's film section, who hated the genre, described such films thus: 'Conceived in the style of a prewar music hall show, they recycle the unbelievable episodes, burlesque scenes and knockabout farce of the café-concert. Repeatedly we see the indulgent colonel, the furious old lady, the ill-tempered officer, the simple-minded country-dweller, the joker enticing maidservants into the bedroom and the adjutant seeking out some poor fall guy among the terrified conscripts.'[62] In 1934, there was controversy over *La garnison amoureuse* (Garrison in love), in which a cavalry squadron earns the nickname 'les cavaliers de l'amour' (the cavalrymen of love) on account of its exploits with women. A new colonel, anxious to restore order, confines the men to barracks. The narrative follows three lieutenants' attempts to get back into the barracks after sneaking out to meet their lovers. A veterans' association and right-wing newspaper editor complained to War Minister Pétain that the film was antimilitarist, anti-French and immoral. The marshal demanded a ban on films showing officers in burlesque scenes – which bore fruit three years later.[63]

In fact, vaudevilles were neither antimilitarist nor pacifist, but dramatised the republican ideal of the citizen-soldier. They portray irreverence, resourcefulness and improvisation, known in French as 'Système D' (for 'se débrouiller', 'muddling through'), rather than the allegedly blind obedience of the old aristocratic or German armies. A more indulgent hierarchy is conventionally restored at the end. In *La garnison amoureuse*, the general arrives to tell the colonel that the uniform will not suffer too much if young officers are allowed to enjoy themselves.

This was the spirit in which NCO Léon Rodier of 146 RIF – a future general – enjoyed such films. He remembered that one of them, *Le train de 8 h. 47* (1934), which also relates young officers' attempts to catch the last train back to barracks, 'created a storm' in his regiment.[64] His own memoir tells of just such antics. As it happens, we know what Rodier's colonel thought of his cadres, for he wrote in 1935 that 'faced by executants without a sense of discipline, cadres do not command with the necessary energy and firmness, out of ignorance of what is necessary and out of fear of provoking incidents'.[65]

To counter vaudevilles, the army sponsored a handful of films that presented its own view of command. The fortifications were central to them, reminding viewers that they were as much a social as a military project. Among them was the film adaptation of the murder mystery *Double crime sur la ligne Maginot* (1937), which mirrors *La garnison amoureuse* in that the three lieutenants who are suspected of murder all sneak out of the *ouvrage* for suspicious purposes. But they all turn out to be model officers – even the murderer, who is also a German spy. Ordinary soldiers figure only as marching automatons. The fictional *ouvrage* is presented as a model of automated hierarchy – another reminder that a purpose of the *gros ouvrage* was to restore command.

Command is central to Jean-Paul Paulin's film *Trois de Saint-Cyr* (1938), which was sponsored and vetted by the army. It tells the story of officers who train together at Saint-Cyr and then find themselves defending a desert fortification while awaiting relief by an armoured column – an obvious parallel to the Maginot Line, where the film-makers had originally hoped to set the movie. The army counselled that 'gaiety and spirit of camaraderie' be introduced into the Saint-Cyr scenes, and that the hero, Mercier, be made more human, for his 'rigidity appears excessive'.[66] In the finished cut, Mercier alternates improbably between clipped military speech and smiling warmth. He teaches his young friend that 'Present arms!' is 'an order, not an invitation'.[67]

In sum, education and popular culture presented diverse views of command and obedience, including the absolute command of the *ouvrage*, traditional paternalism, the republican citizen-soldier and pacifism. But conscripts' views of the army were not simply acquired from above. Their own individual, social and family backgrounds and ideas counted too.

Although the nation was not a traumatised body, individual trauma was widespread. Children living in the occupied north had experienced the Great War at first hand, with the added stigma of suspected collaboration. Most of the young men of Alsace-Lorraine had fought for Germany. Many more conscripts had lost fathers or other close relatives or had lived with diminished or choleric fathers. Others were raised by poverty-stricken mothers, forced to work such long hours that they could not care for their children. At the same time, multiple commemorations organised by schools and churches urged children to be worthy of their fathers' sacrifices. Orphans were often separated and expected to wear black, thus constantly reliving their trauma. It would be difficult to devise a better way to implant a sense of inadequacy in young minds.[68]

This does not mean that one colonel was right to attribute the presence of so many criminals and subversives in his regiment to 'the absence of a father during young years or general postwar slackening'.[69] It is impossible to generalise about the impact of the war. Much depended on whether the child had experienced belonging, care and acceptance and how carers had framed the event, and that is usually beyond the historian's reach. However, teachers and doctors reported speech problems, bedwetting and emotional lability. Juvenile delinquency rose from the beginning of the war, and did not decline until 1929.[70] For years afterwards, stressful situations could trigger the trauma response of fight, flight, freezing or fawning. Whatever the case, trauma complicated personal relations, and potentially disrupted military authority, especially given that recourse to alcohol was a common response to trauma – as it probably was for Daladier.

Interwar France was anyway a time of heavy drinking: over two million adults downed more than two litres of wine a day and the average consumption was 250 litres per year.[71] Alcohol consumption potentially compromises the inhibitions and fear on which obedience may depend, but the cultural expectations of drunken behaviour and individual circumstances matter too. Drinking en route to joining up was expected of the most patriotic soldier. During the Munich crisis, most reserves travelled without solid food, but with abundant alcohol, so it was at least a day before they could be 'used'.[72]

Alcohol and trauma complicated an older culture of violent rivalry between male youths of villages and city neighbourhoods, gangs, and rugby and football teams, often shading into petty crime and brushes with the law.[73] This disorder was perhaps a way for children to assert their individuality and reconcile themselves to the relative lack of life choices. In the army, too, minor indiscipline reconciled manly independence with the reality of relative powerlessness. Acceptance was not inevitable, however. The intense group solidarity of adolescent gangs with their *caids* (bosses), in which individual status depended on character, drinking, and physical and sporting prowess, confrontation with the police and perhaps gaol time, potentially clashed with military rank.

Furthermore, historians have on occasion been misled by the ineffectiveness of communist activity in the army into underestimating its influence among conscripts. Gang rivalry in cities was sometimes politicised. In the working-class Paris suburb of Ivry, schoolchildren fought a 'war' in which belonging was signalled by rings engraved with crosses or the hammer and sickle. Elsewhere, children abused priests in the street. Residents of poor districts joined strikers in fighting the police.[74] Football tournaments and boules matches were organised by political and religious groups of left and right. On the Maginot Line, the divide between French and German speakers was easily politicised.

Whatever some officers said about the benefits of frontier life, service during the long, cold, eastern winters often provoked or aggravated psychological suffering. Although colonels' annual reports nearly always maintained that conscripts' morale was good – otherwise they risked being accused of inability to command – they acknowledged problems. Colonel Denis (162 RIF) reported that long periods guarding *ouvrages* and working in the camps led to 'physical and moral lassitude', without a negative effect on discipline.[75] Colonel Dumotier (2 Génie, RF-Metz) reported that regulation light bulbs in barracks 'emit only a weak light that generates *cafard*'.[76] Furthermore, soldiers living underground were said to suffer from a form of *cafard* specific to the fortifications, known as '*bétonite*' – 'concretitis'.

The right-wing press acknowledged the psychological impact of frontier service, but painted a complacent picture. The journalist André Willemin saw *cafard* as intrinsic to willing self-sacrifice, mitigated by painting false windows with country scenes in underground rooms. His conscripts never admit to *cafard*. A soldier asks his friend, 'Are you suffering from *bétonite*?' The friend replies, 'Me? Never!' – but he stays in bed, face to the wall.[77] Some officers were less optimistic, for they saw *cafard* as provoking poor discipline. Major Curet (75 BAF) stated that his men struggled to cope with solitary mountain posts: 'There's sometimes in them a lassitude that always ends up with nervous letting go and decline.'[78] 'Letting go' often led to summary punishment by corporals and NCOs and in serious cases to military courts.

Punishment

Conscripts were summarily punished for offences such as 'drinking an exaggerated quantity of wine during a night exercise', 'although not drunk suffering an illness that necessitated transport to the infirmary', 'inventing a false pretext to avoid a chore', 'jokingly threatening another comrade with a bayonet', 'failing to care for horses' and 'being in a café in shirtsleeves' – the latter case punished with a week in prison. These cases have left little context in the archives, but the records of military courts provide a precious insight into both individual crimes and obedience and disobedience generally.

To understand broad patterns, I constructed a sample of 498 cases of soldiers from twenty-two fortification regiments who were tried in the tribunals of Nancy and Metz, responsible for the northeast. The first interesting point is that no officer appears in the sample. Officers who committed offences were usually transferred – often to fortification regiments. Offending NCOs were punished with transfer too, but prosecuted if they abandoned their posts or insulted or assaulted superiors.

Secondly, despite complaints of bullying in the left-wing and veteran press, only two sergeants and two artillery corporals (brigadiers) were accused of assaulting and/or verbally abusing subordinates.[79] All four benefited from attenuating circumstances. Three received one month in prison; the fourth, who had also called his victim a 'lazy arsefucker' ('fainéant, enculé'), got three months. The army usually stood behind cadres accused of abuse. Tribunals existed primarily to discipline the troops, but we shall see that corporals could be victims of bullying.

The third general point is that much insubordination and even insolence were routinely tolerated. In fact, cadres and men alike adhered to unwritten rules about what indiscipline was acceptable and what could be expected of soldiers depending on whether they were new recruits – 'bleus' – or 'anciens'. These rules were nevertheless open to interpretation and often broke down.

Around 23 per cent of the sample were prosecuted for abandonment of or sleeping at their post and/or desertion. Rodier remembered that while he and his comrades took their duties seriously, that did not prevent them enjoying unauthorised trips from Longuyon to Longwy, Metz, Nancy and even Paris.[80] Such offences often went unpunished and unrecorded. General Sivot (RF-Metz) reported that troops were apathetic and prone to drunkenness and late returns from leave.[81]

Dispersal of the troops in the fortified zone provided opportunities for local recruits to sneak home. A commander on the northern frontier worried that his men might prove unreliable in a defensive battle, for they were dispersed among friends and family in the strong sociability of the region.[82] Alsace-Lorrainers were particularly likely to absent themselves. Colonel du Bouchet (178 RIF) thought that Alsatians were disciplined soldiers but drank too much and left casemates to visit their wives.[83] Private Sabel (41 RMIC, Régiment de mitrailleurs d'infanterie colonial), a professional soldier with positive evaluations, served over 100 days of punishment between 1934 and 1937 for unauthorised absences. Eventually, he found himself before a tribunal, where he explained that he had been visiting his sick and recently bereaved father in Metz. He was reluctant to reveal what he had done in the city for the rest of the week.[84]

Soldiers were attracted to the many cafés and inns that were still numerous in small villages.[85] Village dances were freer than the tightly regulated events of the past. Reyx reported that in the absence of cinema the men attended local dances, where, he said, euphemistically, 'the idylls begun by some men provoke brawls'.[86] Sneaking away from camp was common. On Christmas night, 1936, Privates Scheltienne and Tremblain were watching a film in the rudimentary surface barracks of PO-Immerhof – this, doubtless, was their lieutenant's attempt to 'organise their leisure' – when they heard from a comrade of a dance in Hettange-Grande, a few minutes' walk away. Unfortunately for them, the duty NCO chanced upon them returning to camp at 2 a.m.[87]

Much more serious were the crimes of Private Pierre Heissat, who was said by the colonel of 23 RIF to have profited from the necessarily relaxed discipline consequent upon the extreme dispersal of early fortification service to commit numerous crimes. As a professional soldier, rejected by his family for precocious alcoholism, Heissat was just the sort of character that Condé feared would lead young conscripts astray in isolated casemates, and indeed his commanding officer reported that he did exactly that. He was sent to a punishment battalion.[88]

Insubordination was the offence most often brought before the tribunals (43 per cent). And 37 per cent of the overall total included physical violence. Most offences took place in small blockhouses, casemates or villages, or sometimes in security barracks. Insubordination also occurred in spaces and at times when conscripts believed themselves beyond the reach of military authority. Thus, General André Corap (2nd Region) reported that promises of reprisals against corporals and NCOs increased in the weeks before liberation from service and that indiscipline was common in trains taking soldiers to and from camps.[89]

In May 1935, three officers were playing bridge with the sub-prefect in a café in Boulay. A soldier of 146 RIF, 'hands in his pockets', wandered over to watch. When Lieutenant Heugas invited the man to return to his seat, another soldier, Private Bussier, protested, 'We're in a public place, free to do what we want.' An argument ensued. Bussier received four months in prison for refusing an order to return to Téting camp.[90] This case is unusual in that it involves direct disobedience of an officer, for they, like sergeants, usually became involved in incidents only when they escalated.

The best way to bring out the complexity of obedience and disobedience is to examine some individual cases. That of Private Rolland exemplifies conflict between military rank and conscripts' own sense of hierarchy and of the reach of command. The incident began when Corporal-of-the-Week Lesquoy (155 RIF) punished his men with a chore for pillow fighting in the dormitory after lights out. As he left, Private Rolland asked, 'Even if we fought for two hours, what the fuck is it to you?' – adding for good measure, 'You're too short to command us.' He warned that they would soon meet in civilian life and challenged the corporal to 'come outside and take off your jacket if you're a man'. Lesquoy declined and informed Rolland that he would be punished. Rolland replied, 'Take that!' and punched him twice in the face. For Rolland, physique and bravery trumped military rank, and the corporal's authority was in any case not valid after lights out. The prosecution asked for the relatively light sentence of five months, while the defence asked for three months because of Rolland's excellent evaluations. The judge went with the defence, perhaps because by then – for reasons unknown – Lesquoy had been stripped of his rank. Poor evaluations of corporals and NCOs often inclined tribunals to leniency and perhaps allowed Rolland to get away with bullying.

In the case of Private Barbier (37 RIF), the accused's upbringing complicated similar issues. One afternoon in July 1936, the duty corporal ordered him to collect a letter from Sergeant Guyollet in the company office and take it to another sergeant nearby in Bitche. Barbier went straight to Guyollet and told him that he could not comply with the order because at 13:00 hours his duty was to wipe the refectory tables and he should not be expected to go to Bitche wearing fatigues rather than his uniform. And as an *ancien* he should not be assigned the task of a *bleu*. When Guyollet ordered him to leave, Barbier replied, 'You can't throw me out like a dog.' Showing his fist, he warned, 'Be careful you don't meet me one evening,' and dared Guyollet to take off his stripes, 'if you're a man'. As he left, he threw the letter on the desk and said he would happily await the lieutenant's report on his punishment.

Barbier did not in principle reject military authority. He appealed to higher priorities – the smooth running of the refectory – while refusal to be seen in town in fatigues showed concern for his military status. He also appealed to unwritten rules regarding the duties that could be given to an *ancien*.

His reaction to the order also suggests childhood trauma. Witnesses, Guyollet included, described Barbier as 'usually a good comrade and soldier', 'sober', but also a 'hothead', 'not in control of his nerves', whom it was best not to upset. They also reported that, when demanding not to be treated as a *bleu*, he trembled, clenched his fists and marched around the desk to confront Guyollet physically. Loss of physical control in response to a minor issue is compatible with transference of the emotions of past trauma into new circumstances. In fact, his peasant father had died in the previous war. He was raised by his mother and stepfather, and from age fourteen he laboured on farms. He joined the army in 1934 for five years because his employer refused to raise his wages and he did not want to live at the expense of his stepfather. His army career disappointed, for he was quickly assigned to 'auxiliary' duties – hence his refectory job. Appointing himself guardian of the functioning of the refectory saved his self-respect, but may also have been a defence against anxiety. His captain speculated that Barbier had become upset at an apparent triviality and insisted on his status as an *ancien* because he had served two and a half years as private second class with no promotion prospects.

Childhood trauma probably contributed to the case of Private Boulair, serving with 168 RIF at Cattenom security camp.[91] In his case, there was also a political dimension. One Saturday evening in December 1937, he arrived at the guardhouse to serve the second night of a week for drunkenness on exercise. He helped himself to four blankets and went straight to bed. The duty corporal ordered Boulair to return three of them. He 'obeyed' immediately, throwing them onto the bed, saying, 'They've never tamed me elsewhere and they won't here. Besides, I'm not French. France disgusts me. I belong to a party dedicated to changing the regime [i.e. the Communist Party]. You can punish me. I don't give a fuck. I'll smash all your faces in. Only mountains never meet.' As he was led into the prison, he threatened while banging on the door, 'Lock me in here and I'll break everything'. The adjutant-chef arrived. Boulair repeated, 'I'm not French,' and claimed that having already served five years of prison, he was not worried by more: 'You can put me up against a firing squad and I'll smash everyone's face in.' He lay down to sleep and muttered unintelligibly.

All the previously mentioned elements are present. Boulair's claim that his behaviour stemmed from anger provoked by *cafard* justified it as a legitimate response to military life. He appealed to unwritten rules – indeed, his colonel confirmed that in some circumstances more blankets might be allowed. Although he was not a war orphan, a childhood of tuberculosis and four years' juvenile incarceration suggests that his overreaction was also rooted in early trauma and transference. His comrades reported that he did not tolerate criticism or jokes.

Boulair expressed a deeply felt sense of his own worth as a man (perhaps concealing the opposite) – the army would not 'tame' him. His individuality and masculinity is graphically illustrated in a haunting portrait found in his kit; whether it was drawn by himself or someone else is not recorded (see Plate 9). Dismissed as a 'caricature' by the investigating officer, it echoed conventional images of male beauty in fitness magazines and asserted working-class masculinity through physical strength and labour, as idealised in communist iconography.[92] Boulair looks directly at the viewer – including at himself either as artist or more likely as recipient of the portrait – thus expressing pride and defiance while looking inward. The visibility of his tattoo underlines rebellion, both in his own eyes and in those of superiors, for whom body art was a sign of marginality. His kepi is worn incorrectly to express individuality, but kepi and identification tag together relate masculine physicality to the army. It is not unequivocally an image of disobedience; officers too wore their headgear incorrectly.

It is difficult to disentangle Boulair's touchy hypermasculinity from his communist sympathies, which were confirmed by the enquiry. As a working-class native of Paris, he was typical of communist supporters without being an activist. His 'communism' was not that of the increasingly nationalist, antifascist party of the late 1930s, but that of its pre-1934 internationalism and violent antimilitarism, which did not vanish from the party. The party's antimilitarist activity may have been a failure, and when Boulair appeared in court the party was anyway advocating 'humane discipline', but communist sympathisers were present in the army. They were probably especially common in RFs Lauter and Metz, for quick reinforcement by rail required manning from the Paris region, where communism was strong.

Organised communist antimilitarism was ineffective. Clandestine cells in barracks faced the obstacle of high conscript turnover, repression and the party's preference for action in the arms industry. At any rate, the party urged members to behave as model soldiers, just as they were expected to be the 'best workers'. Boulair's case suggests that sympathisers did not necessarily behave accordingly. On an individual level, communism sometimes contributed to indiscipline.

At first sight, the fact that 29 per cent of the tribunal cases in our sample concerned theft, largely from other soldiers, suggests that solidarity among conscripts was limited. Indeed, the army saw thieving as a serious threat to unit cohesion, which is why, in 1928, Pétain insisted that military tribunals retain jurisdiction over theft on military premises.[93] Consequently, soldiers were prosecuted for stealing objects of little cash value and quite small sums of money.

Individual cases reveal a complex picture. Take that of Private Abraham, who admitted stealing a razor and fourteen francs from Private Maison. Other soldiers suspected him of thieving a pen, stamps, shoes and a watch. His captain wrote that Abraham opposed inertia to everything requested of him; his morality was doubtful; he was a hypocrite and a liar. Despite recognising that there were extenuating circumstances – his mother had raised her five children alone, having been abandoned after the war, and as a youth Abraham had served time for stealing from his sister – the tribunal gave him three months in prison. His brief escape from custody while awaiting trial probably did not help his case. Yet his comrades were generous; they had collectively questioned him about thieving in the past. He owned up privately to Maison, who told him to keep the razor and said that the next time he was short of money his comrades would chip in.[94]

This was not the only case of generosity to thieves. When Private Lesoing (149 RIF) was found to have stolen fifty francs from Private Picot's kitbag, Picot and his friends confronted Lesoing, who immediately confessed and gave back 41.90 francs. The conscripts reported him to an NCO. Yet Picot described Lesoing as a 'good comrade'. This testimony helps to explain why the court suspended his three months' sentence. That his father, a drinker, had died young probably counted too. Both theft cases suggest that mutual bonds may have been as important as command in ensuring discipline, but they had limits.

Conflict between interior French and Alsace-Lorraine conscripts certainly undermined cohesion. Early in 1936, Private Boulefroy of II/23 RIF allegedly punched the Alsatian Private Feist in the eye and called him a 'Boche' in a quarrel over washing up. A few weeks later, Boulefroy's friend Private Vimont was punished for slapping a sergeant. Meanwhile, another sergeant, Lancelle, punished Feist and another Alsatian, Private Pfister, for drunkenness. Soon afterwards, as the men were marching to a blockhouse construction site at Trimbach, Lancelle saw Feist point to the local cemetery and say, 'If you punish me, I'll smash your face in.' Feist claimed, unconvincingly, to have uttered the words, half in Alsatian, half in French, to a comrade, not to Lancelle.

A couple of days later, Feist and Pfister, along with three more Alsatians and a Lorrainer, encountered Boulefroy and Vimont in a Trimbach café. They immediately got into a dispute, which escalated with the accusation that the Alsace-Lorrainers had been called 'Boches'. Lancelle arrived, and with the help of another sergeant escorted Vimont and Boulefroy from the café. The five Alsatians beat up the two sergeants and conscripts as they left. In this incident, the quarrel between Alsace-

Lorrainers and interior French was conflated by another between the soldiers and the sergeants.

The court was lenient, for it suspended all the sentences. The accused were immediately released and transferred to local regiments. Perhaps decisive was that three of the defendants had lost fathers in the previous war, in which they had served on the German side – no wonder they were sensitive to the 'Boche' insult. The fathers of two more had died afterwards of unknown causes. All of them had troubled pasts. For instance, Kiehl, whose father had been killed in 1914, had been sent to a special school on account of poor school attendance and a predilection for drink. The court congratulated the sergeants on their courageous and perilous intervention.

This examination of command and disobedience in the fortifications confirms the intrinsic impossibility of a fortification project based on the top-down regulation of human beings, machinery and nature. Yet it does not necessarily follow that disobedience entailed rejection of military authority. Soldiers obeyed as often for their own reasons, perhaps because they were nationalists or saw themselves as citizens of the democratic republic, but rarely because they embraced Popular Front antifascism. The peacetime army found this difficult to understand. Its maximalist definition of obedience left little room for nuance – as its response to the problem of border minorities demonstrated.

Part III

THE MAGINOT LINE IN CIVILIAN SOCIETY AND CULTURE

7

THE MAGINOT LINE IN THE BORDERLANDS

In December 1929, the French Communist Party chose Émile Béron to speak in the military budget debate in the Chamber of Deputies. This thirty-three-year-old former metalworker, originally from Alsace, represented the steelmaking constituency of Thionville-West in the Moselle Valley, which the most powerful of the proposed fortifications were designed to protect. His voters were largely germanophone, and many German nationals commuted across the border to work in local mines and steelworks. Béron spoke French as a second language. When he denounced troops' poor conditions and boasted of revolutionary propaganda in the barracks, tempers boiled over, as so often in parliament.

At least one deputy mimicked Béron's pronunciation, provoking the Communists' star speaker, Jacques Doriot, to jump up: 'Somebody here dares to reproach our colleague for his Alsatian accent! We can't accept that he should be treated that way! They didn't ask to become French in 1918. Since you took them, don't criticise their accents.' The sitting was suspended.

When it resumed, Béron reminded 'those who rebuke me for my accent' that he had risked his life fighting German militarism during the annexation, adding that he now claimed the right to join the French proletariat's struggle against the common enemy and turn imperialist into civil war. He denied the validity of national frontiers and recognised only the fluid boundary between capitalism and communism.[1] He also sympathised with the Alsace-Lorraine autonomist movement, which was influential in his constituency. The party regarded national minorities, along with immigrants and colonial subjects, as allies of the proletariat in its struggle against 'capitalism in its imperialist stage'.

A few days later, during the more measured exchanges of the Senate, retired General Stuhl reported the fortification bill from committee. Like Béron, he was a bilingual Moselle parliamentarian. Otherwise, the two men could not have been more different. Stuhl was typical of the returning émigrés who were initially prominent in Alsace-Lorraine politics following the return of the region to France. He was born in 1862 in germanophone Haspelschiedt in the Northern Vosges. To escape service in the German army, he joined the Foreign Legion as a private soldier before attending Saint-Maixent for officer training. As a lieutenant-colonel, he commanded a regiment in the war, retired in 1919, and in 1923 was promoted to reserve general. By then, he had served three years as a senator. For Stuhl, the proposed fortifications marked the boundary between France, committed to using its material resources for the progress of humanity and world peace, and 'certain peoples' whose mentality remained warlike – the Germans.[2]

For the Moselle autonomist and germanophone *Lothringer Journal*, the backing for fortification of nationalists of Stuhl's ilk demonstrated the gulf between the population and its elected representatives.[3] The newspaper exaggerated, for many frontier inhabitants did approve of fortification. Nevertheless, construction caused so much discontent that even nationalists could not ignore it. Their emotional attachment to France confronted the reality that fortification was seen by many Alsace-Lorrainers as a threat to material well-being and to their unique position between France and Germany.

Lucien Febvre, founder of the world-famous Annales school of history, who was then teaching at Strasbourg University, understood this culture well. His history of the Rhine (1935) argued that the river was neither the natural frontier of France, as French nationalists claimed, nor the sacred river of Germany, as German nationalists saw it. It could not truly be a border unless by crossing it one found oneself in a 'different world, among a set of ideas and enthusiasms, surprising and disconcerting to the foreigner'. That was not the case on the Rhine. For Febvre the Rhine was a European river, linking Switzerland, France,

Germany, Belgium and the Netherlands, economically, religiously and culturally.[4]

Porous as the Rhine frontier was, it was the only continuous physical marker of the Franco-German border. From Lauterbourg to Luxembourg, it was possible to cross inadvertently and clandestinely through thick forests, where frontier posts, if they existed at all, had been removed or hidden by vegetation. On the Alpine border, if it was not inaccessible, the notion of private – and military – property was as ill-defined as the national border.

Inhabitants on both sides retained cross-border connections. They shared Flemish, Italian or German languages. People crossed for business, to visit family, attend religious services, shop, visit the hairdresser, cultivate their lands, join the Foreign Legion, pick blueberries or smuggle drugs and tobacco. The border was also populated by hundreds of thousands of immigrants and colonial subjects who worked in the frontier industries. Italians, present on the entire frontier, represented the largest proportion.

Fortifications were meant to mark and defend national boundaries and signal the unity of the national population in a potentially long war. Yet to build and man them, the authorities relied on people whose loyalty they suspected – germanophone Alsace-Lorrainers, Italian and other immigrants and colonial workers and soldiers.

The German Border

In November 1918, French troops received ecstatic welcomes in Metz and Strasbourg. On 8 December, France's military and political leaders arrived in the latter city, the party pausing at the Place de Broglie, where, in 1792, Rouget de Lisle had first performed 'La Marseillaise'. On the steps of City Hall, Clemenceau declared that this mighty demonstration proved that there was no need for a referendum on the future of Alsace-Lorraine. For the French, Alsace-Lorraine's fundamental Frenchness had remained intact through five decades of annexation.

While there is no doubting the enthusiasm, it was probably mixed with relief at the restoration of order and defeat of the revolution that had spread from Germany to Alsace-Lorraine – the red flag briefly fluttered over Strasbourg Cathedral. In northern Alsace (the department of Bas-Rhin) and contiguous Moselle, where German influence was strongest, attitudes towards France were more mixed. Veterans of the German army largely remained aloof from the celebrations.[5] The younger generation had never known French rule.

In 1920, a group of the first Alsatian conscripts in the French army was initially welcomed in Belfort. According to the police, their conversations in dialect attracted no attention – Belfort after all was an Alsatian city. Songs were a different matter, as was drunkenness and shoving people off the pavement. The rumour spread that an Alsatian veteran of the German army had replied to the question 'Would you have shot me if you'd seen me in a trench?' with 'Yes, because that would have been one fewer.'[6] Although untypical, this incident suggested that reintegration of a region with a unique history into the centralised French system would not be straightforward. France and Alsace-Lorraine had both changed since 1871.

Becoming French

In 1870, following Emperor Napoléon III's defeat and capture by the Prussian army, France became a democratic republic. That did not mean abandoning the ambition of previous royal and imperial governments to establish uniform administrative structures and laws (as discussed in chapter 4). Indeed, since the Republic based itself on the sovereign people rather than a monarch, it pushed uniformity further than ever. Whereas monarchies endeavoured to rationalise their administrations – for instance, by ensuring the use of French in the bureaucracy and courts – they hardly cared what language the mass of the population spoke. The democratic republic did.

The Republic was assimilationist. Loyalty to the country was thought to depend on absorbing Frenchness by living within its borders, attending its schools, performing military service, speaking French – still a minority language in the late nineteenth century – and on other cultural indicators such as style of dress. Free compulsory primary education and universal adult male military service were essential to assimilation, especially linguistic assimilation.

Republicans also considered democracy, patriotism and secularism to be interdependent. They distrusted Catholicism for its loyalty to an international power, the papacy, and for its conservatism and obscurantism. By 1905, they had eliminated the Church's privileged position in the state and education. Republicans also saw Catholicism as untrustworthy because it was strong in peripheral areas where the population spoke Basque, Breton, Catalan and Flemish. For republicans, regional languages were 'backward', whereas French was the language of progress. While there was some resistance to linguistic assimilation before 1914, especially in Brittany, the French language progressed, not least because speaking it offered employment and commercial advantages.

Alsace-Lorraine did not fit this story. Prior to German annexation, loyalty to France was strongest among bilingual urban elites; the masses' identity was less certain. Then, simultaneously with nation-building in France, the province experienced German democratisation, schooling and military service. By 1914, French culture contributed more to a sense of difference within the federal German state than to separatism. Indeed, as a federal state, Germany allowed considerable room for difference. Alsace-Lorraine Catholics and Protestants possessed rights they had lost in secularised France. Contestation was largely limited to Catholic demands for rights equal to those of other German provinces, for the 'Reichsland Elsaß-Lothringen' was directly ruled by the Protestant, Prussian militarist Reich.[7] Protestants, especially the Lutherans who were numerous in Bas-Rhin and contiguous Moselle, did not contest the German state and neither even did the francophone minority in Moselle. Over 300,000 men served in the German army during the war, while 18,000 deserted to join French forces.

Nevertheless, for the French authorities, the enthusiasm of 1919 proved that the 'lost sisters' would easily reintegrate into the French nation. They therefore made French the language of schools, courts and administration. Yet most people spoke German dialects corresponding to those across the border – Luxembourgish in the north, middle Franconian further south and closer to Swiss German in southern Alsace. In school, they had learned high German. Only around 4 per cent of adults in Bas-Rhin department and 6 per cent in Haut-Rhin were first-language French speakers. In Moselle, 47 per cent reported

French as their mother tongue, but on the germanophone side of the language line, which split the department in two, the situation resembled that in Alsace.[8] Interior French visitors, to use Febvre's expression, found Alsace-Lorraine 'disconcerting'. In Strasbourg in 1923, the lawyer Maurice Garçon found it 'Boche, well and truly Boche'.[9]

In 1924, the government's plan to introduce all secular legislation in Alsace-Lorraine provoked massive protest and developed into a wider defence of Alsace-Lorraine's difference. From 1927, an organised autonomist movement grew which advocated the maintenance of the Concordat, restoration of German as the foundation of schooling and protection of social rights (more generous in Germany). Autonomists also attacked militarism and depicted Alsace-Lorrainers as a 'people', one that was entitled to protection of its ethnic and linguistic characteristics. The majority of Alsace-Lorraine communists split with the national party to ally with right-wing autonomists.[10]

The government, in the hands of Poincaré since mid-1926, responded with repression. In November 1927, the police arrested twenty-four autonomists. In April 1928, despite imprisonment, two of them, Joseph Rossé in Colmar and Eugène Ricklin in Altkirch, were elected to parliament. In the following month, twenty-two autonomists, including Rossé and Ricklin, were tried at Colmar. The prosecution proved the charge of plotting against the state in only four cases. In the furore, autonomism became the main determinant of political alignment. The francophone elite – including its bevy of retired generals – lost its grip on Alsace-Lorraine parties.[11]

The extent of autonomism, and still more of pro-German sentiment, should not be exaggerated. Nationalists dominated on the French side of the Moselle language line and were present all over Alsace-Lorraine. Explicit autonomism was strongest in the Protestant minority of Strasbourg and in northern Alsace and contiguous Moselle – i.e. in the fortified zone. But Catholics, too, were attached to germanophone culture and language and advocated advanced forms of regional devolution. Even nationalists could not afford to ignore voters' concerns. General Hirschauer, for instance, pressed for the right of conscripts serving outside Lorraine to receive newspapers in German. Both autonomists and nationalists were largely committed to Aristide Briand's policy of reconciliation between France and Germany. Some autonomists were frankly antimilitarist (Figure 11).

Fortification, Nationalism and Autonomism

The decision to fortify the Franco-German border coincided with unrest in Alsace-Lorraine. We have seen that in 1927, at a meeting of the CSG, General Boichut had accused Pétain's proposals for deep defence of endangering the province's security and that a few months later Poincaré told the generals that the Lauter, 'the least certain region in Alsace', must not be abandoned. In February 1929, his government dissolved the autonomist municipal council of Haguenau in the Lauter zone. In 1929, Poincaré reminded Debeney and Painlevé of 'political interest in demonstrating as soon as possible the will to defend Alsace'.[12]

There was nothing new about using fortifications to mark the reach and power of the French state. Those of Vauban were part of the centralising efforts of absolute monarchy; they helped to simplify the tangle of medieval jurisdictions and remind locals that they were subjects of the crown.[13] Two centuries later, fortification again expressed state power in a still contested borderland, as did multiple parades and regimental festivals in border towns and the regional touches on the neoclassical barracks of the security camps.

In the Senate Army Commission, retired Alsace-Lorraine generals, the leaders of Alsace-Lorraine nationalism, pressed for construction to begin. Most prominent was Hirschauer, whose Saint-Avold (Moselle) family had chosen exile in 1871 when he was fifteen. He rose to command the 2nd Army in the Great War and afterwards became supreme commander in Alsace-Lorraine. On retirement in 1920, he was elected to the Senate. He argued that only the deterrence of fortification could prevent Alsace-Lorraine becoming the front line in a new war.[14] Many of his constituents agreed. The mayor and general councillor (the *Conseil général* was the representative body at department level) of Falck (Moselle) asked for extension of the fortifications: 'We know only too well these people's feelings towards us and fearfully imagine being woken one fine night by Pomeranian grenadiers' rifle butts.'[15]

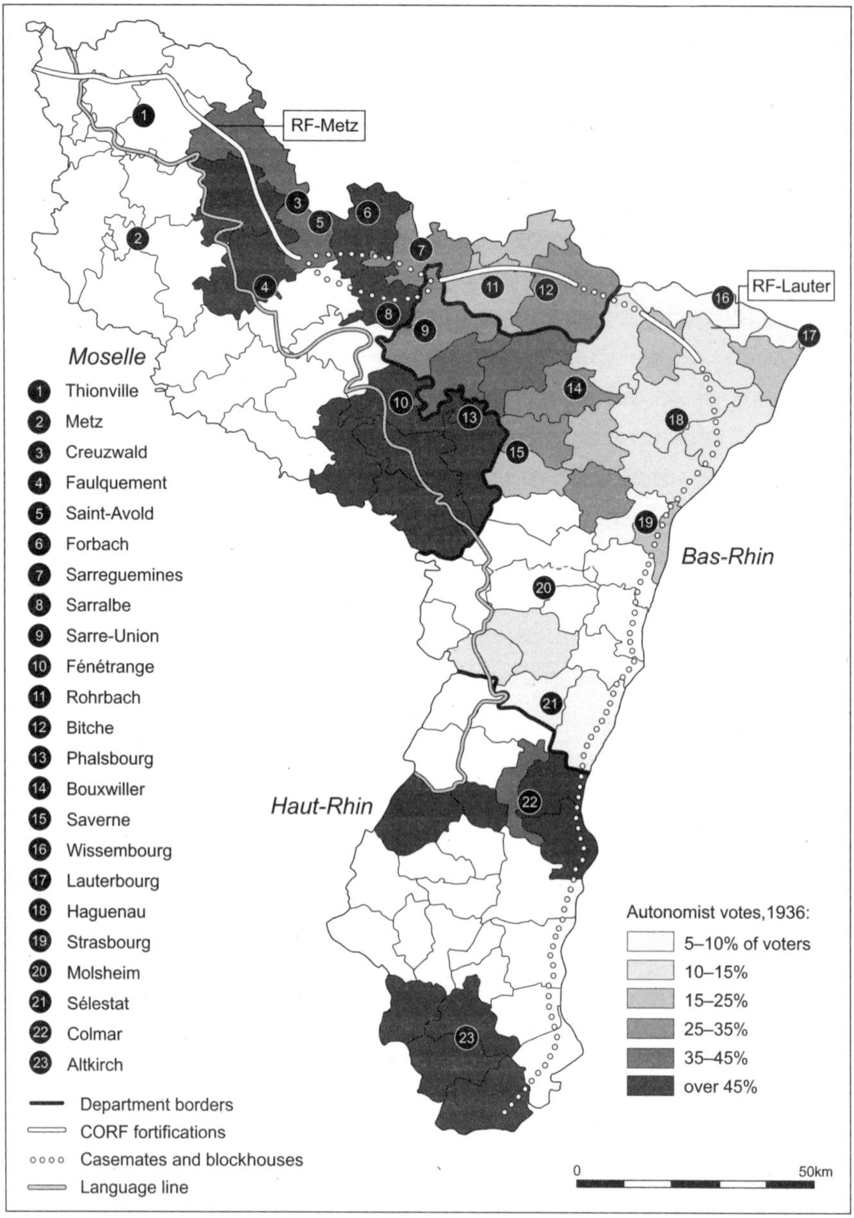

11. Autonomism in the elections of April 1936. In Haut-Rhin votes were for the explicitly autonomist deputies Stürmel and Rossé. In Bas-Rhin the votes were for the explicitly autonomist Landespartei, Fortschrittspartei, and pro-autonomist communists. In Moselle candidates were presented jointly by the autonomists and far-right league, the Croix de Feu.

The appeal of fortification was potentially bolstered by construction contracts and jobs. New military roads and railways benefited local communities. The mayor of Wissembourg successfully lobbied for a road to compensate for loss of trade with its natural hinterland in Germany. Not everyone could win. Military engineers refused the Wœrth commune's request for connection to the narrow-gauge network because doing so would sacrifice equally deserving towns and because its gauge was anyway incompatible with that of the main line.[16] In fact, fortification was so disruptive that even nationalists criticised the army.

In July 1928, Stuhl told the Senate Army Commission that from Boulay to Bitche, people were protesting against fortification works and accusing the government of warmongering.[17] Predictably, the pro-German autonomist Landespartei (Country/Homeland Party) was outraged. Its journalists saw linguistic assimilation and fortification as part of the same attack on the region's special mission to bring France and Germany together and on the province's racial and linguistic identity:

> Not a glacis but a bridge is our solution. Therefore, we protest with all vigour against the insane fortifications, which prepare once again to churn up the blood-drenched earth of Alsace-Lorraine and expel the peasantry from their traditional soil. Since we wish to maintain the people in their place, so that they can play the role we have described, we also protest against the assimilation policy of the French state, which wrests from us the German language and whatever German customs we still have, on the grounds that only then allegedly can peace be guaranteed. Must we then commit intellectual suicide, give ourselves up, and relinquish the precious genetic inheritance from our fathers?[18]

The left-wing autonomist Fortschrittspartei (Progress Party) did not use the same racist biological concepts, but it did ask how the government could evoke the Locarno spirit of reconciliation with Germany while turning Alsace into a glacis.[19] As for the communist-autonomists, they attacked German and French imperialists alike for treating the region as a 'battlefield, bastion and fortified zone'. Their orthodox communist brother enemies anticipated that fortification would provoke a new war in which the population of Alsace-Lorraine would be wiped out.[20] Even the moderate anti-autonomist wing of the Catholic Union populaire républicaine (UPR)/Elsässische Volkspartei agreed that Alsace-Lorraine should not be a glacis for a 'bloody game of soldiers' but 'a bridge, permitting France and Germany, two nations with very developed cultures, to exchange peacefully their intellectual riches'.[21] It also claimed that overspending and construction flaws could have been avoided if regional authorities had been allowed a say.[22] Once construction began, complaints increased.

Expropriation and Easements

In 1935, an autonomist newspaper vividly described the view on the train from 'Metz to F . . . [?Forbach]':

> A quadruple barrier of densely packed barbed wire stretching to the horizon, across roads, meadows, fields and ditches, along forests and watercourses. [It resembles] a vast impenetrable enclosed garden. A similar spectacle is offered to the eyes of a walker on the road from S[aint-Avold] to V[eckring]. It is impossible to evaluate the number of kilometres of barbed wire covering all this zone; we know they used taxpayers' money to depreciate the value of the land of our peasants and render it quasi-useless for agriculture. It is pointless to emphasise the state of mind reigning in the population, to which the military authorities contribute by introducing a sort of state of siege in this region. The population of these localities, situated in a zone rendered inaccessible, can no longer move about, thanks to the large contingent of troops garrisoned in this part of the Lorraine. V[ehl]-E[versing] has been 'militarily' occupied since 12 April 1935. There are twenty-five men in each house. One gets an idea of the enthusiasm of the population.[23]

Statistics on the number of plots of land expropriated for fortification work by the department confirm the impact of fortification. Over half – 33,835 – were in the Moselle alone and over 70 per cent in the

Moselle and Bas-Rhin together (44,401). At Veckring, over half the agricultural land was expropriated. The old Bitche camp, originally constructed by the Germans, already covered 3,500 hectares; the security camps occupied around 300 hectares each.[24] Alterations to buildings in the vicinity of military installations were subject to approval. The Génie archives contain thousands of requests for exemption, of which many were refused.

Expropriations began in mid-1928. Military surveyors identified what they needed and then posted bilingual lists of plots and proprietors outside the town hall and in the local press. A commission chaired by a magistrate, including the mayor, decided the price. Landowners could present their views to the commission themselves or employ experts. They could accept the proposed price within five days or appeal to a slow and uncertain 'expropriation jury'. If they chose the latter procedure, they nevertheless had an interest in allowing construction to begin anyway, for the sum eventually paid would be interest-bearing from that point. In December 1929, the War Ministry drew the attention of the local military authorities to Alsace-Lorrainers' grievances. Although the army countered that landowners did not understand the law, grievances could not be denied.[25]

Expropriation often reduced farmers' plots to tiny dimensions or split them in two, making cultivation impossible. Where the remaining plot was less than a quarter of the original, and no more than 1,000 square metres, the owner could ask for purchase of the whole.[26] Given that many farms were small, expropriations could have serious consequences. At Dalstein-Menskirch (Moselle), for instance, where the land was sufficiently fertile for farmers to live well on seven or eight hectares, farmers wondered what would become of them at the next harvest. The Génie brushed off their complaints, saying that the largest expropriation was only 4.6 hectares across nine lots, but agreed to visit the commune to hear people's concerns.[27] There were many complaints that officers did not know German.[28]

Expropriation for narrow-gauge military railways was a particular problem. Because they required only a few metres' width of land, the low price paid hardly compensated for splitting small fields. In January 1929, the sub-prefect of Wissembourg reported that the inhabitants of the Soultz-sous-Forêts and Wœrth were 'profoundly discontented' about expropriation for the construction of such a railway. He asked the army to consider purchasing whole plots if badly affected.[29] The Génie acknowledged the issue, but stated that the requirement to avoid tight curves and slopes meant that it was not always possible to take account of farmers' concerns. It offered to purchase whole plots even though legally not obliged to do so. Yet it felt that since purchase prices were generous, owners should accept deals lower than those initially offered.[30] Two years later, the ministry ordered reduction of compensation. The army regretted that unrealistic hopes had been raised, but it did not budge. Thirteen of forty-two proprietors accepted the reduced prices.[31]

In November 1936, the Bas-Rhin department's Conseil général – once again – debated expropriation. One councillor said that in the Eichal valley on the border with Moselle, despite land having been militarily occupied for a long time, prices had not been agreed. What is more, the Génie had taken the only good land in the valley to build a barracks that could have been built elsewhere. One smallholder had not been able to plant potatoes because the army owed him 10,000 francs; since the commune would not treat him as an indigent, he 'fell into the greatest misery'. Labourers and smallholders were obliged to borrow money to pay for necessities. Protests against the army's sluggishness were 'increasingly vehement'.[32] In Wissembourg sub-prefecture, opposition may have delayed construction.[33]

The government sided with the army. To speed up expropriation, a 1935 decree stated that in the absence of an amicable agreement for immediate occupation, the Génie could 'temporarily' occupy land as soon as they obtained a declaration of public utility from the prefect. The measure was then extended to permanent works. The whole procedure including expropriation now took two to three months.[34]

There were restrictions around the many firing ranges, airfields and camps. At Hestroff (Bas-Rhin) the Génie erected four kilometres of wire; farmers were initially allowed to enter their fields through openings, but subsequently they were closed, despite the prefect's request for reopening.[35] Huge armoured barriers disrupted travel within frontier towns, raising and lowering them causing houses to shake.[36]

Although the major fortifications had been constructed by 1935, land continued to be expropriated for barbed-wire barriers around the *ouvrages*, antitank obstacles and thousands of blockhouses. Since construction was by then under the control of unit commanders, prone to resent military engineers' 'bureaucratic' procedures, they often occupied land illegally. Monsieur Grabbler of Wineckerthal was not amused that a seven-metre-thick barbed-wire entanglement appeared around a blockhouse, trees had been cut down and an open-air gun emplacement had been dug, all beyond the rightfully expropriated area. The Haguenau Génie chefferie denied knowledge of the works and remarked that there were many such cases. The nationalist Senator Jean de Leusse backed Grabbler.[37]

Conflicts about military use of land were common all over France, but in Alsace-Lorraine they were easily politicised and fed antimilitarism beyond the usual communist culprits. The autonomist *Elsaß-Lothringer Zeitung* newspaper believed that even land of little economic value was too good to be engulfed in a senseless military venture; expropriations prevented towns from expanding and 'disenfranchised and annihilated' the peasantry of the Alsatian lowlands.[38] The Alsace-Lorraine socialists had no sympathy with autonomism, but they too complained that Alsace was becoming a fortified region 'with all the restrictions and dangers that such a situation entails for the inhabitants'.[39]

Fear that discontent fed autonomism obliged nationalists to take up complaints.[40] De Leusse reported that the farmers of Oberroedern (RF-Lauter) were 'extremely upset' because they had only been offered 450 francs per acre, whereas poorer land nearby fetched 550 and even 600 francs on the open market. He urged the authorities to remedy the situation so that autonomists did not exploit it.[41] Also fearing autonomist exploitation, nationalist Deputy Joseph Weydmann backed Lampertsloch (Bas-Rhin) inhabitants' complaints that the army had not repaired damage to their main street caused by military traffic.[42]

Despite the economic benefits of construction, business feared disturbance of cross-border trade and was sensitive to the difficulties faced by farmers. The nationalist *Straßburger Neue Zeitung*, which was supported by business interests, held that brutal military methods and the persistent reduction of arable land undermined 'the entire structure of the economic life of the region'.[43] The pro-French Christian Democrat

Joseph Brom complained that the fortifications prevented recovery from the economic crisis.[44] Disruption probably did serve autonomism.[45] In the troubled Wissembourg sub-prefecture on the Lauter, for instance, Weydmann's lobbying for local farmers did not prevent his losing his seat to a candidate more sympathetic to autonomism.

Immigrant Workers

Alsace-Lorrainers were hostile to the many immigrant workers on the construction sites. Belgians, Luxembourgers, Germans and increasingly North Africans were already common in the steel towns of Longwy and Briey (Meurthe-et-Moselle) and the Moselle Valley, and in the mining towns on the Moselle–Germany border. There was also new Italian immigration along the whole frontier, organised by employers and government in concert with the Italian regime.[46] Italians were especially prominent in the building trades, which were essential for the construction of fortifications – an irony not lost on contemporaries.

From 1930 to 1932, the proportion of foreigners on the fortification construction sites reached 38 to 50 per cent of a workforce that peaked at 32,500.[47] From 1934, foreign labour moved from Alsace-Lorraine to the new fronts in the Meurthe-et-Moselle, Meuse and Ardennes departments.[48] Nowhere were foreign workers ever eliminated, not least because the introduction of the forty-hour week in 1936 accentuated shortages of skilled workers.[49] Initially, most skilled immigrant workers were Italians, often masons. Poles, Czechs, Yugoslavs and North Africans were employed as navvies.

As construction began, military engineers and employers pressed for increased recruitment of foreign labour. Firms not engaged in fortification work backed this demand, so that their own employees would not be enticed by better pay on the fortification sites.[50] The government set up a coordination commission of Génie officers and local civil servants, to which employers were sometimes invited. In March 1930, it agreed that up to 80 per cent of workers could be foreign. Fearful of popular outrage, the government reduced the quota to 51 per cent, a figure that magically corresponded to official figures in 1932.[51]

From 1931, as unemployment rose, so did pressure to reduce the number of foreign workers. A law of August 1932 (enacted by a left-wing government) fixed quotas by department for the proportion of foreigners who could be employed on public contracts, including fortifications. In fact, the number of foreigners was falling, for once concrete pouring was finished, work became less labour-intensive and shifted inside, where only French citizens could be legally employed. It was therefore convenient for employers to lay off foreigners. Employers also promised to train the French unemployed for semi-skilled tasks and improve living conditions on the construction sites so that they would be willing to live away from their families.

Yet local peasants came to construction sites only if work was slack on their own farms and the weather was good.[52] French urban unemployed lacked specialist skills and found navvying too demanding. One contractor told his local deputy that he got better results with foreign workers and so preferred to accumulate fines, leading the outraged deputy to urge the authorities to impose the maximum 7,000 francs. Another deputy suggested that those who refused to work as navvies should have their unemployment allowances cut. The labour inspectorate retorted that only improved pay and conditions would attract French workers; not only was the work hard, but lodgings on remote sites were inadequate. Some lacked sinks and running water for washing dirty work gear and let in the wind and rain.[53]

Despite their compatriots' reluctance to work in such terrible conditions, French workers complained that employers treated foreigners better than citizens who paid their taxes and completed military service.[54] Apart from orthodox communists, all shades of Alsace-Lorraine political opinion resented foreign workers. The independent communist deputy Victor Doéblé (Forbach, Moselle) deposited three reports in parliament complaining about the recruitment of foreigners at a time when 'Alsatians' [*sic*] were unemployed.[55] The nationalist *Metzer Freies Journal* signalled the sacking of 'four good local workers' from the fortification works in the Nied valley at a time when foreign workers were still being hired.[56] Xenophobia usually focused on the economic competition of foreign workers, and, as we shall see in the following chapter, on espionage.

Antisemitism had a long history in Alsace-Lorraine, and it increased from 1933, when refugees from Germany, mostly Jews, sometimes communists, began to pass through the region. From October, the government closed legal routes, but clandestine arrivals continued. Édouard Dreyfus, nationalist mayor of Mulhouse, claimed to speak for all northeastern France when he defended the right of his region to 'remain French'. He demanded that the government persuade Germany to ensure that refugees crossed the border with sufficient funds. The city of Strasbourg voted a resolution to the effect that border areas should not be the sole dumping ground for France's humanitarian tradition.[57] Robert Schuman, deputy for Thionville-Campagne, future founder of the European Union and candidate for beatification, despite his own transnational roots in France, Germany and Luxembourg, advocated revision of naturalisations back to 1919.[58] The full range of racist stereotypes appeared in attitudes to colonial soldiers.

Colonial Soldiers

Just as interwar French industry relied on immigrant labour, so the army relied on colonial subjects, who represented 26 per cent of troops in 1920 and 36 per cent in 1930. The Law on Organisation of the Army (1927) established 'mobile forces' – eight Senegalese, Algerian and Moroccan divisions that could serve either in the colonies or, for the first time in peacetime, on French soil. Of these, the 2nd and 4th North African divisions (DINA – Division d'infanterie nord africaine) served in the northeast and another division in the southeast.[59]

The authorities turned reluctantly to colonial soldiers, for racism was common. Although republicans claimed that empire would civilise 'backward peoples' and enable some North Africans to become officers, they considered civilisation of the mass to be a long way off. The right thought that colonial peoples could not be civilised or assimilated at all. In 1922, during a CSG discussion, Poincaré opined that reliance on colonial troops would produce a half-caste nation ('le métissage de la France').[60] Twelve years later, Weygand, who stood out as a racist in a racist age, considered that the army relied too much on colonial troops for defence of the national soil and that their service in France might reveal to them 'weaknesses and vices of our civilisation' and 'provide weapons with which to fight us when they return home'.[61]

On 28 May 1935, the nationalist Alsatian deputy Alex Wiltzer denounced the presence of colonial troops in his constituency to the war minister. Asked to investigate, General Condé surmised from Wiltzer's vague indications that the incriminated unit must be 28 RTT (Régiment de tirailleurs tunisiens), currently labouring on fortifications in the Bouzonville area. The EMA reassured Wiltzer that Condé's inspections had shown that relations between North Africans and locals were very good and that mayors had made no complaints. The regiment would soon return to barracks and be out of farmers' barns well before the harvest.[62]

Yet Deputy Doeblé backed Wiltzer's story in the press and reported the alleged rape of a woman in Blies-Guersviller by a soldier of 41 RMIC. These articles were immediately reported in German newspapers across the border. The headline 'Black Shame and Barbed Wire in Lorraine' ('Schwarze Schmach und Drahtverhaue in Lothringen') echoed the racist campaign against French colonial troops in the Rhineland and Ruhr occupations of 1923–4.[63]

Five months later, in October, the pro-German autonomist press claimed that the Alsatian population lived in constant fear. It was convinced that tremendous moral ruin would remain after the departure of these 'half-black troops', who are building fortifications and teaching our native people 'civilisation'. It added that the Germans never brought Africans to our country; the 'cultured' French were responsible for that.[64] The orthodox communists agreed that fortifications were a nuisance, but they alone defended their 'fellow proletarians of African descent'.[65]

These allegations were as dubious as those against French troops in occupied Germany had been.[66] The October case probably refers to 23 RTA (Régiment de tirailleurs algériens), whose commanding officer reported that his men had worked 'with devotion' on the fortifications, despite harsh winter conditions. He reported no incidents. At their Morhange barracks, the men of 23 RTA were largely segregated. They frequented dedicated 'cafés maures' and brothels.[67] Sex represented another bone of contention between Alsace-Lorrainers and the army.

Regulated Prostitution

France was a country of regulated prostitution. Women received medical care in return for residence in 'maisons closes'. These establishments were primarily designed not to protect women but to hide 'immoral' sex work from public view and channel men's 'natural urges' safely. (Men could in theory prosecute women who 'infected' them.) The army was especially concerned to regulate the sale of sex, for the unregulated trade undermined discipline and provided opportunities for espionage. Syphilitic bodies were hardly compatible with military effectiveness or manliness. Advertisements for syphilis cures appeared in *La France militaire*. Gamelin was rumoured to suffer from the advanced stages of the disease.

In the interwar years, opposition to licensed brothels grew. Abolitionists in the medical profession, churches and women's groups pointed out that regulation did not prevent the existence of a huge unregulated trade. Furthermore, prostitution corrupted youth and caused public disorder. In Strasbourg, a campaign for abolition was launched after some young Catholics (either hundreds or a few, according to different sources), in town for the 47th National Festival of Gymnastics, visited the establishments of the rue des Pêcheurs. The campaign was backed by the autonomists, who accused the French of importing prostitution and venereal disease.[68] Whereas German licensed brothels were discreet, more visible French establishments were an open affront to the religious sensibilities of the region. Some Catholic officers, notably Stuhl, advocated abolition. In practice, the army was torn between abolitionism, lecturing the troops on sexual restraint (usually to jeers) and furtive pressure on municipalities to regulate sex work – with mixed results.

Five Alsace-Lorraine towns were among the dozen French municipalities that shut their *maisons closes*. The choice to do so normally lay with municipal councils, and exceptionally with the prefect in the case of Strasbourg. Colmar shut its brothels in 1881, despite the opposition of the German army. Military pressure to reopen them continued under French rule, the mayor resisting until 1937. In Strasbourg, the army and civil authorities agreed in 1919 to increase their number in view of the military presence, and there were soon around fifteen establishments. Lucie P.'s in rue des Pêcheurs was reserved for gentlemen and officers, while homosexual prostitution resided – unregulated – at the Hotel Villa Regina. By 1926, thanks to abolitionists, licensed brothels were gone from the city. By 1936, Haguenau, Sarreguemines and Metz had followed suit, in the latter case despite the opposition of the military governor.

There was one area in which the army, abolitionists and autonomists were agreed: *maisons closes* were essential for colonial troops. In the enquiry held prior to their closure in Strasbourg, General Émile Reibell, commander of the city, acknowledged their necessity. An abolitionist retorted, 'Let the army organise one – it has the money and premises.' Both sides saw racial mixing as dangerous and regarded colonial men as prone to rape white women. When Gamelin inspected the fortified zones, officers persuaded him to take up the issue of brothels. The EMA replied that North African women required certificates of morality to come to France to work, which, of course, their occupation made impossible.[69] In 1938, the army asked for permission to open a *maison close* for North Africans at Oberhausbergen, a few kilometres from Strasbourg, but it too encountered obstacles.

In reality, the behaviour of metropolitan troops was more disruptive than that of colonial troops, for they participated in unregulated prostitution in streets, cafés and boarding houses, which shaded into sexual assault. For instance, a rare arrest revealed that sixteen-year-old Paulette, travelling without a railway ticket, had had sex with two airmen in a carriage toilet, and that they had not handed over the promised fifty francs.[70] This was only one aspect of the unsettling impact of interior French troops on the province.

Troops and Civilians

Interior French soldiers arrived in Alsace-Lorraine with mixed ideas about the province. At school, they had learned the official view of it as a thoroughly French, anti-German region, but not that most inhabitants were germanophone. This idealised picture co-existed with more ambiguous notions in middlebrow and popular culture, in which clichés about Alsace-Lorrainers merged into anti-German stereotypes. In film and popular literature, Alsace-Lorrainers were semi-German, dim-witted or militarised authoritarians, such as the Alsatian gamekeeper in Jean Renoir's *Règle du jeu* (1939). If they were heroic patriots, as in *Double crime sur la ligne Maginot*, dramatic tension required doubts about their loyalty.

These clichés did not equip soldiers to meet real Alsace-Lorrainers. As 171 RIF took up position in Neuf-Brisach on the Rhine, its commander reported surprise at the locals' Germanic language. He added that 'some have difficulty in understanding that among a population speaking a backward dialect there are many, very many, especially at Mulhouse, who nourish a profound devotion for France' – implying that not all did.[71] Difficult and distant relations with local civilians were a major reason why officers were reluctant to serve in the fortifications.

Annual reports on units' morale were mixed in regard to relations with locals. Commanders from Sarreguemines in the Moselle to Oberhoffen in Alsace suggested that the army was more respected there than in the interior.[72] Yet autonomism was well represented in the fortified zone, as was sympathy for Germany. Even nationalist Alsace-Lorrainers were attached to their German culture and language, and the term 'Boche' insulted everyone. French soldiers tended to see any dialect speaker as potentially disloyal. Friction was always possible.

Encounters in cafés were problematic. Cafés everywhere are ritualised and emotional sites, within which spaces are differentiated by age and class, and in Alsace-Lorraine differentiation was also by language. In traditional garrison towns, soldiers frequented established military cafés, but on the frontier they were a noisy, francophone presence in germanophone spaces. Arguments about women were common.[73] That too was possible wherever troops were found, but in Alsace-Lorraine quarrels often raised the question of national loyalty – as in the case of the brawl between the men of second battalion 23 RIF in Trimbach described in the previous chapter.[74]

On 11 November in the same year, 1936, in the café du Tigre in Strasbourg, two NCOs of 1 Génie and their wives insisted that the band play the 'Marseillaise' to mark the anniversary of the armistice. Four hundred of 1,300 present remained seated, provoking Adjutant Langlois to get on a chair and shout that those who had not stood were 'Boches'. Not everyone understood French, reports said, but everyone knew what 'Boches' meant. The café owner urged everyone to shout 'Vive la France' to show that there were no Boches present, which everyone supposedly did. There was a commotion; the adjutant was shoved and gestured towards his sabre, while his wife punched a female client. She was thrown out and her companions left with her.[75]

Peaceful discussions in cafés sometimes got out of hand. In March 1935, in Wissembourg, two Alsatians, both employed on the fortifications, were chatting in a bar about the recent remilitarisation of the Rhineland (a few hundred metres away). A French NCO (23 RIF) suddenly jumped up and called the two men 'Boches'. According to the *Écho de Wissembourg*, only the locals' 'solid nerves' and 'restraint' prevented them from immediately 'settling the NCO's account'. Instead, they reported the incident to the Abel-Douai barracks, where one of the complainants was taken into custody at bayonet point because he could not prove his identity, despite being a well-known Wissembourg citizen. The paper complained that it was 'unacceptable that we Alsatians should be called "Boches"'. The incident reached the prime minister's office, which is why it survives in the archives.[76]

In the Catenom–Elzange–Anzeling sector, locals allegedly prevented soldiers from crossing their woods and lands, even if uncultivated and unenclosed, and unjustly accused them of poaching.[77] In 1932, a foreman on a construction site at Saint-Avold told a worker, 'If you speak Boche I won't understand; speak French and I'll reply.' The worker 'flew into a rage' and whacked the foreman with a plank.[78]

The geography of such incidents, together with officers' reports, shows that poor relations with civilians were most likely in northern Alsace and bordering Moselle, where German culture was most visible to troops and autonomism most influential. Street signs were bilingual or in German; advertisements were in German and buildings looked German, though more so in Alsace. German culture was also evident in Strasbourg, and autonomism was well represented there too: from 1929 to 1935 its mayor was a germanophone, pro-autonomist communist.[79]

It does not follow that Alsace-Lorrainers involved in these disputes were necessarily pro-German. In the Trimbach brawl, as the six Alsace-Lorraine soldiers beat up Vimont and Boulefroy, locals egged them on, shouting, 'We aren't Boche, we're Alsatians, we're French like everyone else.'[80] Likewise in the Strasbourg café, locals protested that they were not 'Boche'.

There were few reports of poor relations in Haut-Rhin. A rare example is an intelligence report on the Munich crisis mobilisation, which stated that reservists from the interior were generally satisfied with their welcome in Alsace-Lorraine, but expressed reservations about the Moselle and the Sundgau – the latter being the autonomist Marcel Stürmel's constituency.[81]

Frontier Guards

A campaign to recruit volunteers for the new Gardes frontaliers from 1937 confirms that suspicion of the army was strongest on the fortified northern frontier, and permits us to narrow the focus. These units were recruited from local reserves living near the *ouvrages*, charged with immediate reinforcement of GRM border posts during mobilisation. Garde frontalier service was compulsory for younger reserves and voluntary for those aged forty to forty-eight. In Alsace-Lorraine, the latter were unlikely to speak French and likely to be veterans of the German army. Consequently, the GRM was ordered to acquire 'relevant information concerning physical aptitude, morality, loyalty, relations with Germany etc.' on volunteers – a wide brief.[82] Autonomists, inevitably, opposed the creation of these units, denouncing them as 'lois d'exception', punitive laws applied only to Alsace-Lorraine.[83]

In 1937–8, GRM officers and NCOs toured the frontier to recruit volunteers. To sustain morale, once units were created, commanders set up social circles alongside them (Amicales). It proved possible to recruit volunteers along the frontier from RF-Lauter to RF-Metz, including the Sarre sector in the Moselle. Some volunteers learned French; some voluntarily trained guard dogs; others improvised antitank mines. They participated assiduously in training periods, in the Amicales and in periodic celebrations.

As early as 1931, however, the autonomist press predicted disquiet about this proposal in the Bitche area (also part of the SD-Sarre).[84] It did indeed prove hard to organise a unit there, especially given the sparseness of the population. NCOs were particularly hard to find.[85] Recruitment meetings elsewhere provoked a number of incidents. In the frontier villages of Neunkirchen and Schwedorf (SF-Faulquemont, Moselle), the local Catholic priests, two brothers, warned attendees that pay would be poor and training compulsory, and that those who refused to volunteer would be excluded from work on fortification sites. The priests' politics were complex, but they were not unconditional patriots. The police set nuance aside: 'The *curés* in question do not hesitate to continue their anti-French work from the height of their pulpits, recommending to their flock the exclusive use of German, thus working to delay effectively the complete assimilation of these frontier regions.' They supposedly told troops who wanted sermons in French to switch on the radio.[86]

Of course, antimilitarism and friction between soldiers and civilians were present across France, but they were less frequent elsewhere, less often politicised, and rarely called patriotism into question. That was true of the fortified southeastern frontier, even though it too was relatively recent.

The Italian Border

Nice and Savoie were first annexed by France in 1792, during the Revolutionary Wars, only to be lost to the kingdom of Sardinia-Piedmont under the Treaty of Vienna (1815). In 1860, under the Treaty of Turin, Emperor Napoleon III re-annexed the province as a reward for having assisted Sardinia-Piedmont in the wars of Italian unification against the Austro-Hungarian Empire. Since Savoie was francophone and Italian national feeling was not widespread there, assimilation into France was relatively straightforward. Nice was more problematic, as the nationalist leader Giuseppe Garibaldi, who had been born there, opposed annexation. Many Italian speakers left, and were often sympathetic to irredentism.

Italian nationalists never accepted the loss of Nice and Savoie. After the war, irredentism was exacerbated by anger at France (and Britain) for refusing at the Versailles Conference to deliver all the territory promised in return for Italy's having joined the war on the Entente side. In power from 1922, Mussolini periodically demanded the return of the provinces. In 1929, construction of the fortifications began first in the southeast because Italy was considered the most immediate threat.

There was no autonomist movement in the southeast, but irredentism was present in the immigrant or immigrant-origin population. Italians had traditionally come to the southeast, especially to the Alpes-Maritimes department (including Nice), which had the highest proportion of foreigners of any French department: 20 per cent were Italian, and another 9 per cent were foreigners of other origins.[87] Fascist sympathisers among the Italian population were organised in the Fasci all'Estero (Fascists Abroad), directed by the Nice consulate and its subsidiaries in smaller towns. The consulate protected fascists from the police and encouraged Italians and French of Italian origin to send their children to summer camps in Italy. The émigré newspaper in Nice, *Il pensiero latino*, published violently irredentist articles.[88] The army was never as worried by irredentism, however, as it was about Alsace-Lorraine autonomism. In Alsace-Lorraine, it regarded all those who spoke German or accented French – almost everyone in the fortified zone – as potentially subversive. In the southeast, prejudice focused on a clearly identifiable minority, albeit sizeable, while most of the population was considered loyally French.

Furthermore, expropriation of land had less impact in the southeast than in the northeast. Only in the seventeen kilometres from the Col de Brouis in the Alpine foothills to Menton on the coast, where ten *gros ouvrages* and thirteen smaller works were sited, did it affect relatively densely populated areas with valuable agricultural land. There were some complaints. In the vicinity of the Sainte-Agnès *gros ouvrage* in the foothills, for instance, the army refused a proprietor permission to enlarge his residence within a restricted zone, even though the mayor backed him. The Génie threatened expropriation of the whole property.[89] Generally, however, militarisation affected lightly populated areas. Rimplas, the site of an artillery fort, had only 217 inhabitants in 1938, nine per square kilometre.

Indeed, Rimplas suffered more from expropriation for Italian fortifications, which stimulated French nationalism. The 1860 Treaty of Turin had guaranteed French communal and individual property on the Italian side of the border. Yet from 1935, the Italians forbade pasturing and woodcutting in an ever-expanding military zone. The commune of Isola (population 730 in 1938) lost 7,000 hectares of rich transhumance pasture and forests on the Italian side. Appeals to the treaty and to common sacrifice in the previous war failed to move the Italians. In 1939, ninety-two families were expelled from the chestnut groves and dairy farms of Chastillon in the same commune, of which forty-four were deprived of resources and had to leave Isola. The mayor resigned, condemning the 'inadmissible spoliation' and the silence of the French government. French border communes pressed for the extension of the frontier to include cross-border lands and communications. Given their own claims on French territory, the Italians could hardly accept that. After the Second World War, France annexed the disputed territories.

Tourism was perhaps a greater problem in the southeast than the northeast. Because roads and mountain pathways criss-crossed frontiers, and passports were now required, Italian fortification disrupted mountain climbing in the Haute-Tinée and Haute-Vésubié as well as pilgrimages to Madone de Fenestre. Even tourists with passports were arrested. The police were especially worried that foreign tourists sipped tea and met prostitutes at the Hotel Righi, which was squeezed between the GO-Sainte-Agnès entrance and its combat blocs (see Plate 10).[90] And, of course, Italians and French forbade photography – which was integral to tourism.[91]

Neither did anti-immigrant feeling, though just as strong, have the same consequences in the southeast as in Alsace-Lorraine. Immigrants were numerous in the earlier stages of fortification. In 1935, for instance, 47 per cent of workers at the Monte Grosso *gros ouvrage* were immigrants, while one site director and all three shift leaders were Italian. At Breil, which was near completion, only 11 per cent of workers were foreign, most having returned to their homelands.[92] North African immigrants were probably more numerous in the southeast than in Alsace-Lorraine. In April 1935, there were nineteen on the Borie site in the Breil sector.[93] In the southeast, anti-immigrant feeling contributed to French nationalism, whereas in Alsace-Lorraine it fed both French nationalism and autonomism, for it resonated with German attacks on

French use of colonial troops during the war and subsequent occupation of Germany.

Officers' annual reports on relations with civilians in the southeast were entirely positive. One commander reported that manoeuvres in SF-Dauphiné impressed locals who had not seen troops for thirty years. The arrival of 157 DBAF at Embrun and Jausiers was greeted with enthusiastic demonstrations.[94]

Even in Alsace-Lorraine, fortification rarely, if ever, provoked organised protest. In 1929–33, the communists endeavoured to stir up discontent among fortification workers and expropriated peasants as part of a nationwide campaign to form a broad revolutionary front. Their efforts were no more successful here, however, than elsewhere. It is unlikely that communists were responsible for what little unrest there was on the fortification sites before 1936. Mostly, it was directed against foreign workers.

Expropriated peasants held some meetings, and in some cases refusal to accept proposed prices was organised and premeditated. The mayor of Lembach was so frustrated with the Génie's refusal to open a breach in the antitank barrier during the hay harvest that he ordered communal roadmenders to remove eight rails themselves. The affair was settled amicably, for the commune had the rails repositioned with the help of a pile-driver loaned by the Génie.[95]

More often protest was individual. In 1939, Paul Paquin of Wiesenthal near GO-Otterbiel (SF-Vosges) removed posts himself during the hay harvest and sent the 610 franc bill to the Génie. In previous years, he complained, the infantry had either opened the promised gap so late that half his hay had rotted, or did not do it at all. Again, matters were settled amicably. The Génie was happy that the bill was less than the 1,000 francs it would have cost to restore the rails themselves.[96] One wonders how solid these barriers were. Most often, discontent was channelled through the press and elected representatives. Autonomist parties were too legalistic to engage in subversion.

From 1934 onwards, the struggle between the far-right leagues and antifascist Popular Front displaced autonomism as the primary source of political division in Alsace-Lorraine. The alliance between autonomists of left and right broke down. Simultaneously, the rise of Nazism isolated pro-German autonomists from the rest. Yet although fragmented, autonomism remained popular electorally. In 1936, the last national elections before the war, five of the nine Alsatian deputies were convinced autonomists. In Moselle, autonomism was absent on the French side of the language line, but on the germanophone side two deputies were elected with autonomist backing.[97] The army remained just as concerned that autonomism – which it defined very widely – was a vehicle for German subversion and espionage. Its fears led to the intensification of repression in the province and contributed to an authoritarian turn in the national government.

8

POLICING THE MAGINOT LINE

At 8.30 a.m. on his first day as commander of La Tête de Vieux Fritz, Major d'Espinac climbed the ladder to its highest observation post. He studied the little casemates dotting the slopes to the left and right, entrusted with ensuring that every inch of ground was covered by intense fire. Nested in the terrain, they would be invisible once the concrete had yellowed.

'Yes,' he thought to himself, 'this *ouvrage* is well planned.'

His deputy, Captain Dubois, seemed to read his thoughts.

'Major, it's invulnerable isn't it? They could sacrifice a million men without progressing a foot. We're not about to see the swastika floating over our Vieux Fritz.'

Espinac replied, 'I agree that Vieux Fritz is invulnerable from outside. I'm sure of it. But you see, if I was German, I'd think how to take it from the inside.'

He explained to the stunned Dubois that with cunning the fort could be overcome in fifteen minutes. If the Germans succeeded, 'there would be a breach in the line, and through the breach . . .'.[1]

A few minutes later, Espinac was dead, submachine-gunned as he stepped out of a lift into the fort's lowest level. Investigations established that one of three lieutenants, each originating from a linguistic minority – Alsatian, Flemish, and Breton – must be a murderer and a spy.

The episode is of course fictional: it comes from Pierre Nord's *Double crime sur la ligne Maginot*. Nord was nevertheless typical of those nationalists who thought that dark conspiracies moved world history and manipulated disloyal elements such as communists and linguistic minorities. The three lieutenants' origins are meant to make them capable of treason. The guilty party turned out to be a German officer masquerading as French. The novel contributed to obsession with the potential disloyalty of Alsace-Lorrainers on the Maginot Line.

The army was not exempt. A glossy brochure warned troops in capitals that 'ESPIONAGE IS NOT JUST AN EASY SUBJECT FOR A FILM OR A 3.30 FRANC NOVEL', and that in the few months of 1937 four times as many people had been arrested as in the whole of 1933.[2] Although multiplied in the imagination by prejudices akin to Nord's, espionage on the Maginot Line was real. A remarkable 60 per cent of the 358 espionage cases reported to the Ministry of Justice concerned the Colmar legal jurisdiction responsible for the Alsace-Lorraine–Germany border. Within the province, almost all were in frontier sub-jurisdictions. Another 7.5 per cent concerned the Aix jurisdiction on the Italian border, of which 74 per cent were in the Nice sub-jurisdiction.[3] Elsewhere, espionage cases were rare – even in Paris, despite communist targeting of its war industries.

The major reason for the increase in the number of cases is that the government widened legal definitions of espionage. This was partly in response to the dispersal of fortification in a landscape in which daily life continued, which meant that people encroached inadvertently on fortified terrain. The greater availability of motor vehicles and portable cameras also multiplied possibilities for espionage.

Equally important was mistrust of the inhabitants of Alsace-Lorraine and of the Italian-origin population of the southeast. We have seen that the fortifications were sited in zones with multiple cross-border exchanges and that construction and manning of the fortifications depended on communist workers, German-speaking Alsace-Lorrainers, Italians, North Africans and even Germans. The number of potential enemies was enormous. Spies, like the guilty party in *Double crime sur la ligne Maginot*, were supposedly capable of masquerading as French officers: as an intelligence agency put it, 'The more suspect natives of

Alsace-Lorraine are, the less they appear as such – for instance, linguistically.'[4] Underlying this view was a fixed, biological definition of national identity that conflicted with the official view that people could become French by learning the language and adopting its culture.

Counterintelligence officers and politicians also saw psychological tactics as integral to total war. The collapse of the German home front in 1918 proved for them that victory depended as much on civilian morale as on military hardware. It followed that the Germans would use subversive groups in France to undermine fighting spirit. The Maginot Line was considered particularly vulnerable to treason because it comprised a single line of defence. Treason in one fort opened up the whole country to rapid defeat.

The authorities' prejudice, conspiratorialism and inability to understand communism and autonomism made their task impossible, for they saw almost everyone as a potential spy. They overinterpreted minor intelligence, and struggled against inadequate resources and the tendency of military engineers and contractors to put rapid construction before security. Frustrated, the military and civilian security services pressed the government for increasingly authoritarian legislation.

The 'Enemy Within'

However exaggerated and misconceived, the army's concerns about communist subversion were not entirely without foundation. When construction began in 1928, the Communist Party was strong on the frontier. In the 1928 legislative elections it won well above its national average of 11 per cent from Lille to Colmar, the exceptions being the short borders of the Meuse and Meurthe-et-Moselle with Belgium and Luxembourg. The party won 27 per cent of votes cast in Moselle, 20 per cent in the Bas-Rhin and 13 per cent in the Haut-Rhin. In parliament, a Communist represented Maubeuge North, subsequently the most heavily fortified northern sector.

The party was at that time pursuing an ultra-revolutionary line, advocating political strikes, violence against the police, antimilitarism, support for Alsace-Lorraine autonomists and espionage. High-profile affairs such as the Fantomas industrial espionage case of 1932 kept the issue in the public eye. One general opposed the construction of *gros ouvrages* on the grounds that the technicians required to service their machines would have to be recruited from communist workers.[5] Counterintelligence was convinced, quite falsely, that the party was in the pay of the German government.[6]

Antimilitarist campaigns within the army were ineffective, and most activists refused to engage in espionage. Strike action on the fortification sites was also limited. In 1932, Strasbourg police reported that, having recognised the inadequacy of its antimilitarist efforts in Alsace-Lorraine, the party planned to protest against conditions on the fortification sites and mobilise peasants against expropriations. Workers were hardly responsive; peasants not at all. In 1935, the Alpes-Maritimes police reported that there was little communist activity on the fortification sites.[7]

By that point, the party had joined the antifascist Popular Front and was shifting from antimilitarism to bellicose nationalism. Counterintelligence abandoned the conviction that the communists served Germany, but conspiratorialist anticommunism persisted. One reason was the election of seventy communist deputies in 1936. Another was that June saw the beginning of a huge national strike (against the party's wishes), which soon spread to the fortified zone. Strikes and occupations began in Mulhouse on the 9th, affecting the mines and steelworks of Moselle and Meurthe-et-Moselle. Workers on fortification sites and in the factories that supplied them participated.[8] Work on the new fronts was held up, leading parliamentary inspectors to ask the government to end the strikes by 10 July, in order not to miss the November completion deadline.[9] Completion was possibly delayed by a month.[10] Unrest continued into 1937–8.[11] Although the party attempted to contain the strikes, the unrest convinced the intelligence services that the communists' real aim was to provoke war and thus revolution, as in Russia in 1917. Military intelligence believed that the party possessed a clandestine structure in Paris that was ready to seize power in wartime.

German disinformation intensified fear of communist conspiracy. To encourage appeasers, Hitler attempted to persuade the French that their real enemy was communism. Pétain was especially credulous, passing fake documents on to the Deuxième Bureau and EMA, which issued warnings to units.[12] In December 1936, Major Georges Loustaunau-Lacau, a member of Pétain's staff, formed the Corvignolles, a network dedicated to rooting out communist cells in the army. 'Corvignolles' was the family name of Vauban, whose biography Loustaunau-Lacau was then writing. He did not explain this choice, but he perhaps saw his organisation as an anticommunist fortification within the army – a reminder that the fortifications were built to secure the nation politically as well as militarily.

Notwithstanding the extent of anticommunism, officers' participation in the Corvignolles should not be exaggerated. Many did not see subversion in the army itself as a significant problem. They considered individual communists to be misguided Frenchmen, whom officers were able to turn back to the patriotic path. Alsace-Lorrainers posed a different problem, for they were suspected of not being genuinely French.

The intelligence services believed that even if autonomism was not actually a German invention, they at least controlled it. In reality, few autonomists favoured return to the Reich. Yet successive German governments did attempt to use the minority-rights clauses of the Versailles Treaty to defend Germans lost to the Reich at a time when autonomists in Alsace-Lorraine and Brittany were demanding recognition as minorities under the Treaty.[13] Under the Locarno Treaty (1926), Germany accepted the loss of Alsace-Lorraine, but while the state held back from the Alsace-Lorraine movement, a civil-society organisation, Robert Ernst's Hilfsbund der vertriebenen Elsaß-Lothringer (Aid Association for Alsace-Lorraine Exiles), continued to sponsor German cultural associations and the autonomist press.

For counterintelligence, two plus two made five. A Deuxième Bureau officer stated that the French 'framework was just a sham, and that [autonomists] awaited the moment to throw it off'.[14] In 1929, General Emmanuel Fonville asserted, 'In Silesia, the Italian South Tyrol, as in Alsace, as in Lorraine, they are at work, following a great plan.'[15] In 1938, another military journalist asked, 'Don't you think that if, for example, Austria, Czechoslovakia and Danish Schleswig possessed fortified regions, certain *ouvrages* would already be occupied by secret formations present in the country? It would be advisable to expect the same type of treason on the part of French groups misled by certain subversive theories.'[16]

The arrival of refugees from National Socialist Germany intensified the security services' fears. Closure of legal routes forced them to cross clandestinely through the fortifications.[17] Those who could not afford to move on survived as best they could.[18] For instance, the communist Jacob Marko entered France after completing a prison sentence for fighting the SA. While looking for work in the Moselle, he was arrested in a restaurant in the frontier village of Liederschiedt near GO-Grand-Hohékirkel.[19] In November 1938, Jews fled Italy following the enactment of antisemitic laws there, just as more arrived from Germany in the wake of the Kristallnacht pogrom. In 1919, 1924 and 1933, deputies tabled bills to keep foreigners away from military installations and the border, and in 1938 the government used decree powers to implement a measure for this purpose.[20]

German and Italian intelligence might plausibly have used refugees as cover, but there is only one, rather dubious case among the 358 espionage cases reported to the Ministry of Justice. In May 1933, Thomas Muller, a German resident in Alsace, claimed to have been recruited by German intelligence while visiting relatives in Germany. He was supposedly instructed to pose as a refugee and acquire intelligence on the fortifications.[21] The story is implausible, for he was legally entitled to live in France and refugee status would have made his status more uncertain. Moreover, refugees did not have access to the inside information the Germans needed.

It was in fact the Italians who possessed the stronger 'fifth column' on French soil. The foreign organisation of the Italian Fascist Party, the Fasci all'Estero, worked in tandem or competition with Italian consulates, which used their control over immigrant workers' passports to recruit agents. They also established an effective network of pro-Fascist officers in the Alpes-Maritimes police.[22]

Most spies wanted money. Career criminals involved in drug smuggling and prostitution saw espionage as just another opportunity provided by the border. Take the case of Joseph Drosd, a thirty-eight-year-old German citizen of Polish origin and proprietor of a Saint-Avold café, and his wife, 'la belle Sophie'. Joseph lived in Saarbrücken across the border, having been deported on account of involvement in a vice affair, but he visited France clandestinely. The couple worked for German intelligence in the Saarland. In 1931, one of their clients, the Mosellan Alphonse Choppé, site supervisor at PO-Coume, handed over its plans in return for 22,400 francs. Drosd also persuaded René Plestan, a career soldier in 18 Chasseurs à cheval, to steal a modern light machine gun, which he and Drosd took to Saarbrücken. Plestan's arrest brought down the network: both Drosds, Choppé and Plestan were imprisoned. In 1939, shortly after his release, Choppé was sentenced to a further ten years' hard labour for attempted espionage. In 1940, the Germans released him from prison; he joined the Nazi Party Motor Corps and later the Wehrmacht, but there is no evidence that he was politically motivated.[23]

In 1931, Paul Uhrig began delivering secrets on the fortifications after his timber business collapsed, using cross-border trade to contact German agents.[24] Roger Jacques found his monthly salary at GO-Hackenberg insufficient, so he persuaded his lover to deliver plans to German intelligence. He was arrested after another of her lovers, an NCO in 146 RI (Régiment d'infanterie), denounced him.[25]

By 1936–1937, the Germans had identified the more important *ouvrages*. Good binoculars and the questioning of travellers were enough to determine their general positioning. Aircraft needed only fifteen minutes to enter French airspace and photograph *ouvrages* before recrossing the border, too late for the French to react. Aerial photographs allowed the discernment of *ouvrage* outlines from their antitank obstacles and changes in vegetation, but not always their armaments, fields of fire or mode of operation. Besides PO-Coume, the Germans obtained partial plans of GO-Hochwald and GO-Simserhof. Not everything was correct: the Simserhof munitions entrance bloc did not include its 47mm antitank gun, probably because it was added later. The Germans did not realise that artillery turrets contained twin rather than single 75mm guns. Their capture of Czech *ouvrages* following the Munich agreement proved more dangerous than espionage, for it permitted experimentation with ways of neutralising French fortifications. Whatever the case, the intelligence services barely had the resources to police real, let alone imaginary, espionage.

Impossible Surveillance

In theory, military intelligence, the Deuxième Bureau, was responsible only for gathering intelligence and for counterintelligence abroad, the latter the province of its subdivision, the Section de centralisation de renseignement (SCR). Surveillance and counterespionage on French territory were reserved to the civilian Renseignements généraux, a division of the national police, the Sûreté général (Sûreté national from 1934). In practice, distinctions were blurred, for the Deuxième Bureau surveyed foreign groups with ramifications in France – communism, fascism, Nazism and Alsace-Lorraine exiles.[26] The army was also responsible for keeping a list of 'propagandistes révolutionnaires' (PR), i.e. communists and other subversives in the army.

The Sûreté often investigated on behalf of the Deuxième Bureau, for only in the later 1930s did it possess its own intelligence service.[27] Its *commissaires spéciaux* formed a political police, responsible for monitoring public opinion and countering subversion and espionage. They carried out background checks and issued and checked identity cards, not to mention reporting suspicious flights and fire watching. They also maintained Carnet B, a list of potentially treasonable trade unionists, socialists and autonomists.[28] Yet in 1930, there were only around 700 *commissaires* to cover the country outside Paris, rising to 800 in 1939, only ten per department.[29]

The authorities also disposed of the thinly spread gendarmerie, which was responsible for policing the army and civilian rural areas besides counterespionage. In the 6th Region (Metz) in 1939, there were only 437 officers and men.[30] From 1931, creation of the GRM reinforced surveillance of the frontier.[31] Yet only from 1935, once the Saarland voted to rejoin Germany, was it deployed on the Moselle frontier.[32] And GRM units were absent for months on their other duty – helping the civilian police repress civil disorder.[33]

Militarised customs officials and forest guards also contributed to border surveillance. Neither group was numerous, and there were no customs officials on the Germany–Moselle frontier until 1935. Moreover, the authorities feared that these officials – like all Alsace-Lorraine functionaries, even Sûreté agents – were German auxiliaries.[34] In 1932, following a misunderstanding between a cavalry patrol and a dialect-speaking forest guard at Flistroff (Moselle), the military governor of Metz demanded the inscription on Carnet B of all doubtful guards. The Moselle prefect agreed that the frontier administrations were not 'absolutely guaranteed from the national point of view'.[35] Military units were expected to report unusual occurrences. Yet after three Sûreté inspectors were able to circulate unchallenged around a troop convoy at Veckring near GO-Hackenberg, the command had to remind troops of the secrecy of fortification.[36]

In January 1931, the discovery that unknown individuals had entered the unlocked Judenhof casemate (RF-Lauter) provoked the ministry to review security. In future, guards would be provided from the not yet constructed camps. In the meantime, the ministry recommended beefing up gendarmerie patrols and provided motor vehicles for them, but the distances involved were still too great for continuous surveillance. It also recommended using civilian guards with 'dangerous dogs'.[37] But the sheer scale of the construction sites and fortifications, the number of contractors and military units involved, their integration into surrounding society and the importance of cross-border movement made continuous surveillance impossible.

Economic and political factors ruled out closing the Belgian border, which 100,000 people – mostly Flemish speakers, another minority regarded as anti-French – crossed each day in order to work in France. All that could be done was to regulate the flow. From 1928, workers required a *carte frontalière*, dependent on the approval of the employer and the Belgian and French authorities. In 1935, to protect French employment, movement of *frontaliers* was restricted to a zone ten kilometres either side of the frontier.[38]

On the German border, as international tension dissipated in the mid-1920s, local arrangements enabled people once again to visit family and work and trade across the border. Tacit agreements were formalised in the convention of 25 April 1929. There too, individuals living within ten kilometres of the border could be issued with a *carte frontalière*, allowing them to cross without a visa. The army saw this convention as 'very dangerous for national defence'. Since the victory of National Socialism, it claimed, only politically loyal Germans crossed, and they gathered information about the fortifications. Spies disguised as shepherds allegedly brought flocks to graze in France. The army attempted to use the return of the Saarland to Germany to force recognition 'that the fortifications exist' and revise the convention.[39] The reworked agreement of 1936 restricted mobility of German soldiers and functionaries, and border prefects promised to enforce the 1929 regime more rigorously.[40] Concerns did not disappear, however. The special police were alarmed, for instance, that German border officials asked Frenchmen visiting Germany for their military papers.[41]

The rules governing the Italian border were similar, but meant little in wild mountain spaces. Take the Austrian citizen nineteen-year-old Stephen Otto, who arrived in France via a mountain path, then wandered in search of work. After serving a month in a Marseille prison for vagabondage, he planned to walk back to Italy. He was caught by the GRM on a military road in the Col de Brouis fortified zone.[42]

The intersection between the construction sites and the rest of society was hard to police. Outside them, itinerant, mostly foreign labourers set up makeshift camps. Entrepreneurs built unauthorised canteens there, offering victuals and accommodation. Although many were insalubrious and broke various laws, workers preferred these 'immoral' establishments to the dearer ones run by contractors.

In January 1934, the Breil *commissaire spécial* and Génie commander visited the Col de Brouis site (SF-Alpes-Maritimes) to investigate the presence of unauthorised persons. They entered unchallenged, and found the GRM post empty, with files and provisional access permits littered on the table. They crossed paths with the owner of a canteen irregularly established outside who was illegally delivering goods inside. It turned out that the GRM officer had left his post to buy matches in the cheaper canteen outside. The prefect refused an application to regularise the canteen, but in June it was still there, provoking a retired Sûreté inspector, owner of a competing nearby bar, to demand that closure be enforced.[43]

As war minister in 1934, Pétain urged an end to the 'abuse and danger' of canteens close to fortification sites. In December, his successor banned them within five kilometres of a site.[44] By then, heavy work requiring large numbers of navvies was shifting to the new fronts. As work began in his Montmédy constituency, Deputy André Beauguitte complained that illegal canteens competed with local business and represented a 'permanent danger of espionage'.[45]

Maintaining secrecy on the construction sites was problematic, for work required multiple copies of partial plans. In 1934, a worker was found to have three plans for works in the Hettange-Grand area in a drawer under his dirty washing – souvenirs, he said. He got away with a suspended 100 franc fine because his employer admitted that supervisors could not keep track of thousands of plans.[46] In 1938, officers were still complaining that contractors allowed workers to keep plans after working hours and even after *ouvrages* were complete.[47] To expose the laxness of security, a Deuxième Bureau officer entered a site in the Thionville sector, claimed that he was 'engineer Schlesser' (his real German-sounding name!), and made off with the electrical plans.[48]

Officers were reluctant to show identification to other ranks on fortification sites, and even more so when confronted by civilian security personnel. In one case, officers found looking at a cloche refused to give their names to a civilian site guard. One replied that it was he who should ask a civilian for his papers. His commanding officer backed him.[49]

Night-time surveillance of construction sites was imperfect. The task of watching over the 1,400 metres of underground galleries of GO-Otterbiel fell solely on the sixty-two-year-old shoulders of Alfred Beccia. One winter evening in 1934, he saw a glimmer of light in a gallery. Armed with an iron bar he discovered two men, whom he bravely challenged. One asked, 'What do you want with us?' The other spoke incomprehensibly in German and shot him twice at point-blank range, happily not fatally. Both intruders fled. Investigation revealed the first to be a well-known French smuggler, resident in Germany. The prosecutor-general commented that, as a result of inadequate surveillance, there had been other such incidents.[50]

After completion, many smaller blockhouses were not permanently manned. They were supposed to be locked but not all were, and some locks were broken. The Rhine blockhouses were visible from the opposite bank and more so from boats. The German journalist Fritz Haubold published an article in *Spire* magazine with photographs taken from a boat.[51] German youths swam across and left insulting graffiti in blockhouses.

Completed fortifications could not be isolated from surrounding society. Military railways were sometimes used for commercial transport too. When not on a war footing, *ouvrages* relied on the civilian electricity grid, obliging company employees to read the meters. Military engineers and civilian technicians entered to carry out improvements and repairs. Food and munitions came in; waste went out – in *Double crime*, the spy hid in the waste disposal system.

Because forts were buried and blockhouses disseminated over wide areas, normal life continued around them. Locals wittingly or unwittingly used shortcuts across military terrain. At GO-Schiesseck and PO-Welschhof (SF-Rohrbach) farmers often grazed their sheep on *ouvrage* surfaces, sometimes within the barbed-wire perimeter. That the sector commander feared that these shepherds' attitude to France was 'dubious' probably testifies more to the army's fears than to espionage.[52]

A voluminous file concerning the little village of Gerstheim on the Rhine shows how difficult surveillance was on a relatively small site and how easily it was politicised.[53] The local *commissaire spécial*, Inspector Hansler, had experienced long-standing difficulty in policing border crossings, for the village possessed one of the three boat bridges across the Rhine.[54] (The army preferred more easily policed ferries.) Locals crossed, legally or illegally, for multiple reasons.

From 1930, the construction of two casemates required greater security. Yet the Génie established its office in the customs post, separated only by a locked door from allegedly pro-communist customs officers (there was a graffiti hammer and sickle on the Germany-facing wall). The directors of works lodged and drank at the nearby Au bord du Rhin, a restaurant – still open – owned by Baron Mettern von Zorn de Bulach, brother of a well-known pro-German autonomist. The hotel manager had served in the German army; he and his wife read the autonomist press. Their hostelry was frequented by Germans, including the commander of Gerstheim during the last war. One local, who had been refused a card to work on the fortifications, attacked Hansler in the street. Autonomists and their opponents both petitioned for his removal. Protests reached the government, which urged more tactful enforcement of regulations.

Security remained lax. In August 1931, an officer was surprised to find a party of eighteen people, two with cameras, examining one of the casemates, while a peasant on its roof explained its operation. Hansler had not appeared because there was no surveillance on Sundays. Prosecution was impossible because there was no barrier around the site, and the warning sign leaned casually against a temporary shed. Hansler's difficulties did not end there. Two years later, Louise Fendelsheim gave information on him to her boyfriend, a German customs officer and spy. For that and other espionage offences, she spent two months in prison.[55]

A *France militaire* contributor wrote, 'With the *ouvrages* so numerous and dispersed, exterior surveillance is illusory, despite the vigilance of the police and gendarmerie.' He saw espionage as inevitable: 'The Germans profit from our need to employ foreign workers, just as Alsace-Lorrainers spied on German works for us before 1914.'[56] Nevertheless, with varying degrees of success, the army and security services demanded harsher legal measures to regulate contractors, workers and soldiers.

Italian and German Contractors

Since contractors of Italian origin were omnipresent in the building trades, they were inevitably awarded contracts. In July 1939, an anonymous denunciation complained that, via Italian contractors, 'all the plans for the Metz barracks and perhaps all the *ouvrages* of the region are in Hitler's archives, thanks to his friend, the Duce'.[57] In 1938, M. Agnese, a lieutenant in the Italian army, was prosecuted for pitching for a contract to work on the Rimplas *ouvrage* through a French associate.[58] Yet Italian contractors never became a major political issue. The centre and right-wing press probably refrained from accusing Italians of espionage because it hoped to win Italy as an ally against Germany. A nationalist journalist claimed that Maginot fortified the Italian border in response to the Duce's inflammatory speeches, but used Italian labour to demonstrate that he had not done so as an enemy![59]

Rumours of German involvement in construction were more common but less well founded. They were apparently confirmed by the army's use of war reparation deliveries in kind, such as barbed wire, rails, tools and sheet metal, in fortification construction. In 1933, the army suggested obtaining as much as possible from Germany before the

Dawes Plan for reparations gave way to the less favourable Young Plan. When an Ardennes deputy asked embarrassing questions, the ministry opposed raising the matter in parliament because doing so would risk diplomatic incidents. Another complication was that French industrialists who disliked competition from reparations in kind were often behind accusations of German espionage.[60] And since until 1935 the Saarland was part of the French economic area, its businesses were entitled to bid for civilian, not military, contracts. The distinction was blurred because fortification infrastructure required new roads, railways and bridges.

Stories concerning German contractors largely emerged from overactive journalistic imaginations fed by unlikely informants. A Strasbourg journalist claimed to have learned from an informer living in Italy with contacts in the Italian secret services that the Germans were paying contractors to mix substandard cement with excessive sand, so that damp ground would weaken the concrete. Equally improbably, another contact told this same journalist that, in a train from Saarbrücken, he had overheard a German agent reveal that the Germans invented such rumours to turn Alsatians against France. The Génie found no evidence of sabotage. It suggested that sacked workers invented such stories to harm Alsatian morale.[61]

In 1931–2, the press was exercised by the involvement of two allegedly German firms, Dam-As and Schwertzler, in constructing bridges over the Moselle – military-related projects constructed by civil engineers. Local business complained that Dam-As used reparations contracts to unfairly compete with French business. Deputy Robert Schuman became involved. The affair turned into a national attack on German engineers' and workers' sabotage of the fortifications. Counterintelligence found one example of illegal subcontracting to a German firm, but no sabotage. Nevertheless, Dam-As's distant links to a German firm were enough to bar it from bidding for further contracts, along with two other firms with foreign connections.[62]

Espionage by company agents acting independently was more plausible, though hard evidence was elusive. In 1935, for instance, an employee of a German firm entered the old German Driant fortification in the second line using a pass belonging to a French worker.[63] In another case, the Nuss firm in Strasbourg was prosecuted because it allowed a German technician to take plans for fortification-related work across the Rhine to Kehl to work on at home![64] The Nuss firm was refused further contracts so long as it continued to employ two Germans, one of whom was considered suspect because his brother had sung the German nationalist song 'Watch on the Rhine' in his lodgings.[65] Espionage was not proven in these cases, but pressure for legal restrictions on foreign businesses in Alsace-Lorraine intensified.

In 1934, War Minister Pétain complained that new German factories were appearing in the fortified zone, benefiting, he thought (quite wrongly), from easy naturalisation of German refugees. He also fretted that if the Saarland returned as expected to Germany, firms might relocate to the French border zone so that they could preserve French markets while employing cheaper German labour. He saw such firms as hotbeds of espionage. He backed Haut-Rhin senator General Joseph Bourgeois's proposal to subject opening industrial establishments within thirty kilometres of the border to War Ministry approval.[66] Business organisations, desirous of reducing foreign competition, backed Pétain, but the Foreign Ministry thought it unwise before the plebiscite to give the impression that Saarlanders were unwelcome in France.[67] The plebiscite over, the Senate approved Bourgeois's proposal. Nothing came of it because Chambers of Commerce in Alsace-Lorraine feared damaging the regional economy, while the Foreign Ministry pointed out that the small number of Saarland refugees were anti-Nazi, francophile and perhaps had family in the Moselle. The ministry did agree, however, that it was essential to eliminate the 'veritable German colonies' of workers on reparation-in-kind projects in the Saint-Avold region, for they remained under the orders of Third Reich labour organisations.[68]

Construction Workers

Construction workers probably represented a greater espionage danger than firms themselves, but proved difficult to regulate, for the authorities struggled to reconcile rapid construction of works with security and popular hostility to foreigners. Regulations dating back to 1921 and a ministerial instruction of 8 October 1930 made background checks by the special police and photo ID compulsory for all workers on fortification sites, French or foreign. This was a significant step, for hitherto identity cards had not been required of French citizens in any context. Foreigners could not work inside *ouvrages* at all. It is difficult to know how many people were refused cards. Sûreté files for Breil in 1935 show that around four workers per month were deemed undesirable.[69] Otherwise, only cases that led to prosecution survive in the archives. The mechanic Louis Jost, a germanophone French citizen, was excluded from the sites because at the end of a theatre performance he repeatedly saluted Nazi-style while shouting, 'Heil Hitler!' On appeal, he was given permission to work outside the fortifications, but worked inside anyway, either with the complicity of a foreman or by entering through a cupola. The police found three blocks of melinite and fuses in his home. He was imprisoned.[70]

Contractors and the Génie, whose priority was to complete the works, connived to avoid regulations. On 10 March 1934, the 6th Region command, covering RF-Metz, scolded the Génie for tolerating contractors' negligent attitude to identity cards. Many workers had illegal temporary cards issued by the Génie or none at all, while those dismissed for lack of ID often returned to work. The regional command reminded the Génie that only *commissaires spéciaux* had the right to issue ID. Doubtless as a result of pressure from the engineers, the circular was quickly modified, so that the Génie could authorise foreigners with special skills to work inside *ouvrages*.[71]

In 1934, the government created a coordination commission for labour on fortification sites. It was charged with the contradictory task of avoiding 'harm to general and special interests wherever there are fortification works, while maintaining productivity at its maximum'. The government's priority remained completion, for it urged the commission to avoid meeting.[72] The prefect and army refused an employment-office functionary access to the sites. Prefect and labour inspectorate urged prioritisation of French workers, but made an exception for Belgians, whose employment was 'desirable given friendly relations between our countries'.[73]

Desire for rapid completion also conflicted with the obligation of the *commissaires spéciaux* to enforce legal quotas on foreign labour, gradually introduced in 1932–3. In October 1935, Major Munier, director of works at Longuyon (SF-Crusnes), protested to his superiors that despite there being no French workers available, foreigners were refused cards to work inside the *ouvrages* because quotas had been reached – indeed, the cardless were often deported. Contractors were therefore reduced to hiring the 'undesirables' who hung around construction sites.[74] The Sûreté and Deuxième Bureau refused to budge, and pointed out that fifty-eight workers in the Thionville sector alone were cardless.[75] Contractors continued to employ workers illegally.

In January 1936, legal restrictions on foreign workers were reinforced. The 6th Region brought rules for civilian workers into line with stricter regulations for soldiers in fortification regiments, and a few weeks later the Interior Ministry made this a national requirement. Certain people were automatically excluded from the sites – no longer was an unfavourable background check needed. Automatically excluded were citizens or naturalised citizens with foreign attachments, citizens of Alsace-Lorraine of German origin who had acquired French nationality after 1919, children of foreigners who had been born on French soil and had opted for French nationality in their twenty-second year, anyone naturalised within the last ten years, and people who had lived abroad.[76] To enforce these rules, the special police extended surveillance to the relatives of potential workers.[77] Given that these measures weighed especially heavily on Alsace-Lorrainers, they reinforced their conviction that the French considered them second-class citizens. They remembered that in 1919–20, following the province's return to France, the army had played a leading role in purging tens of thousands of Alsace-Lorrainers with German attachments.[78]

Enforcement remained inconsistent.[79] In 1936, in some 6th Region sectors, all workers were expected to have cards, while in others only workers inside the *ouvrages* had them. To add to the confusion, in December 1936 the command allowed that in view of the urgency of work, the special police could be 'less severe' towards those working on barracks, antitank rails and suchlike.[80] Italians were permitted to install WCs, sinks and door seals at the Col de Brouis *ouvrage* because the work was nearly finished.[81] Two years later, the Sûreté complained that military engineers employed new firms without notifying it. Consequently, inspectors did not know whether workers really were required inside *ouvrages*; the illegible signature of a company director was insufficient and could only facilitate clandestine activity, they warned.[82]

Some contractors employed German workers. A minister informed the Chamber Army Commission that around two hundred of them had been sacked in 1932. Only a handful of German retired foreign legionnaires were allowed to stay after one showed his combat wounds and complained that he had been refused work as if he was a 'Boche'. The police were unsure of the rules: an inspector reported that most Germans in the Wissembourg sector had been sacked, but asked whether the site manager was entitled to remain.[83] The authorities were watchful, for the Germans were known to have confiscated an ex-legionnaire's site permit and were expected to use it to print forgeries.[84] Isolated cases of German citizens working on the sites continued to be uncovered. In 1937, for instance, the German metalworker Paul Singer was sentenced to two weeks for having pretended to be French to obtain work on a site.[85]

There were many dubious cases. In 1937, Tomaso Zanzotto, a hard-up hairdresser of Italian origin, was taken to work on the fortifications by two men he had met in a bar. The Génie gave him a two-week temporary pass for employment inside GO-Fermont, despite his having no obvious aptitude for the work. The special police nevertheless concluded that Zanzotto could remain since background checks were positive.[86] The Strasbourg Sûreté complained that another worker had used a temporary pass for external work to fool military guards into letting him enter *ouvrages* several times. They urged the military engineers to standardise temporary cards.[87]

There were sufficient espionage cases involving foreign workers to stoke the authorities' fears. In 1933, a *commissaire spécial* caught the Italian Antonio Menardi, former site foreman, in the act of breaking into the safe on a construction site at Escherange (Moselle). He fled and was apprehended on the Luxembourg border. He admitted that an unknown Luxembourger had offered him 3,000 francs for the job.[88]

Soldiers

As soon as Alsace-Lorraine returned to France, the authorities devised measures to deal with the many men who had served in the German army who now became part of the French reserve. Initially, they proposed to evacuate of all men of mobilisable age to the 'interior'. Within a few months, they assumed that official purges had removed 'German' elements from Alsace-Lorraine and thus from the army too and that the rest had served Germany unwillingly. Only those who had become reserve or active officers during the war or who had German relations would be evacuated to the interior.[89] In 1925, checks on new reserve-officer candidates ended.[90]

As autonomism grew, surveillance returned to the agenda. In 1928, General Boichut, commander of the 20th Region, warned that although Alsace-Lorrainers were unquestionably loyal, doubtful elements might infiltrate reserve-officer ranks. In Belfort, he recounted, four of ten trainee lieutenant-interpreters, who by nature of their job had access to secret information, were 'suspect from the national point of view'. He feared that they would use their reserve-officer status to pose as patriots while undermining Alsatian loyalty to France.[91] Investigation found ten suspicious interpreters, including one socialist, one with commercial relations with Germany, four autonomists, two pro-Germans, one 'very dubious' ex-officer and a deserter.[92] In Paris, the 4th Section at the War Ministry, normally responsible for surveillance of communists, informed premier Tardieu of several more such cases.

In the following year, the war minister reiterated that all but 10 to 20 per cent of Alsace-Lorraine troops must serve away from their home provinces, if possible in the navy. Those who had a statutory right to serve near home also remained in Alsace-Lorraine.[93] In fact, the Bas-Rhin prefect reported in 1932 that only half served outside the provinces; he saw this as dangerous and a missed opportunity for reintegration. Yet a commander said that Alsatians sent to the interior were bullied and returned hating France.[94] Poincaré thought it better if Alsatians did not serve where 'ultra-regionalist Breton and Flemish movements' were present.[95]

The formation of fortification regiments created a dilemma: to be instantly ready to respond to an attack, reserves must come from no more than ten kilometres away – largely therefore from germanophone Alsace-Lorraine. And to train for their future role, more new Alsace-Lorraine recruits and reserve officers would have to undertake military service in the fortifications. As plans for RIFs and RAPs took shape, autonomists made significant gains in the parliamentary elections of May 1932.[96] The solution was to increase surveillance of Alsace-Lorrainer soldiers.

In 1932, the restrictions currently applied to men of the 1914 to 1917 conscription classes who had served as active or reserve officers in the German army were softened. Henceforth, an annual process removed those designated 'reliable' from the list of suspects. For instance, Theodore Kerner was eliminated because he was a member of a French nationalist party and because gendarmes and customs officers frequented his hostelry. Albert Caven of Saint-Avold benefited because he had spoken French at home since his marriage.[97]

The EMA also discussed ways to eliminate suspect Alsace-Lorrainers from 'special corps' – largely in practice from fortification regiments. The Deuxième Bureau proposed vetting new conscripts and their families and informing the regions of the results. In the CSG, General Gouroud warned that fortress units should not include too many local men. A scribbled note reveals that EMA chief Gamelin was 'of a less absolute opinion'. His staff suggested that Alsace-Lorrainers would not be dangerous if encadred in the *ouvrages* by interior French officers, especially as those due to be incorporated in 1932 had largely experienced French-language schooling. It was therefore sufficient to eliminate doubtful elements such as those whose parents lived in Germany.[98] The upshot was the ministerial instruction of 20 August 1932, which ordered prefects to investigate 'certain elements who are not communist, but who are of doubtful loyalty from the national point of view'. The police were urged to tread carefully, for even pro-French Alsace-Lorrainers were likely to be offended. Each year, investigations turned up a handful of 'dubious' characters, mostly students, for this measure appears in practice to have concerned only reserve-officer candidates.[99]

In March 1933, mobilisation centres were instructed to submit the names of doubtful reservists to fortification units so that they could be eliminated (those already listed as 'propagandistes révolutionnaires' (PR) were dealt with separately). In October, as Daladier pressed for the use of *frontaliers* in the fortifications, the army reassured him that only those 'whose loyalty was certain' would be mobilised there.[100] From 1934, reservists put forward for promotion to NCO were specifically vetted. Surviving files include a communist from Barembach, refused despite having volunteered for service in the French army in 1916, and another man rejected simply because he was of German origin.[101]

In April 1934, Weygand, on inspection of RF-Metz, noted that the proportion of Alsatians permitted to serve as fortification troops was, for 'good political reasons', limited to 10 per cent, but felt that it could be increased to 20 per cent for Moselle conscripts who spoke French well. The general staff accepted 20 per cent in the more francophone Moselle reluctantly, probably because it was aware that the fortified areas were almost exclusively germanophone.[102] Meanwhile, War Minister Pétain warned that Alsatian reservists were lending their ID to Germans so that they could join French regiments.[103]

In 1936, fears intensified again. Remilitarisation of the Rhineland brought German forces to the frontier itself, making the rapid deployment of local reserves even more essential. Recruitment of volunteer Gardes frontaliers was accelerated, and the police were reminded to vet these older, largely germanophone men.[104]

Soon afterwards, the electoral victory of the Popular Front brought anticommunism to the fore, but because immigrant workers were believed to be communists, anticommunism intensified suspicion of all minorities. On 7 July 1936, the War Ministry forbade conscripts with foreign attachments to serve in any unit in a fortified area (see above, p. 220 for the categories concerned). A partial exception was made for married men with children, who were allowed to serve in field regiments in fortified zones, but not in RIFs or RAPs.[105] From 1938, photographs were added to *livrets militaires* (military ID papers) of reservist *frontaliers* posted to *ouvrages*, while reserve officers got a special ID card.[106]

The proportion of Alsace-Lorrainers in regiments remained high. In November 1936, the RF-Lauter command reported that 80–100 per cent of conscripts in the latest incorporation were Alsatian, and that units lacked dialect-speaking NCOs to supervise them.[107] Despite vetting, many were probably autonomists, but there were no prosecutions of Alsace-Lorraine soldiers for espionage.

Some Italian-origin soldiers did engage in espionage. In August 1932, during a routine inspection, incriminating documents concerning the modernisation of the Peira-Cava fortifications (SF-Alpes-Maritimes) were discovered under the mattress of *chasseur alpin* Jacques Semeria. He had been born in France to immigrant parents and his father had returned to Italy. He admitted intending to pass the documents to the Nice consulate, either through an Italian worker he had met on the construction site or through a prostitute of his acquaintance. The affair received considerable press coverage. General Henri Noguès commented in *La France militaire* that while conscripts such as Semeria did not have access to valuable information, they would be dangerous in the event of a surprise attack, 'obviously' by soldiers in disguise. Men of Italian origin, Noguès said, should not serve in the southeast, so that they would not have to fire on relatives. He regretted that fortifications in the southeast were constructed by significant numbers of Italians and those in Lorraine by some Germans.[108]

Despite the greater danger in the southeast, fear of espionage in the northeast was primarily responsible for the intensification of repression, the politicisation of justice and the erosion of legal guarantees against arbitrary prosecution. Alsace-Lorrainers, despite being French citizens in the country of universal rights, were subject to laws of exception.

The Politicisation of Justice

The army had long been unhappy with the treason and espionage laws. Article 76 of the Penal Code punished 'intelligence with the enemy', but only if it could be proved that the accused was attempting to help a foreign power wage war on France – not, for instance, if the motivation was to earn money. Articles 80, 81 and 82 punished people who actually delivered secrets to foreign powers for this purpose, but not those who simply possessed them. Gathering evidence required lengthy surveillance to catch perpetrators in the act of spying and delivery. The law did not punish incitement to espionage, thus leaving 'string-pullers' untouched.[109]

The authorities also disliked the fact that since 1848 treason and espionage had been treated indulgently as political crimes, for in those days treason usually concerned democratic opponents of monarchy and empire. Political status ruled out the death penalty and entitled prisoners to privileges. Moreover, conspiracy and intent were hard to prove and juries were reluctant to convict.

The espionage law of 18 April 1886 partially rectified the omissions by criminalising actions that fell short of treason but represented a danger for the state, such as unauthorised or negligent possession of military material and entry into military sites. However, they were categorised as 'offences' (*délits*) rather than crimes and were tried in lower courts that could not impose harsh penalties. This law too left incitement to espionage unpunished. It also took no account of recent technology such as photography: one could be prosecuted for drawing a fort but not for photographing it.

Anticommunism played a part in security-service pressure for new legislation. The authorities were disappointed that in the Fantomas trial of June 1932 the law proved incapable of decapitating the Communist Party.[110] Nevertheless, with the help of imaginative jurisprudence, around 2,000 communists had been prosecuted under the anti-anarchist *lois scélérates* (wicked laws) of 1893–4. Communist protests that they were not anarchists were disallowed on the grounds that the law criminalised violence that threatened society itself. And since their crime was defined as 'social', not political, communists could not be treated indulgently.

It was harder to deal with autonomists. They could not be prosecuted under the anti-anarchist laws, for by no stretch of jurisprudence did they threaten the foundations of society, and indeed many were highly conservative. In 1928, the Colmar trial of autonomists under Articles 87–89 of the Penal Code for conspiracy to subvert the state, showed how difficult it was to prove treasonable intent. To counter the prosecution's feeble circumstantial tissue, defendants simply quoted expressions of loyalty to France.[111] Furthermore, the trial confirmed juries' reluctance to convict in political cases – especially in Alsace-Lorraine, where people thought that the French treated them as second-class citizens. Only three defendants were found guilty, and disturbances greeted the verdicts. Subsequently, prosecutors were often reluctant to prosecute because of the risk of acquittal and agitation.[112] As a new anti-espionage law was discussed, autonomism was never far from people's thoughts, and neither, secondarily, was Italian irredentism.

On 3 July 1930, against a background of renewed threats to Nice and Savoie from Mussolini, a meeting of Foreign and Interior Ministry officials together with intelligence and other officers recommended the expulsion of foreigners convicted of crimes, a Carnet B for Italians and a new anti-espionage law. A few months later, the Tardieu government approved the measures proposed at Nice, including a 'Carnet spécial' for dangerous Italians, which was extended to all foreigners in 1933 and fused with Carnet B in 1938. The 1930 meeting also asked the minister of justice to hasten discussion of the anti-espionage bill in parliament.[113]

Back in 1922, the general staff had proposed a law expanding the definition of espionage and assuming intent to spy in the case of illegal possession of secrets or entry into a military site. Although the government and the Senate accepted it, the reporter in the Chamber Civil and Criminal Legislation Commission, Robert Schuman, deputy of the Moselle, had objected to the presumption of guilt. Following the return of the right in 1928, the government reintroduced the bill in the Senate. It was part of a flurry of repressive measures, including a bill to criminalise separatism, arrests of communists and the banning of anticolonialist organisations operating in France. The Senate Civil and Criminal Legislation Commission accepted the EMA's preference for presumption of treasonable intent for possession of secret documents or entry into military terrain, but Schuman again criticised 'repression of cases of espionage that were not proven'.[114] Also controversial was Article 9, which made incitement to espionage a crime, even if not followed by acts. The army wanted to assume espionage 'unless the defendant could prove otherwise', arguing that it was in the 'general interest' to do so where proof was difficult.[115]

In 1931, the Deuxième Bureau protested against the long delay. In support, it cited three cases in Alsace-Lorraine. Two civilian draughtsmen working on the Haguenau fortifications had been convicted of selling plans to the Germans. A local civilian caught sketching fortifications at the Pont de Gambsheim was successfully prosecuted, but would not have been had he photographed them. And a site manager in possession of secret plans could not be prosecuted because there was no evidence that he intended to deliver them to the enemy.[116]

In 1932–3, the bill shuttled between the commissions of both houses and the EMA. The army used the Alsatian Senator Eccard to support its case, asking him to stress that 'as representative of a frontier department he was especially interested in the repression of espionage'. In

1933, a compromise text was agreed. Daladier as prime minister and war minister was probably instrumental, for in discussions of the refugee crisis he had proved sympathetic to the army's concern with espionage.[117] The bill became law on 26 January 1934.[118]

It extended the definition of secrecy to plans, documents, texts, objects, installations and diplomatic and economic material. It criminalised intentional or negligent illegal entry into military sites and the war industries. It created new offences including the receipt and/or transmission of secret material and incitement to espionage. Punishments were increased, though not as much as the army wanted, for espionage remained a *délit* tried in lower courts. The compromise removed the assumption of intent to commit espionage, but made it an aggravating factor in punishment: the court had to decide whether possession or trespass was inadvertent or culpable – no easy matter.[119] In the fortified zones the law permitted a substantial increase in prosecution, provoking much discontent.

Particularly problematic was Article 6, which incriminated photography, sketching and other means of recording within ten kilometres of a military establishment. Even topographical surveys and aerial photographs produced for civilian construction projects became secret documents. Furthermore, one could be prosecuted not only for photographing the *ouvrage* itself, but also for taking a photograph with one's back to it, thus revealing its approaches and fields of fire. A member of the Chamber Civil and Criminal Legislation Commission warned that the law was unenforceable and likely to be arbitrary in practice.[120] Before long, even the Deuxième Bureau agreed, for it would mean forbidding photography in much of the frontier provinces.[121] The commander of the 20th Region appealed for flexibility, for he thought (wrongly) that the law made it illegal to carry a camera within fifteen to twenty kilometres of the frontier, including Strasbourg (and indeed Paris as a fortified zone). The Sûreté nevertheless insisted on the danger of espionage.[122] Articles 5 and 7, which punished illegal entry into a military terrain, also had major implications, given the huge number of blockhouses.

As predicted, prosecution was uneven because of the impossibility of continuous surveillance, and arbitrary because the texts did not explain how intent to commit espionage was distinguishable from negligence or curiosity. Social and political criteria, not to say prejudice, determined prosecution and punishment. Thus, when a female dancer and a waitress were caught inside an *ouvrage* with a sergeant, the prosecutor wrote, 'Because of their professions, the two women appear likely to have entered the military *ouvrage* for the purposes of espionage.'[123] In contrast, a business couple who climbed through a gap in the barbed wire surrounding GO-Michelsberg were said to have seen no warning sign and acted from 'pure curiosity'. The prosecutor commented that the rigorous terms of Article 7 should be reserved for those who appeared suspect from a national perspective.[124]

Another case confirms that enforcement was as much about repressing political enemies as countering espionage. Hugo Eberlein, a refugee and leading German communist, was discovered in Strasbourg masquerading as a Danish travelling salesman. In his possession were documents on the self-determination of Alsace-Lorraine and the situation of local communist newspapers. Since that was perfectly legal, the army wanted him charged with unlawfully entering a fortified zone under the 1934 law – namely, Strasbourg! The prosecutor refused because Eberlein had not been asked for a passport on arrival from Paris at Strasbourg airport.[125]

Arrests and prosecutions provoked criticism. Autonomists, not surprisingly, evoked a state of siege and 'military occupation'.[126] Nationalists admitted problems. Senator Gaston Rogé (Meurthe-et-Moselle) wrote to the minister of justice that he had recently witnessed in 'Alsace' (he had actually visited Moselle) that 'the rigour with which espionage legislation is enforced does not increase the authority of the French administration, for it often makes it look ridiculous, sometimes odious, and it's perhaps there that one must look for the reasons for recent autonomist successes'.[127]

Multiple investigations of newspapers for infringing the 1934 law's articles on the publication of militarily sensitive material confirm the politicisation of anti-espionage, despite cases rarely coming to anything. In October 1934, the German-language autonomist *Elsaß-Lothringer Zeitung* was investigated for publishing two poor-quality photographs of *ouvrages* with the comment that French fortifications swallowed unbelievable sums while disarmed Germany was forbidden to construct fortifications. The prosecution collapsed when the defence revealed that the photos had previously appeared in the German picture magazine *Deutsche Illustrierte* and three French periodicals, that had not been troubled by the police.[128] Likewise, the *Journal de Haguenau* was investigated for reporting (in German) that soldiers had been relaxing at a church festival after removing machine-gun nests and barbed wire from the area. This case collapsed when it emerged that the offending article had been reprinted from the nationalist *Dernières Nouvelles de Strasbourg*, which again had not been prosecuted.[129]

The authorities' response was to remedy the law's 'defects'. To circumvent civil-liberties objections, they profited from right-wing governments' increasing use of powers to legislate by decree. Pierre Laval's government (7 June 1935 to 24 January 1936) used powers granted for financial recovery to legislate in tangentially related areas. Thus, a decree of 30 October 1935 stipulated that if an offence under the 1934 law was considered to be motived by espionage, it should be transferred to a military tribunal, where lenience was considered less likely. The Deuxième Bureau did not get all it wanted, however: although in theory military tribunals could impose the death penalty, espionage and treason remained political crimes.[130]

In April 1938, Daladier became prime minister at the head of a right-wing government armed with still more extensive decree powers.[131] His primary enemy was communism, but the period also saw a wave of anti-semitism and xenophobia, accentuated in the fortified zones by the arrival of more refugees from Germany and Italy. By then, the increasingly bellicose left was also suffering from spy fever. The socialists denounced Hermann Bickler of the pro-Nazi autonomist Jungmannschaft (Youth Group) as an Alsatian Konrad Henlein (leader of the pro-Nazi Sudeten separatists in Czechoslovakia). Even the communists advocated stronger security 'in regions as infested with Hitlerist spies, suspicious autonomists and traitorous Françistes [fascists] or Doriotists [the dissident communist Jacques Doriot had moved to the far right] as Alsace and Lorraine are'. The party had moved a long way from advocating self-determination for Alsace-Lorraine.[132]

The decree of 17 June 1938 which reinforced the espionage laws was a product of this climate (though it did allow local military and civil authorities to reduce if appropriate the zone in which photography was banned). It removed political status from espionage and treason, thus making capital punishment possible. It presumed that anyone knowingly in contact with an enemy agent was guilty of attempted espionage; a ministerial instruction issued shortly afterwards explained that this article permitted prosecution in cases where 'damage to the nation', a legal criterion, could not be clearly established.[133] The decree also reinforced restrictions on the divulgation of military information and espionage affairs in the press. Although prosecutors still hesitated to apply harsh penalties for fear of public protest, repeated investigations and the threat of banning meant that by 1939 the autonomist press was semi-muzzled.[134] Ironically, just as the law reduced the definition of political crimes to almost nothing – to a 'peau de chagrin' (a skin of sorrow), as the French colourfully say – the politicisation of justice reached a level not seen since monarchist days.

Tangentially related to fortification, but directly to repression in Alsace-Lorraine, was another decree of 25 May 1938. It punished 'attacks on the integrity of the national territory or the authority of France in territories where this authority is exercised' with up to five years in prison. It had originally been proposed following the failed Colmar prosecutions of autonomists in 1928. Since there was insufficient support for this measure in parliament, only decree powers made it possible.

In September 1938, the Strasbourg prosecutor began to investigate autonomists under this law, but nothing concrete was found.[135] Instead, on 4 February 1939, the autonomist Karl Roos was arrested for offences under the espionage laws. Shortly afterwards, *Der Elsässer*, the mouthpiece of the Alsatian Catholic Party, the UPR, protested that exaggeration of the espionage threat and misuse of the law were liable to turn the Alsatian population against France and undermine the possibility of restoring good relations with Germany.[136]

Decree powers granted on 19 June, as war appeared increasingly unavoidable, were virtually unlimited. Some general measures, such as forbidding the circulation of foreign tracts and bulletins (24 June), were national in scope. Others specifically applied to the fortified zones. The secret decree of 27 March gave regional commanders power to institute a state of siege in the event of enemy preparation for attack, or of 'interior sedition or armed assembly in fortified zones coinciding with foreign threat'. Likening the nation to a besieged fortress was not a rhetorical device.

With hindsight, these laws appear to prepare the way for Vichy authoritarianism. From a republican perspective, however, they could be justified as defending democracy against real danger, even if the threat of autonomism and communism was enormously exaggerated. The repressive trend might well have been reversed had France been victorious. What we can say is that fear of espionage on the Maginot Line contributed to making France more authoritarian than it had been in 1930. Liberties were especially restricted in Alsace-Lorraine.

Indeed, distrust of the frontier population informed plans to evacuate the population of the fortified zone to the southwest in the event of war. When the question came up during a parliamentary inspection in 1936, the nationalist Moselle Senator de Leusse warned officers of the 'doubtful state of mind of certain *frontaliers*', while General Victor-Henri Schweisguth, deputy EMA chief, stressed the importance of an increased budget for counterespionage.[137] While there is no reason to doubt that humanitarian motives were central to evacuation, it was also an admission of the impossibility of policing the fortifications.

9

THE MAGINOT LINE IN POPULAR CULTURE

In 1922, General Guillaumat wrote to Marshal Pétain that his plan for a 'Great Wall of France' was an entirely passive doctrine, one that promoted a false sense of security and fatally dispersed the efforts of the country.[1] His letter apparently sustains the myth that fortification was an emotional prop for a people traumatised by the hecatomb of the Great War, German resurgence and chronic social and political instability; that it was either a symptom or a cause of a passive mentality englobing the high command, politicians and ordinary people. It supposedly encouraged the illusion that modern war could be fought without casualties and blinded the army to the danger of armoured warfare.[2]

That Guillaumat himself was one of the architects of fortification should give us pause for thought. We have seen that passive defence and belief in continuous lines was strong, but that it was also criticised by soldiers from senior officers down to those who manned the fortifications. Furthermore, the army always regarded an armoured German invasion of the Low Countries as more likely than an assault on the Maginot Line; mobile forces had been formed and the regulations modified to prepare for that eventuality.

It is nevertheless possible that the government knowingly misled the public. After all, Daladier told parliament that, thanks to our 'inviolable' fortifications, the army could defend the frontier, but could not 'undertake an offensive across the Flanders plains' – despite knowing that the current Plan D envisaged just such an advance.[3] And he committed little money to the north.[4] On trial in 1942 for his part in the defeat, Gamelin accused journalists of spreading the false notion of inviolable continuous fronts and of calling 'all our frontier organisations the "Maginot Line"'.[5]

In fact, neither government nor army had the means to present a single view to the public. Government action was confined to secret subsidies to favourable newspapers. It did envisage setting up an information commissariat in wartime, with the task of orienting news at home and abroad. In discussion of this measure, General Louis-Antoine Colson, deputy chief of staff, wondered whether politicians could be subtly brought around to introducing political censorship in periods of 'political tension' preceding war.[6]

In 1926, the army reorganised its existing services into a Section cinématographique under the then Captain Calvet, who remained in post through successive promotions to 1940. It was limited to producing training and education films on topics such as the history of the army, physical education and venereal diseases. In 1931, Calvet joined the board of film censors, where his voice was one of several. Recruitment posters and press reports on new weapons, manoeuvres and ceremonies were the army's main positive means of propaganda. In the immediate prewar years, in response to German propaganda, the state increased its power to censor, as the army had wished.

Yet government and army continued to rely on private companies, whose priorities were as much commercial as patriotic. To be marketable, newspapers required sensation, while film and literature had to fit established genres such as the murder-mystery or western, which shaped the message. In any case, depictions of French military capabilities reflected and contributed to disputes about doctrine within the army rather than presenting a coherent view. Arguably, by 1939 public representations of war in popular culture were even more polarised than disputes in the military sphere.

1929–1935: 'Our Fortifications in the East'

While journalists regularly discussed fortification in the context of defence and diplomacy, it was rarely the subject of specific reportage.

Fear of espionage ensured that the army accorded access parsimoniously, for unlike infantry, tanks and planes, the fortifications were sited on the frontier, under enemy eyes, among a population considered unreliable. Furthermore, the shoestring resources of the Section cinématographique and the multiple military interests that had to approve requests for access deterred companies that required immediate news.[7]

The army granted the leading photo-magazine *L'Illustration* only two authorisations before 1938, despite its sympathetic stance. Even then, the army regretted having permitted its correspondent Jean Quatremarre to include photographs in a report of 14 April 1934. Despite precautions, his article allegedly compromised agents who had fed disinformation to the Germans. In December 1935, Quatremarre was again granted access, but when the local command inspected his pictures, it found that he had photographed some tanks. Military engineers agreed reluctantly that the photos of the *ouvrages* could be published if retouched 'within the limits of plausibility' – the thickness of the concrete would be reduced, cloches moved or resized, mounts for machine guns removed and the names of *ouvrages* changed. The published text would say that the photographs had been taken with the agreement of the army and certain details suppressed – otherwise prosecutions for illegal photography under the espionage law would be jeopardised.[8] In fact, we have seen that *L'Illustration*'s pictures did turn up in the French and German press.[9]

Despite their doubts, the authorities used visits – permitted exclusively to the right-wing press – to further their own agendas, and Quatremarre received his authorisation on that condition. Reports therefore mentioned officers' poor housing while lauding conscripts' comfort in the camps. Another constant theme was the technological modernity of the fortifications.[10] They were also said to be happily integrated into border communities – an obvious response to local criticism. Reserves recruited from nearby villages supposedly knew that 'it is their own fields, families and church belltower that they will be defending'.[11]

Journalists compensated for lack of hard information with far-fetched descriptions. A popular science magazine blended apparent technical detail with the invention of *ouvrages* capable of housing whole divisions (15,000 men), each linked to other *ouvrages* by underground galleries. Forts supposedly contained huge vats of wine.[12]

These accounts did not depict the fortifications as invulnerable. Quatremarre evoked massive armoured doors in galleries that could be closed in the event of 'penetration'.[13] Neither did the press claim that the whole frontier had been or should be fortified. Quatremarre explained that once the fortifications were complete, the greatest danger was invasion through Belgium or Switzerland.[14] *L'Illustration*'s first article ruled out a 'high, thick Great Wall of China' on the grounds that it would take sixty years to build.[15] In *Le Matin*, Stéphane Lauzanne evoked a 'defensive chain from Menton to Dunkirk', but saw it as impossible to 'encircle the whole country with an armoured wall'. Typically, his map showed fortification from Switzerland to the Moselle, yet differentiated the light fortification of the Rhine from the two fortified regions.[16] On the northern plains, with their many towns, he wrote, the army relied on little shelters, mobile fortification and, in the last resort, flooding.[17]

Robert Poulaine's series of articles for the highbrow, moderately conservative *Le Temps* saw mobility as the necessary response to a German invasion. Although confident that permanent readiness and the support of interval troops would enable the fortifications to hold out against air and tank assault until relief arrived, he feared that the speed of a German attack and the bombing of French railways might prevent reinforcements from reaching the frontier in time. In the name of the citizen army, he rejected de Gaulle's proposal for a professional heavy-armoured division, and thought that heavy tanks were unmanoeuvrable – rightly, it turned out. He endorsed initial defence, but thought that counterattack by a 'mobile cover' could intervene to 'win the battle or prevent the adversary from winning'. Observing manoeuvres, he explained the transformation of infantry tactics since 1914. He found small camouflaged groups, commanded by corporals, each soldier capable of replacing his leader. He also made a veiled criticism of the reliance of fortification regiments on horse transport.[18]

The left paid little attention to fortification, or indeed to any form of weaponry. The pacifist and satirical *Canard enchaîné* ridiculed descriptions of comfort, suggesting that the Nicolas chain of wine merchants was setting up on the Maginot Line. To satirise the pretension to cover all angles of attack, it claimed that the intelligence services were forecasting the exact arrival of enemy shells.[19] The communists counterposed 'modern comfort' to militarist ill-treatment of vulnerable conscripts. Even they, however, were impressed by the technical achievement. A conscript's letter to the germanophone *Humanité d'Alsace et de Lorraine* described the machinery of a casemate as 'prodigiously modern': a man seated in a cloche had only to press a button and a light machine gun came to hand. He described the electrical supply and the telephone, 'also counting among the modern things'.[20]

The fortifications were not yet known as the 'Maginot Line'. In November 1929, a few days after taking office, Maginot inspected the construction sites. His press communiqué insisted that despite 'certain reports that set M. Painlevé and myself against each other, the programme on which we are working at present, which I shall continue and hasten, is that which was decided and set in motion by my predecessor'.[21]

After Maginot's premature death in January 1932, right-wing tributes emphasised his role in construction and linked it to a nationalist, anti-German foreign policy – not to the spirit of reconciliation that Maginot had invoked at the time. The far-right newspaper *Action française*, which celebrated Maginot's supposed nationalism (and claimed that his opponents had had him murdered by poisoned oyster), was first to use the label 'Ligne Maginot', though it did so only twice in 1932 and eleven times in 1933. Given that many officers read the neo-royalist daily, it is not surprising that the label occasionally appeared in *La France militaire*, where an anonymous writer counselled that 'those in charge of national security will be wise to maintain and perfect the organisation – strictly defensive – that already bears the name, and will conserve it in history, the *Maginot Line*'.[22]

In the Chamber of Deputies, the right-wing Tardieu sparred with Daladier over whether Maginot or Painlevé had been responsible for the fortifications, but did not give them a name.[23] Anyone desirous of political neutrality avoided attributing responsibility altogether. Quatremarre merely praised 'him who undertook the work but died before completion' and credited also Weygand and Belhague.[24] De Gaulle prudently identified fortification with 'Painlevé or Maginot'.[25]

1935–1938: Fortification and Appeasement

In the mid-1930s, as the left urged potentially military resistance to fascism, appeasers began to see retreat behind the fortifications as the alternative to fighting fascism in alliance with the Soviet Union. That the fortifications were at stake in this realignment was clear in the Chamber debate of February 1936 on ratification of the Franco-Soviet Pact:

> M. Foreign Minister [Flandin, a moderate conservative]: The real debate is between those who retain faith in peace guaranteed by collective security, and who in return for its benefits accept its obligations [i.e. the possibility of war], and those who to avoid the threat of war are ready to surrender to force [i.e. to Hitler], sacrificing security to personal guarantees that force [Hitler] has deigned to grant them, at least until now.
>
> They say, 'let Pan-Germanism and Pan-Slavism fight it out; retreat behind the line fortified by Maginot and absorb the blows!'
>
> M. Marcel Héraud: Nobody has said that.
>
> M. Foreign Minister: I beg your pardon. I've heard it said at this very rostrum. *(Applause on the benches of the left and extreme left.)* Impious words, which could cause deep ravages in Europe if they were accepted as the opinion of France. *(Repeated applause on the benches of the left and extreme left.)*[26]

A right-wing journalist in Lyon agreed that 'the left offered only Russian machine guns and their unreliable trains, while we [French] depend on the Maginot Line, which the left once mocked'.[27]

Remilitarisation of the Rhineland reinforced this reasoning, for fortification appeared even more important now that German soldiers were on the border. Most dailies published the letter in which War Minister Maurin denied that France was mobilising and maintained that occupation of the fortifications was sufficient to defend the country.[28] *L'Echo de Paris* reported that fortification provided 'great relief and comfort', and claimed, improbably, that the Germans would not have stopped at the frontier had the fortifications not been completed. The paper launched an appeal to improve fortification troops' comfort. Reporter Jean Clair-Guyot, whom the paper sent to the east, evoked the usual themes of comfort and conscripts' admiration for their officers, though differed from earlier accounts in emphasising the fortifications' powerful armament.[29] A delegation of veterans in the Meuse laid a wreath on the grave of their department's famous son, Maginot, at a time when 'all France, on account of present difficulties, turns its eyes towards the Maginot Line'.[30] Léon Daudet, in *L'Action française*, shouted that the fortifications 'are A GREAT THING, THE ONLY IMPORTANT THING IN THESE IMBECILIC AND SHAMEFUL YEARS'.[31]

Appeasers seized on the fact that the Germans could now fortify their frontier. Clair-Guyot saw the primitive barricades that Rhineland communities erected to counter a possible French riposte as proof that they did not want war.[32] A few weeks later, the Germans poured the first Westwall concrete. The French press reported the mobilisation of 120,000 German workers on construction sites.[33]

Helpfully for sales, Captain André Brouillard, writing as Pierre Nord, published his *Double crime sur la ligne Maginot* just after remilitarisation. The novel had some impact on popular views of the Maginot Line, for it had sold 24,000 copies by July 1937 and probably twice as many by 1939. Many more people read second-hand copies or saw it advertised in booksellers' windows and the press.[34] Despite Nord's far-right sympathies, however, the novel did not derive from the pro-appeasement mood, for it had been written in 1933–4. It depicts Germany as a dangerous enemy; there is no trace either of anticommunism, though hostility to autonomism was implicit.

Also absent is a false sense of security. The novel evokes the possibility of conflict within the fort itself, which is also vulnerable to espionage. And the hero, Captain Ardant, explains that an attack through Belgium is more likely: 'Don't forget that with their motorised divisions, they could be in Brussels in a day. And on the second . . . I prefer not to think of it.'[35] In his military writings, Brouillard/Nord warned against static defence and the continuous front: junior officers should be ready for a war of 'speed and surprise' and to defend themselves 'without the reassuring shoulder of a neighbour or the commander's voice'.[36]

In fact, the Maginot Line setting had more to do with Nord's desire to publish a best-selling murder-mystery than with promotion of a particular doctrine. As an example of 'formula fiction', a crime novel obeys rules that authors must follow if a book is to be marketed appropriately and readers are to get what they pay for. Specifically, it stages a detective's intellectual combat with a criminal in the solution of a mystery, regarding which the reader and investigator possess the same clues. Typically, such a novel unfolds in an enclosed space – an English drawing room or the Orient Express, for instance – so that extraneous characters and events cannot contribute to the solution.[37] A fort fitted the bill perfectly.

The mystery genre also suited Nord's far-right politics and predilection for the conservative top-down command model. Indeed, he probably used the label 'Maginot Line' because he was a reader of *Action française*, the newspaper most likely to use the term.[38] Nord's admiration of the fort as a model of military command shines through the novel, contrasted with the disorganised forest outside. Command is enhanced by the conventions of the murder-mystery. The formula dictates that the murder is an incongruous event in a normally ordered setting such as a country house, that the victim possesses social standing and that unmasking the murderer restores order. In *Double crime*, the commander is the victim. The investigators, a Sûreté inspector and Deuxième Bureau officer Ardant, represent the state. They fight both individual crime and the enemies of society. Order is restored at the end. Or is it?

In fact, mystery novels also present a world of uncertainty. To make the puzzle challenging, the author includes red-herring characters, drawn from the same circle as the unidentified murderer, with apparent motives. Nord's three suspect lieutenants are suspicious simply by virtue of being natives of minority-language-speaking regions, and they all turn out to have something to hide. Lies are exposed only in the final pages. And since the author must ensure that the investigator wins the competition with the reader to find the guilty person, there is a tendency towards improbable solutions – in this case, a German officer masquerading as French.[39] Thus, the novel promotes suspicion of minorities, even of those able to appear perfectly assimilated and French.

Indeed, the espionage subplot unsettles the restoration of order typical of the murder-mystery. In *Double crime*, the guilty man is merely one player in a continuing plot against France. The ambience of imminent danger is never dissipated. Towards the end, Ardant says, 'By cunning they could breach it the Maginot Line and God only knows what will happen.'[40] *Double crime* helped spread rumours that German officers really had infiltrated the fortifications.

In the months following the remilitarisation of the Rhineland, events strengthened appeasers' conviction that France should adopt a purely defensive stance rather than fight 'fascism' in alliance with the Soviet Union: the socialist victory and communist gains in the 1936 elections, the strikes that followed and the outbreak of the Spanish Civil War. In September, the Belgian declaration of neutrality confirmed this logic. The right-wing press welcomed Daladier's promises to reinforce fortification of the north.

Yet most right-wing commentators still accepted that if the Germans invaded Belgium the French must meet and possibly defeat them there, rather than simply form a continuous front. *Figaro* journalist Jean Rivière condemned passive defence and hoped that Daladier's rearmament programme would provide mobile forces able to *defeat* the Germans in Belgium.[41] Retired General Noël de Castelnau, now an influential Catholic journalist, who had been an advocate of all-out attack during the previous war, hoped that new Belgian fortifications would provide French commanders with 'freedom of *decision* and manoeuvre'.[42]

If the left mentioned fortification in these months, it was in relation to the Spanish republicans' defence of Madrid against General Francisco Franco forces.[43] With the exception of the pacifist wings of the Socialist and Radical-Socialist parties, the Popular Front parties remained committed to the eastern allies – Daladier included. They invoked collective security and military force if necessary, yet had little to say about military methods or means other than to approve the Blum government's huge increase in military spending.

Insofar as the socialist and radical-socialist press and politicians were interested in weaponry at all, they advocated continuous light fortification on the whole frontier. Some socialists also castigated the generals for wasting money on motorisation and armour, given that tanks were as vulnerable to defensive weapons as cavalry and infantry. They did not claim, however, that such defences actually existed. They highlighted gaps in the fortifications and criticised the army for *not* having built the 'defensive organisations counselled by the lessons of the war and the technological capabilities of modern weapons'.[44] Radical-Socialist journalists did not forget the Belgian danger. Reserve officer and journalist André Guérin wrote that the first line of defence could not be on the frontier: 'We must study battle lines [in Belgium] and prepare a few fall-back positions.'[45] The communists still hoped that the League of Nations and the Soviet alliance would deter Hitler's expansionism in eastern Europe but were willing to risk war. Weaponry only ever figured in articles about the Red Army.[46]

Meanwhile, left-wing pacifists depicted the fortifications as useless because bombing and chemical warfare made border defence illusory.[47] For pacifist-inclined Alsatian autonomists, news that the German army had tested ballistic rockets proved the uselessness of fortifications. In response, nationalists expressed confidence that the general staff was intelligent enough to have foreseen this problem.[48]

The place of the fortifications in public discourse should not be exaggerated. The historian Ladislas Mysyrowicz shows that in the 1936 election campaign, twenty successful right-wing candidates, four Radical-Socialists and two dissident Socialists lauded them. Around thirty-four more Socialists endorsed disarmament and reduction of military service. These figures, coupled with the diverse perspectives described above, hardly support Mysyrowicz's conclusion that candidates 'chloroformed' public opinion.[49]

Even so, the question of who was responsible for the fortifications was becoming controversial, for the left was keen to prove that it was not antimilitarist or pacifist. In 1935, the mostly right-wing speakers at the unveiling of the Maginot memorial near Verdun did not use the term 'Maginot Line', but they did attribute construction of the fortifications to Maginot.[50] A few weeks after remilitarisation, perhaps thanks to the publication of *Double crime*, the left-wing *L'Œuvre* claimed that 'the "Maginot Line" is nothing less than the "Painlevé Line", for the latter had drawn together years of minute research and begun construction'.[51] Former Prime Minister Édouard Herriot recalled that Painlevé had appointed Foch.[52] For the right, Tardieu defended Maginot's case, and keen for reflected glory, referred to the fortifications that 'Maginot and I constructed'. One right-wing newspaper referred to the 'Ligne Maginot-Tardieu'.[53] An Action française group in Nancy – perhaps annoyed that the parliamentary right had appropriated their label – claimed that neither Painlevé nor Maginot deserved credit: Action française in Nancy, through the Union lorraine pour la protection de la frontière du Nord-Est, had forced the government to act.[54]

Whoever was really responsible, Maginot was a more convincing military symbol for the right than the pacifist non-combatant Painlevé. Maginot's war record and role in the veteran movement had already established his nationalist credentials before construction began. His premature death, just as the right was preparing to reject disarmament, permitted creation of a myth around 'le sergeant Maginot'. In 1935, the snobbish aristocrat, right-wing Catholic deputy and Lorraine forge master François de Wendel perceptively pointed out that the Maginot legend has little to do with who he really was:

> Maginot was not a man of great character. He was a party animal and not entirely reliable in his choice of friends. But he was courageous, possessed a sense of politics, his wound, and the fact of being a deputy of the east, continuer of the tradition of the Meuse. M. Poincaré in a sense made him the incarnation of patriotism and the best rampart against ministers who were weak in the face of Briandist encroachments. It's a fact that politics – we saw it with Barrès and Jaurès – makes people in the eyes of public opinion what they hardly actually are. Nevertheless, the people in question pick up this toy, and they end up acting in conformity with the idea that others have of them. That was the 'Maginot Case'.[55]

In the army Maginot was still not universally admired, thanks to his association with the veteran movement. Shortly after the 1936 elections, probably acting on instruction from Daladier as the new war minister, Paris region Director of Military Engineers General Alleau explained that Painlevé deserved credit for cutting through 'sterile debates'. Maginot had established a special account, but his main contribution was superfluous bureaucracy.[56] Whatever the case, the question of label remained within the political microcosm and was secondary even there. In a lengthy military policy debate in the Chamber of Deputies in January 1937, which included discussion of fortification, there was only one reference to 'what has been called the Maginot Line'.[57]

Only the release on 24 September 1937 of Félix Gandéra's film adaptation of *Double crime sur la ligne Maginot* anchored the label 'Maginot Line' in the popular vocabulary. According to a movie magazine's unscientific poll of cinema managers, it was the sixth most successful film of 1937. Around 417,000 Parisians saw it, and many more did so in the provinces.[58] Within a short time of the movie's release, the term was in general use. Resistance to the 'Maginot Line label' certainly persisted. Officers often called it 'le CORF'. In parliament in February 1938, a member of the late Painlevé's moderate-left party interrupted Flandin with the shout 'Call it the Ligne Painlevé!'[59] Yet the apparently apolitical milieu of the cinema propagated the label and with it the conservative agenda of the film.

The film was partially shaped by the army, for Gandéra submitted the script to the Section cinématographique. In return, he was allowed to visit a fort and was lent 150 rifles, 50 carbines and 10 submachine guns, plus a battalion of infantry in campaign uniform with its band. He assured the army that the film 'entirely honoured France and its army'.[60] As he was not allowed to film inside a fort, the interior was reconstructed in the studio – a cinema-goer noted the thud of boots on wooden boards rather than concrete.[61] Otherwise, the price of military scrutiny was not high. The film is more concerned to promote the attractiveness of the fortifications for officers and the traditional command model than any particular military strategy or doctrine.

Nor does it promote a sense of security. As in the novel, the death of the spy resolves nothing. And at a time when appeasers increasingly justified German expansionism and minimised the threat to France, *Double crime* presents Germany as a dangerous enemy, to a greater extent even than the novel. In the latter, the female lead, Anna, the German wife of Commandant Brouchot (an early suspect), was portrayed relatively positively and her father was a Rhinelander opposed to German nationalism. In the novel, her father becomes a convinced Nazi, while Anna is torn between loyalty to Brouchot and to the spy – who turns out to be her brother. Brouchot, who is promoted to co-investigator, renounces her at the end of the film and marches out of the Maginot Line fort at the head of his men – the image of traditional command.

During the Munich crisis, appeasers saw the fortifications as a defence against communism more than against Germany and attributed the crisis to communist bellicosity rather than to any German threat to France. Consequently, the logic of journalists' accounts of the mobilisation became somewhat convoluted, not to say defeatist. Hubert Tourville detected the resolution of their elders of 1914 in the orderly departure of reservists to the fortifications, despite, he remarked, knowing who was responsible for their departure – that is, the communists. In their train, he implausibly claimed, a German on the way to the Nuremberg rally assured the reservists that his countrymen wanted peace as much as the French.[62] For Colonel Fabry, another appeaser,

> It was towards this tough framework [the Maginot Line] that thousands and thousands of mobilised Frenchmen journeyed from all corners of France. There, in contact with a healthy army, they discovered the virtues of discipline, order, labour, shoulder to shoulder, hierarchy and authority, all that which makes a people great and happy, all that from which the country has been separated during the last two years, and which the reborn 'front' has brought back to life.[63]

The Munich agreement was a major defeat for the communists. The government pushed home its advantage. On 30 November, it mobilised all the means at its disposal to break a general strike called to defend the forty-hours law. Public service workers were placed under military discipline. A conservative newspaper commented that the disobedience of public employees was the equivalent of mobilised reserves en route for the fortifications holding a debate on the merits of Czech policies.[64]

In the right-wing press, the Maginot Line became a general symbol of order and strength. New steel silos in which to stock grain for a long war were a 'Ligne Maginot du blé', 'A Maginot Line of grain'. *Match* magazine described the pronatalist Family Code of 1939 as 'the Maginot Line of tomorrow'. The security services had supposedly erected a 'Maginot Line of counterespionage'. The Excelsior football team was 'too frail to cross the Maginot Line of the Metz defence'.[65] The expression even entered the vocabulary of germanophone Alsatian Catholics, who described the doctrine of apostolate as a 'geistige Maginot-Linie' – a 'spiritual Maginot Line'.[66]

This was not the only view of fortification. Opponents of the Munich agreement depicted the Czechoslovak army and fortifications as major losses for the French. The communists, who had hitherto shown scarcely any interest in French weaponry, berated Daladier for delivering to Hitler, 'on bended knee, the secrets of our Maginot Line along with the 20 billion francs that the Czech fortifications cost us'.[67] Again, no false sense of security.

The Maginot Line and the Authoritarian Turn

In the final two years of peace, appeasers became even more determined to shelter behind the Maginot Line, just as the army acquired greater powers over propaganda and the German government engaged in massive publicity for the Westwall.

The French army's long campaign for censorship bore fruit as part of an authoritarian turn in the late Third Republic. Although Daladier, as a good democrat still ostensibly loyal to the Popular Front, claimed to oppose censorship, he had his military cabinet draw up a proposal.[68] On 25 October 1937, a circular in the name of Edmond See, president of the Commission de contrôle (of cinema), decreed that spy, war and crime films and films ridiculing the army would only exceptionally be approved. Scripts depicting the army, high personalities of state and institutions had to be submitted to the commission before shooting.[69] The budget of the Section cinématographique had already been increased from 1.2 million in 1936 to 2.1 million in 1938.

Serious attention to propaganda awaited late 1938, by which time Daladier was heading a right-wing government. The army would have liked to produce its own propaganda, but since resources were inadequate it confined itself to backing private initiatives – so long as vetting confirmed that partners presented a rounded view of military capabilities, had a sufficient audience and were morally reliable. It urged caution, for 'in this cosmopolitan milieu, the discovery of information of a secret character is considered a feat of professional prowess'. The army expected authors and directors to submit pictures, synopses and scripts for approval.[70]

In February 1938, the army accepted a pitch from the French agent of the London-based March of Time Ltd, a subsidiary of the American newsreel and documentary company Time Inc., for *Derrière la ligne Maginot* (Behind the Maginot line). Despite its title, the documentary met the army's criteria. It promised a balanced view of military capabilities and the company had a global presence. After submitting a script, the company was granted access to the fortifications.[71]

In September of that year, the army charged a new commission with centralising information about ceremonies, manoeuvres and equipment – with the glaring exception of fortification – to show foreigners that France could defend itself. Initially, fortification remained off limits, ostensibly to avoid overburdening the local command. The real reason was in fact fear of espionage, so great that the army even renounced making training films for fortification troops.[72] Moreover, the army advocated a 'broad view of the French army'. 'Fragmentary' newsreel or newspaper reports and photography, especially of the Maginot Line, would not be endorsed. The army wanted documentaries, not newsreel images of the fortifications.[73] Newsreel crews who thought they had permission to film were turned away from the fortifications. However, German propaganda for the Westwall and commercial competition forced a rethink.

The Westwall was vital to Hitler, for he needed to guard his rear as he turned to the remains of the Czechoslovak state and Poland. French journalists closely followed the construction effort, awestruck by the mobilisation of hundreds of thousands of workers in this apparent demonstration of Teutonic efficiency.[74] Fabry detected behind the bluff 'a very strong organisation of terrain that was already difficult for an attacker', with some *Werke* that were fifty metres deep.[75] In November

1938, to deter resistance to their expansionism, the Germans allowed the international press to tour the Westwall. A few days later, newsreels in British and French cinemas included a two-minute sequence on the 'Siegfried Line'.[76] French companies redoubled pressure for authorisation to film the Maginot Line.

They became angry when March of Time published stills from its documentary in *Time* magazine and licensed them to French publications such as *Match*. It also reserved showings of its documentary in Britain and the USA to Gaumont. British companies, the Chamber Army Commission and Finance Ministry, which wished to publicise government bond sales, all pressed for permission to film. As a compromise, the army authorised the newsreel trade association to film on behalf of all its members. The companies promised to use the scenes only in newsreels, not to make a documentary rivalling the army's own projects.[77] The Maginot Line became more visible. What did audiences see?

The anglophone version of *Derrière la ligne Maginot*, sensitive to Anglo-American audiences' prejudices, struck a balance between denying accusations of French 'militarism' and reassurance that France was capable of defending itself. It also countered the perception that the French army was unmilitary. French soldiers might look 'slovenly', the narrator candidly admitted, and discipline was necessarily mild in a citizen army, but soldiers were no less patriotic. Neither were they less efficient, as the modernity of the Maginot Line proved. Images of specialists, tanks and planes were interspersed with others of horse-drawn artillery – not a surprise anywhere in the world.

Of the French version, only reviews and a detailed script with extensive annotations survive.[78] Rather than a coherent doctrine, the script reveals controversies, the desire of each arm for its share of screentime and a recruitment drive. A section on the incorporation of conscripts, obviously designed to attract career soldiers, stresses the advantage in civilian life of learning specialist skills in the army. It also gives a prominent place to military and political leaders. There is a long, slow shot of Daladier lighting a cigarette, a sign of calmness and connection to the people. *Le Matin* commented that the 'great stars of the film were . . . President Daladier and Generals Gamelin and Georges'.[79]

Whereas the anglophone version begins with the Maginot Line, the French version begins with 'peaceful human activities', workers in factories, peasants in the fields, intellectuals in offices and laboratories. It then moves from the incorporation of conscripts to a military parade, heavy artillery, tanks and motorised artillery. A proposed revision to the script describes the infantry as 'queen of the battlefield' and explains that it operates in groups of specialists and that men are expected to use their initiative. Horses are less present than in the anglophone version, and the commentary assigns them to the past. Yet the passage 'the world lived in the reign of the automobile' was replaced with 'the automobile made its appearance in the world'. The section devoted to the air force is far from defensive. The commentary remarks, 'terrestrial defence, even if reputed invulnerable, would not prevent the air force from sowing destruction in the vital centres of the opposing country' – a clear exaggeration of the air force's offensive capability.

The section on the Maginot Line, which appears relatively late, includes the usual themes – modern machinery, specialists and comfortable interior life. The fortifications are not depicted as invulnerable. A description of the Maginot Line as 'a solidly locked gate' was altered to the less certain 'a rampart behind which . . .'. The narrator explains that reserves would quickly concentrate at threatened points and that 'when the moment comes, on the signal of the EMA, all the forces of the nation will embark on a ferocious offensive to throw out the invader and accomplish his defeat'. The state of defences on the northern frontier is vague.

The army also sponsored the better-known documentary *Sommes-nous défendus?* (Are we defended?), made by the newsreel company Ciné-reportage. The script was drafted by a house writer, Emmanuel Bourcier, also vice-president of the Association of Veteran Writers, with 'technical advice' from the army. The EMA found no image or phrase in the finished product harmful to national defence.[80] Its premiere was held on 4 November 1938, just after the Munich crisis. In cinemas, it was usually presented before feature films, and so widely seen.

Sommes-nous défendus? provides the best evidence of a Maginot mentality.[81] It opens with an aerial shot of a picturesque village, viewed through a cut-out of an outline map of France. The map rotates as the camera descends into the village, past the belltower to scenes of farming life. The camera lingers on close-ups of shutters, doors and gates being locked and barred as a storm threatens. The film cuts to a café, where local men play cards. Yet the card game is linked to national and international life by the radio, from which they hear that war is imminent. The players repeat clichés about the shamefulness of war, military decline, equipment shortages and demographic inferiority.

A well-dressed stranger, played by René Lefevre, interrupts the players. He personifies the voice-of-god narrator in the flimsy storyline. He asks rhetorically, 'Do you really think France can be swallowed like an egg?' He replies that just as the villagers have protected themselves against a storm, so France can instantly close its doors. He insists that although defensive, France shows its strength to deter war. At the end of his explanation, the narrator tells the card players to 'work in peace, for we *are* defended'. The army, he assures them, remains that of the Marne, which in 1914 halted two million invaders. Twelve of the documentary's sixty-seven minutes are devoted to the Maginot Line. They depict the usual constant readiness, specialists and comfort, its modernity contrasting with the images of rural life in the opening sequences.

Yet the message is not straightforward. It becomes clear that the Maginot Line is only one of the weapons that defend the nation. A map shows that it protects only the German and Luxembourg frontiers. The Belgian frontier is not mentioned, and on the map the camera pans away from it to the northeast. There is no mention of the Alpine fortifications, but a substantial section displays the physical and technical prowess of the Alpine infantry.

There is no sense of how or where military capabilities were to be used. Motorised infantry and armoured forces are given considerable attention, but their purpose is not explained. Light-armoured divisions, created in 1935 and 1937, are not mentioned. Reassuringly, audiences are informed that anti-aircraft artillery and fighters would counter enemy bombers, yet they may have wondered what the purpose of the French bombers they saw was. They would have been right to do so, for the air force lacked an agreed doctrine.

Right-wing newspapers, which alone reviewed the film, did not mention doctrine or strategy. Only *Le Matin* and *Le Jour* explicitly mentioned the Maginot Line, and while their remarks were positive, they hardly amount to a cult of fortification. They were more concerned to criticise scenes depicting the war industries for hiding communist subversion and mismanagement in the nationalised sector.[82]

In contrast to *Sommes-nous défendus?*, the army's third sponsored project, the feature film *Trois de Saint-Cyr*, explicitly dramatised French strategies and doctrine. The production company, Productions Calamy, pitched it as a celebration of 'the grandeur of our army, the deep roots of its traditions and the souls of those who serve in it'. In return for substantial military participation, it promised to accept 'in advance all the modifications that you judge useful up to the completion of the film'.[83] The army provided eight weeks' access to Saint-Cyr, equipment, troops for battle scenes in Tunisia – actually filmed in Syria – and the band of the Garde républicaine. Calvet and a representative of the Troisième Bureau modified the script and closely followed production.[84] On 31 January 1939, *Trois de Saint-Cyr* was launched at a gala performance at the Olympia cinema in Paris, attended by Daladier. Before the war, an estimated 578,000 tickets were sold in Paris alone.[85]

The film relates the stories of three Saint-Cyr graduates. Pierre Mercier is ranked first of the final-year recruits (the 'major de promotion'); he is from a poor background, and his mother has sacrificed herself for his education. His friend and rival, Paul Parent, is ranked last (the 'système'). Pierre asks Paul to look after a new cadet, Jean Le Moyne, a family friend, who has joined the army against the wishes of his wealthy banking family. The first part of the film depicts the traditions and teaching of Saint-Cyr. In the second part, the three heroes find themselves in Tunisia. Pierre commands a line of outposts, which is threatened by rebels, and Paul and Jean join the relief column sent to his aid, the latter dying a heroic death.

Although strategy and doctrine structured the film, the press focused only on its domestic political implications. The right-wing *L'Intransigeant* thought that the 'abnegation and heroism of French officers' mattered more than its hasty editing and rudimentary script. The fascistic *Liberté* reported that young men left the cinema in step as Saint-Cyriens.[86] The left-wing press hardly noticed the film, but where it did, it too was more struck by its social than its military aspects. *La Lumière* thought that the heroes were bourgeois mediocrities, suited to the conformism and 'good average' of the officer corps.

References to the Maginot Line are neverthless obvious. In fact, the production company wanted to set battle scenes in both the metropolitan fortifications and the colonies, and the screenwriter was authorised to visit the fortifications. In the end the Maginot plan was dropped, perhaps because Calvet – one suspects him of backing appeasement – was reluctant to depict Germans as the enemy.[87]

The film transposes the doctrine of initial defence and armoured counterattack to the colonies. As the rebels prepare to attack, Pierre urges caution while Paul advocates pre-emptive attack. Pierre reminds Paul of a rugby match at Saint-Cyr, in which his futile solo run lost the match. Paul's ill-advised and insubordinate operation goes wrong, and Pierre saves his life. The film also dramatised the nccessity of mobility. Calvet praised the script for showing the army's modern weapons, while the EMA lauded the inclusion of 'a manoeuvre of motorised forces'.[88]

Yet the film did not present the Maginot Line as the primary theatre of operations. In the first part of the film, the cadets attend a lecture on the 'Frontiers of the North and East' illustrated by a map. They hear that an enemy attack across the German frontier would meet several 'obstacles' – i.e. the Maginot Line – and that it is therefore easier to invade France through Belgium. Whereas *Sommes-nous défendus?* provides qualified evidence of defensiveness, *Trois de Saint-Cyr* depicts manoeuvre and victory, again with qualifications.

Polarisation

In 1938, Pétain's warning about the return of the offensive in his preface to Chauvineau's *Une invasion est-elle encore possible?* showed that doctrine was contested in the army. In the months before the war, public differences were sharper still, for the German destruction of Czechoslovakia and renewed Italian claims on Nice, Savoie and Tunisia narrowed the choice to one between war and German hegemony.

On one side stood inveterate appeasers led by Pierre Laval, including Colonel Fabry, Pétain and Alsace-Lorraine autonomists, who continued to advocate understanding with Germany and Italy. More than ever, appeasers saw the Maginot Line as a symbol of France's willingness to fight only if directly threatened. They now presented it as a continuous line from the North Sea to Tunisia, and played down the danger of violation of Belgian neutrality. A particularly far-fetched pamphlet, authored by 'Colonel X', might be at the origin of the myth, shared by some contemporary historians, that all Maginot Line forts were linked by tunnels.[89] Whether appeasers refused to confront the reality of war is more debatable.

True, Paul-Émile Cadhilac reported in *L'Illustration* that an *ouvrage* infirmary did not expect to have to treat wounded, except by accident.[90] Yet for Colonel Fabry, the invulnerability of the fortifications made war more terrible. He did not think the Germans would invade via Belgium, and argued that so long as the Maginot Line was completed as expected in the north, neither French nor German fortifications could be breached. Behind their concrete, the adversaries would strike terrible, non-fatal blows. Dreadful means of destruction would arise from the brains of men and machines. 'Doubtless,' he concluded, governments 'will not want to believe that all this stems from the Maginot Line. It will, however, be true.' He reassured readers that this prospect made the Maginot Line a guarantee of peace, but feared that governments were not yet conscious of this fact.[91]

He was right that others were convinced that Hitler could only be stopped militarily. The communists had long believed this, and now centre and right increasingly agreed. Readiness to risk war did not necessarily also mean abandonment of initial defence or the long-war strategy, but in the public sphere alternatives were suggested.

In *Le Temps*, Jean Ernest-Charles advocated 'powerful expeditionary forces, well equipped, mobile, capable of deployment in the different locations of our vast empire and even in zones of European operations'. He predicted that neutralisation of the northeastern front by the Maginot and Siegfried Lines would impose 'imagination and mobility on our strategists'. Armies would move from Egypt and Boulogne to Ulm, as in the days of Napoleon.[92]

In a different register, similar ideas were dramatised in Commandant Cazal's series of five novels *La guerre! La guerre!*, published from March to August 1939. 'Cazal' was the latest pseudonym of the sixty-two-year-old Adolphe d'Espie, his best-known being Jean de La Hire. He authored hundreds of formulaic novels from romances to westerns. *La guerre!* brought together espionage, colonial and adventure genres with futurology and science fiction. The plot is rudimentary, and the characters are cardboard cut-outs; *Double crime* is highbrow by comparison.[93] The narrative evolved with changing international events, but the genre required French heroism and eventually victory.

In the first volume, probably completed before Hitler's invasion of Czechoslovakia, d'Espie's conservatism, not to say his sympathy for the far right, is to the fore. The communists attempt to profit from the bombardment of Paris to seize power, and French forces are more concerned with fighting them than the Germans. Yet in the second volume, *Maginot-Siegfried*, which appeared after the German destruction of Czechoslovakia, the narrative is radically different. The Soviet Union declares war on Germany and joins the Western allies. There are violent conflicts on the Maginot Line, but French forces encircle fifteen German divisions in Switzerland. In the next volume, *Batailles pour la mer*, Anglo-French forces encircle the Germans again in a colossal war of manoeuvre in Belgium, in which 'crude trenches hastily dug during forced or planned pauses count for nothing'.[94] In *L'Afrique en flammes*, the Italians agree a separate peace following defeats in the Balkans, North Africa and the Mediterranean. In the final novel, *La fin . . . par le pétrole*, German generals overthrow the deranged Führer. After he dies of a stroke, they sue for peace.

This war is not 'clean'. *La guerre!* begins with a graphic description of an air raid on Paris, recalling the frightening images that periodically appeared in the picture press. Maginot Line soldiers are not safe. The crew of one fort hears whistling, then 'all the occupants of Casemate 8, with its twin turrets, pass instantly from life to death, while the clever architecture of the casemate becomes a chaotic iron volcano and the steel guns are transformed into an indescribable magma of scrap metal'.[95] Although, as the adventure genre demands, the outcome of the war is never in doubt, the cost is high.

As in the murder-mystery, formula fiction requires suspense plus a happy ending. In *La guerre!*, this is provided by combining futurology with science fiction. Futurologists such as Jules Verne attempted to project the potential of current knowledge into future realisation. Science fiction, in contrast, depends on a 'novum', an unprecedented, not to say impossible innovation such as time travel or invisibility, which is inserted into an otherwise normally functioning world. In *Maginot-Siegfried*, soldiers on the Maginot Line see a shell fall like a 'shining meteor' and 'streaking through the air like a steel cone', exploding with a flash 'brighter than the sun'. No technical explanation is advanced, so readers are left ignorant of whether the meteor is a novum or an application of known rocket technology.

Army and politicians alike were fearful of technological surprises. In debates about fortifications, officers dismissed certain schemes as 'Jules Verne', without denying that they might be possible in the future.[96] In 1934, Daladier told parliament that nobody knew how technology would evolve: 'certain anticipations of H.G. Wells and even the novels of Jules Verne have proved more clairvoyant than some courses taught at the École de guerre before 1914. Nobody can distinguish utopia from truth.'[97] Weygand too feared that the Germans were preparing technical surprises as dangerous as any tactical innovation.[98]

After all, this was a period of rapid technological evolution, in which the military use of rockets and atom bombs was only half a decade away. Radar was close to deployment. Death rays and rockets were staples of the press and popular fiction.[99] In 1938, the journalist Geneviève Tabouis reported that the Germans had abandoned experiments with electric rays designed to stop the machinery of the fortifications because they had decided on a joint German–Italian invasion through Switzerland.[100] There was no complacency in France about the potential of existing technology and the possibility of future surprises.

On the eve of war, one of the first ever opinion polls found that 76 per cent of French favoured defending Poland. The French did not face the prospect of war with enthusiasm, for they expected bombing of cities and gas warfare and doubted the loyalty of Alsace-Lorraine troops on the Maginot Line. For now, appeasers had to keep quiet. Beyond the conviction that France could not immediately strike Germany, there was less consensus about military strategy and doctrine. Pétain warned that the folly of offensive warfare was returning in the army, while in the public sphere doubts about the Allies' ability to win a long war were emerging.

After Hitler's invasion of the rump Czechoslovakia, the British and French guaranteed Poland's integrity, belatedly seeking military agreement with the Soviet Union. Even appeasers were in favour, if only in the hope that the prospect of a two-front war would deter Hitler. Desperate for a second front, the French came close to offering eastern Poland to the Soviet Union, compensating the Poles with future German territory (which was the outcome after 1945). But Stalin did not trust British appeasers. While negotiations dragged, the Soviet Union and Germany concluded a non-aggression pact, announced on 22 August. Its secret protocol demarcated 'spheres of influence' in Poland. For Hitler, that was the green light. German troops entered Poland at 04:45 on 1 September 1939.

1. Contemporary photograph of the munitions entrance of the Hackenberg *gros ouvrage*. In the bottom left, the narrow-gauge railway line leads directly into the *ouvrage* to an unloading station beyond a curve to cover it from enemy fire. The railway then leads down a slope to barracks and services and to the feet of the combat blocs. The radio antenna is strung along the facade, on the top left of which is an observation cloche armed with an LMG.

2. From left to right, Marshals Pétain, Foch and Joffre wearing their distinctive uniforms at the victory parade of 14 July 1919.

3. This aerial photograph of the construction of GO-Galgenberg shows on the bottom left the personnel entrance bloc. Top left is Bloc 3 with its machine-gun turret. In the middle is Bloc 6, which was to be armed with a 135mm bomb-thrower. Between Blocs 6 and 3 are the site offices and barracks for workers.

4. The machine room at Hackenberg. In the foreground, the officer of 164 RIF instructing a subordinate symbolises command. In the background, the soldier's gesture is integral to the operation of the machine.

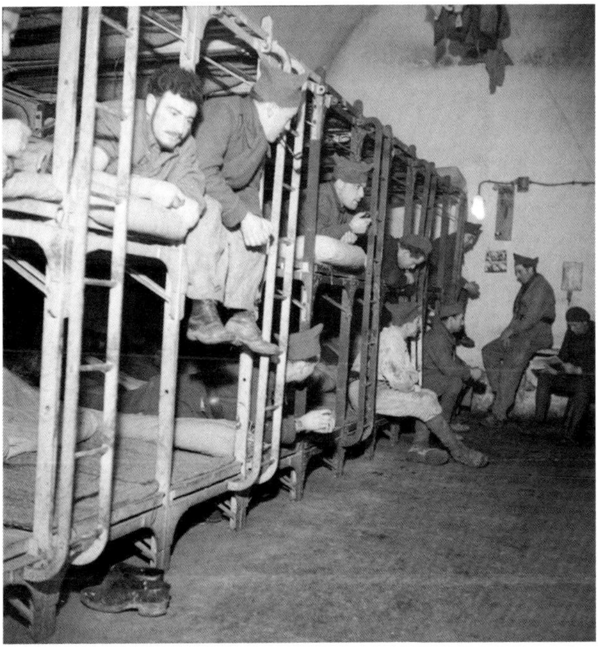

5. Sleeping quarters in PO-Velosnes in SF-Montmédy, crewed by 246 men and 6 officers of 155 RIF and 169 RAP. The bunks were permanently occupied in turn by the men of three 'watches'.

6. On 26 September 1938, at the height of the Munich crisis, Édouard Daladier, Foreign Minister Georges Bonnet and General Maurice Gamelin arrive at 10 Downing Street, London. All three had served at the front during the Great War.

7. In this contemporary photograph of the thirteenth-century Tour de la Poudrière, Wissembourg, it is possible to see two of three LMG embrasures in the blockhouse constructed in its cellar and ground floor.

8. Officers' houses in the Cité des officiers at Elzange security camp in RF-Metz. The larger house on the left did not figure in the initial plans, but was probably constructed once permanent manning under the command of a major had been decided. The houses are now part of a leafy estate.

9. Sketch of twenty-one-year-old Private René Boulair (168 RIF) found in his personal effects prior to his conviction for insubordination.

11. During the winter of 1939–40, a sapper of the 3rd Génie regiment supervises soldiers of 169 RIF in fatigues and in one case wearing the beret of the fortification regiments, as they construct a concrete work in the sub-sector of Œutrange (SF-Thionville).

10 (opposite). Contemporary photograph of the entrance bloc of GO-Sainte-Agnès in the southeast. To the right is the restaurant Righi, which the authorities then considered be an espionage danger. Further right, the artillery casemates (just visible) looked down on Menton, 1,238 metres below.

12. The crew of a Hotchkiss M1914 machine gun on an anti-aircraft tripod, somewhere on the 5th Army advance posts in the Northern Vosges during the phoney war.

13 (opposite, top image). A *corps franc* patrol somewhere in no-man's-land in advance of the 5th Army sector in the Northern Vosges. The lead soldier carries an FM24/29 LMG, while those behind carry Berthier carbines.

14 (opposite, lower image). The view from La Ferté's Bloc 2, northwest towards the village of Villy. On the left is a barbed-wire barrier, in the middle antitank rails and on the right an antitank ditch.

15. The GFM (lookout/LMG) cloche on La Ferté's Bloc 2 showing multiple 88mm impacts. A direct hit on its embrasure, perhaps imperfectly shut, decapitated Sergeant Roger Conraux (thirty-two years, seven months and nine days) and killed privates Paul Gomez (thirty-two years, three months and twenty days) and Joseph Kösters (twenty-two years, five months and two days).

16. German soldiers at La Ferté's entrance shortly after the combat ended. To the left, with its vulnerable high profile, is observation/GFM cloche 8; to the right is the jammed mixed-weapon turret.

17. From left to right, General Weygand, Secretary of the War Council Paul Baudouin, Paul Reynaud and Marshal Pétain. The picture was taken on 10 June 1940. On that day, Italy declared war on France, the Germans broke through the 2nd Army into Champagne to threaten the Maginot Line, and the government left Paris for the southwest.

18. A wounded German soldier is carried away from PO-Kerfent. Multiple infantry assaults failed to take the fort.

19. Bloc 3 of PO-Kerfent, destroyed by 88mm impacts from a range of less than 100 metres, which stripped away the concrete and exposed the steel rods. The 47mm antitank gun is still in firing position in its embrasure.

20. Colonel Fabre, commander of GO-Grand-Hohékirkel, learns that he is considered to be a POW. On the left, General Max von Viebahn, commander of ID 257, looks on.

21. German soldiers inspect a turret somewhere in RF-Metz.

22. Wehrmacht soldiers relax outside Hackenberg Bloc 8. German propaganda attributed the capture of Maginot Line forts to the triumph of brave soldiers over French concrete. The image of muscular, bare-chested German soldiers is also omnipresent in French individual and press accounts of the battle.

Part IV

THE MAGINOT LINE IN COMBAT

10

A PHONEY WAR? LIFE ON THE MAGINOT LINE

The Maginot Line was on a war footing well before Germany invaded Poland. The *disponibles* ('availables' who had just completed their service) had been recalled after the destruction of Czechoslovakia in March. On 21–22 August 1939, Measure 21 set in motion the tripling of fortification regiments as their professional and active cadres transferred to new units. Two days later, the mostly Alsace-Lorrainer *frontaliers* of the B1 reserve were called up, and by 29 August B2 reserves had arrived from further away. Mobilisation proper, from 2 September, brought campaign troops to the frontier. Within two weeks, they had relieved the GRM and Gardes frontaliers in the advance posts and reinforced the intervals.

No fewer than four armies took up position behind the fortifications in Alsace-Lorraine. General Condé's 3rd Army covered RF-Metz, General Édouard Requin 4th Army held the Sarre and General Victor Bourret's 5th Army was on the Lauter. These three armies were part of the 2nd Army Group, commanded by General Prételat. General Garchery's 8th Army on the Rhine belonged to the 3rd Army Group along with the 6th Army, the latter being a reserve unit consisting only of a staff. These two army groups were under the command of General Alphonse Georges, who was Gamelin's deputy for the front from the Channel to Switzerland (Figure 12).

On 1–2 September, as the armies established themselves, church bells gave the largely germanophone civilian population of the 'Red Zone', stretching from the rear of the fortifications to the frontier, a few hours' notice to assemble for evacuation to the southwest. Some

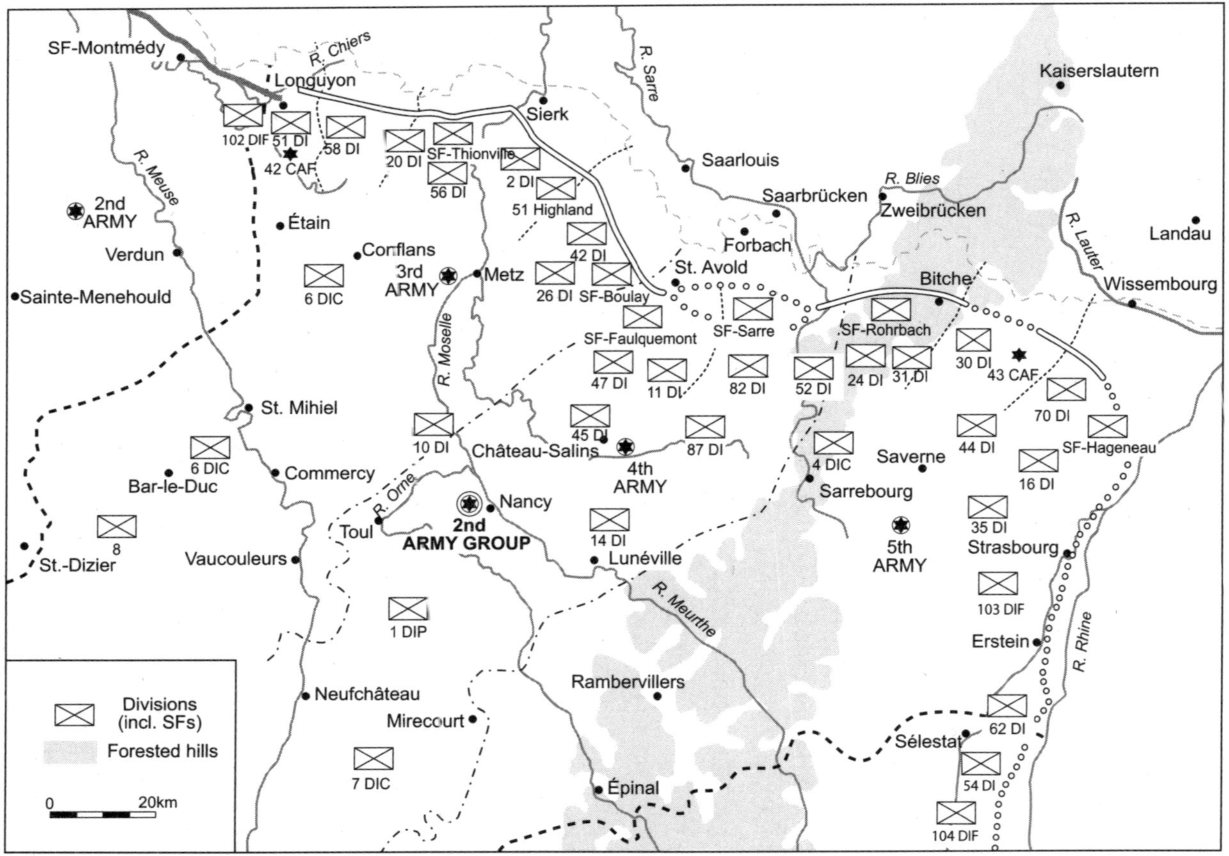

12. Divisions on the Maginot Line, 10 May 1940.

688,000 people were ordered to depart: 45 per cent of Mosellans and 31 per cent of Alsatians, including every inhabitant of Strasbourg. The remaining 1.1 million women, children and older male civilians shared space with around 1 million soldiers, including the equivalent of ten divisions of fortress infantry – nearly half the front-line troops. Non-evacuated Rosheim, with 2,744 peacetime inhabitants, lodged over 2,000 soldiers in homes, barns and fields.[1]

Mobilisation in the southeast followed the same schedule, except that there was no evacuation, for Mussolini declared Italy to be 'non-belligerent but not neutral'. Several Alpine units were transferred, some to Alsace-Lorraine, leaving their elite ski sections, the Section d'éclaireurs skieurs (SES), to patrol the frontier. Operations in the High Alps were anyway impossible from mid-October to the following June.

The Maginot Line had fulfilled its primary purpose of covering mobilisation and the *attaque brusquée* never materialised. From 6 September, its guns supported a token sortie into the Saar to support the Poles. It was soon called off, and the mobile forces involved moved to the Belgian frontier, where more serious events were expected. Yet an attack on the Maginot Line could not be entirely ruled out. During the long, cold, wet winter of the 'phoney war', troops awaited an unlikely attack. In American English, 'phoney' meant 'fake'; the French translation, 'drôle de guerre', additionally signifies 'weird', 'strange' and 'funny'. But to borrow from the subtitle of the Sarreguemines veteran and historian Henri Hiegel's book about the Moselle during the war, it was a joke 'only for those who weren't there'.[2]

According to the decadence thesis, the phoney war undermined the morale of a country already reluctant to fight. This picture relies on a crude concept of morale as a collective state of mind and is easily refuted by demonstrating that French troops often fought bravely. But the opposite view, that the generals' mistakes betrayed the troops, minimises or renders irrelevant the mental and physical toll of the phoney war on the troops and indeed civilians. If poor morale, where it existed, compromised willingness to fight, it will have to be demonstrated when we arrive at May and June 1940. To focus simply on whether 'morale' contributed to the defeat, however, impoverishes the story of the campaign and obscures the history of the Maginot Line.

A useful starting point is with the insights of Jean Crémieux-Brilhac. Critical of the failure of the high command to make sense of the mass of data it accumulated from soldiers' correspondence, he dug deeper. He found that morale was 'excellent' in active units, especially the cavalry and armoured and motorised formations, but only 'good on the whole' in B reserve divisions.[3] He also mentioned in passing that the morale of fortress regiments was shaky.

Digging deeper still reveals that fortress units belonging to the problematic 'good on the whole' category were stationed from RF-Lauter to the Sarre Gap (Figure 13). These areas were inhabited by a poorly mixed cocktail of Alsace-Lorraine soldiers and civilians, divided between nationalists and autonomists, including a few pro-Nazis, and interior French soldiers, divided between nationalists and communists from the Paris red belt. Figure 14 shows that the pro-Nazi autonomist movement, the Jungmannschaft, was strongest in this area and that negative interactions between troops and civilians were most common here. The area witnessed the most military action, the greatest exposure to bad weather, the dampest conditions in the *ouvrages* and the most extensive pillaging of evacuees' homes. The Maginot Line neither restored command, provided troops with habitability nor reassimilated Alsace-Lorraine into the nation.

Mobilisation

The French went to war reluctantly yet willingly, aware that the alternative was German hegemony.[4] In late October, the Deuxième Bureau, responsible for sampling soldiers' letters, found the same 'astonishing morale': 'not enthusiasm, but firm determination to finish things once and for all with [the Germans] of today and tomorrow, a cold anger, and understanding that we are not here to string pearls' (i.e. spend a long time on a boring task).[5] There was no evidence of communist opposition to the war; the Nazi–Soviet Pact divided the party and many activists were imprisoned. Most autonomists agreed that war was the only alternative to German domination. In Haut-Rhin, the Institut d'études européennes (IEE) contrasted the 'seriousness and calm' of the present with the near panic of the Munich crisis. In northern Alsace,

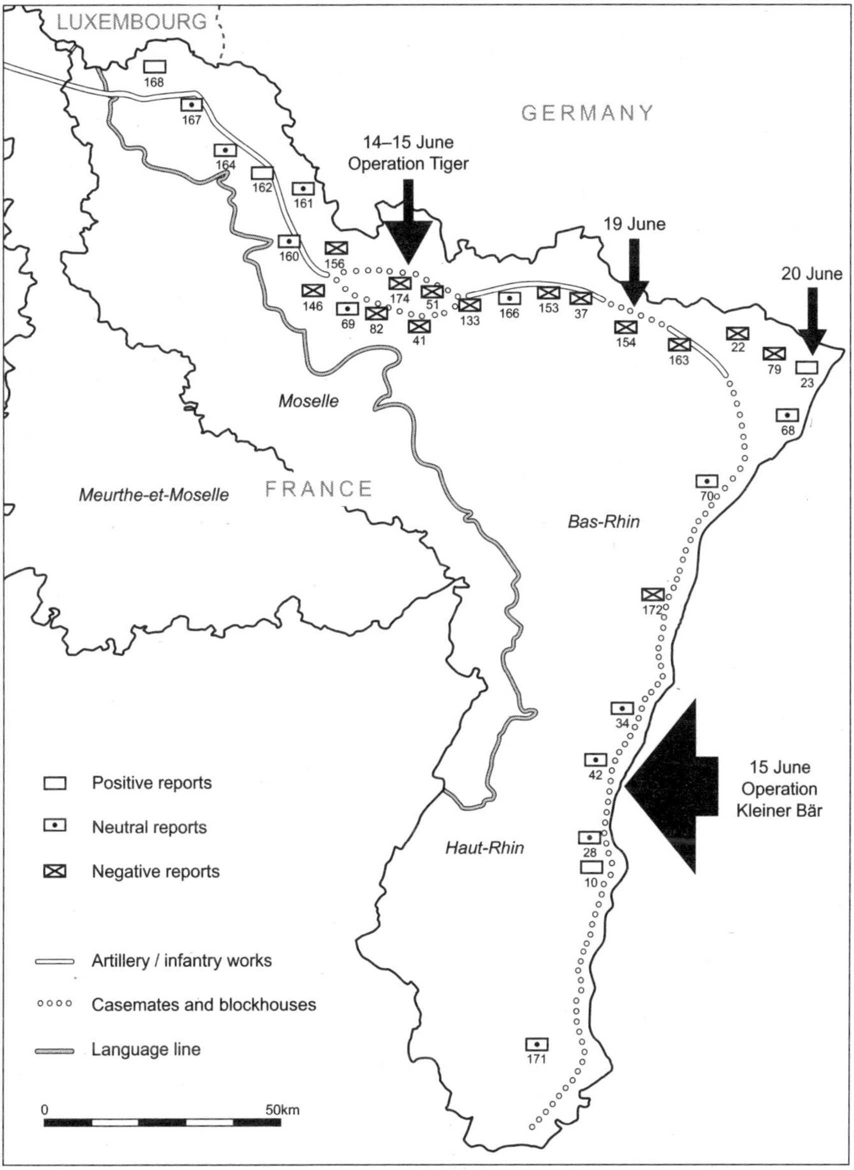

13. Fortress infantry regiments' morale during the phoney war.

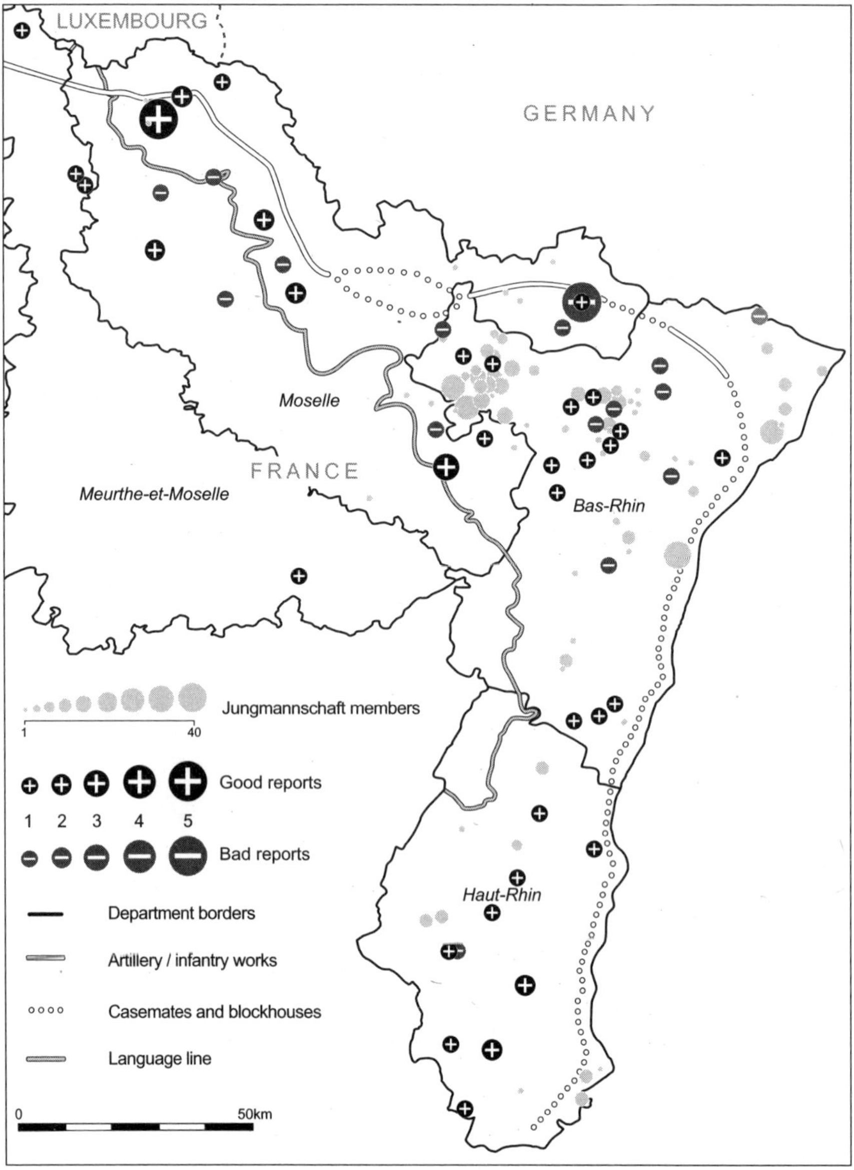

14. Positive and negative relations between soldiers and civilians compared with Jungmannschaft groups.

where pro-German sentiment was stronger, Lieutenant René Balbaud reported that German speakers sang 'God Save the King' on hearing that Britain had declared war.[6]

While neither officers nor men had a sophisticated understanding of Nazism, it is not true, as is sometimes suggested, that they had no idea why they were fighting. Some Catholic soldiers saw themselves as defending Christian civilisation against Hitler, or Catholic Alsace against pagan or Protestant Nazism. A sergeant praised a chaplain whose faith in victory was sustained by the pope's recent encyclical condemning totalitarian states for depriving men of personality and liberty.[7] Non-Catholics also condemned Nazi authoritarianism, personal rule and the blind obedience of the German people. The French, they considered, fought as free citizens of a republic. Yet republican egalitarianism also fed resentment of 'embusqués' (shirkers) – those who were not doing their bit, notably workers assigned to war industries.

This was not a tolerant patriotism. Interior French soldiers were suspicious of Alsace-Lorrainers either for not assimilating or for being racially unassimilable. There was no condemnation of Nazi racism. Antisemitism was traditionally strong in Alsace-Lorraine. The sub-prefect of Mulhouse reported that many soldiers and civilians believed that Jews were either not mobilised or serving in cushy jobs.[8] Neither was antisemitism unknown among officers. The Jewish officer Lieutenant Robert Felsenhardt heard from a captain the old smear that the infantry was too hard for Jews.[9]

Not everyone shared the warrior mentality. Without necessarily approving the idea, some expected politicians to cook up a new Munich, thus avoiding war again. Although rarely unconditional, pacifism had not disappeared. Sapper André Giroud, a pacifist journalist from Lyon, was 'torn' between the equally terrible options of war and servitude. He decided to march without being tempted by the hero role.[10]

There were discordant notes in Alsace-Lorraine. The IEE saw the firing of a Moselle postman for refusing to distribute mobilisation papers as proving 'microbial proliferation' of autonomism.[11] The future Resistance leader Raymond Aubrac, stationed north of Strasbourg, recalled that on hearing that France was at war, older reserves speaking an 'incomprehensible language', who had probably fought for Germany in the previous war, were overcome by great anxiety and got roaringly drunk.[12]

Life above Ground

Initially, the front resembled, one soldier wrote, a 'land of milk and honey'. In the beautiful late summer, mobilised pastry chefs made flans with the abundant flour. Abandoned livestock roamed; cows bellowed for want of milking; apples, pears and mirabelles, the iconic fruit of Alsace, ripened on the trees; game teemed in the forests; the scent of grilling meat wafted through the woods. Officers and men helped themselves to evacuees' property – more on that later.[13] All this made the following months harder to bear.

The winter of 1939/40 was extremely harsh. It first rained on 5 September and from the 12th it did so frequently and heavily. The Moselle flooded cellars. In the Sarre Gap, the same impermeable clay soils that permitted defensive flood works now worked against the French. Before the rain, the men of Sergeant Henri Guizard's 41 RMIC struggled to dig three metres into rock-hard marl soil. By the 17th, they were wading in sticky mud and their trenches and gun emplacements were collapsing. Guizard and his fellow NCOs constructed a shelter from logs and canvas, draught-proofed with straw. Yet in November, it became a swimming pool. For the first time, the men were demoralised.[14] A soldier stationed three kilometres from the Rhine had the impression of living on a sponge.[15]

Then, from 12 December to well into February, came frost and snow. January 1940 was the coldest month since 1838, temperatures plummeting to –24°C in Metz. The north was not much warmer, but interval troops on the Maginot Line were less well protected. Guizard was warm in his shelter, but slept with mice nesting in his straw bedding and scuttling around his head. His men froze in tents, despite each having a stove.[16] Giroud's company, in the same area, scraped the granite-hard soil with picks and shovels.[17] Mail and food supplies were delayed, and wine, bread, vegetables and meat were frozen. Guard duty was a trial.

Relief marches required superhuman effort. Horses fell; lorries slid off the roads. Soldiers illegally cut firewood, provoking complaints that they damaged forests.[18] In early February, the Deuxième Bureau reported that all letters began with accounts of 'intense and rigorous cold, which causes all kinds of suffering'.[19]

Had the men been adequately kitted out, they would have coped better. There were no complaints in the Alps, where equipment was appropriate. In the northeast, parliamentary inspectors reported that troops required hundreds of thousands of boots, blankets, tunics and tents. Soldiers wore civilian clothes into December and beyond, Giroud's unit receiving multicoloured requisitioned civilian sweaters.[20] Families, friends and charities sent woollens and balaclavas. Even men with complete uniforms rarely had anything to change into when wet. In the Sarre Gap, the men of 123 RI found three-hour duties in flooded machine-gun posts impossible because they lacked rubber boots.[21] Even in showpiece GO-Hackenberg, the men had to make do with sky-blue uniforms in such a pitiful state that their commander was reluctant to allow them to go on leave.[22] The soldiers who received khaki found its woollen sweater inadequate, so tunics had to be mass-produced. In November, only the top and bottom buttons of Guizard's second-hand tunic fastened, so that he resembled a man trying to appear slim.[23]

Since freezing weather compromises the immune system, there were many cases of colds, viruses, influenza, colic, mumps, measles and diarrhoea, not to speak of lice. The commander of SF-Haguenau attributed illness to wading in twenty centimetres of water and to a lack of basic medication such as aspirin.[24] 'Illness' is listed as the cause of death of 226 soldiers in the three Alsace-Lorraine departments from the declaration of war to the end of April 1940 (15 per cent of all deaths).

Horses suffered even more than men. Most field infantry and artillery regiments relied on equine transport (as did German equivalents), usually requisitioned – like human soldiers, horses were a reserve force. The RIFs possessed 130 horses for 67 horse-drawn vehicles (plus 250 bicycles, 67 motorbikes with sidecar and 44 motor vehicles). Each of the armies on the Maginot Line possessed around 15,000 horses. Many were dead within a month. Officers responsible for requisition often lacked the knowledge to identify suitable animals or, to meet quotas, took animals that were unfit. Used to eating an oat-heavy diet, horses suffered from a sudden shift to hay, which was in short supply owing to a poor harvest. Parliamentary inspectors were afflicted by the sight of hundreds of horses tied up night and day in a wood under the pouring rain.[25] A veterinary surgeon wrote home that corpses were piling up in the courtyard because it was no longer possible to send them all to the knackers.[26] Subsequently, the army improved shelter, but horses still suffered from lack of exercise, were overworked or were killed by accidents and disease.[27] By March, there was such a shortage of horses that commanders feared manoeuvre would be impossible.[28]

Horses often proxied men's suffering. True, a horse put down after slipping on ice might be dragged back to camp to be eaten.[29] Yet soldiers often expressed concern at the horses' plight.[30] The actor Jean-Louis Barrault related a particularly affecting story. He saw a peasant whispering in his horse's ear as he led it to the requisition centre: 'Then he stopped, pressed his forehead against the horse's long face and spoke face to face. He cried, then sobbed.' The peasants in Barrault's unit went on hunger strike until the officers increased the oats ration. 'Fine men,' he commented, 'who for a moment reconciled me with life.'[31]

Life below Ground

The *ouvrages* provided shelter from the elements but were not designed for long-term occupation, especially as increased armament and crew size further reduced precious space. Shortly before the conflict, General Schickelé, the military physician-general, warned that 'darkness, confinement and humidity' conditioned life underground. The first, he mistakenly thought, could be remedied by electric lighting. Confinement was more problematic, for poorly circulating air was soiled by men and weapons, thus causing 'breathing difficulties, sweating and, in susceptible people, cold sweats and nose, throat and bronchial trouble'. Although ventilation and heating reduced humidity, in most cases 'living in a damp atmosphere will be normal in deeply buried fortified *ouvrages*, and in the long term will result in some harm to the occupants'.[32]

Dignitaries were usually taken to the best *ouvrages*, such as the Hackenberg. In January 1940, British General Edmund Ironside had to visit nearby Mont des Welches because ice made Hackenberg inaccessible. He observed that the men did not seem to suffer from underground life. Excellent ventilation and elaborate means to expel fumes ensured good air quality. Sleeping arrangements, food and water were good too.[33] A few weeks into the war, a soldier writing from an unnamed *gros ouvrage* found life interesting 'in the métro', this 'clean, well-lit, comfortable underground city'. Initially it had been damp, but the situation improved every day.[34] It is true that as the air outside cooled during winter, it no longer condensed inside, while radiators were able to maintain 21°C in sleeping quarters.[35] Yet as the previously quoted parliamentary inspectors found, conditions remained hard in Hackenberg. Galleries still leaked; latrines still stank. At GO-Hochwald, the journalist Roland Dorgelès found a sort of 'fog' in the galleries and puddles on the floor.[36]

Conditions were worse in the *petits ouvrages*. Work to install air conditioning to combat the terrible damp in GO-Velosnes was never completed.[37] At PO-Einseling, where underground installations were also unfinished, the shaft and gallery led only to a WC. A second chamber, excavated in 1940, proved uninhabitable on account of lack of air. The sixty-six-man crew therefore took turns to occupy beds in the combat bloc near the surface, through which a furious freezing wind whistled. They lived in their greatcoats. In one casemate, 'bad smells of enclosed humanity made it hard to breathe' and the least chore caused quarrels between infantry and artillery.[38]

Neither were conditions enviable in the completed Rotherberg infantry shelter, manned by 2/162 RIF. René de Chambrun's graphic description of his attempt to sleep in his tiny damp room below ground is worth quoting at length. Each morning his roommate asked him whether he had slept well:

> The first few mornings I had to answer this question decidedly in the negative. The diesel engines for the blowers circulating fresh air throughout the fort were only turned on three times each day for a total of eight hours. Then, some of the moisture from the walls was

absorbed and we could read, write and breathe almost normally. Regularly, though, at ten o'clock every night the whistle shrieked down the gallery where the engine room was located; within a few seconds the huge dynamos died down gradually, the lights dimmed and faded into complete darkness. The slight vibration of the walls of the fort ceased. In the Stygian darkness, the quiet became oppressive. It felt like being in a submarine lying on the bottom of the ocean without any kind of power.

I shall never forget the first night in that little cell. After an hour or so I began to feel the scarcity of air and to suffer from claustrophobia. Bentz was fast asleep, but I kept lighting matches to look at my watch in the hope that I would discover that their hands had suddenly jumped forward and the morning was approaching. Finally, I could stand it no longer, and decided to get up. Groping my way down the gallery with my flashlight, I came at last to the staircase at the rear of the fort and rushed up the 140 steps – to find the heavy steel door closed and barred. There was just a crack under the door, and I went on the floor flat on my face with my nose as near as possible to the crack and tried to breathe in the outside air. That helped a little. The thought that this war might last several years, and that I would spend night after night like this appalled me. I began to envy all those officers and men from Lorraine who apparently were much tougher than I.

I had not been there five minutes when I heard footsteps in the gallery, soon echoed by the walls surrounding the staircase. It was our Gascon, Saint-Guily, who had come to join me from the depths of his own cavern. He had the same idea as I. We decided that we were not yet *des gars du béton* [concrete lads], and I began to discuss the possibility of volunteering for the Foreign Legion to breathe pure air. But at five o'clock the engines began to rotate, the lights went on, and we forgot how miserable we had been a few hours before.[39]

A 133 RIF soldier in PO-Haut-Poirier, on the damper left of RF-Lauter, mocked press stories of the 'comfortable' lives of Maginot Line soldiers, with their lifts and showers: 'Our room? Four concrete walls covered with lime-based paint that was once white, running with shiny rivulets of shiny condensation. Big drops of water stagnate on the ceiling, which, thanks to the light, resemble shiny pearls . . . Number one enemy is water. The other is cold.'[40]

By late November, the high command was concerned. General Prételat, as 2nd Army Group commander, evoked the 'physical fatigue and moral lassitude' of crews that remained too long underground. The army rightly feared that fortification troops resented being treated as second-rate. Certain *ouvrages* in RF-Lauter – Schiesseck, Otterbiel Grand-Hohékirkel and Lembach – were singled out as problematic.[41] These were precisely the areas in which relations between interior French and Alsace-Lorrainers were poorest.

Pillage and Repression

Alsace-Lorrainers, who constituted between 15 and 60 per cent of mobilised fortification regiments, soon heard that evacuated friends and relatives had endured a hellish journey to southwestern villages. Accommodation there was often poor, employment was lacking and some locals called evacuees 'Boches'.[42] At the front, soldiers' anger was intensified by witnessing the pillage of evacuated homes. Sapper Giroud's notes on what he saw in Volmunster are typical:

> I'm still stunned by the sight of houses with windows and doors open, no piece of furniture not gutted or contents not scattered on the floor. In the kitchens, I walk on broken plates, chairs broken, sinks shattered. In the bedrooms, clothes and lingerie trampled. Drawers thrown on the floor, letters opened, family heirlooms strewn about. Magnificent pieces of furniture caved in. Lovely children's bedrooms are now masses of pink woollens, broken toys thrown around an overturned bed. Anything not used by soldiers is destroyed. So much intimacy profaned! So many memories annihilated! So many loving touches trampled and soiled![43]

In their letters, soldiers reported having seen valuables taken away. Some admitted participation. A soldier of 279 RI promised his parents souvenirs 'like those I've already sent'.[44] Subsequently, pillage happened all over France as the battle spread, but in Alsace-Lorraine it had a special meaning; it varied geographically and corresponded with areas of low morale.

Soldiers treated Alsace-Lorraine as conquered territory. The sight of Germanic residential architecture (less common in Moselle), German street signs, German-language books and newspapers and photographs of men in German uniform in houses all supposedly proved sympathy for the enemy.[45] Adjutant Lavergne (162 RIF) met gunners who thought they were in Germany because they found pictures of 'German' soldiers in homes.[46] Others knew perfectly well where they were: one claimed that men vandalised houses because they 'smell of Germany'.[47]

Often, soldiers destroyed gratuitously, denying inhabitants' humanity into the bargain. Though sometimes the work of roaming pigs, defecation recalled the propaganda of the previous war, which attributed a foul odour to 'subhuman' Germans. While Giroud politely mentioned 'soiling', an Alsatian NCO lamented that in his boudoir 'they sat my lovely dolls in a circle and crapped in the middle'.[48] Sartre explicitly connected vandalism to prejudice: soldiers complained about everything from the language to Alsatian sausages. Everyone had met someone who claimed to be Alsatian first, French or German second. 'Obviously,' Sartre sarcastically concluded, 'this righteous indignation easily leads to shitting in evacuees' beds.'[49]

Soldiers received contradictory signals from the high command. Two days before mobilisation, the government increased the penalty for pillage from hard labour to death.[50] Yet the army ordered soldiers to requisition essentials that it was incapable of supplying itself. Officers turned a blind eye or 'requisitioned' themselves.[51]

The authorities were torn between the belief that pillage stories were fabricated by German agents to weaken the army, and concern that, even if false, they undermined Alsace-Lorraine troops' morale. The high command ordered officers to correct the 'surprise and shock' of badly informed troops that Alsace-Lorrainers 'preciously conserve their dialect'.[52] Yet when two Alsatian parliamentary inspectors voiced moderate concerns about pillage, their socialist colleagues and the accompanying liaison officer doubted their patriotism.[53] In fact, during the previous war one of the Alsatians concerned had deserted the

German army to join the French, while the other had been imprisoned for refusing to supply the army with tobacco. Informed of the incident, 8th Army commander General Garchery opined that the deputies' 'sympathies are with those other elected representatives who are currently imprisoned'.[54]

He was referring to the arrest in October 1939 of 300 activists, including deputies Rossé, Stürmel, the autonomist-communist Jean-Pierre Mourer and the Mosellan autonomist Victor Antoni. Despite the burden of proof having been lowered in previous years, prosecutors failed to build cases under the espionage laws. Nonetheless, Karl Roos, who had been arrested before the war, was convicted under these laws of delivering secrets to German agents and executed in February. In Alsace-Lorraine, reactions were mixed. An Alsatian soldier in 155 RAP saw the arrests as a response to 'rottenness' in 'our dear Alsace'.[55] An Auenheim man, who drunkenly declared that he would lay down his life for Roos, was untypical.[56] However, the IEE again urged the government to combat the widespread view that Roos's crime was not 'opinion', but espionage, 'permitting the Germans to wage a bloody war against the Maginot Line'.[57]

While the fiercest critics of the evacuation did not contest its necessity, security concerns were present there too.[58] Dialect-speaking political-police inspectors accompanied evacuees; letters home were monitored. The Sûreté was pleased that evacuation prevented 'neighbouring [German] propaganda' from penetrating the country.[59]

Alsace-Lorrainers in uniform remained suspect. In July 1939, the CSG rejected as 'contrary to the national interest' a proposal to improve the speed of mobilisation by increasing Alsace-Lorrainers' proportion in fortification units.[60] In October, parliamentary inspectors concluded that Alsatian morale was generally good, but required surveillance so that inaction did not undermine their warrior mentality, especially given that German propaganda might exploit discontent about the evacuation and create doubts about the war.[61] In fact, Alsace-Lorrainers' attitudes to the war and to the interior French varied geographically.

Pillage was most common from RF-Lauter to the River Moselle. This was the theatre of the Saar offensive, during which the looting of German homes was not unknown. Thereafter, soldiers manning advance posts on freezing wet nights lived in fear of German patrols. Rumours spread that German raiders were guided by locals who had crossed the frontier to avoid evacuation.[62] Immediately behind the evacuated area, nationalism was strong, but interior French soldiers were also likely to meet pro-German autonomists and even pro-Nazis.

It is significant that interior French soldiers' criticisms of autonomism were almost exclusively confined to northern Alsace and contiguous Moselle (Figure 14, page 264). Relations between soldiers and civilians were bad in 'unlovely and fairly autonomist' Bitche. One soldier said that inhabitants' manners were 'disagreeable' there, and that shops and cafés coldly refused to serve them.[63] Two soldiers wrote that the inhabitants of Obermodern preferred those who wanted 'living space' to French soldiers. They expected relations with civilians to collapse.[64] Vetting probably ensured that known autonomists were few in fortification regiments. The interior French nevertheless tended to distrust Alsace-Lorrainers, whether autonomist or not, and no Alsace-Lorrainer liked being referred to as 'Boche'.

On the Rhine front, relations between Alsace-Lorrainers and interior French were better. Pillage was sporadic (and absent on the Luxembourg and Swiss borders).[65] The river marked a clear boundary between nations and there was little military action.[66] Furthermore, autonomism in southern Alsace was more Catholic and more anti-German, while French language and French culture were more widespread. In autonomist Sundgau a village might be decked with tricolours, but not in the equally autonomist north.[67]

In the south, civilians were especially likely to welcome French soldiers into their homes, though soldiers sometimes received invitations in the north too. The Deuxième Bureau reported hundreds of positive opinions of host families in southern Alsace and sometimes elsewhere. Soldiers extolled comfy beds, milky coffee and buttered bread for breakfast, convivial dinners with families, Christmas presents and parties.[68] Communication across language barriers was facilitated by bilingual children. Giroud wrote that during a family dinner in Fleisheim in Moselle, the daughter interpreted and everyone had fun.[69] Even in the autonomist Sarre-Union, Drulingen and Petite-Pierre region, a medical officer remembered that men were treated as family members in return for help with farm work.[70] There were many relationships between soldiers and local young women.[71]

Often, however, relations were superficial and equivocal. The IEE intelligence agency reported that 'sympathy for France, polite silences, semi-mutism, and mental reservations hide mixed and worrying sentiments'.[72] Good manners ensured that even Moselle autonomist leader Antoni drank a Glühwein and discussed the war with three officers billeted in his home, one of whom was perhaps a police informer.[73] In other cases, alcohol removed inhibitions. For instance, Alphonse Simon, a fifty-seven-year-old ex-Feldwebel in the German army, was prosecuted for having claimed in a Metz café that 'we were better governed by Germany' and for singing the praises of the Nazis.[74]

Some interior French soldiers did not trust Alsace-Lorrainers, however hospitable. A soldier in Haut-Rhin thought that 'although locals look happy with us, they don't like us, for they sympathise with autonomism'.[75] Another reported that a 'comrade' was 'courageous enough to steal the watch belonging to the young woman who had so nicely welcomed us on our arrival'.[76] Sartre wrote that soldiers were 'lodged free by bourgeois, pampered by pretty girls and applauded by children, yet criticise Alsatians severely'.[77]

Sex remained a bone of contention. Church campaigners in Alsace-Lorraine had secured the closure of many licensed brothels. Yet fortification troops on short leaves in Mulhouse complained of the absence of 'certain distractions'. The local sub-prefect therefore considered reopening public brothels, while rigorously monitoring unlicensed prostitution.[78] The army was divided. Catholic officers often opposed them, as did the Premier Bureau (responsible for manpower), probably on public health grounds, while the Deuxième Bureau thought that licensed brothels limited clandestine prostitution and thus espionage. As a compromise, the EMA laid down in February 1940 that new institutions would be opened only exceptionally and only if the municipalities agreed, and that if municipalities proved negligent, the army itself would vet personnel, monitor public health measures and repress unregulated prostitution. All parties agreed on the need for brothels staffed by colonial women, so that colonial troops did not have relations with French women.[79] In SF-Montmédy, the Catholic Church lent buildings for this purpose.[80] As the Deuxième Bureau feared, the unregulated sex trade flourished in cafés.

In peacetime, cafés had witnessed clashes between interior French and Alsace-Lorraine young men over women and over who was entitled to drink where. Incidents continued in Bitche during the phoney war, where, on one occasion, civilians clubbed soldiers as they left a bistro. The latter responded with their belts and attacked the fleeing civilians.[81] More often, with young Alsace-Lorraine men mobilised elsewhere, cafés became places of the sexual domination of local women.[82] There, the reality was not of ersatz family life, but of infidelity, sexual harassment, paid sex and sometimes violence. Lieutenant Balbaud frequented cafés, where one 'flirts and dances', where girls from the Paris cabarets say that they have come to 'visit boyfriends'.[83] Sartre wrote of 'flattered and bold waitresses at the Écrivisse restaurant, who rub against men and suddenly call them to the cellar, from which they emerge tousled'. The 'unconventional' Sartre did not mention this in letters to his partner, Simone de Beauvoir.[84] Some soldiers appear to have believed that they had a right to sex, just as they had a right to loot. Visiting Sartre in Brumath, de Beauvoir twice experienced unwanted sexual attention from soldiers who assumed that women at the front were 'available'.[85] Even a 5th Army man who condemned infidelity blamed women for their behaviour while their husbands were at the front getting themselves shot.[86]

Within regiments, relations between interior French and Alsace-Lorraine soldiers, problematic in peacetime and worsened by pillage, never recovered. The Deuxième Bureau concluded that in certain units, after nearly seven months of living together, French and Alsatians did not mix, a consequence, it thought, of the latter's 'lack of élan'.[87] In outlying bunkers, French speakers were often a minority.[88] Hermann Bickler, leader of the Jungmannschaft, thought that two 'Altfranzösischen' men in his fifteen-man bunker 'must have felt curiously lost as we spoke German among ourselves'.[89] Two interior French dined each evening in a neighbouring bunker because the Alsatians in their own did not speak French.[90] As far away as Nancy, Georges Sadoul, film historian and communist activist, reported near-fisticuffs between interior French and those they called 'Alsacos'.[91]

The interior French accused Alsace-Lorrainers of offences ranging from praising German methods to speaking German dialects. One soldier complained about those who saw everything done by the French as bad and everything done in Germany as good – 'I sometimes ask whether I'm still in France.' A soldier in 79 RIF thought that Alsatians were completely unlike the French, and reported frequent fights. The censor remarked, 'Camaraderie does not reign among Alsatians and other provincials in this regiment.'[92]

Whereas the interior French did not refrain from criticising their Alsace-Lorraine comrades in their letters, the reverse was less common, probably for fear of prosecution. Some Alsace-Lorrainers expressed patriotic sentiments: on learning that Alsace-Lorrainers were to be granted special leaves, twenty soldiers wrote comments such as 'Vive la France!'[93] Yet abstract France was more appealing than its flesh-and-blood incarnation. Some criticised the interior French from the perspective of affronted patriotism. One wrote, on finding his house pillaged, 'That's what they do to soldiers ready to sacrifice their lives.'[94] A gunner (5th Army) could not understand why evacuees were called 'Boche', given that 'we are more sincerely and patriotically French than those of the interior'.[95] Some condemned the French more categorically. The Alsatians of 133 RIF apparently saw their interior French comrades as pillaging 'hordes', 'savages', 'bandits' and 'Indians'.[96]

That did not rule out tensions among Alsatians. Take for instance 22 RIF, stationed in the Haguenau Forest. Around 80 per cent of the NCOs and men of the regiment were Alsatian, as were 60 per cent of its officers. The 6th Company included no less than five Alsatian Catholic priests – one lieutenant and four sergeants. Most of the Alsatians were also practising Catholics. Their captain, Richard Pierron, however, was the offspring of the bilingual Francophone bourgeoisie of Mulhouse, which was typically nationalist, francophile, secularist, anti-clerical and often Calvinist. Pierron permitted the men to construct small chapels in the forest, yet repeatedly reprimanded them for spending more time tweaking these little edifices than constructing defences. When he threatened to demolish them if the priests continued to preach in German to soldiers who knew French, an argument ensued, Pierron recalled, about the 'too famous "Muttersprache" and the rights of the Alsatian clergy etc.'. Pierron had never accepted that one could be first Catholic, then Alsatian, and then French (that had been the view of Abbé Xavier Haegy, one of the autonomist leaders imprisoned following the trial at Colmar in 1928).[97] We shall see that this quarrel had repercussions during the battle.

Fighting Demoralisation

The high command's efforts to maintain morale were inspired by those that had supposedly ensured victory in the previous war, in which French soldiers had fought on while German morale collapsed.[98] They focussed primarily on improving material well-being, providing leaves and rest and stimulating troops' patriotism. The results were mixed, for the task was enormous and limited by the army's concern with hierarchy.

It was intrinsically difficult to improve life in the *ouvrages* and casemates. Gamelin and Prételat ordered more frequent reliefs and the external accommodation of non-essential personnel. Other suggestions included gymnastics outside the *ouvrages* or Swedish gymnastics inside, improving ventilation and showers, and short tours in the advance posts – perhaps not an enthralling prospect. Evaluation of these measures in February and March 1940 revealed a constant shortage of both trained replacements and of adequate accommodation for rest periods. In SF-Vosges, no CORF casemate crews were resting. No soldiers in 154 RIF were on relief, for there was no room in camps. Parliamentary inspectors regretted that nothing had been planned for long-term occupation. There were no recreation or dining spaces for the men, who were forced to eat in the galleries or on their bunks, and no meeting rooms for officers. The inspectors concluded that the men led a terrible existence.[99]

For those serving in the open air, leaves began in November. By May 1940, most soldiers had benefited from two two-week absences. Supplies of clothing also improved. However, rest in pillaged villages and camps was often less comfortable than in the position, as Lieutenant-Colonel René Rodolphe said of Oberhoffen camp.[100] Fighting boredom was harder than improving material conditions. Tours by the entertainers of the Théâtre aux Armées were valued by those who benefited, but visits were rare and seats were limited, some being reserved for officers and NCOs. Also of limited impact were lectures on elevating subjects – despite General Georges ordering subordinates to identify soldiers able to propagate the moral, social and patriotic ideas presented in lectures given by members of the High Council on Natality.[101]

The army promoted 'front newspapers' to relieve boredom and reinforce cohesion, but feared giving the soldiers a voice. Newspapers had to be authorised by the EMA and were obliged to restrict content to health advice, behaviour on leave, patriotic stories, innocuous cartoons and mildly satirical depictions of military life, without harming the prestige of the army. When the 3rd Army authorised expression of discontent in such a paper, it was quickly slapped down.[102] Some front newspapers nevertheless escaped censorship. Sapper Giroud helped edit a sheet called 'Sape gardée: manuel de savoir parer' – a play on defensive works intended to communicate that the newspaper was designed to help soldiers cope and to annoy officers. It was not antiwar.[103]

A new initiative, insignia for individual *ouvrages*, was also intended to sustain unit cohesion and reinforce hierarchy. Although designed by the officers and men themselves, these too required senior approval. Yet they sometimes provoked discord. At GO-Anzeling, in the spirit of harmony, an infantry lieutenant proposed representing each arm by a crenellated tower, cannon and armoured knight, with Anzeling church in the background. The artillery proposed a casemate with gun.[104]

Since only the largest *ouvrages*, such as Hackenberg, possessed a crew numerous enough to make the manufacture of enamel insignia economically viable, insignia were more usually painted on walls. In shared places, such as the main gallery, they included patriotic images – for instance, the tricolour and slogan 'Vanquish or die' in Bisterberg casemate (RF-Metz). Just as often, murals expressed the identity of specific arms in their own spaces rather than that of the *ouvrage* as a whole. At Latiremont an artillery bloc featured the insignia of the 22nd battery of 154 RAP.

Clubs (*foyers*) for the men and NCOs were more successful because they allowed men some latitude. Consisting of canteens, usually with a wireless and games and reading rooms, they were inevitably of uneven quality. Sadoul described a sorry space in a school classroom where soldiers sat on benches too small for them. Guizard liked his *foyer*, for chairs, magazines on tables, wireless and electricity 'remind us that we have not returned to prehistoric times'.[105] *Foyers* were inaccessible to those who spent months in *ouvrages*, casemates and blockhouses and even more so to those on advance-post duty.

With mixed results, soldiers found their own ways to fight boredom, loneliness, homesickness and fear, perhaps also to reconcile themselves to the necessity of war and the possibility of death, or to vent frustrations about military life and perhaps express antiwar feeling. Many found comfort in religion. Some Catholics, Guizard among them, thought they were witnessing a religious revival in a country that had been precociously dechristianised. Attendance at mass was higher than in peacetime, when male practice was usually low. A lieutenant in RF-Metz remarked, 'It is a beautiful spectacle, these churches filled with reflective men.' Probably correctly, he attributed this revival to service in Christian Lorraine, for church attendance was normal for local men in the regiments. The lieutenant also recognised that consciousness of imminent danger and suffering played a part.[106]

Lieutenant Felsenhardt explained that all the men in his unit were delighted to receive little medals of the Virgin from their new chaplain. He thought the chaplain was wrong to conclude that the war had brought them back to God, who had been dozing in their hearts thanks to easy living: Felsenhardt dared not say that they simply wanted protection against bad luck and insurance for the afterlife.[107] He was probably right in the sense that widespread belief in the power of such tokens reflected superstition as much as attraction to organised religion. Thus, another priest considered that although the men of his regiment esteemed him, they 'displayed complete ignorance of religious truths and worse, fantastic deformations in cases where some knowledge remains'. They saw religion as all well and good, so long as it did not ask anything of them.[108] Yet tokens could also represent stronger links to Catholic teaching and mean more than a passive acceptance of fate. The enormously popular cult of Saint-Thérèse de Lisieux, with its medals, pamphlets and relics, taught that religion was about 'resignation', which to Catholics meant not passivity but winning little victories in one's own domain.[109]

Catholicism was also linked to the traditional belief that France was the Church's favoured nation. A sergeant recounted to his wife a sermon in which the chaplain had assured the men that victory was certain because 'God is with us'. On another level, the many priests who served as sergeants or junior officers probably attenuated homesickness. Guizard was reassured by contact with a priest from Vannes, with whom he shared peacetime acquaintances.[110]

Religion could also divide. Unsurprisingly, given that many were primary-school teachers, not all officers were sympathetic to religion. Felsenhardt's colonel was a freethinker. Guizard's anticlerical captain forbade him to go to mass, and allegedly told another soldier to 'kneel before a tree to pray'.[111] Soldiers without religious faith found other ways to cope.

Soldiers' endless games of the card game belote are usually dismissed in the novelist Louis-Ferdinand Céline's contemptuous remark, 'The French army was expensive. 400 billion to flee [from the enemy], eight months of belote, one month of defeat.'[112] The quotation tells us more about Céline's elitist belief that 'the people had no ideals', only 'needs', than about troops' attitudes.[113] In fact, belote involves bidding for contracts with a partner against another pair. The combination of hope and chance releases dopamine and counters depression, entailing both recognition that one's future depends on being dealt 'good cards' and the ability to play the hand one gets.

Le cafard remained the primary way of labelling and dealing with discomfort. Giroud joked on rejoining his regiment that men drew barracks slang, such as 'Ça me fait chier' (It's pissing me off), from military stores along with their kit.[114] In the *ouvrages*, the term '*bétonite*' (concretitis), denoting lassitude due to inaction and confined air, was ready to be used.[115] Even Sartre, who as an existentialist philosopher held that reliance on clichés was an excuse not to make one's own life, ultimately accepted that the term had some value. The pro-socialist writer and literary critic Claude Jamet remained contemptuous of military slang.[116]

Le cafard retained its old association with homesickness. A soldier in 52 DI wrote, 'What *cafard* again on Sunday! There are days when nothing is right. Why? Undefinable . . . A vague ennui, the impression of loneliness, of inactivity, the sense of mourning for the fine days and hours of the past, a little of all of that, nothing, everything at once . . .

May it come, good God, the most blessed day of all when we are together again.'[117]

Songs retained their ability to provoke *le cafard* without demoralisation, for singing, especially collectively, releases dopamine, oxytocin and serotonin. A soldier remarked that it was not a bad thing that songs at a theatre performance triggered memories and *le cafard*.[118] Guizard celebrated his birthday with food parcels, belote and singing, to which he contributed a rendition of what he called 'Le Grand Nil Bleu' – he probably meant 'La légende du Nil', an escapist and nostalgic song.[119] The composer Olivier Messiaen, mobilised in a pioneer regiment near Sarreguemines, feared that using a pickaxe and carrying unbelievably heavy weights would destroy his keyboard technique. He nevertheless sang morsels of melodies while on guard duty as his feet burned with cold.[120] While it is hardly surprising that Messiaen resorted to music, other soldiers did the same in the most adverse conditions. A soldier in a reconnaissance unit saw 'poor squaddies' going up to the line, their knees in snow, with huge kitbags on their back. Yet they were in good humour and sang as best they could. 'In the end, what can you do?' he asked. 'We have to put up with all this courageously.'[121]

In this sense, soldiers proved their manhood and possibly patriotism by assuming their *cafard*. It is significant, therefore, that the word was not used to describe the experience of the advance posts. As a gunner put it, 'Since we have been ready to fire our guns, I no longer have *le cafard* and wait with a smile.' He remembered his father who had served before him.[122]

Roland Dorgelès, reporting for the weekly *Gringoire*, used the term 'cafard' in this same optimistic sense. He admitted that the men suffered from *bétonite* on account of the damp, poor air quality and the absence of women. But he and the *ouvrage* doctor agreed that, like *le cafard*, *bétonite* was curable by a glass of wine, a song or a letter.[123] Lieutenant-Colonel Rodolphe, probably one of the officers Dorgelès consulted, saw the article as 'remarkable'.[124] Jamet, who read it just before he visited GO-Billig, thought it fine for members of the Académie Goncourt (i.e. Dorgelès) to find it all charming, but 'the medical profession will have much to say about what becomes of men subjected to such strange conditions – physical state, moral state. Humidity, insipid heat, overpressure, blinking lights, isolation in this cave and idleness in this tube.'[125]

In fact, 'cafard' also gained a new, perhaps more negative meaning, linked to a state of chronic low physiological arousal as a result of inactivity, compounded by the slowing of bodily and mental functions consequent upon cold weather. Soldiers expressed this form of *cafard* to outsiders as boredom to the point of stupidity and emptiness. Sartre wrote, 'When I write that I'm tired, it's wrong. I am simply empty and turned into a moron.'[126] An adjutant in 22 RIF wrote that after six months without relief, he had given up all socialising and was living as a brute with an immense sorrow and no occupation to divert the flow of his thoughts.[127] Another soldier wanted the photographer responsible for 'cute magazine photos of the Maginot Line' to swap places and would not tell her/him that he would emerge an 'illuminé', a play on the association in French between light and madness.[128] One 153 RIF officer was evacuated for depression; another, who saw enemies everywhere, turned a submachine gun on his fellows – fortunately he was overpowered before hurting anyone.[129] In the most extreme cases, soldiers took their own lives, the Deuxième Bureau attributing suicide to 'extreme *cafard*'.[130] There were fifty-eight such tragedies in Alsace-Lorraine between the declaration of war and 30 April 1940.[131]

Songs did not necessarily unite. Sadoul wrote that on hearing Alsatian soldiers sing beautiful hymns, the interior French asked why they could not sing in French like everyone else.[132] Sadoul also remembered that in singing George Brassens's 'Le revenant', soldiers screamed out with 'frenetic anger' the line 'Ah, c'qu'on s'émmerd'ici!' (Oh, how pissed off we are here!). The piano in the café frequented by Sadoul's unit was mostly used to play popular songs. The occasional singing of the communist anthem 'The Internationale' was met by indifference, but the 'Marseillaise' provoked shouts of 'Shut up, dirty brown-noser!'[133] Some troops were antipatriotic, but the male taboo about expressing emotion extended to patriotism. And ridiculing patriotism allowed soldiers to obey while preserving their sense of self.

Often accustomed to heavy drinking in peacetime, soldiers also resorted to alcohol. The army supplied a daily ration of 25cl – far less than the litre per day allowed at the end of the previous war. The wine lobby, which presented wine, beer and cider as 'healthy drinks', agitated for increased rations, but did not prevail against the public-health lobby. Soldiers stationed away from the front nevertheless bought wine – 'pinard' in military argot – in cafés, shops and military cooperatives. In long evenings, drinking was one of the few available pastimes.[134] In February, the Deuxième Bureau reported that alcoholism was multiplying in labour battalions, pioneer regiments and fortified sectors. In the *ouvrages*, drunken soirées were not unknown in the officers' mess.[135]

Alcohol consumption initially suppresses inhibitions and reduces anxiety in situations from social interaction to combat. Often, therefore, drinking provoked arguments and fights. Soon, however, alcohol's depressant effects lead to anger, morosity and depression. Regular consumption leads to a vicious cycle in which alcohol's power to reduce anxiety is attenuated, leading to more drinking. In the cold weather, the heaviest drinkers probably withdrew into themselves. In April 1940, the Deuxième Bureau saw the alcoholism noted in many units as the only dark point in generally good morale reports – to the point, it wrote, that doctors were concerned about the future of the race. Soldiers deprived of drink during their front-line tours often spent their entire combat bonus on drink afterwards, provoking one soldier to remark that, thanks to falls and fights, there were more wounded than on the front line.[136] And as always, alcohol complicated discipline.

Discipline

The few comments about officers in letters written during the first months of hostilities were mainly positive, but included some negative remarks. One correspondent, for instance, remarked that an 8th Army captain was 'très gentil'; another that discipline was too harsh in 107 BCA (Bataillon de chasseurs alpins), stationed at Le Queyras in the High Alps.[137] In late November 1940, a 3rd Army lieutenant was said to have loaned one soldier money and had his mother send a food parcel to another needy man.[138]

Soldiers were especially complimentary about their officers over Christmas and New Year. At this time of family togetherness, when homesickness was particularly strong, officers' distribution of presents, such as woollens knitted by their wives, sometimes created a father–son bond between officers and men. It is also possible to find a sense of equality. An NCO in 23 RAMF wrote that officers and men, who were all 'just big kids', joined together in snowball fights.[139]

As winter progressed, criticism of officers grew, especially on the front from the Sarre to the Lauter. A soldier in 22 RIF, for instance, complained that he had returned to his casemate from leave to find the same 'bastard who's beginning to seriously get on my nerves'.[140] The men of 71 RI, in the freezing Sarre advance posts, complained that some had been sent to the guardhouse for wearing their collars turned up or having a dirty greatcoat.[141] Even Guizard found it 'abusive' that a 'good little bloke' had copped a week for not having saluted a lieutenant.[142]

Sadoul recounted several cases in which soldiers expressed a desire to kill their officers. Given that threats of violence, usually drunken, were so often prosecuted in military tribunals in peacetime, and were part of the ritual of liberation from service, these cases are plausible. As a communist, Sadoul was on the lookout for class consciousness, but recognised that these threats stemmed from other motives. He himself distinguished between good and bad officers.[143]

Sartre's observations are informative. He wrote that wherever he went, he found 'the same hatred of officers, a hatred reasoned and profound . . . which has nothing in common with antimilitarism'. At Detwiller, he heard from men who were angry that a captain had punished some comrades by making them stand facing a wall for two hours; they would have preferred four days in prison to this insult to their dignity as men. They warned that officers would not get away with this for ever. Yet they did not question the war.[144]

The dissonance between the high command's view of discipline and the soldier's attachment to the republican idea of the patriotic citizen-soldier emerges clearly from one letter. The writer was prepared to make enormous sacrifices, but could not accept being treated as a 'digestive tube', easily satisfied with cheap wine and a military social club, 'as if that served to fill the heart and mind; we wish to be treated as men, to be spared bureaucratic bullying and officers' brusque behaviour'.[145] The common criticism of officers as 'skirt chasers' also betrayed the egalitarian assumption that soldiers too had a 'right' to women.[146]

Some reserve officers probably embraced the republican command model. Roland de Margerie, a high-ranking diplomat who served in 152 RI on the Maginot Line, recalled that reserve officers were more intimate with the troops than the professionals, a fact he attributed to reserve officers' demagogy, egalitarianism and shared amateurism.[147] Professionals' distance, particularly pronounced in the 'organised' fortifications, was confirmed by another reserve officer, who described them as 'bureaucrats'.[148] Soldiers certainly responded differently to reserve officers. Giroud related that a private had told a reserve lieutenant who threatened him with a military tribunal not to take himself for an active or an adjutant.[149] A 5th Army pioneer wrote home that they were commanded by recalled men who 'allow a certain liberty, which makes us almost forget that we are soldiers'.[150]

Indiscipline varied with time and place. There was much disobedience in the confusion of mobilisation, when units in the process of formation were often left to their own devices. Giroud and his friends, first stationed in SF-Briançon, took an unauthorised trip to Lyon. They met their lieutenant on the way, but refused his order to return. He was in no position to insist, given that officers' wives were sharing their lodgings.[151]

Pillage undermined discipline. An officer remembered that having sacked the village of Sierck, the men of 57 RI resembled a 'savage horde as much as a team of removal men'. Some carried bulging suitcases, others pulled carts filled with objects and others still led dogs, cows and pigs. All the men were wearing balaclavas and some sported women's furs or blankets. The colonel stripped the men of their prizes and ordered them to parade.[152]

At the front, disobedience was rare, and not simply because desertion and disobedience in the face of the enemy were serious offences. Those manning the advance posts lived on their nerves during the night, and slept and worked during the day. Indirect evidence suggests that the usual requirements for buttoning greatcoats and saluting were relaxed as junior officers and men lived together.

Further back in the intervals, desertion and unauthorised absence were often excused. Guizard, stationed on the third line, noted that his captain ignored his having returned a day late from leave.[153] With the tacit approval of their officers, the Alsatians of a labour battalion habitually left for home on Saturday evenings and returned the next day after mass.[154] Sanctions were more likely in aggravated cases. A sergeant in 37 RIF in SF-Vosges received a week for having given an Alsatian a false pass to visit his family. He did not regret having helped a man who had gone three months without seeing his family only twenty-two kilometres away.[155] Sartre witnessed the trial of a cyclist messenger who had spent ten unauthorised days with his pregnant girlfriend. His lieutenant, although terribly intimidated by the court, spoke on the accused's behalf, but could not save him from a year in prison.[156]

Indiscipline was most common in the rear. Whereas officers saw it as essential to 'take back in hand' units whose discipline had been relaxed at the front, the men saw manoeuvres and revues as 'inappropriate', because they had earned their rest and were not 'novices' (*bleus*). Some wrote home that they had been happier at the front.[157]

Desertion cases prosecuted in the tribunals largely concerned the depots and service units. The one surviving series of tribunal records – fifty-three in SF-Boulay for the eight months of the phoney war – shows a substantial drop in direct refusal of orders from 43 per cent in the prewar sample to 21 per cent.[158] Overwhelmingly, tribunals dealt with desertion, which increased from 11 to 38 per cent. All but three of 168 depot troops prosecuted in the 20th Region were accused of desertion.[159]

In the *ouvrages*, isolation from the exterior, strict work routines and confined space reduced opportunities for disobedience. Most visitors commented on the orderliness of *ouvrages*, and barely distinguished men from machines. Jamet saw GO-Billig as an 'incredible war machine' in which 'everything has been foreseen . . . Everything except human life. Iron discipline keeps the crew upstanding, fixed! No matter where – kitchen, infirmary . . .' – at least as long as the officer is looking.[160] The qualification suggests that all was not always as it semed.

On 10 October 1939, the commander of SF-Faulquemont asked *ouvrage* and casemate commanders for lists of men unsuited to service. In return, he received a veritable rogues' gallery of individuals serving in Laudrefang, Bambesch, Einseling, Teting and Kerfent in SF-Faulquemont and in Mottenberg and Coume in SF-Boulay, along with a few members of casemate crews. Some were physically unfit, but most were bad influences. At Bambesch, for instance, four men accomplished their tasks with ill-will, only under constant surveillance and threat of punishment. At Kerfent, eight men on detachment from the regimental depot had long histories of punishment and prison. Given that Alsace-Lorrainers were vetted before being allowed to serve in the *ouvrages*, it is not surprising that the overwhelming majority of those listed were interior French.[161] However, when *ouvrage* crews were sent for rest, Alsace-Lorrainers could not resist visiting their relatives. Rodolphe remembered that prison sentences rained down.[162]

Opposition to the War?

Officers' assessment of communist danger in the army was mixed.[163] As in peacetime, many considered that their ability to command brought out the patriotism of these misled Frenchmen. Few saw an organised communist danger within regiments. For instance, despite RIFs being off limits to communist activists, Auguste Lecœur, a high-ranking party member from the Pas-de-Calais, was assigned to a fortification regiment at the end of a spell in prison for attempting to reconstitute the banned party. His captain promised that he would be treated like any other soldier so long as he behaved as they did.[164] Communist slogans – unlike pacifist ones – were rarely picked up by postal censors.[165] Yet Rodolphe contrasted discipline in the *ouvrages* with 'the sad slackness of certain groups, due to mediocre leadership and unrestricted demagogy', blaming both poor leadership and political agitation.[166]

Crémieux-Brilhac is probably right that communist themes circulated in private conversations, where they converged with more traditional left-wing pacifism. Giroud, for instance, a socialist pacifist, hesitated between antifascism and seeing the war as a struggle between the British and the Nazis as the communists did. He recorded several political discussions in the unit, in which, for instance, Sapper Narboud espoused the whole communist line without being a member of the party.[167]

Communist sympathisers were most common in northern Alsace and Moselle, for to take advantage of rapid rail links, RFs Metz and Lauter recruited significantly from the Paris and northeast regions and

Moselle steel towns where the party was influential. Several of the soldiers listed by SF-Faulquemont as unfit for *ouvrage* service were probably communists.[168] Given that troops pillaged officers' houses and military property as well as Alsace-Lorrainers' homes, it is possible that communist antimilitarism and class resentment sometimes motivated it.[169] And only on this border, in SF-Vosges, is there an example of French soldiers initiating fraternisation with the Germans, which was party policy (the Germans usually took the lead). In this case, responsibility lay with two interior Frenchmen, while Alsatians initially 'hung back'.[170] Also in this area, in GO-Michelsberg, the chance discovery of a communist tract in a book led to the arrest of men involved in distributing propaganda and even turned up a plot to destroy the *ouvrage* – perhaps as a response to French plans to support the Finns in their war with the Soviet Union, which had just begun. Several soldiers expressed satisfaction at the arrests in their letters home, while prudently claiming not to have suspected anything themselves.[171]

Anticommunism was probably stronger than communism among the troops. The Nazi–Soviet Pact was widely condemned. Some soldiers had not forgotten the 'crimes' of the Popular Front, when communists' impossible wage demands had supposedly pushed France to the edge. And now, they thought, communist workers remained in the factories while the 'flower of youth' got itself killed for ten sous a day.[172] A few correspondents were ready to volunteer to fight for Finland. A soldier in 37 RIF concluded that the Russians, 'even more than the Boche, are the evil genies of Europe'. Another asked why Thorez, Marty and other communist leaders had not been shot.[173] Anticommunism was shared by many Alsace-Lorrainers and linked to antipathy for Hitler. One wrote that 'everyone is returning to religion and there are no more communists among us'. He did not want a 'Moscow peace', only a 'peace that allowed us to live as men, not in the Hitler style'.[174]

Not surprisingly, few Alsace-Lorraine soldiers expressed autonomist or anti-French sentiments in their letters. One, however, wrote to an evacuated friend that freedom depended on chasing the Jews from Alsace and that he could not regard the French as liberators.[175] A soldier in 60 RAMF (Régiment d'artillerie mobile de forteresse, SF-Vosges) wrote that the treatment of evacuees caused him to lose all respect for France; he dreamed of leaving the country.[176] More optimistic for the future of autonomism, an artillery corporal (bombardier) thought that the ignoble treatment of refugees would reinforce Alsace-Lorrainers' 'ties and feeling', with positive results after the war.[177] Alphonse Vollmer was prosecuted for declaring while on leave in the southwest that German soldiers were better, and that if he was ordered to attack, he would put a bullet in his own leg.[178]

The Deuxième Bureau claimed that since the Germans knew that the Maginot Line was inviolable, they would attempt to circumvent it by undermining the morale of the people.[179] German propaganda themes were simple: Germany had no quarrel with France and no claim on Alsace-Lorraine; the war was being fought for the British Empire and City of London; the French were on the front line while the British seduced their wives. On 6 October 1939, Hitler reiterated in a major broadcast that he wanted peace with France.

The Germans dropped thirty million leaflets. Loudspeakers on the banks of the Rhine reached a limited audience, but German radio was widely listened to.[180] French radio was highbrow and intermittent, while German radio continuously broadcast popular music interspersed with 'news' in French. Radio Stuttgart broadcast shows written by the far-right Frenchman Paul Ferdonnet, which were especially popular. Furthermore, there was hardly any German-language programming on French radio, for Radio Strasbourg had been evacuated to Paris, from where it retransmitted national programmes in French – including Parisian local news. Alsace-Lorrainers listened instead to German radio, which was not forbidden in cafés until March.[181]

The impact of this propaganda is difficult to measure. Loudspeaker propaganda and banners were often mocked, and provoked jocular replies. The anti-British slogan 'La France aux Français', for instance, was answered by 'La Pologne aux Polonais'. Sadoul wrote that Alsace-Lorrainers chuckled during speeches by Goering and Hitler, dismissing them as the 'same old stuff'. A soldier in 10 RIF, probably Alsatian, wrote that we 'know this band of pigs and mock their crazy ravings'; he had only to remember 'Herr Schulmeister's cane'.[182] Some soldiers recognised that the Germans were attempting to divide the Allies.

German propaganda struck a chord with others. After all, only a few months previously, during the Munich crisis, many had been ready to believe Hitler's reassurances. The conviction that British troops were fighting to the last Frenchman was a recurrent theme in letters home. Nazi propaganda attacks on British imperialism and capitalism converged with communist themes.[183]

Hitler's reassurance that he had no designs on Alsace-Lorraine resonated in the province, for appeasement had been particularly strong there. Once war broke out, the belief spread that German failure to bombard Alsace proved Hitler's goodwill.[184] The IEE reported that in Colmar, Haguenau and northern Bas-Rhin there was a potentially dangerous 'muted anxiety', stirred up by German radio.[185] Alsatians in SF-Vosges were said to hope for a 'prompt solution to the present war'.[186] They were not alone. As the winter progressed, soldiers became convinced that their leaders were secretly negotiating peace. It did not necessarily follow that they wanted peace on any terms, but the Deuxième Bureau was concerned.

Morale Improves . . .

From late February, as the first sunny days began to melt the snow, morale improved. *Ouvrage* crews were delighted to be able to take the air, practise sports and work on external defences.[187] Better weather also brought the expectation of active operations, preoccupation with which began to jostle in soldiers' letters with speculation about a compromise peace.[188]

Attitudes fluctuated with the weather and the international situation. In late March and until mid-April, the mood darkened again as the rain returned and the visit of the American diplomat Sumner Welles to the Vatican, Rome and Berlin provoked belief that peace was near – though not necessarily that it would solve anything. Indeed, soldiers perceived peace between Finland and Russia (12 March) as a new Munich.[189] The replacement of Daladier at the head of the government by Paul Reynaud (21 March) was largely seen as a political distraction, though some expected more energetic prosecution of the war.

The German occupation of Denmark and Norway (8 April) and the Allied response, the Deuxième Bureau testified, 'whipped up morale' again.[190] Guizard commented that events disproved German radio's claim that the 'English' don't fight.[191] Soon afterwards, spring arrived for good. On 19 April, Guizard wrote that 'rays of sun are brightening up the woods. It's easier to hear the birds sing, and for two days, cuckoos have been calling.'[192] Anti-German sentiment remained strong. A sergeant in southern Alsace claimed to prefer death rather than live under the heel of a band of bloodthirsty savages and liars.[193] The idea of a compromise peace disappeared, though outlooks fluctuated as news good and bad arrived. Even the Sarre Gap, where units had been discouraged by pillage in November, no longer attracted Deuxième Bureau attention. Its final summary before the battle began concluded, 'One feels that the army will rediscover, when the moment comes, all its élan.'[194]

. . . but Not Everyone's

In fact, morale remained problematic in the heavily fortified zone from SF-Haguenau to SF-Vosges. In late March, the intelligence services reported that while many Alsace-Lorrainers were for 'total victory', fear that fighting would bring further evacuation, pillage and sacrifice provided openings for autonomists.[195] The morale of several *ouvrages* was also said to be low in this area.[196] It would be a mistake, however, to detect a simple divide between interior French patriotism and Alsace-Lorraine doubts.

Take 172 RIF, stationed in the Strasbourg sector from which around 30 per cent of the regiment's men hailed. On the one hand, in an area in which part of the bourgeoisie was traditionally bilingual, ties developed between regulars and locals in associations of reserve officers and NCOs. On the other hand, Strasbourg was a stronghold of pro-autonomist communism. The Deuxième Bureau stated that morale was especially low among Alsatians in the regiment. Infantry Sergeant Kuntz, who was punished for 'anti-French views', protested his Frenchness and threatened retribution against the sappers who had denounced him. A lieutenant doubted that his men would hold under fire. A captain decried the quality of other officers. Depression was widespread and there was at least one suicide.[197]

The CDF's expectation in 1926 that fortification would restore traditional command, provide habitable conditions through improvement of the physical environment and help reintegrate Alsace-Lorraine into the nation had not been realised. Dispersal of the troops, antipathy between interior French and Alsace-Lorrainers and the inability to control geology, air quality and hydrology, not to speak of the weather, all ensured that these objectives were not met. Morale as measured by the army suffered, and problems particularly affected the heavily fortified northern Alsace and contiguous Moselle.

Yet the army's maximalist definition of morale as 'faith in the grandeur and destiny of the country, conviction in fighting for a just cause, confidence in one's leaders, one's comrades and one's own value' did not help it understand that Alsace-Lorrainers might attack France for not recognising their patriotism or that republicans might fight Nazism (and perhaps communism too) as republican citizens.[198] The point, however, is not to prove that the French were not decadent after all, but to understand how soldiers on the Maginot Line put their experience into words. Whether and how these inconsistent, diverse and shifting outlooks mattered in combat is only one aspect of the question, and it depended on, amongst other things, how units were deployed and the actions of the enemy, to which we now turn our attention.

11

CONTACT

In its 1926 proposal for fortified regions, the CDF had envisaged 'an organisation permitting important economies in manpower' on the German and Italian frontiers, thus permitting the mass of the French army to be deployed in the north. The CDF wanted the interval between RFs Lauter and Metz kept open to trap the enemy and considered that a second line was unnecessary, for in the unlikely event of a breakthrough in the fortified zones, field armies would counterattack. Potential intervention in Belgium remained central to all French plans subsequently, and in the later 1930s reform of the regulations, mechanisation and motorisation widened the tactical possibilities.

Yet the organisationalist principles of the fortifications, the commitment to top-down command and the desire to cover all angles of attack created increasing demands for manpower and weaponry. The tendency towards stasis and bureaucratisation increased because Pétain and the left prioritised organisation of defences for a long attritional war, and were more cautious about intervention in Belgium. They were responsible for dividing the whole frontier into defensive and fortified sectors manned by a growing number of immobile fortification units.

On the eve of war, the army planned both for a long war and for intervention in Belgium and/or Switzerland, the precise purpose of these operations remaining uncertain. Gamelin saw the Belgian theatre as decisive, and had always advocated manoeuvre in defence and attack, while his deputy Georges was more cautious. Officers generally preferred service in manoeuvrable field units to the fortifications, without necessarily having clear ideas about doctrine. In the public sphere, doubts about whether France could win a long war emerged, while Pétain warned against the return of offensive doctrine.

During the phoney war, conflict over strategy and doctrine intensified. The French deployed huge forces on the Maginot Line and began constructing new defences, yet developed plans for ever more ambitious operations from the Arctic to the Caucasus and for assistance to the Belgians, Dutch and Swiss. To improve the field army's capacity for manoeuvre, the army attempted to reform the fortifications' command structure and convert RIFs into campaign units. On the Maginot Line, junior officers pressed for new methods. Yet as a bureaucracy and interest group, the fortifications resisted reform and weighed heavily on French choices, which were in any case limited.

Options

The army was well aware that initial defence permitted the enemy to concentrate overwhelming force on a weak point, and that fortifications always succumbed if the enemy devoted sufficient means and paid the price. The generals knew that Oberstleutnant Walter Spannenkrebs had written a book claiming that the Maginot Line's small number of *ouvrages* and lack of depth made it vulnerable to frontal attack with heavy tanks and assault engineers.[1] Since Germany did not possess heavy tanks, such an attack was unlikely. The French knew from intelligence reports, however, that German experiments on captured Czech forts revealed them to be more resistant than expected to conventional artillery and aerial bombing, but vulnerable to high-velocity 88mm antitank fire against embrasures.

The long-war strategy was also dangerous. Some feared that the Allied economic blockade of Germany would force Hitler into an early attack on France before the Allies acquired material superiority. They were right: the war's catastrophic effect on the German economy persuaded Hitler to throw caution aside, whatever the economic consequences. Alarmed, his generals plotted but did not act.[2]

In France, although the intelligence services reported German difficulties, doubts that the Allies were better placed than the Germans to fight a long war grew. Polish resistance did not last. The Nazi–Soviet Pact appeared (misleadingly) to provide Germany with vast new resources and the blockade seemed ineffective. Paul Morand, a diplomat responsible for blockade policy in London, wrote in January 1940, 'I think that presently and until spring, time works for us, but afterwards, it will be the opposite, for the Germans will organise the Russians, once the latter have stopped skidding on the spare wheel.'[3]

To hasten German collapse, some politicians and generals urged peripheral operations. Weygand, recalled to command in the Levant, championed a Balkan operation, for he thought it impossible to defeat Germany 'on the little Rhine–Moselle front' and that time favoured communism.[4] This scheme foundered in the face of opposition from the British and Gamelin. In December 1939, when war broke out between Russia and Finland, some favoured combining help for the Finns with interrupting transport of Swedish iron ore through Norway to Germany. The Allies also considered bombing Russian oil-producing facilities at Baku. Gamelin largely prioritised intervention in the Low Countries and ultimately invasion of Germany. He was pessimistic about the long term.

The French made an enormous effort. They initially mobilised twenty-nine classes of conscripts, though in the oldest classes only reserve officers in their forties remained under the colours.[5] Germany mobilised only seven classes. In January, Gamelin reminded Daladier that France had reached its limit, whereas Germany presently disposed of 135 divisions on the western front and would soon have 160. In reality, it deployed 135 in May, by which time France had 100 divisions, including 10 in training and 10 British. Gamelin saw the coming year as potentially 'decisive and difficult', and whatever happens, he added, 'it must seal the failure or impotence of Germany'. He accepted that British support would increase and that twenty Belgian and ten Dutch divisions redressed the balance numerically, but he doubted their quality.[6] These fears help to explain why Gamelin's plans became bolder.

Assaulting the Westwall (the Siegfried Line)

Despite extravagant promises to the Poles, Gamelin never planned more than a token offensive into the Saar. He warned that it must not compromise intervention in the Low Countries and/or Switzerland. In July 1939, trials on mock-ups of Westwall bunkers under General Condé's auspices anyway concluded that the army lacked the necessary air superiority, heavy artillery, shells with base fuses able to explode after penetrating concrete and equipment for crossing antitank obstacles.[7] In reality, the Allies cynically counted on six months of Polish resistance to allow their war industries to mobilise. Gamelin instructed Georges merely to plan a 'methodical' engagement with German defences.[8]

Polish setbacks prompted Gamelin to bring the operation forward to 7 September, earlier than the twenty-one days originally thought necessary. If the operation was quicker off the mark, however, execution was pitifully slow compared to the German advance in Poland. Under cover of Hochwald's 75s, nine divisions crawled five kilometres forward on a fifteen-mile front on either flank of the Forbach and Stiring-Wendel salient. Mines, the real surprise weapon of 1940, were an unexpected hazard. Booby traps were attached, one soldier wrote home, to apples on trees, dead hares and gendarmes' kepis.[9] Field commanders were asked to designate parts of the Westwall for experimental attack, but that was all.

Although the purpose of the offensive was ostensibly to divert German forces from Poland, Gamelin used the first sign that divisions were moving west as an excuse to scale it down. On 14 September, troops were ordered to adopt a defensive stance, and from the 16th they disengaged when confronted with limited counterattacks. A rearguard remained on German soil until 16–17 October, when it withdrew entirely in the face of a larger counteroffensive.[10] In their letters home, soldiers reported (falsely) that the Germans had been lured onto French 75s, suffering thousands of casualties.[11]

Some French commanders saw halting the Saar offensive as a missed opportunity, but the Westwall was a tough nut. At the time of Munich, a paltry 517 bunkers had been complete; now, there were 11,283, interspersed with minefields.[12] General Paul-Henry Gerodias, commanding

29 DIA at Forbach, thought it impossible to create a pocket in the Westwall because the further one advanced, the narrower the front became.[13] The shortness of the frontier made it hard to mount diversionary attacks. The Westwall proved its strength in late 1944, when it inflicted a major defeat on the Americans in the Hürtgenwald.

Nonetheless, the French planned a diversionary action in 1940 to be put into effect in the event of German violation of Belgian neutrality and a full-scale assault in 1941. Condé's 1939 study concluded that by 1 July 1940 the army would have sufficient artillery and B1 bis heavy tanks to open a gap of four kilometres, eleven kilometres by October 1940 and twenty-eight kilometres by 1 March 1941.[14] In January 1940, Prételat's staff produced a plan to overwhelm the Westwall advance posts and break through on a front of twenty to twenty-five kilometres using forty-five infantry divisions, twenty battalions of tanks and two heavy-armoured divisions (DCrs – Divisions cuirassées).[15] Georges ordered training on mock-ups of the Westwall in special camps, not in the rear of the army zone. In spring 1940, for instance, 36 DI left the RF-Metz advance posts to begin such training at Mailly Camp.[16]

As so often, tactical instructions were divided between control, method, mobility and dispersal. In July 1939, regulations for breaching fortified fronts laid down that in the first stage, specialised units would infiltrate, outflank and overwhelm enemy advance posts. In the second, 'method' and frequent pauses would take over. Artillery would destroy bunkers and demoralise defenders. Self-propelled artillery and heavy B1 bis tanks able to cover churned-up ground would then fire at embrasures before infantry attacked them. During the Saar offensive, guidance was updated. Rather than pause once blockhouses had been neutralised, assault infantry would immediately move on to the next blockhouses, leaving following infantry to finish them off. The guidance emphasised coordination at battalion level, and warned against excessive dispersal while allowing it in some circumstances. Light tanks would exploit the breach.[17] Of course, we cannot know how the assault planned for 1941 would have proceeded in practice. We only know that discussion among senior commanders continued and that views were evolving.

De Gaulle, for instance, no longer advocated using armoured divisions to seize bargaining chips across the border. As commander of 5th

Army tanks, he persuaded army commander General Bourret to plan a mass armoured counterattack against a German assault on the Lauter and to allow him to study a future offensive.[18]

In January 1940, visiting 5th Army HQ with Reynaud, de Gaulle maintained that an immediate attack on the Westwall was feasible. Bourret and his chief of staff, the future Marshal Jean de Lattre de Tassigny, objected that the army lacked aviation, heavy artillery and heavy tanks. Even if they broke through, 100 Allied divisions would soon face 180–200 German – a commander who ordered such an assault would be hanged![19] A few days later, in a famous memorandum to Weygand, Gamelin and Georges, de Gaulle showed that he had listened. He accused them of watching passively through the observation slits of their fortifications while Hitler enslaved Europe, and predicted 'movements, surprises, irruptions and pursuits, of which the scale and rapidity will infinitely surpass the most dazzling events of the past'. Yet he also accepted that both sides' fortifications were currently invulnerable, even to the light tanks used by the Germans in Poland. He recommended the development of heavy tanks of 100 metric tonnes able to break through successive lines (way beyond the technology of the day and French productive capacity) for a future offensive. Gamelin later claimed to have discussed deploying heavy tanks against the Westwall with de Gaulle. True or not, their ideas had converged.[20]

Meanwhile, General Charles Huntziger, commander of the 2nd Army, suggested replacing artillery preparation with surprise aerial bombing to stun the defenders and disrupt fields of fire by churning up the ground rather than destroy blockhouses, immediately followed by assault infantry alone, for tanks would be unable to cross bomb craters. The procedure would be repeated for the second line, and the breach would be exploited by infantry and horse cavalry, followed when possible by armoured and motorised divisions. Huntziger asked how worried the French would be if they thought that the Germans intended such an attack against the Maginot Line.[21] Of course, they did plan one in his sector, but did not have to worry about a second line, because it was incomplete.

Defending the Maginot Line

On mobilisation, the Maginot Line constituted a single line without a second line. Some *ouvrages* were incomplete. The intervals lacked trenches and concrete shelters; advance posts had to be constructed from scratch. The flooding and light fortification in the Sarre Gap remained vulnerable. An attack southward through the Marville Gap between SF-Montmédy and RF-Metz might knock over the *ouvrages* like dominos. Lightly fortified sectors – the Sarre Gap, southern Alsace and the Jura on the Swiss border and most of the Luxembourg–Belgium border – required improvement. There was no second line anywhere besides the old Verdun–Metz complex and the former German fortifications of Mutzig–Molsheim. How and what to prioritise was controversial.

Gamelin had always seen discontinuous moles as compensation for the weakness of continuous lines and their lack of depth, thus eliminating the need for a second line. Yet he imposed his preferences intermittently. Consequently, existing defences mixed continuity and moles. On mobilisation, he instructed subordinates to work within existing plans, while constructing advance posts and adding depth to the resistance position with 'durable field fortification'.[22]

In October 1939, Gamelin told Georges that outside the CORF fronts, units must prepare strongpoints and even 'veritable bridgeheads' in advance of the resistance line, able to delay and counterattack the enemy. He claimed that the 'unimaginative' German attackers must be set puzzles and urged subordinates to 'conduct' rather than 'endure' (*subir*) the battle, for only on CORF fronts could the French hope to hold the Germans on the resistance line.[23] Yet he told Senator Jacques Bardoux that, since it was discontinuous, even the Maginot Line was not invulnerable: 'I do not believe in a war like 1914–18: two immobile fronts. There will be salients, because armies now dispose of the means to make a breakthrough and use it. When one launches armoured divisions through a gap, one cannot know where they will halt.'[24]

Georges thought that Gamelin expected the French to fight in open country. He saw second lines as essential everywhere – even behind the Maginot Line. He passed on Gamelin's 'suggestions' to his subordinates as commands, ordering them never to 'whirl around' or 'surge back' if bypassed by tanks, and instructed them to hold out while awaiting counterattacks from a second line. Projects were to be submitted to him, so that they did not upset prepared fire plans.[25]

On 4 September, Gamelin established a Commission d'études des zones fortifiées (CEZF), charged with providing army commanders with technical advice on fieldworks and with constructing a second line along the entire frontier using private contractors' industrial equipment and labour. To preside over the CEFZ, he recalled from retirement General Belhague, former president of the CORF, and General Ferréol Lefort former director of engineers – 'the very team that had realised the Maginot Line', Gamelin later wrote.[26] Yet in 1935 Gamelin had not backed Belhague in his battle to prevent field commanders undermining the coherence of his system.

Belhague soon accepted that the CEZF had little influence over the advance posts and resistance position. Field commanders countermanded his orders to their engineers. Ninth Army commander General Corap told Belhague that work on the second position must not disrupt work on the resistance line.[27] Belhague complained to Gamelin that army group commanders had sabotaged his instruction to protect embrasures by ensuring that blockhouses fired only to the flanks. He refused to be 'responsible for an organisation that escapes me and for which I am only a constructor'.[28] Yet by late November he had still not communicated his plans to the army groups.[29]

On the second line, the CEFZ planned 600 kilometres of works in four tranches consisting of trenches, gun emplacements, antitank obstacles, a six-metre-wide barbed-wire barrier and 1,200 blockhouses.[30] Work on the first tranche – Cassel in the north, the Sarre and the Jura – was supposed to begin at once, but was delayed until spring. The other tranches never began, on account of bad weather and lack of labour and material. Field commanders often refused to release troops to work on the second position, objecting that their men were fully engaged in patrolling and maintaining the first.[31] There were quarrels over the allocation of precious gravel and sand, labour and mechanical diggers.[32]

Gamelin did not support the CEZF. On 15 January, Belhague was included in a cull of older, supposedly less dynamic generals. Although

Gamelin's principal motive was probably to replace the major-general at GQG with General Joseph Doumenc, more loyal to himself, he did not regret Belhague's departure. Georges, in contrast, was displeased by the loss of the 'great engineer who gave us the Maginot Line and who was in the process of doubling it with a second'.[33] The two men continued to tussle. In April, Gamelin scolded Georges for not having constructed the strongpoints in advance of the resistance line that he had ordered back in October – including those at Sedan. These were more important, he said, than the second position.[34]

With Belhague gone, the CEZF, now under General Philippe, inspector of engineers, was confined to overseeing the first tranche of second-line works. Georges and Gamelin both ordered army commanders to assist the CEZF's work, but the results were uneven.[35] At Cassel, only eight of twenty-six STG casemates were constructed. Sixteen Corps refused to provide engineers and labour for the works because they were engaged on the first position. Weapons and cloches never arrived.[36]

In the Sarre Gap, Belhague wanted eighty casemates in a first line and eighty-four more 1,500 metres further back along the Albe river. Visiting the Sarre–Union sector in January, Ironside was pleased to see 'pillboxes in irregular lines and barbed wire in all directions dividing the battlefield to confuse the enemy advance'.[37] Sergeant Guizard, who visited the second line for reassurance, thought it 'uncrossable'.[38] Indeed, although few of the second-line STG casemates were completed, the combination of blockhouses and flooding created a resistance line stronger than anything constructed by field commanders.

The latter still relied on intuitive feeling for the terrain and for the 'art of war' rather than on the engineers' abstract formulae. Prételat's enthusiasm for radiesthesia was undimmed. Although official investigations ended with the outbreak of war, he continued them himself. His experiments were not 'absolutely convincing', he told Georges, but they revealed 'troubling concordances with reality', such as German troop movements near Lake Konstanz. He gave his three army commanders lists of diviners. Following a protest from the Académie des sciences, the ministry forbade further experiments, but Prételat informed Georges that he would continue anyway. Meanwhile, a radiesthesist reported that the Germans had built a tunnel under the Rhine, which neither the diviner nor military engineers could locate.[39] Sartre heard from a chasseur that his captain sat in his office and used his pendulum to check whether the machine-gun sections were in their assigned places. The chasseur, Sartre continued, 'spoke slowly and scrupulously. When he finished, he added in the same tone, "He's a twat [*con*]".'[40] When new units arrived at the front, they often modified fieldwork to their own liking.[41]

Whoever was responsible for construction, they faced serious obstacles. Aubrac, constructing blockhouses on the Rhine, had to heat the concrete before use.[42] The army's demand for gravel, sand, armoured doors and cloches expanded just as mobilisation deprived quarries and factories of labour. In some blockhouses, special concrete had to be substituted for reinforced concrete.[43] The multiplication of models of blockhouse and weapons made mass production of standardised parts impossible. Belhague complained that the latest embrasure protection fitted only the earliest 25mm antitank gun, not the two more recent models. He recognised in September that most armour for the new works would not be supplied until April 1940.[44]

Labour was in short supply, as civilian contractors lost labour to mobilisation. Demobilising older men decimated the Régiments régionaux de travailleurs (RRTs, Regional Labour Regiments). Precious resources were wasted on new barracks for labour battalions constituted from Spanish refugees and International Brigaders, many of whom were German, for they were considered too dangerous to lodge close to the troops. Yet the army acknowledged that these men were productive, resistant to cold and unfazed by bombardment.[45]

In view of these problems, the Troisième Bureau advised prioritising the first position and constructing a second only where the first was weak. In February, the director of engineers urged scaling down the whole programme.[46] After the defeat, the army was accused both of devoting insufficient resources to fortification and of constructing defences at the expense of training.[47] Evaluation of the charge is difficult, for fieldworks include everything from substantial STG blockhouses to simple trenches. Some conclusions are nevertheless possible.

Concrete works were labour-intensive (see Plate 11). A small, 170-cubic-metre bloc required 4,850 man-hours of labour from transport of materials to completion, the equivalent of digging four kilometres of trenches. Construction was primarily the responsibility of peripatetic Génie regiments such as Sapper Giroud's. Specialist labour units did the heavy lifting and digging. The CEZF disposed of 16,500 labourers in twenty battalions, thirty-five companies of Spanish labourers, nine of International Brigaders and twenty-four of North African Pioneers. Another 180,000 men were recruited from line regiments and a further 1,750 from reserve labour battalions, making 248,250 in total. Civilian contractors and labour were also employed. The battle over, the Génie estimated that campaign units had assigned around one-third of their manpower to constructing concrete works.[48] That estimate fits with Georges's order that regiments should normally assign one battalion to fieldwork and two to training.[49]

Of course, commitment varied. A 2nd Army Group circular complained that while soldiers fought well, they constructed field fortification less ardently. It instructed that troops must combine training with construction, and that all arms must contribute, even armoured units.[50] Roland de Margerie, serving with 152 RI, spent much of November digging an antitank ditch on the Swiss frontier, which he retrospectively saw as futile, but he also describes periods of intense training.[51]

As for cost, in October 1939, 250 million francs were allocated for the rest of the year and 1,770 million for 1940, of which 900 million went to the CEZF, not including the cost of armament or armoured cloches. On 1 April 1940, the Senate Army Commission reported a total cost of 6.2 billion francs for all the CORF *ouvrages* up to the outbreak of war, 900 million for MOM works and 400 million for improvements to the *ouvrages*. It commented that it was 'very little' at a time when the war was costing one billion a day.[52]

For these sums, the Sarre and Cassel positions had been improved to different degrees, new positions were built in advance of Longwy and moles were constructed on the right flank of RF-Lauter at Wissembourg. The army completed 2,729 blockhouses between mobilisation and May 1940. A further 821 were incomplete. The effort was uneven, however. The British Expeditionary Force (BEF) finished 86 per cent of the 300 blockhouses required in its sector, and the 9th Army completed

52 per cent of the 377 in its sector. The 2nd Army, which included Sedan, constructed only 9 per cent of the required 660 blockhouses.[53]

Whatever the case, French efforts were in line with those of the enemy. Rolling out the usual stereotypes, General Aubert Frère reported that native German vigour was displayed primarily in 'organising the terrain', and that once their patrols captured ground, they immediately 'organised it'.[54] German troops on the Belgian frontier spent much time improving the Westwall. Neither French nor German works matched the immense fieldworks that the Russians constructed at Kursk in 1943.[55] Field fortifications were, and remain, a standard part of the military repertoire.

Weaknesses in the French works cannot be denied, at least with hindsight. On the Maginot Line proper, no second line was ever built. Even Georges thought that it was sufficiently strong not to require one. Yet the *ouvrages* were very vulnerable to attack from the rear, where they lacked artillery.

On mobilisation, the Sedan–Mézières defences were still limited to Barbeyrac's single line of weak blockhouses plus antitank obstacles with gaps to allow cattle through. They were set up to two kilometres back from the river to avoid flooding and troubling navigation, so hardly covered crossing points. The GQG's proposal for defences in advance of Sedan town was ruled out as too costly. Two more lines of blockhouses were therefore planned on the left bank of the Meuse. Thirty-three of sixty-six were complete by May; thirteen more were largely finished, and eighteen others would be by 18 June. Most new blocks lacked armoured doors, embrasure protection, and the rock, earth and grass covering normally piled in front (*rocaillage*) that protected and camouflaged them. Only one bloc, Vaux-Dessus, possessed 75mm artillery. Unfortunately, too, modification in light of 1st Army Group's plans created a disturbing gap in the second line between the Pepinière casemate in the north and Côte-du-Pré-de-Meuse to the south.[56]

In March, parliamentary inspector Pierre Taittinger notoriously described the Sedan defences as 'rudimentary, not to say embryonic'. He saw little anti-aircraft protection. He feared that Belgian resistance might be symbolic, that the *maisons fortes* on the frontier would be quickly overcome and that troops could easily infiltrate through the woods close to Sedan. He had little faith in the Meuse: 'not very wide, not very deep, and for several months its current is fairly slow'. In the previous war, the Germans had crossed it multiple times.[57]

Huntziger dismissed the report as 'ill-informed'. He reiterated the standard thinking that the forest and Meuse would slow the enemy advance and concluded that 'no urgent measure was needed'.[58] Although neither Gamelin nor Daladier saw the report itself, they probably learned about it, but dismissed it for political reasons. Taittinger had annoyed Gamelin by opposing his appointment and labelling him a 'bureaucrat in a kepi', while Daladier remembered Taittinger as one of the leaders of the far-right demonstrations of 6 February 1934 that had forced his resignation.[59] Taittinger's status as a war veteran and self-appointed expert did not improve his credit in the army.

Gamelin had also dismissed Prételat's map exercise of 1938, which concluded that two armoured and one motorised division could reach Sedan in three days. He responded that he would have time to bring up reserves. Prételat himself probably did not foresee how quickly the Germans would cross the river once they arrived. The reorganisation of fortification command not only confirmed that Sedan was not a priority, but further weakened its defences.

Reorganisation

Strengthening the quantity and manoeuvrability of the field army was one of the high command's priorities. That meant transferring divisions away from the Maginot Line and converting RIFs into more manoeuvrable field regiments. And since the latter required fewer personnel, reorganisation potentially facilitated the formation of new divisions. Reorganisation also promised to meet field commanders' long-standing desire to establish control over the fortifications. Inevitably, there was opposition.

The high command recognised that the Maginot Line had not economised manpower, for it was impossible to rule out an attempt to assault it or outflank it from the north or south. The Deuxième Bureau consistently overestimated the number of German divisions in the Eifel between Aachen and the Moselle. Since they never detected their orientation towards the southwest, it appeared possible that they could attack either Belgium and Luxembourg or the fortifications.

Consequently, no fewer than three armies were positioned behind the RFs and another on the Rhine, including thirty-one fortress infantry regiments. Mussolini's declaration of non-belligerence permitted transfer of forces from the southeast, where the 6th Army was downgraded to the Army of the Alps, with only three B series infantry divisions and three fortified sectors. Yet 29 and 30 DIA and part of 4 Génie, Giroud's unit, spent months on the Maginot Line. The possibility that the enemy might move from Belgium and Luxembourg to encircle the fortifications caused the 2nd Army to privilege defending the fortifications' northern flank rather than Sedan.[60]

The high command also recognised that the command structure on the frontier was confused. To ensure that they mobilised quickly, fortified sectors and regions were organisationally independent of slowly mobilising campaign units. Once mobilisation was complete, this independence tangled the chain of command. Sometimes fortress troops were commanded by campaign units; sometimes the contrary; sometimes – horror of horrors – an officer could be commanded by another with less seniority.

In May 1939, Prételat had already proposed that once mobilisation was complete, fortification regiments should be converted into 'northeast type' campaign units.[61] On 28 September, he urged abolition of the fortified regions and reduction of fortified sectors to 'technical services' under the authority of campaign units alongside the artillery, infantry, engineers and so forth, and the transfer of young career officers from the fortifications to field units.[62]

On 25 November, Gamelin ordered the implementation of Prételat's proposal, but included what proved to be an unfortunate compromise. In active sectors, campaign divisions would command. These included the right flank of RF-Lauter, the Rohrbach plateau, the Northern Vosges and the Sarre. 'Passive' sectors with strong natural defences and/or permanent fortifications could be defended by static fortress units and B divisions. They were meant to be able to survive alone if campaign troops advanced or retreated. They included the Jura mountains, Belfort, the Rhine, the eastern Vosges, the Crusnes sector of RF-Metz, Maubeuge and . . . Sedan–Mézières (see Figures 12 and 17).[63]

Reform provoked widespread and often bitter opposition from the fortification command. Lieutenant-Colonel Heme, head of the RF-Metz staff, told a 2nd Army Group staff officer that fortification troops were once again 'ignored and sacrificed' by the campaign army. As proof, he cited a soldier sent to serve a prison sentence in an *ouvrage* and a division commander who wanted to rest his infantry in another. The new 'technical' fortification units would be too weak to protect their 'interests'.[64] SF-Rohrbach feared that amputation of personnel would compromise construction of defensive works and make it impossible to hold out if campaign troops departed.[65] Quarrels between fortification and field units extended down to unit level. Captain Dupont at Montmédy grumbled that field officers, ignorant of the ABC of fortification, modified fire plans established in peacetime.[66]

On 24 December, Georges confirmed Gamelin's plan, which was implemented from January to March 1940. Thus, SF-Sarre, in an active zone, answered to XX Corps. In 'passive' areas, Corps d'armée de forteresse (CAFs) and Divisions d'infanterie de forteresse (DIFs) or field units, usually B series, commanded combinations of fortification and field units. At Sedan, for instance, 147 RIF, which held the front line, was under the command of the B series 55 DI and above that of X Corps. The new CAFs and DIFs differed from normal corps and divisions in having reduced services such as artillery and transport. Gamelin saw transfer of divisional artillery away from units in the Ardennes specifically as reinforcing other units' capacity for manoeuvre.[67] Corap, commander of the 9th Army, responsible for Mézières, protested in vain about the weakening of his defences.[68]

Despite most officers favouring the conversion of RIFs into field regiments, that reform came to nothing. Senior commanders opposed disruption of fire plans on the eve of the expected German offensive. General Requin, 4th Army commander, doubted efficiency savings, for to maintain established fire plans with more lightly armed campaign divisions, extra divisions would be required on the frontier.[69] Anyway, there was insufficient equipment for existing units, let alone for new ones then being created.[70] On 9 February, Georges abandoned conversion.[71]

Nevertheless, on 1 March he ordered an exchange of personnel between fortification and B regiments. The rationale was that the young, active cadres of the RIFs – who had been forced to serve in them! – were better suited to revitalising reserve units, while mature, less emotional, more solid men were more appropriate for defence.[72] Formal orders were issued only on 7 April. Transfers began, but officers had little time to integrate into their new units before action started. For instance, 71 DI at Sedan exchanged 600 men and 20 officers with 132 RIF only a fortnight before the German offensive. As part of this exchange, 38 RA sent horse drivers to a fortification artillery regiment that had no transport.[73]

Few campaign divisions were transferred away from the Maginot Line. There is no supporting evidence for Georges's claim that Prételat's resistance was responsible. In fact, in early April, Prételat released three divisions to Georges's reserve, and three more were to follow on 10 May.[74] Georges himself hesitated to do more, for he considered that fortification work took priority.[75]

In Contact

Another reason for overmanning was that on 5 November 1939 the GQG ordered campaign units to acquire combat experience in the Maginot Line advance posts.[76] All but three active divisions served tours there, as did eighteen of twenty A series, seven North African and six colonial, but only five of eighteen B series divisions. Only in March did Georges inform Prételat that the practice would end.[77]

The advance posts consisted of rudimentary strongpoints constructed from felled trees and earth, surrounded by barbed wire, manned by at least a combat group with a light machine gun (LMG). Their task was to prevent the Maginot Line coming under heavy-weapon fire, warn of an attack and delay it. Initially, they would retreat first to the strongpoints of the 'ligne de recueil' (retreat line), which was expected to resist until explicitly ordered to pull back to the *ouvrage* line.[78]

The advance posts were also charged with patrolling to prevent German infiltration and reconnoitre German positions. In daytime, patrols were to destroy or capture any German patrols they encountered. At night, they were to ambush, reconnoitre and listen.[79] At least 1,385 men were killed in action on the Franco-German frontier during this not-so-phoney war (see Plate 12).[80]

Soldiers' experience was shaped as much by stereotypical views of Germany as by fear and discomfort in the advance posts. French prejudices concerning Germany were equivocal. Mindlessly obedient to authority, Germans supposedly lacked the imagination of the liberty-loving French. This stereotype informed the earliest soldiers' letters, which reported that during their 16–17 October Saar counteroffensive, thousands of Germans were mown down as a consequence of their habit of advancing in close order shouting, 'Long live Hitler!'[81] The view was soon displaced by the other side of the stereotype – admiration for German military prowess. German fanaticism and obedience made them audacious, brave soldiers.[82]

By late November, fear of German patrols was widespread. The most positive sampled letter mentioned 'poor devils' who had lost several wounded repelling a German raid that took twelve comrades prisoner.[83] Pierre Taittinger claimed that while he was inspecting the 5th Army, a few ranging shots from German artillery provoked a panicked retreat of officers and men alike along eleven miles of front. The men abandoned their equipment and screamed, 'Voilà les tanks!'[84]

Certain themes recurred in letters home. First, the Germans could be heard hooting like owls or yelping like dogs as rallying cries. They were accompanied by well-trained wolfdogs with collars that exploded if captured.[85] The Germans did use dogs, but fears hardly matched reality.[86] Identification of the Germans with animals owed more to the depiction of them as subhuman barbarians in the propaganda of the previous war. Secondly, the Germans could always see the French, but the French could never see the Germans. A lieutenant (85 RI) wrote, 'My impression is that the Boche see us, but we don't see them, and there is a lack of audacity on our part which demoralises our best soldiers.' Another officer was visited nightly by 'men in black with dogs, whom he'd never managed to see'.[87]

It can hardly be doubted that duty on dark, damp, freezing nights was frightening, or that distinguishing intruders from wildlife through the rain and the sound of the wind howling in trees was difficult. High alertness in conditions of extremely unpleasant cold and damp interferes with cognition. But how soldiers interpreted physiological experiences depended on individual outlook and cultural expectations.

Sergeant François Mitterrand, future president of the Republic, told his father of 'living on two trembling feet, with a body that shivers and ends up tasting fear, cold and delicious sensations of danger'.[88] Most French soldiers saw nothing delicious about their circumstances, not least because their views of their adversaries were shaped by a stereotypical belief in German daring and efficiency – from which a few historians have not been immune.

In fact, the units of German Army Group C opposite were second-rate. It is true that during the winter the Wehrmacht engaged in intensive training, designed to correct poor reconnaissance skills and a predilection for continuous defensive lines observed in the Polish campaign. Yet this programme prioritised units earmarked for the *Sichelschnitt* through Belgium and Luxembourg, not those of Army Group C. The latter was ordered simply to hold the line and improve fortifications, while planning a possible offensive in the second stage of the battle.[89] The thirteen divisions patrolling the Saar and Northern Vosges consisted of a mixture of frontier guards, depot troops and older reserves who had often received little training owing to Versailles restrictions. Sixty Infanterie Division (ID), for instance, was hastily formed from Danzig Brownshirts.[90]

Like the French, the Germans devoted much effort to constructing defences, and time for training varied.[91] Army Group C commander, General Wilhelm Ritter von Leeb, thought that his troops' morale was good, but dependent on the fortifications and the expectation of imminent peace.[92] Leeb did not inspire full confidence in his subordinates. General Geyr von Schweppenburg, commanding XXIV Corps, preferred the flexible 'mission-oriented' tactics associated with Erwin Rommel, whereas Leeb remained committed to methodical artillery-infantry operations. Indeed, Leeb opposed war against France and was vaguely involved in plotting against Hitler.[93]

German patrols were sometimes daring (perhaps thanks to consuming amphetamines). They secretly placed microphones in French posts to assess their morale and observe their routines so that raids could catch them off guard.[94] One night, a sergeant and two men of 154 RIF on lookout on the lower floor of a *maison forte* at Brementelle saw a group of Germans run up the outside stairs to the upper floor. The French soldiers on the ground floor attempted to warn their two comrades eating their meal above, but had to watch helplessly as the Germans made off with them. The officer and NCOs at the post were sanctioned for negligence.[95]

Such escapades were exceptional. The Germans usually approached close enough only to make the French reveal their positions. And they avoided clashes in the hope of persuading the French that their quarrel was with the British. German artillery was ordered not to fire into France, and French sources confirm that they seldom replied to French barrages.[96] In December, however, Hitler ordered attacks on newly arrived British units to undermine their morale and compromise them in the eyes of the French. The letters home of 2nd Lieutenant A.W. Gason of the Duke of Cornwall's Light Infantry (DCLI), stationed in an area he likened to a large-scale Cotswolds, show that British troops were just as jumpy as the French. In early March, the DCLI suffered a particularly effective German raid, in which, Gason said, they lost some fine men – two dead and fourteen prisoners.[97]

Some French officers recognised that such incidents were unusual. The commander of SF-Vosges told subordinates that most German approaches were nothing compared to the nightly fusillades to which flimsily protected soldiers were subjected in the colonies. Troops must no longer respond to minor incursions with barrages sufficient to stop divisions.[98]

In a widely circulated report, Colonel Jean Manhès, veteran of the previous war and commander of 30 DIA in the Northern Vosges, claimed that most raids were figments of 'a war psychosis'. His men had been 'asphyxiated' by predecessors' stories of 'culotted Germans each evening visiting unspeakable buffoonery on the French'. Manhès verified only three 'prudent' German approaches to 600 metres in one month, which, once the French fired, 'honourably' withdrew. To an officer who asked why trees were riddled with German ammunition, he showed five deformed bullets from a French model 92 revolver, a prodigious quantity of brass hammers from French F-1 grenades and some triggers from French O.F. grenades. Intelligence showed that the German troops were young, inexperienced infantry, who were just as likely as the French to unleash volleys of fire at imaginary infiltrators. Manhès concluded that although Germans and French were equally brave, both feared the dark and preferred to fight shoulder to shoulder. There was no need to 'let the Germans take the piss'.[99] Manhès's superior agreed – the Germans had executed only two real raids and the French had countered with three, one of which had captured two soldiers.[100]

In fact, the French were not wholly unsuited to this war. The much-criticised 1921 regulations for commanding large units accepted the principle of devolved command, albeit subject to strict rules. In 1935–9, revised regulations had increased space for initiative, partly in response to junior officers' unhappiness with the infantry's lack of manoeuvrability.[101]

French infantry did not neglect training. The GQG issued multiple circulars on topics from machine-gun operation to combined-arms tactics. Men were to be conditioned for the attack by running, jumping, hiding and climbing in full kit on varied terrain.[102] Soldiers' letters and diaries frequently complained that time away from the front was devoted to difficult training.[103] Undoubtedly, terrible weather hampered training, as it did for the Germans.[104]

Training probably depended on officers' background, age and familiarity with the evolving regulations. An evaluation of the officers of 7 DIC (Division d'infanterie coloniale) is revealing: Lieutenant-Colonel Louis Crapon achieved excellent results by organising small training patrols, whereas Lieutenant-Colonel Boivin was 'a know-all who had had to make an effort to adapt to the circumstances of the present war'.[105] This diversity explains why initiatives to form French equivalents of the *Stoßtruppen* came from both above and below.

Traditionally, the French army rejected the formation of elite units, for the principle of the nation in arms taught that the best troops must be spread through the whole army. This conception appeared to have been vindicated in 1918 by the victory of good average French units, once the enemy's minority of elite units was exhausted. Specialist patrolling and raiding groups had nevertheless been formed during the conflict, and some of the men involved fought again in 1939–40, such as Joseph Darnand (24 BCA), who had participated in the famous raid of 14 July 1918.

After the war, memory of raiding was sustained by the street-fighting far right – the rather less violent equivalent of the Italian Arditi and German Freikorps. In the 1920s, the anticommunist Ligue des chefs de section (Platoon Leaders' League) explicitly evoked devolved command. Darnand belonged to several such groups, and on the Maginot Line served under the orders of his far-right friend Félix Agnély.

Within the army, small-group tactics were far from unknown. Many officers had served in the colonies, where irregular tactics were the norm. Retired Lieutenant-Colonel François de La Rocque, leader of the far-right Croix de Feu during the 1930s, took pride in having led Moroccan irregulars (*goumiers*). On the Maginot Line, an officer in an Algerian regiment wrote home that his men were expert ambushers. Alpine infantry, chasseurs (light infantry) and small parachute units prided themselves on mobility and initiative. Divisional and Corps reconnaissance groups (GRDI and GRCA respectively) embraced an ethos of daring. A lieutenant in one described his men as 'marvellous', performing honourably in clashes and bringing back intelligence.[106] We may assume that the reserve officers from Alsace-Lorraine in the fortification regiments who had served in the German army had not entirely forgotten the importance of using initiative to complete their missions.

In November, infantry units began to organise specialist patrolling groups known as '*groupes francs*' or '*corps francs*'. The colonel commanding 56 DI in RF-Metz ordered that while only the high command could formally establish them, each battalion must recruit volunteer 'scout-patrollers'. That the 56th was a B division composed of older reservists warns against generalisation about fighting quality.[107] The notoriously immobile fortress units did not stand aside. Groups recruited from 146 and 156 RIF were permanently based on the *ligne de recueil* rather than rotated to the advance posts for the usual ten-day tour. Even the crew of the huge Hochwald fort created one.[108] General Joseph Hassler (22 DI) in SF-Thionville encouraged subordinates to 'respond [to enemy raids]. It's the job of junior cadres. It's the front that leads. The rear registers and coordinates afterwards.'[109] A reserve officer (101 RI, 41 DI) wrote, 'Everything is done by section leaders. Orders do not come from above at all, but are suggested, sometimes imposed, by us.'[110]

Results varied. On 18 December, Lieutenant Tambourini led groups from II and III/154 RIF and 13 BCA on a patrol of enemy posts on the slopes of Haute-Reissen in Germany. They were to advance silently within sight of each other, and if one came under fire the two others were to attack enemy flanks. When II/154 RIF was halted by submachine-gun (SMG) fire, Tambourini ordered suppressing fire while he led 13 BCA around the enemy right flank, capturing two officers and two NCOs. The II/154 RIF group, which ran to assist the chasseurs, was met by fire from the re-established German line. Meanwhile, III/154 RIF attacked the enemy's left flank, where its commanding lieutenant and two corporals were killed and another lieutenant was wounded and captured. The men, temporarily disoriented by the loss of their leaders, recovered when Tambourini returned.[111] These tactics were a far cry from the stereotype of methodical frontal attack (see Plate 13).

Other groups performed less well, but not necessarily because they were defensive and passive, as the capture of a whole platoon of 2 RI north of Bitche shows. General Bourret attributed this setback to the fact that some days previously 6 GRDI, holding the section, had abandoned the position in the face of a mere threat – one squadron was reduced to a crowd of 'haggard' men milling around the village of Hanviller. It had been replaced by 2 RI. Since the latter was 'fatigued', corps ordered it to avoid combat. Yet on his own initiative a company commander mounted a little operation with artillery support to establish advance posts further forward, which resulted in the loss of the platoon in question. Bourret transferred a GRDI officer, but noted that French raiding parties had captured prisoners and gathered valuable intelligence.[112]

After a failed ambush carried out by a 99 RIA group, the patrol's commanding officer said that lying in wait in the wet, freezing forest was extremely trying. The men required leather clothing, trousers with padded knees, and boots capacious enough for thick woollen socks. Patrollers had carbines, easier to manipulate in the undergrowth than rifles, but lacked SMGs, which were ideal for forest combat and which the Germans possessed.[113] Such shortcomings encouraged the high command to act.

Gamelin condemned passivity. He warned Georges against static defence, and urged 'varied reconnaissances and active patrols'.[114] Georges did indeed prioritise control, for he ordered commanders to submit plans for raids to him for approval. Prételat, who saw this requirement as stifling initiative, asked permission for local commanders to submit scenarios in advance so that they could respond before the Germans took countermeasures.[115]

In the first week of December, the results of an enquiry into German tactics arrived. VIII Corps (5th Army) concluded that German units' effectiveness varied, but that they all displayed the characteristics of the 'race' (prejudice again): painstaking method, deception, surprise, booby traps, vigorous patrolling and 'organisation of the terrain'. RF-Lauter's response described improbable night-long firefights, yet admitted that next morning it was rare to find a spent cartridge. General Henri Vernillat (43 DI) felt that the passive French stance ceded the advantage to the Germans. He called for the creation of units able to match the *Stoßtruppen*.[116]

Georges gave way. On 11 December, he told Prételat that since the beginning of November the enemy had identified fifteen French divisions and taken 118 prisoners, compared to nine identifications and seventeen prisoners for the French. He attributed French inferiority to their 'defensive spirit' and alleged preference for continuous positions (in fact they were usually discontinuous, but might be linked by barbed wire). Consequently, 'dynamic' German patrols simply advanced to find French posts. He ordered the creation of specialised patrol units and also endorsed the aforementioned Manhès's preference for improving whole units' patrolling skills.[117]

Prételat was as reluctant to establish *corps francs* as Georges. He feared that they would monopolise and kill the most combative, while consigning the rest to second-rate status. Yet he also accepted that French troops were 'resigned' to inferiority, if sometimes tempered by a 'spirit of glorious sacrifice'. He recognised shortcomings – overmanning of the advance posts and positions too easily located by the enemy. The Germans, in contrast, occupied many advance posts only in daylight and did not necessarily return to the same location. French raids often found them empty.[118]

Prételat conceded that since the best men were assigned to patrolling anyway, units might as well be organised officially. He ordered constitution of *corps francs* in twenty divisions, then in thirty more. They would serve one-month tours based on the *ligne de recueil*. He insisted that they should neither carry out combined operations with other *corps francs* nor recruit too many corporals, and that regiments as a whole must continue to patrol.[119] Meanwhile, Gamelin reiterated the need for *corps francs*, beginning a letter to Georges, 'I am very annoyed, and I know that they are very annoyed in high places too, about the recent series of incidents on your front.'[120]

As Prételat feared, *corps francs* soon became an elite. His own orders stated that they would raise morale and dominate the enemy, and that they must be detached from parent regiments and placed at the disposition of fortified sectors.[121] Georges's staff admitted that they would stay together for long periods and carry special equipment, including carbines, SMGs, daggers, torches and insulated wire-cutters. Experiments began to replace notoriously ill-fitting uniforms with clothing adapted to individuals.[122] *Corps francs* received special training: intensive physical exercise in the mornings, then shooting, tracking and infiltration under fire; lessons in German tactics in the afternoon, unless involved in a night exercise.[123] Several groups unofficially designed their own enamel insignia – the general commanding SF-Haguenau authorised 22 RIF to wear one depicting a black Gallic winged helmet. One *corps franc* described itself as 'an elite group that manoeuvres the best, obeys blindly but intelligently, and is exemplary at the front and in camp'.[124] The high command claimed that *corps francs* had improved reconnaissance.[125]

The *corps francs* usually found sufficient volunteers. Margerie's unit was a partial exception, for while most junior officers in his unit volunteered, none of the other ranks did. The men who were assigned to them nevertheless performed well.[126] Several soldiers in other units wrote home that they had enthusiastically volunteered. In 167 RIF, volunteers were offered promotion and decorations, and five times more came forward than were required.[127] A soldier in 12 RIC (Régiment d'infanterie colonial) described *corps francs* as 'splendid chaps, tattooed, loud, drunken but brave boys all the same, and it works; they don't like the Boche'.[128]

Some, such as Darnand, Agnély and the former Jeunesses patriotes activist Captain Stéphane Pighetti (67 BCA), had far-right pasts.[129] Others, such as the former school teacher Lieutenant-Colonel Léon Sinais, were republican. The republican Maginot's 1914 jottings were published in 1940 as *Carnets de patrouille* (Patrol notebooks). He became the man of the people who acted where the high command had failed.

Prételat remained unconvinced by the need for specialised units. He ordered that in the first tour, *corps francs* alone would patrol and raid, while the rest of the men improved defences. In the second, all troops must demonstrate their patrolling nerve.[130] In April, 2nd Army Group reaffirmed that all infantry must be trained in shooting, fieldcraft and manoeuvre.[131] Practice varied. In 22 GRDI, the *corps francs* operated separately, but the rest of the unit also took turns to patrol.[132]

The overwhelming majority of patrols passed off without incident, for their purpose was to locate the enemy rather than fight.[133] One soldier wrote home that even when patrols met, they fired in the air and moved on.[134] Serious combat also occurred. At Apach on 22 February, German attackers blew up a house serving as a 47 RIF strongpoint before being forced back by small arms and artillery. Three men in the house disappeared, and one 'certain' German death was reported. At Manderen, six kilometres away, the French captured a prisoner.[135]

The best-known clash took place on 8 February in the streets of evacuated Forbach, where the *corps francs* of 24, 25 and 65 BCA and 65 RIF confronted the '*Stoßtruppen*' of 23 ID. As the French observed enemy activity, two Germans, probably bent on looting, entered a house where the French were hiding. In the ensuing retreat under fire, Agnély was among the nine killed. Darnand returned with two men to bring back his corpse, a deed for which he earned the accolade 'Best Soldier in France' and made the front cover of *Match*.[136]

Another albeit disastrous example confirms that the French were far from passive.[137] The 127 RI *corps franc* was charged with taking prisoners at an enemy post. Finding that the position had been reinforced with troops, barbed wire and mines, the French should have retreated. Instead, the captain sent one group forwards and another to outflank the post, which became trapped in a minefield. Ten or thirteen were killed and twenty-six men wounded. The captain was criticised for 'too ardent' action and losing sight of his 'prepared mechanism'.[138]

The French admittedly suffered from disadvantages. In the forest, the French LMG, the FM-29, proved reliable in ambushes and could be fired on the move. It was lighter than the German MG 34, but fired more slowly and was no match for SMGs in chance encounters.[139] On 12–13 February, an LMG group prematurely ambushed a German patrol, claiming at least three dead. Three Germans replied with SMGs, hitting the lieutenant and killing two others. The commanding colonel commented that 'the enemy benefited from the advantage incontestably accorded by SMGs in close combat'.[140] The French only began mass production of their MAS-38 in May 1940. Prételat, who had begged for supplies, claimed during the June 1940 debacle to have discovered a stock in a factory.[141]

Of course, if judged by abstract standards, all armies fall short. What mattered was that relative to the Germans in these circumstances, French efforts were respectable. General Condé concluded that on the 3rd Army front from October 17 1939 to 9 May 1940 there were five substantial clashes between patrols, four French raids on German posts, and thirteen German raids on the French. Six of the German raids occurred in the few weeks before the 10 May offensive.[142]

Evaluations of divisions that served on the Sarre front concluded that six were excellent, seven were good and thirteen were fine once they had overcome their nervousness (24 and 45 DIs).[143] Huntziger, responsible for Sedan, explained in response to Taittinger's criticism that the middle-aged reserves defending his sector did not require special training – despite having told Gamelin a few days earlier that tours on an active front would revive their warrior spirit.[144]

The military experience of the phoney war on the Maginot Line showed that despite challenging conditions, French troops were capable of adapting to new tactical conditions, and that the tendency towards devolved command persisted. Yet the fortifications remained overmanned. Attempts to free troops for active sectors and to make fortification regiments more mobile failed. Defences were strengthened in some areas, such as the Sarre Gap, but weakened in others, notably from Sedan to Mézières. There was no second line behind the CORF *ouvrages*. It is not enough to list strengths and weaknesses. Whether they mattered in combat depended on whether the Germans were able to take advantage of their relative strengths.

12

THE MAGINOT LINE AND CASE YELLOW

The assumption that French military doctrine and practice derived from decadence, a Maginot mentality or Great War thinking makes it difficult to understand why Gamelin ordered the fateful advance into the Low Countries – the Dyle–Breda operation. One unsatisfactory solution is to stretch the definition of 'defensive' so far that it makes little sense of events. To see linking up with the Belgian and Dutch armies as evidence of an outdated obsession with continuous fronts means forgetting that the operation required armoured units to beat the enemy to objectives up to 200 kilometres from French lines and only 100 kilometres from German bases.

Also inadequate is the suggestion that the Dyle–Breda plan was so discordant with Gamelin's supposedly cautious character and with French defensiveness that the Allies or politicians must have imposed it. In fact, French politicians and British generals both deferred to the French army in operational matters. In the absence of a reasonable explanation, it has even been suggested that Gamelin's mind was clouded by secondary syphilis.[1] The operation is less surprising if we recall that Gamelin stood on the side of manoeuvre in a long controversy about doctrine and military plans, and that these disputes intensified during the phoney war.

Gamelin himself was not, and was not known as, a doctrinaire of static defence. Remember that Weygand had once compared him to Foch and that in 1932, in a contentious CSG meeting, the two generals had pushed for ambitious action in Belgium against Pétain's caution. On the eve of the battle, General Georges Misserey (XIII Corps, Colmar) likened him to the active Foch and Georges to the defensive Pétain.[2] Gamelin did not imagine the great encircling movements advocated by General Erich von Manstein, who devised the German plan for the invasion of France. But the Dyle–Breda operation was far removed from the methodical, conducted artillery-infantry advance of the 1921 regulations.

Basil Liddell Hart exaggerated in suggesting that Gamelin did not understand defence at all.[3] In fact, in the debates about fortification described in previous chapters, Gamelin consistently advocated manoeuvre around strongpoints (moles) and lacked confidence in defensive lines. In September 1939, he advised Georges that where fortification was not available, or if armour-air forces broke through, 'the battle might take the form of a mêlée that we did not experience in the last war'. We should, he added, 'attempt to avoid such an eventuality but we must foresee it'.[4] Georges and Prételat, in contrast, preferred continuous first and second lines. Gamelin's counterattacking outlook has perhaps been obscured by his notoriously elliptical way of approaching matters, his tendency to 'suggest' rather than order and refusal to assume responsiblity. While he did impose the Breda variant on Georges he expected him to conduct the battle and assume responsibility for it.

Plans for entering the Low Countries became progressively more ambitious.[5] During the Saar offensive, the northern armies waited on the frontier fortifications, such as they were. Then, on 24 October, Gamelin issued orders for a potential move forward to the Escaut/Scheldt line to cover the Lille conurbation and save a fragment of Belgian territory – provided the Belgians called on Allied help in time and the Germans entered central and northern Belgium as expected. Yet Gamelin had always wanted more. On 1 September, he told Daladier that Italian neutrality made a move to the Albert Canal and even to the German border feasible, but he still saw a Belgian request for assistance as a condition of any operation.[6]

In late October, Gamelin used Deuxième Bureau reports of a possible German move against the Netherlands alone to press for more extensive operations. He and Georges agreed that the 7th Army should protect the port of Antwerp by occupying the Dutch side of the Escaut/Scheldt estuary. Gamelin saw this as a step to linking with Dutch forces, and on 9 November he told his staff: 'I continue to believe that the best thing for us now is a battle of movement on the left in Belgium, in successive coordinated bounds; I did not desire this two months ago, but today the tool is ready' – i.e. armoured and motorised divisions.[7] Georges was cautious about the Dyle plan and frankly opposed the Breda variant. Gamelin pressed ahead regardless because Belgian attitudes seemed to be evolving. German press attacks on neutral countries and trustworthy intelligence suggested possible violation of their neutrality.

On 10–13 November, the Belgians and French 'exchanged information'. Gamelin learned that the Belgians preferred reinforcement on the Albert Canal, but that the conditions for advance to the Antwerp–Dyle–Namur line were also present: permanent mobilisation of the Belgian army, a possible appeal for assistance and construction of an antitank barrier in the Gembloux Gap, the weak point in the Dyle line. Georges was more cautious, writing in his diary of restraining the ardour of General Henri Giraud (7th Army commander) and General Gaston Billotte (1st Army Group commander). Georges later claimed to have been 'perplexed', but at the time his practical objections were confined to the familiar problem of coordination with the Belgians. Like most commanders, he thought that the advantages of advance to the Dyle (but not Breda) outweighed the dangers.[8]

On 15 November, Gamelin's Instruction personelle et secrète (IPS, Personal and Secret Instruction) no. 8 ordered preparation for an advance to the Dyle, including a possible push to Breda. Three days later, the Allied Supreme Council confirmed the order. Georges's own IPS no. 8 was limited to General Maurice Blanchard's 1st Army seizing the lightly fortified Dyle Line. Further south, in a secondary operation, General Corap's 9th Army left would advance to the Belgian Meuse at Dinant, while its right would remain in a defensive stance on the French Meuse from Monthermé to Sedan (see Figure 5, page 8).

Over the following weeks, Gamelin's plans became grander. On 23 November, he met senior commanders – Georges was not invited! – and instructed them to prepare studies for moves to Breda and to the Albert Canal if the Belgians still held it.[9] When informed of the plan, Georges warned that a German move into central Belgium might be a feint designed to divert attention from a powerful attack further south between the Meuse and Moselle. Georges and General Gaston Billotte, 1st Army Group Commander, particularly opposed sending the 7th Army to Breda, for it was the sole reserve army. Gamelin appeared to agree.[10]

Yet a month later he ordered Georges to have his staff prepare studies for moving beyond the Dyle. 'We must not', he wrote, 'allow minds to crystallise around dispositions which, even with the corrective of a march forward into Belgium, are inspired in the end by a defensive conception'. Options included, after a pause on the Dyle line, moving to eastern Luxembourg, outflanking the Germans on the left to take the Albert Canal and an offensive from Moselle northwards. He urged subordinates to prepare for rapid action when the time was ripe.[11]

Gamelin accompanied his note with some 'reflections', which provoked an exchange with Georges that showed how far apart their ideas were. Gamelin distinguished an attack on the Westwall using the destructive power of artillery from an 'encounter battle' involving tanks and aircraft. Although, he opined, the latter might be glimpsed in 1914 and 1918, its nature was 'unforeseeable'. He allowed that the French had an interest in accepting the first shock on a prepared position, but in the first stages and in exploitation, when there was no coherent front, rapidity was more important than order. Gamelin's reflections were compatible with the 1936 IGU's paragraphs concerning avoidance of an encounter battle when two sides were moving, but which advocated sudden and brutal action rather than order where the enemy was less well established, and reminded commanders that at some point, the enemy's front would have to be broken.[12] However, Gamelin's use of 'unforeseeable' and knowledge of Gamelin's various plans meant that Georges took them as departing from the spirit of the regulations. His handwritten annotations asked whether French forces would be caught in no-man's-land. His considered reply reminded Gamelin of article 201 of the IGU, which warned that an encounter battle must be avoided at the beginning of the battle and that young, inexperienced troops must only be deployed methodically with maximum artillery support. Georges reasserted the necessity also of a second defensive position.[13]

The British were alarmed by Gamelin's plans. Liddell Hart doubtless heard of them on the grapevine, for he wrote after the war that everyone behind the scenes knew that the high command was full of schemes for taking the offensive. Captain Paul de Villelume, chief of Reynaud's military cabinet, learned from many conversations with Gamelin that he imagined 'the attack that will one day destroy the Third Reich'.[14] Georges reassured the British that these studies were hypothetical. When he warned Gamelin of British fears, Gamelin suggested that the French should move to the Albert Canal alone, leaving the British to cover the Dyle.[15]

At this stage, Giraud, whose 7th Army would undertake any Dutch operation, remained enthusiastic. In January, General Henry Pownall (BEF chief of staff) wrote in his diary that Giraud had 'great hopes of fighting a grand battle with a "mass manoeuvre" on our left rear when we advance. He's a fire-eater and doesn't like being edged in on.'[16]

Gamelin again considered advancing to the Albert Canal and a flanking counterattack as a possibility if the Belgians held out long enough in his 'War Plan 1940' of 26 February. Georges, in contrast, proposed taking advantage of the growing number of British divisions to extend their front to the left, thus permitting the 7th Army to return to the strategic reserve.

On 6 March, Gamelin formally revived the Breda option. His IPS no. 11 of six days later ordered Georges to plan and implement an operation he opposed. Georges's own IPS no. 9 of 20 March justified it by the existence of defences at Gembloux, the build up of British forces and the improvement of the French armies. In the following weeks, Georges, Billotte and now Giraud too attempted to persuade Gamelin of the danger of the operation. They cited lack of coordination with the Dutch, exposure of 7th Army columns to air attack and the loss of the 7th Army from the strategic reserve. Gamelin told the Belgians that advance to the Albert Canal was possible only if they called the Allies in pre-emptively, so that a battle en route could be avoided.[17] Yet he persisted with the Dyle–Breda operation. Why?

Although the plan itself was not imposed by politicians, Gamelin was under political and military pressure to break the eight-month stalemate. His opposition to a Balkan front annoyed Daladier, his political patron. In January, de Gaulle accused military and political leaders of watching through observation apertures on the Maginot Line while Europe burned. The views of this still obscure colonel mattered less than Reynaud's demand for an operation in Scandinavia to halt iron ore deliveries to Germany and/or in the Caucasus to interrupt supplies of Russian oil. In February, Pownall noted, 'Gamelin feels that he will be for the high jump unless something happens soon in the military sphere.' Pownall saw calls for 'action' as vague, and worried that a half-baked operation would be launched simply for the sake of doing something.[18]

Since Daladier was also criticised for 'inaction', Gamelin feared that if, as seemed likely, Daladier fell and was replaced by Reynaud, he would lose his own position to Georges. Indeed, he issued his Breda instruction on the day on which Daladier finally resigned.[19] The Dyle–Breda plan specifically was not imposed by politicians, but related political and military considerations encouraged Gamelin to act. Doing so affirmed his authority over Georges, and at least among initiates it refuted accusations of passivity.

However, the decision was not simply a response to immediate political considerations. Gamelin had long favoured the maximum possible advance into Belgium, and the operation was made tactically possible by the shift in resources since 1935 from fortification to the DLMs and motorisation and by revision of the regulations. More specifically, the plan was to send the DLMs deep into Belgium and the Netherlands, from where they would fight delaying actions back to the lightly fortified Dyle and Gembloux position, on which, by then, the main force would have established itself.[20] Billotte's instructions for the Breda operation entailed linking with the Dutch and threatening the German flank.[21] Gamelin was willing to risk an encounter battle, telling a senator that he knew that Gembloux was not properly fortified, 'whatever the Belgians said'.[22]

Rather than reflecting a 'Maginot mentality' or obsession with continuity, Gamelin's plan rejected passivity and Georges's preference for methodical advance, and used the fortifications as the hinge for an ambitious manoeuvre. Another, neglected, reason that Gamelin gave for preferring 'a battle of movement' was to sustain 'the offensive spirit of the troops, the morale of the troops and of the interior'.[23] This remark makes sense in the light of the Deuxième Bureau's multiple reports that passivity and falling morale were undermining the troops' warrior spirit. For Gamelin, the Dyle–Breda plan was the antidote to passivity and defensiveness. Yet since the army still considered an attack on the Maginot Line to be possible, it consumed huge resources and limited French options if the Dyle–Breda plan failed.

Gamelin's plan may have been unrealistic, reliant on faulty intelligence, marked by wishful thinking about the defensive value of the Ardennes and hamstrung by the weight of the Maginot Line. Passive and unimaginative it was not. It was the half-baked outcome of a long-running politicised battle within the army concerning tactics, in which Gamelin imposed his will over the more cautious Georges in the context of fears that Germany was better placed to win a long war.

Had the Germans stuck to their original scheme to push through central Belgium to the coast, Gamelin's plans might not have provoked immediate disaster, though whether the ultimate outcome would have been different cannot be determined. Yet in Germany, as in France, a battle of wills was taking place. Manstein, ultimately backed by Hitler, prevailed over more cautious generals, and ensured adoption of the plan to assault the Meuse: the Manstein Plan – Case Yellow. In May 1940, both sides risked everything on a single throw of the dice.

Case Yellow

At 4:00 on 10 May, a few hours after the Germans had entered the Low Countries, Gamelin ordered implementation of the Dyle–Breda manoeuvre. By 3:00 on 11 May, the 7th Army's advance guard had reached Breda by sea, rail and road, while General René Prioux's cavalry corps (2 and 3 DLMs and motorised infantry) had reached Gembloux. Further south, also preceded by cavalry, the 9th Army's left moved more ponderously to the Belgian Meuse, while its right remained on the French Meuse. Further upstream, the 2nd Army covered Sedan to the Maginot Line (see Figure 5, page 8).

The first shock occurred immediately: German paratroops and glider forces seized the bridges over the Albert Canal and the modern fort of Ében-Émael guarding its northern flank. Unlike Maginot Line forts, Ében-Émael was not an *ouvrage palmé* and so it fell as soon as its centre was taken. General Erich Hoepner's Armee-Korps XVI (3 and 4 Panzer) quickly exploited the breaches and headed for Gembloux. The 7th Army risked being cut off in the Netherlands. In any case, it had been unable to liaise with Dutch forces, which despite initial successes were crumbling. On the 12th, Giraud was ordered to support the battle in Belgium – in other words, to retreat.[24]

Debate resumed about the wisdom of the Dyle–Breda manoeuvre. Demonstrating again that French plans were not fixed, positions had reversed. Previously cautious Georges and Billotte advocated pushing the DLMs forward to the Albert Canal, while Prioux preferred to cancel the operation altogether, for he found no antitank barrier in the Gembloux Gap.[25]

Despite these setbacks, the operation went to plan. The cavalry corps pushed on past Gembloux, and on 12–14 May it clashed in a huge armoured battle with General Hoepner's Panzers at Hannut. The outnumbered DLMs fulfilled their mission of delaying the enemy long enough for the main force to establish itself at Gembloux. There, on the 15th, the French repelled the Panzers, which had attacked without awaiting infantry support. This was a rare occasion during the campaign on which armoured forces spearheaded an assault on the French, and it was beaten off by antitank and field artillery. The DLMs, held in reserve, did not intervene. This success counted for little, however, for the main German effort was concentrated in the Ardennes. The French took some time to realise that, not least because the enemy carried out diversionary attacks on the Maginot Line.

On 12 May, Armee-Korps (AK) XIII (XIII Corps, part of Armeeoberkommando (AOK) 16 and Army Group A) assaulted the Longwy salient, which the Germans feared was a potential departure point for a counterattack northward. In fact, the French never planned more than a delaying action there. After a day of intense combat, they withdrew under cover of the Latiremont and Fermont *ouvrages*.

Meanwhile, battalion-strength groups attacked Maginot Line advance posts and attempted to secure observatories. On 11 May, for instance, the Black Watch platoon (51st Highland Division) holding the position at Betting in advance of GOs Michelsberg and Hackenberg was surrounded by soldiers allegedly of the SS.[26] Bren-gun carriers quickly persuaded the Germans to retreat. The next day, the Germans bombarded the whole front, and their infantry made gains against the Highlanders and French positions on their right. Betting, surrounded again, burned. Snipers in the woods harassed 1st battalion Black Watch. A relief effort by the 51st's divisional tanks was bogged down in the wet ground and suffered losses. On the 16th, the division was still holding on, but because the Gordons' D company was cut off, General Fortune ordered a limited retreat. Then, the whole 51st, along with the French divisions on its flanks, was ordered to fall back to a position five kilometres in front of the Maginot Line.

The largest diversion was a three-division advance code-named Operation Fackel (torch), designed to overrun the outposts in the Sarre Gap and seize observatories. It was a classic infantry affair preceded by a fifteen-minute artillery barrage. Total surprise ensured that many posts did not resist, but others held out until the end of the day.

Georges's preference for fighting on the fortifications prevailed over Gamelin's for manoeuvre in advance of them. Commanders authorised retreats, in some cases before contact. Operations ended on 15 May, once the Germans knew that the Meuse operations had succeeded. For a month, action on the Maginot Line was limited to intensified patrolling and skirmishing in no-man's-land. Nevertheless, fear that the Germans intended to turn south to encircle the Maginot Line compounded the errors of the Dyle–Breda manoeuvre.

Sedan, Field of Misfortune

On 12–13 May, the Germans concentrated high-quality armoured and air forces against the weakest part of the French line. At Dinant, on the Belgian Meuse, the inadequately motorised 9th Army arrived at more or less the same time as the Germans, obliging it to fight a near encounter battle on the river. Further south on the French stretch of the river, General Werner Kempf's 6 Panzer's attempted crossing at Nouzonville, its initial target, was beaten off. It overcame stiff resistance at Monthermé, but failed to debouch from the town up the steep wooded slopes. In neither case was the initial assault carried out by tanks. After preliminary bombardment by Stukas and tanks firing as artillery, elite assault infantry and engineers crossed the Meuse in rubber boats and neutralised the blockhouses on the other side. The next day, armoured forces crossed on pontoon bridges.

The same tactics were used at Sedan – the town at which the French armies had been encircled and captured in the war of 1870, and where, on 26 August 1914, the Germans had again established a bridgehead. Events there require a little more attention, because reorganisation of the fortress troops had weakened Sedan's defences and compromised counterattacks.

None of the conditions that were supposed to delay the enemy approach to Sedan were met.[27] Rather than link with the French, Belgian Chasseurs ardennais retreated northwards, away from French forces. The handful of groups that the retreat order failed to reach showed what might have been possible, for at Bodange a few chasseurs held up 1 Panzer for a day. Belgian destructions hardly retained the Germans, for they were not covered by fire; they delayed the French more, for unlike the Germans they did not have the equipment required to overcome them. French cavalry failed to delay the Germans, either because they met the main German thrust or because they overestimated more limited forces. The *maisons fortes* on the frontier only slowed the enemy a little. By the evening of 12 May, the Germans were in Sedan town.

As a 'passive' sector, Sedan and Mézières were held by B divisions and fortress corps and divisions of the 2nd and 9th Armies respectively. These units had lost much of their artillery in the reorganisation of fortress command. They had been disrupted by exchanges of personnel between fortification and field units and by a series of partial reliefs. Sedan itself was held by the B series 55 DI, with 147 RIF on the front line. The division had not experienced contact on the Maginot Line outposts.

The assault mounted by 1, 2 and 10 Panzer updated the Napoleonic principle of concentrating overwhelming force at weak points. It proceeded more quickly than the two or three days that the French had predicted because Stuka bombardment made it unnecessary to await horse-drawn artillery. For eight hours, a few artillery pieces plus tanks firing as artillery bombarded the French positions while 88mm anti-tank guns fired at embrasures. Bombardment by 500 aircraft shredded the nerves of the infantry in their blockhouses, cut phone lines, disrupted fields of fire and provided cover for infiltration through shell holes. Then, behind a smokescreen, infantry crossed the river in rubber boats. Stunned defenders were incapable of serious resistance. On the flanks, Donchery to the west and Wadlincourt to the east, 147 RIF resisted well. However, Regiment Großdeutschland's success in the centre undermined defence on the flanks. No blockhouse covered a 1.5-kilometre gap at Gaulier, where the Germans had crossed in 1914.

Concentration on a narrow 2,800-metre front permitted rapid deep exploitation. By the evening, infantry were approaching the intact second position on the heights at Boulette and the Bois de Marfée. Units at the front were holding out. Yet some men fled as far as heavy-artillery batteries, where their cry that the enemy had crossed the Meuse quickly became the rumour that tanks were at Bulson, nine kilometres from the bridgehead. (In reality, no tanks crossed that day.) Panic was spread as much by senior officers on the telephone as by fleeing men. Although hardly engaged, 55 DI fled, as did part of 71 DI, positioned to the right, out of the firing line. The panic disrupted telephone communication and artillery support for the front. By 23:00, the Germans held the second line and were pushing into the junction of the 2nd and 9th Armies on the River Bar and the Ardennes Canal.

On the afternoon of 13 May, General Pierre Grandsard, whose X Corps was responsible for Sedan, ordered his reserves to 'push back' the enemy. Meanwhile, GQG allocated to Huntziger its own reserves – 3 DIM (Division d'infanterie motorisée and 3 DCr, organised as XXI Corps under General Jean Flavigny.[28] The airforce was ordered to bomb the crossing, then consisting of one pontoon bridge. These ripostes all failed.

The next morning, Allied bombers experienced huge losses and missed the Sedan bridges. Tenth Corps's counterattack was hampered by lack of intelligence on German whereabouts, disrupted communications and the difficulty of moving through retreating troops. German aerial reconnaissance quickly spotted the small force of obsolete French tanks, which was destroyed by antitank guns. An armoured counterattack pursued the retreating French, thus threatening the flank of the neighbouring 71 DI and completing its disintegration.

That afternoon, XXI Corps found it just as hard to get to its start line, its difficulties compounded by bombardment and the need to refuel its tanks. By 16:00, the force was aligned, with 130 B1 bis and Hotchkiss tanks in front and the motorised infantry and artillery behind – exactly as the regulations prescribed. Yet Flavigny cancelled the counterattack and dispersed his tanks to assist with the containment (*colmatage*) of German attempts to break out to the west.

On an individual level, Flavigny's decision is hard to fathom. More generally, it encapsulates not the primacy of defence over attack but the dilemmas of French doctrine.[29] Huntziger's orders were contradictory, in that they ordered both *colmatage*, implying dispersal, and counterattack, implying concentration.[30] In practice, Flavigny first deployed for counterattack but then decided to block on a wide front. Whether this decision changed the course of the battle is hard to say, given that with air and numerical superiority in the sector, the Germans would probably have been able to counterattack. And the enemy was anyway breaking out upstream. Yet the chance was lost to inflict a major blow on the enemy flank and perhaps to strengthen the hand of the cautious party in Oberkommando der Wehrmacht (OKW).

Just as Flavigny avoided orders to counterattack, so General Guderian disobeyed General Ewald von Kleist's order to consolidate the Sedan bridgehead before heading for the channel. Meanwhile, Rommel broke out at Dinant, which in turn caused the collapse of defences at Monthermé, where General Georg-Hans Reinhardt (XXXI Panzerkorps) also disobeyed orders.

That evening, Huntziger approved Flavigny's decision. On the 15th, pressed by the furious Georges, Huntziger renewed the counterattack order. Yet it proved impossible to bring 3 DCr back together. Huntziger then compounded French problems by withdrawing his right from the Chiers to block a move southwards towards the Maginot Line. Georges's orders of the 14th were to prevent the enemy moving west and south, but Huntziger chose to prioritise the south. On 16 May, Huntziger told a staff officer that his greatest fear was being 'rolled up' (*me laisser enrouler*).[31] His army occupied the Bretelle d'Inor. (A 'bretelle' is a position perpendicular to the front.) The officers of 136 RIF, astonished considering they were not heavily engaged, went in search of a written order. They were also annoyed that the units commanding them did not understand how difficult retreat was, given that they were spread over a two-kilometre front and needed time to dismount the weapons in their casemates. Some were left behind and never joined the bulk of the regiment behind the Bois d'Inor. Thus, to protect the fortifications, the 2nd Army left the route to the rear of the 9th Army and the Channel open.[32]

La Ferté

Ironically, given Huntziger's desire to cover the Maginot Line, withdrawal from the Chiers exposed its last fort, PO-La Ferté. The troops of 3 DINA, which held the 2nd Army's right, withdrew so quickly from their blockhouses in advance of La Ferté that they left their heavy weapons behind. Theoretically, the Bretelle d'Inor covered La Ferté, but it consisted only of some antitank ditches and forest clearings.

The *ouvrage* was sited on the slopes of a hill between the little villages of Villy and La Ferté, from where it dominated the Chiers valley (see Plate 14 and Figure 15). Originally planned as a three-bloc *ouvrage* with a gallery leading to an entry bloc, it consisted merely of two casemates linked by a narrow gallery which led to a first-aid station, a command post, stores and a kitchen. In the absence of a gallery leading to a rear entrance bloc, there was no emergency escape route and air intakes were positioned in the fort itself. Owing to the lack of an

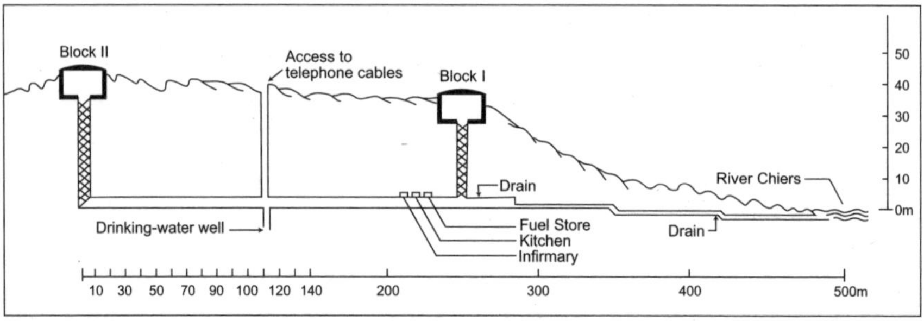

15. La Ferté section.

ammunition lift able to bring excavated rock to the surface, no sleeping quarters were constructed at the lowest level. They were situated in the blocs themselves, directly exposed to the reverberations of artillery impacts. Conditions were far from 'modern comfort'. They were frankly dangerous.

Bloc 1 was armed with three cloches, one with a 47mm antitank gun, the others with combinations of machine guns, 25mm antitank guns and LMGs. Bloc 2 was armed with a modernised turret from Verdun with two 25mm guns and two heavy machine guns firing to the flanks or frontally and three cloches of various types. The left was largely uncovered. There were no howitzers or mortars to cover dead ground, but the fort was supported by two artillery casemates near the village of Villy (Villy-Est and Villy-Ouest) just to the northwest of the fort, manned by 169 RAP. Defence of the above-ground perimeter left something to be desired, perhaps because it was used for football matches and to avoid troubling the two badgers kept in the antitank ditch. In March 1940, 2nd Army engineers proposed linking the two casemates to the *ouvrage* and constructing a gallery to the rear at a time to be decided.[33]

La Ferté was garrisoned by two officers, nine NCOs and ninety-four soldiers, mostly of the locally recruited 155 RIF.[34] Their commander Lieutenant Bourguignon, a Saint-Maixentais, had arrived at La Ferté only on 25 March.[35] The surrounding area was defended by troops of 155 RIF and the *marsouins* (colonial troops) of 23 RIC, fortified in blockhouses constructed in the cellars of dwellings using rails and concrete. The right flank, defended by 3 DIC and 155 RIF, was relatively secure in a line of blockhouses on the Sedan–Montmédy road. Among defenders there was François Mitterrand, who described his position as an 800-metre line of antitank rails and narrow escape trenches. He asked his father for hessian sacks with which to construct a shelter, plus some rum or cognac.[36] The artillery of the next *ouvrage* in the line, Le Chesnois, also covered the right. It could not reach the left, where I/23 DIC defended Hills 226 and 311.

Weak as La Ferté was, its guns represented an obstacle to General Eugen Ritter von Schobert's AK VII's mission of extending the Sedan bridgehead into the Chiers valley and thus to confuse the French about the direction of the main effort. The attack began with shelling of the advance positions on the Chiers in the early hours of 15 May. The following infantry were surprised to find empty blockhouses and weapons abandoned by 3 DINA. On their own initiative, pioneers crossed the Chiers in inflatable boats.[37] French shelling intensified as they approached the interval troops and *ouvrage*. Then, the 75s of the Villy-Ouest casemate opened up. In the latter, Lieutenant Tyckozinki, veteran of the previous war, sent packing a captain from 155 RIF who wanted to know who had authorised him to open fire. Tyckozinki fired 800 of his 1,500 shells – against regulations, which permitted only 200 per day.[38] The Germans halted, safe in former French positions, while they awaited the arrival of 210mm Mörser artillery from Belgium.

In the early hours of 16 May, a first attack on Bloc 2 preceded by artillery and then Stuka bombardment failed. The Germans realised that they must first defeat the interval troops. A new bombardment began at 13:00. A diversionary assault on the right was beaten off by the artillery of Le Chesnois and the Villy-Est casemate. On the dangerous left, the Germans overcame courageous resistance to take Hill 226, but could not cross the open ground in advance of Villy. During the night of 16th/17th, artillery duels continued (Figure 16).

At 10:00 and 13:00 on the 17th, infantry advancing behind a rolling barrage again failed to take Villy. Yet La Ferté's two casemates were abandoned in the wake of the erroneous news that Villy had fallen and the correct news that enemy troops were progressing towards Hill 311 on the left. Shells rained down on the *ouvrage* and opened paths through the rails and barbed wire. At Villy, exhausted defenders were running short of ammunition and water. In the afternoon, the Germans managed to infiltrate the village and by 16:00 resistance had ceased. By the evening, they controlled Hill 311, having reduced its substantial STG blockhouse with a flamethrower. The way to the fort was open.

On the 18th, the men inside wrote letters for sending with the daily supply chenillette. They reassured families that although exhausted by lack of sleep and subject to incessant bombardment, they were holding firm. La Ferté's doctor told his parents that the men had total faith in their *ouvrage*. At midday on the 18th, Bourguignon requested that 155s cease firing on the *ouvrage* surface because observers in the cloches

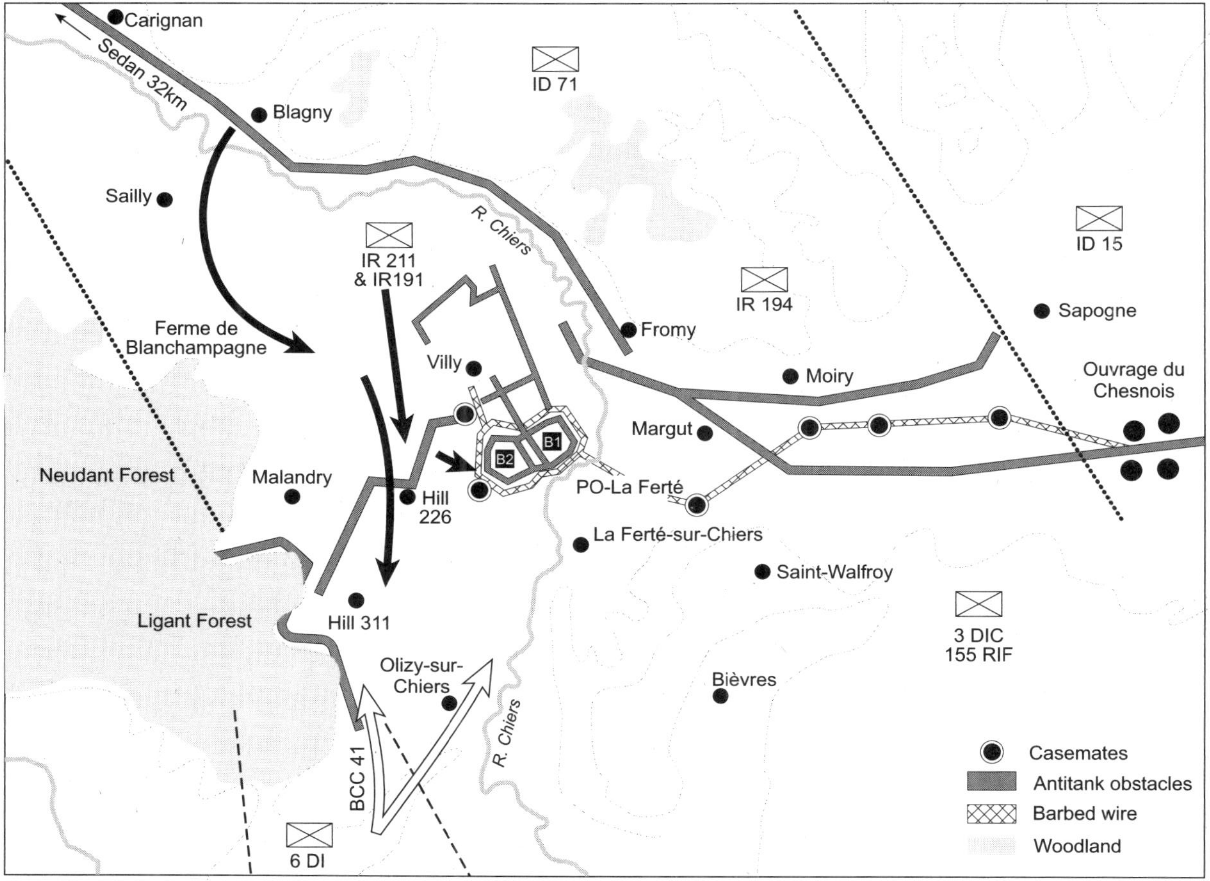

16. The attack on La Ferté.

could not stand the reverberations. An enemy shell ricochet hit the embrasure of the GFM cloche on Bloc 2, decapitating Sergeant Conraux and killing two others. Shortly afterwards, for reasons unknown, Bloc 2's turret jammed in firing position (see Plates 15 and 16).

From 17:00 to 18:10, artillery fired at the *ouvrage* to create shell holes for infiltration, after which smoke shells blinded French units on the right. At 18:10, 88s fired at the cloches for just ten minutes, not to pierce them, but to create holes into which explosives could be placed. As soon as shelling ceased, assault pioneers approached Bloc 2 through a moonscape of 210mm howitzer craters up to four metres deep and nine metres long. An observatory five kilometres to the rear of the *ouvrage* saw the pioneers, but its requests for artillery were refused, possibly because guns had been diverted to support a relief attack. In ten minutes, the pioneers finished off its GFM cloche and damaged the turret's embrasure before destroying the other two cloches. They threw explosives inside, setting off fires; the crew did not call down artillery because they attributed the explosions to German shells. Inside, machinery collapsed and bedding caught fire. The men fled down the spiral staircase to the lower level without closing the door that isolated the gallery from the bloc. Bourguignon, unaware that fires prevented the enemy from entering Bloc 2, ordered defence of the gallery.

Bourguignon's superiors reassured him that a relief operation was underway. A group of B1 bis tanks approached the fort, but withdrew because the infantry of 6 DI had been stopped at Hill 311 with heavy casualties. Yet the route to the fort was undefended! Meanwhile, preceded by a new artillery barrage, the pioneers moved to Bloc 1. From around 23:00, they blew up three out of four cloches, causing enormous damage and more fires. The crew of Bloc 1 joined their comrades in the gallery. Their attempt to buttress the airtight door with crates of victuals failed thanks to ammunition explosions. Blasts in Bloc 1 then breached the airtight doors, establishing a flow of toxic air through the gallery into the bloc. The men wore gas masks, but they were ineffective against carbon dioxide.

Since the *ouvrage* remained in telephone contact, senior officers were well aware of the horror below ground. What happened during the final hours is contested. Some years later, radio-operator Joly at GO-Le Chesnois claimed that Captain Aubert, commander of Le Chesnois, told Bourguignon that an *ouvrage* commander does not surrender – he goes down with his ship. Although this idea had certainly been expressed in the past, Aubert actually urged evacuation, and the rest of Joly's story is implausible.[39] It is certain that Bourguignon repeatedly requested permission to evacuate. It would seem that the fortification hierarchy – Aubert and General Maurice Burtaire, commander of SF-Montmédy – pleaded his case. The final decision lay with General Falvy, commander of 3 DIC. At 03:40, he hesitated but did not intervene, not even to authorise evacuation of those not required to serve the one remaining weapon, which was inaccessible as a result of damage within the fort and anyway pointed in the wrong direction. The ignorance, perhaps prejudice, of infantry officers regarding fortification, seen so often in previous years, probably played a part. Were the fortifications not manned by privileged troops, who were supposed to resist when surrounded?

By that point, evacuation was in any case problematic. Masks that were ineffective after forty-five minutes had already been worn for hours. The least movement was an effort: some attempted to climb the stairs, but most slipped into torpor and slumped against the gallery walls. One of the first to die was the *ouvrage* doctor. The last message arrived at 05:00 on the morning of the 19th from radio officer Sailly: 'We're stifling . . . the lieutenant is next to me, we are going to try to get up the steps.' There were no survivors. When it was finally possible to enter the *ouvrage*, most of the dead were in the gallery; some were on the steps and Bourguignon was seated in his office.

What had happened? The assault had implemented lessons learned on captured Czech *ouvrages*. It was facilitated by Huntziger's withdrawal to the weak Inor position, which uncovered La Ferté's left, the breakdown of the turret and failure to shell the pioneers. Once toxic gases invaded the gallery, the absence of a safe exit was fatal. Infantry officer Falvy understood neither that the fort was effectively disarmed nor the danger of asphyxiation.

News of the fate of the La Ferté crew quickly spread through the fortified zones, permanently shaking confidence in the *ouvrages*. For the rest of the campaign, German loudspeakers and tracts warned crews that their forts were 'mass graves', and that like their comrades at La

Ferté, they would die like 'rats in a hole in the depths of their concrete'.[40] The French high command's circular on the lessons of La Ferté graphically warned that while *ouvrages* were proving resistant to artillery, the enemy might throw explosives or other dangerous material into the *ouvrage* through damaged embrasures.[41]

The Northern Fortifications

As the tragedy at La Ferté unfolded, the Panzers advanced westwards from their bridgeheads. Once they had broken through at Sedan and Monthermé, Panzerkorps Kleist and Reinhardt had an almost open road until elements of 1 and 10 Panzer met de Gaulle's 4 DCr at Montcornet and Laon. Panzergruppe Hoth, moving from Dinant in Belgium, had to confront the fortifications of the north.

The high command saw these works as a fallback position for use if the intervention in Belgium turned out badly, but expected troops to retreat there in reasonably good order and to be reinforced by fresh units. Gamelin had warned that irruption of tanks through continuous French lines could cause a mêlée in the rear. He therefore advocated construction of strongpoints able to resist if passed, from which armoured counterattacks could be launched. Yet he did not force subordinates to abide by his instructions. Defences therefore consisted of the *petits ouvrages* of SF-Maubeuge, for Gamelin the 'Môle de Maubeuge', the casemates of the Mormal Forest to the north and the continuous line of blockhouses of SF-Maubeuge and SF-Ardennes southwards to Hirson and the Forest of Saint-Michel. The Panzers avoided the Maubeuge strongpoint and took on the blockhouses to the south.

The southern extremity of this line in the Forest of Saint-Michel on the frontier, north of the towns of Hirson and Saint-Michel, was defended by a mixture of weak Barbeyrac blocs and stronger but unfinished STG blocs constructed during the war.[42] The high command considered blockhouses necessary because the forest was still regenerating after destruction by the Germans during the Great War and was therefore crossable by tanks. The blockhouses had limited fields of fire owing to their small number of embrasures, the forest cover and the choppy terrain.

On 15 May, the Saint-Michel blocs were mostly unmanned, for 22 DI had advanced to the Belgian Meuse, where it collapsed in an encounter battle for which it was entirely unfitted. The military police rounded up around 300–400 exhausted 22 DI men, who had fallen back in disorder to their starting point without their heavy equipment. They were reinforced by a few pioneers, a reconnaissance group and a retreating battalion of R35 light tanks. They followed orders to form a mole in a part of the forest rather than defend the whole front. The first line was on the frontier, the second three kilometres back. By 17 May, they were surrounded. Some men fled from the blockhouses into the woods, while the R35s had the worst of an engagement with infantry and antitank guns. The next day, the Germans took one frontier blockhouse which had run out of ammunition, and then the rest of the front line from the rear. The Barbeyrac forest blockhouses, with their masonry walls, proved vulnerable to heavy mortar fire.

A few kilometres further north, still in the Ardennes sector, the blocs of the Anor sector were also empty. They consisted only of two larger blocs and a few light works around Anor town. The static 102 DIF attempted to extend its front to the area, while 1 DINA arrived in dribs and drabs from the reserve. The defenders nevertheless held out for a day against German infantry divisions.

Further north again, defences in the Maubeuge sector consisted of a line of blocs without depth, designed and constructed in 1937 by the engineers of the 1st Region. Dismountable machine-gun turrets were positioned close to them. On 16 May, in the Solre-le-Château region, General Erwin Rommel's 7 Panzer faced a position defended by 84 RIF, consisting of four blockhouses, four turrets and six improvised posts. Antitank fire and Stukas failed to dislodge the French. Since antitank obstacles blocked all other routes, Rommel attempted to force a passage through a single road. He succeeded only when the French artillery ran out of ammunition. Two blockhouses fell, allowing the Panzers to speed through the gap. The delayed 5 Panzer followed shortly afterwards. The next day it helped infantry reduce the rest of the blocs and then headed west, while detaching some units to assist IDs 8 and 28 (AK VII) in attacking the Maubeuge *petits ouvrages*.

Like La Ferté, these works did not have the solidity of the Maginot Line proper, for they had been built on the foundations of Séré de

Rivières forts. La Salmagne, Bersillies and Sarts were two-bloc infantry works, similar to La Ferté, except that some turrets were armed with 50mm mortars. Boussois *ouvrage* had three blocs and a second turret. The forts were supported by seven casemates. Further west on the north bank of the Sambre were the eight machine-gun and antitank casemates of the Mormal Forest. The fortifications were manned by 84 and 87 RIFs and 161 RAP, commanded by 101 DIF.

ID 28 moved to the south and east towards the *ouvrages*. One detachment, supported by a penny packet of tanks detached from 5 Panzer, captured the Maubeuge town citadel. Artillery bombardment on casemates south of the Sambre, although supported by Stukas, did little damage. On 20 May, ID 8 attacked the casemates west of Maubeuge using the same methods. The 87 RIF defenders put up a heroic resistance before succumbing.

Meanwhile, artillery and Stuka bombardment cratered the terrain and created gaps in the barbed wire around PO-Boussois. The absence of interval troops and the need to retract turrets for their protection permitted the Germans to fire 88mm antitank rounds at the cupolas at a range of 500 metres. Dust and noxious gases enveloped the *ouvrage*. As at La Ferté, the fort depended for fresh air on one intake per bloc, rather than through a gallery to the rear, and the filters could cope for only twenty-four hours. Also, the blast of explosions countered the over-pressure that was supposed to keep toxic air out. The defenders improvised a ventilator linked to the *ouvrage* drain and fought off infantry assaults on 20 and 21 May. On the 22nd, however, Stuka bombs buried Bloc 2's air intake. Immediately afterwards, infantry used smoke and shell-hole cover to throw charges into the fort and block the last air intake completely.[43] The crew surrendered before toxic fumes could kill them. The Germans subsequently overcame the La Salmagne, Bersillies and Sarts *petits ouvrages* using the same tactics.

To close this story, it remains to mention the fate of the remnants of 1 DINA and other units that had taken refuge in the Mormal Forest area. Although surrounded by 5 Panzer to the north and 7 Panzer from the south, many escaped after bitter fighting thanks to the intervention of 1 DLM, which had returned from Breda. The Mormal Forest casements, which had been so controversial in the early 1930s, did not play a significant part in the battle.

There is a pattern in these defeats: cost-cutting and technical flaws in the forts, their unfinished state, the absence of supporting infantry, the unsuspected effectiveness of German 88mm Flak guns, which were used more effectively than at La Ferté, and the impossibility of covering all angles of attack, especially in the hilly, thick Saint-Michel forest. The lack of depth in the northern fortifications, whether blockhouses or *petits ouvrages*, meant that if one line fell, the rest were vulnerable from the rear. Strongpoints fared no better. Maubeuge was vulnerable from the rear, as was the improvised resistance centre in the Saint-Michel Forest. That said, once the Panzers were in the rear of the French armies it is doubtful whether better defensive organisations could have saved them.

To Dunkirk

We need not linger further on the failure of the Allies to halt the Panzers' drive to the sea, except insofar as it casts light on the myth of the Maginot mentality. Although the French often fought more stubbornly than at Sedan, the odds were against them. The advance into Belgium, coupled with the unbalanced distribution of reserves and fear of an attack on the fortifications, made it impossible to mount more than limited counterattacks designed to fill gaps or delay the Panzers. In Belgium and northwest France, on the northern flank of the German breakthrough, the pressure of Army Group B prevented the 1st Army and BEF from disengaging sufficiently for a counterattack southwards. On the southern side of the salient, forces were too weak and scattered to concentrate sufficiently, as shown by the failure of Colonel de Gaulle's initially promising operations with the recently formed 4 DCr at Montcornet on 17 May and at Laon on the 19th.

In theory, a pincer attack from north and south represented a serious danger. On the 19th, aware that he was about to be replaced by Weygand, Gamelin ordered such an operation. On the 21st, the new Generalissimo confirmed that the operation would go ahead on the 25th. Its failure provoked Weygand to accuse the British of heading forty kilometres northwards to the ports. In fact, the plan encountered the obstacles already described. Unknown to Weygand, on 21 May, the day on which he confirmed the operation, a predominantly British counterattack southwards to Arras initially frightened the Germans. However, British tanks were decimated by antitank guns. A threat to the British right forced withdrawal not towards the ports but twenty-five kilometres northeast. The British still planned to participate in the offensive, but danger to the rear made it impossible. As for the French, they simply did not have the forces to strike north, not least because the Germans had established bridgeheads on the far side of the Somme. Weygand cancelled the operation, and on the 25th the BEF began to deploy for evacuation.

It would be erroneous to attribute these failures to an exaggerated attachment to the doctrine of *colmatage* – first 'containing' a breakthrough and then counterattacking – a method lacking the rapidity necessary to counter armoured exploitation.[44] The verb 'colmater', which rarely appears in the regulations, applies specifically to *local* enemy successes and the instruction is actually to 'squeeze' the flanks of a salient, not simply contain it. In the event of large breaches, in which the line had to be re-established, the IGU prescribed 'immediate counterattacks before the enemy recovers', and then counterattacks with reserve corps, which necessarily took longer to develop since they came from further away.[45]

Most of the operations mounted after Sedan were counterattacks without prior blocking. At Sedan, X Corps, in conformity with the regulations, ordered an immediate counterattack without any mention of containment, while XXI Corps first deployed for counterattack and then dispersed its tanks into defensive positions. De Gaulle's operations were both counterattacks, while the Arras operation was both counterattack and (feeble) breakout attempt. Weygand's operation was a classic pincer movement intended to encircle the Panzers. In any case, blocking breaches in a front is not intrinsically erroneous. On the eastern front, the Wehrmacht remained faithful to echeloned, continuous defences, resorting to isolated strongpoints only when it had no choice. In the second stage of the Kursk battle, it struggled to plug gaps opened by Soviet armour.

The lack of appropriate skills to make decisions in high-pressure complex circumstances is underlined by continuing recourse to radiesthesia. On 22 May, Georges and Doumenc allowed General Léon Cointet to use his pendulum on their map. This polytechnician was a previous chief of the Deuxième Bureau, to which, it seems, he still provided information. Doumenc claimed that he and Georges exchanged dismayed glances during this 'comical' episode. Yet they verified his claims – after all, Georges had not opposed Prételat's experiments – and found that his intelligence was sometimes exact but more often not.[46]

In both armies, decisions were the outcome not of 'mentalities' but of doctrinal differences and power struggles among commanders, contingencies on the battlefield and incomplete information, the gaps being filled by intuition, guesswork and sometimes prejudices. One might object that it is not accidental that caution determined the outcome on the French side and daring on the German. Yet circumstances would have been very different had Gamelin not imposed the adventurous Breda variant on his cautious subordinates.

German leaders continued to quarrel. Fearful for the Panzers' flanks, von Rundstedt and Hitler delayed them on 17–18 May. They also rejected a bold plan to leave the remnants of the northern armies to Army Group B so that Army Group A could turn west to smash French forces assembling on the Somme–Aisne line. Then, on the morning of 25 May, as Guderian prepared to move on Dunkirk, just twelve kilometres away, another order halted the advance for two days. Had Maginot Line divisions concentrated for a push northwards with Huntziger's 2nd Army, rather than transfer piecemeal to the north, the course of the battle would certainly have changed. The French did not know that each of the enemy halt orders was a response to minor or imaginary threats from the south. As it turned out, however, Hitler's halt order provided precious breathing space for the Allies to create a perimeter at Dunkirk and work on a new line along the Somme and Aisne to the Montmédy fortifications and thence to the Maginot Line. Now the fortifications were directly involved in the battle.[47]

13

TRAGIC DESTINY

As the Allies evacuated from Dunkirk, the French aligned new forces along the River Somme via the Ailette Canal to the River Aisne, anchored on their right to SF-Montmédy and thence to the Maginot Line. Among the units deployed were new Polish and Czech divisions and fourteen 'light' divisions formed from retreating soldiers and men repatriated from Dunkirk. One, 2 and 4 DCrs were partially refitted. Further units were transferred from the Maginot Line. On 20 May, the 51st Highlanders left the Sarre for the Somme, while Giroud's 4 Génie left southern Alsace for the Marne. Giroud and his comrades journeyed forty to a wagon, rendered idiotic by heat, strawdust, stink and lack of sleep, 'dumbfounded that they would soon be part of this vast battle of armoured steel and flesh'. On arrival, they dug trenches behind the river.[1] On 26 May, the entire XXIV Corps moved from SF-Crusnes to the Somme and two days later the 4th Army left for the Aisne, leaving behind XX Corps as the 'Sarre Detachment'. The Deuxième Bureau's postal samples showed that the troops' morale was elevated, and that they were confident in their tanks and artillery. Publicly, Weygand was positive too.[2]

Privately, he was not. Most units were under-equipped. German advance guards, which arrived on the Somme at the same time as the French, established bridgeheads on the left bank at Abbeville, Amiens and Péronne from which they could not be dislodged. The weakness of French air reconnaissance made the enemy difficult to locate, and raiding and patrolling skills honed in the Maginot advance posts could not compensate.[3] Only a few days into his appointment, Weygand had not abandoned all hope. His mood fluctuated between predicting defeat and ordering measures such as completion by July of the training of the latest contingent of conscripts.[4] He told anyone who would listen, however, that in the likely event of a breach of the line, the government must assume its responsibilities – an armistice.

Weygand's tactical choices were inseparable from political considerations. Rather than echeloned defence, his Order no. 1 stipulated construction of strongpoints on a loaded front, designed to block the Panzers at important road junctions, usually in villages. These 'Weygand hedgehogs' were to be capable of 365-degree defence and were expected to resist when bypassed and await counterattack. Whether Weygand's decision owed more to fidelity to Foch's opposition to echeloned defence or to his desire to fight a single battle for honour prior to an armistice is unclear. Probably both. Nevertheless, lack of depth made it hard to continue the battle once the enemy had broken through. On 24 May, four days after assuming command, Weygand told Paul Baudouin, secretary of the Comité de guerre (which brought together Weygand as general in chief with ministers reponsible for the war effort, including Pétain), that his defences were a dyke of sand and that no retreat line was possible. After a 'combat for honour', the war must end.[5] The next day, he told the Comité de guerre itself that the alternative of 'methodical retreat' to successive positions was impossible.[6] While such a retreat was undeniably difficult, it is telling that Pétain said nothing, given that this doctrine had made his reputation. Ironically, given the conventional association of echeloned defence with outdated doctrines of the last war, the only senior officer known to have suggested it was de Gaulle, who wished to continue the war from a redoubt in Brittany.[7]

Weygand's attention was turning to the army's future role in the government. Having explained the likelihood of defeat, he informed the Comité de guerre that the country would pay the price of having declared war without adequate equipment and doctrine, and that honour gained in the coming battle would aid national recovery. For the first time, ministers considered an armistice, albeit hypothetically (see Plate 17).

After the war, Weygand claimed that by ensuring the Germans did not invade the empire, the armistice had permitted North African troops to contribute to the liberation of French soil. That was not his plan in June 1940. At the time, even the British planned to bomb, blockade and starve Germany into submission, not to invade the continent. In June 1940, 'armistice' did not mean a respite to prepare resistance, but a temporary cessation of hostilities prior to peace, as it had in November 1918. Once the battle was lost, Weygand obstructed all proposals in regard to continuing the war – Churchill's suggestion of guerrilla war, the Breton redoubt and transfer of the government and remaining forces to North Africa. He responded to the latter idea with a racist slur. He considered that young conscripts sent to North Africa would die like flies, and doubted whether the Anglo-Americans could match the Luftwaffe.[8] He also tried to persuade the government (not the high command) to await the Germans in Paris – another way to hasten an armistice.[9]

Weygand's problem was that key figures – de Gaulle, Reynaud and President of the Republic Lebrun – were convinced that Allied and American resources would ultimately prevail. Weygand was perhaps misled into underestimating their determination by Reynaud's own wavering. In a private briefing on 24 May, Reynaud appears to have been half-persuaded by Weygand's arguments until, on 26 May, a visit to Churchill restored his morale.[10] Even after that date, Weygand's illusions were encouraged by the hesitation of the anti-armistice party between ill-defined 'resistance to the end', a Breton redoubt and transfer of the government to North Africa. Weygand contrasted himself as a 'realist' with politicians who lacked the 'balls' to confront the truth.[11] That he was wrong is less relevant than that their opposition conflicted with his expectation of a rapid armistice. Once the government made the request, the Germans delayed their response while they captured the Maginot Line and the Italians won some territory.

Maginot Line troops became pawns in the battle over the armistice. Weygand feared that early abandonment of the fortifications to save men from capture would undermine his orders to resist on the Somme–Aisne line, prolong the battle and delay the armistice. Like other senior officers, Weygand also feared that the communists possessed an organised apparatus in Paris, ready to seize power amidst defeat.[12] In reality, thanks to repression following the Nazi–Soviet Pact, the party was incapable of organising a small bread riot. Nevertheless, the Maginot Line, once seen as buttressing order, now appeared to endanger it.

How would fortification units, whose morale had often been low, hold up? Would the many Alsace-Lorrainers in their ranks prove loyal? Would disharmony within units undermine fighting capacity? Would the fortifications ensure firm command? Would the integration of advanced technology and human and natural power represented by the fortifications prevail against a numerically stronger enemy (Figure 17)?

Retreat?

On 18 May, Gamelin had transferred Huntziger's 2nd Army from the 1st Army Group to Prételat's 2nd Army Group in order, he said, to allow its reinforcement with underemployed divisions behind the fortifications.[13] Two days later, in a telephone conversation, Weygand pressed Prételat to ensure that Huntziger adopted a more aggressive stance.[14] Prételat did send reinforcements to Huntziger, and urged counterattack. But Prételat was increasingly inclined to abandon the fortifications. His purpose was not only to prevent encirclement, but to ensure that troops were able to keep order. He too feared a communist coup and favoured an armistice.[15]

On 26 May, Prételat visited Weygand and Georges at La Ferté-sous-Jouarre, where, to avoid the hubbub of the GQG, they sat together on a bench in the grounds. Prételat feared that once the Aisne defences broke, Panzers would cross the open Champagne countryside and encircle his forces. He asked permission to withdraw from the Maginot Line.Weygand refused. He did not want to give others an excuse to retreat, and fortification troops anyway lacked transport. Retreat was pointless, he reassured Prételat, for the previous day (at the Conseil de guerre meeting) he had agreed with the government to stake everything on this line. The two generals later disagreed over whether Weygand uttered the word 'armistice'.[16] It hardly matters, for the possibility was in everyone's minds, and Weygand implied – optimistically – that it would quickly follow loss of the battle.

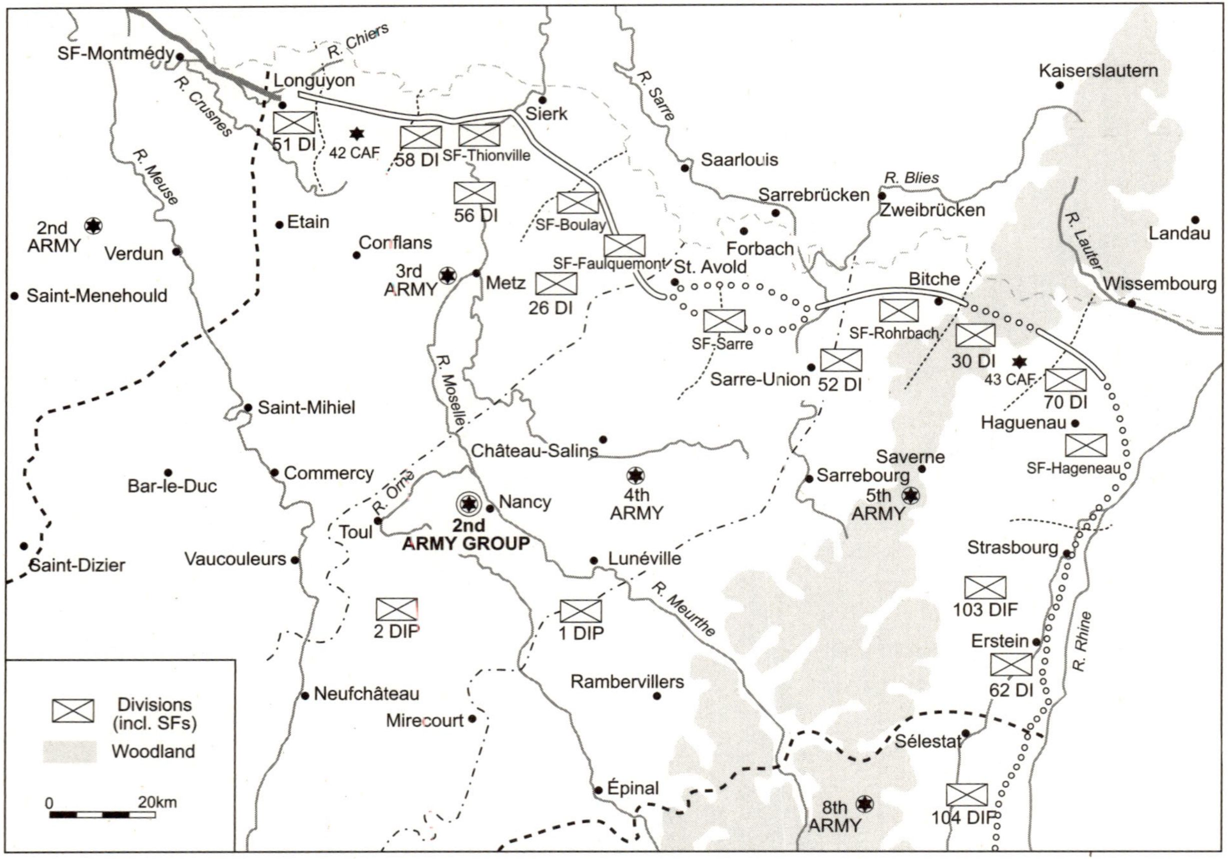

17. Divisions on the Maginot Line, 10 June 1940.

On 27 May, Prételat met Huntziger and Condé (3rd Army) at the Château d'Hattonchâtel, a neo-Renaissance pastiche on the site of a medieval castle destroyed in 1918. Prételat and Huntziger agreed on the need to abandon the fortifications and save the army to keep order, but differed on the means. Prételat urged Huntziger to echelon his defence in order to counterattack the enemy flanks. Huntziger reluctantly agreed to remain in line as long as possible with the 10th Army on his left and SF-Montmédy on his right. He would then, if necessary, withdraw to the Marne on his left and to Longuyon on the right flank of RF-Metz, thus abandoning the Montmédy fortifications. But to preserve forces to counter 'hard popular movements', Huntziger would have preferred a rapid move 100 kilometres west to the Morvan plateau without fighting. In his diary, he wrote, 'We must save the armies – that which is living – resign ourselves to what's dead, the CORF, since the Germans aren't attacking it.'[17] He thought that Prételat did not understand the pace of modern warfare. In fact, Prételat proposed ordering his subordinates to study retreat from the Maginot Line, but to prevent dislocation, he envisaged a fighting retreat in regulation 'bounds', covered for as long as possible by the *ouvrage* crews.[18]

Condé objected that retreat was impossible for immobile fortification regiments and harmful to France's image in Alsace-Lorraine. General Raymond Tessier, his chief of staff, added that any disorder would probably be directed at Huntziger for 'abandoning this fortress for which France has spent so many billions, and which the people are used to seeing as an unbreachable safeguard'.[19] In his diary, Condé worried, 'if we can't hold out with part of our forces on the fortifications, we will hold out even less successfully in open country with a few B divisions and fortress troops with no training for a war of movement. And we will be drowned in the population reflux, which risks turning into a total mess.'[20]

On 2 June, Huntziger and Prételat again failed to convince Weygand that retreat from the Maginot Line was vital. Weygand was closer to Prételat's than Huntziger's views on tactics, however, for he approved the limited retreat of the 2nd Army right to Montmédy then Longuyon and a counteroffensive into the flanks of enemy armour debouching from the Aisne.[21]

After the meeting, Prételat ordered his army staffs to study disengagement and ways to make fortress units more mobile. Tessier, responsible for this 'depressing and unsatisfying' task in the 3rd Army, arrived at a more or less acceptable battalion composition. But lack of transport meant that machine guns and antitank guns must be left behind. Most artillery could only go by rail, but there were few trains. Military engineers would have to leave everything. Stocks of food and ammunition would be distributed or abandoned.[22] He did not mention that the loss of so many horses further reduced mobility.

Prételat's fears intensified on 3 June. Georges informed him by telephone that Weygand had decided to put Huntziger at the head of a new 4th Army Group comprising the 2nd and 4th Armies, charged with defending the Champagne region. Prételat was understandably angry that the matter had not been raised the previous day, even though it must already have been decided. Prételat did not believe Huntziger capable of resistance.[23] Nevertheless, the following day, Georges confirmed Prételat's plans to reinforce and protect 2nd Army Group's flank. Georges and Weygand saw defeat as likely, but still not inevitable.

That was how matters stood when, on 5 June, the day after the Dunkirk battle ended, German Army Group B attacked French forces from the Somme to the Ailette Canal. The French inflicted heavy casualties on the enemy, forcing abandonment of the plan to head straight for Paris. Yet French forces soon retreated to the Seine, in effect to a second line – with the disadvantage that since the front line had been loaded, there were insufficient reserves to hold it or counterattack.[24] Kleist's Panzers then transferred east to support the attack on the Aisne. Huntziger's 4th Army Group was quickly broken on its left, where the 6th Army ceded as a result of the crisis on the Somme. On Huntziger's right, the 2nd Army, now under General Henry Freydenberg, held out better, but was hard pressed. On 10 June, a counterattack by forces previously deployed there by Prételat for such an eventuality inflicted heavy losses. At Vonq on the Aisne, *Stoßtruppen* sowed confusion deep into French lines without regard for their flanks. However, the *corps franc* of 36 DI, Robert Felsenhardt's unit, participated in counterattacks with armour that mopped up many of the infiltrators.[25]

That day, Prételat phoned Georges to ask how to harmonise his plans with Weygand's and warned of the danger of encirclement if Huntziger withdrew. Georges responded that Prételat had no right to complain because his fortress troops were better off than those on the Aisne. He nevertheless promised no retreat beyond the 'Argonne enclosure' – the current line.[26] Georges underestimated Huntziger's weakness, as the experience of Crémieux-Brilhac's 47 RI (20 DI, 42 CAF) shows. On 10 June, it was sent by rail to the Marne, losing nearly 200 killed and wounded to aerial bombing en route. Crémieux-Brilhac's battalion was surrounded and captured the next day at Jaulgonne. The rest of the regiment retreated east on foot.[27]

That night, Huntziger pulled his right back to a line with SF-Montmédy on its right. Yet whereas Prételat expected further delaying actions and counterattacks, Huntziger anticipated the general retreat he expected Weygand to order. Huntziger was as little concerned for the fortifications as he had been for the 9th Army four weeks previously.[28] Huntziger's reputation in high places remained mysteriously intact, for the following day, de Gaulle, on behalf of Reynaud, asked him to replace Weygand. Whether Huntziger accepted is not known, and Reynaud did not sack Weygand. By 12 June, Guderian, now leading his own Panzergruppe with four armoured divisions, was at Châlons-sur-Marne. The Montmédy fortifications were abandoned.[29]

On 11 June, Weygand signed preparatory orders for the general retreat of all six armies from the Channel to the Rhine, which became effective the next day. At the same time, Paris was declared an open city. There would be no more delaying actions behind natural or artificial obstacles, let alone counterattack. Weygand's objective was 'to regroup our large units in the best possible condition' in the south and west, avoid combat if possible and thus remain safe from capture before the armistice was concluded.[30] On the same day, he explicitly asked the Council of Ministers to request an armistice, which it refused to do. The armistice was not requested for another five days and not implemented for nine days beyond that.

The retreat order reached the 2nd Army Group at 15:00 on 12 June. En route, it crossed with Prételat's own preparatory retreat orders, which he had sent to Weygand to force his hand. Weygand, Huntziger and Georges expected Maginot Line troops to retreat quickly southwest via Sarrebourg, Épinal and Dijon to the Morvan. Prételat, as he told Weygand's staff on the telephone, considered it too late to disengage and that only an armistice could save the fortification troops, but nevertheless planned staged disengagement.[31]

After receiving the orders, Prételat summoned Tessier to discuss retreat of the 3rd Army. The latter repeated Condé's reservations. He asked only whether the high command was aware of the 'grave consequences of these orders'. Prételat assured him that retreat had been agreed with the Council of Ministers. (In fact, the council did not discuss retreat and rejected Weygand's armistice proposal.) Tessier expressed his sadness at abandoning Lorraine and Metz without fighting and launching the army 'into the tragic unknown'. As news arrived of a possible attack on the Sarre and of enormous concentrations of tanks northeast of Reims, a delegation of staff officers tried to persuade Tessier that if the GQG knew the real situation it would defend Alsace and Lorraine to the end.[32] There was nothing to be done. At 17:30, Weygand ordered retreat from the Maginot Line to begin and Prételat sent out his own orders soon after.

The plan was for a staged retreat. The next night, the 3rd Army's interval troops would withdraw in line seventy kilometres south to the Marne–Rhine Canal, where, as Condé put it, they would 'face the enemy'. The artillery, including casemate crews, would leave on the 14th/15th, and *ouvrage* crews on the 15th/16th, having first sabotaged them. The SF-Sarre troops would also leave in three stages beginning a night later on 14/15 June, reinforcing the Marne–Rhine Canal line. 5th Army's schedule differed in that its forces would not fight on the canal, but simply recuperate there before moving on. And because of the 5th Army's position facing north and east, it would leave battalion-strength interval troops behind together with *ouvrage* crews to cover retreat. On the Rhine, 8th Army troops would leave a skeleton force to support the Rhine casemates, while the bulk of forces would move west to hold the Vosges Mountains crossing points. There, they would cover 5th Army's retreat southwest, then head west themselves. To cover 2nd Army Group's western flank, further reinforcements would move to the Marne–Rhine Canal west of Nancy to link with the 2nd Army.

Prételat made a last attempt to persuade Weygand that it was too late to retreat. On 13 June, he made the 600-kilometre round trip to see Weygand at GQG, now at the Château de Vaugereau near Briare in the southwest. He aimed to urge Weygand to fulfil his 'promise' of 26 May concerning an armistice. Since Weygand had left for a Comité de guerre meeting, Prételat was met by General Doumenc, major-general at GQG, who remembered finding himself 'nose to nose with a man pale with fury, spitting out clipped phrases' to the effect that it would be criminal to obey Weygand's impossible order and that he would be netted like the armies at Dunkirk. Doumenc 'calmly' replied that Prételat would have been better advised to visit Georges at the nearby Château de Beauvoir. 'Not on my life,' replied Prételat. 'I'd strangle him.' Doumenc reassured Prételat that the government was aware of the situation, that Huntziger's forces were holding firm and that the enemy was running out of steam. That evening, Georges urged Prételat by telegram to hasten his withdrawal and noted in his diary that he had ordered him to move rapidly, not in bounds. The next day on the telephone, Prételat accused Georges of 'inertia' regarding the armistice.[33]

Corps, divisional and regimental commanders agreed that retreat was impossible. They advanced the familiar objections: weakening of the line, months of wasted work, lack of transport and the absence of a clear objective. General Fernand Lescanne, commanding XLIII Corps in the Vosges-Haguenau sector, saw retreat as 'nonsense', for he would probably arrive on the Moselle, his destination, with 'Germans on my arse'.[34]

In the *ouvrages*, consciousness of their predicament was intensified by shelling and infiltration, which now affected the Luxembourg border too. Late on 12 June, Lieutenant Graveel and the other Bréhain *ouvrage* bloc chiefs were called to the commander's room. Over a glass of wine, they learned the 'stupefying news' that 58 DI would leave at 21:30 that very evening. They devised plans to defend neighbouring casemates and their own surface themselves. Since rumours were spreading, Graveel gave his own turret crew the news: 'Consternation. A poignant silence. My eyes wet, but I recover.' Graveel urged the men to have confidence in him and put France first. As the men resumed work, he went to his room, threw himself on his bed, and wept. He then returned to drink the usual aperitif. Now that the *ouvrage* was surrounded, life was harder. The bread and wine rations were reduced; waste was no longer evacuated but stocked in an empty magazine.[35]

At *gros ouvrage* Michelsberg the loss of external power, consequent on the Génie's destruction of a generating station, enhanced the sense of isolation. The commander of Kerfent *petit ouvrage*, Captain Broché, saw no protection between his front and the German frontier. The departure of troops protecting the entrance bloc in the woods was another 'hard blow'.[36]

On the evening of the 13th, interval troops began to leave. Prételat ordered requisition of whatever horses, motor vehicles and carts remained, except that, for reasons unknown, the vehicles of the Briey factories were off limits. Major Dupas (1st battalion 156 RIF) recalled that his unit lacked carriages for transporting machine guns and antitank guns and that he had only five operational vans. In 37 RIF, neither dead horses nor broken-down vehicles were ever replaced. Despite heroic efforts by mechanics, only thirty-three of the regiment's seventy-six lorries and vans were serviceable. The men were not used to marching, especially those who had spent so long underground.[37] Those who had lived on their nerves in the advance posts were exhausted before they left.

Retreat was painfully slow, hampered by the flight of civilians and by other units. Officers and men, despite orders, took non-essentials accumulated over nine months. Georges Sadoul carried the manuscript of his history of the cinema. Even if units possessed wheeled transport, it was often inadequate. Colonel Orgebin (164 RIF) received carts from SF-Boulay, but they were partially loaded with items such as metallic beds. At 03:00, he saw his men pass, 'collars open, dark with sweat'. Each horse was pulling two carts, in one case a repainted hearse. The cortege included a cow fitted with a cacolet.[38] Things soon got worse. On the 14th, General Erwin von Witzleben's AOK 1 launched Operation Tiger in the Sarre Gap, from which defenders were due to leave in the evening.

Operation Tiger

In November 1939, the Germans drew up plans to attack the Sarre Gap and to cross the Rhine as soon as the Panzers arrived in the vicinity of

Langres (where they actually arrived on 15 June). Aware that the French might abandon the Maginot Line, they continuously probed their lines, and on 2–6 June, after bitter fighting, they forced withdrawal from the Sarre advance posts.

The marshy sector was defended by planned flooding covered by blockhouses. Many were incomplete, but there were hundreds of them and the STG casemates among them were solid. Since the departure of the 4th Army, the region had been defended by SF-Sarre, consisting of 69, 82 and 174 RIF and the colonial machine-gun regiments, 41 and 51 RMIC, supported by a Polish division. Casualty figures suggest that around 20 per cent of the fortification troops were Alsace-Lorrainers.

At 06:00 on 14 June, six German divisions, followed by three more in the second echelon, attacked from Saint-Avold to Puttelange. It was a classic frontal assault, preceded by the most intensive artillery bombardment of the campaign. As shells rained down on Lieutenant René Didelot's 174 RIF near Puttelange, his major panicked and sent men in all directions for news. The men looked at each other, pale and tense.[39] Back on the third line, shells fell on Guizard's sector, churning up soil, shredding trees, covering his shelter and riddling tents.[40] Then, Stukas came. As bombs fell, Captain Dupont saw civilians looting a tobacconist and a headless motorcycle rider beside his machine.[41] At 09:00, the infantry attacked, pushing antitank guns to fire at embrasures. They quickly overcame advance posts and took the HQ casemate at Kalmerich Wood, but did not breach the resistance position. At Holving, where Guizard had admired 41 RIMC's defences, blockhouses, an antitank ditch and clearance of a whole wood for a field of fire prevented the enemy from progressing.[42]

Although French units fought well, in one well-documented case Moselle soldiers proved disloyal. On the evening of the 14th, as the resistance of Captain Daubenton's 6th machine-gun company of II/174 RIF manning the Kalmerich casemate drew to an end, Sergeant Briot, a germanophone Mosellan, arrived with 'orders' from the Germans to surrender or die. In itself, that was unproblematic, for the Germans often used bilingual Alsace-Lorrainers as intermediaries. Threatened by Daubenton, however, Briot admitted that his men had left their casemate to fraternise with the Germans and agreed not to fire on their 'brothers'.[43] The incident was exceptional, but not inexplicable. The pro-Nazi Jungmannschaft counted members in the region and Bickler briefly served there. Lieutenant von Bleichert, a German artillery observer, commented that during the evening several Alsace-Lorrainers were among the prisoners taken from Daubenton's sector: 'They hope to see their homeland again very soon. Even the real Frenchmen [*echten Franzosen*] do not hide their joy that the war is over for them.'[44]

Despite this local success, neither interior French nor Alsace-Lorrainers panicked as troops at Sedan had. In the evening, Witzleben was ready to call off the operation, but documents on a captured lieutenant revealed the French plan to withdraw. With the Germans in hot pursuit, retreat became rout. Didelot's and Guizard's units retreated as part of the Groupement Dagnan (named after its commander). As Didelot's men fell back through the empty second-line casemates, they merged with a chasseur unit in a tangle of vehicles. Now they were convinced that they were 'fucked'.[45] Guizard's men were initially 'outraged': 'How can we so easily leave a position on which we've worked so hard? Yes, the attack was strong, but we were capable of resisting and could have received reinforcements.' That night, despite a painful knee and bruised feet, Guizard marched forty-six kilometres to Saint-Jean-de-Bassel. Men who had been ready to fight ferociously now believed all was lost.[46]

Operation Kleiner Bär

On the Rhine, AOK 7's objective was to pierce French defences on the 15 June, cross the Alsatian Plain and seize the entrances to the Vosges Mountains. AOK 7 was not well equipped or trained, but benefited from the support of field artillery, ten batteries of 88s and some assault engineers. The main effort was on a thirty-kilometre front from Schœnau to Neuf-Brisach.

The sector was held by 104 DIF, which was already preparing to leave. The forces remaining on the Rhine consisted only of two battalions each of 28 and 42 RIF, 242 RI, 9 and 10 BCPyr (Bataillon de chasseurs pyrénéens). Substantial CORF casemates covered the major crossing points, while lighter blockhouses constructed under the command of the general of that name were positioned on the banks. About a mile from the river were some stronger casemates and fortified villages. Northwards from Schœnau to Rhinau and beyond was a second position consisting of CORF casemates and fortified strong-points in the so-called 'Village Line' along the main north–south road.

During the night, commanders along the Rhine reported that the Germans were clearing passages in their barbed wire to bring up boats and 88mm guns. They asked in vain for artillery fire, but most guns had just been withdrawn – only three batteries of 170 RAP remained. On 15 June, at 09:00, a ten-minute, 300-gun bombardment rained down. The weather prevented use of Stukas, but for another ten minutes antitank guns fired directly at the embrasures and cloches of the Rhine casemates 400 metres away. Reply was difficult because the defenders lacked field artillery, their casemates fired only to the flanks and there were few turrets able to fire frontally. Eighty-eight fire went straight through the walls of the Garchery blockhouses, one of which collapsed into the Rhine; 37mm antitank guns were sufficient to destroy their weapons. The CORF casemates were more resistant, but ultimately they too were doomed to be pierced by 88mm shells. Officers' antiseptic reports do not convey the horror of the experience.[47] Besides the risk of injury from being thrown about, and of internal injuries, from ruptured eardrums to intestinal perforation and pulmonary haemorrhages, blast causes short-term disorientation and long-term traumatic brain injury. It was safest to evacuate during bombardment, but some fled in disorder to the second line, while others remained in the casemate until, inevitably, a shell exploded inside.

That was the fate of Rhine casemate Fort-Mortier in the 28 RIF zone. To suppress its fire, the Germans first targeted its cloche, in which they opened a breach. Another shell entered through the hole just as three men were attempting to block it with sandbags, killing one and wounding the others. Casemate commander Adjutant-chef Welsch vainly called for artillery to silence the German guns. The men could hear lumps of concrete detaching from the exterior. After another breach was made in the wall, a shell exploded in the main chamber.

Private Alphonse Ehresmann gasped in agony on the floor before dying. The ventilation system failed and the chamber filled with smoke.[48]

At 09:20, covered by smoke shells, the Germans sent seven divisions across the Rhine in 700 motorised assault boats. They took less than half a minute to cross, and although several were sunk, most made it to the French bank. The enemy quickly appeared behind Fort-Mortier casemate, but were beaten off with mortars from neighbouring casemates. The crew succeeeded in repairing an LMG, which fired on boats still crossing the river until the enemy put it out of action. The crew retreated to the second line.[49] On the French left, at Schœnau, ID 218 found most casemates neutralised to the north, but was pinned to the banks by fire from damaged Schœnau-Sud, which held out for another twenty-seven hours. Further south still, where blockhouses were less dense, down to Marckolsheim, ID 218 and 221 made short work of any casemate still capable of resisting. They infiltrated into the forest and approached the second line. Initially, ID 239 achieved similar success against 9 BCPyr, but a counterattack from the third line pushed them back. On the French right, at Neuf-Brisach, blockhouses were more numerous and well camouflaged and French artillery was stronger. Counterattacks by 28 RIF caused serious losses and abandonment of the crossing.

In contrast, ID 557's secondary attack, beginning at 13:00 at Rhinau in the 103 DIF sector (5th Army) to the north, occupied the banks with little opposition. Despite the continuing resistance of the Rhinau-Sud casemate, they progressed through the forest towards the Village Line. There, at 17:00, they took the Ziegelhof casemate, thus threatening its neighbours from the rear. By the evening, this was the only point at which the Germans were approaching their day-one objective, the Rhône–Rhine Canal.

Many of the troops defending the casemates were Alsatians, often commanded by teachers or priests. Their morale had been unproblematic during the phoney war. There had been relatively little pillage or military action, and although autonomism was strong in this Catholic area, there was little or no sympathy for Germany. That did not prevent the scapegoating of Alsatian soldiers. In captivity, certain officers of 42

RIF claimed that the Alsatian Lieutenant Paduch abandoned casemate Sponeck-Sud and led the Germans to second-line defences. In fact, Paduch had wisely ordered his men out of the casemate during the bombardment, and reoccupied it once the Germans began crossing the Rhine. Since the enemy had not destroyed the embrasures, the crew sank four boats, probably drowning many of the occupants, before an 88 began to fire on the casemate embrasures. At 10:30, enemy assault troops threw grenades through a shellhole in the cloche, but were fought off with grenades. An audacious German rushed the door and sprayed the occupants just as one defender was about to throw a grenade. It exploded, killing two men. Half the ten known deaths were of locals. Witnesses confirmed that after the casemate's surrender, the Germans pushed Paduch, without his helmet, ahead of them as a shield, not as a guide. It seems that officers projected unease about their own conduct onto Paduch – a pattern to be repeated.[50]

Since their artillery was in the process of repositioning and the infantry's own heavy weapons had not yet arrived, the Germans postponed further operations against the French. The next day, Stuka bombardment blinded the casemates and stunned their defenders, allowing pioneers to destroy their embrasures. In the Marckolsheim sector, the Germans then pushed into the forest, but were delayed by snipers in the trees and found it difficult to deploy their LMGs in the thick brush.[51] Further south towards Neuf-Brisach, Stukas and artillery destroyed casemates and easily crossed the Rhône–Rhine Canal, for it was dry thanks to the Génie having blown up the locks to prevent them serving as crossing points![52] By the evening of the 16th, when the defenders were ordered to retreat to the Vosges, the Germans had still not broken out, but the trap around the Maginot Line troops was closing on all sides.

Retreat Orders Modified

The Sarre and Rhine offensives, combined with the crisis of the 2nd Army in the west, compromised the already difficult disengagement from the fortifications. On 13 June, Guderian reached Saint-Dizier, thus splitting the 4th from the 2nd Army. On the 14th and 15th,

16 AOK pushed the 2nd Army off the old Verdun battlefield, where its latest batch of prisoners included François Mitterrand. OKW saw an opportunity quickly to seize the Lorraine steel complex intact and encircle the 2nd Army Group. Possibly, OKW realised that fortress troops' immobility made them easier to encircle than Huntziger's forces. Halder ordered Guderian's Panzers to the Swiss frontier.

Not only was Freydenberg's 2nd Army cut off from Huntziger's command, but Freydenberg himself had lost contact with his Corps. Prételat and Georges agreed by phone that these corps should come under 3rd Army orders. Freydenberg and his staff then sped south. To reinforce the western flank of the Maginot Line troops, Prételat ordered SF-Haguenau to send reinforcements. Eight battalions drawn from six RIFs plus artillery units formed the 'Groupe Regard' (after its commander) destined for the Chaumont region. On the night of 14/15 June, some left by road, while others waited at railway stations, for trains were difficult to assemble.[53]

At 13:10 on 15 June, in response to yet more outdated orders from GQG, 2nd Army Group secured modification of the interval troops' retreat itinerary. Rather than head southwest to the Morvan, units would form a redoubt in the Vosges. Those retreating south from the fortifications would form the north face on the Marne–Rhine Canal with their left at Nancy and Toul. Those heading west would reinforce the 2nd Army on the Moselle and Meurthe. The southern and eastern Vosges passes would constitute the other faces. Over 400,000 men, including 22,000 in the *ouvrages*, were caught in the second mass encirclement of the campaign after Dunkirk, but with no hope of rescue. Although the generals did not specify the purpose of this deployment, it was to hold out until the armistice. That evening, Condé and Bourret met near Épinal. Unable to contact Prételat, they pressed Georges to inform the government of their plight (Figure 18).[54]

The Germans now directly threatened the *ouvrages* from the rear and cut off the crews' retreat. Profiting from the 2nd Army's retreat from Montmédy, AOK 16 sent units to the rear of the northern flank of RF-Metz. On 15 June, GO-Latiremont fired on huge convoys of vehicles on the Route nationale, blowing up horses and men, while others ran into the fields. GO-Fermont harassed ID 183 as it moved south

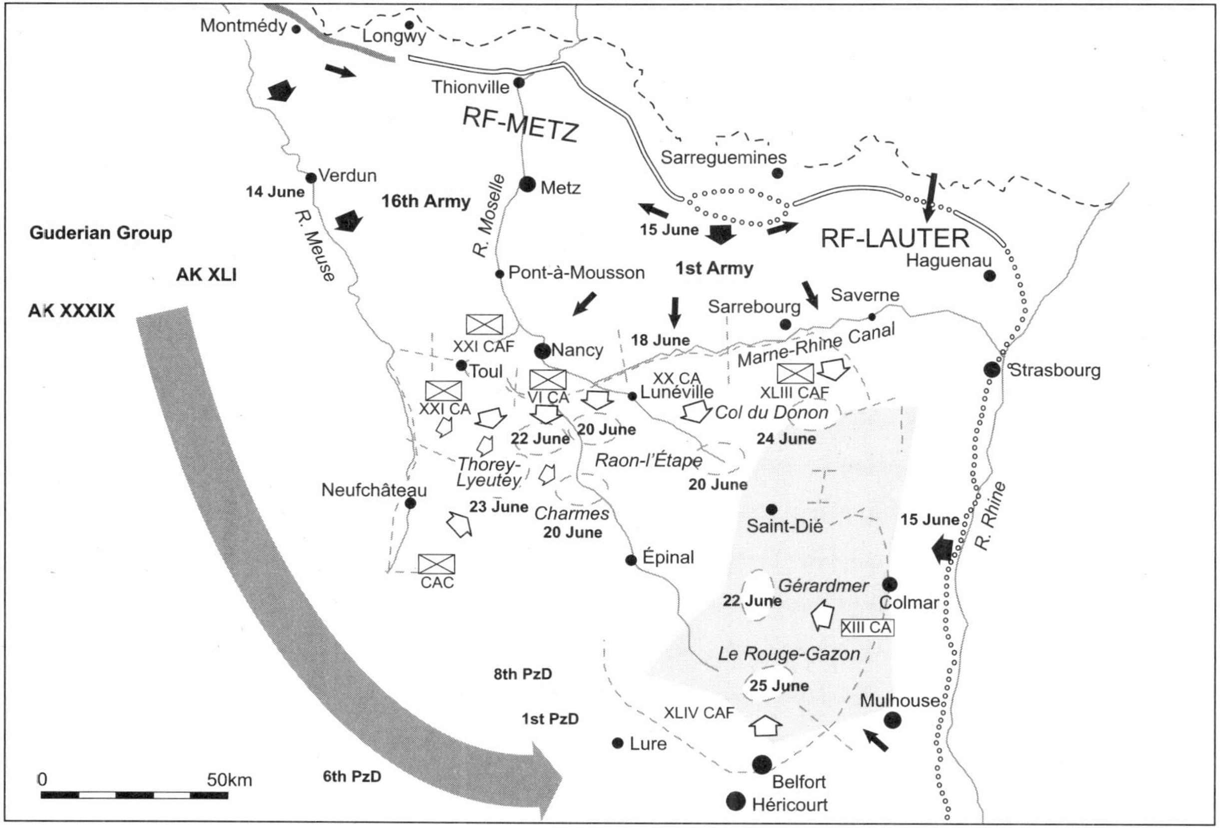

18. Retreat to the Vosges.

from Longwy. Meanwhile, Witzleben's AOK 1 fanned out from the Sarre Gap to the rear of the *ouvrages* on either side. On the evening of the 16th, German horsemen were in the vicinity of the first *ouvrages* in SF-Faulquemont. To the east, two members of a patrol from PO-Rohrbach were killed in an ambush. One was carrying the orders for retreat that night, which is probably why the advance posts were attacked as the artillery retreated.

On the night of 15/16 June, despite the presence of the Germans behind them, fortress artillery (the RAPs), interval casemate crews and remaining riflemen disengaged as timetabled. They were joined by 40 per cent of the *ouvrage* crews in SF-Thionville, which was judged to be particularly threatened. Lacking transport, many artillery units had to destroy their guns and ammunition. Their men were ill suited to marching, for mobilisation centres often assigned the flat-footed and arthritic to the artillery. Few had sidearms other than revolvers. En route, they faced not only German patrols but also bridges blown by those retreating ahead of them. Locals sometimes refused to shelter them for fear of attracting the Germans.

Many were quickly captured. Others wandered and hid, sometimes fighting off German patrols. At 23:00, a seventy-strong detachment led by Captain Jean Réquiston left PO-Immerhof. Slowed by unbroken new boots, the men passed through the destroyed village of Hettange-Grande before finding a barn to sleep in. The following night's march was still more painful. On 17 June, a German patrol discovered them sleeping in another barn.[55]

Sometimes, discipline collapsed. The casemate crews of SF-Faulquemont were reluctant to march at all, especially once they had left the road for open fields to avoid patrols. A lieutenant brandished his revolver to persuade them to continue after a halt, but some melted away. Others refused to cross an eight-metre-wide river. On the night of 17/18 June, they managed only eight kilometres in wet, muddy clothes, despite leaving behind those who had fallen by the wayside. They survived on cherries until they managed to kill a cow. On 22 June, a sergeant who had been captured looking for food brought news that armistice negotiations were underway.[56] The war was not over, but options changed.

The Armistice

The struggle of Reynaud and de Gaulle (in the government since 5 June) against the pro-armistice party led by Weygand, Pétain and a growing number of politicians had reached its climax. By 15 June, Reynaud had come round to the idea of capitulation in France and continuation of the war from the empire, without taking practical steps in that direction. Weygand, however, threatened resignation rather than the 'dishonour' of capitulation – despite units having capitulated all over the front. On 16 June, at a meeting of the Council of Ministers in Bordeaux, Pétain forced the issue by threatening his resignation unless the government concluded an armistice. At the end of the afternoon, in a second meeting, Reynaud – to his eternal regret – resigned rather than defend his own preference. Pétain became prime minister with Weygand as minister of defence. Now occupying a political post, Weygand left conduct of the battle to his subordinates. Had politics always been his unacknowledged ambition?

At 00:30 during the night of 16/17 June, the government, now under Marshal Pétain, asked the Germans via the Spanish embassy for 'the immediate cessation of hostilities and to make known the conditions of peace proposed by Germany'. That it asked not for the terms of an armistice as the government had agreed, but for those of peace, reveals the true stakes in the conflict of the preceding days.

At 12:30 on the next day, Pétain broadcast a short message: 'It is with heavy heart that I tell you we have to cease fighting.' This unfortunate formulation implied that the French should lay down their arms, perhaps even capitulate! Yet the Germans had not even replied to the request for an armistice. Newspapers subsequently added '*attempt* to cease combat'; Weygand instructed the army to keep fighting, and Pétain stressed in subsequent speeches that the armistice had not been concluded. Yet as Guderian's Panzers rushed southwards towards the Swiss frontier, they passed through towns in which mayors had pasted notices informing residents of the armistice and in which French troops were hanging about in cafés. As they moved towards Belfort, resistance increased, probably because the true situation was becoming known. Many French soldiers wished either to continue fighting or at least to avoid capture.[57]

Hardly any officers were aware that having been sacked from the government, de Gaulle had flown to London from where, on the 18th, he appealed on the BBC for the French people to continue the war. Apart from the practical obstacles to hearing the broadcast, de Gaulle was not popular in the army. It is well known that none of his own subordinates in 4 DCr answered his appeal, but not that its men also held him in low esteem. In its 7 June summary of morale, the postal censor took the unprecedented step of identifying him by name as the object of rank-and-file soldiers' criticism.[58] It is plausible that many of those fighting might have responded to an appeal from another high-ranking general to move to the Mediterranean ports for evacuation to North Aftrica. No such officer was to be found.

Initially, German commanders ordered their units to avoid needless casualties. On the evening of 17 June, however, the Führer ordered them to pursue the beaten enemy without respite and reoccupy the territory of the old Reich as far as Belfort, Toul and Verdun. Halder ordered Guderian to swing north from the Swiss border to pursue the French into the Vosges. It is possible that half of the 1.8 million men who became POWs were captured between the request for an armistice and its implementation.[59]

In the absence of a response from Germany, Pétain's government revived the plan to transfer part of the government to North Africa. Ministers were ready to leave during the night of 19/20 June. The next morning, aware of the danger that the French might after all continue the war, the Germans replied to the armistice request. Weygand insisted on an immediate cabinet meeting, thus preventing the ministers' departure.[60] On the Maginot Line, the battle continued.

SFs Vosges and Haguenau

On 19 June, ID 215 attacked the Northern Vosges Gap, where morale had been especially poor. A single line of blockhouses and casemates in the dense forest, in which trees had been cleared to provide narrow fields of fire, was defended by 165 RIF. Steep slopes and ravines prevented mutual support and hampered spotting for the artillery of GO-Four-à-Chaux, rendering ineffective the 1,680 artillery and mortar rounds that the *ouvrage* loosed off. Interval troops had gone.

The attack began with unsuccessful attempts by Stukas to suppress Four-à-Chaux artillery. However, air superiority permitted the Germans to deploy normally vulnerable observation balloons. The familiar combination of air, artillery and antitank bombardment damaged or blinded the blockhouses and dazed their defenders. In the absence of interval troops, infantry easily infiltrated the French position. They climbed onto two of the casemates' roofs and dropped grenades inside; pioneers then attacked the others from behind. Three casemates held out until the afternoon.[61] The military odds were more than usually loaded against the defenders, so it is hard to say whether low morale undermined their determination.

French defences resisted more effectively the following day on the right flank of SF-Haguenau. The morale of 22 and 79 RIF had been poor during the winter, but it was good in 23 RIF, on which the main blow fell. In the latter, we saw, there were solid personal ties between some interior French active and Alsatian reserve officers. Furthermore, on 7 June Colonel Regard informed his superiors that the course of the war and contact with the enemy in the advance posts had actually increased the troop's determination, especially as 'suspect elements' had 'mostly' been eliminated.[62] The balance of forces was also more favourable to the French. General-Lieutenant Erich Denecke's ID 246 comprised very young and rather old troops, neither well trained nor well equipped. The threatened casemates were stronger than those in the Northern Vosges, for they were mutually supporting and armed with antitank guns as well as machine guns. There was also a second line of infantry shelters. Well-placed observatories directed artillery from Hochwald and Schœnenbourg *ouvrages* to their left. Defenders were more numerous, for to support eight companies of casemate crews the 5th Army had left behind one battalion of fortress troops per sector, two Génie and transmissions companies and, against the wishes of 70 DI's commander, 81 BCP. The defenders benefited from a complete staff at Pfaffenhoffen, and a determined commander in the person of fifty-two-year-old Lieutenant-Colonel Jacques Schwartz, born in annexed Mulhouse and educated in France before entering Saint-Cyr.[63]

Denecke aimed to overcome casemates Aschbach-Ouest, Aschbach-Est, Oberrœdern-Nord and Oberrœdern-Sud, held by 79 RIF, in which morale had been difficult. Neither the usual artillery and Stuka bombardment nor antitank fire on embrasures and cupolas broke the defenders' will – not even at Oberrœdern-Sud, where a soldier in a cupola was decapitated. Infantry assaults were beaten off by fire from the *ouvrages* and casemates. Only at Oberrœdern-Nord did the Germans get close. Denecke ordered a Stuka bombardment on the casemates and *ouvrages* to cover withdrawal.

The defenders were nevertheless encircled, for ID 215, once through the Northern Vosges, wheeled east to their rear. To their right, SD-Bas-Rhin unexpectedly retreated, thus closing the trap. By the time of the armistice, Schwartz controlled a strip of territory from the Lembach *ouvrage* to the Rhine. Within it, Lieutenant Ollivier commanded forty-three determined Alsatians and two Parisians in the vicinity of GO-Hochwald. Their morale remained 'very high', despite storms, cold and mosquitos.[64]

Dernier carré

Meanwhile, together with the remnants of the 2nd Army, Maginot Line troops formed a last square, bounded by the Moselle and Meurthe rivers facing west, the Marne–Rhine Canal facing north and the Vosges Mountains facing east and south. Insofar as anyone commanded, it was Condé at 3rd Army HQ in Gérardmer, 225 kilometres from Prételat's HQ at Lons-le-Saunier until 16 June, then 275 kilometres from Bourg-en-Bresse thereafter. Condé assumed responsibility for the 5th Army, once it had retreated, for the 2nd Army, now officially removed from Huntziger's command, and on 16 June for the 8th Army.

Nothing illustrates the attachment of the generals to the preservation of 'command' better than the story of Prételat's counteroffensive order. On the evening of the 16th, under the mistaken impression that German armour was not yet in force on 2nd Army Group's western flank, he ordered Condé's 3rd Army to attack southwards from Nancy, supported by XXXXV Corps (formerly part of the 8th Army) moving west from southern Alsace towards Belfort and Mâcon. To 'stimulate energies', Prételat attempted to go to Belfort – an odd destination, given that Condé was in Gérardmer. Having been refused a plane, he left with his senior officers and orderly crammed into two cars. After ninety kilometres, he chanced upon the two officers he had sent to inform Condé of the attack order. They told him that his road was blocked, so he returned to Bourg-en-Bresse.[65]

Condé implemented the order – despite asking his diary how he could possibly attack southwards while covering himself in all directions, and despite having responded to Pétain's ceasefire speech by ordering troops to avoid needless bloodshed. Assembling units for the offensive succeeded only in disorganising defences on the western face of the redoubt, just as German pressure increased there. At 11:30 on 18 June, Condé cancelled the offensive, only for Prételat to pass on an order from the even more isolated Georges at GQG to summon 'last energies' and 'save honour'. Condé's rejoinder is worth quoting:

> Many units without bread, munitions or petrol. With their remaining not yet exhausted fractions, nearly all our corps contain the enemy with difficulty. Never a friendly plane, no intelligence. Enemy bombardment frequent. Any movement to the south, a movement one might call 'an offensive', could complete the collapse. As for saving the troop's honour after announcement of the end of the struggle, encircled, not supplied, fighting for six weeks in open countryside, it's done.[66]

Yet Condé launched the offensive and sent far-fetched reports on its progress.[67]

As Prételat and Condé conducted imaginary counteroffensives, interval troops retreated towards the Marne–Rhine Canal, where they lined up facing north with their backs to the Vosges Mountains. Among them was Didelot's 174 RIF, many men of which had either deserted or thrown their weapons away by the time they reached the canal. Yet the birds sang. A few men bucked up and sang too.[68] On 18 June, the Germans launched a frontal artillery-infantry attack in the fog. Despite a successful counterattack by 133 RIF, the Germans broke through in the 37 RIF sector. The next day, all units retreated into the Vosges.

Guizard, on the left of the canal with 41 RMIC, was disappointed to have to retreat again without fighting. He got his wish the next day at Avricourt, where his unit installed their machine guns in a house covering a bridge behind the first line. After a day of being forced into ditches by shelling, he slept that night in damp clothes. Unable to restrain a few tears, he prayed, clutched a medallion and 'thought of his mother, alone in this torment'. In the action next day, the battalion left at least ten dead behind.[69]

Reinforcements sent by rail and road to the west-facing flank rarely fought as coherent units. The dispersed elements of the Groupe Regard, which had left SF-Haguenau on 13/14 June, put themselves at the disposition of units wherever they found themselves, nearly 180 kilometres apart. The particularly well-documented story of one element, 1st battalion 22 RIF, merits a closer look, for its battle at Héricourt against the advance guard of 1 Panzer exposed many of the military, political and social tensions that have been followed through this book.[70]

Certain facts are clear. After the battalion left by train for Chaumont, its commander, Major Robert Babault, learned that that the enemy was already there. The train diverted towards Vesoul, but was blocked at Lure by a hospital train which had run out of water, on which there were hundreds of casualties including thirty dying young men. After burying those already dead, there was no choice but push the hospital train onwards, leaving it at Montbéliard. En route, Babault phoned the fortress city of Belfort for new orders. He was told to halt at Sainte-Evette, from where he made the short journey to report to the Belfort commander, General Louis-Germain Girol. Babault was ordered to defend the roads along which 1 Panzer was expected to advance to Belfort, with his most important detachment twelve kilometres south-west of the city in the small town of Héricourt (see Figure 18, page 361).

On 17 June, Babault set up his HQ in the Château Schwob I in the centre of the town, while Captain Richard Pierron's 25mm antitank and machine guns defended the southern exit to Lure and Besançon with his HQ in the Château Schwob II. Lieutenant Chazelle's company held the northern exit towards Belfort. Several vehicles passed through the darkness, some belonging to a retreating Polish unit, of which one man was accidentally shot dead in the confusion. Another vehicle contained two German plenipotentiaries on their way to seek Belfort's surrender.

Between midnight and 01:00 on the 18th, Pierron's company destroyed an armoured car, a Kübelwagen (the equivalent of a jeep) and an antitank gun, and captured two prisoners, all belonging to 1 Panzer's reconnaissance unit, Aufklärungs-Abteilung 4 (AA 4). An hour later, two more plenipotentiaries under a white flag arrived at Pierron's post and also asked to go through to Belfort. Pierron telephoned General Girol, who agreed to see the envoys and ordered the battalion to retreat to reinforce the defence of Belfort. Pierron phoned Babault, who declared this order 'stupid', and obtained Girol's permission to remain at his own risk.

At 06:00, the Germans attacked Pierron's group again. Another armoured car was destroyed and the commander of a French antitank gun was killed. Pierron and his men were captured. Depending on the source, the Germans withdrew in good order either because their mission was only to reconnoitre, or because Babault rallied a hotchpotch force that threw them back.

On 25 June, the day that the armistice entered force, Babault reported Pierron's 'cowardice' to his superiors.[71] He charged that on arrival at Héricourt, Pierron had been reluctant to unload his weapons, that he had invented Girol's withdrawal order, and that during the 06:00 hours combat, he found Pierron retreating in two columns with his machine guns having abandoned his antitank guns. Babault claimed to have physically forced Pierron to advance prior to his capture. Babault's accusation was followed up by a commission created by the Vichy regime to investigate 'suspect retreats'. We do not know the outcome, but on 13 June 1947, Pierron found himself before the judges of the Paris Military Tribunal, accused of 'abandonnement de poste'. He was acquitted, for Girol confirmed that he had ordered the battalion to retreat to Belfort. Even with the help of German documents that were not available to the court, the whole truth is uncertain, for the testimonies are inconsistent and incomplete. But it is possible to extrapolate some wider points.

The incident revealed complex tensions between and among Alsatians and interior French. Babault mentioned almost in passing that Pierron was a former reserve officer in the German army. He had indeed been incorporated in 1915 aged twenty as a Gefreiter (private), fought on the eastern and western fronts, and ended the war as a lieutenant with an Iron Cross.[72] Given, as we saw, that Alsatians made up most of the soldiers and NCOs and a majority of the officers in 22 RIF, he was probably not the only ex-German officer.[73] The Deuxième Bureau had described the regiment's morale as problematic in January and April, as it was in several units on that front.[74] That interior French–Alsatian relations were strained in the regiment is suggested by the fact that on 16 May, a squad of Alsatians sent out from GO-Hochwald to repair an antitank barrier complained that they were 'sacrificed' – an echo of the refrain that Alsace-Lorraine was the 'glacis' for others' fights. Their lieutenant blamed the inability of their drunken interior French chief-corporal to command Alsatians.[75] Pierron stated that Babault hated all things Alsatian and that he twice accused Alsatians of 'speaking Boche'.[76] Pierron's accusation is plausible. Yet Babault was married to a French-born germanophone woman of Alsatian origin.[77]

Whatever the reality of Babault's views, Pierron spoke as an affronted patriot. Indeed, he shared interior French suspicion of certain fellow Alsatians. He first appeared in this book as the anticlerical captain who reprimanded the five Catholic priests among his subordinates for preaching in German. Pierron thought that this dispute explained why one soldier-priest, Lieutenant Busser, testified against him in 1947.[78]

No evidence confirms one witness's claim – he was probably not an eyewitness – that only the 'Alsatian element' surrendered.[79] German after-action reports do not mention that the prisoners were Alsatian or that Pierron expressed pro-German sentiment. On the contrary, they made Pierron and Lieutenant Patay (of Pierron's company) stand for hours and threatened to shoot them if their envoys did not return from Belfort (they eventually did). In fact, German troops were as suspicious of Alsatians as the French. After-action reports lump Alsatians together with 'Emigranten' supposedly in the area, a pejorative term covering Volksdeutsche (Germans outside the Reich, including Alsatians), Polish fighters and International Brigaders. These documents also accuse Alsatians of cowardly acts, such as at Montbéliard a few miles away, of firing on an officer who was carrying a white flag and beating him up.[80]

There was also a social element to the conflict between Babault and Pierron. Another officer remembered that relations between reserve and regular officers in 22 RIF were 'not all they should have been'.[81] Pierron probably identified with active officers who, we have seen, were often dismissive of reserve officers and Saint-Maixentais. Years later, when Roger Bruge's book raked over the Héricourt battle, Pierron wrote to a friend that Babault was an overexcited, vulgar, uneducated 'bloke risen from the ranks', who should never have been an officer.[82] Babault's own file reveals that successive commanders had indeed described him as a brave soldier, but also as incapable and lacking education. In February 1939, he had left the army on the grounds of unfitness to serve.[83] Pierron had also risen from the ranks, but the difference was one of class too. When Babault arrived in the regiment, he offended Pierron by addressing him using the familiar 'tu', which, Pierron replied, he only allowed his friends to do.[84]

From a military perspective, Pierron considered himself a better soldier than Babault, perhaps because of his training in the German army. Pierron's elegiac evaluations describe him as 'very military' and show that he was an assiduous attendee at reserve-officer training. In 1947, he told his interrogator that Babault was a fine soldier of the Great War who had learned nothing since Verdun – yet Babault's otherwise negative evaluations praise his military knowledge. Pierron claimed in self-defence that at Héricourt he 'had the right and duty to take initiatives in order to fulfil his mission, which was to prevent the Germans entering Héricourt' – his words reflect German mission-oriented doctrine as much as the new emphasis on resourcefulness in revised French field manuals. Pierron admitted withdrawing his machine guns before the 06:00 battle and leaving his antitank guns uncovered, but said that he had done so because Babault's deployment was defective and that he only left the 25mm guns because their horses had bolted into the centre of town. He obeyed Babault's order to advance and was taken prisoner. Lieutenant Patay confirmed this account.[85]

Finally, given that both Babault and Pierron fought in 1914–18, one suspects the impact of traumatic stress. Research suggests cautiously that soldiers who had experienced that conflict were particularly likely to come before the commission investigating suspicious retreats.[86] As always, individual cases are impossible to prove. Yet Babault stated that when ordered to advance, Pierron replied, white as a sheet, 'I'm too frightened. We'll die' ('*Je n'ai pas le courage. On va mourir*'). Two civilian witnesses confirmed this account. The battalion medic stated that Pierron and Patay were 'cool' and 'brave' and favoured resistance, but doubted their men's determination. The medic was not an ocular witness to the battle, but wondered whether a fine man experienced a momentary lapse. As for Babault, Pierron described him 'shouting and gesticulating like a madman', and several witnesses confirmed his hotheadedness. Babault's evaluations state that after serious wounds in 1917, he was prone to mood swings, and was 'unbalanced', 'hot-headed' and 'unreliable'.[87]

The affair affected the course of the engagement, and perhaps caused unnecessary casualties, though whether Pierron's untimely retreat or Babault's initial deployment was at fault is impossible to say. Most likely the exhausted, tense officers misunderstood each other in a frightening, confused situation in which rumours abounded, as the rest of the day confirmed.

At 16:00, AA 4 attacked again, this time in force from the north. Although on the Maginot Line the Germans did not engage in the 'war of extermination' then beginning in Poland and evident in France in the massacre of Senegalese troops, the old fear of '*francs tireurs*' (sharpshooters)remained alive. Their anger at the 'rabble' (*Gesindel*) of 'Alsatians and international emigrants' who were supposedly responsible for the disappearance of their envoy, was compounded by the death of one of their oldest NCOs. A civilian who appeared in a window was shot dead. Civilian hostages accused of being *francs tireurs* were used as shields. The French fell back, except for a mortar section positioned in a farm, captured because only one man (an Alsatian) dared follow orders to retreat. The enemy's first attack was repelled with losses of men and vehicles. Under mortar cover, they then surrounded the HQ in Schwob I. Babault capitulated. The Germans claimed eighty French dead. The real number was eight, of whom five were Alsatian. The Germans lost four killed. Babault's stand did not protect Belfort, for 1 Panzer had already by-passed Héricourt to take Belfort from north and south, thus sealing the fate of the 8th Army.[88]

After the war, the 8th Army's commander, General Laure, was much criticised for not following his staff's advice to cross into Switzerland. That was still possible on 17 June, but on hearing that his old mentor,

Pétain, had announced a ceasefire, he followed Condé's order to retreat into the Vosges where he hoped to hold out until the armistice. Several years of service in Pétain's various cabinets had hardly prepared him for such responsibility. It is probably not a coincidence that shortly after Pétain joined the government, Laure replaced Garchery, who was close to Gamelin. Several witnesses remarked that Laure appeared overcome by events. He knew that Belfort covered movement into either the Vosges or Switzerland, but did not reinforce the city. He urged Girol to sabotage its modernised outer forts and defend only the unmodernised citadel. On the 18th, as Belfort fell, Weygand authorised crossing the frontier, but only some 45,000 troops made it.[89]

By 21 June, the remnants of 2nd Army Group were dispersed or isolated in pockets. The future Resistance leader Henri Frenay, a member of 43 CAF staff, marvelled that while career officers fought on because they had learned discipline at Saint-Cyr, peasants, workers, office staff and engineers, men who had left reluctantly for the frontier, 'fought courageously and sometimes fell despite safety being so near'. Here and there, however, he saw gendarmes stopping men fleeing.[90] Guizard's unit continued its fighting retreat into the Vosges, despite the men being convinced that they were surrounded and experiencing momentary panics. Guizard disarmed a drunk who was firing at his own men.[91]

As some units disintegrated, Alsace-Lorrainers often deserted, simply because they were closer to home. Those of 104 DIF on the Rhine, for instance, departed while the rest of the division withdrew to the Vosges.[92] Downstream, Aubrac's unit retreated, minus a few Alsatian peasants, whom he did not blame for leaving a routed army.[93] It is plausible that in 172 RIF, antipathy between officers and men, interior French and Alsace-Lorrainers played some part in the decision to stay or leave.[94] In the Vosges at Waldersbach, the regiment's third casemate-crew company was charged with defending the HQ of General Frédéric Vallé, commander of 103 DIF. They promised to hold out to the last cartridge, but an Alsatian lieutenant fled with three other Alsatians. The rest ambushed and counterattacked the German advance guards before capitulating on 22 June.[95]

In one case, discipline broke down entirely. On 20 June, hundreds of gunners belonging to 23 RAMF found themselves in an orchard in the village of Tantamont on the Moselle. Given that the men had followed orders to render their guns inoperable, officers and men alike were surprised when their commander, Colonel Joseph Charly, ordered them to deploy for a final combat. In the ensuing dispute, Charly may have drawn his revolver and ordered an NCO to organise a firing squad. He did order Gunner Fernand Burier, hitherto a model soldier, to gather abandoned ammunition. Burier supposedly replied, 'If I do go, I'll drop him.' Then, as Charly walked with another officer, Burier shot him in the back. Eight years later, a military tribunal convicted Burier, but took an indulgent view, officially because he had acted without premeditation, unofficially because the whole unit was complicit.[96]

On 21 June, General René-Paul Dubuisson (2 DIC) asked the Germans for a ceasefire; Laure (8th Army) ordered a ceasefire on the 22nd; Lescanne (43 CAF) followed suit on the 23rd. On the same day, the Groupement Dagnan capitulated in the Vosges, Didelot and Guizard among its ranks.[97] On the 24th, Condé himself surrendered. Only the *ouvrages* held out.

The *ouvrages*

Since 16 June, the presence of the enemy in the rear of most of the *ouvrages* made abandonment and retreat dangerous. The infantry officers and one cavalry officer, Major Paul Bonlarron, left behind to oversee the evacuation of the artillery, casemates and *ouvrages,* did not wish to disobey orders, but neither did they want to be captured.[98] Against them were ranged some *ouvrage* commanders and many junior officers, torn between desire to avoid POW status by holding out and fear of sharing the fate of La Ferté. Tensions mounted. In PO-Haut-Poirier, the crew resented Major André-Charles Jolivet, responsible for SF-Sarre, who had set up his HQ in the *ouvrage*, for his lack of fortification experience. Cochinard, who had established his HQ in GO-Anzeling, was said to have 'neutralised' the fort's commander, Major Ernest Guillebot, and compromised its close defence. Cochinard himself supposedly sank into despair. Major Denoix, for whom establishing an HQ in PO-Laudrefang was his first experience of a fort, left matters largely to a junior lieutenant, for the *ouvrage* commander was ill.[99]

Rumours abounded. Haut-Poirier officers thought that Jolivet must be a German in disguise. Rodolphe wrote that at Hochwald, at 'all levels', stories concerning parachutists and La Ferté 'created an atmosphere favouring acceptance of the most far-fetched information'.[100] At 06:30 on 16 June, Bréhain *ouvrage* unleashed several barrages at imaginary tanks.[101] At Anzeling, where there had been quarrels for months between arms, the mood was tense, just as reliance on the fort's own generators reduced ventilation. The return of warm weather made damp 'once again master of the blocs'.[102]

Alsace-Lorrainers were nervous. The army had supplied those among them who had fought for France in the last war with false papers to ensure that they were not executed for treason if captured. Some still feared that having been born in Germany, they might be shot as spies. According to Sapper Robert Reignier in Grand-Hohékirkel, one such Alsatian, 'a fine fellow but nervous', was smuggled out with the help of an officer who stole papers for him from another soldier.[103]

The enemy arrived in SF-Crusnes so early that abandonment was never seriously considered. In neighbouring SF-Thionville, the danger was considered so imminent that the *ouvrages* were partially evacuated early. Further east in SF-Boulay, Cochinard suspended the order on the 16th, but did not annul it (PO-Bousse was abandoned in the confusion). Commanders in SF-Faulquemont and SF-Rohrbach refused to cancel the order without approval from their uncontactable superiors. At PO-Laudrefang, officers believed they would not be able to cross their own barbed wire.

On 17 June, Pétain's ceasefire broadcast and news that the Germans were on the Swiss frontier changed things. In the afternoon, sector commanders annulled the retreat order – unaware that at 12:00 Condé had done likewise for the 3rd Army, perhaps knowing that Pétain was about to broadcast. If the *ouvrage* crews were to remain in situ, it was not clear why. Did Pétain's speech mean that the *ouvrages* must be handed over to the victor? Should they be defended in the event of attack?

There is little evidence that the refusal of Maginot Line troops to capitulate meant rejection of the armistice. More important was the understandable desire to avoid POW status. The *ouvrages* therefore refused invitations from enemy envoys to surrender. Cochinard broadcast the message 'All *ouvrages* from the Moselle to the Sarre holding firm.' At Bréhain, Graveel approved the rejection of German overtures because he expected the Germans to scale down their attacks now that they 'had France'.[104] In fact, the Germans were determined to assault the forts.

The *gros ouvrages* of RF-Metz would probably have proved a tough but not uncrackable nut had the Germans persisted. In SF-Crusnes, on 17 June, two 88mm Flak guns out of sight on a reverse slope fired 160 rounds at Fermont's Bloc 4. Four hours later, there was a one-metre hole in the casemate wall. One shot landed inside, without causing serious damage. Since the Flak gunners were unaware of their success, they ceased firing, thus giving the crew the opportunity to repair the breach with armoured plates.[105]

Infantry-artillery assaults were less successful. On 21 June, the Germans attacked Fermont again and PO-Ferme-Chappy. A two-hour heavy-artillery bombardment did no damage, even a direct hit on a turret, but the purpose was probably to suppress French artillery. Machine-gun and mortar fire from the *ouvrages* themselves plus artillery from neighbouring forts beat off infantry attacks. Leeb annulled further operations.[106] The only other *gros ouvrage* subjected to land assault was Michelsberg, which the Germans bombarded with 88s. The density of defences, however, made it impossible to position the guns close enough to damage the fort.

Well armed with direct- and indirect-fire weapons and supported by flanking *ouvrages*, the *gros ouvrages* were well placed to resist infantry-artillery assaults. Antitank guns were a major threat, though the high profile of the 88mm made it vulnerable. *Petits ouvrages* were less able to resist.

To the west of the Sarre Gap, the Germans faced the *petits ouvrages* of SF-Faulquemont, armed with machine guns and antitank guns and mostly lacking rear entrance blocks for ventilation and escape. Vichy's suspect retreats commission uncovered evidence of discipline problems in Bambesch, Einseling and Laudrefang, but the surviving documents provide little detail (see Figure 2, page 4).[107]

On 16–17 June, ID 167 profited from the absence of interval troops to infiltrate through the woods to the rear of Bambesch. Since the *ouvrage*'s indirect-fire 81mm mortar turret had never been constructed and the interval troops had departed, the Germans were free to deploy an 88mm in a ravine previously covered by an abandoned casemate (the Germans knew it to be abandoned because a casemate commander set fire to his diesel reserves, creating a column of black smoke). On the 19th–20th, antitank gunners destroyed Bloc 2, and then turned their attention to Bloc 3. In the absence of rear ventilation, toxic air from Bloc 1 flowed into the galleries. The *ouvrage* machine-gun turret, which covered both front and rear, was hit and jammed but continued to fire. The attacking infantry were beaten off once but subsequently got close enough to throw grenades into the air intakes. The *ouvrage* commander surrendered. The next day, the Germans repeated these tactics at Kerfent, which suffered from similar deficiencies. Antitank guns destroyed the blocs, allowing infantry to enter. They were repelled by an LMG firing through the embrasure in the armoured door. Again, the crew surrendered because destruction of the exhaust system for the *ouvrage* motors poisoned the air (see Plates 18 and 19). At nearby PO-Laudrefang, which had been attacked at the same time, the Génie constructed an additional exhaust in the postern door in the ditch around Bloc 1, which helped the *ouvrage* to hold out.[108]

On 22 June, the Germans failed to reduce Einseling *ouvrage*. The crew reoccupied certain casemates to fool the Germans into thinking that others were active. The enemy divided their assaulting infantry, which were repelled by machine guns in Einseling itself and reoccupied casemates. Crucially, the defenders benefited from Laudrefang's 81mm mortars, which were able to fire into dead ground. They kept 88mms distant enough to ensure that their fire was inaccurate, while mortars and machine guns put enemy infantry to flight.[109]

On the east of the Sarre Gap, the Germans faced three similar *petits ouvrages*, and there too morale was faltering (see Figure 3, page 4). On news of the armistice request, Major Bonlarron, responsible for SF-Rohrbach, ordered *ouvrages* not to fire on small enemy groups and on larger ones only if ordered by the government! He added that the *ouvrages* must be clean pending an armistice.[110]

The first *ouvrage* to be assaulted, PO-Haut-Poirier, was originally planned as an artillery fort with 75s and 135mm howitzers. It actually consisted of three linked machine-gun casemates, Bloc 2 also having a mixed-arm turret.[111] Its 50mm mortars had been delivered without supports. The *ouvrage* sappers managed to install one in a cloche, but there was no way to expel its gases.

Profiting from cover provided by abandoned French trenches and blockhouses, including one illegally constructed to cover the entrance, the Germans approached from the rear.[112] Assault troops were beaten off. But from early afternoon, they bombarded Bloc 3 with 105mm and 150mm artillery, for they lacked 88s. Enemy guns were invisible to Haut-Poirier's own weapons and out of range of Simserhof, the nearest artillery work. A heap of gravel prevented the weapons of Bloc 2 from covering the rear. The crew were helpless. Every five or six seconds they heard screeching as shells penetrated the concrete, then huge explosions. Eighty-one impacts each removed a fragment of concrete and exposed and twisted the steels. By the end of the afternoon, the concrete had been reduced by one metre. At around 18:30, a shell passed through the weapon chamber into a second chamber where it caused hundreds of mortar bombs and antitank shells to explode. Most of the crew were at the lower level eating, but the three men inside died instantly. For the rest of his days, bloc commander Lieutenant Robert Bonhomme's nights were disturbed by memories of the explosions and the sight of burned uniforms, blood, morsels of flesh and detached limbs.

The officers plus Jolivet met to discuss the situation. The *ouvrage* was still functioning, and there was some talk of fighting in the gallery. Doing so risked explosives being thrown in, however, as at La Ferté, while blocking the gallery with rails and concrete would cut off the power plant and therefore light and ventilation. An officer at neighbouring Welschhof heard from an Haut Poirier officer that German plenipotentiaries had told them that the armistice had been signed and that they had therefore stopped firing. Jolivet and *ouvrage* commander Captain Joanin Gambotti agreed that capitulation was justifiable because the *ouvrage* had resisted beyond 17 June, the Germans already controlled much of France and the armistice was signed (though not implemented). The one officer who objected quickly rallied to the majority. Late that evening, Haut-Poirier surrendered. If there was any sabotage of the *ouvrage*, it was very limited. Jolivet ordered crews of neighbouring casemates to leave them 'clean and in order'. After the war, the surrender provoked a polemic, of which the details remain obscure. Jolivet's authority may have covered a decision about which officers felt some guilt, for surrender exposed neighbouring *ouvrages*.

ID 262 turned its attention to the third fort in the line, Rohrbach. This *ouvrage* had the same weaknesses as its neighbours, but was covered by GO-Simserhof, which easily dealt with an infantry assault. On 23 June, General Edgar Theissen therefore reoriented his forces towards Welschhof and its interval casemates.[113] While he understood that, covered by Simserhof's artillery, it was likely to resist strongly, reconnaissance revealed that Welschhof itself had no artillery and that empty blockhouses could be used to shelter antitank guns. First, however, he sent a plenipotentiary to inform the defenders that the armistice had been signed.

Morale had been weak in the PO-Welschhof during the phoney war. After hearing Pétain's broadcast, Captain René Lhuisset assembled the men in the gallery, where he told them that their mission was defence without thought of retreat.[114] In fact, he packed his personal effects for departure and drew up an order advising his men how to behave towards the Germans. His lieutenants, after a painful discussion, persuaded him not to issue it, but the news got out. Through their embrasures, the crew could hear the Germans ringing church bells and see them letting off fireworks in neighbouring towns and villages to celebrate the signing of the armistice. On the radio, they heard Haut-Poirier surrender. Welschhof had similar weaknesses. Its 50mm mortars lacked supports. Simserhof's artillery could reach the fort only when the wind was favourable. The crew was obliged to remain quasi-permanently at their posts because some men had been sent to occupy abandoned blockhouses.

In the early hours of the 23rd, guns positioned beyond Simserhof's range began firing. By 08:30, the three flanking casemates had surrendered, for they were unable to defend themselves to the rear. For the rest of the day, three 150mm shells per minute hit Bloc 1 like huge jackhammers. The observation cloche, in which several men were injured by slivers of metal, was uninhabitable. From other blocs, it was possible to see that the roof slab had been reduced from 2.5 to 1.5 metres thick. Direct hits completely destroyed the twin machine guns and embrasure, leaving a gaping hole and jamming the armoured door leading to the interior. Although the bloc's 47mm in its second weapons chamber was intact, it pointed away from the attackers. Lieutenants Louis Haite (a bilingual Lorrainer born in Meurthe-et-Moselle department), Gaston André and Aloyse Fritz filled the hole with sandbags and knocked holes in the armoured door so that they could grenade anyone who entered.

As at La Ferté, the air was becoming unbreathable. To compensate for disruption of Bloc 3's air intake by bombardment, sappers opened an airflow from Bloc 1, but the blast of explosions disrupted or reversed it. Carbon dioxide built up in the western part of the *ouvrage*. Lhuisset feared that infantry would approach through dead ground to block the all too visible outlet for contaminated air.

The crew was divided. Lhuisset advocated capitulation on the grounds that the quantity of munitions stored in the galleries ruled out combat there and that the crew risked suffocation – the only emergency exit was through the drain. Furthermore, the *ouvrage* was of no use to its neighbours. Most of the junior officers, led by Haite, were determined to hold out for the short time remaining before the armistice, thus saving honour and their own freedom. Two pro-resistance NCOs caught Lhuisset preparing white flags. He agreed to delay capitulation until the next day, but ordered a white flag to be placed in Bloc 1 in case the Germans entered during the night. Lieutenants Herment, Caraman, Fritz and Haite, backed by the crew, insisted on defending the bloc anyway, for if the Germans reached the shaft they could throw explosives into the fort. They organised watches and made sure of the support of officers in the other blocs. The men kept their spirits up by endlessly listening to their phonograph.

The next morning, unknown to the resistance party, a corporal imparted to Lhuisset the false news that the Germans had entered Bloc 1. Lhuisset had white flags hoisted and reported to Bonlarron at Simserhof that it was no longer possible to hold out and that he was destroying documents; in fact, to avoid adding to CO_2 levels, they were not burned.

Although the *gros ouvrages* of SF-Haguenau and SF-Vosges were not subjected to ground assault, Hochwald and Schœnenbourg endured frightening heavy artillery and Stuka bombardment. Major Rodolphe, commander of Hochwald's artillery, recounted the experience. The men heard a growling, which grew in volume to the point where it rendered them mute. Then a strong explosion shook the bloc. Everything went out. The bloc trembled and oscillated as if shaken by a giant's hand. Shells stacked by the turret collapsed and rolled noisily into the neighbouring casemate. A torrent of water gushed towards the ammunition lift. Panicking, the men scrambled towards the staircase and stumbled down. Superficial damage was quickly repaired, and the men came back upstairs. Having seen that the roof remained intact, they regained confidence in their concrete.[115]

Rodolphe probably underestimated the psychological impact of bombardment. Flight from an *ouvrage* was not easy and was possibly more dangerous than remaining, but it did happen. At GO-Mont des Welches, which experienced shelling from 21 June, electro-mechanic Sergeant C. lost possession of his faculties, crossed the antitank ditch and fled. The explosion of an 81mm shell inside the *ouvrage*'s Bloc 1 caused only minor injuries but did nothing to calm fears. The next day, three more men deserted. After the armistice, it was discovered that fifteen men had left a nearby casemate.[116]

Grand-Hohékirkel also had a history of poor morale. According to a junior officer, its commander Major André Fabre literally wept on hearing Pétain's speech. He told his officers that despite the armistice the *ouvrage* would resist until all means were exhausted, and any casemate crew that left would be shelled. The letters of an ordinary soldier, Sapper Reignier, reveal that the crew had been dismayed at the abandonment order, for they expected certain death if they left, but that Fabre's determination was also unpopular. As the *ouvrage* fired in support of neighbouring casemates and was itself shelled, rumours spread that if the *ouvrage* surrendered, troops could return home, but if it resisted, one in three would be executed. Officers' authority collapsed and they were supposedly as panicky as their men. Fabre wandered the gallery like a lost soul. Reignier's claim that some men advocated vengeance against him is plausible, for such threats were common in peace and war. Reignier's letters also show that tension between Alsace-Lorrainers and interior French increased.[117] Neither officers nor men were aware that the delay in signing the armistice was due to Hitler's desire to take them prisoner and to the resistance of the *ouvrages* of the southeast.

Italy

As combats ended in the northeast, they began in the southeast.[118] Although Italy declared war on 10 June, it was in no position to carry out an offensive, for its forces were deployed defensively behind its fortifications. Consequently, combat was initially limited to exchanges of fire between fortified artillery and skirmishing, in which the French elite ski sections, the SES, held the initiative. On 21 June, the Italians nevertheless attacked all seven of the Alpine routes that were practical for motor vehicles along the 400-kilometre frontier. The notional objective was Marseille, but the real purpose was to take as much land as possible and arrive at the sea before the Germans.

Each pass was defended by a strong line of platoon- and sometimes company-manned concrete advance posts close to the frontier, which had no equivalent in the northeast. Further back, covering the advance posts, were twenty-two *gros ouvrages* and fifty-four other concrete works.

In the northern sector, the Italian 4th Army hardly got beyond the advance posts – vindication, perhaps, of General Degoutte's insistence on building them, despite the CORF's resistance. The main effort in the High Alps was through the La Seigne, Petit-Saint-Bernard and Col du Mont passes (SF-Savoie, SSF-Tarentaise) defended by the modernised Redoute-Ruinée and Séloges advance posts. Both held up the advance. Italian attempts to encircle them were incomplete by the armistice. Forty kilometres south, the Italians mounted subsidiary attacks through the Lac Mont Cenis region (SSF-Moyenne-Maurienne). Here the French counted on strong artillery works, advance posts and two B divisions. The Italians succeeded in taking the little fort of La Balme, but elsewhere slowly moving columns were halted by artillery and machine guns (Figure 19).

In the south (SF-Alpes-Maritimes), Italian units moving through the passes were supposed to link with a land and amphibious assault on the coast. In the mountains, however, gains were limited to the Haute-Maurienne (SF-Savoie), where, benefiting from the cover of a heavy fog, the Italians captured the unfinished Arcellins advance post. Forces advancing through the Ubaye valley towards the *ouvrages* of

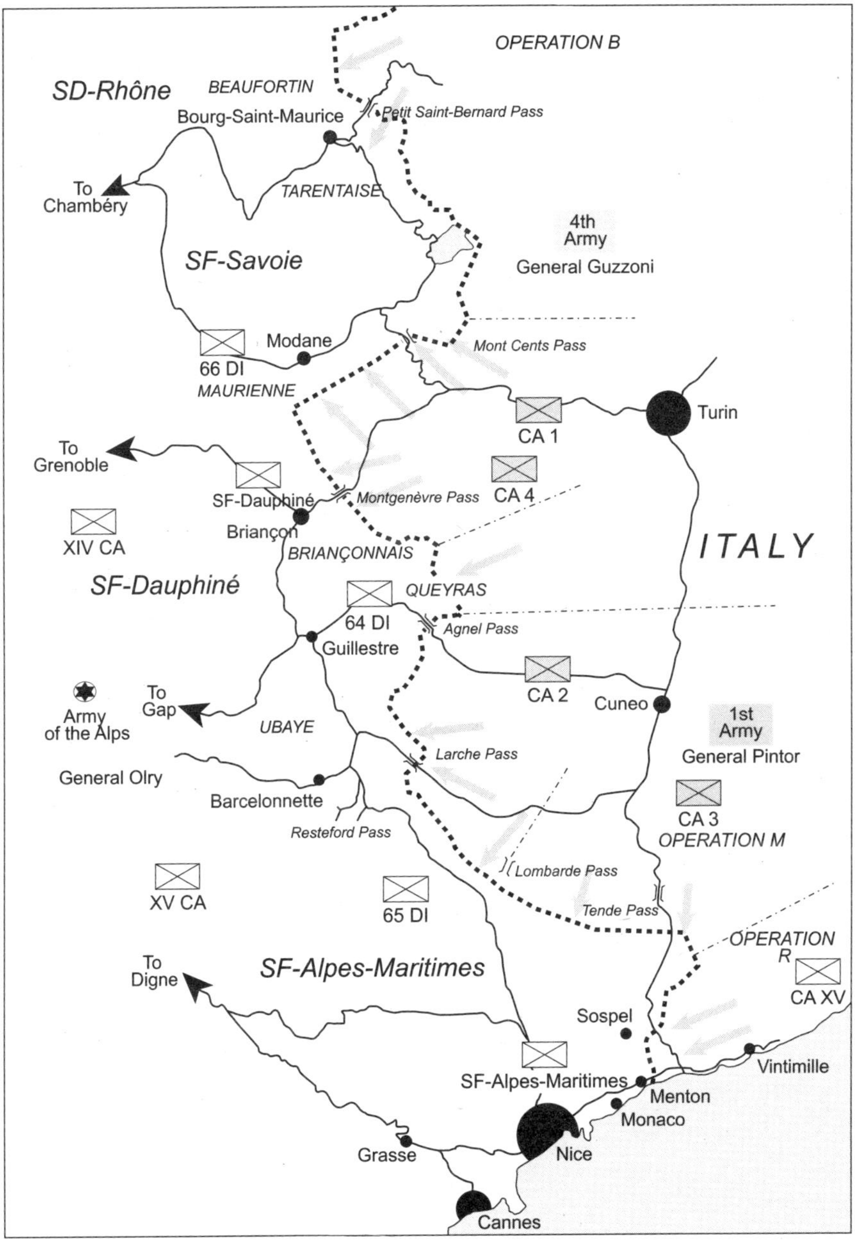

19. The Italian war.

SF-Dauphiné were so hampered by snow, fog and supply problems that they did not reach their destination before the armistice. The amphibious assault was called off on account of shortage of boats, high seas and strong moonlight. Land forces surrounded Menton, from which the French withdrew after street fighting. Against 40 French deaths, 84 wounded and 145 prisoners, the Italians lost 642 killed, 2,631 wounded and 1,141 prisoners. Furthermore, 2,151 Italians were incapacitated by frostbite. That French units were able to cope with the cold underlines how much better equipped French mountain troops were compared not only to the Italians but also to their own comrades in the northeast.

Hitler's patience ran out. He feared that excessive Italian demands would cause the French to reject the armistice and sail their fleet to British ports. The armistice established a fifty-kilometre demilitarised zone along the Italian frontier. The *ouvrages* were evacuated and left in the hands of guardians. The Italians did not feel able to treat the undefeated French as POWs, but the Germans did.

The End

Late on 24 June, French radio broadcast the terms of the armistice. France was to retain a theoretically sovereign government, its empire and its fleet, but the north and Atlantic coasts were to be occupied. Article 7 stated that fortifications situated in occupied territory, as those in the northeast were, must be handed over intact. The fate of the crews was less certain. Whereas Article 1 required encircled troops to lay down their arms, which amounted to capitulation, Article 4 stipulated that troops stationed but not captured in the future occupied zone should be moved to the unoccupied zone and Article 20 stated that captured troops must remain POWs. When the armistice came into force, the crews of most *ouvrages* had not been captured, and so they expected to move to the future unoccupied zone, just as those of Belfort and Bitche had in 1871.[119]

On the morning of 26 June, crews left the *ouvrages* to take the air and to inspect and photograph the marks of battle. They were physically and emotionally exhausted by weeks of extreme tension but grateful to be alive and in the open air. At Bréhain, Graveel joyfully walked among the trees, picked flowers and heard birds sing. Some trees had been scythed by his 'terrible shells', but 'bizarrely' he could not find the tank he imagined he had destroyed.[120]

Both sides were uncertain. The evening before the armistice became effective, French sector commanders forbade individual negotiation with the Germans, but their own dealings with plenipotentiaries varied. Schmidt in SF-Haguenau was most peremptory, agreeing only to send back German prisoners in return for the evacuation of French wounded. O'Sullivan in SF-Thionville was least so: he forbade damage to the *ouvrages* and speculated that crews would be 'sent to the rear'. The following day, German emissaries were sent packing from former RF-Lauter, the French refusing to negotiate on the grounds that their own high command had not informed them of the terms of the armistice. But in former RF-Metz, sector and *ouvrage* commanders began negotiations. Exchanges were confused because French communications had often broken down and the Germans received contradictory orders. During the afternoon of 26 June, Leeb, as commander of Army Group C, informed his subordinates that *ouvrage* crews were destined for POW camp. Yet some of his senior subordinates wished to apply Article 4, for they feared that if crews were forced to surrender, they would destroy the *ouvrages* and deprive the Germans of booty. To resolve the situation, Leeb asked the French high command to send officers to order surrender once the new armistice commission at Wiesbaden had resolved matters.

Meanwhile, the Germans persuaded the commanders of former RF-Metz to evacuate the *ouvrages* and march the crews to security camps pending the Wiesbaden commission's decision, to be personally delivered by a French staff officer. On the 27th, Graveel marched with the officers and men of GO-Bréhain to the Morfontaine security camp, where they blushed when the Germans showed them the damage inflicted by interval troops before they left. Graveel then returned to the *ouvrage* to clear mines and unexploded shells – a condition of the armistice – a task which cost one man his life.[121] Speculation about whether the men would be sent to POW camp or to the unoccupied zone spread across the fortified zone.

At GQG, Georges instructed the three staff officers charged with attending the armistice commission to make the case for the application of Article 4. On 28 June, they arrived at German 1st Army HQ at Lunéville. Both sides stood their ground, and so the French moved on to Wiesbaden. There, they briefed Huntziger, who had just arrived to take up his position as French delegate to the commission. Humiliatingly, Huntziger had to make the case to a mere major, who passed it on to Commission President General Carl-Heinrich von Stülpnagel. The next day, Stülpnagel informed the French by letter that they must personally order the *ouvrages* to surrender, and that failure to do so would breach the armistice. If the French refused, Lyon, Clermont-Ferrand and Saint-Étienne would remain occupied. They were not informed that German forces had been ordered to prepare to move towards Toulouse.

The Germans' case was dubious. Not only had they encouraged the French high command to believe that only a few *ouvrages* were resisting surrender, but Stülpnagel's letter also falsely asserted that Article 4 applied only to troops that had freedom of movement. Its claim that commanders in former RF-Metz had accepted the German position was excessive, for they had handed over the *ouvrages* but left the fate of the crews in suspense. Roger Bruge criticised RF-Metz commanders for providing the Germans with a pretext, but in fact the OKW had probably already made its decision. The three French staff officers left to deliver the bad news to sector commanders, who, without exception, protested against the decision to make prisoners of them (see Plate 20). Major Pophillat, commander in SF-Crusnes, admitted a few days later that premature evacuation of the *ouvrages* had deprived the French of bargaining power.

Bruge's suggestion that Weygand and Huntziger gave way too easily is more convincing. He argues that their long-standing indifference to fortification troops led them to underestimate how many *ouvrages* had refused to surrender. When they arrived in the fortified zone, the three staff officers were shocked to discover that almost all the *ouvrages* were intact. One of them told Cochinard that they would make another appeal on their behalf. Back at Lunéville, they telegrammed Huntziger to say that the entire Maginot Line from Rochonvillers to Saint-Avold and from Rohrbach to the Rhine was concerned. Huntziger's diary shows that despite Bruge's doubts that he had really done so, he did in fact make the request. He received another refusal from Stülpnagel. Weygand sent a telegram to the *ouvrages* congratulating them for resisting until the high command informed them of the ceasefire. In reality, commanders were well aware of the ceasefire and rather than 'resist' they had simply refused to leave the *ouvrages*. Bruges doubts that the Germans would have jeopardised the armistice and risked the French fleet and air force joining the British camp just to capture 22,000 more prisoners. Whatever the case, Weygand and Huntziger had been desperate for an armistice, and were unlikely to do anything to endanger it. At about the same time, Huntziger ordered surrender of a fort on the Swiss border that had not even been surrounded.[122]

On 1 and 2 July, the crews left for POW camp. Those of the unfortunate class of 1935 were to spend almost their entire twenties away from home. Having completed their military service from September 1936 to August 1938, only to be recalled during the Munich crisis in September, they returned again in March 1940, their service often ending only with liberation from POW camp in 1945. For many of the senior officers, this was not their first experience of captivity. Cochinard and Fabre had both been captured in August 1914, the former in the terrible defeat at Morhange, the latter with the surrender of the Maubeuge citadel (see Plates 21 and 22).

CONCLUSION: MYTH AND HISTORY

Pétain's Vichy regime attributed the defeat to republicans, communists, socialists, pacifists, the British, Freemasons and Jews. Under Vichy's antisemitic laws, around 96 Jewish officers were expelled from the land army; the War Ministry, held at the time by General Huntziger, secured a special dispensation to additionally exclude at least 216 NCOs. Jews were forbidden to join as ordinary soldiers.[1] Lieutenant Robert Felsenhardt, who had escaped from captivity, refused the chance to remain in the army, for he rightly expected that his Jewish origin would soon result in his expulsion. He joined a Resistance network that ultimately became Libération-Nord. He survived the war and went on to become a famous radiesthesist.[2]

One of Vichy's first acts was to establish a high court to judge the 'guilty'. The Riom legal jurisdiction drew up charges against Daladier, the former air minister Guy La Chambre and Léon Blum, along with Robert Jacomet, secretary-general at the War Ministry, and Gamelin. Daladier was arrested at the home of André Borie, head of the firm that had constructed so much of the Maginot Line. Reynaud was also arrested, but never prosecuted at Riom because a trial would only have highlighted his and de Gaulle's campaign for armoured divisions.

Meanwhile, the previously mentioned commission established by Defence Minister Weygand to investigate 'suspicious retreats' compiled nearly 6,000 dossiers.[3] The commission was kept secret for fear of exacerbating division within the army and undermining the case against politicians. It rarely troubled senior generals, not least because Huntziger served as war minister for eleven months from September 1940. Prételat was not investigated, despite Commission President General Frère considering that an officer of his rank should have risked his life to rejoin his men. These suspicions did not prevent Prételat from being appointed president of another commission responsible for stripping Vichy's enemies of their citizenship. Condé, who had remained with his men, was investigated but cleared.[4]

Vichy's leaders never attributed the defeat to the Maginot Line. To avoid appearing to repudiate the armistice, its tame press made little of the *ouvrage* garrisons' refusal to capitulate. In the Riom trial, in which fortification could not be avoided, prosecutors and witnesses saw the problem as too little fortification, not too much; they depicted it as one more example of underfunding and criticised failure to extend the Maginot Line to the north. General Laure, who rejoined Pétain's inner circle once released from POW camp, wrote in his 1942 biography that 'this gigantic work, to which nothing could be compared, carries in every way the mark of [Pétain's] mind and will'.[5] Yet delving too deeply into the fortifications' history might have revealed that Pétain had long resisted the construction of *gros ouvrages*, had opposed fortification of the Belgian border and had joined Daladier in pressing for cuts that had compromised the resistance of several *petits ouvrages* in June 1940.

Ultra-collaborationists, the pro-Nazis who criticised Vichy and its governments for rejecting total integration of France into Germany's New Order, were more critical of the fortifications. One such journalist claimed that even if they had been extended to the north, Germany's superior forces would have broken through. Yet he also praised Pétain for recognising that the fortifications lacked depth.[6]

The Resistance, particularly the followers of de Gaulle, was primarily responsible for the Maginot myth. It was easy for the Resistance to contrast de Gaulle's advocacy of mobile armoured warfare and resistance with Pétain's pessimism, defeatism during the 1940 campaign and collaboration. In 1944, in a tendentious anti-Pétain pamphlet, the Gaullist Albert Bayet condemned the 'old men of the general staff . . . the imbecilic doctrinaires who clung on to the theory of inviolable lines' inherited from the Great War. With 'Pétain at their head, they opposed their senile and stubborn orthodoxy to de Gaulle and the innovators, the theorists of the tank and the aircraft'.[7] Reynaud wrote from his prison cell to Pétain: 'Do we believe that the French people will remain unaware that the high command insisted that a continuous front from the sea to Switzerland was invulnerable and that the enemy could only create salients in it, which, the deeper they were, would be the more dangerous for him?'[8] The report of the postwar parliamentary enquiry into the defeat, authored by one of de Gaulle's pre-1939 parliamentary allies, saw the general staff's 'static conception of defence' as the primary cause of defeat.[9]

After the war, Gaullists reshaped the Maginot Line myth. De Gaulle's enemy was now the Fourth Republic, which he saw as perpetuating the error of the Third in establishing a powerful parliament and weak presidency of the Republic. In his memoirs, written in 1954, he claimed that since the politically unstable parliamentary republics were unable to give clear direction to the army, its ageing commanders rejected manoeuvre for the obsolete continuous front. Furthermore, de Gaulle held that defensiveness and passivity emanated from the 'stagnant' mentality of the whole nation.[10] In 1958, as a result of what can only be described as a coup, de Gaulle became president of the new Fifth Republic. Numerous TV documentaries presented the Maginot Line as a symbol of 'decadent' parliamentary government, to be implicitly contrasted with the modern presidential constitution, the latter equated with armoured warfare and soon an independent nuclear strike force.

Academic historians buttressed the myth. An obligatory reference point was Marc Bloch's *L'étrange défaite* (Strange defeat). The author was a world-famous social historian and veteran of both wars, executed by the Germans in 1945 for Resistance activities. His manuscript, published posthumously in 1946, argued that although a republic (in France, republic and democracy are synonymous) was the best form of government, it had become 'decadent'. His book is a long indictment of the intellectual failings and egoism of all classes of French society. He unwittingly echoed de Gaulle in claiming that the parliamentary regime had allowed too much power to the old-fashioned 'feudal' general staff, which had sunk excessive money in concrete at the expense of tanks and planes. We were taught, he wrote, to 'place all our confidence in the Maginot Line, built at great expense with a great outpouring of publicity, only to make it too short on the left, thus allowing it to be outflanked'.[11] Bloch's book became a pillar of the decadence thesis.

There would be little point in simply piling up evidence that the French were 'not decadent', for that would mean replacing one easy generalisation about 'the French' with another. The problem is with the concept of a national mentality itself. More convincing explanations of the defeat show that specific problems mattered in relation to German plans. They largely agree that Allied weakness in the air, their consequent inability to locate the enemy and therefore take the initiative, inadequate telecommunications and the advance deep into the Low Countries and failure to divine the German plan explained the defeat. Whether a different strategy would have brought victory or avoided defeat, we cannot say. Notwithstanding, had the troops behind the Maginot Line reinforced a 2nd Army advance northwards rather than committing them piecemeal, the resulting course of events would have been different, especially given that we now know how much Hitler feared such an attack. Likewise, had the Germans stuck to their original plan of driving through central Belgium to the sea, the Allied deployment would have made more sense. But could they have held off a stronger attack than that which they resisted at Gembloux?

The Maginot Line's contribution to the defeat was mixed. Some myths are easily disposed of. It was not 'in the wrong place': it blocked the easiest routes to Paris, into Alsace and towards Nice. The French did not consider the fortifications invulnerable. However, the Germans concluded that they would not be ready to assault them frontally until 1941 and therefore risked everything on violation of the neutrality of Belgium, the Netherlands and Luxembourg. Indeed, the fortifications were constructed, from the strategic to the tactical level, to force the Germans to take this route, and thus guarantee British intervention, which at the time of construction was far from certain.

The fortifications were not an enormous burden on French arms spending. Between 1920 and 1934, the army received 77 billion of credits, of which no less than 67 billion simply maintained the troops. Of the remaining 10, the CORF special account received 5.4 billion up to 1936 (not counting armaments). Researching, testing and manufacturing new equipment received 2.5 billion. In addition, up to June

1938, the regions received 1,801 million for field works.[12] Although until 1936 fortification accounted for almost all spending on modern weapons, tanks and especially aircraft mass-produced at that time would have been obsolete by 1938, let alone 1940 – yet obsolete German tanks proved capable of sowing chaos in the French rear. Technology on its own was not decisive.

Once it was clear that Gamelin had sent the best French forces into a trap, overmanning of the Maginot Line compromised the ability to counterattack the German armoured divisions. Gamelin and Prételat had foreseen that the Maginot Line undermined the manoeuvrability of the field army, but attempts to reorganise fortification troops either came to nothing or further weakened defences at the decisive points on the Meuse.

A major reason for the failure to deal with overmanning is that the fortifications had become a powerful interest within the army. Although or because fortification troops were so often treated as second rate, they stubbornly defended their system and their 'interests'. As in any top-down management system, the desire to foresee everything and the focus on the 1 per cent of things that might go wrong, especially when combined with cost-cutting, creates a self-sustaining bureaucracy with a vested interest in identifying system-endangering problems and solutions. Bureaucratisation often stems from 'efficiency savings'.

Rather than speculate on different outcomes, it is more illuminating to remember the immense difficulties the French faced, with a more powerful enemy, unreliable allies, few offensive possibilities and a long, vulnerable frontier. Comparison of France in 1940 with German options in 1944 reveals multiple comparisons with Sedan. Unable to take the initiative against a superior foe, the Germans suffered the intrinsic weakness of initial defence – the ability of the enemy to concentrate overwhelming force at a weak point. To compensate, the Wehrmacht devoted extensive resources to fortifications from Trondheim to Bordeaux – not to speak of east Prussia – to which they transferred guns from the Maginot Line. German generals disagreed on how to resist an Allied invasion – Rommel pushed for immediate beach defence, while Geyr von Schweppenburg favoured a delayed, massive armoured counterattack. Misled by Allied deception, OKW expected the main attack at Pas-de-Calais and hesitated when Normandy was invaded, unsure if it was a diversion. The 21st Panzer Division's counterattack was delayed by tangled command chains and Allied air superiority. Most of its tanks were destroyed by British forces; panic spread among rear troops after false reports that Caen had fallen. OKW delayed deploying stronger Panzer divisions, and the Das Reich division took seventeen days to reach Normandy due to bombings, Resistance sabotage and halts to massacre civilians. In Normandy, armour was dispersed to hold the line. Das Reich's counterattack on 28 June failed against British forces.

To underline the point, German success in 1940 depended not only on their plan, but on circumstances and French deployment and actions. The relatively small theatre of northern France meant that Guderian's decision to push on ahead of the slow-moving infantry did not have the negative consequences of similar actions in Russia. Had the Germans lost in 1940, it would have been possible with hindsight to point to 'deep causes' such as plots against Hitler, tension between OKH and OKW, disagreement on the tank–infantry relationship, the late formation of several German armoured divisions, the inability of German industry to manufacture the Panzer IV in sufficient quantity, the poor training of infantry reserves, and so on.

The history of the Maginot Line throws a more novel light on a related, surprisingly neglected question: *why* did the army engage in such a risky operation in the Low Countries? The answer proposed here is that Gamelin's decision to impose the Dyle–Breda manoeuvre, or at least the Breda variant, on Georges, was part of a politicised power struggle between the two generals. While historians have recognised the political and military pressure on Gamelin to take decisive action, they have not related the Dyle–Breda operation to his long-held preference for defensive manoeuvre and counterattack rather than continuous fronts. The issues were not new. They dated back at least to Colonel Pétain's opposition to offensive doctrine before 1914. The controversy shaped patronage and promotions and was materialised in the Maginot Line and in motorised and mechanised forces. These conflicts were complicated by questions such as the introduction of short military service, republicanisation of the army, tactical devolution of command, officers' dislike of fortification service and the appearance of faster aircraft, tanks and infantry and artillery transport.

The outcome of these struggles varied over time. Until around 1927, the French planned to advance from occupied Germany to meet the eastern allies. Fortification was a low priority, but debates about future plans revealed the extent of doctrinal conflict. The Maginot Line emerged from the brief period of international détente and relative financial health from 1927 to around 1931. Then, when Weygand and Gamelin replaced Pétain and Debeney, construction of the Maginot Line coincided with moves towards mobility, at first constrained by resources, but which developed quickly from 1936. By 1938–9, the picture is of polarisation, expressed most starkly in Pétain's warning, albeit exaggerated, that offensive doctrine was re-emerging. The advance of motorisation and mechanisation contrasted with appeasers' desire to remain behind the Maginot Line rather than support Czechoslovakia. One may certainly find evidence of a 'Maginot mentality' in this period in public culture too, but it coexisted with imaginings of decisive victories in France or elsewhere. Polarisation increased during the phoney war, as some generals and politicians began to doubt that France could win a long war. Plans were hatched for interventions in peripheral theatres. The (misunderstood) crisis of morale during the phoney war increased pressure on Gamelin to 'do something'.

That brings us to the Maginot Line as a response to the challenges of democracy, communism, autonomism and tactical devolution of command. The fortifications were built on the centralising, calculable principles of the classical tradition, updated with organisational science and modernism and with the latest technology. They were conceived as a hierarchical, rationalised system of interdependent parts. Soldiers, the terrain, air and water were formless and dangerous unless 'organised' by an elite. Reality proved them wrong.

Firstly, despite the legend of the 'forteresse invaincue', the Maginot Line's military record was mixed. Besides hundreds of blockhouses, the Germans overcame nine of thirty-two *petits ouvrages*: La Ferté, four at Maubeuge, two in SF-Faulquemont and two more in SF-Sarre. Two *gros ouvrages*, Le Chesnois and Velosnes in SF-Montmédy, were abandoned, as was PO-Bousse; Fermont, Schœnenbourg and Hochwald were damaged by heavy artillery, though their armament was intact.

Although the Génie designed forts resistant to the heaviest artillery, their casemates proved vulnerable to repeated bullseyes, not only from high-velocity 88s, which had not been foreseen in 1926, but also from light field artillery firing anti-concrete shells. Five *petits ouvrages* were neutralised by artillery alone – Sarts, Bambesch, Kerfent, Haut-Poirier and Welschhof. The other four – La Ferté, Bersillies, La Salmagne and Boussois – succumbed to infantry, which infiltrated sufficiently close to neutralise ventilation systems and/or weapons.

Design flaws were magnified by the departure of interval troops, who might have been able to keep infiltrators at bay and locate enemy artillery. At La Ferté, however, significant interval troops remained. Covering troops on the Chiers further forward were withdrawn but not those defending the *ouvrage* itself, and the 2nd Army mounted an unsuccessful armoured counterattack. The dependence of the fortifications on supporting troops, moreover, worked against resource economy. It should also be remembered that the fortifications were confronted by second-rate German forces without tanks and sometimes without 88mm guns.

Cost-cutting was a major reason for the weaknesses in the Maginot Line. Many *gros ouvrages* were not built at all, and those that were built were more widely spaced than originally planned and deprived of some of their weapons. La Ferté, Bambesch, Kerfent, Haut-Poirier and the blockhouses of the Northern Vosges Forest all paid the price of too-distant artillery cover. Yet building the originally planned number of *gros ouvrages* was impossible for an army that could barely clothe its men.

Philippe Truttmann and Frédéric Lisch are probably right that the grandiosity of the CORF's plans was responsible for the contrast between the strength of the central *ouvrages* in RF-Metz and the frailty of its flanks. They suggest, for instance, that replacement of separate personnel and munitions entrances with single blocs in RF-Metz would have economised the 57 million francs necessary to equip each *petit ouvrage* on the right flank with artillery turrets, thus saving them from capture.[13]

Secondly, even if more money had been available, it was never feasible to 'organise the terrain' in the sense meant by the CORF. Before the war, the forest and water authorities had somewhat constrained the army's ability to do as it wished. During the phoney war, the AEF may have delayed permission for clearing fields of fire around some *ouvrages*, but in wartime soldiers often ignored such constraints, cutting down trees to construct strongpoints and to clear fields of fire. The crew of Grand-Hohékirkel doused Wolschachen Wood with petrol and set off incendiary grenades.[14]

Yet as Alléhaut predicted in 1928, bombardment altered the terrain by creating shell holes through which infantry infiltrated and brought up antitank guns. None of the captured *ouvrages* possessed howitzers or mortars able to fire into dead ground. PO-Einseling and PO-Laudrefang, in contrast, were saved by the latter's mortars. In a futile attempt to cover all dead ground and approaches, multiple cloches were added during construction. Little more than high-profile, fixed tank turrets, they proved very vulnerable and deadly for some occupants.[15] The floods and flow of the Rhine made it impossible to properly camouflage the Rhine casemates and fatally exposed them.

The elaborate systems designed to bring in fresh air, counter gas attack and expel fumes from weapons, kitchens and latrines were more easily disrupted under attack than had been foreseen, especially in *petits ouvrages* without intakes in rear galleries. The blast of explosions, let alone breaches in the fort's fabric, disrupted the system of over-pressure and movement of air inside the entire *ouvrage*. It had originally been thought that the *palmé* design would allow isolation of compromised blocs from the rest of the *ouvrage*; in fact, the dependence of the whole on a single power system made that difficult – as at Welschhof. The consequences were most deadly at La Ferté, but poisoned air also contributed to capitulation at Welschhof, La Salmagne and Boussois. Of course, *gros ouvrages* were better armed and possessed rear escape routes and ventilation. Yet at GO-Fermont, only the Germans' ignorance of their success in blasting a hole in a casemate wall prevented them from exploiting it.

Thirdly, fortification relied too heavily on relatively untested delicate technology. Large or small, *ouvrages*' weaponry had many moving parts susceptible to breakdown at the best of times. At Bréhain, the automatic ammunition loaders (norias) in Graveel's turret often malfunctioned, necessitating the transport and loading of shells by hand. On 14 June, an antitank shell dented the sheath through which the barrel of the 81mm mortar moved; chisels, files and polish ensured that it was repaired in half an hour.[16] At Hochwald, Stuka bombs dislodged the safety clips on a turret, causing it to oscillate between eclipse and fire positions, hitting each with a dull thud. It still worked, but stiffly.[17] These mishaps had no serious consequences, but at La Ferté and Sarts, turrets jammed in semi-eclipsed position, while that at Bambesch malfunctioned.

There is a wider point here. Advanced technology was sometimes decisive in the Second World War, notably in the air, but not inevitably and rarely alone. Thus, the best French tanks, the B1 bis, were technologically superior to those of the Germans – at the price of being harder to manufacture – hence the delayed establishment of the DCrs. They were also difficult to deploy and manoeuvre and were vulnerable to breakdown. German victory in 1940 depended largely on obsolete tanks. Indeed, French defenders often faced only advance guards with motorcycles and armoured cars alone. In 1942–3, as the numbers moved against Germany, the Wehrmacht turned to technology, often overengineered. At Kursk, premature deployment of breakdown-prone Panther tanks with poorly trained crews proved as disastrous as the B1 bis counterattacks on the Meuse. As the military situation worsened again, the Germans developed wonder weapons; however advanced they were, they sucked up scarce resources and could not have been manufactured in sufficient quantities to turn the tide. The Germans, like the French in 1940, were defeated by technically inferior mass-produced weapons. These remarks call into question the myth that the 'modern' Blitzkrieg confronted the 'old-fashioned' Maginot Line. In its own way, the Maginot Line was modern too, for its advanced technology and manning systems were designed to provide a rapid, economical response to a surprise armoured attack.

Fourthly, the objective of providing better conditions for troops and thus of improving 'productivity' under fire was only partially achieved. Material conditions in the Maginot Line *ouvrages* and larger casemates improved on Verdun, but became oppressive over the eight months of the phoney war. The much more numerous interval and advance-post troops endured very harsh conditions. Morale suffered, causing psychological problems, withdrawal from social life or tension between men. It also aggravated endemic unease between and among interior French and Alsace-Lorrainers. Morale as the Deuxième Bureau measured it declined during the winter and did not always recover, especially in the Northern Vosges and Haguenau sectors. Whether that compromised willingness to fight is debatable, for interval troops often fought bravely until disorganised by the retreat order and Pétain's 'ceasefire' broadcast and even thereafter.

It would seem that morale suffered most in the *ouvrages*. It is striking that during the phoney war soldiers' letters were initially filled with references to 'confidence in their concrete'. This faith was perhaps reflected in the fatal willingness of the men of La Ferté to obey orders in desperate circumstances. The confidence expressed in their final letters contrasts with the readiness of soldiers at La Salmagne, Boussois and Welschhof to surrender once the air was soiled.

That is one reason why death and injury were low in the *ouvrages* – 105 men died at La Ferté, but only a handful in other *ouvrages*. The toll among interval troops was much greater. In the Moselle plus the two departments into which interval troops mostly retreated, Meurthe-et-Moselle and Vosges, at least 4,400 men died from all causes, plus around 600 more in the two Alsatian departments. These figures did not equal casualty numbers in the five most fought-over northern departments (23,500) or the three departments in the forefront of the Somme–Aisne battle (13,500).[18]

Fifthly, hierarchical command was never established in the way imagined in 1926. For one thing, officers did not always present a united front, especially in the *ouvrages*, where there was a clear spatial boundary between the artillery, Génie and infantry. As the *ouvrages* were surrounded, tension between fortification officers and the infantry and cavalry officers assigned to command sectors was common. Field officers' failure to understand the nature of the fortifications probably contributed to the La Ferté disaster and to the fatal delay in ordering abandonment of the Maginot Line – remember Georges's comment to Prételat that his situation was enviable by comparison with that of the field army.

Traditional command came closest to realisation in the *gros ouvrages*. Even there, soldiers often escaped officers' gaze, and rejected the work discipline of the factory-fort. In the intervals, troops were too dispersed to be subject to their officers. Reserve officers and men often espoused the republican principle of the citizen-soldier. Soldiers themselves brought their own hierarchies to the army, notably the male culture of physical strength, sometimes their politics, communist or autonomist, and sometimes their personal traumas.

French doctrine and practice were not entirely dictated from above. In the advance posts, officers demonstrated tactical initiative and the army modified its opposition to elite units. Yet officers had little idea of how to harmonise tactics, circumstances and orders. Lacking guidance such as the Military Decision Making Process, used in the contemporary British army, they relied on clichés about the 'art of war' and even radiesthesia.[19] The immediate legacy of this conflict was the irregular warfare between the Resistance and its enemies and of the Algerian War. In 1943, Darnand, now an SS officer and head of the collaborationist, paramilitary Milice, organised his most committed followers into 'Francs-gardes'. The Resistance simultaneously organised '*corps francs*'. Colonel Albert Lacaze of 99 RIA, which had been so active on the Maginot Line, became intelligence chief of its armed branch, the Armée secrete. Felsenhardt's commanding officer, Colonel Sinais, who had trained the 36 DI *corps franc*, was arrested in 1944 while organising Resistance combat groups in Brittany. He died in Bergen-Belsen. A rather different example is 23 RIF sergeant and *corps franc* volunteer Marcel Bigeard, who, via the Resistance, went on as a colonel to lead 'unconventional warfare' in Algeria. There, he struggled to overcome other commanders' preference for battalion-strength actions.[20]

Despite the limits of the top-down command model, troops largely obeyed. The fortifications did not witness an equivalent of the mass panic at Sedan. There were, however, several examples in which units arguably retreated or surrendered too readily – the usual reason was that an adjacent unit had given way. Sergeant Guizard wrote that his lieutenant, whom he referred to as a 'little girl', was 'not up to it' and hid in a cellar when the first shells hit.[21] Didelot made similar complaints about his major.[22] Yet most often discipline broke down only when the battle was clearly lost. Resentment of officers, including death threats, reappeared. Alsace-Lorrainers were among the first to desert, for they were closest to home. Others were in the forefront of resistance, but were nonetheless the targets of French prejudice, which contributed to undermining the place of Alsace-Lorraine in the nation.

Sixthly, the fortifications neither defended Alsace-Lorraine militarily nor reintegrated its inhabitants into the nation. The interior French, from the government and general staff to ordinary soldiers, idealised Alsace-Lorraine but suspected that it remained German. The army relied on these supposedly excellent soldiers for rapid reinforcement of fortification units, but never trusted them. Ordinary soldiers' hostility to Alsace-Lorrainers persisted in defeat. The Zouave Gaston Folcher, whose diary contains multiple references to Alsatian disloyalty, wrote that in POW camp each evening Alsatians paraded a swastika flag while 'singing hymns in German that we could not understand'.[23] Sapper Reignier claimed that Alsace-Lorrainers who had advocated resistance in GO-Grand-Hohékirkel now 'prostrated themselves' before the enemy. One suspects that, for Reignier, targeting Alsace-Lorrainers' 'treason' covered shame at his own capitulation and indeed respect for German military qualities. He reported approvingly that during the last days before the armistice, the Grand-Hohékirkel chaplain gave lectures on French decadence and German superiority, which obviously prefigured the Vichy regime and its policy of collaboration with Germany. Reignier himself almost wished that Germany would 'take on the direction of everything, cleansing as necessary. We would suffer, perhaps, but ultimately it would be a great good for the people.'[24]

Alsace-Lorrainers, nationalist or autonomist, all disliked being referred to as 'Boche' and resented legal discrimination, the treatment of their evacuated friends and relatives, and pillage of their houses. Their mild protests fed ever-stronger repressive laws targeted explicitly or implicitly at them. The truth was that only a minority of Alsace-Lorrainers were pro-German to the extent of wanting return to the Reich. Many more were Alsatian first or at least equivocal, but that did not necessarily entail unwillingness to fight for France or at least against Germany. Vetting limited the numbers of the politically unreliable serving in fortifications regiments, especially the *ouvrages* – many were nationalist and some were more committed to resistance than the interior French, notably at GO-Grand-Hohékirkel and PO-Haut-Poirier.

Colonel Schwartz at SF-Haguenau was the most inflexible of the sector commanders.

The attitude of Alsace-Lorraine civilians to attitude to defeat varied. While an old farmer fled because he had seen enough of the Germans over forty years, another said that he would never forget that the French had abandoned Alsace without a fight.[25] Civilian reactions largely corresponded to the political geography of the province. Graveel's men, marching through nationalist Metz to a POW camp, heard 'Vive la France' from all sides.[26] Guizard, retreating from the Sarre Gap through Hazembourg, Fénétrange and Berthleming, thought that many in the region would find it easy to welcome the invader.[27] A German artillery officer who passed through the area soon afterwards met a civilian who showed him his Iron Cross, which he could now wear proudly.[28]

As soon as hostilities were over, the Germans effectively re-annexed Alsace-Lorraine. Some of the most pro-German autonomist leaders accepted minor positions in the Third Reich. To the Lutheran minority in the northern Bas-Rhin and nearby Moselle villages, Nazi rule perhaps initially looked like the return of the old Reich, permitting them another blow in their long struggle against Catholics. At least 2,428 Alsatians volunteered for the SS and Wehrmacht. They originated particularly from these areas and Strasbourg canton, where autonomism was also influential.[29] Many evacuees returned home, a sign perhaps of a crisis of national sentiment.[30] Alsace-Lorraine POWs were released, on condition that they signed a declaration confirming their desire for German citizenship. Yet no sooner was the Alsatian Captain Pierron, the accused of Héricourt, released from POW camp than he was re-arrested by the Gestapo for spying for the French twenty years previously. Having seen names in a file during an interrogation, he rightly believed that he had been denounced.[31] Paduch, falsely accused of treason on the Rhine, joined the Free French in North Africa. Attitudes towards Nazi rule soon changed. Eighty thousand francophone Mosellans were expelled to France. Jews were deported to the death camps. Catholics were alienated by denunciation of the Concordat. Everyone resented the forced incorporation of 130,000 young men into the Wehrmacht.[32]

Pétain, as head of the Vichy state, effectively gave up on Alsace-Lorraine – the same Pétain, it will be remembered, who was accused of surrendering national territory during the Great War and whose fortification plans had been criticised for abandoning the province. When it was Pétain's turn to stand trial in 1945, abandonment of Alsace-Lorraine was a principal charge against him.

Vichy pushed to extremes the erosion of legal guarantees that had begun with the 1934 espionage law and subsequent decrees, which the army saw as essential to counterespionage on the Maginot Line. Laws designed to fight communism were more widely used against the Resistance, but when jurists explained the origins of Vichy's new laws, they situated the rupture not in July 1940 but with the espionage law of 1934 and the decrees of the late 1930s.[33] Pétain's condemnation to death (commuted to life imprisonment in a fortress) under Article 75 of the Penal Code was possible only because a decree of 17 June 1938 had finally realised the army's desire to withdraw political status from espionage and treason.

In the dark days of May and June 1940, although the Maginot Line was part of a movement to restore traditional military and social hierarchy and fight communism and autonomism, it became, in the eyes of the senior generals, a danger to their desire to preserve the army as the agent of national recovery. Weygand's insistance on fighting a last battle on a single line prior to a quick armistice condemned 400,000 men to five years of prison camp.

By then, the Maginot Line was wrecked. The Germans used it as target practice, experimented on it, stripped it of valuable metals and sent its guns to the Atlantic Wall. They sabotaged the *ouvrages* they had repurposed as command centres as the Americans approached. The Americans too shelled Maginot Line casemates.

From 1947, as the Cold War began, the army began to investigate what parts of the fortifications might be saved for defence against the Soviet Union. In 1951, the government approved a 2 billion franc modernisation programme. Three moles were planned at Rochonvillers, Bitche and Haguenau with more to follow. *Gros ouvrages* Hochwald, Billig, Bréhain, Four-à-Chaux and the Sarre flooding system once again became building sites, supervised by officers with pre-1940 experience. However, the outbreak in 1954 of the Algerian War, coupled with the NATO command's reliance on nuclear deterrence, put an end to these plans – although the Americans and Canadians used Rochonvillers and Kerfent respectively as command centres.

Technological obsolescence mattered too. Casemates were quickly abandoned, for they were even more vulnerable to modern tanks than they had been to 88mm antitank guns. Cloches had proved their dangerousness. Thanks to France's departure from NATO in 1963, some *ouvrages* continued to figure in French plans. Some, notably Rochonvillers, were refurbished as atomic war command centres. Some *ouvrages* continued to be used for military purposes into the 1980s and even the present.

The process of turning the Maginot Line into a site of memory was well underway. Captain Philippe Truttmann, the last professor of fortification at the Génie's technical school, was responsible for making Simserhof into a museum owned by the army. Much more frequently, local councils acquired *ouvrages*, which were restored by voluntary associations. Until the 2000s, Maginot Line veteran associations were heavily involved in them. Roger Bruge, notwithstanding his quality historical work, provided the mythical narrative of the 'unvanquished fortress' and redemption through resistance – his pentalogy, *Les combattants du 18 juin*, refers to de Gaulle's BBC broadcast for resistance.[34]

The remains of the Maginot Line are situated on what is now an open border at the heart of the European Union. The fortifications are one of the many sites at which French, Germans and Italians meet. Yet people of the Moselle, of the two Alsatian departments and of the southeast are as divided as their interwar forebears, for the two dominant political parties are that of the ultra-European President Macron and the far-right Rassemblement National (RN). Immigration and borders remain as divisive in these regions now as they were then. When a pro-European politician mocked the RN policy of re-establishing border controls as 'The Maginot Line. A formidable frontier on paper, but a paper frontier,' the RN leader replied in a speech at Oxford University that she had no intention of surrounding the country with barbed wire – borders should be filters, not walls.[35]

Historians have no special ability or right to decide what frontiers, if any, a society requires. That is a moral question for everyone in a free society. Historians do have the training and knowledge to confront myth with evidence, as this book has attempted to do. Perhaps more important still, historians' special skill lies in understanding the multiple perspectives and experiences of people in the past, whether they are sympathetic to us or not. On the one hand that means recognising that the particularly hubristic nature of the Maginot Line fortifications had major consequences for the soldiers who manned them and for civilians of the militarised zone – not least for Jewish refugees – and that the impossibility of 'organising' humans, machines and the natural world contributed to the growth of authoritarianism in French society. On the other hand, empathetic understanding also entails recognising that those who elaborated French military plans and doctrine confronted unprecedentedly difficult circumstances, even if their understanding was sometimes warped by prejudices of the worst kind: unreliable allies, an enemy with superior resources, and, from 1933, a militarist Nazi dictatorship committed to the racial and racist reorganisation of Europe.

GLOSSARY

Casemate	Concrete work containing fixed artillery and/or machine guns. Could be a single work or one of the blocs in an *ouvrage palmé*. In the latter case, weapons usually fired to the flanks.
Chefferie des travaux de fortification	Engineer offices within fortified sectors responsible for project management, turning the plans drawn by Directions des travaux de fortification into construction plans, expropriation of land and supervision of individual construction sites.
Cloche/GFM cloche	Fixed armoured bell sunk in concrete with niches for lookout and/or weapons. A Guetteur Fusil-Mitrailleur cloche was for both lookout and close defence, armed with a light machine gun (fusil-mitrailleur).
Combat bloc	Individual concrete bloc at surface level linked to the galleries below by lifts and steps. Blocs could take the form of casemates or they could contain turrets.
Direction des travaux de fortification	(Fortification Works Directorate) Local emanation of the CORF, responsible for deciding the precise emplacement of *ouvrages*, their individual plans and coordination of construction sites.
Embrasure protection	Armoured protection for weapons embrasures was provided by inward-pointing funnel-shaped armour (*trémies*), with or without steps, which permitted the weapon to be traversed. In bunkers, protection was usually provided by armoured plates, but the multiplicity of designs and huge demand meant that few had been fitted by May 1940.
Gallery	Tunnel within a fort.
Ligne de recueil	Literally meaning 'gathering-in line', best translated as 'retreat line'. This line was sufficiently well manned to 'gather in' troops retreating from the advance posts. In French military parlance, the verb *recueillir* was used to designate retreat to any position that was already manned and defensively organised.

Maison forte	Fortified house, consisting of a ground-floor blockhouse with antitank and sometimes machine guns, with masonry quarters above, built in the style of a forest dwelling. Sited on the frontier, their task was to delay the enemy by destroying vehicles that had been halted by cratering of the roads or other obstructions. Some, which were fitted with raisable barriers, also served as posts for the GRM.
Military Regions	Twenty territorial divisions, each responsible for administering military units, recruitment, training, mobilisation of a corresponding army corps, and relations with the civilian authorities (notably the prefects). They were also responsible for constructing field defences and, following dissolution of the CORF, for all fortification in their region. In wartime, the regions were responsible for the depots and interior, while General Headquarters (GQG) was responsible for the army zone.
Munitions entrance	(*Entrée munitions*) Principal entrance bloc for men and munitions at ground level, ideally in a small valley, permitting narrow-gauge railways to bring supplies directly into the *ouvrage*'s main gallery. Some forts were supplied by lorry rather than rail. Some entrances led directly to shafts.
Ouvrage palmé	Type of large fortification consisting of a series of combat blocs and entrance blocs at surface level, linked to underground barracks, power plants and other services by shafts and galleries.
Personnel entrance	(*Entrée des hommes*) Bloc in an *ouvrage* armed with fixed light weapons in niches and cloches. Despite its name, it was actually an emergency entrance to a shaft with a munitions lift for use in the event that the munitions entrance became unusable. The men entered by the munitions entrance.
Resistance line	The line on which the army planned to accept full-scale battle – the line of *ouvrages* on the Maginot Line.
Security camp	(*Camp de sûreté*) Housing for cadres and barracks for troops situated close to the *ouvrages*.
Shelter	(*Abri*) Concrete protection for infantry up to company size. Some contained no fixed weapons or permanent crew, only niches for the infantry's own weapons. Like small blockhouses, they would be occupied as required.
Turret	Armoured weapon mount rotatable through 360 degrees, retractable when installed in a Maginot Line fort, for 75mm artillery, mortars and/or machine guns.

NOTES

Introduction

1. Robert Lavergne, *Journal de guerre du Hackenberg: Mes deux années passées dans un ouvrage Maginot août 1939–août 1941*, ed. Alain Hohnadel (2007), 34–5, 10–11 May 1940.
2. Archives du Sénat (AS) 68S11, Charles Riebel, 'Rapport', 2–5/11/1939; Robert Varoqui, *Du béton et des hommes: Ouvrage A19 Hackenberg* (1995), 78.
3. Gérard Giuliano, *Les soldats du béton: La Ligne Maginot dans les Ardennes et en Meuse, 1939–1940* (1986), 23–4.
4. René Goeminne, *Villy-La Ferté: Souvenirs 39–45* (1985), 23.
5. Goeminne, *Villy-La Ferté*, 23–4.
6. 'No Wall Is Impenetrable – Just Ask the French', *Washington Post*, 31/7/2015; 'The U.S. Military Is Not Ready for the New Era of Warfare', *New York Times*, 13/9/2024; 'Ukraine's Maginot Line Is About to Crumble', *Telegraph*, 16/5/2024; 'UE: taxer les véhicules électriques chinois, et après?', *Le Monde*, 8/10/2024.
7. 'Jude Bellingham: Very Good Footballer, Very Lucky Boy', *Guardian*, 25/3/2025.
8. Jean-Louis Crémieux-Brilhac, *Les Français de l'an 40* (2 vols, 1990).
9. 'En septembre 1940, j'ai décidé de m'évader', *Le Monde*, 9/4/2015, https://www.lemonde.fr/disparitions/article/2015/04/09/en-septembre-1940-j-ai-decide-de-m-evader_4612409_3382.html.
10. Julian Jackson, *The Fall of France: The Nazi Invasion of 1940* (2003), 197–211.
11. Martin S. Alexander, *The Republic in Danger: General Maurice Gamelin and the Politics of French Defence, 1933–1940* (1992); Jeffery A. Gunsburg, 'The Battle of the Belgian Plain, 12–14 May 1940: The First Great Tank Battle', *Journal of Military History*, 56 (1992), 207–44; Martin S. Alexander, 'In Defence of the Maginot Line: Security Policy, Domestic Politics and the Economic Depression in France', in Robert W.D. Boyce, ed., *French Foreign and Defence Policy, 1918–1940: The Decline and Fall of a Great Power* (1998), 164–94; Ernest R. May, *Strange Victory: Hitler's Conquest of France* (2000); Jeffery A. Gunsburg, 'The Battle of Gembloux, 14–15 May 1940: The "Blitzkrieg" Checked', *Journal of Military History*, 64 (2000), 97–140; Philippe Garraud, 'L'ombre portée de 1914–1918

dans les années 1930', *Vingtième siècle*, 104 (2009), 17–27; Martin S. Alexander, 'Radio-Intercepts, Reconnaissance and Raids: French Operational Intelligence and Communications in 1940', *Intelligence and National Security*, 28 (2013), 337–76.

12. See, for instance, the opposition between Philip Nord, *France 1940: Defending the Republic* (2015), and Douglas Porch, *Defeat and Division: France at War 1939–42* (2022). See also Don W. Alexander, 'Repercussions of the Breda Variant', *French Historical Studies*, 8 (1974), 459–88.
13. Karl-Heinz Frieser, *Blitzkrieg-Legende: der Westfeldzug 1940* (1996); Marco Sigg, *Der Unterführer als Feldherr im Taschenformat: Theorie und Praxis der Auftragstaktik im deutschen Heer 1869 bis 1945* (2014).
14. Roger Bruge, *Les combattants du 18 juin* (5 vols, 1982–9).
15. Gaston Prételat, *Le destin tragique de la ligne Maginot* (1950).

1 The Disputed Lessons of the Great War

1. Général Debeney, 'Armée nationale ou armée de métier?', *Revue des deux mondes* (September 1929), 241–76 at 268.
2. Garraud, 'L'ombre portée de 1914–1918'.
3. Charles de Gaulle, 'Rôle historique des places françaises', *Revue militaire française*, n.s., 17 (October–December 1925), 356–83 at 358.
4. Peter Sahlins, 'Natural Frontiers Revisited: France's Boundaries since the Seventeenth Century', *American Historical Review*, 95 (1990), 1423–51.
5. Jean-Paul Amat, 'Guerre et milieux naturels: les forêts meurtries de l'est de la France, 70 ans après Verdun', *L'espace géographique*, 16 (1987), 217–33.
6. On French research in the period, see Pierre Richard, *Commandant Mougin, Henri-Louis-Philippe: 1841–1916, précurseur des cuirassements français* (2003).
7. Allain Bernède, 'L'enseignement de la fortification à l'École supérieure de la guerre avant la première guerre mondiale', in *Actes du colloque Séré de Rivières* (1999), 61–84 at 63.
8. Elizabeth Greenhalgh, *Foch in Command: The Forging of a First World War General* (2011), 9.
9. Bernède, 'L'enseignement de la fortification', 73–6.
10. Henri Ortholon, 'L'état-major français et le grand état-major allemand face au système Séré de Rivières de 1870 à 1914', in *Actes du colloque Séré de Rivières* (1999), 46–57 at 50.
11. Danielle Delouche, 'Cubisme et camouflage', *Guerres mondiales et conflits contemporains*, 171 (1993), 123–37; Frédéric Thiery, '"La première veste de camouflage de guerre du monde" est inventée par Louis Guingot', *Guerres mondiales et conflits contemporains*, 227 (2007), 7–21.
12. Martin Barros, 'La deuxième ligne dans le système Séré de Rivières 1872–1914', in *Actes du colloque Séré de Rivières* (1999), 202–44.
13. Edmond Buat, *Journal du général Edmond Buat: 1914–1923*, ed. Frédéric Guelton (2015), 8/6/1916.
14. Greenhalgh, *Foch in Command*, 9–139.
15. Greenhalgh, *Foch in Command*, 91–8.
16. Buat, *Journal*, 22/1 to 21/2/1915.
17. Buat, *Journal*, 7–10/8/1915.
18. Buat, *Journal*, 22/2 to 19/3/1915.

19. Bénédicte Vergez-Chaignon, *Pétain* (2014), 77.
20. Raymond Poincaré, *Au service de la France: Neuf années de souvenirs* (1930), 312.
21. Adolphe Guillaumat, *Correspondance de guerre du général Guillaumat: 1914–1919*, ed. Paul Guillaumat (2006), 22–23/3/1916.
22. Vergez-Chaignon, *Pétain*, 84–93.
23. Paul Jankowski, *Verdun: The Longest Battle of the Great War* (2014), 139–41.
24. César Méléra, *Verdun (juin–juillet 1916)* (1925), 34–5.
25. Guillaumat, *Correspondance de guerre*, 15–16/3/1916.
26. Henri Bordeaux, *La délivrance de Verdun* (1933); Jacques Péricard, *Verdun: Histoire des combats qui se sont livrés de 1914 à 1918 sur les deux rives de la Meuse* (1933). See Ian Ousby, *The Road to Verdun: France, Nationalism and the First World War* (2002) and Jankowski, *Verdun*, 141, on conditions in the fortresses.
27. Henry Morel-Journel, *Journal d'un officier de la 74e division d'infanterie et de l'armée française d'Italie (1914–1918)* (1922), 24/10/1916.
28. Elizabeth Greenhalgh, *The French Army and the First World War* (2014), 151.
29. Michel Goya, *La chair et l'acier: L'armée française et l'invention de la guerre moderne (1914–1918)* (2004), 261–6.
30. Greenhalgh, *Foch in Command*, 164–5; Vergez-Chaignon, *Pétain*, 95.
31. Joe Lunn, '"Les races guerrières": Racial Preconceptions in the French Military about West African Soldiers during the First World War', *Journal of Contemporary History*, 34 (1999), 517–36.
32. Emmanuel Saint-Fuscien, *À vos ordres? La relation d'autorité dans l'armée française de la Grande Guerre* (2011), 243.
33. Greenhalgh, *The French Army*, 125.
34. Saint-Fuscien, *À vos ordres?*, 209–11.
35. Marc Sorlot, *André Maginot (1877–1932): L'homme politique et sa légende* (1995), 9.
36. Sorlot, *André Maginot*, 56–9.
37. Élisabeth du Réau, *Édouard Daladier: 1884–1970* (1993), 31–3.
38. Du Réau, *Édouard Daladier*, 31–3.
39. Commandant Jibé (pseud. Henry Mordacq), *L'armée nouvelle, ce qu'elle pense, ce qu'elle veut* (1905); Jean Jaurès, *L'armée nouvelle* (1911).
40. Yves Cohen, 'Fayol, un instituteur de l'ordre industriel', *Entreprises et histoire*, 34 (2003), 29–67 at 47–8.
41. Cohen, 'Fayol, un instituteur de l'ordre industriel'; Stéphane Rials, *Administration et organisation: De l'organisation de la bataille à la bataille de l'organisation dans l'administration française* (1977), 158–60.
42. Greenhalgh, *The French Army*, 150.
43. *L'Opinion*, 28/12/1916.
44. Yves Gras, *Castelnau ou l'art de commander, 1851–1944* (1990), 302.
45. Buat, *Journal*, 11–14/5/1916.
46. Buat, *Journal*, 28/1/1917.
47. Buat, *Journal*, 27/3/1916, 28/1/1917; Hubert Bonin, 'La leçon de Buat en 1914–1920: du bon général au bon manageur', *Revue historique des armées*, 293 (2019), 76–95.
48. Gilles Néret, *Fernand Léger* (1993), 66.
49. Fernand Léger and Léonce Rosenberg, *Correspondances: 1917–1937*, ed. Christian Derouet (1996), hors série, October 1916; Christopher Green, *Art in France, 1900–1940* (2003), 153–4; Delouche, 'Cubisme et camouflage'.

50. Saint-Fuscien, *À vos ordres?*, 243.
51. Abel Ferry, *Les carnets secrets d'Abel Ferry (1914–1918)* (1957), 27/4/1915.
52. Guillaumat, *Correspondance de guerre*, 15–16/3/1916.
53. Buat, *Journal*, 6–21/1/1915; Ferry, *Les carnets secrets*, 27/4/1915, 29/2/1916.
54. Sorlot, *André Maginot*, 60–71, 77–8; Vergez-Chaignon, *Pétain*, 115–16.
55. Saint-Fuscien, *À vos ordres?*, 227–37.
56. Goya, *La chair et l'acier*, 224–7.
57. Goya, *La chair et l'acier*, 226; Greenhalgh, *The French Army*, 298–9.
58. Vergez-Chaignon, *Pétain*, 148.
59. Goya, *La chair et l'acier*, 397–401.
60. This view was expressed by General Marie-Émile Fayolle in his *Cahiers secrets de la Grande Guerre, 1914–1918* (1964), 1/7/1918; Jean de Pierrefeu, *G.Q.G., secteur I, trois ans au grand quartier général* (1920), vol. 2, 225–6 on Buat's role at GQG.
61. Colonel Paoli, 'Le coup du main du 366e R.I. 14 juillet 1918', *Revue historique des armées*, 93 (1968), 51–60.
62. *L'Écho de Paris*, 9/12/1918; *L'Humanité*, 12/12/1918.

2 The Decision to Fortify, 1919–1930

1. *Journal official: Débats parlementaires: Chambre* (henceforth JODC), 11/11/1918, 3000.
2. *L'Écho de Paris*, *Le Matin*, 12/11/1918.
3. JODC, 16/3/1922, 860.
4. Christian Benoît, 'La symbolique de l'Armée de terre: de l'usage à la réglementation de l'usage', in André Thiéblemont, ed., *Cultures et logiques militaires* (1999), 51–83 at 63.
5. Edmond Ruby, *Sedan, terre d'épreuve, avec la 2e Armée, mai–juin 1940* (1948), 18.
6. Buat, *Journal*, 14/6/1920, 1/5/1920.
7. Buat, *Journal*, 13/7/1922.
8. Jadwiga Attier-Zmudka and Jean-Marie Sérot, 'A Particularly Tragic Case of Possible Alzheimer's Disease, That of Marshal Pétain', *Journal of Alzheimer's Disease*, 71 (September 2019), 399–404; Nol Swaddiwudhipong, David J. Whiteside, Frank H. Hezemans, Duncan Street, James B. Rowe and Timothy Rittman, 'Pre-diagnostic Cognitive and Functional Impairment in Multiple Sporadic Neurodegenerative Diseases', *Alzheimer's and Dementia*, 19 (2023), 1752–63.
9. Jean-Yves Mary and Alain Hohnadel, *Hommes et ouvrages de la ligne Maginot*, vol. 2 (2001), 12.
10. Ladislas Mysyrowicz, *Anatomie d'une défaite: Cinq études sur les origines profondes de l'effondrement militaire français, 1919–1939* (1973), 39.
11. JODC, 15/6/1934, 1531; Prételat, *Le destin tragique*, claimed falsely that the infantry had advocated *gros ouvrages*.
12. Auguste Isaac, *Journal d'un notable lyonnais, 1906–1933*, ed. Hervé Joly (2002), 19/10/1919.
13. Robert J. Young, '*L'attaque brusquée* and Its Use as a Myth in Interwar France', *Historical Reflections*, 8 (1981), 93–114.

14. Philippe Garraud, 'La construction de la ligne Maginot alpine et son emploi en 1940: un système défensif novateur et efficace', *Guerres mondiales et conflits contemporains*, 259 (2015), 93–114.
15. Adam Tooze, *The Wages of Destruction: The Making and Breaking of the Nazi Economy* (2007), 135–40.
16. This is the thesis of Adam Tooze, *The Deluge: The Great War and the Remaking of Global Order, 1916–1931* (2015).
17. SHD 7N3764/1, General Henri Alby, 'Note pour l'EMA', 19/2/1921; Clemenceau to Pétain, 25/2/1919; Buat to Clémenceau, 26/2/1919. According to Buat, *Journal*, 15/5/1919, the EMA in Paris asked Pétain's GQG at Chantilly to draw up the report.
18. SHD 7N3764/1, 'Exposé d'une organisation des nouvelles frontières de la France', 15/5/1919.
19. Responses collected in SHD 7N3764/1.
20. SHD 7N3763, Note, 7/7/1919; SHD 7N3764/1, 11/7/1919.
21. SHD 7N3764/1, 19/11/1919, 13/12/1919.
22. *Règlement de l'infanterie: Service en campagne* (1929); *Manuel du gradé d'infanterie* (1931).
23. SHD 9N306/3, Duport to war minister, 4/9/1925.
24. IPGU, 74–81.
25. Gérard Saint-Martin, *L'arme blindée française*, vol 1: *Mai–juin 1940! Les blindés français dans la tourmente* (2nd edn, 2011), 9–12.
26. SHD 1K130/9, Fonds Weygand, Foch, Diary, 3/1922, 16/8/1924.
27. SHD 7N3764/4, Lefèbvre, Instruction, 5/3/1920; Buat to Président du conseil, 4/8/1920; Berthelot to Président du conseil, 31/12/1920.
28. SHD 7N3664/2, 'Exposé d'une organisation des Frontières de la France', undated, late 1919/early 1920. This is a heavily revised version of the document of the same title of 15/5/1919. See note 18 above.
29. Buat, *Journal*, 16–18/1/1922.
30. SHD 7N3673/1, 'Historique des études'.
31. SHD 1N23/4, 'Rapport de présentation: Bases générales de l'organisation defensive du territoire nationale', May 1920, and 'Procès verbal de la séance'.
32. SHD 7N3763/1, Foch to Pétain, 3/5/1920.
33. SHD 7N3763/1 contains correspondence and the individual reports.
34. SHD 7N3763/1, Nivelle report, 20/10/1920.
35. SHD 7N3763, Instruction, 10/12/1920 (including draft annoted by Pétain); SHD 7N3763/1, Buat to Humbert, 10/12/1920. Paul-Émile Tournoux, *Haut commandement, gouvernement et défense des frontières du Nord et de l'Est, 1919–1939* (1960), 23–4 wrongly describes the instruction as Buat's project.
36. SHD 1N25/4/1, Pétain to CSG, 13/2/1922.
37. SHD 1N25/4/1, 'Projet de note sur l'organisation défensive du territoire', 13/2/1922.
38. SHD 1N25/4/1, Buat to Pétain, 1/3/1922.
39. SHD 1N25/4/1, Debeney to Pétain, 1/3/1922; Mangin to Pétain, 8/3/1922.
40. SHD 1N25/4/2, Pétain, Note, 20/3/1922.
41. SHD 1N25/4/2, Buat to Pétain, 24/2/1922; Guillaumat to Pétain, 29/3/1922.
42. Buat, *Journal*, 15/1/1922.
43. Buat, *Journal*, 15/1/1922.
44. Buat, *Journal*, 18/1/1922.

45. Buat, *Journal*, 26/5/1923.
46. SHD 1N/50/3, Pétain to Buat, 11/4/1922; ?Coliot, Note, 13/5/1922.
47. SHD 1N25/4/1, 'Note sur l'organisation défensive du territoire'; Guillaumat to Pétain, 1/3/1922 (Pétain's marginal note reads 'alors que faut-il faire?'); Buat, *Journal*, 21/5/1922.
48. Buat, *Journal*, 20–23/5/1922. For the minutes of the meeting, see SHD 1N25/4/3.
49. SHD 1K130/9, Fonds Weygand, Foch, Diary, 6/1922.
50. SHD 1N25/4 bis, Pétain, Note, 12/7/1922.
51. SHD 1N50/2, 'Ordre du jour', 15/6/1922.
52. SHD 1N50/2, PV CDT, 19/6/1922.
53. SHD 1N25/4 bis, Pétain, Note, 12/7/1922.
54. Buat, *Journal*, 10/9/1922; Tournoux, *Haut commandement*, 31–2.
55. SHD 9YD648, Dossier Guillaumat, 'XXX'; Buat, *Journal*, 14/5/1919, 5–8/3/1921, 13 and 29/12/1922.
56. SHD 1N28/8, Guillaumat to war minister, 8/11/1926.
57. Tournoux, *Haut commandement*, 42–3.
58. SHD 1N50/4/2, 'Examen de l'ordre du jour', 23/11/1922; PV, Séance, 23/10/1922; Buat, *Journal*, 30/10/1922.
59. Buat, *Journal*, 17/2/1923; SHD 1N27/7, 'Rapport au Ministre', 27/3/1923.
60. SHD 7N3763/3 and 1N27/7, 'Organisation défensive du territoire', 16/3/1923; Tournoux, *Haut commandement*, 44–5; Buat, *Journal*, 20/12/1923.
61. Buat, *Journal*, 20/12/1923.
62. Vergez-Chaignon, *Pétain*, 197–200.
63. Tooze, *The Deluge*, 456–7.
64. Peter Jackson, *Beyond the Balance of Power: France and the Politics of National Security in the Era of the First World War* (2013).
65. SHD 1N27/7, 'Questions posées au CSG', 15/12/1925; SHD 7N3781/2, ministry to Hellot, 29/6/1924.
66. Jean-Michel Guieu, 'Paul Painlevé et la paix', in Claudine Fontanon and Robert Frank, eds, *Paul Painlevé, un savant en politique* (2005), 119–31.
67. Charles à Court Repington, *After the War: A Diary* (2005), 6/3/1921.
68. SHD 7N2368/5, Painlevé to Hellot via Debeney, 13/5/1925.
69. SHD 7N3764/4, Messimy to war minister, 19/1//1925.
70. AN Fonds Painlevé 313 AP 230, 'Note sur le désarmement', 3/1/1929.
71. SHD 1N28/8, Doumergue's opening remarks in PV CSG, Séance, 17/12/1926.
72. SHD 1N27/7, Debeney, 'Note sur l'organisation défensive', 26/5/1925.
73. SHD 1N27/7, Painlevé to Guillaumat, 31/12/1925; SHD 7N3764/5.
74. Located at Lille, Metz, Strasbourg, Grenoble, Briançon and Nice.
75. Émile Laure, *Pétain* (1941), 281.
76. Tournoux, *Haut commandement*, 332–4.
77. AN Fonds Painlevé 313 AP 213, Foch to Painlevé, 24/4/1926.
78. SHD 1N20, PV CSG, 14/12/1927.
79. The Law on the General Organisation of the Army (13 July 1927) laid down the number of units and their composition in terms of metropolitan and colonial troops. The Cadres Law (28 March 1928) set out the proportions of officers, NCOs and other ranks. The Law of 31 March 1928 introduced one-year universal male conscription in the metropole and for citizens in North Africa (native conscripts were chosen by ballot for longer terms).
80. *L'Action française*, 1/4/1936.

81. *Le Figaro*, 22/6/1927; SHD 7N3771, Vœu, 7/11/1927; *Fédération des pays envahis: Union lorraine pour la protection de la frontière du Nord-Est* (1927).
82. SHD 7N3757/2, PV CDF, 12/10/1926; SHD 1N28/8, 'Rapport au ministre', 6/11/1926.
83. SHD 1N28/8, PV, Séance, 17/12/1926.
84. Tournoux, *Haut commandement*, 86–9.
85. SHD 7N3757/3, PV CDF, 3/3/1927; SHD 1N29/3, 'Note lu au CSG', 4/7/1927.
86. SHD 1N29/3, 'Note sur les formes de la fortification', 16/5/1927.
87. Laure, *Pétain*, 282.
88. SHD 1N20, 'Séance préparatoire', 2/7/1927; Tournoux, *Haut commandement*, 103.
89. SHD 1N29/4, unsigned, undated note to Bineau, ?October 1927.
90. SHD 1N29/3, PV CSG, Séance, 4/7/1927.
91. SHD 1N52/5, PV CDF, 5/7/1927; SHD 1N29/3, Guillaumat to Painlevé, 8/8/1927.
92. SHD 7N3771/1, 'Note pour l'EMA', 29/8/1927.
93. Laure, *Pétain*, 285–8, quotes Pétain in the CSG meeting of 9/9/1927, but Pétain actually appropriated an expression taken from Guillaumat's report.
94. Notably in his long intervention in the CSG meeting of 17/12/1926 in SHD IN28/8, PV CSG.
95. SHD 1N29/3, 'Note sur les formes de la fortification', 16/5/1927.
96. See p. 000.
97. SHD 1N52/4, 1/8/1927; SHD 7N3757/2, PV CDF, 27/5/1926; SHD 7N3757/3, PV CDF, 3/2/1927.
98. SHD 1N28/8, 'Rapport au ministre', 6/11/1926, 55.
99. SHD 1N54/1, 'Conférence dans le bureau de Pétain', 10/5/1930.
100. SHD 1N29/4, 'Note sur les formes de la fortification', 9/9/1927; SHD 1N20, 'Réunion préparatoire', 11/10/1927; SHD 1N29/4, PV CSG, 12/10/1927.
101. SHD 1N52/1, 'Instruction sur le fonctionnement de la CORF', 27/9/1927.
102. SHD 1N29/4, PV CSG, 12/10/1927.
103. SHD 7N3781/1/10–11, 'Les fortifications', Humbert to Debeney, 25/7/1928; 'Note du général Normand', 31/7/1928, and 'Suite à note', 6/8/1928.
104. SHD 7N3781/1/10–11, Note, Humbert to Debeney, 25/7/1928; Normand, Rapport, 31/7/1928. Although Pétain had at one time opposed *gros ouvrages*, other interventions show his determination that all should stick to the agreed programme: SHD 7N3781/1, Pétain to Debeney 17/10/1929; AS 69S10, 1924–7, Audition Painlevé, 5/7/1928.
105. Pierre Hoff, *Les programmes d'armement de 1919 à 1939* (1982), 72.
106. AN Fonds Painlevé 313 AP 230, 'Note pour les présidents des commissions', 7/1/1929; SHD 7N3764/8, 'Historique des études', 8/1929.
107. AN Fonds Painlevé 313 AP 230, Painlevé, Note, 4/1/1929.
108. SHD 7N3796/6, 'Note pour le EMA', 26/5/1928; SHD 7N3771/1, 'Réponse au Sénat', 5/12/1928; Cabinet Ministre de la guerre, Note, 19/9/1930.
109. Sabine Jansen, *Pierre Cot: Un antifasciste radical* (2002), 53–120.
110. Pierre Cot, 'Des fortifications ou des mitrailleuses? Vauban ou Hotchkiss', *La Renaissance* (November 1928), 6–9.
111. Laure, *Pétain*, 287–8.
112. Antoine Targe, *La garde de nos frontières* (1930).

113. JODC, 28/11/1928; André Tardieu, 'La ligne Maginot et la Défense nationale', *Gringoire*, 24/4/1936.
114. SHD 7N3780/5, 22/11/1928.
115. *La France militaire*, 22/12/1928.
116. *La France militaire*, 3/1/1929.
117. AN Fonds Painlevé 313 AP 230, 7/1/1929.
118. AN Fonds Painlevé 313 AP 230, Painlevé, Note, 7/1/1929.
119. SHD 7N3781/1/, 'Note sur les formes techniques', undated, for meeting of 12/1/1929.
120. AN Fonds Painlevé 313 AP 230, Painlevé, undated note, early 1929.
121. SHD 7N3764/8, Pétain, 'Bases sur lesquelles', 26/1/1929; Belhague to minister, 31/1/1929; 'Historique des études', 8/1929; AN Fonds Painlevé 313 AP 230 for individual notices.
122. AN Fonds Painlevé 313 AP 230, Painlevé to Chéron, 24/1/1929.
123. AN Fonds Painlevé 313 AP 323, Note, 1/1/1929 (Directive 31 October).
124. SHD 7N3796/6, Belhague to minister, 22/11/1929.
125. SHD 7N3771, Painlevé to Rollin, 19/9/1929; AN Fonds Painlevé 313 AP 230, Note, 1/10/1929; secretary-general to Painlevé, 21/10/1929.
126. *L'Écho de Paris*, 21/11/1929; SHD 7N3796/7, Maginot to Chéron, 2/4/1930.
127. JODC, 29/12/1929, 4232–5.
128. Tournoux, *Haut commandement*, 336–7.
129. SHD 7N3796/7, Maginot to Chéron, 2/5/1930; SHD 7N3796/8, Maginot to finance minister, 24/3/1931.
130. JODC, 156/1934, 1531.
131. *Journal officiel: Débats parlementaires: Sénat* (JODS), 28/12/1929, 1369.

3 Organising the Frontier, 1930–1935

1. Cecil O. Smith, 'The Longest Run: Public Engineers and Planning in France', *American Historical Review*, 95 (1990), 657–92.
2. SHD 7N3757/1, 'Organisation défensive', 25/11/1929.
3. SHD 7N3762/1–3, correspondence of 1927–31.
4. SHD 7N3672/3, EMA 3e Bureau, 'Instruction sur le fonctionnement de la CORF', signed by Painlevé, 26/10/1927.
5. Rials, *Administration et organisation*; Jackie Clarke, *France in the Age of Organization: Factory, Home and Nation from the 1920s to Vichy* (2011).
6. Yves Cohen, *Le siècle des chefs: Une histoire transnationale du commandement et de l'autorité* (2013).
7. François Monnet, *Refaire la république: André Tardieu, une dérive réactionnaire, 1876–1945* (1993), 93–4; Vergez-Chaignon, *Pétain*, 295–8.
8. SHD 1N28/8, CDF, 'Rapport au ministre', 26/11/1926, 4–5; SHD 7N3796/7, War Ministry to Finance Ministry, 2/5/1930; SHD 1N54/1/3, Weygand to commander 6th Region, 18/10/1932; AN C14982, Chamber Army Commission, 7/12/1932, Audition Bernier; Pierre Saly, *La politique des grands travaux en France, 1929–1939* (1977), 151–2.
9. Pétain, preface to Paul Vauthier, *La doctrine de guerre du général Douhet* (1935), xiii.
10. Quoted in Guy Pedroncini, *Pétain: La victoire perdue* (1995), 31–5.

11. The Law on the General Organisation of the Army (13/7/1927) laid down the number of units and their composition in terms of metropolitan and colonial troops. The Cadres Law (28/3/1928) set out the proportions of officers, NCOs and other ranks. The Law of 31/3/1928 introduced one-year universal male conscription.
12. AN Fonds Painlevé 313 AP 239, 'Critique du projet Painlevé', ?1926.
13. Rouquerol, 'La cohésion dans l'armée moderne', *La France militaire*, 1/2/1933.
14. Debeney, 'Armée nationale ou armée de métier?', 253–4. For figures see SHD 7N2323/7, 'Militaires de carrière', 14/3/1935.
15. JODC, 29/3/1923, 1664–5, and 18/3/1923, 1355; SHD 7N3764, GQG, April 1919; SHD 1N28, 'Rapport au ministre', 6/11/1926; SHD 7N3796/6, 'Note EMA', 25/5/1928.
16. Debeney, 'Armée nationale ou armée de métier?', 253–4.
17. Marie-Eugène Debeney, 'La guerre moderne et les machines', *Revue de la semaine*, February 1922, 123–61.
18. SHD 1N29/3, 'Note sur les formes techniques de la fortification', 16/5/1927.
19. Robert Poulaine, *Le Temps*, 26/7/1935.
20. SHD 1N55/1/1, 'Note sur l'armement', 16/3/1928.
21. SHD 1N55/5, CSG, 'Séance d'études', 13/7/1932; SHD 1N55/1, CSG, Note, 18/4/1933; SHD 7N3781/2, Instruction, 26/3/1935; Fabry (3e Bureau) to commanders 6th and 20th Regions, 21/6/1935.
22. Romy Golan, *Modernity and Nostalgia: Art and Politics in France between the Wars* (1995), 41, 155.
23. Le Corbusier, 'Pour batir, standardiser et tayloriser', supplement to *Bulletin du redressement français*, 3:9, 1/5/1929, 1–8.
24. Mary McLeod, '"Architecture or Revolution": Taylorism, Technocracy, and Social Change', *Art Journal*, 43 (June 1983), 132–47 at 137.
25. McLeod, '"Architecture or Revolution"'.
26. Jean-Louis Cohen, *Architecture en uniforme: Projeter et construire pour la Seconde Guerre mondiale* (2011), 23.
27. Paul Vauthier, *Le danger aérien et l'avenir du pays* (1930); Pierre Vago, 'Défense passive', *L'architecture d'aujourd'hui*, 8 (June 1937), 2–33.
28. Louis Bance, 'Fortification et architecture', *La Nature*, 1/8/1931.
29. SHD 7N3796/1, CORF, 'Note relative aux marchés', 12/1/1927; SHD 7N3762/5, PV CORF, 9/12/1927.
30. *Le Figaro*, 22/6/1927; SHD 7N3771, Vœu, 7/11/1927; *Fédération des pays envahis*.
31. Mary and Hohnadel, *Hommes et ouvrages*, vol. 1, 41.
32. SHD 7N3796/1, 4e Direction to Secrétariat général, 29/4/1929.
33. André Borie and Camille Bouché, *Les travaux publics et les problèmes économiques et financiers* (1933).
34. Mary and Hohnadel, *Hommes et ouvrages*, vol. 1, 40–50.
35. AD Meuse 2R53, Conseil de prefecture interdépartemental, 'Conclusions', 19/11/1936 and 10/3/1937.
36. SHD 7N3796/1, CORF, Note, 12/11/1927.
37. SHD 1N28/8, Report, 6/11/1926.
38. SHD 1N54/1/1, 'Protection du Bassin de Briey', 25/4/1930; Weygand to Pétain, 29/7/1930; 'Note sur la protection', 30/4/1930.
39. SHD 1N54/1/1, Weygand to Pétain, 18/3/1930; Pétain to minister, 28/3/1930.

40. SHD 7N3771/1, Belhague to war minister, 29/7/1931; Comité des forges to Président du conseil, 23/5/1931.
41. This section relies on Kevin Passmore, 'Organizing the Terrain: The Maginot Line, 1919–1939', *Environmental History*, 29 (2024), 86–117.
42. SHD 7N3763/3 and 1N27/7, 'Organisation défensive du territoire', 16/3/1923, 6; Santiago Gorostiza, '"There Are the Pyrenees!": Fortifying the Nation in Francoist Spain', *Environmental History*, 23 (2018), 797–823 at 798, 802, shows that Spanish engineers also endeavoured to 'perfect nature'.
43. SHD 7N3764/1, Klein, 'Étude sur l'organisation de la frontière', 31/3/1919, 11.
44. SHD 7N3764/1, Klein, 'Étude', 9–10.
45. SHD 7N3822/5, Requin to ministry, 19/7/1937.
46. Louis Chauvineau, 'L'organisation du terrain et ses conséquences', *Revue militaire française*, n.s., 35 (January–March 1930), 246–73 at 258.
47. Clément-Grandcourt, 'Lignes continues, places rondes et villes ouvertes II', *La France militaire*, 7–8/1/1934; SHD 7N3673/1, Pétain, Note, ?1920; SHD 7N3765, Note, 1/12/1934; Maurice-Gustave Gamelin, *Servir*, vol. 1: *Les armées françaises de 1940* (1946), 43–4; Ruby, *Sedan, terre d'épreuve*, 19–21; Ladislas Mysyrowicz, *Autopsie d'une défaite: Origines de l'effondrement militaire français de 1940* (1973), 43–4.
48. SHD 7N3781/10–11, Normand, 'Les fortifications', 25/7/1928.
49. Benoît Boutefeu, 'L'aménagement forestier en France: à la recherche d'une gestion durable à travers l'histoire', *Vertigo*, 6 (2005), 1–8.
50. JOCD, 20/11/1928, 2715; Jean-Jacques Dubois, 'Influences humaines sur l'évolution des paysages et des limites de la Forêt de Mormal', *Hommes et terres du nord*, 2 (1973), 73–106; Jean-Paul Amat, 'L'arbre et la forêt, témoins du champ de bataille', in Gérard Canini, ed., *Mémoire de la Grande guerre* (1989), 299–312.
51. SHD 7N3771/1, 'Réponse', 3/4/1936; SHD 7N3675/2/2, Pouille to mayor, 23/4/1936, and Direction Génie to DG EAF, 17/6/1936; SHD 7N3770/6, General Mussel, 'Visite de la Commission de l'Armée', 19–20/3/1936.
52. SHD 1N54/1/1, Pétain, Note, 7/11/1930.
53. Mark Cioc, *The Rhine: An Eco-biography, 1815–2000* (2003), 3.
54. Albert Demangeon and Lucien Febvre, *Le Rhin: Problèmes d'histoire et d'économie* (1935), 151, 164–5, 172; Cioc, *The Rhine*, 48–67.
55. A. Desaunais, 'Le bief de Kembs, premier tronçon du grand canal d'Alsace', *Géocarrefour*, 9 (1933), 143–8; Cioc, *The Rhine*, 51–4; Christoph Bernhardt, *Im Spiegel des Wassers: Eine transnationale Umweltgeschichte des Oberrheins* (2016), 375–87.
56. AD Bas-Rhin 98AL244, Dossier presse, *Rhein-Westfalen Zeitung*, 6/7/1933.
57. SHD 1N28, CSG, 17/12/1926; SHD 7N3769, 2e Bureau, Note, 26/12/1929; Brécard to war minister, 16/2/1931; miscellaneous correspondence, 1937–8.
58. SHD 1N54/1, Belhague to ministry/EMA, 20/3/1930.
59. Capitaine du génie Alheilig, *École d'application de l'artillerie et du génie: Cours de fortification: La fortification après 1885 (officiers-élèves du génie)* (1911), 82.
60. SHD 14YD480, Dossier personnel.
61. Robert Normand, 'Nos grandes écoles: L'École du génie', *Revue des deux mondes*, March 1929, 183.
62. Normand was probably responsible for the ministerial circular of 10/7/1928, *Revue du génie militaire*, 63 (1928), 371–2. See also 'Architectes militaires italiens', *Revue du génie militaire*, 60 (1927), 394–425.

63. SHD 1N28, 17/12/1927.
64. SHD 1N29/3, 'Note sur les formes techniques', 16/5/1927.
65. SHD 1N29/3, Note, 4/7/1927; SHD 1N29/4, PV CSG, 12/10/1927; Tournoux, *Haut commandement*, 86–9; Mary and Hohnadel, *Hommes et ouvrages*, vol. 1, 18.
66. SHD 7N3760, CORF, 'Note sur les formes techniques', 12/3/1928, 12–13.
67. Pierre Rocolle, *Le béton a-t-il trahi? Historique de la ligne Maginot et de la ligne Mareth* (1950), 21.
68. SHD 7N3762/5, PV CORF, 1/7/1929; SHD 7N3822/8, correspondence and plans; Philippe Truttmann and Frédéric Lisch, *La muraille de France ou La ligne Maginot: La fortification française de 1940, sa place dans l'évolution des systèmes fortifiés d'Europe occidentale de 1880 à 1945* (2009), 362-3.
69. Robert Brice, *L'ensemble fortifié du Hochwald* (1988); Mary and Hohnadel, *Hommes et ouvrages*, vol. 1 (2000), 54–6.
70. Truttmann and Lisch, *La muraille de France*, 362–3.
71. Brice, *L'ensemble fortifié du Hochwald*, 14–15.
72. SHD 7N3762/3, 'Rapport au ministre', 13/5/1929.
73. SHD 7N3762/3, Note, 25/6/1934.
74. Gérard Monnier, *L'architecture en France: Une histoire critique (1918–1950)* (1990), 345.
75. André Metz, 'Gustave Umbdenstock: Membre de l'Institut', *Revue du génie militaire*, 75 (1936), 593–616 at 594.
76. Gustave Umbdenstock, *Cours d'architecture* (2 vols, 1930), vol. 2, 57–117; Monnier, *L'architecture en France*, 345.
77. Camille Mauclair, *La crise du panbétonnisme intégral: L'architecture va-t-elle mourir?* (1933), 20, 93.
78. *Le Matin*, 15/10/1930, 14/9/1939.
79. Quentin Hughes, *Military Architecture* (1974), 225–30.
80. SHD 1N53/1/1, CORF, Note, 24/5/1928; SHD 7N3796/6, Painlevé to Senate Army Commission, 29/7/1929.
81. SHD 7N570 supplément, Gandéra to war minister, 7/4/1937; AN Fonds Moscou 199404963, Intérieure to Défense, 30/4/1937.
82. SHD 1N29/4, PV CSG, 12/10/1927.
83. Robert Didio, 'Note au sujet de la fortification permanente', *Revue du génie militaire*, 73 (1934), 5–42 at 33–4.
84. Pierre Nord, *Double crime sur la ligne Maginot* (1936), 24, 217.
85. Didio, 'Note', 33–4.
86. Christopher Wilk, 'Sitting on Air', in Christopher Wilk, ed., *Modernism, 1914–1939: Designing a New World* (2006), 225–48.
87. SHD 1N29/3, CDF, 'Note pour le CSG', 16/5/1927, 8.
88. Brice, *L'ensemble fortifié du Hochwald*, 21–2.
89. Löic Glad, 'Un petit ouvrage de la ligne Maginot: L'Einseling', *Le Cahier du pays naborien*, 2004, 66.
90. SHD 7N3781/2, 'Note ITTF', 17/9/1935; Ministère de la guerre to general commanding the ITTF, 25/7/1935.
91. SHD 2V1 (STG), Dossier étanchéité, 'Notice provisoire', 19/5/1932.
92. M.-J.-A. Schickelé, 'Le service de santé dans les régions fortifiés', *Archives de médecine et de pharmacie militaires*, 109 (1939), 179–247 at 192.
93. SHD 7N3766/6, 'Questions soulevées', 14/6/1935.

94. SHD 7N3781/2, Fabry to governor of Metz, 25/7/1935.
95. SHD 7N3770/4, 'Observations', undated, August 1935; SHD 7N3770/10, 'Éléments de repose', 5/3/1936.
96. Émile Alléhaut, *Être prêts: Puissance aérienne, forces de terre: Doctrine, organisation, moral* (1935), 154.
97. Robert Poulaine, 'Trois mois avec l'armée', *Le Temps*, 6/8/1935.
98. [Lucien Souchon], *Feue l'armée française* (1929), 48–51.
99. Bernadette Bensaude-Vincent, 'Des rayons contre raison? L'essor de la radiesthésie dans les années trente', *Sciences et société*, January 2002, 201–26.
100. André Metz, 'Enquête sur la radiethésie', *Revue du génie militaire*, 74 (1935), 87–100.
101. Prételat, *Le destin tragique*, 9–11.
102. SHD 1N54/1/1, Correspondence Pétain–Weygand–Degoutte, April and May 1930, and Conférence bureau de Pétain, 10/5/1930; Mary and Hohnadel, *Hommes et ouvrages*, vol. 4 (2009), 8–10.
103. SHD 7N3757/2, Guillaumat to ministry, 8/1/1926; SHD 7N3781/1, draft Debeney to Pétain, 6/11/1929; Pétain to Debeney, 18/11/1929.

4 Fortification Contested

1. Sorlot, *André Maginot*, 215–20.
2. Philip Bankwitz, *Maxime Weygand and Civil-Military Relations in Modern France* (1967), 207–34.
3. SHD 1N34/2, Weygand to Gamelin, 12 and 15/1/1934; 1N34/1–10bis, Weygand to Gamelin, 10 and 18/1/1934; SHD 1N34/6, Weygand, Résumé, 15/12/1934.
4. SHD 7N3765/1/5, 'Note sur la couverture', 26/5/1934; Maxime Weygand, *Le journal du général Weygand, 1929–1935*, ed. Frédéric Guelton (1998), 15/5/1930; Porch, *Defeat and Division*, 37.
5. Weygand, *Le journal*, 72–7, 204–18.
6. Émile Mayer, *Nos chefs de 1914: Souvenirs personnels et essais de psychologie militaire* (1930), 14–15; Henri Lerner, 'Le lieutenant-colonel Émile Mayer et son salon (1851–1938)', in Olivier Forcade, Éric Duhamel and Philippe Vial, eds, *Militaires en république 1870–1962* (1999), 503–6; Jean-Jacques Becker, 'Vers l'armée de demain', in Vincent Duclert, ed., *Le colonel Mayer: De l'affaire Dreyfus à de Gaulle* (2007), 285–94.
7. Bruno Chaix, 'De Gaulle et le débat doctrinal du début des années trente', in Fondation Charles de Gaulle, ed., *Charles de Gaulle: Du militaire au politique 1920–1940* (2004), 91–101; Bruno Chaix, 'Le général Alléhaut, un théoricien militaire ignoré de l'entre-deux-guerres', *Guerres mondiales et conflits contemporains* (1996), 69–83.
8. Letter of 17 April 1935, reprinted in Chaix, 'Le général Alléhaut'.
9. Maxime Weygand, 'L'état militaire de la France', *Revue des deux mondes*, October 1936.
10. Colonel Charras, quoted in Weygand, *Le journal*, 20.
11. Buat, *Journal*, 14/4/1919.
12. Weygand, *Le journal*, 88.
13. SHD 1N34/2, Weygand to Gamelin, 12 and 15/1/34, 21/3/1934.
14. SHD 1N28/8, 'Rapport au ministre', 6/11/1926, 27.

15. SHD 1N28/8, Rapport, 6/11/1926; SHD 1N29/1, PV CSG, 18/1/1927, and Instruction, 3/2/1927.
16. SHD 7N3765/1/3, Hirschauer to minister, 13 and 24/9/1932.
17. SHD 1N32/4, Note, 27/6/1932; SHD 7N3771/1, 'Projet de réponse', undated; SHD 7N3771/2, miscellaneous motions; SHD 7N3770/6, Chamber of Commerce of Nancy, 23/6/1934.
18. SHD 7N3771/2, ministry to Rotours, 13/12/1928; SHD 1N29/1, PV CSG, 18/1/1927; SHD 1N31/10, 27/9/1930; SHD 7N3771/1, EMA to Messimy, 27/71929; EMA to Dumont, ?1930; Painlevé to Chamber of Commerce of Douai, 3/11/1930.
19. SHD 1N54/1/2, Colonel Larcher, Compte-rendu, 9/9/1931; Maginot to Pétain, 28/9/1931.
20. SHD 1N32/3, Messimy to Maginot, 23/12/1931.
21. SHD 7N3771/1, Gamelin to Messimy, 24/12/1931, and ministry to Messimy, undated; SHD 5N583/1, draft response from War Cabinet, 15/1/1932.
22. SHD 7N3765/2, Messimy to unnamed general.
23. SHD 1N32/3, PV CSG, 28/5/1932 and Pétain, 'Note sur la défense de la region-frontière du nord', 2/5/1932.
24. SHD 7N3765/1, 'Rapport de Présentation', 11/4/1932.
25. SHD 1N54/1/3, Gamelin to Weygand, 10/6/1932.
26. Laure, *Pétain*, 336–40.
27. SHD 1N42, Pétain, Note, 2/5/1932.
28. Weygand, *Le journal*, 125.
29. SHD 1N32/3, PV CSG, 28/5/1932.
30. SHD 1N32/4, PV CSG, 4/6/1932; Weygand, *Le journal*, 58–64.
31. SHD 5N583/1, Note, 20/11/1933.
32. SHD 7N3765/1/2, Note, 30/6/1932.
33. Quoted in Du Réau, *Édouard Daladier*, 91.
34. Weygand, *Le journal*, 13/2/1933, 10/6/1933, 25/9/1933.
35. SHD 29N179, Instruction, 21/11/1931.
36. SHD 1N334/4, miscellaneous correspondence, including Daladier, 'Note pour l'EMA', 15/6/1933.
37. SHD 1N34, Weygand to Gamelin, 12/1/1934.
38. SHD 7N3765/2/1, Messimy to Gamelin, 12/5/1933.
39. SHD 7N3765/1/4, Note, 15/9/1933.
40. SHD 7N3765/1/4, Note, 25/10/1933.
41. SHD 7N3781/1/1033, Belhague to Daladier, 26/10/1933.
42. SHD 5N581/3, 'Principales réalisations du président', 5/1/1937; JODC, 19/12/1933, 4698–703; Tournoux, *Haut commandement*, 164.
43. SHD 1N33, War Ministry to EMA, 15/6/1933.
44. AS 69S12, Audition Daladier, 22/3/1933.
45. JODC, 15/6/1934, 1530–1.
46. Jules Moch speech in JODC, 14/6/1934, 1934; General Denain, JODC, 15/6/1934, 1432; Pétain, preface to Vauthier, *La doctrine de guerre*, viii.
47. This paragraph depends on Vergez-Chaignon, *Pétain*, 132–3, 211–12.
48. SHD 5N577/1/2, military cabinet to Gamelin, 26/3/1934.
49. Laure, *Pétain*, 378–82; Alfred Conquet, *Auprès du maréchal Pétain* (1970), 27–65.
50. JODC, 14/6/1934, 1496.
51. SHD 7N3796/12, EMA Note, 31/12/1935.

52. Tournoux, *Haut commandement*, 167.
53. Laure, *Pétain*, 382–5.
54. SHD 7N3765/1/5, Instruction, 19/3/1934; Laure, *Pétain*, 382–5.
55. SHD 1N34/2, Weygand to Gamelin, 12 and 15/1/1934, 21/3/1934.
56. Henry Dutailly, 'Une puissance militaire illusoire 1930–1939', in Guy Pedroncini, ed., *Histoire militaire de la France*, vol. 3: *De 1871 à 1940* (1992), 351–4; Jean Perrier-Cornet, 'Le maréchal Pétain, ministère de la Guerre (9 février–8 novembre 1934)', in Olivier Forcade, Éric Duhamel and Philippe Vial, eds, *Militaires en république 1870–1962* (1999), 235–44.
57. AN C//14983, PV Chamber Army Commission, 21–22/11/1934.
58. SHD 1N34/6, Weygand, Résumé, 15/12/1934.
59. Robert Doughty, *The Seeds of Disaster: The Development of French Army Doctrine 1919–1939* (1985), 185; Bruno Chaix, *En mai 1940, fallait-il entrer en Belgique? Décisions stratégiques et plans opérationnels de la campagne de France* (2005), 50.
60. Alexander, *The Republic in Danger*, 13–33.
61. Conquet, *Auprès du maréchal Pétain*, 23.
62. SHD 7N3765/1/5, Notes, 18/3/1935, 3/4/1935.
63. SHD 1N29/4, PV CSG, 12/10/1927.
64. SHD 5N583, 'Crédits alloués', 9/9/1938.
65. SHD 7N3770/4, Belhague to Gamelin, 4/7/36; Alleau, Note, 20/7/1936.
66. SHD 7N3762/6, Fabry to Belhague, 3 and 30/7/1935; SHD 7N3770/4, Belhague to Gamelin, 4/7/1936; Alleau, Note, 21/8/1936; Prételat, *Le destin tragique*, 9–10; Gamelin, *Servir*, vol. 2: *Le prologue de drame: 1930–août 1939* (1946), 184–5.
67. SHD 5N581/2, Fabry, JMO, 6/1935.
68. SHD 5N581/2, Fabry, JMO, 7/10/1935, 6/1/1936.
69. Peter Jackson, *France and the Nazi Menace: Intelligence and Policy Making 1933–1939* (2000), 158–9.
70. SHD 33N95/9, Note de Service, 1/8/1936.
71. Alexander, *The Republic in Danger*, 257–60; Jackson, *France and the Nazi Menace*, 161–77.
72. SHD 7N3770/5, War Ministry response to Army Commission, 18/3/1936; Tournoux, *Haut commandement*, 261; Gamelin, *Servir*, vol. 2, 241–3.
73. SHD 7N3781/1, Huré to Daladier, 1/12/1936.
74. SHD 33N95/1, War Ministry to commander 20th Region, 7/3/1936; SHD 33N95/8, 20th Region to 3e Bureau EMA, 16/7/1936; SHD 33N95/1, 20th Region, Instruction, 25/11/1936.
75. Jean-Baptiste Duroselle, *La décadence: 1932–1939* (1985), 176; Anthony Eden, Earl of Avon, *The Eden Memoirs* (1960), vol. 1: *Facing the Dictators*, 338–73.
76. Gamelin, *Servir*, vol. 2, 197.
77. Julian Jackson, *A Certain Idea of France: Charles de Gaulle* (2017), 86.
78. François Cochet, 'La société militaire en France: réalité et perception par Charles de Gaulle (1919–1940)', in Fondation Charles de Gaulle, ed., *Charles de Gaulle: Du militaire au politique 1920–1940* (2004), 17–32 at 25–6.
79. SHD 7N3434/1, 'Le problème militaire français', 1/6/1936; Jackson, *France and the Nazi Menace*, 186–9.
80. Doughty, *The Seeds of Disaster*, 35; Alexander, *The Republic in Danger*, 121–2; for a qualified criticism, see Kevin Passmore, 'Au Contact: French Infantry Tactics in the Maginot Line Advance Posts During the Phoney War, 4 September 1939 to 10 May 1940', *War in History*, 26/3/2025, https://doi.org/10.1177/09683445251329056.

81. SHD 9N306/3, Dufieux, Note, 27/1/1936.
82. SHD 7N2676, 'Le nouveau règlement', 28/12/1935. The manual in question was probably the *Ausbildungsvorschrift für die Infanterie*.
83. Général Barrard, 'Réflexions sur nos règlements d'infanterie: le groupe et la section de F.-V.', *La revue d'infanterie*, 45 (August 1935), 189–97; 'Études et notes sur notre règlement', *La revue d'infanterie*, 88 (April 1936), 598–666; 'Études et notes sur notre règlement', *La revue d'infanterie*, 89 (December 1936), 1107–218.
84. *Instruction sur l'emploi tactique des grandes unités* (1936), article 4, paragraphs 223–4; *Instruction sur le service en campagne* (1939), 45–6.
85. SHD 7N4003, Gamelin, 7/10/1936.
86. 'Instruction du 6 June 1938 sur le service en campagne', *La France militaire*, 6/6/1939.
87. *Règlement de l'infanterie: Instruction technique* (1939); *Règlement de l'infanterie: Combat* (1939); *Manuel du gradé d'infanterie* (1939); ABC, 'Règlement de l'infanterie', *La France militaire*, 7, 8, 24/5/1939, 1 and 17/6/1939.
88. Lieutenant-Colonel Kuntz, 'Le compartiment du terrain', *La France militaire*, 4/1/1939.
89. SHD 7N3796/13, minister of national defence, 26/10/1936.
90. Pierre Vanderputten, 'L'organisation fortifiée de la frontière ardennaise', in Maurice Vaïsse, ed., *Ardennes 1940* (1991), 15–32.
91. SHD 5N/583, undated, probably September 1936; SHD 7N3796, 26/11/1936; SHD 7N3697, 12/12/1936.
92. SHD 7N3796/13, minister of national defence, 26/10/1936.
93. AN C//14643, PV, Séance, 17/12/1936.
94. Alexander, *The Republic in Danger*, 196–9.
95. JODC, 29/1/1937, 258.
96. Jonathan Zorach, 'Czechoslovakia's Fortifications: Their Development and Role in the 1938 Munich Crisis', *Militärgeschichtliche Zeitschrift*, 20 (1976), 81–94.
97. Gamelin, *Servir*, vol. 2, 316.
98. SHD 7N3771/1, Bordereau, 2/4/1938.
99. SHD 7NN2131/1, Renseignement, 25/8/1938; UK Paramount newsreel, 16/11/1937; Christoph Rass, 'Die Bedeutung des Westwalls für die nationalsozialistische Politik und Kriegsführung', in Karola Fings and Frank Möller, eds, *Zukunftsprojekt Westwall: Wege zu einem verantwortungsbewussten Umgang mit den Überresten der NS-Anlage* (2008), 49–58; John D. Heyl, 'The Construction of the *Westwall*, 1938: An Exemplar for National Socialist Policymaking', *Central European History*, 14 (1981), 63–78.
100. SHD 31N62/Archives diverses, Messages téléphoniques, 30/9/1938.
101. AN F^{60} 174, 'Les grandes manoeuvres allemandes', 18/8/1938; Robert J. Young, 'Le haut commandement français au moment de Munich', *Revue d'histoire moderne et contemporaine*, 24 (1977), 110–29; Talbot Imlay, *Facing the Second World War: Strategy, Politics, and Economics in Britain and France 1938–1940* (2003), 32–3; Simon Catros, 'Le haut commandement et l'éventualité d'une guerre franco-allemande en 1938–1939 à partir du journal inédit du chef d'escadron de Villelume', *Revue historique des armées*, 15 (2014), 83–94.
102. SHD 7N4040/2, 13/12/1938.
103. Vergez-Chaignon, *Pétain*, 315.
104. Vanderputten, 'L'organisation fortifiée', 21–2.

105. Prételat, *Le destin tragique*, 12.
106. AN 2W5, 'Historique des questions particulières', undated, ?1942; Mary and Hohnadel, *Hommes et ouvrages*, vol. 1, 37–8; Prételat, *Le destin tragique*, 11–16; Vanderputten, 'L'organisation fortifiée', 21–2.
107. Prételat, *Le destin tragique*, 14.
108. SHD 1N54/1/1, ministry circular, 29/4/1930.
109. Ruby, *Sedan, terre d'épreuve*, 23.
110. 'Un certain disparate: Entretiens avec François Le Lionnais', Oulipo, accessed 6/6/2022, https://blogs.oulipo.net/fll/.
111. SHD 28N15, Prételat circular, 18/10/1939; Prételat to Georges, 20/10/1939, 19/11/1939.
112. SHD 7N3770/5, 'Note pour l'EMA', 5/3/1936; SHD 7N3770/8, 'Commandement et encadrement', undated; SHD 7N3770/10, 'Importance des déboisments à faire', 26/4/1933.
113. SHD 7N3824, Colson to 20th Region, 24/9/1938, 7/11/1938.
114. SHD 33N108/4, Colonel Touchard, Note, 15/7/1937.
115. SHD 33N108/4, unsigned manuscript note, 15/5/1937, probably chef de bataillon of III/37 RIF.
116. SHD 7N3775/2, 'Notice technique', 11/3/1935, referring to Daladier's approval on 27/7/1933; SHD 33N96/1, 20th Region, 26/10/1937; AN C//14643, PV, Séance, 17/12/1936.
117. Léon Noguéro, *Soldat en Alsace-Lorraine, 1939–1940*, ed. Henri Noguéro (2017), 54, 25/10/1939.
118. SHD 7N3770/4, Pinson, Compte-rendu, undated.
119. SHD 7N3766/3, Direction génie, Note, 1/4/1939.
120. Ruby, *Sedan, terre d'épreuve*, 23.
121. SHD 33N108/3, Colonel Creskens, Note de Service, 1/6/1937.
122. SHD 33N108/4, Combet, commander SS-Bitche to colonel 37 RIF, 25/7/1939.
123. Paul Marque, *La ligne Maginot aquatique* (1989), 13–18; Mary and Hohnadel, *Hommes et ouvrages*, vol. 3 (2003), 116–21; Emmanuel Chiffre, Denis Mathis and Grégory Weimerskich, 'Les hydrosystèmes défensifs: des paysages militaires atypiques de la Ligne Maginot', *Revue de géographie historique*, 10–11 (2017), 13.
124. SHD 7N3770/8, Inspection, undated, 1936; SHD 33N108/4, General Vielliard, Note, 24/12/1938.
125. SHD 33N108, 37 RIF, Compte-rendu, 15/4/1937; Creskens to Génie, undated, ?August 1937.
126. SHD 7N3770/2, Pétain, 'Observations', 24/8/1937.
127. Ruby, *Sedan, terre d'épreuve*, 23.
128. Prételat, *Le destin tragique*, 13.
129. Prételat, *Le destin tragique*, 14; Mary and Hohnadel, *Hommes et ouvrages*, vol. 1, 36–8.
130. Gamelin, *Servir*, vol. 1, 116–17, Notes, 8/2/1938, 12/10/1938.
131. AS 69S13, Commission de l'Armée, 8/2/1939.
132. Vergez-Chaignon, *Pétain*, 308–18.
133. Gamelin, *Servir*, vol. 1, 128, Note, 12/10/1938.
134. Jackson, *A Certain Idea of France*, 102; Imlay, *Facing the Second World War*, 243.
135. Louis Chauvineau, *Une invasion est-elle encore possible?* (1939).
136. SHD 7N3757/1, 'Rapport au ministre', 3/6/1939.

5 Officers and NCOs on the Maginot Line, 1933–1939

1. *La France militaire*, 31/1/1929.
2. For a list of specialisms, see SHD 1N32, PV CSG, Annexe 2, 4/6/1932.
3. *La France militaire*, 10/4/1919.
4. SHD 1N24/5, PV CSG, 26/10/1921.
5. Tim Benton, 'Building Utopia', in Christopher Wilk, ed., *Modernism, 1914–1939: Designing a New World* (2006), 149–73 at 158.
6. SHD 7N3770/8, 6th Region, Rapport, 24/2/1936.
7. Jean-Émile Cadilhac, 'Sur le front et dans les entrailles de la Ligne Maginot', *L'Illustration*, 7/1/1939.
8. SHD 7N4037/1, General Cousse, Rapport, 23/121935.
9. SHD 7N3822/4, Belhague to ministry, 30/8 and 29/10/1929; 'Note sur l'organisation d'un quartier', 5/2/1930.
10. C. Rougeron, 'Le bombardement des immeubles d'habitation', *Revue de l'armée de l'air*, 8 (1936), 661–74; Efi Markou, 'Militaires et urbanistes durant les années trente: l'aménagement urbain et la menace aérienne', *Les annales de la recherche urbaine*, 91 (2001), 18–26 at 22–3; Romy Golan, *Modernity and Nostalgia: Art and Politics in France between the Wars* (1995), 77–8; Monnier, *L'architecture en France*, 353–4; Benton, 'Building a New World', 155.
11. Henry Dutailly, 'L'architecture militaire', in Guy Pedroncini, ed., *Histoire militaire de la France*, vol. 3: *De 1871 à 1940* (1992), 364–5.
12. AD Moselle 29J3–4. On the barracks generally, see Truttmann and Lisch, *La muraille de France*, 303–11.
13. Stéphane Perréon, 'Les fortifications de Vauban au cœur de l'architecture et de l'art du Grand Siècle', in Jean Baechler, ed., *La guerre et les arts* (2018), 235–51.
14. *L'Humanité d'Alsace et de Lorraine*, 1/1/1933. See also *Le Matin*, 8/4/1936, and *L'Intransigeante*, 3/6/1938.
15. Henry de Montherlant, *L'équinoxe de septembre* (1938), 92–3. Montherlant wrote in the context of his opposition to appeasement.
16. SHD 7N3770/4, Captain Pinson, 'Compte rendu de visite', 21/1/1935 or 1936.
17. SHD 7N3770/4, Belhague to Gamelin, 4/7/1936.
18. SHD 7N3781/2, Fabry to governor of Metz, 25/7/1935.
19. *Le Matin*, 8/4/1936.
20. *L'Intransigeant*, 8/4/1936.
21. SHD 7N3822/5, Gamelin to 20th Region, 8/12/1933.
22. SHD 7N3770/4, 'Additif au rapport', 17/11/1933.
23. *Le Matin*, 8/4/1936.
24. SHD 7N3770/4, Médecin-commandant Poiteau, Compte-rendu, 20–21/2/1936.
25. SHD 7N4040/1, Colonel Balourdet, 4/12/1935.
26. SHD 7N3770/4, Captain Poitou, 20–21/2/1936.
27. SHD 7N4039/1, Chef de bataillon Pirot, 20/11/1935.
28. AS 69S95 (95 probably coding error for 97), 'Notes, visite sur la frontière de l'est', 31/3/1936, 1/4/1936.
29. Léon Rodier, 'Un témoignage sur la ligne Maginot 1937–1940', in Guy Pedroncini and Pierre X. Stroh, eds, *De l'oppidum à l'enfouissement: L'art de la fortification à Verdun et sur les marches de l'Est* (1996), 287–97 at 293.
30. SHD 7N4040/2, 10/12/1938.

31. SHD 7N3765/1/4, Gamelin, 'Note pour le ministre', 25/10/1933; SHD 7N3770/1, Note (inspection Weygand), 25/10/1934; SHD 7N3770/4, Pinson, Rapport, undated, 1935/6; SHD 7N3822/4, minister to commander 20th Region, 3/7/1935.
32. SHD 7N2322/1, 'Note sur les cadres . . . de région de forteresse', 5/2/1936.
33. SHD 7N2380/1, Instruction, 17/8/1933; 'Note sur les spécialistes', 12/11/1933; undated note, late 1936; *Journal officiel: Lois et décrets* (JOLD), 22/7/1937, 8298.
34. SHD 7N4040/2, Colonel Chomereau, 13/12/1938.
35. SHD 7N4040/1, Colonel Alaurent (153 RIF), 9/12/1935; SHD 7N4039/1, Chef de bataillon Purch (7 BCA), 13/12/1935; SHD 7N4039/Rapports d'ensemble, General Garchery, 10/2/1937.
36. Albert Laumonier, *Mémoires d'un prisonnier de guerre: De Brigueil-le-Chantre à Kobierzyn, en passant par la Ligne Maginot* (2019), 19–26.
37. SHD 7N4040/1, Colonel Herique, 11/12/1935.
38. SHD 7N4040/1, commander SF-Rohrbach, 10/12/1935.
39. SHD 7N4040/1, 28/11/1935.
40. SHD 7N4039/1, 157 DBAF, 9/12/1935; 72 and 73 BAF, 11/12/1935.
41. SHD 7N4037/1, 6th Region, 10/12/1938.
42. Stéphane Jonas, 'Les jardins d'Ungemach à Strasbourg: une cité-jardin d'origine nataliste (1923–1950)', in Paulette Girard and Bruno Fayolle-Lussac, eds, *Cités, cités-jardins: Une histoire européenne* (2019), 65–85; Paul-André Rosental, *Destins de l'eugénisme* (2016), 109.
43. 'Cité des officiers', www.Maginot.org/metrich/elsange12-010_fr.htm.
44. SHD 7N3765/1/4, Gamelin, 'Note pour le ministre', 25/10/1933; SHD 7N3770/4, 'Analyse du rapport Guitry', 13/9/1934; SHD 7N2322/1, 'Note sur les cadres . . . de région de forteresse', 5/2/1936; SHD 7N3765/1/4, Note, 25/10/1933; SHD 7N3781/2/2, 'Instruction provisoire sur le service dans les ouvrages', 7/10/1937, 1.
45. SHD 7N4037/1/, Colonel Caille, Rapport, 14/12/1935.
46. Charles de Gaulle, 'La condition des cadres dans l'armée' (1930/1), *Espoir* (1975), 8–60; Judith M. Hughes, *To the Maginot Line: The Politics of French Military Preparation in the 1920s* (1971), 30–4; Jean Doise and Maurice Vaïsse, *Politique étrangère de la France: Diplomatie et outil militaire, 1871–1991* (1992), 284–5; Jackson, *A Certain Idea of France*, 89.
47. SHD 7N4039/2, 157 RAP, 12/1935; Jean Lopez, *Heinz Guderian* (2025), 21.
48. SHD 7N4039/2, Rapport, 1935.
49. SHD 7N4040/1, Colonel Herique, 11/12/1936; General Lemoine, 12/12/1935.
50. SHD 7N4037/2, Colonel Potier, 21/11/1935.
51. SHD 7N4037/2, Colonel Fonlupt, 15/11/1938.
52. SHD 7N4037/1, Colonel Caille, Rapport, 14/12/1935.
53. SHD 7N4040/1, 28/11/1935.
54. *La France militaire*, 5/7/1928, 4/1/1929; Hughes, *To the Maginot Line*, 30–4.
55. Raoul Girardet, *La société militaire de 1815 à nos jours* (1998), 242–3.
56. De Gaulle, 'La condition des cadres'; Hughes, *To the Maginot Line*, 30–4; Doise and Vaïsse, *Politique étrangère de la France*, 284–5; Jackson, *A Certain Idea of France*, 89.
57. SHD 7N4039/Rapports d'ensemble, General Garchery, 10/2/1937.
58. SHD 7N4039/1, Colonel Dessaux, 9/12/1935.
59. SHD 7N4040/1, Colonel Creskens, 9/12/1935.

60. SHD 7N4040/1, Colonel Herique, 11/12/1936; General Lemoine, 12/12/1935.
61. SHD 3K131, Témoignage Albéric Vaillant.
62. SHD 5N583/1, Notes, 17/12/1933.
63. SHD 7N4040/1, Colonel Creskens, 13/12/1936.
64. SHD 7N4037/1, 6th Region, General Sivot, état-major, RF-Metz, 28/12/1938, and SF-Thionville, 13/12/1938; SHD 7N4040/1, General Ducasse, Rapport, 20/12/1935.
65. SHD 7N4040/1, 22/12/1935.
66. SHD 7N4037/1, Colonel Dumotier, 2/12/1935.
67. SHD 7N4037, Colonel Labretoigne de Mazel, 9/12/1935; Colonel Courboulin, 163 RAP, 9/12/1935.
68. SHD 7N4033/2/11, 'Note pour l'EMA', undated, ?December 1933.
69. SHD 7N4037/1, Rapport, Baudouin, 13/12/1936.
70. SHD 7N4034/1/2, 'Note analysant . . . morale 1936', 17/3/1937, and responses; SHD 7N 4034/1/3, 'Note analysant . . . morale 1937', undated, c. March 1938; SHD 7N4039/Rapports d'ensemble, General Garchery, 10/2/1937.
71. SHD 7N4034/1/3, 'Note analysant . . . morale 1937', undated, c. March 1938.
72. SHD 7N4037/1, Colonel Tournade, 10/12/1938.
73. SHD 7N4040/2, Lieutenant-Colonel Reyx, Rapport, 10/12/1938.
74. SHD 7N4037/1, Colonel Grisot, 1/12/1938.
75. SHD 7N4037/1, 10/12/1938.
76. SHD 7N4037/1, Colonel Cochinard, 29/11/1938; 10/12/1938.
77. Roger Bruge, *On a livré la ligne Maginot* (1975), 115–22.
78. SHD 7N4040/2, Colonel Chomereau, 13/12/1938.
79. SHD 7N3766/3, IEE, 'Remarques récentes sur la situation le long de la Ligne Maginot', 19/1/1939.
80. SHD 7N4037/1, Colonel Cochinard, 29/11/1938.
81. SHD 7N4037/1, Colonel Grisot, 1/12/1938.
82. SHD 7N4037/1, Colonel Tournade, 10/12/1938.
83. SHD 7N4037/2, Colonel Fonlupt, 15/11/1938.
84. SHD 7N4037/1, 28/12/1938.
85. SHD 7N4037/1, Colonel Tournade, 10/12/1938.
86. SHD 7N3770/3, Capitaine de frégate Desjardin, 30/9 to 4/10/1938.
87. Jean-François Staszak, '"On n'est pas un bon légionnaire quand on n'a pas le cafard": enjeux médicaux, culturels et politiques d'un sentiment géographique (1880–1930)', *Carnets de géographes*, August 2016.
88. SHD 7N4037/1, 29/11/1938.
89. SHD 7N3766/3, IEE, 'Remarques récentes sur la situation le long de la Ligne Maginot', 19/1/1939.
90. SHD 7N4040/1, 10/12/1935.
91. SHD 7N4037/2, Colonel Potier, 21/11/1935.
92. SHD 7N4040/2, 10/12/1938.
93. SHD 7N4034/1, untitled, undated, extracts from a 'magazine article'.
94. SHD 7N4037/1, Colonel Chateignon (149 RIF) 28/11/1938.

6 Command and Disobedience on the Maginot Line

1. SHD 7N3781/1/1933, PV CDF, Extrait, 27/5/1926; Extrait, 3–4/2/1927.
2. SHD 7N3780/5, 'Réponse à Pierre Cot', 22/11/1928.

3. Humbert Ricolfi, *Le code de justice militaire du 9 mars 1928* (1928), 74.
4. *La Voix du combattant*, 10/3/1928; Buat, *Journal*, 19/4/1923.
5. *La France militaire*, 6/2/1929.
6. Charles de Gaulle, *Vers l'armée de métier* (1934), 86–8.
7. SHD 7N4037/1, 21/11/1935.
8. SHD 7N4039/2, 157 RAP, Rapport, unsigned, 'année 1935'.
9. SHD 7N3776/3, General Guitry to ministry, 20/7/1935; SHD 7N3781/2, 3e Bureau, Note, 11/1/1939; Bordereau, 5/2/1939, and undated ministerial instruction.
10. SHD 7N3778/4, Hubert, Note, 9/4/1936.
11. SHD 7N3770/4, Pinson, Rapport, undated, 1935/6; SHD 7N3781/2, Note, unsigned, 4/12/1935; SHD 7N3781/2, 'Instruction provisoire sur la service dans les ouvrages', 7/10/1937.
12. SHD 7N3781/1/1933, 'Constitution des dossiers d'ouvrages', 18/6/1934; 7N3781/2, EMA, 'Note sur l'organisation des ouvrages', 11/1/1937.
13. SHD 7N3781/2, 'Instruction provisoire sur la service dans les ouvrages', 7/10/1937.
14. SHD 5N581/2, 'Mesures prises', 7/6/1935 to 25/1/1936.
15. Christian Benoît, 'La symbolique de l'Armée de terre: de l'usage à la réglementation de l'usage', in André Thiéblemont, ed., *Cultures et logiques militaires* (1999), 51–83 at 66–73.
16. 'Insignes régimentaires', *Le Passepoil*, 19 (1939), 97–8.
17. *Bulletin officiel des Ministères de la guerre, des pensions, primes et allocations de guerre*, 1935, no. 105-1, Parti permanente, 2981; 1937, 4663; no. 32, 1938, 2872–3; Benoît, 'La symbolique de l'Armée de terre', 66–73.
18. SHD 33N95/6, Colonel Vohl, Rapport, 18/7/1938.
19. SHD 7N3770/4, Captain Pinson, 'Compte rendu de visite', 21/1/1935 or 1936.
20. SHD 7N3781/2, 3e Bureau, Note, 11/1/1939; Bordereau, 5/2/1939, and undated ministerial instruction.
21. SHD 7N4037/1, Rapport, 24/12/1938.
22. SHD 7N4039/1, 71 BAF (SF-Savoie), Chef de bataillon de Parseval, 4/12/1935.
23. SHD 7N4039/1, 6/12/1935. See also SHD 7N4040/2, Creskens, 13/12/1938.
24. SHD 7N4037/2/1935, Potier (171 RIF), 21/11/1935.
25. Crémieux-Brilhac, *Les Français de l'an 40*, vol. 1: *La guerre, oui ou non?*, 88–92; Mona Siegel, '"History Is the Opposite of Forgetting": The Limits of Memory and the Lessons of History in Interwar France', *Journal of Modern History*, 74 (2002), 770–800; Hugues Marquis, 'Un aspect de l'implication de l'École dans la Grande Guerre: l'hommage aux "maîtres morts pour la France" dans l'académie de Poitiers (1914–1930)', *Annales de Bretagne et des Pays de l'Ouest: Anjou, Maine, Poitou-Charente, Touraine*, 122 (2015), 119–37 at 131.
26. Dominique Fouchard, *Le poids de la guerre: Les poilus et leur famille après 1918* (2013), 325.
27. [Souchon], *Feue l'armée française*, 133–6.
28. SHD 7N4040/2, 10/12/1938.
29. SHD 7N4040/1, 17/1/1936.
30. SHD 7N4037/1, 1/12/1938.
31. SHD 7N4036/2, 11/1/1938.
32. SHD 7N2020/1, 9/12/1935. See also 7N4039/1, 71 BAF (SF-Savoie), Chef de bataillon de Parseval, 4/12/1935.
33. SHD 7N4040/2, Colonel du Bouchet, 13/12/1938.

34. SHD 7N4034/1, untitled, undated, extracts from a 'magazine article'.
35. AD Bas-Rhin 286D98, 'Incidents militaires', Boichut report, 8/4/1928.
36. *La France militaire*, 11/6/1932.
37. AD Bas-Rhin 286D98, 'Incidents militaires', statistics, 2/7/1935.
38. *Elsaß-Lothringer Zeitung*, 29/6/1934; AD Bas-Rhin 286D98, 'Incidents militaires', 27/8/1934.
39. SHD 33N95/3, Note de Service, 7/10/1936; AD Bas-Rhin 286D98, Préfet to Inspecteur de l'Académie, 4/5/1933.
40. SHD 7NN2062/408, DGSN report, 29/10/1938; SHD 7N3766/3, IEE, 'Remarques récentes sur la situation le long de la Ligne Maginot', 19/1/1939.
41. SHD 7N3770/3, Capitaine de frégate Desjardin, 30/9 to 4/10/1938.
42. SHD 33N95/7, War Ministry, 17/11/1938.
43. SHD 7N3770/4, Médecin-commandant Poiteau, 20–21/2/1936.
44. SHD 7N3770/3, Capitaine de frégate Desjardin, 30/9 to 4/10/1938; Schickelé, 'Le service de santé', 192.
45. SHD 7N4040/1, Rapport, 17/1/1935.
46. *La France militaire*, 12/1/1929, 15/12/1932.
47. SHD 7N4040/1, Colonel Balourdet, 4/12/1935.
48. SHD 7N4037/1, 19/12/1935.
49. SHD 7N3770/4, Captain Poitou, 20–21/2/1936.
50. SHD 7N4039/Rapports d'ensemble, General Garchery, 10/2/1937.
51. Joan Tumblety, *Remaking the Male Body: Masculinity and the Uses of Physical Culture in Interwar and Vichy France* (2012), 82.
52. SHD 7N4039/Rapports d'ensemble, General Garchery, ?January 1938.
53. SHD 7N4040/2, Lieutenant-Colonel Reyx, Rapport, 10/12/1938.
54. Noguéro, *Soldat en Alsace-Lorraine*, 62, 5/11/1939.
55. *La France militaire*, 12/1/1929, 15/12/1932.
56. SHD 7N4040/1, Colonel Herique, 11/12/1935.
57. Reports in SHD 7N4040/1/12/1935.
58. Antoine Prost, 'Les représentations de la guerre dans la culture française de l'entre-deux-guerres', *Vingtième siècle: Revue d'histoire*, 41 (1994), 23–31.
59. Fouchard, *Le poids de la guerre*, 245.
60. SHD 3R145, e.g. Calvet, Compte-rendu, 3/9/1937; Jean-Pierre Jeancolas, *Histoire du cinéma français* (2011), 207–11.
61. Jeancolas, *Histoire du cinéma français*, 219–24.
62. SHD 3R145, Calvet, Rapport, 8/4/1937.
63. SHD 3R145, Calvet, Rapport, March 1934; unsigned, probably Calvet, 14/3/1934; 'Une parisienne' to Pétain, 7/10/1934; Note, 8/10/1934.
64. Rodier, 'Un témoignage sur la ligne Maginot', 291–2.
65. SHD 7N4037/1, Colonel Chateignon, 21/11/1935.
66. SHD 3R145/1, Calvet to Calamy, 1/9/1937.
67. *L'Action française*, 3/2/1939.
68. Olivier Faron, *Les enfants du deuil: Orphelins et pupilles de la nation de la Première Guerre mondiale, 1914–1941* (2001), 202–32; Manon Pignot, *Allons enfants de la patrie: Génération Grande Guerre* (2012), 378–400; Fouchard, *Le poids de la guerre*, 104–32.
69. SHD 7N4040/1, Colonel Roton (151 DI), 9/12/1935.
70. Fouchard, *Le poids de la guerre*, 111.
71. Eugen Weber, *The Hollow Years: France in the 1930s* (1995), 71.

72. SHD 7N3770/3, Capitaine de frégate Desjardin, 30/9 to 4/10/1938; SHD 7N4040/2, 13/12/1938.
73. Éric Marlière, 'Socio-histoire de la délinquance juvénile d'un ancien quartier ouvrier de "banlieue rouge" en mutation: de l'entre-deux-guerres aux années 2000', *L'homme et la société*, 191 (2014), 71–94.
74. Laura Lee Downs, *Childhood in the Promised Land: Working-Class Movements and the Colonies de Vacances in France, 1880–1960* (2002), 243; Stéphane Audoin, 'Le parti communiste français et la violence: 1929–1931', *Revue historique*, 269 (1983), 365–83 at 379.
75. SHD 7N4037/1, 16/12/1937.
76. SHD 7N4037/1, 21/12/1935.
77. *L'Intransigeant*, 31/5 to 1/6/1938.
78. SHD 7N4039/2, 18/10/1938.
79. DCAJM, Sergeants Carpy and Ravier and Brigadiers Lapointe and Leroy.
80. Rodier, 'Un témoignage sur la ligne Maginot', 291–2.
81. SHD 7N4037/1, General Sivot, 28/12/1938.
82. SHD 7N4036/1, General Doumenc, 12/12/1936.
83. SHD 7N4040/2, 13/12/1938.
84. DCAJM, Dossier Antoine Sabel, 2/4/1911.
85. Jean-Claude Richez and Léon Strauss, 'Tradition et renouvellement des pratiques de loisirs en milieu ouvrier dans l'Alsace des années trente', *Revue d'Alsace*, 113 (1987), 217–38 at 218–20.
86. SHD, 7N4040/2, Rapport, 11/12/1938.
87. DCAJM, Dossier Tremblain et al., 10/3/1937.
88. SHD 9NN1-1730/1-11131, Dossier Heissat, correspondence, July and August 1938.
89. SHD 7N4036, 9/1/1939.
90. DCAJM, Tribunal militaire de Metz, Dossier Bussier, 30/5/1935.
91. DCAJM, Tribunal militaire de Metz, Dossier Boulair, 6/1/1917.
92. Tumblety, *Remaking the Male Body*, 17–44; Luc Capdevila, 'L'identité masculine et les fatigues de la guerre (1914–1945)', *Vingtième siècle: Revue d'histoire*, 75 (2002), 97–108.
93. Pétain to Ricolfi, 9/2/1928, cited in Ricolfi, *Le code de justice militaire*, 89–91.
94. DCAJM, Tribunal militaire de Metz, Dossier Abraham, 11/4/1917.

7 The Maginot Line in the Borderlands

1. JODC, 10/12/1929, 4228.
2. JODS, 28/12/1929, 1371.
3. 'Der Grenzschutz', *Lothringer Journal*, 20/1/1931.
4. Albert Demangeon and Lucien Febvre, *Le Rhin: Problèmes d'histoire et d'économie* (1935), 129; Alison Carrol, *Borderland: The Return of Alsace to France, 1918–1939* (2018), 186.
5. Joseph Schmauch, 'Marseillaise, paradis tricolore et drapeaux par milliers', *Revue d'Alsace*, 141 (2015), 297–320 at 316–17.
6. AN F^7 13/014, Directeur de la sûreté Belfort to prefect, undated, 1920.
7. François Roth, *Les Lorrains entre la France et l'Allemagne: Itinéraires d'annexés* (1981); Christian Baechler, *Le parti catholique Alsacien: Du Reichsland à la République jacobine* (1982).

8. Carrol, *Borderland*, 144–59.
9. Maurice Garçon, *Journal: 1912–1939*, ed. Pascal Fouché and Pascale Froment (2022), 23/12/1923.
10. Jean-François Colas, 'Les droites nationales en Lorraine dans les années 1930: acteurs, organisations, réseaux' (PhD, Paris X Nanterre, 2006), 336–46; Christopher J. Fischer, *Alsace to the Alsatians? Visions and Divisions of Alsatian Regionalism, 1870–1939* (2010), 195–200.
11. Carrol, *Borderland*, 95–112.
12. SHD 1N29/1, PV CSG, 18/1/1927; SHD 1N29/3, PV CSG, 4/7/1927; SHD 1N29/4, PV CSG, 12/10/1927; SHD 7N3763/3, Painlevé to Poincaré, 17/1/1929.
13. Sahlins, 'Natural Frontiers Revisited', 1423–51.
14. SHD 7N3765/1/3, Hirschauer to war minister, 13/9/1932.
15. SHD 5N583/1, Knaff to Wiltzer, 22/12/1932; Wiltzer to war minister, 16/3/1933.
16. AD Bas-Rhin 286D100, mayor of Wœrth to prefect Bas-Rhin, 11/1/1929; Ingénieur Thiry to prefect, 22/1/1929.
17. AS 69S10, 1924–7, Audition Painlevé, 5/7/1928, 27.
18. *Elsaß-Lothringer Zeitung*, 19/12/1929.
19. *Die Freie Zeitung*, 9/11/1929.
20. *Die Neue Welt*, 28/10/1930; *L'Humanité d'Alsace et de Lorraine*, 21/9/1932, 29/5/1932.
21. *Der Elsässer*, 9/10/1928.
22. *Elsässer Kurier*, 3/2/1934.
23. *Jung-Lothringen*, 19/10/1935; *Elsaß-Lothringer Zeitung*, 30/10/1935.
24. Henri Hiegel, *La drôle de guerre en Moselle* (1983), vol. 1: *3 septembre 1939–10 mai 1940*, 11; Laurent Miclo, 'La Lorraine et la Ligne Maginot', *Annuaire de la Société d'histoire et d'archéologie de la Lorraine*, 73 (1973), 143–62 at 154.
25. AD Bas-Rhin 286D100 (Sector Gerstheim), Chef de bataillon Reverdy to prefect Bas-Rhin, 18/12/1929.
26. See, for instance, *La République*, 22/12/1929 (in German).
27. AD Bas-Rhin 98AL244, war minister to labour minister and DGSAL, 23/5/1930.
28. *Die Freie Presse*, 21/1/1930.
29. AD Bas-Rhin 286D100, sub-prefect Wissembourg to prefect Bas-Rhin, 31/1/1929.
30. AD Bas-Rhin 286D100, Colonel Froissard to prefect, 6/2/1929.
31. AD Bas-Rhin 286D100, prefect to Colonel Reverdey, 29/5/1931; prefect to mayor of Soultz, 13/6/1931.
32. AD Bas-Rhin 98AL244, Conseil général du Bas-Rhin, extract from deliberation, 26/11/1936.
33. AD Bas-Rhin 286D98, General Ducasse to prefect, 9/10/1935.
34. SHD 7N3766/3, Ministère de la défense nationale, 'Prise rapide des terrains', 17/7/1939; see also 7N3766/3, 'Publicité relative aux opérations d'expropriations', 15/2/1938.
35. AD Bas-Rhin 98AL244, mayor of Hestroff to war minister, 26/4/1936; prefect Moselle to SCAL, 9/6/1936.
36. SHD 31N63, Zone avant, Garde des routes, Wiltzer to Directeur des douanes, 8/8/1935; SHD 7N3771/1, Schuman to minister, 30/10/1935.
37. SHD 33N108/4, correspondence, August 1937.

38. *Elsaß-Lothringer Zeitung*, 10/1/1930.
39. SHD 7NN2119, Commissaire spécial Strasbourg, 10/12/1928.
40. *Le Lorrain*, 5/3/1931.
41. AD Bas-Rhin 286D100, de Leusse to [illegible], 24/8/1931.
42. AD Bas-Rhin 286D100, Rapport, 10/8/1931; prefect to General Lefort, 15/9/1931; [unsigned] to Weydmann, 10/10/1931.
43. *Straßburger Neue Zeitung*, 28/11/1929; see also *Dernières Nouvelles de Colmar*, 3/2/1932.
44. Conseil général du Haut-Rhin, Procès-verbal, 7/5/1936.
45. François-Georges Dreyfus, *La vie politique en Alsace: 1919–1936* (1969), 259–60.
46. Pierre George, 'L'immigration italienne en France de 1920 à 1939: aspects démographiques et sociaux', *Publications de l'École française de Rome*, 94 (1986), 45–67.
47. AN C14982, Chamber Army Commission, 7/12/1932.
48. AD Ardennes 1M101, PV Commission de coordination (Meuse), 26/11/1934, 22/3/1935, 4/1/1936.
49. AD Ardennes 1M101, PV Commission de coordination (Meuse), 4/1/1936.
50. AD Bas-Rhin 98AL244, 24/10/1930.
51. AN C14982, Chamber Army Commission, 7/12/1932.
52. AD Bas-Rhin 98AL244, Commissaire spécial, Rapports de police, 4/8/1930.
53. AD Ardennes 1M101, PV Commission de coordination (Meuse), 26/11/1934, 22/3/1935, 4/1/1936.
54. AD Bas-Rhin 98AL244, Commissaire spécial, Rapports de police, 16/10/1930.
55. AN C14982, Chamber Army Commission, 7/12/1932.
56. *Metzer Freies Journal*, 4/3/1931.
57. Timothy Maga, 'Closing the Door: The French Government and Refugee Policy, 1933–1939', *French Historical Studies*, 12 (1982), 424–42 at 432.
58. Vicki Caron, 'The Antisemitic Revival in France in the 1930s: The Socioeconomic Dimension Reconsidered', *Journal of Modern History*, 70 (1998), 24–73 at 50, 57.
59. SHD 1N36/4, General Georges, 'Emploi des contingents coloniaux', 13/6/1936; SHD 1N36/4, Rectificatif, 22/6/1936.
60. SHD 1N25/2, PV CSG, 20/2/1922; SHD 1N25/5, PV CSG, 13/7/1922; Buat, *Journal*, 27–29/1/1921.
61. SHD 1N34/2, Weygand to Gamelin, 15/1/1934.
62. SHD 7N3771/1, correspondence Wiltzer, Condé, Loizeau, May–June 1935.
63. *Saarbrücker Zeitung*, 4/6/1935.
64. *Jung-Lothringen*, 19/10/1935; *Elsaß-Lothringer Zeitung*, 29/10/1935; AN BB[18] 6097/BL/510, Autonomism, 5/11/1935; AD Bas-Rhin 286D101, 3/11/1935.
65. *L'Humanité d'Alsace et de Lorraine*, 31/10/1935.
66. Sally Marks, 'Black Watch on the Rhine: A Study in Propaganda, Prejudice and Prurience', *European Studies Review*, 13 (1983), 297–334.
67. SHD 7N4040/1, 23 RTA, 2/12/1935.
68. Patricia North, 'Les amours tarifiées à Strasbourg durant l'entre-deux-guerres', in *De la prostitution en Alsace: Histoires et anecdotes* (1996), 173–94.
69. SHD 7N3770/10, 'Élements de réponse', 5/3/1936.
70. AD Moselle 304M; Hélène Duffuler-Vialle, 'L'évolution de la réglementation de la prostitution durant l'entre-deux-guerres: l'exemple du Nord de la France' (PhD, Lille II, 2015); Laurent Erbs, 'Cachez ce commerce que je ne saurais voir! Prostitution et société messine', *Clio: Histoire, femmes et société*, 31 (2010), 267–86; North, 'Les amours tarifiées à Strasbourg'.

71. SHD 7N4037/2, Rapport, 21/11/1935.
72. SHD 7N4040/1, various reports.
73. SHD 7N4040/2, Lieutenant-Colonel Reyx, Rapport, 10/12/1938.
74. Dépot central des archives de la justice militaire, Tribunal militaire de Nancy, Dossier Petit et al., date de naissance 11/10/1914.
75. AD Bas-Rhin 286D98, Commissaire 4e Arrondissement, 16/11/1936.
76. AN 7NN2131/1, *L'Écho de Wissembourg* and Commissaire spécial Wissembourg to prefect, 28/3/1935.
77. SHD 7N4037/1/, Rapport, 14/12/1935.
78. AD Bas-Rhin 98AL244, Rapports de police, Sûreté Boulay, 22/10/1932.
79. Hiegel, *La drôle de guerre en Moselle*, 346; Laird Boswell, 'Franco–Alsatian Conflict and the Crisis of National Sentiment during the Phoney War', *Journal of Modern History*, 71 (1999), 552–84 at 563.
80. Dépot central des archives de la justice militaire, Tribunal militaire de Nancy, Dossier Petit et al., date de naissance 11/10/1914.
81. SHD 7N3766/3, IEE, 'Remarques récentes sur la situation le long de la Ligne Maginot', 19/1/1939.
82. SHD 33N95/8, 20th Région militaire, Note, 25/6/1937.
83. SHD 33N95/6, Colonel Vohl, Rapports, 24/4 to 20/7/1938.
84. *Lothringer Journal*, 20/1/1931.
85. SHD 33N95/8, 'Projet d'instruction', 18/9/1936.
86. SHD 31N63, incidents, correspondence and reports, 14/1 to 8/8/1937.
87. George, 'L'immigration italienne en France'.
88. AN BB[18] 6095 20/BL/405, Belloni case, 1933; Ralph Schor, 'La surveillance des Italiens dans les Alpes-Maritimes 1919–1939', in *La frontière des Alpes-Maritimes de 1860 à nos jours: Ruptures et contacts* (1992), 87–93; Olivier Minvielle, 'Le renseignement français et l'Italie dans les années trente', in Olivier Forcade, ed., *Le secret et la puissance: Les services spéciaux et le renseignement aux XIXe et XXe siècles* (2007), 94–105.
89. Jean-Yves Mary, *La Ligne Maginot: Ce qu'elle était, ce qu'il en reste* (1980), 18.
90. AD Alpes-Maritimes 04M1355, Commissaire spécial to Prefect, 6/6/1934; Commissaire spécial report, 26/1/1935.
91. Georges-Dominique Oberti, 'Les litiges frontaliers franco-italiens dans le département des Alpes-Maritimes' (PhD, Aix-Marseille, 1939), 52–87, 98; Jean-Louis Panicacci, 'La militarisation de la frontière', in *La frontière des Alpes-Maritimes de 1860 à nos jours: Ruptures et contacts* (1992), 75–86 at 84.
92. AN C14982, Chamber Army Commission, 7/12/1932; AD Alpes-Maritimes 04M1355, Commissaire spécial Breil, 8/1 and 8/8/1935; AD Ardennes 1M101, PV Commission de coordination (Meuse), 1/2/1935.
93. AD Alpes-Maritimes 04M1355, Commissaire spécial, Rapport, 4/4/1935.
94. SHD 7N4039/1, General Godfroy, EMA 14th Region, 9/1/1936.
95. SHD 33N108/4, correspondence, 7/1937.
96. SHD 33N108/4, especially Paquin to Génie Hagenau, 12/3/1937, and to SF-Vosges, 27/12/1937; Génie Saverne to Mahé, 19/4/1939.
97. Louisa Zanoun, 'Interwar Politics in a French Border Region: The Moselle in the Period of the Popular Front, 1934–1938' (PhD, LSE, 2009), 65, 122–3.

8 Policing the Maginot Line

1. Nord, *Double crime sur la ligne Maginot*, 36–7.
2. SHD 9N359/3, 'Quelques procès' and Note, 12/4/1938.
3. The cases are in AN BB[18] 6093–6100.
4. AD Bas-Rhin 98AL649, IEE, 8/9/1939.
5. SHD 1N29/4, PV CSG, 12/10/1927.
6. AD Bas-Rhin 98AL244, Rapport de police, Commissaire générale de la police d'Alsace-Lorraine to Commissaire spécial, 12/10/1932; AN BB[18] 6093 20/BL/349; AN BB[18] 6093 20/BL/348, January–March 1932.
7. AD Alpes-Maritimes 04M1355, several reports in 1935.
8. Zanoun, 'Interwar Politics in a French Border Region', 161–4.
9. SHD 7N3675/2/1, Chamber Army Commission (unsigned) to Daladier, 27/6/1936, and undated manuscript note.
10. SHD 7N3770/4, Belhague to Gamelin, 4/7/1936.
11. SHD 7N3822/3, Requin to 20th Region, 19/11/1937.
12. Georges Vidal, *L'armée française et l'ennemi intérieur* (2015), 117–18.
13. 'La politique des minorités nationales', *La France militaire*, 3–4/2/1929; 'Encore la question des minorités', *La France militaire*, 16/10/1937.
14. SHD 7NN2119, 'Les fonctionnaires d'origine allemande', undated, ?1927/8; SHD 7NN2119, Commissaire spécial Strasbourg, 10/10/1928.
15. 'La politique des minorités nationales', *La France militaire*, 3–4/2/1929; 'Encore la question des minorités', *La France militaire*, 16/10/1937.
16. 'Utilisation des places fermées anciennes', *La France militaire*, 26/4/1934.
17. Maga, 'Closing the Door'.
18. Maga, 'Closing the Door'.
19. SHD 33N95, Allain, Rapport, 19/8/1936.
20. Ralph Schor, 'La police et la surveillance de la frontière des Alpes-Maritimes de 1919 à 1939', in Marie-Claude Blanc-Chaléard, ed., *Police et migrants: France 1667 à 1939* (2001), 275; Maga, 'Closing the Door'; Caron, 'The Antisemitic Revival in France', 36–7.
21. AN BB[18] 6094 20/BL/399, Dossier Muller, 1933.
22. AN BB[18] 6093 20/BL/369, Commissaire divisionnaire Nice, 6/9/1932; BB[18] 6095 20/BL/405, Belloni case, 1933; Marie Vogel, 'Une police d'état à la frontière: la Direction de la police d'État à Nice, 1927–1939', *Cahiers de la Méditerranée*, 55 (1997), 187–202.
23. AN BB[18] 6095 429, 1933–4; AD Bas-Rhin 98AL244, 'Rapport trimestriel', 26/4/1934; AN Direction générale de la Sûreté nationale 20160181/100, Dossier Choppé; *Le Temps*, 14/10/1933.
24. AN BB[18] 6095 20/BL/328, 1931.
25. AN BB[18] 6095 20/BL/425, 1933.
26. Vidal, *L'armée française*, 178.
27. The Contrôle général de la Surveillance du territoire.
28. AD Alpes-Maritimes 04M1355, Moyrand to commander 15th Region, 26/3/1935.
29. René Lévy and Jean-Marc Berlière, *Histoire des polices en France: De l'ancien régime à nos jours* (2011), 266–94.
30. AD Alpes-Maritimes 04M1355, Moyrand to commander 15th Region, 26/3/1935.

31. SHD 7N3765/1/5, Note, 23/8/1935.
32. SHD 33N96/1, 20th Region, Note, 5/11/1936.
33. SHD 7N3765/3, Hirschauer to ministry, 13/9/1932; EMA, Note, 14/10/1932; 7N3770/10, 'Eléments de réponse', 5/3/1936; 7N4037/1, 'Rapport sur l'état d'esprit', 8/12/1938.
34. SHD 7NN2119, 'Les fonctionnaires d'origine allemande', undated, ?1927/8; 7N3770/6, 'Questions soulevées', 14/6/1935.
35. SHD 7NN2131/1, Vaulgrenant to prefect Moselle, 2/6/1932; interior minister to war minister, 29/7/1932.
36. SHD 31N62/2, 2e Bureau, undated, ?1936.
37. SHD 7N3822/4, war minister to 20th Region, 20/1/1931; 3e Bureau, Note, 31/1/1931.
38. Firmin Lentacker, 'Les frontaliers belges travaillant en France: caractères et fluctuations d'un courant de main-d'œuvre', *Revue du Nord*, 32 (1950), 130–44.
39. SHD 31N63, Régime frontalière, Guitry to prefect Moselle, 1/10/1935; manuscript note, ?April 1936; Compte rendu Misson Henry to Paris, 6/11/1935; Lescanne to prefect, 30/9/1935; Condé to ministry, 2/10/1935.
40. SHD 31N63, Régime frontalière, Daladier to governor Metz, 4 July 1936; foreign minister to Président du conseil, 19/3/1936.
41. SHD 31N62/2, Commissaire divisionnaire de police spécial, 30/1/1936; 2e Bureau, Note, 1/2/1936.
42. AD Alpes-Maritimes 04M1355, 5/1/1935.
43. AD Alpes-Maritimes 04M1355, Commissaire spécial Breil, 27 Janaury 1935, and Dossier Col de Brouis.
44. AN C14982, Chamber Army Commission, 7/12/1932; AD Ardennes 1M101, PV Commission de coordination, 4/1/1936.
45. AN BB[18] 6096 20/BL/490, Beauguitte to Chamber Army Commission, 19/11/1934; Pétain to Ministry of Justice, 15/9/1934.
46. AN BB[18] 6096 20/BL/486, August–December 1934.
47. SHD 31N62/2, 22/1/1936; 6th commander, 8/7/1938; Génie Metz-Ouest, Rapport, 8/4/1939.
48. Paul Paillole, *Services spéciaux 1935–1945* (2 vols, 1978), vol. 1, 109–10.
49. SHD 31N62/2, Captain Henry to Chef des travaux, 17/8/1933.
50. AN BB[18] 6996/AL/448, Procureur général Colmar to Ministry of Justice, 7/2/1934; AD Bas-Rhin 98AL244, 'Communication téléphonique', 30/1/1934.
51. *La France militaire*, 15/12/1932.
52. SHD 31N62/2, 6th Region, Note de Service, 6/6/1938; SHD 33N108/4, Colonel Creskens to Génie, 5/7/1937; André to Pierron, 25/6/1936; AN BB[18] 6099 20/BL/642, May–July 1936.
53. AD Bas-Rhin 286D100 (Sector Gerstheim), correspondence, 1930.
54. SHD 7N3768/3, War Ministry to Ministry of Public Works, 30/11/1927.
55. AN BB[18] 6095/BL/436, November 1933–February 1934.
56. *La France militaire*, 15/12/1932.
57. Minvielle, 'Le renseignement français et l'Italie'.
58. Mary, *La Ligne Maginot*, 18.
59. Paul Lévy, *Aux Écoutes*, 16/1/1932.
60. AN Fonds Painlevé 313 AP 230, Dossier finance, 'Note pour le ministre', 26/6/1933; Saly, *La politique des grands travaux*, 147–58.

61. *Le Matin*, 14/1/1934; AD Bas-Rhin 98AL244, [illegible] to Valot, 25/1/1934; SHD 7N3770/5, Inspection, 1934; SHD 7N3770/5, war minister visit, 'Malfaçons', ?1934.
62. See the voluminous correspondence in AD Bas-Rhin 98AL244, 1931–2.
63. SHD 31N62/2, correspondence, September 1935.
64. AN BB[18] 6100 16/BL/707, correspondence, April–May 1938.
65. AD Bas-Rhin 286D101, Commissaire divisionnaire to Surveillance du territoire, 29/3/1935.
66. AN BB[18] 6096 20/BL/490, Pétain to CSDN, 21/7/1934; Confédération générale de la production française to Ministry of Labour, undated; SHD 5N583/1, Pétain to Messimy, 7/11/1934.
67. AN BB[18] 6096 20/BL/490, Interior Ministry to Ministry of Justice, 16/8/1934; Ministre du commerce et de l'industrie to justice minister, 6/11/1934.
68. AN BB[18] 6096 20/BL/490, Ministry of Foreign Affairs to Ministry of Justice, 20/9/1934; 'Comptes rendus des séances du Conseil Municipal de la Ville de Strasbourg, 130e séance', 10/12/1934, 870–86, cited in Carrol, *Borderland*, 132.
69. AD Alpes-Maritimes 04M1355, Commissaire spécial Breil, 5/6/1935.
70. SHD 31N62/2, Commissaire spécial to Contrôleur général, 27/10/1938.
71. SHD 31N62/2 (Pièces de principe), Note de Service, Vaulgranant, 10/3/1934; modifications of 26 March and 26 April. The staff of RF-Metz could also issue passes for officers to visit the *ouvrages* to perform their duties.
72. AD Ardennes 1M101, ministry to prefect Meuse, 19/10/1934, for the organisation of these bodies.
73. AD Ardennes 1M101, PV Commission de coordination (Meuse), 26/11/1934, 22/3/1935, 4/1/1936.
74. SHD 31N62/2, correspondence, Munier to Grenat, 23/10/1935; Grenet to RF-Metz.
75. SHD 31N62/2, correspondence, 2e Bureau, 16 and 19/11/1935.
76. SHD 31N62/2, circular, 22/4/1938.
77. SHD 31N62/2, Commissaire spécial Thionville to commander 6th Region, 14/12/1936.
78. Laird Boswell, 'From Liberation to Purge Trials in the "Mythic Provinces": Recasting French Identities in Alsace and Lorraine, 1918–1920', *French Historical Studies*, 23 (2000), 129–62; Carrol, *Borderland*, 57–63.
79. SHD 31N62/2, 6th Region, 2e Bureau, 20/1/1936, 17/3/1938.
80. SHD 31N62/2, 6th Region, Note de Service, 24/12/1936.
81. AD Alpes-Maritimes 04M1355, Adjutant Brun, 8/1/1935.
82. SHD 31N62/2, letters of commander 6th Region and Sûreté, 1 and 4/2/1937.
83. AN C14982, Audition Bernier and Lefort, 7/12/1932; AD Bas-Rhin 286D100, Tableau, 1/8/1931.
84. SHD 31N62/2, 2e Bureau, Note, 7/2/1936.
85. AN BB[18] 6100/BL/691, August–December 1937.
86. SHD 31N62/1, Commissaire spécial Longwy, 10/12/1937.
87. SHD 31N62/2, Contrôleur général des services de police d'Alsace et de Lorraine, 17/11/1938.
88. AN BB[18] 6095/BL/403, May 1933; *Le Temps*, 1/6/1933.
89. SHD 7NN2119, Buat, Instruction, 26/7/1920.
90. SHD 7NN2131/1, Boichut to war minister, 13/7/1928.
91. SHD 7NN2119, Boichut to war minister, 13/7/1928.

92. SHD 7NN2119, 'Liste des officiers de réserve', 7/12/1928; Codechèvre to EMA 2e Bureau, 2/7/1928, and multiple reports of December 1928.
93. SHD 7NN2119, Note no. 2, 10/12/1927, War Ministry to Poincaré, 26/7/1928.
94. SHD 7NN2119, undated note, probably 1932; AD Bas-Rhin 286D98, prefect Bas-Rhin, undated, c.1928.
95. SHD 7NN2131/1, Direction générale des services d'Alsace et de la Lorraine to War Ministry, 4/8/1928.
96. AN C15164, 'Organisation defensive', undated, ?1931; 'Note sur les régions fortifiés', JOLD, 26/6/1931, 6914.
97. SHD 7NN2131/1, Minister of War to military governors of Metz and Strasbourg, 14/4/1932; 'Feuille de renseignements', 27/12/1932; Blanchard to ministry, 29/8/1936; prefect to commander 20th Region, 10/7/1935.
98. SHD 7NN2131/1, manuscript note, 7/6/1932; unsigned, undated, June 1932; 2e Bureau to minister, 21/6/1932; 2e Bureau to Interior Ministry, 13/8/1932; SHD 1N32/5, PV, 'Questions soulevées', 13/7/1932.
99. AD Bas-Rhin 286D103, prefect to Commissaires spéciaux, undated, and Directeur des services de police, 12/9/1932.
100. SHD 7N3765/1/4, Note, 25/10/1933.
101. SHD 33N95/1/3 (Frontaliers), Note de Service, 11/8/1937.
102. SHD 1N54/1/3, note of Weygand's remarks, 4/4/1934; note État-major (then Gamelin), 7/4/1934.
103. SHD 7NN2131/1, Pétain circular, 12/9/1934.
104. SHD 33N95/4, war minister to 20th Region, 18/1/1937, plus replies.
105. The instruction is summarised in SHD 33N95/1/3 (Frontaliers), Giraud to Commissaire-général de la police d'Alsace-Lorraine, 28/1/1938.
106. SHD 33N95/5, Instruction, 19/5/1938.
107. SHD 33N95/3, Note de Service, 7/10/1936, and responses to request; SHD 33N95/6, 'Plan de ramassage des frontaliers', 29/3/1939.
108. *Le Matin*, 14/8/1932; *La France militaire*, 7/12/1932.
109. AN BB[18] 6093 20/BL/638, Commissaire divisionnaire Nice, Rapport, 6/9/1932; Olivier Forcade, *La République secrète: Histoire des services spéciaux français de 1918 à 1939* (2011), 62–3.
110. AN BB[18] 6093 20/BL/358, Procureur de la République, ?December 1932, and SCR reply for complaints that simple possession could not be prosecuted.
111. Dreyfus, *La vie politique en Alsace*, 133–6.
112. AN BB[18] 6851, Procureur général to Garde des sceaux, 24/6/1931.
113. SHD 7NN2270, Président du conseil to Garde des sceaux, 18/8/1930; Minvielle, 'Le renseignement français et l'Italie'.
114. AN C14905, Commission de la justice et de la législation criminelle, PV, 21 and 28/11/1928.
115. SHD 7NN2270, especially 'Note au sujet du projet de loi', 20/9/1930; Secrétariat général, war minister, Note, 13/3/1930; AN BB[18] 6093 20/BL/329.
116. SHD 7NN2270, 'Note pour le Secrétariat général', 22/9/1931; AN BB[18] 6093 20/BL/329 and 333.
117. SHD 7NN2270, especially 'Note au sujet du projet de loi', 20/9/1930; Secrétariat général, war minister, Note, 13/3/1930, 13/7/1932, 30/11/1933; EMA, Compte-rendu, 11/7/1932; AN BB[18] 6093 20/BL/329, *Le Populaire*, 18/3/1933.

118. AN C15010, Commission de législation civile et criminelle, Séances 16, 23/6/1933, 10/1/1934; SHD 7NN2270, 'Note pour le Secrétariat général', 30/11/1933; Forcade, *La République secrète*, 61–70.
119. SHD 7NN2270, Deuxième Bureau Service de renseignment-Section de centralisation du renseignement (SR-SCR), Note, undated.
120. AD Nord M149 34, prefect to mayors, 29/4/1937; SHD 7NN2270, Amendement Ramadier and SCR, 'Note pour le Secrétariat général', 25/2/1929 and 17/12/1931; Chamber of Deputies, 'Rapport supplémentaire', 11/2/1932.
121. SHD 7NN2270, 'Note au sujet du rapport', undated, mid-1933.
122. AD Bas-Rhin 98AL244, Rapports 1, Contrôleur général to Directeur Sûreté, 2/3/1934; Jean Alteirac, 'La Loi du 26 janvier 1934 sur la répression de l'espionnage' (PhD, Faculté de droit, Lyon, 1935), 71; Virginie Sansico, *La justice déshonorée 1940–1944* (2003), 62–6.
123. AN BB[18] 6100 20/BL/680, August–December 1937.
124. AN BB[18] 6096 20/BL/484, Procureur général to Garde des sceaux, 31/7/1934.
125. AN BB[18] 6099 20/BL/607, SCR to Drappier, 28/11/1935; Procureur Strasbourg to Procureur Colmar, 16/3/1936.
126. *Jung-Lothringen*, 19/10/1935; *Elsaß-Lothringer Zeitung*, 30/10/1935.
127. AN BB[18] 6099 20/BL/637, Thiriet to Rogé, 29/4/1936; Rogé to Garde des sceaux, 30/4/1936.
128. AN BB[18] 6097/BL/510, especially Procureur to interior minister, 29/10/1934.
129. AN BB[18] 6099 20/BL/660, correspondence, August 1936 to March 1937. For a similar case, see BB[18] 6100 696, Procureur général, 17/12/1937.
130. SHD 7NN2270, SCR to EMA, 27/1/1936.
131. Gilles Le Béguec, 'L'évolution de la politique gouvernementale et les problèmes institutionnels', in René Rémond and Janine Bourdin, eds, *Édouard Daladier: Chef de gouvernement* (1977), 55–64.
132. *L'Humanité*, 7/12/1938; Christian Baechler, 'L'autonomisme alsacien dans l'entre-deux-guerres', *Historiens et géographes*, 347 (1995), 249–55.
133. JOLD, 29/6/1938, 7472; SHD 7NN2270, Président du conseil, Bureau de la Justice militaire, Instruction interministérielle, 10/7/1938.
134. SHD 7NN2270, Président du conseil, Bureau de la Justice militaire, Instruction interministérielle, 10/7/1938.
135. AN BB[18] 6386, Dossier Rossé, Procureur général Nancy, 24/9/1945.
136. *Der Elsässer*, 25/2/1939.
137. SHD 7N3770/6, Visite parlementaire, 14/6/1936.

9 The Maginot Line in Popular Culture

1. SHD 1N25/4/2, Guillaumat to Pétain, 29/3/1922.
2. Yves Berthelot, 'La Ligne Maginot ou le béton et le papier: opinions, attitudes, mentalités françaises et la question de la défense des frontières: 1919–1940' (PhD, Lyon II, 1992), 204, 268.
3. JODC, 15/6/1934, 1429, 1532.
4. Chaix, *En mai 1940, fallait-il entrer en Belgique?*, 28–9.
5. SHD Fonds Gamelin 1K224/7, 'La question du système fortifié à créer sur notre frontière de Belgique', 3, 9.

6. Maurice Mégret, 'Les origines de la propagande de guerre française: du Service général de l'information au Commissariat général a l'information (1927–1940)', *Revue d'histoire de la Deuxième Guerre mondiale*, 11 (1961), 3–27 at 8.
7. SHD 7N568/1, 3e Bureau, Note, 11/3/1938.
8. SHD 7N3770/7, correspondence EMA, commander RF-Metz, Quatremarre, 9/1 to 26/3/1936.
9. AN BB[18] 6095 433, Procureur général to Garde des sceaux, 2/1/1934; AN BB[18] 6099 BL 654, correspondence of ?/9/1936; AN BB[18] 6097 510, Procureur général to Garde des sceaux, 12/12/1934; AD Bas-Rhin 286D100/1, Commissaire spécial to Directeur Services général de la police d'Alsace-Lorraine, 13/5/1930.
10. 'L'armature défensive de la France', *L'Illustration*, 9/9/1933; *Le Matin*, 14–22/10/1930; *La Nature*, 15/4/1935.
11. 'La protection de nos frontières', *L'Illustration*, 14/4/1934; *Le Matin*, 15/10/1930.
12. Pierre Coutureaud, *La science et la vie*, 1/7/1936, 35–41.
13. 'L'armature défensive de la France', *L'Illustration*, 9/9/1933.
14. 'La protection de nos frontières', *L'Illustration*, 14/4/1934.
15. *L'Illustration*, 22/2/1930.
16. *Le Matin*, 15/10/1930.
17. *Le Matin*, 20 and 22/10/1930.
18. *Le Temps*, 24 and 26/7/1935, 6 and 14/8/1935.
19. *Canard enchaîné*, 22/10/1930.
20. *L'Humanité d'Alsace et de Lorraine*, 25/5/1933, in AN BB[18] 6093 20/BL/374.
21. *L'Écho de Paris*, 21/11/1929; JODC, 28/12/1929, 4775.
22. *La France militaire*, 3/12/1932.
23. JODC, 19/12/1933, 4701.
24. 'L'armature défensive de la France', *L'Illustration*, 9/9/1933.
25. De Gaulle, *Vers l'armée de métier*, 49–51.
26. JODC, 23/2/1936, 582.
27. *Le Nouvelliste*, 28/3/1936, cited in Berthelot, 'La Ligne Maginot', 294.
28. *Le Matin*, 12/3/1936.
29. *L'Écho de Paris*, 17, 22, 28/3/1936.
30. *L'Action française*, 20/3/1936.
31. *L'Action française*, 1/4/1936.
32. *L'Écho de Paris*, 28/3/1936.
33. Heyl, 'The Construction of the *Westwall*', 64–5.
34. L'Institut Mémoires de l'édition contemporaine (IMEC), Dossier Librairie des Champs-Élysées (LCE) 291; Brouillard to Pigasse, 5/9/1936, and Rapport, 7/7/1937; LCE 102, Dossier Droits d'auteurs.
35. Nord, *Double crime sur la ligne Maginot* (1936), 214, 219.
36. André Brouillard, 'Cas concret de défense contre les chars', *La revue d'infanterie*, 46–7 (1937), 879–907, 1165–201.
37. Régis Messac, *Le 'detective novel' et l'influence de la pensée scientifique* (1929), 9–10; Yves Reuter, *Le roman policier* (2009), 1144.
38. SHD Dossier d'officier, GR 2000 Z 200 9496, Brouillard; Alain Griotteray, *1940, la droite était au rendez-vous: Qui furent les premiers résistants?* (1985), 134.
39. John G. Cawelti, *Adventure, Mystery and Romance: Formula Stories as Art and Popular Culture* (1976), 15–17.
40. Nord, *Double crime sur la ligne Maginot*, 167.

41. Kerillis in *L'Écho de Paris*, 15/10/1936; Castelnau in *L'Écho de Paris*, 16/10/1936; *Le Figaro*, 16/10 and 10/12/1936.
42. *L'Écho de Paris*, 19/10/1936; Lieutenant-Colonel G. Thomasson, 'Les conséquences militaires de la neutralité belge', *Frontières*, November 1936, 574–81; Berthelot, 'La Ligne Maginot', 303–4.
43. *L'Humanité*, 16/10/1936; *Le Populaire*, 16/10/1936; Alexander, *The Republic in Danger*, 196–9.
44. *Le Populaire*, 8 and 9/3/1935, 24/4/1935.
45. *L'Œuvre*, 22/3/1936.
46. *L'Humanité*, 15/3/1936, Thorez speech.
47. Roxanne Panchasi, *Future Tense: The Culture of Anticipation in France between the Wars* (2009), 92–101.
48. *Elsaß-Lothringer Zeitung*, 12/6/1934; *La République*, 13/6/1934; *Bürger-Zeitung* (Moselle), 14/6/1934.
49. Mysyrowicz, *Autopsie d'une défaite*, 271–2.
50. Gamelin, *Servir*, vol. 2, 184, n. 1.
51. *L'Œuvre*, 23/3/1936.
52. *L'Ère nouvelle*, 1/4/1936.
53. Tardieu, 'La ligne Maginot et la Défense nationale'; *L'Ami du peuple*, 15/3/1936, quoted in Berthelot, 'La Ligne Maginot', 292.
54. *L'Action française*, 1/4/1936.
55. Jean-Noël Jeanneney, *François de Wendel en République* (1976), 242–3.
56. SHD 7N3765/1/6, 23/3/1936.
57. JODC, 2/2/1937, 297.
58. *La Cinématographie française*, 27/9/1937; Colin Crisp, *Genre, Myth, and Convention in the French Cinema, 1929–1939* (2002), 325.
59. JODC, 26/2/1938, 645. Paul-Boncour, also of Painlevé's group, called it the 'Ligne Painlevé-Maginot', for like all human things it was a collective work: JODC, 14/3/1940, 17.
60. AN Fonds Moscou 199404963/3/83; SHD 7N570 supplément, Gandéra to war minister, 7/4/1937.
61. *Cinémonde*, 464, 6/10/1937, letter from Henri Helbing.
62. *L'Intransigeante*, 9/9/1938.
63. *Gringoire*, 26/1/1939.
64. *Le Jour–L'Écho de Paris*, 28/11/1938.
65. *Le Matin*, 16/4 and 14/11/1938; *Match*, 13 and 27/7/1939.
66. *Der Elsässer*, 17/9/1938.
67. *L'Humanité*, 13/10/1938.
68. SHD 3R145, Films d'espionnage, 'Analyse', 29/5/1937 summarises 2e Bureau, Note, 26/5/1937. Manuscript annotations express Daladier's view.
69. SHD 3R145, Films d'espionnage, Edmond See to film companies, 25/10/1937.
70. SHD 3R145/3, Calvet, Note, 3/9/1937; SHD 7N572/1, Préaud, Note, 31/8/1938; SHD 7N572/1/4, Note, 31/8/1938; Bordereaux, 19/10/1938.
71. SHD 7N572/1/4, Note, 31/8/1938.
72. SHD 3R145/3, Cabinet to Chambre syndicale française de la presse filmée, 15/9/1938.
73. SHD 3R145/3, Buisson to Chambre syndicale française de la presse filmée, 6/10/1938.

74. SHD 7NN2131/1, Renseignement, 25/8/1938; *Le Matin*, 25/7/1938, 16 and 25/8/1938.
75. *Gringoire*, 2/2/1939.
76. Gaumont-Pathé Archive, 3800ENU29697, 3900GM 07698.
77. SHD 3R145/3, correspondence, November 1938.
78. SHD 7N571, March of Time, 'Modifications . . .', undated.
79. *Le Matin*, 1/12/1938; *Cinémonde*, 17/12/1938.
80. SHD 7N571, Bordereau, 28/4/1938; ministry to Bourcier, 28/4/1938; Bourcier to Buisson, 17/7/38; undated PV following film showing on 7/11/1938.
81. Jeancolas, *Histoire du cinéma français*, 213–15.
82. *Je suis partout*, 18/11/1938; *Le Figaro*, 12/11/1938; *L'Œuvre*, 21/11/1938; *Le Jour*, 12/11/1938; *Le Matin*, 17/11/1938.
83. SHD 3R145/1, Calamy to minister, 7/1/1937, 3/9/1937.
84. SHD 3R145/1, Correspondence, November 1937–August 1938.
85. Crisp, *Genre, Myth, and Convention*, 327.
86. *L'Intransigeant*, 3/2/1939. The review in *Le Figaro*, 8/2/1939, is along the same lines.
87. SHD 3R145/1, Calamy to minister, 7/1/1937; Analyse, 4/2/1937; SHD 7NN571, Analyse, 21/1/1937.
88. SHD 3R145/1, Bordereau, 24/8/1937.
89. Colonel X, *La Ligne Maginot: Bouclier de la France* (1939), 73.
90. *L'Illustration*, 7/1/1939.
91. *Gringoire*, 2/2/1939.
92. *Le Temps*, 4/1/1939. Mysyrowicz, *Autopsie d'une défaite*, 147–8, travesties this article, quoting only the section on fortification, and misinterpreting Ernest-Charles's opposition to the professional corps as endorsement of the existing structure of the army.
93. Marie Puren, 'Jean de La Hire: biographie intellectuelle et politique (1878–1956)' (PhD, École nationale des chartes, 2016), 424.
94. Commandant Cazal, *Batailles pour la mer* (1939), 204.
95. Jean de La Hire, *Maginot-Siegfried: Roman de demain* (1939), 80.
96. For instance, SHD 1N29/3, Fillonneau, 'Note lu au CSG', 4/7/1927.
97. JODC, 14/6/1934, 1530–1.
98. SHD 1N42, Weygand to Pétain, 8/6/1934.
99. William J. Fanning Jr, *Death Rays and the Popular Media, 1876–1939: A Study of Directed Energy Weapons in Fact, Fiction and Film* (2015).
100. Geneviève Tabouis, *Chantage à la guerre* (1938), 197.

10 A Phoney War? Life on the Maginot Line

1. AD Bas-Rhin 98AL649, IEE, 1/9/1939.
2. Hiegel, *La drôle de guerre en Moselle*, vol. 2.
3. Crémieux-Brilhac, *Les Français de l'an 40*, vol. 2: *Ouvriers et soldats*, 522–4.
4. Crémieux-Brilhac, *Les Français de l'an 40*, vol. 2, 425–7; François Cochet, *Les soldats de la drôle de guerre: Septembre 1939–mai 1940* (2004), 43–50.
5. SHD 27N69/2/2a, 1/11/1939.
6. René Balbaud, *Cette drôle de guerre (Alsace-Lorraine, Belgique, Dunkerque, 26 août 1939–1er juin 1940) telle que je l'ai faite . . .* (1941), 14.
7. SHD 27N69/2/2a, 1/11/1939; SHD 27N69/2/2b, 24/11/1939.

8. AD Bas-Rhin 98AL635, 'Rapport sur la morale', 25/1/1940.
9. Robert Felsenhardt, *1939–1940 avec le 18e Corps d'armée* (1972), 55–6.
10. André Giroud, *Le journal d'un sapeur rebelle pendant la drôle de guerre* (2001), 2/9/1939.
11. *Der Elsässer*, 31/8/1939; AD Bas-Rhin 98AL649, 8/9/1939; Kurt Hochstuhl, *Zwischen Frieden und Krieg: Das Elsaß in den Jahren 1938–1940* (1984), 170–2.
12. Raymond Aubrac, *Où la mémoire s'attarde* (1996), 57–8.
13. D. Barlone, *A French Officer's Diary, 23 August 1939–1 October 1940*, trans. L.V. Cass (1942), 11–12, 11/9/1939; René Didelot, *Drôle de guerre: Les carnets retrouvés, 1939–1940* (2000), 21–3.
14. Henri Guizard, *La drôle de guerre du sergent Henri Guizard sur la ligne Maginot*, ed. Geneviève Déhu (2010), 17/9/1939, 2, 14, 23/10/1939, 19 and 27/11/1939.
15. SHD 27N69/2/2a, 26/10/1939.
16. Guizard, *La drôle de guerre*, 29/12/1939, 11/2/1940.
17. Giroud, *Le journal d'un sapeur*, 11/1/1940.
18. Cochet, *Les soldats*, 99.
19. SHD 27N69/2/2d, 2/2/1940.
20. Giroud, *Le journal d'un sapeur*, 6/9/1939.
21. André Dufilho, *'Mon lieutenant, un blessé vous demande': La 35e division d'infanterie dans la guerre de 1939–1940* (2002), 29.
22. AS 68S11, Charles Riebel, Rapport, 2–5/11/1939.
23. SHD 3K32, Témoignage oral Crémieux-Brilhac; Crémieux-Brilhac, *Les Français de l'an 40*, vol. 2, 430–1; Guizard, *La drôle de guerre*, 19/11/1939.
24. SHD 27N69/2/2a, 1/11/1939.
25. AN 2W7/Commission de l'armée, Rapports, 17–21/10/1939, 5/11/1939.
26. SHD 27N69/2/2a, 26/10/1939.
27. AN 2W7/Commission de l'armée, Rapport, 31/1/1939 to 4/2/1940.
28. AN 2W7/Commission de l'armée, Rapport, 31/1/1940, 4/2/1940, 8/3/1940; AN C15160, Mazerand, Rapport, 9/12/1939; SHD 28N48/2, Roton to army group commanders, 16/4/1940; SHD 5N588/2, 'Réponse à M. Taittinger', 29/4/1940.
29. Balbaud, *Cette drôle de guerre*, 30/12/1939.
30. SHD 27N69/2/2c, 26/12/1939; Guizard, *La drôle de guerre*, 26/8/1939; Giroud, *Le journal d'un sapeur*, 28/12/1939.
31. Jean-Louis Barrault, *Souvenirs pour demain* (2010), 156–8.
32. Schickelé, 'Le service de santé'.
33. William Edmund Ironside, *The Ironside Diaries, 1937–1940*, ed. Denis Kelly and Roderick Macleod (1963), 10/1/1940.
34. SHD 27N69/2/2a, 26/10/1939.
35. René Rodolphe, *Combats dans la ligne Maginot* (1949), 78.
36. See above, p. 1; Roland Dorgelès, *La drôle de guerre, 1939–1940* (1957), April 1940; Robert Varoqui, *Du béton et des hommes: Ouvrage A19 Hackenberg* (1995), 78.
37. Giuliano, *Les soldats du béton*, 22.
38. SHD GR 3K13/1, General Alberic Vaillant, interviewed 1–3/4/1997 Albert Masson, *La Veille inutile* (1985, first published, 1942), 22.
39. René de Chambrun, *I Saw France Fall: Will She Rise Again?* (1941), 30–1.
40. SHD 27N69/2/2d, 2/2/1940.
41. SHD 29N290, Lescanne to 5th Army, 'Morale des RIFs / Rapports', 1/3/1940.
42. SHD 27N12, 'Note sur la situation en Alsace', 10/11/1939; Hochstuhl, *Zwischen Frieden und Krieg*; Boswell, 'Franco-Alsatian Conflict'; Mathieu Dubois, Olivier

Forcade and Johannes Großmann, eds, *Exils intérieurs: Les évacuations à la frontière franco-allemande (1939–1940)* (2017).

43. Giroud, *Le journal d'un sapeur*, 21/1/1940.
44. SHD 27N69/2/2d, 18 and 29/1/1940; SHD 27N69/2/2c, 4th Army, 16/12/1939.
45. Hiegel, *La drôle de guerre en Moselle*, 345–6.
46. Lavergne, *Journal de guerre*, 10, 11, 15/9/1939; Henri Gousset, *Dites à la Kommandantur que je l'emm . . .: Une ville et son maire en zone interdite, 1940–1944* (1980), 34; Claude Jamet, *Carnets de déroute* (1942), 13/10/1940.
47. SHD 27N69/2/2c, 8/12/1939.
48. Jean-Paul Sartre, *Carnets de la drôle de guerre: Septembre 1939–mars 1940*, ed. Arlette Elkaïm-Sartre (1995), 18/2/1940; Didelot, *Drôle de guerre*, 23–5; SHD 27N69/2/2a, 6/10/1939.
49. Sartre, *Carnets*, 23/11/1939.
50. JOLD, 2/9/1939, 10971; SHD 33N114, Combet to SF-Vosges, 7/9/1939; SHD 33N114/3, 16/9/1939.
51. Hiegel, *La drôle de guerre en Moselle*; Boswell, 'Franco-Alsatian Conflict', 161–4.
52. SHD 27N69/1/1b, GQG, 'Note pour les armées', 30/11/1939.
53. SHD 27N13/6, Captain Thuy, Rapport, 18/11/1939; AD Bas-Rhin 98AL283, draft reports; Saint-Venant to Burrus, 3/11/1939.
54. SHD 27N13/6, Garchery to major general, undated, probably November 1939.
55. SHD 27N69/2/2a, 19/10/1939.
56. AN F^7 14822, Peters to Surveillance du territoire, 15/4/1940.
57. *Der Elsässer*, 26/4/1939; AD Bas-Rhin 98AL647, IEE, 20/2/1939; SHD 98AL156, IEE, 14/2/1940.
58. Hochstuhl, *Zwischen Frieden und Krieg*, 264.
59. AN Fonds Moscou 19940500/73/1413, Note, 1938/9.
60. SHD 1N38/4, 11/7/1939.
61. SHD 5N588, Miellet, Rapport, 12–13/10/1939.
62. SHD 27N69/2/2a, 1/11/1939 (29 DI); 27N69/2/2f, 17/3/1940 (96 RIA); AN C15160, Mission aux armées, September 1939; Dufilho, *'Mon lieutenant'*, 1/11/1939.
63. SHD 27N69/2/2a, 24/10/1939, 6.
64. SHD 27N69/2/2b, 24/11/1939.
65. AD Bas-Rhin 98AL283, draft reports; Crémieux-Brilhac, *Les Français de l'an 40*, vol. 2, 441, n. 1.
66. AN C15160, Rapports 1939–40 including Mazerand, 29/11/1939; AD Bas-Rhin 98AL283, Préfet Bas-Rhin to Vice-Présidence du conseil, 18/10/1939; Préfet Bas-Rhin to Vice-Présidence du conseil, 13/10/1939; SHD 27N69/2/2e, 23/2/1940.
67. Georges Sadoul, *Journal de guerre: 2 septembre 1939–20 juillet 1940* (1977), 11/11/1939.
68. SHD 27N69/2/2a, 10/11/1939; AS 68S11, 'Rapport de présentation', 1/3/1940.
69. Giroud, *Le journal d'un sapeur*, 2/3/1940.
70. Dufilho, *'Mon lieutenant'*, 58–62.
71. Laumonier, *Mémoires d'un prisonnier de guerre*, 29; Sartre, *Carnets*, 634.
72. AD Bas-Rhin 98AL156, IEE, 8/2/1940; SHD 27N69/2/2a, 3rd Army, 26/10/1939, 13/11/1939.
73. Victor Antoni, *Grenzlandschicksal – Grenzlandtragik: Lebenserinnerungen und menschliche Betrachtungen eines Lothringers zu den politischen Irrungen und Wirrungen seiner Zeit* (1957), 155.

74. AD Moselle 53U1/590, September 1939–February 1940.
75. SHD 27N69/2/2c, 8th Army, 8/12/1939.
76. SHD 27N69/2/2a, 1/11/1939 (soldier 24 GRDI).
77. Sartre, *Carnets*, 23/11/1939.
78. AD Bas-Rhin 98AL635, 'Rapport sur la morale', 25/1/1940.
79. SHD 27N65, Notes, 26/2/1940, 24/4/1940.
80. AN 2W7/Visites parlementaires, Framond and Taittinger, Rapport, 8/3/1940.
81. SHD 27N69/2/2a, 24/10/1939, 6; SHD 33N14/5, André, Note de Service, 29/9/1939.
82. AD Moselle 304M196; AD Bas-Rhin 98AL635, prefect Haut-Rhin, 23/1/1940.
83. Balbaud, *Cette drôle de guerre*, 14, 24–7, 33–5. Giroud, *Le journal d'un sapeur*, 29/2/1940, mentions soldiers so hungry on arriving at Petite-Pierre (Bas-Rhin) that they put food before 'girls looking for love'.
84. Sartre, *Carnets*, 16/3/1940; Gilles Ernst, 'Sartre et l'Alsace en 1939–1940: l'identité à l'épreuve de l'évacuation', *Études sartriennes*, 21 (2017), 177–222 at 187.
85. Simone de Beauvoir, *La force de l'âge* (1960), 7–29, 423–4; Sartre, *Carnets*, 23/11/1939.
86. SHD 27N69/2/2g, 30/4/1940.
87. SHD 27N69/2/2f, 17/3/1940.
88. SHD 27N69/2/2b, 28/11/1939; SHD 27N69/2/2b, 26/11/1939; Sadoul, *Journal de guerre*, 6/9/1939.
89. Hermann Bickler, *Ein besonderes Land: Erinnerungen und Betrachtungen eines Lothringers* (1978), 275.
90. SHD 27N69/2/2f, 17/3/1940.
91. Sadoul, *Journal de guerre*, 23/9/1939.
92. SHD 27N69/2/2e, 2/3/1940; SHD 27N69/2/2e, 2/3/1940 (159 RAP); SHD 27N69/2/2f, 17/3/1940; SHD 27N69/2/2g, 15/4/1940 and second week of April; Jamet, *Carnets de déroute*, 13/10/1939.
93. SHD 27N69/2/2a, 13/11/1939 (35 RI); SHD 27N69/2/2c, 2/1/1940.
94. SHD 27N69/2/2c, 21/12/1939.
95. SHD 27N69/2/2a, 13/11/1939.
96. SHD 27N69/2/2c, 28/12/1939.
97. SHD 8YE61605, Pierron dossier, untitled document, date illegible, possibly March 1947.
98. Maude Williams and Bernard Wilkin, *French Soldiers' Morale in the Phoney War, 1939–1940* (2018), 62–81.
99. AN 2W7/Visites parlementaires, Frémond-Tattinger, Rapport, 8/3/1940.
100. SHD 29N290, Gamelin, 27/11/1939; SHD 28N14/1, Note, 16/12/1939; Dentz and Lescanne to 5th Army, 1/3/1940; SHD 29N138/2, 'Note pour les armées', 14/2/1940; SHD 27N69/2/2e, Contrôle postal, 23/2/1940; Rodolphe, *Combats*, 79.
101. SHD 29N130/6, Georges, 'Note pour le 3e armée', 28/3/1940.
102. SHD 29N130/Opinion/Journaux de front; SHD 29N67/3.
103. Giroud, *Le journal d'un sapeur*, 23/12/1939, 2 and 5/1/1940.
104. SHD 34N156/162 RIF, 'Rapport d'un officier', 20–1.
105. Sadoul, *Journal de guerre*, 7/3/1940; Guizard, *La drôle de guerre*, 27–28/11/1939.
106. Guizard, *La drôle de guerre*, 23–24/9/1939.
107. Felsenhardt, *1939–1940 avec le 18e Corps d'armée*, 46–7.

108. SHD 27N69/2/2g, 15/4/1940.
109. Vesna Drapac, 'French Catholic Men at War 1939–1940: A Study of Faith and Masculinity in the Field', *Gender and History*, 34 (2022), 458–75.
110. SHD 27N69/2/2b, 24/11/1939; SHD 27N69/2/2g, 30/4/1940; Guizard, *La drôle de guerre*, 23–24/9/1939.
111. Guizard, *La drôle de guerre*, 23/9/1939, 15/10/1939, 5 and 7/11/1939.
112. Louis-Ferdinand Céline, *Les beaux draps* (1941), 6, 39.
113. Société d'études céliniennes, *Actes du Colloque international de Toulouse L.-F. Céline* (1991), 269.
114. Giroud, *Le journal d'un sapeur*, 6/9/1939.
115. SHD 27N69/2/2c, 2/1/1940.
116. Jamet, *Carnets de déroute*, 12/11/1939.
117. SHD 27N69/2/2e, 4/2/1940.
118. Eric Deroo and Pierre de Taillac, eds, *Carnets de déroute, 1939–1940: Lettres et récits inédits* (2010), 97–8.
119. Guizard, *La drôle de guerre*, 5/11/1939.
120. Christopher Brent Murray, 'Nouveaux regards sur le soldat Messiaen', in Marine Branland and David Mastin, eds, *De la guerre dans l'art, de l'art dans la guerre: Approches plastiques et musicales au XXe siècle* (2010), 243–65 at 247; Christopher Dingle, *The Life of Messiaen* (2007), 67–70.
121. SHD 27N69/2/2e, 4/2/1940.
122. SHD 27N69/2/2e, 4/2/1940.
123. Dorgelès, *La drôle de guerre,* April 1940.
124. Rodolphe, *Combats*, 83.
125. Jamet, *Carnets de déroute*, 30/11/1939.
126. Sartre, *Carnets*, 29/11/1939, 22/12/1939.
127. SHD 27N69/2/2e, 1/3/1940.
128. SHD 27N69/2/2d, 14/1/1940.
129. Jean Nard, *Souvenirs de guerre et de captivité: De la ligne Maginot à la Libération* (1965), 30.
130. SHD 27N69/2/2a, 14/10/1939; Lavergne, *Journal de guerre*, 27/9/1939.
131. See the Mémoire des hommes database: www.memoiredeshommes.sga.defense.gouv.fr.
132. Sadoul, *Journal de guerre*, 23/12/1939.
133. Sadoul, *Journal de guerre*, 13/12/1939, end of January 1940. Sadoul mistakenly attributes the line to 'La chanson des maccabées'.
134. Crémieux-Brilhac, *Les Français de l'an 40*, vol. 2, 463–75.
135. SHD 27N69/2/2g, 15 and 30/4/1940; Sadoul, *Journal de guerre*, 22/2/1940.
136. SHD 27N69/2/2g, 15 and 30/4/1940.
137. SHD 27N69/2/2a, 2 and 12/10/1939.
138. SHD 27N69/2/2b, 24/11/1940.
139. SHD 27N69/2/2d, 15/1/1940.
140. SHD 27N69/2/2d, 15/1/1940.
141. SHD 27N69/2/2d, 29/1/1940.
142. Guizard, *La drôle de guerre*, 25/3/1940.
143. Sadoul, *Journal de guerre*, 12, 14, 17/12/1939, 22/3/1939.
144. Sartre, *Carnets*, 17/2/1940.
145. AN BB^{30}, Clermont, 5/3/1940, letter of 18/2/1940.
146. Sadoul, *Journal de guerre*, 13 and 22/1/1940.

147. Roland de Margerie, *Journal: 1939–1940* (2010), 45–6; Charles Graveel, *Souvenirs de guerre du lieutenant Charles Graveel sur la ligne Maginot, 10 mai–2 juillet 1940* (2012), 15/5/1940.
148. Dufilho, *'Mon lieutenant'*, 61–2.
149. Giroud, *Le journal d'un sapeur*, 4/12/1940.
150. SHD 27N69/2/2b, 16/11/1939; Sadoul, *Journal de guerre*, 12/12/1940.
151. Giroud, *Le journal d'un sapeur*, 25/10/1939.
152. Felsenhardt, *1939–1940 avec le 18e Corps d'armée*, 84.
153. Guizard, *La drôle de guerre*, 24/3/1940.
154. SHD 33N114/5, Regard, 4/10/1940.
155. SHD 27N69/2/2b, 28/11/1939.
156. Jean-Paul Sartre, *Lettres au Castor et à quelques autres* (1983), 25/4/1940.
157. SHD 27N69/2/2f, 31/3/1939; SHD 27N69/2/2g, 12/4/1939.
158. DCAJM, Minutier SF-Burtoncourt / SF-Boulay, 1939–40.
159. SHD 31N142/18, 20th Region Bureau central de renseignment, CR, 25/3/1940.
160. Jamet, *Carnets de déroute*, 30/11/1939.
161. SHD 14P13, 'État de personnel', 14/10/1939 and following.
162. Rodolphe, *Combats*, 79.
163. Georges Vidal, 'Le haut commandement et le craint de "l'ennemi intérieure" en juin 1940', in Christine Levisse-Touzé, ed., *La campagne de 1940* (2001), 357–88.
164. Auguste Lecœur, *Le partisan* (1963), 124.
165. Crémieux-Brilhac, *Les Français de l'an 40*, vol. 2, 477–97.
166. Rodolphe, *Combats*, 81.
167. Giroud, *Le journal d'un sapeur*, 1/12/1939.
168. SHD 14P13, 'État de personnel', 14/10/1939 and following.
169. SHD 27N69/2/2f, 2–8/3/1940 (57 GRDI); SHD 33N114/6, Regard to SF-Vosges, 7/11/1939; Regard to commandant 37 RIF, 11/12/1939; SHD 34N51, Branchard, Rapport, undated, 1945.
170. SHD 27N69/2/2c, 21/12/1939; Williams and Wilkin, *French Soldiers' Morale*, 96–8, shows that German sources confirm the incident.
171. SHD 34N156/162 RIF, 'Rapport d'un officier', undated, probably 1945; SHD 27N69/2/2g, 30/4/1940.
172. SHD 27N69/2/2a, 24/10/1939.
173. SHD 27N69/2/2c, 2/1/1940; SHD 27N69/2/2d, 6/1/1940; SHD 31N142/18, 20th Region, 'Rapport sur le moral', 25/3/1940.
174. SHD 27N69/2/2a, 14/11/1939.
175. AD Bas-Rhin 98AL283, Contrôleur-général de la sûreté nationale to Directeur-général de la sûreté nationale, 22/12/1939. This carton contains several similar expressions of autonomism.
176. SHD 27N69/2/2b, 26/11/1939.
177. SHD 27N69/2/2d, 6/1/1940, 2/2/1940.
178. AD Bas-Rhin 98AL288, DGSN, 15/2/1940; SHD 27N69/2/2d, 6/1/1940, 2/2/1940; Gilles Morin, 'Paroles de "défaitistes": communistes, pacifistes et protestataires pendant la "drôle de guerre"', *Vingtième siècle: Revue d'histoire*, 128 (2015), 105–18 at 116.
179. SHD 29N69/1/1a, Deuxième Bureau, 'Conservation du moral', 25/11/1939.
180. Williams and Wilkin, *French Soldiers' Morale*, 94–105.

181. AN C15164, correspondence 1940, [unsigned] to prefect Haut-Rhin, 16/10/1939.
182. SHD 27N69/2/2g, 30/4/1940.
183. Crémieux-Brilhac, *Les Français de l'an 40*, vol. 2, 477–81.
184. AD Bas-Rhin 98AL156, IEE, 14/2/1940; Dufilho, *'Mon lieutenant'*, 58–62.
185. AD Bas-Rhin 98AL156, IEE, 8/2/1940.
186. SHD 27N69/2/2b, 27/11/1940.
187. SHD 27N69/2/2f, 2–8/3/1940.
188. SHD 27N69/2/2f, 17/3/1940.
189. SHD 27N69/2/2f, 25/3/1939.
190. SHD 27N69/2/2g, 15/4/1940.
191. Guizard, *La drôle de guerre*, 20/4/1940.
192. Guizard, *La drôle de guerre*, 20/4/1940.
193. SHD 27N69/2/2g, 30/4/1940.
194. SHD 27N69/2/2g, third week of April and 30/4/1940; Guizard, *La drôle de guerre*, 20/4/1940.
195. SHD 31N142/18, 20th Region Bureau central de renseignment, 25/3/1940.
196. SHD 29N290, Lescanne to 5th Army, 'Morale des RIFs / Rapports', 1/3/1940.
197. SHD 27N69/2/2c, 23/12/1939; SHD 27N69/2/2d, 2/2/1940; SHD 7N4040/2, Rapport, 13/12/1938; SHD 34N399, JMO, 20/1/1940.
198. *Règlement de l'infanterie: Combat*, 27.

11 Contact

1. Walter Spannenkrebs, *Angriff mit Kampfwagen* (1939); Jacques Bardoux, *Journal d'un témoin de la Troisième* (1957), 28/2/1940.
2. Tooze, *The Wages of Destruction*, 334–72.
3. Paul Morand, *Journal de guerre*, ed. Bénédicte Vergez-Chaignon (2020), 4/1/1940; Talbot Charles Imlay, 'A Reassessment of Anglo-French Strategy during the Phony War, 1939–1940', *English Historical Review*, 119 (2004), 333–72.
4. Gérard Chauvy, *Le drame de l'armée française: Du Front populaire à Vichy* (2009), 338.
5. Cochet, *Les soldats*, 30–4.
6. SHD 27N12, Gamelin to Daladier, 7/1/1940.
7. SHD 27N156/1, 'Conclusion de l'étude . . . Condé', summer 1939; Gamelin, *Servir*, vol. 2, 426; Gamelin, *Servir*, vol. 3: *La guerre, septembre 1939–19 mai 1940* (1947), 26–32; Prételat, *Le destin tragique*, 75.
8. Alexander, *The Republic in Danger*, 306–20; Prételat, *Le destin tragique*, 49–54.
9. SHD 27N69/2/2a, CP, 4th Army, 12/10/1939.
10. SHD 27N12/4/4, Gamelin, IPS no. 2, 9/9/1039; IPS no. 3, 10/9/1939; IPS no. 4, 12/9/1939; IPS no. 5, 15/9/1939; Note, 21 and 30/9/1939; IPS no. 6, 29/9/1939; Prételat, *Le destin tragique*, 62–70.
11. SHD 27N69/2/2a, CP, 24–29/10/1939.
12. Jackson, *A Certain Idea of France*, 203; Williamson Murray, 'The Strategy of the "Phoney War" Revisited', *Military Affairs*, 45 (1981), 13–17 at 15.
13. Bardoux, *Journal d'un témoin*, 4/4/1940.
14. SHD 27N156/1, 'Conclusion de l'étude . . . Condé', summer 1939.
15. SHD 27N156/1, 3e Bureau, GQG to Prételat, 9/1/1940.

16. SHD Fonds Georges 1KMI26, manuscript note, 10/11/1939; Felsenhardt, *1939–1940 avec le 18e Corps d'armée*, 103.
17. SHD 27N84, 'Note sur l'attaque', 7/7/1939; Additif, 10/9/1939; SHD 29N220, 'Plan de manœvre de la Ve armée', Annexe II, 25/2/1940.
18. Paul Gaujac, 'Le colonel de Gaulle commandant les chars de la Ve Armée (septembre 1939–mai 1940)', *Revue historique des armées*, 179 (1990), 57–71.
19. Victor Bourret, *La tragédie de l'armée française* (1947), 72–3.
20. Charles de Gaulle, 'Mémorandum adressé par le colonel Charles de Gaulle aux généraux Gamelin, Eygand et Georges et à MM. Daladier le 26 janvier 1940', in Charles de Gaulle, *Trois études* (1945), 49–70; Saint-Martin, *L'armée blindée française*, vol. 1, 98–9; Gamelin, *Servir*, vol. 3, 75, n. 2.
21. SHD 27N84/4, Huntziger, 'Rupture des front fortifiés', 9/1/1940.
22. SHD 29N52, Gamelin, 29/8/1939; Georges, 15/9/1939; SHD 29N52, 3e Bureau, 'Annexe à la note du 11 Octobre', undated.
23. SHD 27N12/4/4, Gamelin, Note (for Georges), 4/10/39; 'Réflexions', 27/12/1940.
24. Bardoux, *Journal d'un témoin*, 31/10/1939.
25. SHD 29N52, Georges, Note, 15/10/1939.
26. SHD 27N12/4/4, Note, 4/9/1939.
27. Max Schiavon, *Corap: Bouc émissaire de la défaite de 1940* (2017), 236.
28. SHD 27N144/4/4a, Belhague to Gamelin, 26/11/1939.
29. SHD Fonds Georges 1K95/7, diary, late November 1939.
30. Mary and Hohnadel, *Hommes et ouvrages*, vol. 3, 40.
31. SHD 27N84/4/, ministry to Georges, 24/9/1939; SHD 9N52, Georges, Note, 11/10/1939.
32. SHD 29N52, Tuczkiewicz, 'Note sur les travaux', 3/1/1942.
33. SHD 27N144/4/4a, Belhague, Compte-rendu, 6/10/1939; Belhague to Gamelin, 26/11/1939; SHD Fonds Gamelin 1K224/8/7, 22/12/1939; Paul de Villelume, *Journal d'une défaite: 23 août 1939–16 juin 1940* (1976), 18/1/1940.
34. SHD 27N12/4/4, Gamelin, Note (for Georges), 21/4/1940.
35. SHD 29N150, Gamelin, Note, 19/1/1940; Georges to Huntziger, 29/1/1940.
36. SHD 27N144/4/4b, Colonel Guerin, Rapport, 17/10/1939; Fagalde to Belhague, 12/10/1939; Mary and Hohnadel, *Hommes et ouvrages*, vol. 3, 62–3; Jerry Murland, *Cassel and Hazebrouck 1940: France and Flanders* (2017), 76–9.
37. SHD 5N5831/15–20, Cabinet ministre, 'Développement', 22/1/1940; Ironside, *The Ironside Diaries*, 10/1/1940.
38. Guizard, *La drôle de guerre*, 15/5/1940.
39. SHD 28N15, Prételat circular, 18/10/1939; Prételat to Georges, 20/10/1939, 19/11/1939; Bardoux, *Journal d'un témoin*, 5/4/1940.
40. Sartre, *Carnets*, 17/2/1940. 'Con' has the same misogynist meaning in French.
41. SHD 27N144/4/4a, 'Note sur l'importance des travaux d'organisation défensive [*sic*] exécutés par les Armées françaises de la frontière Suisse à la Mer du Nord de Septembre 1939 à Mai 1940', undated, c. September 1940.
42. Aubrac, *Où la mémoire s'attarde*, 58–60.
43. SHD 29N52, Georges to Billotte, 17/12/1939; 4e Bureau, Note, 26/12/1939.
44. SHD 27N144/4/4b, Belhague to Gamelin, 27/9/1939; SHD 27N144/4/4a, CEZF, 'Note fixant les directives techniques . . .', 4/10/1939; SHD 27N144/4/4c, Belhague to Gamelin, 27/11/1939.
45. SHD 29N52, Tuczkiewicz, 'Note sur les travaux', 3/1/1942.

46. SHD 27N144/4/4b, 3e Bureau, 'Note sur l'extension', 30/12/1939; Tetevuide to Condé, 10/2/1940.
47. Crémieux-Brilhac, *Les Français de l'an 40*, vol. 2, 453.
48. SHD 27N144/4/4a, 'Note sur l'importance des travaux', undated, c. September 1940.
49. SHD Fonds Georges 1KMI26, manuscript note, late November 1939.
50. SHD 29N138/2, 2nd Army Group, Note, 16/2/1939.
51. Margerie, *Journal*, 47.
52. SHD 27N144/4/4b, Daladier to 3e Bureau, 13/10/1939; Philippe to 3e Bureau, 30/1/1940; *Journal officiel de la République française: Débats parlementaires: Édition spéciale*, 2/8/1948, Comité secret du Sénat, 16/4/1940, 37–8.
53. SHD 27N144/4/4a, 'Note sur l'importance des travaux', undated, c. September 1940.
54. SHD 28N19, Procédés de combat, Frère, Rapport, 12/12/1939.
55. Roman Töppel, *Kursk 1943: The Greatest Battle of the Second World War* (2018), 74.
56. SHD 29N27/?2, 'Organisation du secteur de Sedan', undated, March 1940; Vanderputten, 'L'organisation fortifiée', 26.
57. SHD 29N27/?2, Taittinger, Rapport, 8/3/1940 and following.
58. SHD 29N27/?2, Huntziger to Georges, 8/4/1940; Pierre Rocolle, *La guerre de 1940* (1990), vol. 2: *La défaite*, 49–52.
59. Martin S. Alexander, 'Prophet without Honour? The French High Command and Pierre Taittinger's Report on the Ardennes Defences, March 1940', *War and Society*, 4 (1986), 53–71.
60. SHD 27N12/4/4, Gamelin, Note, 11/11/1939.
61. Prételat, *Le destin tragique*, 109–13.
62. SHD 29N14/1, Prételat to Georges, 28/9/1939.
63. SHD 27N12/4/4, Gamelin to major-general, 9/11/1939; SHD 29N290, Gamelin, Note, 25/11/1939; SHD 29N52, Note, 8/12/1939.
64. SHD 28N14/1, Colonel Heme, Compte-rendu, 15/12/1939.
65. SHD 29N290, Colonel Conran to commandant VIII Corps, 16/12/1939.
66. Nard, *Souvenirs de guerre*, 33–4.
67. SHD 27N13/6, 'Voyage de Gamelin', 23/11/1939; SHD 27N12/4/4, Gamelin, Avis, 15/12/1939.
68. Schiavon, *Corap*, 261–2.
69. SHD 27N84/4, 'Compte rendu d'un mission', 27/12/1938; SHD 29N290, Frère to Bourret, 18/12/1939; SHD 28N14/1, Requin to Gamelin, 22/12/1939.
70. SHD 5N584, Daladier to Chef d'EMA, 27/2/1940.
71. SHD 29N290, Georges, Note, 9/2/1940. In fact, there had also been opposition within the GQG – see 27N156/1, Préaud, 'Note pour le 1e Bureau', 2/10/1939; Prételat, *Le destin tragique*, 121–3.
72. SHD 7N150, Georges, Note, 1/3/1939.
73. AN 2W54/1, Baudet, Rapport, undated, 1941/2.
74. *CEP*, vol. 3, 687; Rocolle, *La guerre de 1940*, vol. 1: *L'Illusion*, 288. SHD 28N14/1, Prételat to Georges, 16 and 26/2/1940, contains a request to retain a small number of forces.
75. JMO Georges, cited in Max Schiavon, *Le général Georges: Un destin inachevé* (2020), 289–90.
76. SHD 27N156/Orders/1, Georges, Note, 5/11/1939.

77. *CEP*, vol. 3, 697.
78. SHD 29N138/1, GQG, IPS 2 for 2nd Army Group, 30/9/1939; SHD 33N14/10, 3rd Army, General Order 1, 5/10/1939; SHD 34N156/12, especially SF-Vosges, 'Ordre particulier No 11', 12/10/1939, and 46 DI, 'Ordre particulier No 11', 17/10/1939.
79. *Règlement de l'infanterie: Instruction technique*, Articles 357–61; *Manuel du gradé d'infanterie*, paragraphs 19, 49, 357–61.
80. I sampled casualties in the three frontier departments and added those who died in Germany, as listed in the Mémoire des hommes database: www.memoiredeshommes.sga.defense.gouv.fr. An unknown number of those wounded in the advance posts died elsewhere in France. AN C15162, Daladier to Commission, 21/2/1940, reports 862 men as 'disappeared', a figure including POWs, men who had been killed in Germany and deserters from colonial units.
81. SHD 27N69/2/2a, November 1939.
82. SHD 27N69/2/2c, December 1939.
83. SHD 27N69/2/2c, December 1939.
84. Pierre Taittinger, *Les leçons d'une défaite: Ce que le pays doit savoir: Précisions nécessaires par un membre de la Commission de l'armée* (1941), 32. The communiqué was published in all dailies.
85. SHD 27N69/2/2b, 20/11/1939.
86. Leo Freiherr Geyr von Schweppenburg, 'Saar 1940', *Zeitschrift für die Geschichte der Saargegend*, 15 (1965), 220–42 at 220–4.
87. SHD 27N69/2/2a, 28/11/1939.
88. Pierre Péan, *Une jeunesse française: François Mitterrand, 1934–1947* (1994), 119, 121.
89. Williamson Murray, 'The German Response to Victory in Poland: A Case Study in Professionalism', *Armed Forces and Society* 7 (1981), 285–98; Lopez, *Heinz Guderian*, 223.
90. Franz Halder, *The Halder Diaries (The Private War Journal of Generaloberst Franz Halder, from 14 August 1939 to 24 September 1942)*, ed. Arnold Lissance (1976), 18/1/1940; Schweppenburg, 'Saar 1940', 222–3; Georg Tessin, *Verbände und Truppen der deutschen Wehrmacht und Waffen-SS im Zweiten Weltkrieg 1939–1945* (1977), vol. 1: *Waffengattungen – Gesamtübersicht*, 43–7; Siegfried Westphal, *Heer in Fesseln: Aus den Papieren des Stabschefs von Rommel, Kesselring und Rundstedt* (1950), 109–10; Murray, 'The Strategy of the "Phoney War" Revisited', 15; Marc M. Romanych, Martin M. Rupp and John White, *Maginot Line 1940: Battles on the French Frontier* (2010), 24–6.
91. SHD 34N69/11/2, Zorn, 'Le franchissement du Rhin', translated from *Die Wehrmacht*, 12/3/1941; Halder, *The Halder Diaries*, 13/12/1939, 28/12/1939.
92. Halder, *The Halder Diaries*, 3/10/1939.
93. Halder, *The Halder Diaries*, 14/9/1939, 18/5/1940.
94. SHD 33N67, Lacaze to commander 55 Brigade d'infanterie alpin, 23/12/1939; Schweppenburg, 'Saar 1940', 226.
95. SHD 33N67/2, commander RF-Lauter and Lieutenant-Colonel Bourgeois, 26/11/1939.
96. SHD 27N69/2/2c, 21/12/1939; Guizard, *La drôle de guerre*, 23/10/1939.
97. Bodmin Keep, Cornwall's Army Museum, A.W. Gason Papers, letters to parents, 1/2/1940, 11/3/1940; National Archives (UK), WO167/734, BEF War Diaries DCLI, 1939–40; SHD 27N65/5, Bulletin Quotidien, 7/3/1940; Chambrun, *I Saw France Fall*, 44–5.

98. SHD 34N156/11, SF-Vosges, Note de Service, 13/10/1939.
99. SHD 28N19, Manhès, Rapport, 28/12/1939.
100. SHD 28N19, Duron, Enseignements, December 1939.
101. See chapter 5.
102. SHD 29N138/1, Gamelin, Note, 27/11/1939; SHD 29N138/2, Georges, Note, 15/2/1939; 2nd Army Group, Note, 16/2/1940.
103. SHD 27N69/2/2d, 6/1/1940; Guizard, *La drôle de guerre*, 4/5/1940; Margerie, *Journal*, 49. See also SHD 34N69/4/5, Guilloton and Lemée, Rapports, 23/6/1940.
104. SHD 29N138/1, Note, 16/2/1940.
105. SHD 29N220, Rapport, undated, probably April 1940.
106. SHD 27N69/2/2a, 11, 24, 29/10/1939; SHD 27N69/2/2b, 20/11/1939.
107. SHD 32N257/5, Legros, Note de Service, 29/10/1939; 'Projet d'instruction', undated.
108. Mary and Hohnadel, *Hommes et ouvrages*, vol. 3, 34.
109. SHD 32N257/5, Hassler, 'Réflexions', 21/11/1939.
110. SHD 27N69/2/2b, 28/11/1939.
111. SHD 33N67/2, 'Reconnaissance', 16/12/1939; Bourgeois, Rapport, 18/12/1939.
112. SHD 29/N/286, correspondence 13–15/11/1939.
113. SHD 33N67/2, Hau, 'Compte-rendu de patrouille', 16/12/1939.
114. SHD 27N12/4/4, Gamelin, Note, 12/10/1939.
115. SHD 28N14/1, Prételat to Georges, 19/11/1939.
116. SHD 28N19, Dossier 'Procédés de combat', 10/1939 to 12/1939.
117. SHD 27N156/1, Georges to 2nd Army Group, 11/12/1939.
118. SHD 32N257/5, 'Note relative au contact', 27/9/1939; SHD 27N156/1, Prételat to Georges, 12/12/1939; Prételat, *Le destin tragique*, 89–95.
119. SHD 27N156/1, Prételat to Georges, 12/12/1939.
120. SHD 27N12/4/4, Gamelin to Georges, 21/12/1939.
121. SHD 32N169, VIII Corps, Note de Service, 3 and 8/1/1940.
122. SHD 27N156/1, Bourgeois, Note, 14/2/1940; Roton to Georges, 3e Bureau NE Front, 22/1/1940; SHD 27N156/1, Roton, Note, 3/3/1940; Du Mezel, Note, 18/3/1940; Mary and Hohnadel, *Hommes et ouvrages*, vol. 3, 36–7.
123. SHD 32N227, Delmas, 'Programme d'instruction', 22/4/1940.
124. SHD 32N277/5, 'Projet d'instruction des GF de la 56e Division', 26/3/1940.
125. Mary and Hohnadel, *Hommes et ouvrages*, vol. 1, 89.
126. Margerie, *Journal*, 50–1.
127. SHD 27N69/2/2f, 17/3/1940.
128. SHD 27N69/2/2e, undated, late January or early February 1940.
129. SHD 3N67/2, Bethouar to SF-Vosges, 5/1/1940.
130. SHD 32N169, VIII Corps, Note de Service, 3 and 8/1/1940.
131. SHD 32N227/1, Bourret, Note, 13/4/1940 (explaining the note of 10 April).
132. SHD 27N69/2/2d, 18/1/1940.
133. The most extensive discussion of the *corps francs* in combat systematically exaggerates French failures and losses: Mary and Hohnadel, *Hommes et ouvrages*, vol. 3, 34–5.
134. SHD 27N69/2/2e, 2/3/1940.
135. SHD 29N130/2, 'Confirmation de message', 22/2/1940; SHD 27N12, Gamelin, Note, 20/2/1940. The Mémoire des hommes database lists four 47 RIF killed that month: www.memoiredeshommes.sga.defense.gouv.fr.

136. SHD 27N12, Gamelin, Note, 20/2/1940; SHD 32N185, Dossier Darnand; Patrick de Gmeline, *Les corps francs, 39/40* (1999), 67–86. The figure of seventeen French dead reported in Mary and Hohnadel, *Hommes et ouvrages*, vol. 3, 35, appears to refer to the seventeen German dead claimed by Darnand.
137. Mary and Hohnadel, *Hommes et ouvrages*, vol. 3, 35.
138. SHD 29N130/2, 'Confirmation de message', 16/4/1940; SHD 32N227/1, Prételat, Note, 23/4/1940.
139. SHD 32N169, Schwarzenbach, Compte-rendu, 12–13/2/1940; Gmeline, *Les corps francs*, 57, 76–8.
140. SHD 32N169, 'Rapport . . . 12–13 février 1940'; SHD 28N19, 4th Army, 'Ordre de recherche', 4/10/1939.
141. Prételat, *Le destin tragique*, 92.
142. SHD 32N169/7DI/2, Carmejane-Vesc, Rapport, 3/3/1940.
143. SHD 29N220, Responses to Troisième Bureau, April 1940.
144. Alexander, 'Prophet without Honour?'.

12 The Maginot Line and Case Yellow

1. Henri Michel, *La seconde guerre mondiale* (1977), 1, 62; Alexander, *The Republic in Danger*, 336–7; Chaix, *En mai 1940, fallait-il entrer en Belgique?*, 123–4, 183–4; Chauvy, *Le drame de l'armée française*, 89–91; Porch, *Defeat and Division*, 135–6.
2. Bardoux, *Journal d'un témoin*, 5/4/1940.
3. Liddell Hart Centre for Military Archives, LH 1/256, Liddell Hart to Earle, 24/4/1948.
4. SHD 27N12/4/4, Gamelin, Note, 21/9/1939.
5. Chaix, *En mai 1940, fallait-il entrer en Belgique?*, 99–199; Alexander, *The Republic in Danger*, 322–48.
6. Reproduced in Gamelin, *Servir*, vol. 3, 8–16.
7. Quoted in Chauvy, *Le drame de l'armée française*, 347.
8. SHD Fonds Georges 1KMI26, Agenda, 11/11/1940; SHD Fonds Georges 1K97/7, 'Intervention en Belgique', 7; Chaix, *En mai 1940, fallait-il entrer en Belgique?*, 120–2; Schiavon, *Le général Georges*, 250–1.
9. SHD 27N13/6, 'Voyage de Gamelin', 23/11/1939.
10. SHD Fonds Georges 1K97/7, 'Intervention en Belgique'; SHD 27N157/6/6, Georges to Gamelin, 5/12/1939; Chaix, *En mai 1940, fallait-il entrer en Belgique?*, 130.
11. SHD 27N12/4/4, Gamelin, Note (for Georges), 26/12/1939.
12. Paragraphs 219–226 of the *Instruction sur l'emploi tactique des grandes unités* leave much to the commander's judgement.
13. SHD 27N12/4/4, Georges, 'Remarques sur . . . Réflexions', 6/1/1940.
14. Villelume, *Journal d'une défaite*, 10/5/1940; Claude Paillat, *Dossiers secrets de la France contemporaine*, vol. 4: *Le désastre de 1940*, part 2: *La guerre immobile, avril 1939–10 mai 1940* (1984), 215–16.
15. SHD Fonds Georges 1K97/7, 'Intervention en Belgique', 7.
16. Henry Pownall, *Chief of Staff: The Diaries of Lieutentant-General Sir Henry Pownall*, ed. Brian Bond (1972), vol. 1: *1933–1940*, 24/1/1940.
17. Chaix, *En mai 1940, fallait-il entrer en Belgique?*, 170.

18. Pownall, *Chief of Staff*, 9/2/1940; General Bourret, in his *La tragédie de l'armée française*, 83, agreed that Gamelin was attempting to save his position; Chaix, *En mai 1940, fallait-il entrer en Belgique?*, 184.
19. Imlay, 'A Reassessment of Anglo-French Strategy'.
20. *Instruction sur l'emploi tactique des grandes unités*, 75.
21. Chaix, *En mai 1940, fallait-il entrer en Belgique?*, 181; Gamelin, *Servir*, vol. 3, 228–40; Marcel Lerecouvreux, *L'armée Giraud en Hollande (1939–1940)* (1951), 51; Joseph Doumenc, *Les papiers secrets du général Doumenc: 1939–1940*, ed. François Delpla (1992), 204; *CEP*, vol. 3, 684–5; SHD 28N8/3, Billotte, IPS no. 11, 27/3/1940.
22. Bardoux, *Journal d'un témoin*, 20/2/1940.
23. Quoted in Chauvy, *Le drame de l'armée française*, 347.
24. Lerecouvreux, *L'armée Giraud en Hollande*, 217–37; Chaix, *En mai 1940, fallait-il entrer en Belgique?*, 223–4, 231.
25. Gunsburg, 'The Battle of the Belgian Plain'; Gunsburg, 'The Battle of Gembloux'; Chaix, *En mai 1940, fallait-il entrer en Belgique?*, 232–3, 273–4.
26. The following account relies on Eric Linklater, *The Highland Division* (1942), 7–21.
27. The fullest account is Frieser, *Blitzkrieg-Legende*, 145–97. See also, Ruby, *Sedan, terre d'épreuve.*
28. XXI Corps had hitherto consisted of a staff and organic elements without fighting units.
29. Frieser, *Blitzkrieg-Legende*, 202, wrongly states that Flavigny planned first to block and then to counterattack.
30. Frieser, *Blitzkrieg-Legende*, 202–3.
31. Roger Bruge, *Le sang versé* (1982), 50.
32. SHD 34N134/14, Vinson, Rapport, 23/5/1940; Chaix, *En mai 1940, fallait-il entrer en Belgique?*, 258.
33. SHD 29N21, Vennat, Rapport, 8/3/1940.
34. For accounts of the battle see Roger Bruge, *Faites sauter la ligne Maginot: La forteresse invaincue* (1985), 210–69; Giuliano, *Les soldats du béton*, 73–114; Michel Truttmann and Jean-Robert Gorce, *La ligne Maginot au combat* (2 vols, 2022), vol. 1, 131–64.
35. Bruge, *Faites sauter la ligne Maginot*, 212.
36. Péan, *Une jeunesse française*, 119, 121; Éric Roussel, *François Mitterrand: De l'intime au politique* (2015), 75.
37. AD Ardennes 1J575/1, 'Version allemand des faits', translated from *Der Landser Grossband*, No. 513 (1980).
38. AD Ardennes 1J360, André to Collin, undated, letter from POW camp.
39. Mary and Hohnadel, *Hommes et ouvrages*, vol. 3, 177.
40. Bruge, *Faites sauter la ligne Maginot*, 266.
41. SHD 29N52, Georges, Note, 6/6/1940.
42. The following paragraphs rely on Mary and Hohnadel, *Hommes et ouvrages*, vol. 3, 160–4; and Pierre Vanderputten, Claude Girault and Roger Dutry, *Sur les traces de Maginot* (2004).
43. Rocolle, *Le béton a-t-il trahi?*, 64.
44. This is the view of Chaix, *En mai 1940, fallait-il entrer en Belgique?*, 250.
45. *Instruction provisoire technique sur le camouflage* (1936), Articles 268–71, 426.

46. Doumenc, *Les papiers secrets*, 22/5/1940.
47. Frieser, *Blitzkrieg-Legende*, 252–60, 286–301; Lopez, *Heinz Guderian*, 243, 249–51, 255, 259.

13 Tragic Destiny

1. Giroud, *Le journal d'un sapeur*, 23/4/1940.
2. Martin S. Alexander, 'After Dunkirk: The French Army's Performance against "Case Red", 25 May to 25 June 1940', *War in History*, 14 (2007), 219–64.
3. Alexander, 'Radio-Intercepts, Reconnaissance and Raids'.
4. SHD 27N50, Weygand to Reynaud, 25/5/1940.
5. Paul Baudouin, *Neuf mois au gouvernement* (1948), 24/5/1940.
6. SHD 2N26, Comité de Guerre, 25/5/1940; Maxime Weygand, *Recalled to Service*, trans. E.W. Dickes (1952), 95–7.
7. Dominique Leca, *La rupture de 1940* (1978), 6/6/1940.
8. Charles Serre, ed., *Rapport fait au nom de la Commission chargée d'enquêter sur les événements survenus en France de 1933 à 1945 par M. Serre* (2 vols, 1951–2), 7 Rollin deposition, 1401; Charles Reibel, *Pourquoi et comment fut décidé la demande d'armistice, 10–17 juin 1940* (1940), 18–19.
9. Leca, *La rupture de 1940*, 26/5/1940.
10. Thibaud Tellier, *Paul Reynaud: Un indépendant en politique* (2005), 585–95; Margerie, *Journal*, 26/5/1940.
11. Weygand, *Recalled to Service*, 140, 220.
12. Vidal, 'Le haut commandement', 363–5.
13. Doumenc, *Les papiers secrets*, 18/5/1940.
14. SHD 28N12, 2nd Army Group, JMO, 20/5/1940.
15. Prételat, *Le destin tragique*, 161–8; Vidal, 'Le haut commandement', 363.
16. According to Pierre Renauld, 'La fin de la deuxième groupe d'armées', *Bulletin trimestriel de l'Association des amis de l'École supérieure de guerre*, 43 (1969), 45–70 at 47, the generals discussed creation of a 4th Army Group but the plan was then forgotten.
17. SHD 28N12, 2nd Army Group, JMO, 27–28/5/1940; Charles Huntziger, *Les carnets secrets du général Huntziger, 1938–1941*, ed. Max Schiavon (2019), 28/5/1940.
18. Prételat, *Le destin tragique*, 172–3; Huntziger, *Les carnets secrets*, 28 and 29/5/1940.
19. SHD Fonds Bruge 1K594/8, 'Notes sur les Carnets du Général Tessier', 27/5/1940.
20. Quoted in Bruge, *Faites sauter la ligne Maginot*, 296–7.
21. Prételat, *Le destin tragique*, 178–9; Huntziger, *Les carnets secrets*, 2/6/1940.
22. SHD Fonds Bruge 1K594/8, 'Notes sur les Carnets du Général Tessier', 27/5/1940.
23. Prételat, *Le destin tragique*, 179–82.
24. Weygand, *Recalled to Service*, 127.
25. Bruge, *Le sang versé*, 48–53.
26. SHD 28N12, 2nd Army Group, JMO, 10/6/1940.
27. SHD 34N75, multiple reports of which the most informative is that of Chef de Bataillon Buisson, 10/7/1940; SHD 3K32, Témoignage oral Crémieux-Brilhac.
28. Rocolle, *La guerre de 1940*, vol. 2, 271.
29. Renauld, 'La fin de la deuxième groupe d'armées', 51–2.
30. Weygand, *Recalled to Service*, 145–8.

31. SHD 28N12, 2nd Army Group, JMO, 12/6/1940.
32. SHD Fonds Bruge 1K594/8, 'Notes sur les Carnets du Général Tessier', 12/6/1940.
33. Prételat, *Le destin tragique*, 184–205; Doumenc, *Les papiers secrets*, 13/6/1940; Schiavon, *Le général Georges*, 371–2,
34. Bruge, *Faites sauter la ligne Maginot*, 310–16.
35. Graveel, *Souvenirs de guerre*, 12/6/1940.
36. Bruge, *Faites sauter la ligne Maginot*, 320–1.
37. Bruge, *Faites sauter la ligne Maginot*, 306.
38. Bruge, *Faites sauter la ligne Maginot*, 332–47.
39. Didelot, *Drôle de guerre*, 14/6/1940.
40. Guizard, *La drôle de guerre*, 15/6/1940.
41. Nard, *Souvenirs de guerre*, 49–51.
42. Rocolle, *Le béton a-t-il trahi?*, 44.
43. SHD 14P, Rapport complémentaire, 21/10/1941; SHD 34N162/174 RIF, Daubenton, Rapport, undated, 1945. Bruge, *Faites sauter la ligne Maginot*, 311, n. 2, states that a 174 RIF officer accused another officer of ordering a rifle company to abandon its post without firing a shot. This 'affaire de Puttelange' was supposedly reported to the suspect retreats commission, but there is no trace of it in the archives.
44. Erich Wolfram von Bleichert, *Als Artillerie-Beobachter durch die Maginot-Linie* (1942), 37, 57.
45. Didelot, *Drôle de guerre*, 57–9.
46. Guizard, *La drôle de guerre*, 15/6/1940.
47. SHD 34N69/11, Arbus, Rapport, 15/9/1945.
48. Roger Bruge, *Offensive sur le Rhin* (1977), 161–3, 168–9; thanks to Bethany Keenan for information on the physiological and psychological effects of bombardment.
49. Bruge, *Offensive sur le Rhin*, 161–3, 168–9.
50. SHD 14P9, Bruge, Note, 9/11/1976; Bruge, *Offensive sur le Rhin*, 178–80; Alain Hohnadel and Jean-Yves Mary, *Juin 1940, les allemands passent le Rhin* (2006), 48.
51. SHD 34N69/9, Lt Colonel Manitius (Commander Wehrmacht IR 386), 'Le franchissement du Rhin', 20/4/1959.
52. SHD 34N69/11/3, Aullen, Rapport, 25/9/1945.
53. SHD 28N12, 2nd Army Group, JMO, 15/6/1940; *The Halder Diaries*, 14/6/1940.
54. SHD 28N12, 2nd Army Group, JMO, 15/6/1940 (Ordres généraux d'opérations 19 and 20).
55. Bruge, *On a livré la ligne Maginot*, 37–8.
56. Bruge, *On a livré la ligne Maginot*, 45–6.
57. Alexander von Scheele, 'Unsere Division und Abteilung im Rahmen der Operationen des Westfeldzuges', in Leutnant Helmut Schiebe, ed., *Die Panzer-Aufklärungs-Abteilung 4 im Westfeldzug* (1942), 6–90 at 82.
58. AN 2W57, CP, 7/6/1940.
59. Yves Durand, *Les prisonniers de guerre dans les Stalags, les Oflags et les Kommandos 1939–1945* (1994), 25; *The Halder Diaries*, 17/6/1940.
60. Christiane Rimbaud, *L'affaire du Massilia, été 1940* (1984), 82–3.
61. Bruge, *On a livré la ligne Maginot*, 191–9; Rocolle, *Le béton a-t-il trahi?*, 40–1.
62. SHD 33N125/12, Regard to XII Corps, 7/6/1940.
63. SHD 34N51/22 RIF/10/1, Miconnet, Rapport, undated; Bruge, *On a livré la ligne Maginot*, 115–22.
64. SHD 34N51, Ollivier, Rapport, 23/6/1945.

65. Renauld, 'La fin de la deuxième groupe d'armées', 60–1, includes a scathing account of this episode.
66. Renauld, 'La fin de la deuxième groupe d'armées', 54–62; SHD 28N12, 2nd Army Group, JMO, 20/5/1940, dates the telegram to the 20th.
67. SHD 28N12, 2nd Army Group, JMO, 17/6 to 21/6/1940.
68. Didelot, *Drôle de guerre*, 69–79.
69. Guizard, *La drôle de guerre*, 16–18/6/1940.
70. The following four paragraphs rely on Bundesarchiv, RH 27-1-7, 1 Panzer, Gefechtsberichte, 17–19/6/1940; RH 27-1, Einsaß West, 17–18/6/1940; Schiebe, *Die Panzer-Aufklärungs-Abteilung*, 1–96; SHD 34N51, Rapports Richardin and Saul; 14P9 (22 RIF), Babault report, 25/6/1940; Bruge, *Les combattants du 18 juin*, vol. 2, *Les derniers feux*, 474–9, relies on Babault and the German sources alone.
71. SHD 14P9 (22 RIF), Babault report, 25/6/1940.
72. SHD GRYE61605, Pierron dossier.
73. SHD GRYE61605, Pierron dossier.
74. SHD 27N69/2/2d, 13/1/1940; SHD 27N69/2/2g, 15/4/1940.
75. SHD 34 N 51, Rapport Ollivier, 23 June 1945.
76. SHD 8YE61605, Pierron dossier, untitled document, date illegible, possibly March 1947.
77. SHD 8YE110456, Babault dossier, 'Faits postérieure à la proposition . . .', undated c.1945–6.
78. See above, p. 277; SHD 8YE61605, Pierron dossier, untitled document, date illegible, possibly March 1947.
79. Bruge, *Les combattants du 18 juin*, vol. 2, 478.
80. Schiebe, *Die Panzer-Aufklärungs-Abteilung*, 82, 85, 92.
81. Robert Forquin, *Souvenirs de captivité* (2023): www.wikiMaginot.eu/_documents/2023-04/_wiki_docs/1-1681206552.pdf.
82. SHD 8YE61605, Pierron dossier, Pierron to Charly, 15–16/3/1985. This letter also reveals that Pierron wrote to Bruge to correct the latter's version of events.
83. SHD 8YE110456, Babault dossier, summary of evaluations, 1916 to 1940.
84. SHD 8YE61605, Pierron dossier, Pierron to Charly, 15–16/3/1985.
85. SHD 8YE61605, Pierron dossier, untitled document, date illegible, possibly March 1947; Acte d'accusation, 17/5/1947.
86. Robin Leconte, 'Comprendre la défaite: La commission d'enquête sur les repliements suspects 1940–1944' (Mémoire de Master 2, Paris I, 2013), 175.
87. SHD 8YE110456, Babault dossier, summary of evaluations, 1916 to 1940.
88. Schiebe, *Die Panzer-Aufklärungs-Abteilung*, 92; SHD 14P9 (22 RIF), Babault report, 25/6/1940.
89. Rocolle, *La guerre de 1940*, vol. 2, 312.
90. Henri Frenay, *La nuit finira* (1973), 19–21.
91. Guizard, *La drôle de guerre*, 19/6/1940.
92. SHD 14P6 (104 DIF), Esclaibes, Rapport, 14/7/1940.
93. Aubrac, *Où la mémoire s'attarde*, 63. See also SHD 34N52, Machère, Rapport, undated, 1945.
94. See above, p. 292. SHD 27N70/2, 13/6/1940; SHD 34N162, Langsnickel, Rapport, undated, probably late August or September 1940.
95. SHD 34N399, JMO, 30/5/1940.

96. See *Le Monde*, 27/4/1949, and *Le Figaro*, 28/4/1949. There are several inaccuracies in Henri Amouroux, *La vie des Français sous l'Occupation* (2012), 44. The Mémoire des hommes database, which classifies Charly as 'Mort pour la France', wrongly assigns him to 163 RAP: www.memoiredeshommes.sga.defense.gouv.fr.
97. Didelot, *Drôle de guerre*, 75; Guizard, *La drôle de guerre*, 223.
98. Bruge, *Faites sauter la ligne Maginot*, 329.
99. André Perrin, *Evadé de guerre via Colditz* (1975), 15–17.
100. Rodolphe, *Combats*, 139.
101. Graveel, *Souvenirs de guerre*, 16 and 25/6/1940.
102. Perrin, *Evadé de guerre via Colditz*, 15–17.
103. Antoine Bruneau, ed, *A demain, ma chérie. Lettres de la ligne Maginot* (2018), 40–2, 22/6/1940.
104. Graveel, *Souvenirs de guerre*, 16 and 20/6/1940.
105. Bruge, *Faites sauter la ligne Maginot*, 78–81.
106. Bruge, *Faites sauter la ligne Maginot*, 129–38.
107. See above, p. 287.
108. SHD 34N152/1, Hendy, comments on Vincent, Rapport, 27/11/1940
109. SHD 34N152/1, Hendy, comments on Vincent, Rapport, 27/11/1940; SHD 3K13-1, Alberic Vaillant, 1–3/4//1997.
110. Bruge, *On a livré la ligne Maginot*, 56–7.
111. SHD 9NN4-4-458, plans and specifications for PO-Haut-Poirier.
112. SHD 34N158/3, 'Note sur les conditions dans lesquelles les ouvrages de Ht-Poirier et du Welschhhof ont été pris . . .', undated, probably 1945; Bruge, *On a livré la ligne Maginot*, 177–87; Rocolle, *Le béton a-t-il trahi?*, 68.
113. The following account is from SHD 34N158/3, 'Note sur les conditions dans lesquelles les ouvrages de Ht-Poirier et du Welschhhof . . .'; SHD 34N158, Journal de Bord, undated, 1945; Bruge, *Faites sauter la ligne Maginot*, 189–97.
114. The following account relies on SHD 34N158/2, Welschhof, Journal de Bord, 17/6/1940; SHD 24N158, Rapport Caraman, undated, 1945.
115. Rodolphe, *Combats*, 132–3.
116. Jean-Bernard Wahl, *Jours tranquilles et bruits de guerre au Mont des Welches: Août 1939–juillet 1940: Petite histoire, la Drôle de guerre sur la ligne Maginot* (2007), 22/6/1940.
117. Bruneau, *A demain, ma chérie*, 18 to 25/6/1940; SHD 34N151/6, Fabre, Rapport, 1945.
118. Philippe Garraud, 'La politique de fortification des frontières de 1925 à 1940: logiques, contraintes et usages de la "Ligne Maginot"', *Guerres mondiales et conflits contemporains*, 226 (2007), 3–22; Garraud, 'La construction de la ligne Maginot alpine'; Giorgio Rochat, 'La campagne italienne de juin 1940 dans les Alpes occidentales', *Revue historique des armées*, 250 (2008), 77–84; Emanuele Sica, 'June 1940: The Italian Army and the Battle of the Alps', *Canadian Journal of History*, 47 (2012), 355–78.
119. Unless otherwise indicated, the following account relies on Bruge, *On a livré la ligne Maginot*, 241–330.
120. Graveel, *Souvenirs de guerre*, 25/6/1945.
121. Graveel, *Souvenirs de guerre*, 27/6/1940.
122. Huntziger, *Les carnets secrets*, 28 and 30/6/1940.

Conclusion: Myth and History

1. Laurent Joly, *L'état contre les Juifs: Vichy, les nazis et la persécution antisémite (1940–1944)* (2018), 256, n. 81.
2. Felsenhardt, *1939–1940 avec le 18e Corps d'armée*, 185–6.
3. Leconte, 'Comprendre la défaite'.
4. SHD 14P48, Frère to Ministry, 7/9/1942, and 14P4, Capitulation Prételat.
5. Laure, *Pétain*, 385.
6. Paull Allard, 'La Ligne Maginot'; *Le Matin*, 6 and 8/12/1940; Claude-Armand Masson, *La Ligne Maginot, Bastion inutile* (1942).
7. Albert Bayet, *Pétain et la cinquième colonne* (1944), 28, 65.
8. AN 2W6/B IX 12 and 13, Reynaud to Pétain, 5/4/1941.
9. Serre, *Rapport fait au nom de la Commission*, vol. 1, 51.
10. Charles de Gaulle, *Mémoires de guerre* (1954), vol. 1: *L'appel, 1940–1942*, 11–22.
11. Marc Bloch, *L'étrange défaite* (1957), 80.
12. SHD 5N583/1, 'Crédits alloués', 9/9/1938; Robert Frank, *Le prix du réarmement français 1935–1939* (2017), 62; Alexander, 'In Defence of the Maginot Line', 174–5.
13. Truttmann and Lisch, *La muraille de France*, 368.
14. Bruge, *On a livré la ligne Maginot*, 55.
15. Rocolle, *Le béton a-t-il trahi?*, 22.
16. Graveel, *Souvenirs de guerre*, 4 and 14/6/1940.
17. Rodolphe, *Combats*, 133.
18. These figures are available on the Mémoire des hommes database: www.memoiredeshommes.sga.defense.gouv.fr.
19. Major J.E. Passmore, 'Decision Making in the Military', *British Army Review*, 126 (2000–1), 43–9.
20. Felsenhardt, *1939–1940 avec le 18e Corps d'armée*, 189–90; Barnett Singer and John W. Langdon, *Cultured Force: Makers and Defenders of the French Colonial Empire* (2004), 267–345.
21. Guizard, *La drôle de guerre*, 18/6/1940.
22. Didelot, *Drôle de guerre*, 14/6/1940.
23. Gustave Folcher, *Les carnets de guerre de Gustave Folcher, paysan languedocien: 1939–1945*, ed. Rémy Cazals (1981), 24–5.
24. Bruneau, *A demain, ma chérie*, 22/6/1940.
25. Pierre Miquel, *L'exode: 10 mai–20 juin 1940* (2003), 220–1.
26. Graveel, *Souvenirs*, 2/7/1940.
27. Guizard, *La drôle de guerre*, 15/6/1940.
28. Bleichert, *Als Artillerie-Beobachter*, 57.
29. Geoffrey Diebold, 'Les volontaires alsaciens dans les troupes du IIIe Reich', *Union rationaliste*, 3 (2019), 79–87.
30. François Roth, *Alsace-Lorraine: Histoire d'un 'pays perdu': De 1870 à nos jours* (2010), 180.
31. SHD Caen AC 21P661060, Dossier Pierron.
32. Lothar Kettenacker, *La politique de nazification en Alsace* (1978).
33. Sansico, *La justice déshonorée*, 112.
34. Michaël Séramour, 'Histoire de la ligne Maginot de 1945 à nos jours', *Revue historique des armées*, 247 (2007), 86–97.
35. 'Le FN absent quand il s'agit de protéger les Français', *Ouest France*, 24/11/2015; 'Discours de marine Le Pen à l'Université d'Oxford', 6/2/2015, https://rassemblement-national.fr/discours/discours-de-marine-le-pen-a-luniversite-doxford.

FURTHER READING AND SOURCES

Little research published in English deals directly with the Maginot Line. The excellent article by Martin S. Alexander, 'In Defence of the Maginot Line', in Robert W.D. Boyce, ed., *French Foreign and Defence Policy, 1918–1940* (1998), 164–94, is written from a revisionist perspective. Otherwise, published research deals primarily with technical military matters. The best examples are William Allcorn, *The Maginot Line* (2003), and J.E. Kaufmann and H.W. Kaufmann, *Fortress France* (2007). Despite its title, Judith M. Hughes, *To the Maginot Line* (1971), is primarily a history of security policy.

In the voluminous anglophone literature on the fall of France, the Maginot Line plays only a secondary role. Alistair Horne, *To Lose a Battle* (1979), Robert Doughty, *The Seeds of Disaster* (1985), and Elizabeth Kier, *Imagining War* (1997), present the decadence thesis. Douglas Porch, *Defeat and Division* (2022), criticizes revisionists' neglect of social context and is especially interesting on the fortunes of the army under the Vichy regime. Ernest R. May, *Strange Victory* (2000), and Philip Nord, *France 1940* (2015), blame the defeat almost entirely on the generals. Other works bring together social, political and military history, notably Martin S. Alexander, *The Republic in Danger* (1992), and Julian Jackson, *The Fall of France* (2003). The best attempts to demonstrate the way that the structures and doctrines of the army influenced the course of the battle itself are Martin S. Alexander, 'Radio-Intercepts, Reconnaissance and Raids', *Intelligence and National Security*, 28 (2013), 337–76, and Jeffery A. Gunsburg's two articles, 'The Battle of the Belgian Plain', *Journal of Military History*, 56 (1992), 207–44, and 'The Battle of Gembloux', *Journal of Military History*, 64 (2000), 97–140. Maude Williams and Bernard Wilkin, *French Soldiers' Morale in the Phoney War, 1939–1940* (2018), is an excellent social history of the army during the phoney war, which focuses especially on the Maginot Line front.

For the context of French security policy see Peter Jackson, *France and the Nazi Menace: Intelligence and Policy Making 1933–1939* (2000), and Talbot Imlay, *Facing the Second World War: Strategy, Politics, and Economics in Britain and France 1938–1940* (2003). For the global dimension of the interwar crisis, see Robert Boyce, *The Great Interwar Crisis and the Collapse of Globalization* (2009), and Adam Tooze, *The Deluge: The Great War and the Remaking of Global Order, 1916–1931* (2015).

FURTHER READING AND SOURCES

The military history of the Maginot Line is more extensively treated in French. Most important are Roger Bruge's eight volumes, based on extensive interviews and correspondence with protagonists: *Faites sauter la ligne Maginot* (2nd edn, 1985), *On a livré la ligne Maginot* (1975) and *Offensive sur le Rhin* (1977), and the five volumes of *Les combattants du 18 juin* (1982–9). Also vital are Jean-Yves Mary and Alain Hohnadel, *Hommes et ouvrages de la ligne Maginot* (5 vols, 2000–10), Philippe Truttmann and Frédéric Lisch, *La muraille de France ou La ligne Maginot* (2009), and Michel Truttmann and Jean-Robert Gorce, *La ligne Maginot au combat* (2 vols, 2022). These works are all lavishly illustrated and well documented, but contain only vague indications of the sources used. Special mention must be made of WikiMaginot.com, a mine of information on the fortifications.

The best and most relevant academic works are those of Philippe Garraud, including 'L'ombre portée de 1914–1918 dans les années 1930', *Vingtième siècle*, 104 (2009), 17–27, and 'La politique de fortification des frontières de 1925 à 1940', *Guerres mondiales et conflits contemporains*, 226 (2007), 3–22. François Cochet, *Les soldats de la drôle de guerre* (2004), is a nuanced wider study open to revisionism.

Like their anglophone equivalents, most francophone histories of the fall of France pay little attention to the Maginot Line other than as a symbol of the inadequacy of French doctrine. Jean-Baptiste Duroselle, *La décadence: 1932–1939* (1985), is the classic exposition of the decadence thesis. Pierre Rocolle, *La guerre de 1940* (2 vols, 1990), takes the traditional view. It uses Pierre Renauld, 'La fin de la deuxième groupe d'armées', *Bulletin trimestriel de l'Association des amis de l'École supérieure de guerre*, 43 (1969), 57–70, to cover the final days of the Maginot Line. The best books are Jean-Louis Crémieux-Brilhac, *Les Français de l'an 40* (2 vols, 1990), and Bruno Chaix, *En mai 1940, fallait-il entrer en Belgique?* (2005). See also Christine Levisse-Touzé, ed., *La campagne de 1940* (2001).

Published Primary Sources

Annuaire des officiers d'infanterie
État du corps du génie
Journal officiel de la République française: Débats parlementaires: Chambre
Journal officiel de la République française: Débats parlementaires: Sénat
Journal officiel de la République française: Lois et décrets
Charles Serre, ed., *Rapport fait au nom de la Commission chargée d'enquêter sur les événements survenus en France de 1933 à 1945 par M. Charles Serre: Annexes (Témoignages)* (9 vols, 1951)

Published Diaries and Memoirs

Journal du général Edmond Buat: 1914–1923, ed. Frédéric Guelton (2015)
Maurice-Gustave Gamelin, *Servir* (3 vols, 1946–7)
Charles Huntziger, *Les carnets secrets du général Huntziger, 1938–1941*, ed. Max Schiavon (2019)
Gaston Prételat, *Le destin tragique de la ligne Maginot* (1950)
Maxime Weygand, *Recalled to Service*, trans. E.W. Dickes (1952)

FURTHER READING AND SOURCES

Principal Archival Sources

Archives départementales (AD)

Alpes-Maritimes: 04M Surveillance de la frontière
Ardennes: J La Ferté; M Affaires militaires
Bas-Rhin: 98AL Fonds Valot; 286D Cabinet du Préfet
Meuse: M Police; R Affaires militaires
Moselle: J Génie; M Police; R Affaires militaires; U Tribunaux de Première Instance
Nord: J Génie; M Police; 2R Affaires militaires

Archives nationales (AN)

2W Procès de Riom
AP Archives privés (Édouard Daladier, Paul Painlevé, Paul Reynaud, Victor Schweisguth)
BB^{18} Justice division criminelle
BB^{30} Ministère de la Justice
C Archives parlementaires
F^{7} Police générale
F^{60} Services de la présidence du conseil
Fonds Moscou

Archives du Sénat (AS)

69S Commission de l'armée

Bodmin Keep: Cornwall's Army Museum

A.W. Gason Papers

Bundesarchiv-Militärarchiv (Freiburg im Breisgau)

RH 27-1-7

Dépot central des archives de la Justice militaire (Le Blanc) (DCAJM)

Minutiers for Nancy and Metz juridictions 1933–9
(Individual case files are cited in the endnotes.)

Liddell Hart Centre for Military Archives

Liddell Hart Papers

FURTHER READING AND SOURCES

National Archives (UK)

BEF War Diaries

Service historique de la Défense (Vincennes) (SHD)

1K Archives privées
1K97 Fonds Georges
1K130 Fonds Weygand
1K224 Fonds Gamelin
1K594 Fonds Bruge
3K Témoignages oraux
1N Conseil supérieur de la guerre
2N Conseil supérieur de la défense nationale
5N Cabinets du ministre
7N État-major des armées
8N Directions
27N Grand quartier général
28N Groupes d'armées
29N Armées
31N Régions militaires
32N Divisions
33N Secteurs fortifiés
34N Infanterie, artillerie, génie
7NN Fonds de Moscou – Deuxième Bureau
9NN Fonds de Moscou – Direction de l'infanterie
14P Commission d'enquête sur les repliements suspectes
2009 PA Fonds Prételat
3R Films, propagande
2 V Service technique du Génie
8Y Dossiers d'officiers
YD Dossiers des généraux

INDEX